D1120178

*The Unabridged*

# MARILYN

*Her Life from A to Z*

# *The Unabridged*
# MARILYN
## *Her Life from A to Z*

RANDALL RIESE AND NEAL HITCHENS

BONANZA BOOKS
New York

This 1990 edition is published by Bonanza Books, distributed by Crown Publishers, Inc., 225 Park Avenue South, New York, New York 10003, by arrangement with Contemporary Books, Inc.

Manufactured in the United States of America

Library of Congress Cataloging-in-Publication Data

Riese, Randall.
The unabridged Marilyn: her life from A to Z
by Randall Riese and Neal Hitchens.
p. cm.
Reprint. Originally published: New York:
Congdon & Weed, c1987.
ISBN 0-517-69619-3
1. Monroe, Marilyn, 1926-1962 – Dictionaries, indexes, etc.
2. Motion picture actors and actresses – United States – Biography-Dictionaries. I. Hitchens, Neal. II. Title.
[PN2287. M69R54 1990]
791.43'28'092 – dc20

ISBN 0-517-69619-3
h g f e d c b a

# Contents

# ACKNOWLEDGMENTS

We thank the following:

☆ Mark Goins, Chris Esposito, Aaron Kass, and Linda Laucella—for creating an environment of family, friendship, and inspiration.

☆ Jack Artenstein, Nancy Crossman, Angela Hynes, and Donavan Vicha—for their belief in us, for their belief in the project, and for their conviction to do it right.

☆ The authors would also like to thank the individuals listed below, who have generously lent their contributions to this work: Nancy Artenstein, Sylvia Barnhart, Chris Basinger, Dick Biegert, Leo and Frances Caloia, James and Rita Dougherty, T. R. Fogli, Alan France, Jack Gillan, Ray Van Goeye, Sabin Gray, Jack Hanson, James Haspiel, Demetrie Kabbaz, Bill McLean, Joe Martinez, Richard Meryman, Patrick Miller, William Moore, Lionel Newman, Q Pearce, Hal Schaefer, Greg Schreiner, Robert Slatzer, Mickey Song, Bob Thomas, Maxine Thomas, and William Travilla.

☆ A very special acknowledgment to Jack Cardiff, a gentleman in the truest sense, for his stunning cover photograph; and, to all of the other photographers, named and unnamed, whose work we are proud to include herein.

☆ One final, personal note of thanks—to Bernicia Carreira and Sydney Fleming, both of whom, like the subject of this book, are women with a compassion for all living things.

# INTRODUCTION

Nineteen-eighty-seven marks the 25th anniversary of the death of Marilyn Monroe. Amazing, when you think about it. *One quarter of a century.* It doesn't seem possible that we've been without her for that long a time. And yet, somehow, she has never really left us. She has become a part of our collective memory. Her striking and unparalleled blonde luminosity; her hair thrown back in defiance and ecstacy; her lips suggestively parted; her breathy, baby-voiced whisper that seduced us with its innocence; her infectious mirth; and her transparent vulnerability that touched something deep in us all. We understood her pain, because we recognized it in ourselves. No other entertainer—with the possible exceptions of Elvis Presley or Ronald Reagan—has had as much of an impact on popular culture. Marilyn Monroe has become an icon, a symbol of all that is good and bad, of tragedy, and, most importantly, of hope.

There have been many books and millions of words written about Marilyn, and yet there is not one single source that has listed the facts, the quotes, the anecdotes, and the little-known trivia tidbits in a clear, concise, easy-to-read, easy-to-use manner. Over a year of extensive research went into this project. In that time, several hundred books were studied and literally thousands of newspaper and magazine articles, tracing back over *forty years*, were investigated. *The Unabridged Marilyn* does not attempt to be a biography. That has already been done, and done exceptionally well in some cases (primarily, the works of Maurice Zolotow, Anthony Summers, and Fred Lawrence Guiles). Instead, *The Unabridged Marilyn* has been developed as the ultimate personality encyclopedia. Featured is every known fact about MM, including a complete filmography; discography; index of her fashions; reviews of her films; reviews of the films, books, and plays *about* her; a periodical guide to important articles written about her; 100 significant MM dates; information about her relationships to and with other celebrities; and much, much more.

This is *the* indispensable Marilyn Monroe bible—not just for the legions of fans who remember Marilyn from the fifties; but, also for the new generation of fans who have discovered her after her death, and for the fans who have yet to discover her.

Throughout her career, Marilyn Monroe used to adamantly insist that it was *not* the movie executives or the 20th Century-Fox publicity machinery that had made her a star. Instead, Marilyn said, repeatedly, that it was *the people* who had made her a star. Well, twenty-five years after her death, the people have *kept* her a star, a star more revered than ever before.

This book is for the people.

Randall Riese

# *The Unabridged*
# MARILYN
## *Her Life from A to Z*

If a man has a talent and cannot use it,
he has failed.
If he has a talent and uses only half of it,
he has partly failed.
If he has a talent and learns somehow
to use the whole of it,
he has gloriously succeeded,
and won a satisfaction and
a triumph few men ever know.

Thomas Wolfe

THE SYLVIA BARNHART COLLECTION

Hair ad, Frank and Joseph's Salon, circa 1947.

## THE A-1 LOCK AND SAFE COMPANY

On March 15, 1962, MM hired the A-1 Lock and Safe Company (1962 address: 3114 Wilshire Boulevard) of Santa Monica, California, to change the locks in her Brentwood home. On August 15, 1962, the Marilyn Monroe Estate rehired the same company to change the locks in MM's home—one last time.

## RAYMOND J. ABERNETHY

The head toxicologist of Los Angeles County, who examined Marilyn's blood, kidney, liver, et al., on Monday morning, August 6, 1962. His subsequent "Report of Chemical Analysis" claimed that Marilyn had 4.5 mg percent barbiturates in her bloodstream, although no trace of the drugs was found in any of her organs.

## ABORTIONS

Much has been written about Marilyn's many alleged abortions. A good deal of the speculation claims that MM had more than several of these abortions early in her career, which later resulted in her inability to have children. In his 1973 tome, *Marilyn* (Grosset & Dunlap), Norman Mailer dispensed with the usual subtleties.

> [Milton] Greene claims she once had a fearful abortion that made it impossible for her to be pregnant. . . . What may be the best explanation, from a friend who knew Marilyn well, is that she had had many abortions, perhaps so many as twelve! And in cheap places—for a number of these abortions came in the years she was modeling or a bit player on seven year contracts—thus her gynecological insides were unspeakably scarred.

And there are those who agree with Mailer's contentions. In 1955, Marilyn supposedly confided to both Amy Greene and Henry Rosenfeld that she had just had "another" abortion and that this most recent operation brought the cumulative total to thirteen abortions! This figure seems inflated (though not entirely impossible) when you consider that, in 1955, Marilyn was only twenty-nine years old.

The last of these alleged abortions, so the story goes, took place just two weeks before Marilyn's death. This account contends that MM secretly entered Cedars of Lebanon Hospital on July 20, 1962, and that John F. Kennedy was the "would-be-father." Others who have allegedly impregnated MM (and which resulted in abortions) are Charlie Chaplin, Jr. (Sir Charles's son) and Fred Karger.

**THE ACADEMY OF MOTION PICTURE ARTS AND SCIENCES**

An indispensable library, housing a wealth of information on the movies in general and movie personalities in particular (especially Marilyn!) can be found at the Academy of Motion Picture Arts and Sciences, located in Beverly Hills (address: 8949 Wilshire Boulevard; telephone: 278-4313).

**ACCOUNTANT**

Joseph Carr was the New York accountant who assisted Milton H. Greene, et al., in the formation of Marilyn Monroe Productions circa 1954–55.

**JOHN D. ACKELSON**

John D. Ackelson was one of three writers who scripted the 1980 "In Search Of" television segment about MM entitled "The Death of Marilyn Monroe."

**THE ACTORS LAB**

In the summer of 1947, before she had ever even heard of Natasha Lytess, Marilyn began taking acting lessons at the Actors Lab in Hollywood. Located at 1455 North Laurel, just off Sunset, the lab was operated by Morris Carnovsky and his wife, Phoebe Brand.

Initially, 20th Century-Fox subsidized starlet Marilyn's lessons; however, in August 1947, the studio dropped Marilyn's option. Nonetheless, she continued her lessons with the scraps of money she accumulated by modeling.

Marilyn studied at the Actors Lab for approximately two years, but its impact on her overall training seems comparatively minor.

**THE ACTORS STUDIO**

> "I must say I haven't noticed any improvement, however, since she took those elaborate acting lessons. I have always said she should have gone to a train engineer's school instead to learn something about arriving on schedule."
>
> Billy Wilder on MM's
> acting lessons from
> the Actors Studio, 1962

In the 1950s, the Actors Studio was *the* premier acting school in the United States. Helmed by Lee Strasberg, the studio gained prominence for its revolutionary teaching of "The Method" style of acting and worldwide notoriety for its star-studded list of alumni.

In 1955, Marilyn Monroe vowed to put frivolous Hollywood fluff behind her—she was determined to become a Serious Actress. She severed her ties with 20th Century-Fox, moved to New York, befriended the intellectuals, courted Arthur Miller, formed her own production company, and enrolled in Tuesday and Friday classes at the Actors Studio.

Marilyn brought more fame and publicity to the Actors Studio than any other member—with the possible exception of Marlon Brando—since its inception. Curiously, though, she was never elected an "official" member (in the mid-1950s, over a thousand actors auditioned for membership; approximately ten were chosen annually). She was simply another pupil, albeit a famous pupil, who sat at the back of the classroom and kept to herself.

Marilyn attacked her studies at the Actors Studio with a religious vengeance. It was the same fervor that she had applied to conquering Hollywood just a few years before. And, in retrospect, there is little doubt that she succeeded triumphantly. Forget that 1962 Billy Wilder remark. Forget the often snide remarks made by her many detractors. Forget those "Busty Bernhardt" jokes that were tossed from coast to coast in the mid- to late 1950s. To determine what effect the Actors Studio training had on MM's acting talent, all one has to do is take another look at the films she made after 1955. In *The Prince and the Showgirl* (1957), *Some Like It Hot* (1959), and *The Misfits* (1961), she gave superlative performances. And her work in *Bus Stop* (1956) must stand, admirably, among the finest performances ever given.

In the 1960s, and through the 1980s, the Actors Studio lost much of its original prestige. Actors like Marlon Brando, Montgomery Clift, and James Dean seemed to *belong* to the 1950s. Marilyn, of course, died in 1962. And Lee Strasberg passed away in 1982, which ended an era.

In March 1963, the Actors Studio initiated the Marilyn Monroe Fund and campaigned to solicit one hundred founders to contribute a minimum of $2,500 each. The proceeds were expected to go to a new studio rehearsal hall, in addition to a scholarship fund for aspiring young actors. The Marilyn Monroe Theatre can be seen today at the Strasberg Institute in West Hollywood, California.

**Star Alumni of the Actors Studio**

Marlon Brando
Ellen Burstyn
Montgomery Clift
Robert de Niro
James Dean
Sally Field
Jane Fonda
Julie Harris
Steve McQueen
Paul Newman
Al Pacino*
Geraldine Page
Maureen Stapleton
Rod Steiger

*Pacino was rejected the first time he auditioned for the studio. He was accepted the second time.

**Stars Rejected by the Actors Studio**

Jack Nicholson
George C. Scott
Barbra Streisand

## ACTRESSES WHO HAVE PORTRAYED MM OR MM-BASED CHARACTERS

Perhaps this category should be retitled "Actresses Who Have *Attempted* to Portray MM. . . ." This constantly expanding list includes the following:

| | |
|---|---|
| Carroll Baker | *Come on Strong* (1962) |
| Ellen Barber | *Fame* (1974) |
| Brigitte Bardot | *And God Created Woman* (1956) |
| Belinda Bauer | *Winter Kills* (1979) |
| Hortensia Colorado | *The White Whore and the Bit Player* (1973) |
| Beverly D'Angelo | *Hey, Marilyn!* (1975 radio play) |
| Candy Darling | *The White Whore and the Bit Player* (1973) |
| Judy Davis | *Insignificance* (1982 play) |
| Rebecca de Mornay | *And God Created Woman* (1987 remake) |
| Sondra Dickenson | *Legend* (1974) |
| Patty Duke | *The Goddess* (1958) |
| Faye Dunaway | *After the Fall* (1974 TV movie) |
| Constance Forslund | *Moviola: This Year's Blonde* (1980) |
| Jane Francis | *Public Property* (1979) |
| Catherine Hicks | *Marilyn, The Untold Story* (1980) |
| Joyce Jameson | *Venus at Large* (1962) |
| Linda Kerridge | *Fade to Black* (1980) |
| Shirley Knight | *Kennedy's Children* (1975) |
| Katie Labourdette | various television and stage productions |
| Linda Lavin | *Cop-Out* (1969) |
| Stephanie Lawrence | *Marilyn!* (1983) |
| Barbara Loden | *After the Fall* (1964 play) |
| Julie London | *The Eleventh Hour: Like a Diamond in the Sky* (1963) |
| Kate Mailer | *Strawhead* (1986) |
| Jayne Mansfield | *Will Success Spoil Rock Hunter?* (1957) |
| Amanda Powers | *The Hardest Part of It* (1978) |
| Alyson Reed | *Marilyn, An American Fable* (1983) |
| Misty Rowe | *Goodbye Norma Jean* (1976) |
| Theresa Russell | *Insignificance* (1985 movie) |
| Kim Stanley | *The Goddess* (1958) |
| Connie Stevens | *The Sex Symbol* (1974) |
| Heather Thomas | "Hoover vs. The Kennedys" (1987) |
| Judy West | *Turn On The Heat* (1967) |
| Lenore Zann | *Hey, Marilyn!* (1979 stage play) |

### MM Trivia Quiz #1

During her stardom years, MM considered portraying the life stories of several actresses. Which film project did she *not* express interest in? (Answer on page 577.)

a) The Clara Bow Story
b) The Betty Grable Story
c) The Jean Harlow Story

## HAROLD ADAMSON

In 1952, this American lyricist was partnered with Hoagy Carmichael to write some additional songs for *Gentlemen Prefer Blondes.* They came up with "When Love Goes Wrong" and "Ain't There Anyone Here for Love?" Adamson, whose usual partner was Jimmy McHugh, died in 1980.

THE SABIN GRAY COLLECTION

Constance Forslund, "Moviola" (1980) NBC Television.

THE SABIN GRAY COLLECTION

Jayne Mansfield, played MM-based character, circa 1957.

THE SABIN GRAY COLLECTION

Misty Rowe, *Goodbye, Norma Jean*, 1976, feature film.

THE SABIN GRAY COLLECTION

Catherine Hicks, "Marilyn, The Untold Story," 1980 ABC Television.

THE SABIN GRAY COLLECTION

Linda Kerridge, *Fade to Black*, 1980.

**ADEL PRECISION PRODUCTS**

The plant where Doc Goddard, one of Norma Jeane's foster parents, worked and where Norma Jeane had her first date. In December 1941, the Adel Precision Products Company sponsored a Christmas dance. Doc's wife, and Norma Jeane's guardian, Grace McKee Goddard, asked a neighbor, Mrs. Ethel Dougherty, if her son would escort NJ to the dance. Because he had recently broken up with his girlfriend, young Jim Dougherty agreed. He also arranged a date for Doc's daughter, Beebe, and the four of them double-dated. Norma Jeane was fifteen.

**BUDDY ADLER**

Maurice Adler, more commonly known as "Buddy," is the producer who replaced Darryl Zanuck in 1956 as the chief of production at 20th Century-Fox. In 1955, Adler was intent on lassoing Marilyn Monroe, the studio's wandering money-maker, back to the lot. Subsequently, MM *was* re-signed to Fox (on *her* terms), and Adler produced her in *Bus Stop* (1956). Adler also produced such other notable films as *From Here to Eternity* (1953), *Love Is a Many Splendored Thing* (1955), *Anastasia* (1956), *South Pacific* (1958), and *The Inn of the Sixth Happiness* (1958). He died of a heart attack in 1960.

**ADVERTISEMENTS**

Beginning in the mid-to-late 1940s, and extending until well after her death, Norma Jeane Dougherty/Marilyn Monroe appeared in numerous print advertisements. Her photographs have been used to promote such companies as:

American Airlines
City Club Shoes for Men
Close-Up Perfect Kiss-Tested Lipstick
Hilton Hair Coloring
Jantzen Swimwear
Kyron Way Diet Pills
Louis Creative Hairdressers
Lustre-Creme Shampoo
Max Factor Cosmetics
Maxell Tapes
Monroe Systems For Business
Rayve Shampoo
Roi-Tan Cigars
Tar-Tan Suntan Lotion
True-Glo Make-Up by Westmore Cosmetics

THE T. R. FOGLI COLLECTION

### *AFTER THE FALL*

*After the Fall* was the first play that Arthur Miller wrote following Marilyn's death in 1962. It is presumed that he wrote the play for therapeutic purposes. At any rate, it became one of his most commercially successful plays. However, at the time of its opening, Miller was critically lambasted for his unpopular and thinly disguised characterization of Marilyn as Maggie. Wrote Robert Brustein in *The New Republic*:

> . . . a confessional autobiography of embarrassing explicitness . . . a three and one half hour breach of taste.

Critic Walter Kerr, in *The Herald Tribune,* agreed:

> *After the Fall* resembles a confessional which Arthur Miller enters as a penitent and from which he emerges as the priest. It is a tricky quick change . . . but it constitutes neither an especially attractive nor especially persuasive performance.

The play contains what are assumed to be very personal references to the Miller-Monroe marriage. For example:

> QUENTIN/MILLER: The first honor was that I hadn't tried to go to bed with her! She took it for a tribute to her "value," and I was only afraid! God, the hypocrisy!

And . . .

> QUENTIN/MILLER: I should have agreed she was a joke, a beautiful piece, trying to take herself seriously! Why did I lie to her, play this cheap benefactor?

*After the Fall* was directed by Elia Kazan and produced by Robert Whitehead for the Lincoln Center Repertory Company. It was first performed on January 23, 1964, at the ANTA-Washington Square Theatre in New York City.

After its Broadway debut, *After the Fall* was planned to be an MGM feature film, produced by Carlo Ponti and toplined by Sophia Loren and Paul Newman. When those plans disintegrated, Paramount took over the project in 1967. It was announced that Abby Mann would produce the film. At that time, Mann reported that both Sophia Loren and Brigitte Bardot wanted to play the MM-based role. He also mentioned Candice Bergen, Kim Novak, Julie Christie, Vanessa Redgrave, and (moronically) Elizabeth Taylor as being considered for the part.

However, the Paramount version never materialized either. Perhaps this was because Miller refused to allow Marilyn Monroe's name to be used in the film's publicity. He also retained "final approval" rights over the actress who was selected for the role of Maggie. Apparently, Miller didn't want the actress to bear a resemblance to MM.

At any rate, ten years after its Broadway opening, *After the Fall* was produced as a television movie for NBC. Aired on December 10, 1974, it was produced and directed by Gilbert Cates and was adapted for the medium by Miller himself. It starred Christopher Plummer in the role of Quentin and, Faye Dunaway as Maggie.

### THE AGENTS

In Hollywood, it is a commonly accepted practice for movie stars to change agents as frequently as they change automobiles. When stars get tired or dissatisfied with their agents, they simply exchange them for more prestigious, more powerfully *connected* ones. Marilyn Monroe was no exception. The following is a chronological list of the Hollywood agencies and agents who represented her:

| | |
|---|---|
| The Blue Book Model Agency | Emmeline Snively |
| National Concert Artists Corporation | Helen Ainsworth |
| | Harry Lipton |
| The William Morris Agency | Johnny Hyde |
| Famous Artists Agency | Charles Feldman |
| | Hugh French |
| | Jack Gordeen |
| MCA | George Chasin |

### RAY AGHAYAN

Ray Aghayan was one of the creators and writers of the stage musical, *Movie Star,* which opened in Los Angeles in 1982. The play featured, in a brief role, a Marilyn Monroe-based character.

### LLOYD AHERN

The cinematographer on *Love Nest* (1951) and *O. Henry's Full House* (1952).

### HELEN AINSWORTH

Helen Ainsworth headed the West Coast branch of the National Concert Artists Corporation, Norma Jeane's first theatrical agency. It was Ainsworth, in tandem with Harry Lipton, who got Norma Jeane her initial interview with Ben Lyon at 20th Century-Fox.

### THE AIRLINES

☆ After doing some location shooting for *Niagara* in 1952, MM went to New York City to spend a week with Joe DiMaggio. She then boarded an Eastern Airlines flight to Atlantic City, where she participated in the Miss America parade.

☆ MM returned to Los Angeles from Atlantic City via American Airlines on September 3, 1952.

☆ On January 29, 1954, MM and Joe DiMaggio boarded Pan American's flight #831 en route to Tokyo, with a stop in Hawaii for refueling.

☆ On September 8, 1954, MM flew via TWA to Idlewild Airport in New York to shoot location scenes for *The Seven Year Itch.*

☆ On September 16, 1954, MM returned to Los Angeles from New York on another TWA flight.

☆ Marilyn returned to Hollywood—victoriously—following her sit-down strike against 20th Century-Fox, on February 25, 1956, to begin work on *Bus Stop.* She flew via American Airlines.

☆ In March 1956, the *Bus Stop* company flew to Phoenix, Arizona, to do some location shooting. As was typical for her, Marilyn was late and missed the plane. However, she boarded the next available flight—on TWA.

THE T. R. FOGLI COLLECTION

☆ On June 2, 1956, MM returned to New York via American Airlines after completing work on *Bus Stop*.

☆ In February 1962, MM took Eastern Airlines flight #605 to Florida to be with Joe DiMaggio.

**MM Trivia Quiz #2**

In what film(s) was MM seen aboard an airplane? (Answer on page 577.)

**ZOE AKINS**

Akins wrote the play *The Greeks Had a Word for It,* which became one of the sources for *How to Marry a Millionaire* (1953).

**KATHERINE ALBERT**

Miss Albert cowrote the play *Loco,* which became one of the sources for *How to Marry a Millionaire* (1953).

**LOLA ALBRIGHT**

Director John Huston's first choice to play the part of "Angela Phinlay"—one of the pivotal roles that launched MM—in *The Asphalt Jungle* (1950) was tough-talking, Stanwyck-like Lola Albright. Fortunately for MM, Albright was "not available" and second-choice Monroe made cinema history.

**BILL ALEXANDER**

Alexander was the owner of The Mart, a collector's shop on Santa Monica Boulevard in West Hollywood, circa 1962. On Wednesday, August 1, 1962, Marilyn purchased a coffee table there, along with a wall hanging that depicted Adam and Eve. According to Eunice Murray, who was shopping with MM, Bill Alexander did not at first realize that it was a famous movie star shopping in his store. However, after MM signed a check to pay for her purchased items, Alexander was sufficiently moved to ask Marilyn impulsively for her hand in marriage. Instead of being offended, Marilyn was touched by the offhanded proposal, and she promised Alexander that she would think it over. Three days later, she was dead.

**LOUIS ALHANTI**

Alhanti, owner of the Parisian Flower Shop in 1962, was the man who arranged the floral casket blanket for Marilyn's funeral. He was also the man whom Joe DiMaggio contracted to send red roses to MM's crypt "twice a week, forever."

***ALL ABOUT EVE*** ★★★★

1950 138 minutes Black and White
20th Century-Fox
Directed by: Joseph L. Mankiewicz
Produced by: Darryl Zanuck
Screenplay by: Joseph L. Mankiewicz, adapted from the story and radio play, *The Wisdom of Eve,* by Mary Orr.
Photographed by: Milton Krasner
Cast: Bette Davis, Anne Baxter, George Sanders, Celeste Holm, Gary Merrill, Hugh Marlowe, Thelma Ritter, Marilyn Monroe

One of the finest American movies ever made, *All About Eve* is a witty, venomous, backstage tale about a ruthless stage actress named Eve and her tainted rise to Broadway stardom. The film won numerous 1950 Academy Awards, including the "Best Picture" Oscar.

It was Johnny Hyde who coerced Joseph Mankiewicz into hiring MM for the small showcase role of Miss Caswell, student of "The Copacabana School of Dramatic Art." It was a small part, and she was acting in heavyweight company, but Marilyn stole her few scenes by making every moment count. After seeing the daily rushes, Darryl Zanuck was so impressed by MM that he signed her to another contract.

THE RAY VAN GOEYE COLLECTION

With Bette Davis, Anne Baxter, and George Sanders, in *All About Eve*, 1950.

**RUPERT ALLAN**

In 1952, Allan was the West Coast editor of *LOOK* magazine. It was Allan, in tandem with Fox publicist Roy Craft, who was responsible for MM's first *LOOK* cover. In time, Allan became Marilyn's friend, art counselor, and personal publicist. In 1960, toward the end of *The Misfits* shooting, Allan left his post with MM for "a more lucrative" job offer.

**ANGELA ALLEN**

Director John Huston's longtime script supervisor. During the 1960 shooting of *The Misfits,* AA and MM did *not* become the best of friends. In fact, at that time, Miss Allen was quoted as commenting, "I think she's rather vulgar." However, following the shoot, Miss Allen seemed to soften her attitude toward Marilyn. As quoted in Fred Lawrence Guiles's biography, *Norma Jean: The Life of Marilyn Monroe* (McGraw-Hill, 1969):

> "When I saw her up there, it was nearly incredible. The legend, which I thought a kind of joke in questionable taste, suddenly made sense. I could understand why all the fuss had been made, why the crowds went out of their minds whenever they caught a glimpse of her. It's a kind of magic . . . I never came to really like her, but I realized her worth as an actress, her value to any production."

**JUNE ALLYSON**

Born Ella Geisman in 1917, June Allyson became one of the most popular movie stars of the 1940s. In 1945, she married actor Dick Powell. In 1950, Mr. and Mrs. Powell starred in an MGM film, *Right Cross,* which featured starlet MM in a bit part.

**ROBERT ALTON**
In 1954, producer Sol C. Siegel hired Alton to choreograph *There's No Business Like Show Business.* However, Marilyn objected to Alton, and another choreographer, Jack Cole (MM's favorite), was hired to do her dance numbers.

**AMAGANSETT, LONG ISLAND**
Following the difficult England shooting of *The Prince and the Showgirl* (1957), the still newlywed Millers sought out privacy. They rented a cottage retreat in Amagansett, Long Island, where they stayed off and on from early 1957 until July 1958.

**ROD AMATEAU**
Rod Amateau directed *Venus at Large,* a stage comedy that featured a Marilyn Monroe-based character. The play opened at the Morosco Theater on Broadway in April 1962.

**THE AMBASSADOR HOTEL**
In 1945, Emmeline Snively's Blue Book Model Agency had its offices in the Ambassador Hotel (address: 3400 Wilshire Boulevard) in Los Angeles. It was here that nineteen-year-old Norma Jeane had her first interview with Miss Snively. During 1945–46, NJ made frequent visits here for support, advice, and modeling interviews.

Sadly, and somewhat ironically, the Ambassador was also where Robert Kennedy was assassinated twenty-three years later.

**AMERICAN AIRLINES**
Norma Jeane's first advertising assignment as a model (1945) was to pose with a new Douglas Airliner DC-4 Flagship for American Airlines.

Years later, Marilyn was *still* promoting, albeit unintentionally, American Airlines.

THE SABIN GRAY COLLECTION

### THE AMERICAN FILM INSTITUTE

The AFI paid homage to MM with a tribute at the Kennedy Center in Washington, DC, from September 4 through October 6, 1973. Also being feted at that time were French director René Clair and William Shakespeare.

### *AMERICAN PHOTOGRAPHER*

The July 1984 cover of *American Photographer* magazine featured Richard Avedon's famous photograph of Marilyn posing as actress Lillian Russell. Included in the accompanying photo feature was Marilyn and Avedon's interpretation of Jean Harlow, Theda Bara, Marlene Dietrich, and Clara Bow.

### *THE AMERICAN WEEKLY*

In the 1950s, *The American Weekly* published two important series of articles on MM. The first of these was "The Truth About Me," which began running in the November 16, 1952, issue. The articles were "written" by Marilyn, "as told to" Liza Wilson. The second, more informative series of articles, began running in the September 25, 1955, issue. The articles were entitled "The Mystery of Marilyn Monroe" and were written by Maurice Zolotow. This series became the impetus for Zolotow's excellent biography, *Marilyn Monroe,* which was published in 1960.

### THE ANABAS LOOK BOOK SERIES

In 1985, the England-based Anabas Books published a high-gloss, cover-to-cover magazine about Marilyn Monroe. Written by Roger St. Pierre, the publication was subtitled "Marilyn Monroe: an Independent Story in Words and Pictures." It was twenty-seven pages in length, and was sold only in record stores. It's copy price was $5.95.

### *AND GOD CREATED WOMAN*

This popular 1956 French film originated as an homage to MM by director/writer Roger Vadim and actress Brigitte Bardot. The plot revolved around Bardot, an orphan, who is placed in a foster family. To earn her keep, Bardot waits on tables. Almost desperate for love, she gives her heart to animals, children, and nearly every responsive male. When she is threatened with the prospect of being returned to the orphanage, Bardot marries the nice, young, upright man in the community, Jean-Louis Trintignant. (Sound familiar?)

*And God Created Woman* was considered revolutionary at the time of its release, particularly in its casual treatment of sexual mayhem. And it firmly established Bardot as Europe's MM counterpart. Wrote *The Beverly Hills Citizen* on January 2, 1958:

> Uncle Sam may have his Marilyn Monroe . . . and England may have her Diana Dors, but France does not have to take a back seat to either nation in respect to femme charms. After all, La Republique has Bardot.

*And God Created Woman* was remade in 1987 with Rebecca de Mornay in the Marilyn Monroe–based role. The remake was directed by Roger Vadim, and produced by George Braunstein and Ron Hamady for Vestron Pictures.

**ERNEST ANDERSON**
One of the publicists on *The Misfits* (1961).

**JANICE ANDERSON**
Journalist/author who has specialized in books in the fields of travel and the movies. Anderson wrote the 1983 book *Marilyn Monroe,* which was published by the Hamlyn Publishing Group.

**KEITH ANDES**
Born in 1920, Andes was MM's love interest in *Clash by Night* (1952). He made several films and had a couple of television series, but he never quite found popularity as an actor.

**LUCIEN ANDRIOT**
The French-American cinematographer who shot *Hometown Story* (1951).

**ANGELUS TEMPLE**
In 1926, Della Monroe Grainger insisted that her grandchild, Norma Jeane Baker, be baptized at the Foursquare Gospel Church in Sister Aimee Semple McPherson's Angelus Temple, which was located in Los Angeles.

**ANN-MARGRET**
Swedish-born (1941) Ann-Margret Olsson was the heir apparent to the Monroe throne in the early 1960s. And while no one ever replaced Marilyn, Ann-Margret certainly did give a new, raw vitality to the term *sex symbol.*

It was Ann-Margret who came closest to capturing that MM mixture of glamour and vulnerability in the early 1970s.

THE AUTHOR'S COLLECTION

Interestingly, there have been several parallels in the careers of MM and A-M. Most obviously, of course, they were both stereotyped sex symbols, who fought to change their images and become accepted as Serious Actresses. With two Oscar and three Emmy nominations to her credit, A-M has succeeded impressively; Marilyn, on the other hand, did not—at least not in her lifetime.

Following Marilyn's death, and her own subsequent rise, Ann-Margret requested the services of Evelyn Moriarty, MM's former stand-in. At various times, A-M also employed the services of two of MM's hairstylists, George Masters and Sidney Guilaroff.

The MM/A-M Connection was particularly strong in the early 1970s. Ann-Margret paid tribute to MM in her formidable nightclub act with a song called "Does Anybody Here Love Me?" She also paid tribute to Marilyn by turning down offers to star in *After the Fall* (which Faye Dunaway later accepted) and *The Sex Symbol* (which Connie Stevens later *attempted*). She also declined an opportunity to star on Broadway in a musical version of *Some Like It Hot.*

> She was a very healthy girl when she came on the scene, physically and mentally. Years went by, people picked on her. She was terribly abused, for no reason. She became sick—and posthumously they gave her acclaim.
>
> Ann-Margret on Marilyn Monroe,
> *LIFE,* 8/71

It's obvious today that *no one* will ever replace Marilyn Monroe. But, of all the contenders, would-be-contenders, blondes and bleached blondes, it was the redheaded Ann-Margret Olsson who possessed the prerequisite beauty, talent, vulnerability, and uncommon, indescribable, glowing flirtation with the camera. Among A-M's films: *State Fair* (1962), *Bye Bye Birdie* (1963), *Viva Las Vegas* (1964), *Carnal Knowledge* (1971), *Tommy* (1975), and, on television, *Who Will Love My Children?* (1983) and *A Streetcar Named Desire* (1984).

### *ANNA CHRISTIE*

Eugene O'Neill play, famous in the cinematic annals as the film (1930) in which Greta Garbo talked for the first time.

In February 1956, Marilyn Monroe performed the opening barroom scene before the members of the Actors Studio. Maureen Stapleton played opposite her. The scene lasted twenty minutes. The "reviews" ranged from pleasantly surprised to overwhelmingly ecstatic.

### BART ANTINORA

Physical Education instructor from Northridge, California. On May 21, 1954, at the corner of Sunset Boulevard and Beverly Drive in Beverly Hills, Marilyn accidentally rammed her 1952 Cadillac convertible into the rear end of Antinora's MG sports car. Antinora, represented by attorney Fred J. Martino, sued MM and Joe DiMaggio (who was a passenger in the car) for $3,000 each. The case was eventually settled out of court in August 1955 for a "mere" $500.

**RAY ANTHONY**

In 1952, Ray Anthony recorded a song on Capitol Records about Marilyn Monroe entitled "Marilyn." The song was written by Ervin Drake and Jimmy Shirl, and was presented to MM by Ray Anthony and Mickey Rooney at Anthony's Hollywood home.

THE RAY VAN GOEYE COLLECTION

With Ray Anthony, 1952.

***THE APARTMENT***

Excellent, Oscar-winning Billy Wilder film that contains a brief bit featuring a blonde, breathy MM impersonator. In one scene, set at a bar, Ray Walston says to Jack Lemmon: "Listen, kid, I can't pass this up; she looks like Marilyn Monroe!"

***APPLES, KNOCKERS AND COKES***

Aka *Apples, Knockers and the Coke Bottle,* this is an X-rated film that many people believed was one of Marilyn Monroe's earliest movie vehicles. However, in 1982, *Playboy* magazine dispelled the speculation by revealing that the "actress" in *Apples* was none other than its 1954 playmate, Arlene Hunter.

**ARBOL STREET**
On October 20, 1934, Gladys Baker purchased a house on Arbol Street, off of Highland Avenue in Hollywood, for her daughter, Norma Jeane, and her to share. However, within a few months, Gladys suffered a nervous breakdown and was institutionalized. Consequently, the house on Arbol Street was sold.

**ARCHWOOD STREET**
Following her stay at the Los Angeles Orphans Home Society, Norma Jeane Baker lived, for a period, with the Doc and Grace Goddard family at 14743 Archwood Street in Van Nuys, California. Several years later, Norma Jeane and her husband, Jim Dougherty, moved into the Dougherty family home at 14747 Archwood Street, also in Van Nuys.

**ELIZABETH ARDEN**
In 1962, beauticians from the Elizabeth Arden Salon in Beverly Hills paid a visit to MM's Brentwood home and spent hours indulging her with a complete head-to-toe "treatment."

**EVE ARDEN**
Wisecracking, likable comedy actress who spent a whole film career playing those "supporting sister" roles in a slew of movie hits. Born Eunice Quedens in 1912, Miss Arden has appeared in such pictures as *Stage Door* (1937), *Cover Girl* (1944), *Mildred Pierce* (1945), *Anatomy of a Murder* (1959), *The Dark at the Top of the Stairs* (1960), and *Grease* (1978). She garnered additional fame for her television programs, "Our Miss Brooks" (1952–56) and "The Mothers-in-Law" (1967–68).

In 1952, Eve Arden costarred in the Fox comedy, *We're Not Married,* which also featured rising star, Marilyn Monroe.

**HARRY ARENDS**
Producer of the 1988 television documentary, "Remembering Marilyn."

**ROONE ARLEDGE**
ABC news chief who caused controversy by "killing" the October 1985 "20/20" segment that examined the confusing circumstances surrounding Marilyn's death. The segment also investigated, and reportedly confirmed, Marilyn's intimate relationships with both John and Robert Kennedy. Arledge, in addition to being ABC news chief, is also, it seems, a close, longtime friend of Ethel Kennedy.

**CHARLOTTE ARMSTRONG**
Writer of the *Good Housekeeping* suspense serial "Mischief," that *Don't Bother to Knock* (1952) was based on.

**LOUIS ARMSTRONG**
When the London press asked MM what kind of music she liked, she replied: "I like, well, jazz, like Louis Armstrong."

**ARMY AIR CORPS**

In 1945, the Army Air Corps sent photographer David Conover to the Radio Plane Company to shoot a pictorial of women working to benefit the war movement. Conover, of course, selected Radio Plane employee Norma Jeane Dougherty as his model. The photographs subsequently appeared in *Yank* magazine. It was Norma Jeane's first professional photo session.

**ALAN ARNOLD**

Alan Arnold was an English publicist who was assigned—by orders from Buckingham Palace—to arrange a meeting between the royal family and Marilyn Monroe during the latter's 1956 "business trip" to England. As a matter of procedure, Arnold put in the royal request to Sir Laurence Olivier, who was the director of *The Prince and the Showgirl*. Reportedly, Olivier, who was not getting along with Marilyn, promptly disregarded the request. Nevertheless, a meeting was eventually arranged, and the introduction of the two queens took place in late October 1956. (*See* ROYAL COMMAND PERFORMANCE.)

**DOROTHY ARNOLD**

Dorothy Arnoldine Olson was born on November 21, 1917, in Duluth, Minnesota. An actress by profession, Dorothy Arnold met Joe DiMaggio on the set of *Manhattan Merry-Go-Round* (1937) a movie in which both she and DiMaggio had bit parts. They were married in 1939, and had one child, Joe DiMaggio, Jr. In 1944, Dorothy DiMaggio filed for divorce from her famous husband who, ten years later, would marry Marilyn Monroe. Miss Arnold died in Palm Springs, California, in 1984.

**EVE ARNOLD**

In 1960, photographer Eve Arnold was hired by the Magnum Agency to shoot behind-the-scenes photos of *The Misfits* shooting. Later, on October 29, 1960, Arnold obtained a private session with Marilyn, which took place at the Paramount photo studio in Hollywood. This session included some seminude shots of MM, as did a follow-up session in mid-1961.

In her 1977 book, *The Unretouched Woman*, which included a chapter on MM, Arnold said: "She [Marilyn] was the only woman I ever worked with who photographed ten pounds lighter than she was." In 1987 Alfred A. Knopf published Arnold's book of photographs, *Marilyn Monroe: An Appreciation*.

**MAX ARNOW**

Arnow was the head of talent at Columbia Pictures in 1948, when Marilyn was signed to a six-month contract by that studio. Reportedly, Arnow saw the star potential in MM and gave her a screen test. For whatever reason, studio chief Harry Cohn disregarded the test, and Marilyn's option was dropped after the six-month period. Significantly, it was Max Arnow, in tandem with *Ladies of the Chorus* (1948) producer Harry Romm, who was responsible for teaming Marilyn with Columbia's acting coach at the time, Natasha Lytess.

## ART: MARILYN'S COLLECTION

Marilyn Monroe was an aspiring art collector and displayed a developing appreciation of art. For example:

☆ In 1951, MM took an art appreciation class at UCLA.

☆ In 1952, she had reproductions of Dürer, Fra Angelico, and da Vinci in her Hollywood apartment.

☆ In July 1955, MM purchased a bust of Queen Nefertiti for her Waldorf-Astoria apartment in New York City.

☆ In October 1955, MM told Earl Wilson that she was a fan of Goya.

☆ Also in 1955, MM told other reporters that her favorite artists were Goya, Picasso, and El Greco.

☆ In late 1955, MM attended a Rodin exhibition at the Metropolitan Museum of Art. Reportedly, MM fell in love with two pieces, *Pygmalion and Galatea* and *The Hand of God.*

☆ At her East 57th Street apartment in New York City, MM had a Toulouse-Lautrec in her reception room.

☆ Also at her East 57th Street apartment, Marilyn had a large, nude, black metal statue by artist William Zorach.

☆ The year of her death, MM purchased three paintings from the Byrna Art Gallery in Mexico City for her Spanish-flavored Brentwood home.

☆ A couple of months before her death, MM bought a Rodin statue of a man and woman locked in passionate embrace. MM displayed this work in the living room of her Brentwood Home.

## ARTISTS WHO HAVE INTERPRETED MM OR HER IMAGE

There are sure to be other works of art that we are not familiar with, but here is a selective, alphabetized list.

Martin Alton: Color graphic, head and chest of a typical MM pose
George Bevan: Black-and-white graphic
Mick Brownfield: Color collage, using photos and headlines
Mori Bund: *BonBon Marilyn*, color graphic
Dennis Carmichael: *Greetings from Hollywood*, color graphic
Tim Clark: *The Misfits*, cartoon graphic of MM and Gable
Lance Collins: Charcoal and/or pencil sketching
Oscar da Costa: Cartoon graphic, featuring MM in a bubblebath
William de Kooning: *Marilyn Monroe*, color abstract, 1954
Monte Dolack: Cartoonlike graphic, featuring MM in *The Misfits*
Rosalyn Drexler: *Marilyn Pursued by Death*, black-and-white graphic, featuring MM pursued by a man in sunglasses
Michael Faure: *Marilyn Monroe—Vague à lamé*, Color graphic, featuring MM from 1962 *Vogue* layout
*Marilyn Monroe—Sensitive*, color graphic, featuring MM in a ballet dress
*Marilyn Monroe—Sortilège*, color graphic, featuring MM in *Asphalt Jungle*
*Marilyn Monroe—Star*, color graphic, featuring MM in a typical glamour pose
*Marilyn Monroe—Reflection*, color graphic, featuring MM in *Some Like It Hot*
Stanislaw Fernandes: Color graphic, with MM as a robot striking her nude calendar pose, 1980
Leon Garcia: Color graphic, featuring MM in gold lame dresś

COURTESY OF DEMETRIE KABBAZ

Painting, Demetrie Kabbaz, 1986.

Pepe Gonzalez: Color graphic, from Bert Stern's *The Last Sitting*, 1980
Charcoal and/or pencil sketching, from Bert Stern's *The Last Sitting*, 1980
Charcoal and/or pencil sketching collage, featuring MM in various poses, 1979
Mark Harfield: *One in Every Crowd*, color graphic, featuring MM in a crowd of choir boys
Philip Hays: *Marilyn at 50*, color graphic
Paul Huf: *Marilyn on Sunset Boulevard*, color graphic
Jan Hunt: *Marilyn as Cherie*, color graphic, featuring MM in *Bus Stop*
Claude Jackson: *The Red Kimono* color graphic, featuring MM in a red kimono, 1975
Just Janice: Color patchwork wall hanging, featuring MM in a leopard outfit
Demetrie Kabbaz: various larger-than-life-size "cut-outs"
Carl Kain: Black-and-white graphic, highlighted with Color Pastels, featuring MM looking over one shoulder
Dennis Magdich: Color graphic, featuring MM's face at night and day, 1979
Leroy Marsh: Charcoal and/or pencil sketching, from Milton Greene's *Ballet Dress* series
Brad Marshall: *Life, Liberty and Pursuit . . .* , color graphic, featuring MM as the Statue of Liberty
William Moore: various pencil illustrations
Earl Moran: Numerous color illustrations, featuring MM 1946–1950
Olivia: Color graphic, featuring MM in fishnet stockings and leopard outfit, 1983
Color graphic, MM as Santa, 1979
David Oxtoby: Charcoal and/or pencil sketching, featuring MM and Elton John
Dilys Powell: *Punch at the Cinema*, color graphic
Clothilde Nadel: color graphic, featuring MM in *The Seven Year Itch*, 1981

Illustration, William Moore, 1983.

COURTESY OF WILLIAM MOORE

Kenton R. Nelson: color graphic, head and chest of MM
David Resson: color graphic featuring MM in *The Seven Year Itch* skirt scene
Robert Sherriffs: Black-and-white cartoon graphic, featuring MM as a snake from *Niagara*, 1953
Miki Slingsby: Charcoal and/or pencil sketching, featuring MM and Elton John
Nigel Splain: Color graphic, head and shoulders of a typical MM pose
Daniel Tarantola: Semiabstract painting, featuring MM applying makeup
Color painting, featuring MM in a low-cut red gown
Roger Taylor: Charcoal and/or pencil sketching, featuring MM from 1962 *Vogue* layout
Tom T. Tomita: Color graphic: featuring MM in a black cardigan sweater
Vincent Topaio: Color graphic, featuring MM wrapped in white sheet
Vartan: *Look of Beauty*, color graphic
Ben Verkaaik: Black-and-white graphic, featuring MM in a typical MM pose
Mary Vickers: various oil paintings
Jean-Paul Vroom: Color graphic, featuring MM with a big nose
David Ward: Charcoal and/or pencil sketching, featuring MM from April 1952 *LIFE* cover
Andy Warhol: *Marilyn*, color silk screen graphic, featuring eight different-colored MMs
Martin Weld: *Over 21*, pastel sketching, featuring MM painting her nails and carrying packages
Jon Whitcomb: Color graphic, featuring MM in floppy hat with red flowers
David Willardson: Color graphic, featuring MM in a typical MM pose
Wizard and Genius: *Where have all the good times gone?* color graphic, featuring MM and Joe DiMaggio, 1982.

Illustration, Romeo Lopez, 1980.

COURTESY OF ROMEO LOPEZ

Corey Wolfe: *The Legend*, color graphic, featuring MM in *Niagara*, 1983
Color graphic, featuring MM as half leopard and half MM, 1983
Punz Wolfe: Color graphic, featuring MM holding a birthday cake
Kathy Wyatt: Color graphic, featuring MM getting into bubblebath

### *ART AND MRS. BOTTLE*

A play produced by Van Nuys High School that Norma Jeane Baker auditioned for—and didn't get. Years later, Marilyn told biographer Maurice Zolotow, "I wanted to be in it because a boy I had a crush on, Warren Peek, was playing the lead."

### *AS YOUNG AS YOU FEEL* ★★½

1951 77 minutes Black and White
20th Century-Fox
Directed by: Harmon Jones
Produced by: Lamar Trotti
Screenplay by: Lamar Trotti, from a Story by Paddy Chayefsky
Photographed by: Joe MacDonald
Cast: Monty Woolley, Constance Bennett, Thelma Ritter, David Wayne, Jean Peters, Marilyn Monroe, Albert Dekker

Comedy about an aging employee (Woolley), who, due to company policy, is forced to resign. However, instead of resigning, he impersonates the company president and saves the firm from bankruptcy.

This was MM's first film at Fox, under the new contract that Johnny Hyde had negotiated for her before his death. In it, Marilyn played Albert Dekker's secretary. This film is notable because, for the first time, shrewd motion picture exhibitors began to place the name Marilyn Monroe on their theatre marquees. The film was also a first directorial effort by Harmon Jones, and the first Paddy Chayefsky story to reach the screen.

### *THE ASPHALT JUNGLE* ★★★★

1950 112 minutes Black and White
MGM
Directed by: John Huston
Produced by: Arthur Hornblow, Jr.
Screenplay by: Ben Maddow, John Huston, from the novel by W. R. Burnett
Photographed by: Harold Rosson
Cast: Sterling Hayden, Sam Jaffe, Louis Calhern, Jean Hagen, Marilyn Monroe, James Whitmore

Excellent, revolutionary film about an elderly criminal, recently released from prison, who assembles a gang and stages one last robbery.

Pivotal film in the career of Marilyn Monroe, because it was the first time that she was noticed by the public. It was also the first time that Hollywood began to stand up and take notice of MM—following the release of *The Asphalt Jungle,* Hollywood producers began *asking* for Marilyn's services. In the film, MM played Louis Calhern's "niece" (the word *mistress* couldn't be said on the screen in 1950). She was blonde, beautiful, and blossoming with youth. Marilyn's performance elicited all the appropriate wolf whistles, and everybody began to ask, "Who's the blonde?" Her acting wasn't bad, either. Marilyn's harshest critic—herself—would later say that *The Asphalt Jungle* contained her finest dramatic performance.

**MM Trivia Quiz #3**

Where did MM want to go for a vacation in *The Asphalt Jungle*? (Answer on page 577.)

### ASTROLOGY

Marilyn's feelings about astrology were mixed, which seems only appropriate—she was a Gemini. Said MM:

> "I was born under the sign of Gemini. That stands for the intellect."
>
> *LIFE,* 4/7/52

**Famous Geminis**

Joan Collins
Douglas Fairbanks
Ralph Waldo Emerson
Norma Talmadge
Walt Whitman
Peggy Lee
George Bernard Shaw
Hubert Humphrey
Henry Kissinger
John Wayne
Bob Hope
John F. Kennedy
Clint Eastwood
Joe Namath
Brooke Shields
Paul McCartney
Dean Martin
Cole Porter
Jane Russell
Judy Garland

**ATTORNEYS**

As seems common for many public figures, Marilyn Monroe was frequently in need of an attorney. Over the years, Marilyn hired a variety of attorneys, for various reasons, both in Los Angeles and in New York. She also hired not one but two lawyers to handle her 1961 Mexican divorce from Arthur Miller. The following is a chronological list of Marilyn Monroe's attorneys, and, the approximate year that they were hired.

| | | |
|---|---|---|
| Lloyd Wright | General | 1954 |
| W. Claude Fields, Jr. | Traffic Violation | 1954 |
| Jerry Giesler | Divorce | 1954 |
| Raymond G. Stanbury | Car Accident | 1955 |
| Frank Delaney | Corporate | 1955 |
| Irving Stein | | |
| Arturo Sosa Augilar | Divorce | 1961 |
| Aureliano Gonzalez | | |
| Aaron Frosch | General | 1961 |
| Elliot Lefkowitz | | |
| Milton "Mickey" Rudin | | |
| Martin Gang | General | 1962 |
| Roger Richman | Licensing Agent | 1982 |

**ARTURO SOSA AUGILAR**

One of the Mexican attorneys who handled MM's divorce from Arthur Miller on January 20, 1961, in Juarez, Mexico.

**"AUNTS"**

Marilyn didn't have a real mother to raise her, but she did have a succession of women who "mothered" her. Among those in this group were three "aunts" who functioned as guardians. They were:

1. "Aunt" Ida Bolender
2. "Aunt" Grace McKee Goddard
3. "Aunt" Ana Lower

**GEORGES AURIC**

French composer who presented Marilyn with the coveted Crystal Star award, given by the French film industry, as "Best Foreign Actress" of 1958.

**AUSTRALIA**

In 1955, during her hiatus from filmmaking, Marilyn was offered $200,000 to do a twenty-five-day tour of Australia, in which she was to headline her own stage show. The offer was made by Lee Gordon and was reported in the August 17, 1955, issue of *Variety.* MM *did not* accept the generous offer, despite the fact that it was a whopping $190,000 more than she would have earned at 20th Century-Fox during the same twenty-five-day period.

**AUTOPSY**

The autopsy of Marilyn Monroe was conducted at 10:30 A.M. on August 5, 1962. It took place on Table #1 in the autopsy room of the Hall of Justice.

Controversial coroner Thomas Noguchi conducted the operation. He was assisted by Eddy Day. Noguchi's findings were as follows.

> ***External examination:*** The unembalmed body is that of a 36-year-old well-developed, well-nourished Caucasian female weighing 117 pounds and measuring 65½ inches in length. The scalp is covered with bleached blond hair. The eyes are blue. The fixed lividity is noted in the face, neck, chest, upper portions of arms and the right side of the abdomen. The faint lividity which disappears upon pressure is noted in the back and posterior aspect of the arms and legs. A slight ecchymotic area is noted in the left hip and left side of lower back. The breast shows no significant lesion. There is a horizontal 3-inch long surgical scar in the right upper quadrant of the abdomen. A suprapubic surgical scar measuring 5 inches in length is noted.
>
> The conjunctivae are markedly congested; however, no ecchymosis or petechiae are noted. The nose shows no evidence of fracture. The external auditory canals are not remarkable. No evidence of trauma is noted in the scalp, forehead, cheeks, lips or chin. The neck shows no evidence of trauma. Examination of the hands and nails shows no defects. The lower extremities show no evidence of trauma.
>
> ***Body cavity:*** The usual Y-shaped incision is made to open the thoracic and abdominal cavities. The pleural and abdominal cavities contain no excess of fluid or blood. The mediastinum shows no shifting or widening. The diaphragm is within normal limits. The lower edge of the liver is within the costal margin. The organs are in normal position and relationship.
>
> ***Cardiovascular system:*** The heart weighs 300 grams. The pericardial cavity contains no excess of fluid. The epicardium and pericardium are smooth and glistening. The left ventricular wall measures 1.1 cm. and the right 0.2 cm. The papillary muscles are not hypertrophic. The chordae tendineae are not thickened or shortened. The valves have the usual number of leaflets which are thin and pliable. The tricuspid valve measures 10 cm., the pulmonary valve 6.5 cm., mitral valve 9.5 cm. and aortic valve 7 cm. in circumference. There is no septal defect. The foramen ovale is closed.
>
> The coronary arteries arise from their usual location and are distributed in normal fashion. Multiple sections of the anterior descending branch of the left coronary artery with a 5 mm. interval demonstrate a patent lumen throughout. The circumflex branch and the right coronary artery also demonstrate a patent lumen. The pulmonary artery contains no thrombus.
>
> The aorta has a bright yellow smooth intima.
>
> ***Respiratory system:*** The right lung weighs 465 grams and the left 420 grams. Both lungs are moderately congested with some edema. The surface is dark and red with mottling. The posterior portion of the lungs show severe congestion. The tracheobronchial tree contains no aspirated material or blood. Multiple sections of the lungs show congestion and edematous fluid exuding from the cut surface. No consolidation or suppuration is noted. The mucosa of the larynx is grayish white.
>
> ***Liver and biliary system:*** The liver weighs 1890 grams. The surface is dark brown and smooth. There are marked adhesions through the

STATE FILE NUMBER 62-096657 CERTIFICATE OF DEATH
STATE OF CALIFORNIA DEPARTMENT OF PUBLIC HEALTH
LOCAL REGISTRATION DISTRICT AND CERTIFICATE NUMBER 7053 17716

DECEDENT PERSONAL DATA
1a. NAME OF DECEASED—FIRST NAME: Marilyn
1c. LAST NAME: Monroe
2a. DATE OF DEATH: August 5, 1962
2b. HOUR: 3:40 a.
3. SEX: Female
4. COLOR OR RACE: Cauc.
5. BIRTHPLACE: Los Angeles, Calif.
6. DATE OF BIRTH: June 1, 1926
7. AGE: 36
8. NAME AND BIRTHPLACE OF FATHER: unk unk.
9. MAIDEN NAME AND BIRTHPLACE OF MOTHER: Gladys Pearl Baker - Mexico
10. CITIZEN OF WHAT COUNTRY: United States
11. SOCIAL SECURITY NUMBER: 563-32-0764
12. LAST OCCUPATION: Actress
13. 20
14. NAME OF LAST EMPLOYING COMPANY OR FIRM: 20th Century-fox
15. KIND OF INDUSTRY OR BUSINESS: Motion Pictures
16. none
17. Divorced
18a. NAME OF PRESENT SPOUSE
18b. PRESENT OR LAST OCCUPATION OF SPOUSE

PLACE OF DEATH
19a. PLACE OF DEATH—NAME OF HOSPITAL
19b. STREET ADDRESS: 12305 -5th Helena Drive
19c. CITY OR TOWN: Los Angeles
19d. COUNTY: Los Angeles
19e. LENGTH OF STAY IN COUNTY OF DEATH: 36
19f. LENGTH OF STAY IN CALIFORNIA: 36

LAST USUAL RESIDENCE
20a. LAST USUAL RESIDENCE: 12305 -5th Helena Drive
20b. x
20c. CITY OR TOWN: Los Angeles
20d. COUNTY: Los Angeles
20e. STATE: Calif.
21a. NAME OF INFORMANT: Mrs. Inez C. Melson
21b. ADDRESS OF INFORMANT: 9110 Sunset Blvd.

PHYSICIAN'S OR CORONER'S CERTIFICATION
22a. PHYSICIAN
22b. CORONER: autopsy
22c. PHYSICIAN OR CORONER SIGNATURE: Theo J. Curphey M.D. Coroner, By Lionel Grandison, Deputy
22d. ADDRESS: HALL OF JUSTICE LOS ANGELES
22e. DATE SIGNED: 8-28-62

FUNERAL DIRECTOR AND LOCAL REGISTRAR
23. Entombment
24. DATE: Aug. 8, 1962
25. NAME OF CEMETERY OR CREMATORY: Westwood Memorial Park
26. EMBALMER: Charles Waldron
27. NAME OF FUNERAL DIRECTOR: Westwood Village Mortuary
28. SEP 1 2 1962
29. LOCAL REGISTRAR: George M. Uhl, M.D.

CAUSE OF DEATH
30. CAUSE OF DEATH PART I. DEATH WAS CAUSED BY IMMEDIATE CAUSE (A): ACUTE BARBITURATE POISONING
DUE TO (B): INGESTION OF OVERDOSE
APPROXIMATE INTERVAL BETWEEN ONSET AND DEATH

OPERATION AND AUTOPSY
31. OPERATION
32. DATE OF OPERATION
33. AUTOPSY

INJURY INFORMATION
34a. SPECIFY ACCIDENT, SUICIDE OR HOMICIDE: Probable Suicide
34b. DESCRIBE HOW INJURY OCCURRED: As Above
34c. TIME OF INJURY: PRIOR TO 3:40 a. 8-5-62
34d. INJURY OCCURRED
34e. PLACE OF INJURY: Home
34f. CITY, TOWN OR LOCATION: Los Angeles L.A. Calif.

omentum and abdominal wall in the lower portion of the liver as the gallbladder has been removed. The common duct is widely patent. No calculus or obstructive material is found. Multiple sections of the liver show slight accentuation of the lobular pattern; however, no hemorrhage or tumor is found.

***Hemic and lymphatic system:*** The spleen weighs 190 grams. The surface is dark red and smooth. Section shows dark red homogeneous firm cut surface. The Malpighian bodies are not clearly identified. There is no evidence of lymphadenopathy. The bone marrow is dark red in color.

***Endocrine system:*** The adrenal glands have the usual architectural cortex and medulla. The thyroid glands are of normal size, color and consistency.

***Urinary system:*** The kidneys together weigh 350 grams. Their capsules can be stripped without difficulty. Dissection shows a moderately congested parenchyma. The cortical surface is smooth. The pelves and ureters are not dilated or stenosed. The urinary bladder contains approximately 150 cc. of clear straw-colored fluid. The mucosa is not altered.

***Genital system:*** The external genitalia shows no gross abnormality. Distribution of the pubic hair is of female pattern. The uterus is of the usual size. Multiple sections of the uterus show the usual thickness of the uterine wall without tumor nodules. The endometrium is grayish yellow, measuring up to 0.2 cm in

thickness. No polyp or tumor is found. The cervix is clear, showing no nabothian cysts. The tubes are intact. The right ovary demonstrates recent corpus luteum haemorrhagicum. The left ovary shows corpora lutea and albicantia. A vaginal smear is taken.
***Digestive system:*** The esophagus has a longitudinal folding mucosa. The stomach is almost completely empty. The contents is brownish mucoid fluid. The volume is estimated to be no more than 20 cc. No residue of the pills is noted. A smear made from the gastric contents and examined under the polarized microscope shows no refractile crystals. The mucosa shows marked congestion and submucosal petechial hemorrhage diffusely. The duodenum shows no ulcer. The contents of the duodenum is also examined under polarized microscope and shows no refractile crystals. The remainder of the small intestine shows no gross abnormality. The appendix is absent. The colon shows marked congestion and purplish discoloration.

The pancreas has a tan lobular architecture. Multiple sections shows a patent duct.
***Skeletomuscular system:*** The clavicle, ribs, vertebrae and pelvic bones show no fracture lines. All bones of the extremities are examined by palpation showing no evidence of fracture.
***Head and central nervous system:*** The brain weighs 1440 grams. Upon reflection of the scalp there is no evidence of contusion or hemorrhage. The temporal muscles are intact. Upon removal of the dura mater the cerebrospinal fluid is clear. The superficial vessels are slightly congested. The convolutions of the brain are not flattened. The contour of the brain is not distorted. No blood is found in the epidural, subdural or subarachnoid spaces. Multiple sections of the brain show the usual symmetrical ventricles and basal ganglia. Examination of the cerebellum and brain stem shows no gross abnormality. Following removal of the dura mater from the base of the skull and calvarium no skull fracture is demonstrated.

Liver temperature taken at 10:30 A.M. registered 89° F.
***Specimen:*** Unembalmed blood is taken for alcohol and barbiturate examination. Liver, kidney, stomach and contents, urine and intestine are saved for further toxicological study. A vaginal smear is made.

T. NOGUCHI, M.D.
DEPUTY MEDICAL EXAMINER
8-13-62

**RICHARD AVEDON**

Noted photographer who shot the now famous series of Marilyn posing as Lillian Russell, Jean Harlow, Theda Bara, Marlene Dietrich, and Clara Bow. The session took place in New York City in 1958, and the photos originally were published in *LIFE* magazine, December 22, 1958. Said Avedon: "She gave more to the still camera than any actress—any woman—I've ever photographed."

**AVON STREET**

According to Robert Slatzer, Marilyn Monroe lived at 131 South Avon Street in Burbank, California, in 1947.

## THE AWARDS
### For MM

☆ While in school, Norma Jeane was awarded a fountain pen for an essay she wrote, entitled "Dog, Man's Best Friend."

☆ While working at the Radio Plane Company in the mid-1940s, Norma Jeane Dougherty was awarded an "E" Certificate, for excellence on the job.

☆ "Miss Press Club" of 1948 by The Los Angeles Press Club

☆ "Miss Cheesecake of the Year," 1951, *Stars and Stripes*

☆ "The Present All GIs Would Like To Find in Their Christmas Stocking," 1951

☆ "The Best Young Box Office Personality," the Henrietta Awards, 1951

☆ "The Girl Most Likely to Thaw Alaska," the Soldiers in the Aleutians

☆ "The Girl Most Wanted to Examine," The 7th Division Medical Corps

☆ "The Girl They Would Most Like to Intercept," the All Weather Fighter Squadron Three of San Diego

Crystal Award for *The Prince and the Showgirl*, Best Actress, 1959.

THE RAY VAN GOEYE COLLECTION

☆ "Cheesecake Queen of 1952," *Stars and Stripes*

☆ "Most Promising Female Newcomer" of 1952 *Look* Magazine Achievement Awards

☆ "The Most Advertised Girl in the World," the Advertising Association of the West, February, 1953

☆ "Fastest Rising Star of 1952," *Photoplay* magazine awards, March 9, 1953

☆ "Best Young Box Office Personality," *Redbook* magazine awards, March 1953

☆ "The Best Friend a Diamond Ever Had," the Jewelry Academy, July 1953

☆ "World Film Favorite," the Golden Globe Awards, 1953

☆ "Best Actress," *Photoplay* magazine awards, March 1954, for *Gentlemen Prefer Blondes* and *How to Marry a Millionaire*

☆ "The Thank-God Award: To Marilyn Monroe, who in a sweeping public service has made no movies this year," the *Harvard Lampoon*, 1958

☆ "Best Foreign Actress of 1958," the David di Donatello Prize (the Italian Oscar), 1959, for *The Prince and the Showgirl*
☆ "Best Foreign Actress," the Crystal Star Award (the French Oscar), March 1959, for *The Prince and the Showgirl*
☆ "Best Actress in a Comedy," 1959, the Golden Globe Awards, March 8, 1960, for *Some Like It Hot*
☆ "World Film Favorite," 1961, the Golden Globe Awards, March 1962

**For the Movies**
*All About Eve, 1950*
☆ "Best Picture," the Academy Awards
☆ "Best Picture," the British Academy Awards
☆ "Best Picture," the New York Film Critics
☆ "Second Best Picture," the National Board of Review
☆ "Ninth Best Picture," *The New York Times*
☆ "Tenth Best Picture," *Time* magazine

*The Asphalt Jungle*, 1950
☆ "Third Best Picture," the National Board of Review
☆ "Fourth Best Picture," *Time* magazine

*Gentlemen Prefer Blondes*, 1953
☆ "One of the Ten Worst Films of the Year," the *Harvard Lampoon*

*How to Marry a Millionaire*, 1953
☆ "One of the Ten Worst Films of the Year," the *Harvard Lampoon*

*There's No Business Like Show Business*, 1954
☆ "One of the Ten Worst Films of the Year," the *Harvard Lampoon*

*Bus Stop*, 1956
☆ "Fourth Best Picture," *The New York Times*
☆ "Tenth Best Picture," the National Board of Review

*Some Like It Hot*, 1959
☆ "Best Picture," *Time* magazine
☆ "Seventh Best Picture," the National Board of Review

**GEORGE AXELROD**
Very successful American comedy writer who wrote the screenplay for *The Seven Year Itch* (1955), which was based on his hit Broadway play. Axelrod also wrote the screen adaptation of *Bus Stop* (1956) the following year. Interestingly, Axelrod also wrote Jayne Mansfield's hit play *Will Success Spoil Rock Hunter?* (1955), which many aficionados believe was based on MM. Later, Axelrod scored with *Breakfast at Tiffany's* (1961), *The Manchurian Candidate* (1962), and a film that Fox wanted MM to do, *Goodbye Charlie* (1964), which was based on Axelrod's stage play.

# B

## *BABY DOLL*

Nineteen fifty-six Warner Brothers movie that Marilyn had wanted to star in. Based on a play by Tennessee Williams, the film was directed by Elia Kazan and starred Karl Malden, Eli Wallach, and Carroll Baker in the role that made her famous. Although she did not get the part, MM showed no bitterness as she served as an usherette at the *Baby Doll* benefit for the Actors Studio on December 4, 1956.

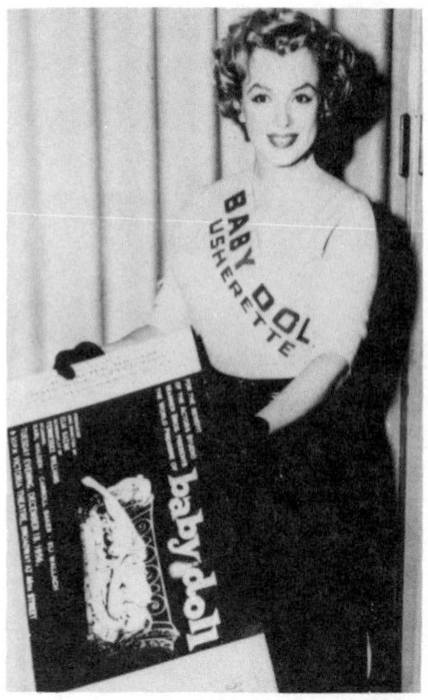


COURTESY OF CINEMA COLLECTORS

Actors Studio Benefit, 1956.

## BABYSITTING

As part of its publicity ploy, 20th Century-Fox, in 1947, marketed its newly signed starlet, MM, as the sweet young neighborhood babysitter, who was "discovered" by one of her clients—who just happened to be a Hollywood talent agent.

**MM Trivia Quiz #4**

In what film did MM portray a babysitter? (Answer on page 577.)

## LAUREN BACALL

In 1944, "Betty" Bacall sizzled in her screen debut (*To Have and Have Not*) opposite Humphrey Bogart, whom, of course, she later married. By 1953, however, Bacall's star had dimmed somewhat, and Marilyn walked off with *How to Marry a Millionaire,* in which Bacall costarred.

During the shooting of *How to Marry,* Bacall once invited MM to the Holmby Hills mansion that she shared with Bogart. Yet several sources maintain that, during the shooting, Bacall was coldly polite to MM—and nothing more. Said Bacall in her autobiography, *By Myself* (Knopf, 1979):

> During our scenes she'd look at my forehead instead of my eyes; at the end of a take, [she'd] look to her coach, standing behind Jean Negulesco, for approval. If the headshake was no, she'd insist on another take. A scene often went to fifteen or more takes, which meant I'd have to be good in all of them as no one knew which one would be used. Not easy—often irritating. And yet I couldn't dislike Marilyn. She had no meanness in her—no bitchery. She just had to concentrate on herself and the people who were there only for her.

Bacall also recalled a time when MM once tried to strike up a conversation (not too successfully) with Bacall's young son, Steve:

> MM: How old are you?
> STEVE: I'm four.
> MM: But, you're so big for four. I would have thought you were two or three.

Born on September 16, 1924, Bacall has proven herself to be one of the most durable performers in show business. Following her impressive debut in *To Have and Have Not,* Bacall starred in such motion pictures as *The Big Sleep* (1946), *Key Largo* (1948), *Written on the Wind* (1957), *Sex and the Single Girl* (1964), *Harper* (1966), *Murder on the Orient Express* (1974), *Health* (1979), and *The Fan* (1981). In addition to her film successes, Miss Bacall won a 1970 Tony Award as the "Best Actress" for her musical performance in *Applause!* And, in 1981, she scored yet another Broadway success with *Woman of the Year,* for which she won another Tony Award.

**JULIAN BACH**

Remember, at the end of *The Seven Year Itch* (1955), when Marilyn Monroe leans out of an apartment window, clutching Tom Ewell's shoes? Well, in actuality, the apartment was owned by Julian Bach, who lent out his home for location shooting. For his generosity, Bach was paid $200 worth of whiskey, and, reportedly, a kiss from MM. Bach's apartment was located at 164 East 61st Street in New York City.

**JAMES BACON**

> "HOLY GOD! She's so exciting. . . . There was *something* about this girl. The moment you met her you *knew* she was going to make it!"
>
> James Bacon, on first meeting MM in 1948

Hollywood columnist and author of *Hollywood Is a Four Letter Town* (Avon, 1976), who purported to be MM's lover for a brief period. According to Bacon, they first met in 1948 at the old Naples Restaurant in Hollywood. In 1977, Bacon wrote a "kiss and tell" article entitled "The Night I Made It with Marilyn Monroe." Therein, Bacon claimed that he visited Marilyn while she was living at Joe Schenck's guest house in the Holmby Hills section of Los Angeles. Bacon has also claimed that Marilyn once told him that she *was* one of the girls who looked after Joe Schenck's failing sexual prowess. Said Bacon:

> I knew she was promiscuous in those early days. She admitted it helped, and I had no illusions that MM was after me. She liked me, sure, but she was also after all the newspapers my syndicated column appeared in.

Following Marilyn's death, Bacon raised a few eyebrows by claiming that he was in MM's Brentwood bedroom the morning of August 5, 1962—while her body was still on the bed.

**BERNICE BAKER**
*See* BERNICE MIRACLE.

**CARROLL BAKER**
MM had wanted the role in *Baby Doll* (1956) that went to the relatively unknown Carroll Baker from Johnstown, Pennsylvania. Born on May 28, 1931, Baker started her career as a dancer before studying at the Actors Studio under the direction of Lee Strasberg. In 1965, Baker starred in the long-planned film, *Harlow,* the role that Marilyn had repeatedly turned down many years before. Baker's other film appearances include *Giant* (1956), *The Carpetbaggers* (1964), and *Star 80* (1983).

THE SABIN GRAY COLLECTION

**GLADYS BAKER**
Aka Gladys Mortenson (also spelled Mortensen), aka Gladys Eley.

> "She was a beautiful woman, one of the most beautiful women it was ever my privilege to know. She had a good heart and was a good friend and was always happy until she got this sickness."
>
> Mrs. Leila Fields,
> Gladys's former coworker at RKO,
> on Gladys Baker
> *Marilyn Monroe* by Maurice Zolotow
> (Harcourt Brace, 1960)

THE ROBERT SLATZER COLLECTION

Mother and daughter, circa 1930.

Born Gladys Pearl Monroe in C.P. Diaz, Mexico, May 24, 1900, Gladys Baker was Marilyn Monroe's mother.

Born into a family with a history of emotional disturbance, Gladys married for the first time while still a teenager. Little is known about her husband, except to say that his name was Jack Baker and that he fathered Gladys's first two children—Hermitt Jack and Bernice. By the time Norma Jeane (the original spelling) was born in 1926, Jack had long since disappeared, with both of the Baker kids in tow. Gladys's second husband, Edward Mortenson—one of two men thought to be Norma Jeane's father—had also left town. While working as a film cutter at Consolidated Film Industries in Hollywood, Gladys had an affair with one of her fellow employees, a C. Stanley Gifford—the second man speculated as being Norma Jeane's father. At any rate, Gladys became pregnant, and Gifford flew the proverbial coop.

Gladys Baker (the name she used most commonly), was only in her mid-twenties at the time Norma Jeane was born, and she was pretty. Some sources have said that she resembled Gloria Swanson and Norma Talmadge. Being that young and that pretty was simply not conducive to working a full-time job and raising, singlehandedly, an infant child—particularly not in Hollywood. Logically, Gladys decided to pay a foster family from Hawthorne $5 a week to take care of little Norma Jeane. Meanwhile, Gladys plotted to use her youth and good looks to obtain a house, a husband, and a father for her child.

During the next several years, Gladys worked on her plan, in addition to working as a film cutter at Columbia and then RKO Studios. On Saturdays, Gladys would take a trolley to Hawthorne, spend the day with her rapidly growing daughter, and then usually rush back to Los Angeles for some promising Saturday night date. This routine varied just once. It was the time that Norma Jeane became sick. In a sudden, overwhelming display of motherly affection, Gladys took off from work, and for three weeks she lived at the Bolender home and nursed her child back to health. This was to be one of the longest stretches of time that mother and daughter would ever spend together.

By 1934, when Norma Jeane was eight, Gladys had saved enough money for a down payment on a home. It was a bungalow, located off Highland Avenue in Hollywood. Gladys rented out all of the rooms except for the two she retained for Norma Jeane and herself. Thus, after years of planning, Gladys had the house—if not the husband and father—and, for the first time since birth, Norma Jeane moved in with "the lady with the red hair."

However, familial bliss was short-lived. Within several months, Gladys had a nervous breakdown. In January 1935, Gladys was carted off to Los Angeles General Hospital (where NJ was born) before being "put away" at the Norwalk State Asylum (where Gladys's own mother, Della, had died). At Norwalk, Gladys was diagnosed as a paranoid schizophrenic—the disease that had destroyed both of her parents and her brother.

Gladys would not live with Norma Jeane again for twelve years. It was 1945, and Gladys was considered well enough to reenter society. By then, Norma Jeane had met and married Jim Dougherty; she was also preparing to divorce him. Norma Jeane was also beginning to make a name for herself in modeling. In fact, she used her modeling savings to rent a two-room apartment in West LA, below "Aunt" Ana Lower's, for her and Gladys to share. However, this second attempt at some semblance of family life was not much more successful than the first. Too much time had elapsed. By then, cover girl Norma Jeane had a fast-paced life of her own. She did not need anyone, including Gladys and Jim, to hold her back and pull her down. There were times when Norma Jeane would take off, a month at a time, on some extended modeling assignment, which left Gladys alone. Finally, after seven months of forced "togetherness," NJ moved into the Studio Club in Hollywood, and Gladys requested to be recommitted to the Norwalk State Asylum.

By 1952, Norma Jeane Baker had grown into the role of Marilyn Monroe and was on the verge of worldwide superstardom. Up until that time, Marilyn had been telling the press that both of her parents were dead. It was easier than a full-blown explanation, it was less embarrassing, and it made good copy. When it was discovered that she had been lying, Marilyn took advantage of the situation by humbly explaining that her mother was an invalid, that she had never had the opportunity to get to know her, and that she had "lied" because she didn't want to put her vulnerable mother in the glaring public spotlight.

Also, in 1952, Gladys, apparently aware of her daughter's newfound celebrity, sent MM the following note from Norwalk:

> Dear Marilyn,
> Please dear child I'd like to receive a letter from you. Things are very annoying around here and I'd like to move away as soon as possible. I'd like to have my child's love instead of hatred.
> Love, Mother

The following month, Gladys was transferred to the country club-like Rockhaven Sanitarium in Verdugo, California, where she remained for nearly fifteen years. Before Marilyn died, she provided a $100,000 trust fund for her mother. Of this, $5,000 was to be drawn annually for Gladys's maintenance at Rockhaven.

After Marilyn's death, Gladys became increasingly disturbed. Reportedly, she attempted suicide by stabbing herself with hairpins, and, when that failed to produce the desired result, she tried stuffing bed sheets down her throat. Also in 1963, Gladys reportedly escaped from Rockhaven by lowering herself from a closet window. She then walked fifteen miles to the Lakeview Terrace Baptist Church in the San Fernando Valley. She was discovered, twenty-four hours later, by the Reverend J. Brian, who found her holding a Bible in one hand and a Christian Science handbook in the other. Gladys was then transported back to the sanitarium.

Three years later, Gladys Eley (she had remarried on one of her brief excursions away from the hospital) made one final exodus from Rockhaven. This time, she was successful. She contacted her daughter, Bernice, who sent her a one-way ticket to Florida and became her legal guardian in 1967. By 1970, Gladys was considered well enough to move to a retirement home, not far from Bernice, where she was able to establish her first independent residence since 1935. In 1982, Gladys was seen outside of her home, riding on a red tricycle, which featured a red danger flag on its handle bars.

Due to legalities and an alleged lack of funds, Gladys did not receive a payment from the Marilyn Monroe estate until December 1976.

For years, Gladys has refused to talk about Marilyn. Said Inez Melson, Gladys's former guardian: "We seldom talk of Marilyn, with Mrs. Eley's belief in the hereafter, she does not regard her [Marilyn] as dead, but, rather, in heaven."

Gladys herself once put it this way: "I'm not interested in material things. I'm interested only in God."

Gladys Baker died of heart failure on March 11, 1984, in Gainesville, Florida. Her last known home address was 330 S.W. 27th Street in Gainesville. She outlived her famous daughter by more than twenty years.

**HERMITT JACK BAKER**

According to Robert Slatzer in his investigative *The Life and Curious Death of Marilyn Monroe* (1974), MM had a half-brother named Hermitt Baker, who was born on January 24, 1918, and died of tuberculosis in the early 1920s.

**JACK BAKER**

Gladys's first husband and the father of Bernice and Hermitt Jack Baker, according to James A. Hudson, in his 1968 book *The Mysterious Death of Marilyn Monroe,* was a gas station attendant who, after leaving Gladys, became a successful businessman. Robert Slatzer reported that Baker was born in Kentucky in 1891. Slatzer then proceeded to document that Baker married Gladys in 1917. Also according to Slatzer, Baker divorced Gladys on June 14, 1921.

What is known is that—for whatever reason—Baker left Gladys and took the children with him to a southern city, probably in Kentucky.

**ROY BAKER**

British director, born in 1916, who directed MM in her first starring role, *Don't Bother to Knock* (1952).

**HANSON BALDWIN**

Despite its overwhelming success, not everyone was thrilled with Marilyn's charitable 1954 tour of Korea. Hanson Baldwin, a military expert for *The New York Times,* wrote a scathing editorial that claimed that the Military needed to:

> . . . correct the weakness in service morale epitomized by the visit of Miss Monroe to Korea. On two occasions during the visit of the motion picture actress, troops rioted wildly and behaved like Bobby-Soxers in Times Square, not like soldiers proud of their uniform.

**KRIS BALDWIN**

Kris Baldwin wrote the foreword of Milo Speriglio's book *Marilyn Monroe: Murder Cover-Up* (1982). At that time, Kris was the special events coordinator of the International Marilyn Monroe Fan Club. Also, in April 1982, Kris was named a first runner-up at 20th Century-Fox's MM Lookalike Contest.

**LUCILLE BALL**

Lucille Ball, the Queen of Comedy, impersonated Marilyn Monroe, the Queen of Cheesecake, in an episode of the "I Love Lucy" television series. The episode, entitled "Ricky's Movie Offer," first aired November 8, 1954.

**LUCIEN BALLARD**

American cinematographer who shot *Let's Make It Legal* (1951) and *Don't Bother to Knock* (1952). In his long, productive career, Ballard was also responsible (along with Joseph La Shelle) for the photography in *Laura* (1944) as well as for the exemplary work in *The Wild Bunch* (1969).

**BALLONA ELEMENTARY AND KINDERGARTEN SCHOOL**

From September 14, 1931, until June 17, 1932, young Norma Jeane Baker attended Ballona Elementary and Kindergarten School (address: 4339 West 129th Street) in Hawthorne, California. The school, which is still in existence, has since been renamed the Washington Elementary School.

**ANNE BANCROFT**

Following some work in television, actress Anne Bancroft made her film debut in 1952's *Don't Bother to Knock,* in which MM starred. For the next five years, Bancroft floundered in mostly ineffective features before scoring a smash hit on Broadway in *The Miracle Worker.* Following her stage success, Bancroft returned to films and won an Oscar for the screen version of *The Miracle Worker* (1962). She followed that success with some fine performances in such excellent movies as *The Pumpkin Eater* (1964), *The Graduate* (1967), and *The Elephant Man* (1980).

**THE BANFF SPRINGS HOTEL**

Hotel where Marilyn lived (Room 816) during the 1953 location shooting of *River of No Return* in Banff, Canada.

**MAGGIE BANK**
Jack Cole's assistant choreographer, who worked closely with Marilyn on the dance routines in *Let's Make Love* (1960).

**BANKS**
At the time of her death in 1962, Marilyn Monroe had two active bank accounts. The banks were:

Irving Trust Bank, New York City
City National Bank, Beverly Hills

**BAPTISM**
Marilyn's grandmother, Della Monroe Grainger, and her "aunt," Ida Bolender, had MM baptized at the age of six months, at the Foursquare Gospel Church, in Sister Aimee Semple McPherson's Angelus Temple in Los Angeles. Marilyn was baptized Norma Jeane Baker on December 6, 1926.

**THEDA BARA**
Theda Bara was the first "vamp" of the American screen. Born Theodosia Goodman in 1890, Bara rose to, and fell from, stardom before 1920. Marilyn "portrayed" her in Richard Avedon's photo series for *LIFE*, December 22, 1958.

**ELLEN BARBER**
Actress who portrayed MM in the ill-fated 1974 Broadway play, *Fame*.

**BRIGITTE BARDOT**
From the mid-fifties on, Bardot was Marilyn's European counterpart. Born Camille Javal Bardot on September 28, 1934, Bardot started out as a ballet dancer/model. Discovered by Roger Vadim (whom she later married), Bardot made her film debut in *Act of Love* (1953). A few years later, she and Vadim

COURTESY OF CINEMA COLLECTORS

concocted *And God Created Woman* (1956), which was originated as a homage to Marilyn.

At Marilyn's royal command performance for the Queen of England on October 29, 1956, Bardot was also presented to the queen. Reporters tried to stir up a feud between the transcontinental sex symbols and dubbed her "royal" performance "The War to the Last Wiggle." However, Bardot was undaunted and unaffected. At that time, BB called MM "charming, beautiful, vulnerable, fragile."

**BILLY BARNES**
Billy Barnes was one of the creators and writers of the 1982 stage musical, *Movie Star*, which opened in Los Angeles. The play featured, in a brief role, a Marilyn Monroe-based character.

**BARNEY'S BEANERY**
Popular, inexpensive Hollywood restaurant (address: 8447 Santa Monica Boulevard) that MM frequented during her starlet period. In fact, after shooting those infamous calendar photos in 1949, MM went to Barney's and ate a bowl of chili.

**SYLVIA BARNHART**
Sylvia Barnhart was the hairdresser who straightened Norma Jeane Dougherty's hair in 1946. More importantly, she was the hairdresser who turned Norma Jeane into a blonde. In 1946, Miss Barnhart was a stylist at the Frank and Joseph's Beauty Salon on Hollywood Boulevard. She styled Norma Jeane/Marilyn Monroe's hair for several years, before MM began her ascent to stardom. Of the struggling starlet, Miss Barnhart has said:

> She'd come in like two or three hours late and still expect to be taken care of. If the truth be known, she was a user. I don't think she cared who she walked over. [But] she was just magnificent, breathtaking to look at.

Today, Sylvia Barnhart lives in Van Nuys, California. She is a Marilyn Monroe collector, and has several rare photographs of early Marilyn Monroe.

**GEORGE BARRIS**
Photographer/writer who shot some of the last photos ever taken of MM. The 1962 Barris session, included in the Norman Mailer book, *Marilyn* (1973) and the Gloria Steinem book, *Marilyn* (1986), contains shots of MM on Santa Monica Beach in a variety of outfits and poses—wearing an oversized sweater, wearing what looks to be a terrycloth parka, and barely wearing a beach towel (while sipping champagne).

In addition to the photographs, Barris interviewed Marilyn for a proposed biography of her life. The interview material was subsequently published in the August 13, 1962, edition of *The New York Daily News*.

THE SYLVIA BARNHART COLLECTION

With Sylvia Barnhart at Hair Show, circa 1947.

**LIONEL BARRYMORE**
Celebrated American character actor and brother of Ethel and John, who made a multitude of films, beginning in 1909. In 1950, Barrymore made what was to be one of his last films. The film was *Right Cross,* and it featured, in a bit part, a starlet named Marilyn Monroe.

**RENO BARSOCCHINI**
A friend of Joe DiMaggio who served as the best man at the DiMaggio/ Monroe wedding in January 1954. Later that year, it was Barsocchini who helped DiMaggio pack and move out of the North Palm Drive home, following DiMaggio's separation from MM.

**BASEBALL**
Up until the time that she met Joe DiMaggio, the closest MM had come to an actual baseball game was her 1951 publicity shot with Chicago White Sox player Gus Zernial. Marilyn finally saw her first baseball game on March 17, 1952. That day, the Hollywood Stars were playing the Major League All-Stars at Gilmore Field, in a benefit for the Kiwanis Club for Children. It was the only time that Marilyn saw Joe DiMaggio play baseball. Joltin' Joe hit a single and a home run.

**CHRIS BASINGER**
Originally from Hawesville, Kentucky, Chris Basinger is an MM collector, and a member of the Marilyn Remembered Fan Club. He started his MM collection in 1959, after seeing the film *Some Like It Hot.* Today, Basinger has an extensive MM collection that includes more than 500 still photographs, videos, and magazines. He is also a serious collector of both Clara Bow and Mae West.

**ROBERT BASSLER**
Bassler produced *A Ticket to Tomahawk* (1950) and *Let's Make It Legal* (1951), both for 20th Century-Fox. Bassler's most noted film was *The Snake Pit,* starring Olivia de Havilland, in 1948.

**JOHN BATES**
Bates is the wealthy attorney who claimed that Robert Kennedy spent the weekend of August 4, 1962, at his ranch in Gilroy, California. However, Bates has admitted that he could *not* account for Kennedy from 11:00 P.M. on August 4 through 8:00 A.M. on August 5, 1962. Note: Gilroy is located three hundred miles north of Los Angeles and sixty miles south of San Francisco.

**KENNETH BATTELLE**
Known simply as "Kenneth," Battelle is the noted "Hairdresser to the Stars," who began doing MM's hair at the tail end of the *Some Like It Hot* shooting in 1958. Based in New York, Kenneth continued to do MM's hair on and off until her death in 1962.

**BELINDA BAUER**
In William Richert's film version of *Winter Kills* (1979), actress Belinda Bauer portrayed Yvette Malone, a character reportedly based on MM.

**JOHN BAUMGARTH**
Baumgarth was the original buyer of *the* famous MM nude shot that was used in the 1950 calendar, "Golden Dreams." At that time, Baumgarth paid photographer Tom Kelley a mere $500 for the shot. As of 1956, *Time* magazine estimated that Baumgarth had made approximately $750,000 from that one photo! Marilyn, of course, received the gargantuan sum of $50 for the entire series of photos.

**GREGSON BAUTZER**
Hollywood socialite who, according to Fred Lawrence Guiles's *Norma Jean: The Life of Marilyn Monroe* (1969), confronted MM at the David Selznick party in 1960. At that time, Joe Schenck, one of Marilyn's earliest benefactors, was in the hospital and possibly dying. Reportedly, Bautzer was quite hostile to Marilyn and accused her of not caring about Schenck's ill health. Marilyn, who attended the party with Yves Montand, broke down crying and pleaded her innocence. Bautzer died in November 1987.

**ANNE BAXTER**
Born in 1923, actress Anne Baxter appeared in fifty-plus movies, including such fine works as *The Magnificent Ambersons* (1942); *The Razor's Edge* (1946), for which she won an Oscar; and *All About Eve* (1950). In addition to *Eve,* Baxter starred in two other films that featured budding starlet MM: *A Ticket to Tomahawk* (1950) and "The Last Leaf" segment from *O. Henry's Full House* (1952). Interestingly, Baxter was to have starred in *Niagara* (1953). Perhaps she backed out when it became apparent that Marilyn Monroe was to be the actual star of the film. Miss Baxter died of a stroke in New York City on December 12, 1985.

**BEACH STREET**
Following their 1954 wedding, Mr. and Mrs. Joe DiMaggio lived, for a few months, at the DiMaggio family home at 2150 Beach Street in the Marina District of San Francisco.

**MRS. GAVIN BEARDSLEY**
In 1945, Mrs. Beardsley taught nineteen-year-old Norma Jeane Dougherty all about the ramps and ropes of fashion modeling—without much success. NJ quickly abandoned fashion modeling in favor of photo work.

**CECIL BEATON**
Noted British photographer (1902-1980) who also served as an advisor on such films as *Gigi* (1958) and *My Fair Lady* (1964). Beaton is also responsible for one of the most beautiful photographs ever taken of MM. Shot in 1956 in

New York, the photo shows Marilyn in a white gown, lying on what appears to be a bed of white sheets. She is shown gently clasping a long-stemmed flower to her breast. Apparently, the photo was one of Marilyn's personal favorites—she kept it on her living room wall in her East 57th Street apartment in New York.

### BEAUTY MARKS

Marilyn had a mole on her upper lip and another one four inches below her right clavicle.

### BEAUTY REGIMEN

> "You don't just wake up in the morning and wash your face and comb your hair and go out in the street and look like Marilyn Monroe. She knows every trick of the beauty trade."
>
> Milton Greene on MM

- ☆ While living on Catalina Island, Jim Dougherty remembers that Norma Jeane used to rinse her face fifteen times after every wash.
- ☆ At varying times, MM would smear Vaseline, cold cream, or hormone cream over her face.
- ☆ While not wearing makeup, MM would apply lanolin or olive oil to her face as a protecting agent.
- ☆ MM would sometimes take "ice baths," prepared by her masseur, Ralph Roberts, to which MM would invariably add Chanel No. 5.
- ☆ From countless hours of practicing in front of a mirror, MM learned how to lower her smile in order to camouflage an excessively high gum line.
- ☆ MM would always have several full-length mirrors in her home. At some of her homes, she had a dressing room in which she would have wall-to-wall mirrors installed.
- ☆ Occasionally, especially during her struggling period, MM would slap saliva on her cheekbones to give then added shine.
- ☆ Marilyn told photographer Bert Stern in 1962 that she always used Nivea Skin Moisturizing Lotion.

### HERMAN M. BEERMAN

The doctor who delivered Norma Jeane Mortenson into the world on June 1, 1926, at Los Angeles General Hospital. When contacted in 1986, Dr. Beerman had the following to say about his famous delivery:

> She looked like any other baby that I delivered. She was the same as the rest.

### THE BEL AIR HOTEL

Marilyn lived at the Bel Air Hotel (address: 701 Stone Canyon Road) in 1948, during her six-month contract with Columbia Pictures and again in 1952, when her star was definitely on the rise. In 1952, MM paid the then extravagant rent of $750 a month for her poolside suite. In 1958, MM's New York friend Norman Rosten, received a letter from her while she was staying at the Bel Air in Suites 133–135 (perhaps, during the Los Angeles shooting of *Some Like It Hot*). MM was at the Bel Air again in June 1962 for the Bert

Stern "Last Sitting" photo session. The first shooting took place in Suite 261; the second session, held soon after, took place in Bungalow 96.

**ARNOLD BELGARD**
The writer responsible for *Dangerous Years* (1947).

**CONSTANCE BENNETT**
Glamorous film star of the 1930s who costarred in the 1951 movie *As Young as You Feel,* which featured MM in one of her most substantial early roles.

**JACK BENNY**
Born Benjamin Kubelsky (1894–1974), Benny presented Marilyn in her television debut. The landmark appearance took place on the opening segment of the 1953–54 "The Jack Benny Show."

Benny, the "thirty-nine"-year-old star of radio, television, and film, occasionally accompanied MM and friend Jeanne Carmen to a massage parlor on Sunset Boulevard for facial treatments. Also, he once accompanied MM and Carmen to a nude beach. According to Anthony Summers's *Goddess: The Secret Lives of Marilyn Monroe* (1985), Benny donned a beard for the occasion, while MM wore a black wig. According to Carmen, they went unrecognized.

THE AUTHOR'S COLLECTION

On "The Jack Benny Show," 1953.

**MAC BENOFF**

The cowriter of the Marx Brothers' *Love Happy* (1950).

**"BENSON"**

An episode of the television program "Benson" featured a blonde goddess named Norma Jeane. The episode was entitled "Boys Night Out" and it initially aired on February 4, 1983. The Marilyn Monroe-based dreamgirl was portrayed by Katie Labourdette.

**HAL BERG**

Berg was the photographer who shot a series of MM photos for the October 9, 1955, issue of *The American Weekly* magazine.

**BERNARD BERGLASS**

Dr. Bernard Berglass was the gynecologist who gave the pregnant Marilyn Monroe a check-up at Doctors Hospital in New York in mid-April 1957. A few months later, on August 1, 1957, Dr. Berglass assisted Dr. Hilliard Dubrow with Marilyn Monroe's emergency surgery which resulted, tragically, in a miscarriage.

**SAMUEL BERKE**

Johnny Hyde's business manager and close friend. Berke was one of the few Hyde associates who did not resent Marilyn. In fact, after Hyde's death in 1950, Berke was one of the few Hyde intimates who insisted that MM be allowed to attend the funeral.

**MILTON BERLE**

Born in 1908, Milton Berlinger (aka Mendel Berlinger), became known as "Mr. Television" and "Uncle Miltie" for his popular TV series that ran from 1948 to 1956.

Berle first met Marilyn on the set of *Ladies of the Chorus* (1948). He was dating the film's star, Adele Jergens, at that time. According to Berle, he and MM had a brief affair.

> Marilyn was on the climb in Hollywood, but there was nothing cheap about her. She wasn't one of the starlets around town that you put one meal into then threw into the sack. Maybe she didn't know exactly who she was, but she knew she was worth something. She had respect for herself. Marilyn was a Lady.
>
> from *Milton Berle: An Autobiography* (Delacorte, 1974)

In 1955, Berle served as ringmaster at the Madison Square Garden Circus in which MM rode atop a pink elephant. Their only other known association, after MM became a star, was Berle's guest appearance in the 1960 film *Let's Make Love.*

**IRVING BERLIN**

Born in 1888, Israel Baline (aka Isador Baline) became one of the most prolific and most popular composers of all time. Twentieth Century-Fox paid "tribute" to Berlin with its splashy 1954 musical *There's No Business Like Show Business,* in which MM costarred. Reportedly, Berlin was quite pleased by her unique interpretation of his songs, despite the fact that most of the critics were not.

**MELVIN BERNHARDT**
Melvin Bernhardt directed *Cop-Out,* two one-act plays that featured actress Linda Lavin as a Marilyn Monroe-based character. *Cop-Out* opened at the Cort Theatre in New York on April 7, 1969.

**MEL BERNS**
Berns did the makeup on *Clash by Night* (1952).

**WALTER BERNSTEIN**
Bernstein was one of the screenwriters involved with the messy, uncompleted 1962 production of *Something's Got to Give.* Unimpressed by Marilyn, Bernstein lashed out against the mounting "Monroe Myth" in his July 1973 article for *Esquire* magazine. Wrote Bernstein:

> She was not glamorous; she was not even pretty; but her appeal was genuine, a child's appeal, sweet and disarming.

Bernstein went on to script such uninspired works as *The Money Trap* (1966), *Semi-Tough* (1977), and *The Betsy* (1978).

**BESSEMER STREET**
Early in 1943, the newly wed Mr. and Mrs. Jim Dougherty packed their belongings and moved from Vista Del Monte Street to a house on Bessemen Street, located in Van Nuys, California.

**ALVAH BESSIE**
Born in 1904, Alvah Bessie is the novelist/screenwriter who was blacklisted in 1949 as one of the Hollywood Ten. In 1966, Random House published Bessie's *The Symbol,* which was a fictionalized biography about Marilyn Monroe (although this was denied by Random House). *The Symbol* was subsequently adapted into a television film retitled *The Sex Symbol* (1974), which starred Connie Stevens as the Marilyn Monroe-based character.

**ANNETTE MARIE BETTIN**
One of the three writers who scripted the 1980 "In Search Of" television segment about MM entitled "The Death of Marilyn Monroe."

**BEVERAGES**

> "If there's one thing I have a weakness for, it's champagne."
>
> Marilyn Monroe to Tom Ewell
> in *The Seven Year Itch* (1955)

MM's favorite beverage, of course, was champagne—particularly Dom Perignon 1953 (the year her career shot somewhere into the stratosphere). She also drank an excessive amount of coffee (black, thank you ever so). She was also known to drink a little vodka here and a little vermouth there. The following is a compilation of *recorded* beverages that MM swilled, sipped, and out-and-out guzzled over the years.

1. Champagne: at her wedding reception, 1942
2. Ginger Ale and Root Beer: on Catalina Island, 1943
3. Herbal Tea: at Ana Lower's home, 1945
4. Beer and Champagne: with David Conover, 1945
5. Milk: during her "struggling years"
6. Coffee: during her "struggling years"
7. Coffee: at Schwab's Pharmacy, 1947
8. Ginger Ale: at the Columbia Christmas Party, 1948
9. Coffee: after shooting the nude calendar photo, 1949
10. Dom Perignon: Christmas with Bob Slatzer, late 1940s
11. Daiquiris: MM's favorite drink during 1950
12. Marsala: on her first date with DiMaggio, March 1952
13. Martinis: at Doheny apartment, April 1952
14. Champagne: on her birthday, 1952

15. Scotch: at the General Brock Hotel, with Bob Slatzer, 1952
16. Margaritas: at the Rosarita Beach Hotel with Bob Slatzer, 1952
17. Italian wine: at Doheny apartment, with DiMaggio, 1953
18. Carrot Juice: every morning at Stan's Drive-In in Hollywood, circa 1953
19. Martinis: during the shooting of *How to Marry a Millionaire*, 1953
20. Vodka (a double): during the shooting of *River of No Return*, 1953
21. Bourbon and Soda: the night of the *How to Marry a Millionaire* premiere, 1953
22. Champagne: during shooting of *The Seven Year Itch*, 1954
23. Champagne: at Romanoff's party, November 1954
24. Mumm's Champagne: at a New York Chinese restaurant, with Truman Capote, April 1955
25. Vodka and Vermouth: at Waldorf-Astoria, 1955
26. Red wine: at Petite Couvee Restaurant, New York, 1955
27. Champagne and a Martini: in *The Seven Year Itch*, 1955
28. Champagne: during shooting of *Bus Stop*, 1956
29. Tea with Gin (or vice versa): at 9:00 A.M., during shooting of *The Prince and the Showgirl*, 1956

30. Cognac: at Connecticut ranch, with Arthur Miller and Norman Rosten, 1957
31. Champagne: from a paper cup, in Rosten's car, 1957
32. Bloody Marys: a daily morning ritual at East 57th Street apartment, 1957
33. Champagne: a daily noontime ritual at East 57th Street apartment, 1957
34. Vermouth: at East 57th Street apartment, 1957
35. Vermouth: from a thermos, during shooting of *Some Like It Hot*, 1958
36. "Milk Punch": a home-mixed concoction of chocolate syrup, milk, and Marsala, in New York, late 1950s
37. Champagne: at David Selznick's party, 1960
38. Scotch (on the rocks): during shooting of *The Misfits*, 1960
39. Bourbon (straight): at the end of *The Misfits* shooting, 1960
40. Champagne: New Year's Eve 1961–62, with DiMaggio
41. Sherry: during interview with Margaret Parton, New York, 1961–62
42. Vodka: to wash down Valium, during *Something's Got to Give*, 1962
43. Champagne (a few glasses): before singing "Happy Birthday" to President Kennedy, May 1962
44. Dom Perignon: at Fox, MM's birthday celebration, June 1962
45. Dom Perignon: during first Bert Stern session, 1962
46. Dom Perignon (spiked with 100 proof vodka): during second Bert Stern session, 1962
47. Milk: to wash down her pills, 1962
48. Grapefruit juice: the morning before her death, 1962

**MM Trivia Quiz #5**
In what film was MM a beer drinker? (Answer on page 577.)

**THE BEVERLY CARLTON HOTEL**
Marilyn first lived at the Beverly Carlton Residential Hotel (address: 9400 West Olympic Boulevard) sometime during her six-month contract with Columbia in 1948. She returned there after Johnny Hyde's death, in December 1950, and also lived there during a good portion of 1952.

**BEVERLY GLEN**
Marilyn, along with her friends (at that time) Milton and Amy Greene, rented a house in the Beverly Glen section of Los Angeles to live in during the shooting of *Bus Stop*. MM began shooting the film in March 1956 and completed it in early June that year. The house was at 595 Beverly Glen Blvd.

**THE BEVERLY HILLS HOTEL**
Marilyn had a long association with the Beverly Hills Hotel (address: 9641 West Sunset Boulevard), and, judging by her actions over the years, it was her favorite hotel in Los Angeles. In 1950, Johnny Hyde escorted MM to Betty Hutton's party for Louis Sobol at the hotel's Crystal Room. By Thanksgiving, 1952, Marilyn was living at the hotel in a room on the third floor. Following her split from Joe DiMaggio, MM sought refuge at the Beverly Hills before she bade Hollywood good-bye and defected to New York. When MM returned to Los Angeles to shoot *Some Like It Hot* in the summer of 1958, she stayed at the Beverly Hills once again. It was also here that Mr. and Mrs. Arthur Miller resided during the lengthy shooting of *Let's Make Love*, which began in February 1960. And, as widely reported, it was here that the adulterous affair

took place between MM and her *Love* costar, Yves Montand. The Montands and the Millers occupied Bungalows 21 and 22 of the hotel. After Marilyn's subsequent divorce from Miller, and after her psychiatric hospitalization for "emotional exhaustion," MM once again sought refuge at the Beverly Hills Hotel. She lived there—alone—for a couple of months, beginning in April 1961. Marilyn's last known visit to the Beverly Hills Hotel took place in 1962, when she met writer Alan Levy for an interview that would later appear in the August 1962 issue of *Redbook* magazine.

**BIOGRAPHIES ISSUED BY STUDIOS**
**Issued by Harry Brand**
**20th Century-Fox, December 30, 1946**

Eighteen-year-old Marilyn Monroe, 20th Century-Fox discovery, is being ballyhooed as sort of a junior Lana Turner, and like the famous star, she's a Hollywood-born-and-bred youngster who didn't have to leave town to attract the attention of the talent scouts.

Once named as the "Oomph" girl of Emerson Junior High School, Marilyn nevertheless had no screen ambitions. She wanted instead to be a secretary, went to work for a defense industry owned by Reginald Denny after her graduation from Van Nuys High School, and there was discovered by army public relations officers who asked her to do some army motion pictures.

As a result of that, she went to work as a photographer's model, worked for some of the biggest agencies in the Los Angeles area, and appeared on some of the fanciest magazine covers.

A short time later Miss Monroe, to add to her income, went to the home of a 20th Century-Fox talent scout to sit with the baby. He was so impressed with her beauty he arranged for her to have a screen test in black and white film. This was so good she was then tested in Technicolor and signed to a long-term contract.

That's fast action in Hollywood, where such behavior is usually considered "impulsive," but the studio execs didn't want to take a chance on a youngster they consider a terrific bet for stardom.

To date, Marilyn has no picture assignments; she's down for six months of intensive grooming before she faces a camera, with dramatic lessons, dancing lessons, and voice training.

She was born on June 1st. Her father died in an automobile accident a year later, and as her mother was too ill to take care of her, she was adopted by Mr. and Mrs. E. S. Goddard, family friends in the manufacturing business. Her real name is Norma Jean Daugherty [sic], which the studio changed because it's too long for a marquee; and they expect her name to land on a lot of them.

***Personal data:*** Loves swimming, horseback riding, yachting, but has a tendency to get seasick . . . writes poetry, but won't show it to anyone . . . loves music, from the classics to boogie-woogie . . . hobby is photography, until her movie career hoped to become a woman photographer of baby animals, kittens, puppies, et cetera . . . hates untidiness, careless drivers, closed places, and cowboy music.

And she loves movies.

**VITAL STATISTICS**
REAL NAME: NORMA JEAN DAUGHERTY [sic]
BIRTHPLACE: Los Angeles California
BIRTHDAY: June 1st
FOSTER MOTHER: Mrs. E. S. Goddard
FOSTER FATHER: E. S. Goddard
HEIGHT: 5 feet 5½ inches
WEIGHT: 118 pounds
HAIR: Blonde
EYES: Blue
EDUCATION: Emerson Jr. High, Los Angeles
Van Nuys High, Van Nuys, California

**Issued by Harry Brand**
**20th Century-Fox, February 7, 1951**

One night not long ago Marilyn Monroe, beautifully groomed and dressed in expensive good taste, was escorted to a premiere at the Circle Theatre on El Centro Street in Hollywood by Charles Chaplin, Jr.

As they neared the theatre someone in the party called attention to a severe frame building sitting back from the street.

"That's the Los Angeles Orphanage," someone said. "You know, where they keep the kids that nobody wants."

Marilyn kept right on walking. She makes no effort to conceal the fact that her early life was spent in a series of private homes and in the orphanage as a ward of Los Angeles County, but this period of her life she prefers to forget. Her eyes are on a bright future in the make-believe world of the films, where anything can come true, and where it really is coming true for Marilyn. At 22, she ranks as one of the cinema's most promising newcomers and her studio, 20th Century-Fox, is building her into a top-bracket star.

Big, sprawling Los Angeles County did the best it could for Marilyn but it's a pretty impersonal sort of father and mother, and even though the various families who kept the little girl in their homes were good to her, she learned early in life to be self-sufficient and to make the best of whatever environment in which she found herself. Perhaps that accounts for the equanimity with which she faced the early disappointment of her Hollywood career after being "discovered" by a studio and then being dropped to await discovery all over again.

Marilyn's real name was Norma Jean Baker [sic] and her mother was a helpless invalid and her father was killed in an automobile accident shortly after her birth. Marilyn has never known either. She spent her childhood in a series of private homes as a ward of the County, and even now she finds it a trifle confusing to remember all of them.

The first home with which she was placed was in Hawthorne, California. She remembers little about them as the family moved east when she was five and Marilyn was placed with a family of British actors who had emigrated to Hollywood and were playing bits in pictures. Marilyn picked up a decided British accent and got her first lessons in knife-throwing, juggling Indian clubs and other vaudeville specialties which might prove valuable in after [sic] life.

At 7½ she moved in with a Hollywood studio worker and his wife and shed the British accent. They lived in a big house on a hill and were kind to her but there were no children around, so she found herself relying mainly for companionship on a collection of exotic birds.

They, too, could not keep her and at 9 Marilyn was taken by the County to the Los Angeles orphan's home. The superintendent, a Mrs. Dewey, was "wonderful and sweet" but there were so many children to care for that the matrons found it impossible to give any of them the affection children need. Here Marilyn had her first job—helping in the pantry and setting tables at 5¢ a month. These nickels were carefully hoarded by the kids so that at Christmas time they could cross the street to the drugstore and buy gifts for each other of writing tablets, pencils, etc. After serving in the pantry at 5¢ a month, Marilyn later had her salary doubled. She was promoted to washing dishes in the kitchen at 10¢ a month. It was during this period, at the age of 9, that Marilyn and other youngsters from the orphanage were Christmas guests of RKO studios. They were shown a movie on the lot and were given a string of imitation pearls as a gift. Marilyn says this was one of the great thrills of her childhood and it may have whetted her appetite for the movies.

Before she was ten, Marilyn was again placed as a boarder with a Los Angeles family, this time in the San Fernando Valley. Then there was another move, this time to a family made up entirely of women; a great-grandmother, grandmother, mother and three young daughters. She stayed there but a short time.

Then came a move which was to have its most important effect upon Marilyn. She was taken in by Mrs. E. Anna Lower, of West Los Angeles, whom Marilyn still thinks of as "Aunt Anna." Mrs. Lower was the nearest thing to "family" that Marilyn has ever known. This wonderful woman, who has since died, treated Marilyn like a daughter and within the limits of her ability provided her with things she needed, plus an abundance of love and affections.

She was with "Aunt Anna" for two years and lived in what was then called the Sawtelle District, regarded by the more favored youngsters from Bel Air and Brentwood as the "wrong side of the tracks."

While living with Mrs. Lower she began to emerge from her shell and spend more time with other children. She took an interest in the school plays and being a lanky girl found herself playing boy's parts both in the school plays and in the out-of-school activities such as the little "radio" shows which she and her Sawtelle friends improvised. It was her fate to play the young prince when such productions as Jack and the Beanstalk were undertaken.

During one period of Mrs. Lower's illness, Marilyn lived for a time with a lawyer and his wife in Westwood, and at another period lived with a family which included three other children in the San Fernando Valley. However, "Aunt Anna's" home remained her real base until the death of that fine woman.

At 15 and in high school, Marilyn experienced a short-lived marriage which she prefers to forget. Both were immature youngsters, the thing didn't work out, and the boy is now happily remarried and has a family.

After completing her schooling at Van Nuys High School in the San Fernando Valley, Marilyn went to work for the Radio Plane Co. inspecting parachutes for target planes. The firm was owned by Reginald Denny.

While working at the plant she augmented her income by modeling and one month had her picture on four magazine covers. Howard Hughes, then convalescing from an airplane accident, saw them and became interested in her but before he could arrange a screen test, 20th Century-Fox had given her a color test and signed her for a year.

Marilyn worked in one picture, "Scudda Hoo! Scudda Hay!" but her tiny part ended up, in the best Hollywood tradition, on the cutting room floor. A year at 20th in which no suitable parts were found and Marilyn was dropped.

Columbia then signed her for a 9-day musical, "Ladies of the Chorus," in which she played a burlesque queen, and Marilyn was again dropped.

Things were tough. She decided she had better supplement her natural charms with acting ability, and engaged the coaching services of Natasha Lytess, one of Hollywood's best and who coincidentally is now a coach at 20th and continuing Marilyn's lessons.

Marilyn engaged a room at the Studio Club, home of many an aspiring starlet, and limited herself to two meals a day. She eked out a living by modeling clothes and posing for fashion and cover photographers.

One day she was approached by an agent who told her Lester Cowan was producing "Love Happy" and needed a blonde for Groucho Marx to chase. She rushed over and was hired on the spot. The scene lasted for a full minute. It didn't get cut, either.

When the picture was released, Cowan persuaded Marilyn to go on tour and plug the picture in Chicago, Detroit, New York and other cities. She did everything—press interviews, TV appearances, charity shows, and picked up a lot of poise in the process.

When she returned from the tour, 20th sent for her again and gave her a part in "Ticket to Tomahawk," in which she played a dancing girl. The picture was filmed in Colorado and the day she returned she received a call from Arthur Hornblow, MGM producer, asking her to read for Director John Huston for a role in "Asphalt Jungle."

She got the part, and meantime had been taken into her home by Lucille Ryman, MGM talent director who had suggested her to Hornblow.

In "Asphalt Jungle" she played the "niece" of Louis Calhern, a wide-eyed young lovely interested in an older man. The role was a minor one but when Marilyn came on the screen it made the audience gasp. Probably her greatest satisfaction came when Huston told her at the end of the picture, "You know, Marilyn, you're going to be a good actress."

Following the "Asphalt Jungle" role, 20th's Joseph Mankiewicz looked at the picture and picked her to play Miss Caswell in "All About Eve." It is another fat part since she appeared in support of

Bette Davis, Anne Baxter, George Sanders and Celeste Holm.

When Darryl Zanuck saw the rushes he sent for Marilyn's agent and signed her to a long-term contract. Her first picture on the new road to stardom was "Will You Love Me in December?" in which Monty Woolley, Constance Bennett, David Wayne, Jean Peters and Thelma Ritter complete the starring cast.

Marilyn is blue-eyed, blonde, 5 feet 5½ inches tall, and weighs 118 pounds.

After having grown up in an atmosphere of uncertainty and change, she is completely poised and takes each day's problems in stride.

Now, with a big studio behind her, a comfortable apartment, nice clothes and a world of friends, she is able to forget the early hardships.

Hollywood, which is often the scene of heartbreak, has been the scene of her success. It hasn't been easy, but at 22 Marilyn has little to complain about.

**Issued by Perry Lieber**
**RKO Radio Studios, November 30, 1951**

| | |
|---|---|
| DATE OF BIRTH | June 1, 1928 [sic] |
| BIRTHPLACE | Los Angeles, California |
| REAL NAME | Norma Jean Baker [sic] |
| HEIGHT | 5 Feet, 5½ Inches |
| WEIGHT | 118 Pounds |
| HAIR | Silver Blonde |
| EYES | Blue |

From lonely orphan to sought after motion picture star is the true life Cinderella story of Marilyn Monroe.

When Marilyn was nine years old she lived at the Los Angeles Orphan's Home, a single city block from the RKO Radio Pictures studios. From an upstairs window in the orphanage she could see the studio's big water tank, with the RKO Radio insignia. It was only a symbol, but it fired her child's imagination with dreams of what must be transpiring in the nearby glamourland.

Then came an unforgettable experience, one which doubtless influenced Marilyn's entire life. The children at the Orphanage were invited to a Christmas party at the RKO Studios. They were shown a movie on the lot, and each of the girls was given a string of imitation pearls as a gift. To Marilyn this party was sheer magic, and from that day she knew what career she meant to follow.

Fittingly, it was to the same RKO Radio Studios that Miss Monroe returned in the early Autumn of 1951 to play her first starring role in motion pictures. She had, during the years that had intervened since the memorable Christmas party, won a foothold in pictures and become recognized as a personality to reckon with. Twentieth Century-Fox has placed her under contract, and was grooming her for stardom. It remained, however, for Jerry Wald and Norman Krasna to star her the first time in their picture, "Clash by Night." In that drama, produced for distribution by RKO Radio, Marilyn Monroe's name is placed above the title along with those of Barbara Stanwyck, Paul Douglas and Robert Ryan.

Thus the big film plant at Gower Street and Melrose Avenue was directly associated with a second major thrill in the life of a girl who can match every big moment of success with a heartache from a lonely childhood.

Marilyn's real name is Norma Jean Baker, but she has no memory of the parents who bestowed it upon her. Her mother was a hopeless invalid and her father was killed in an automobile accident shortly after Marilyn's birth in Los Angeles on June 1, 1926. From infancy until the day she began earning her own living, Marilyn lived in a series of private homes, with an interlude in the orphanage already mentioned, as a ward of the county.

The first home in which she recalls being placed was in Hawthorne, Calif. She remembers little about this, as the family moved East when she was five. Marilyn's next move was to the home of British actors who had settled in Hollywood and were playing bits in pictures. She was picking up a British accent when she was again given a "new home," this time with a studio worker and his wife. They lived in a big house on a hill and were kind to her, but there were no other children around, and Marilyn found herself relying mainly for companionship upon a collection of exotic birds.

The kindly studio workers couldn't keep the little girl, and at the age of nine, the much buffeted Marilyn was taken to the Orphan's home. The superintendent was wonderful and sweet, the matrons were conscientious and kindly, but they simply couldn't provide enough motherly love to go around for so many children.

Before her tenth birthday, Marilyn was again placed as a boarder with a Los Angeles family, this time in the San Fernando Valley. Then there was another move, to a family made up entirely of women—a great-grandmother, grandmother, mother and three young daughters. She stayed there but a short time.

Then came a move which was to have a most important effect upon the migratory child. She was taken in by a Mrs. Anna Lower, of West Los Angeles. Mrs. Lower was the nearest to "family" Marilyn has ever known. This fine woman, who has since died, treated her like a daughter, providing her with the love for which she was so starved. Marilyn remained with "Aunt Anna," as she still remembers Mrs. Lower, for two years. During that time she began to emerge from her protective shell and spend more time with other children. Remembering the wonderful Christmas party at the RKO studios, and still burning with the ambition to become a film actress, she took a lively interest in school plays.

At 15 and while still in high school, Marilyn experienced a short-lived marriage which she prefers to forget. For two immature youngsters, marriage simply didn't work out. After completing her schooling at Van Nuys High School in San Fernando Valley, Marilyn went to work for the Radio Plane Company, owned by former film star Reginald Denny. Her job was inspecting parachutes. While working at the plant she augmented her income by modeling. In one month her picture adorned four magazine covers.

It was during this period that Marilyn adopted an attitude toward so-called "cheesecake photography" which she insists she'll never abandon. Most of her modeling was done in bathing suits, shorts and sweaters and playsuits.

The photographs, reproduced in magazines, attracted the attention of film scouts. Marilyn was tested by 20th Century-Fox, and signed to a year's contract. And that is why she insists she'll never refuse to do "cheesecake" pictures, so long as they are in good taste, no matter how big a dramatic star she may become. They gave her her big chance, and she isn't the kind who forgets.

In that first stop at 20th Century-Fox, Marilyn worked in one picture, "Scudda Hoo! Scudda Hay!" but her tiny part ended up, in familiar Hollywood tradition, on the cutting room floor. At the end of the year, her contract was not renewed.

Columbia then signed her for a musical, "Ladies of the Chorus," in which she played a burlesque queen. Then again, Marilyn was dropped.

At this point, she decided she had better supplement her natural charms with acting technique, and she engaged the coaching service of Natasha Lytess.

Deadly serious in her determination to become an actress, Marilyn took a room at the Hollywood Studio Club, home of many an aspiring starlet, limited herself to two meals a day and eked out a living by modeling clothes and posing for fashion photography.

One day she was approached by an agent who told her Lester Cowan was producing a picture called "Love Happy," and needed a blonde for Groucho Marx to chase. Marilyn rushed over, was hired on the spot. The scene lasted for a full minute, but it wasn't cut out of the picture. When the film was released, Cowan engaged Marilyn to go on tour and plug it in Chicago, Detroit, New York and other cities. She did the complete routine—press interviews, TV appearances, radio shows and charity benefits. In doing so, she acquired confidence and poise.

When she returned from the tour, 20th sent for her again and gave her the part of a dancing girl in "Ticket to Tomahawk." The picture was filmed in Colorado, and the day she returned she received a call from MGM to read for Director John Huston for a role in "Asphalt Jungle." She got the part, which proved the real starting point of her film career.

In "Asphalt Jungle," she played the niece of Louis Calhern. Her role, that of a wide-eyed lovely interested in older men, was comparatively minor, but when Marilyn came on the screen, audiences gasp. A new personality had "arrived."

Following "Asphalt Jungle," Marilyn got her second important chance in "All About Eve." Again, her role was comparatively minor, but she appeared in support of such stars as Bette Davis, Anne Baxter, George Sanders and Celeste Holme, and even in that fast company made herself noticed favorably.

When 20th's Darryl Zanuck saw the rushes of "All About Eve," he promptly signed Marilyn to a long-term contract, and ordered a stellar buildup for her. She appeared in three more pictures for her home studio before being borrowed by Jerry Wald and Norman Krasna for her first starring part in "Clash by Night."

The return to RKO studios ended a cycle in Marilyn's life, opened the doorway to another one in which the heartaches of the past will be remembered only as inspiration for the future.

**LADY PAMELA BIRD**
Lady Pamela Bird was the owner of the residential villa in Moon Point, Jamaica, where Arthur and Marilyn Miller vacationed during their delayed honeymoon in early 1957.

**BIRTH**
Norma Jeane Mortenson was born to Gladys Pearl Mortenson on June 1, 1926, at 9:30 A.M. in the Charity Ward of Los Angeles General Hospital.

**MM Trivia Quiz #6**
In what film(s) did MM give birth? (Answer on page 577.)

**MRS. VIRGINIA BLAGSEN**
Mrs. Blagsen was the owner of the Hollywood building complex where the infamous "Wrong Door Raid" scandal took place in November 1954. The raid involved Joe DiMaggio, Frank Sinatra, and two private detectives, all of whom followed Marilyn Monroe to Mrs. Blagsen's building complex—presumably, to catch MM "in the act" with one of Mrs. Blagsen's tenants. However, the group miscalculated, and they broke into the wrong apartment, which traumatized that apartment's tenant, Florence Kotz. At the subsequent hearing in 1957, Virginia Blagsen was called in to testify that she had witnessed both Joe DiMaggio and Frank Sinatra at the scene. (*See* THE WRONG DOOR RAID.)

**JULIAN BLAUSTEIN**
Producer, born in 1913, of mostly ineffectual films, including *Don't Bother to Knock* (1952).

**THE BLISS-HAYDEN MINIATURE THEATRE**
In 1947, after she was dropped by 20th Century-Fox, twenty-one-year-old Marilyn Monroe became a member of the Bliss-Hayden Miniature Theatre acting company. During her eight-month membership at the theatre, Marilyn appeared in at least two stage productions, *Glamour Preferred* and *Stage Door*. The theatre, which was owned and operated by Lela Bliss and Harry Hayden, was located at 254 South Robertson Boulevard in Beverly Hills. Today, it is known as The Beverly Hills Playhouse.

**BLOOMINGDALE'S**
In 1983, Bloomingdale's purchased the licensing rights, from the Marilyn Monroe estate, to open and operate Marilyn Monroe Clothing Boutiques in twelve of its stores. Incidentally, Bloomingdale's in New York was one of Marilyn's favorite stores.

***THE BLUE ANGEL***
After the completion of *The Prince and the Showgirl* shooting toward the end of 1956, 20th Century-Fox wanted Marilyn to star in a remake of *The Blue*

*Angel.* The original *Angel* was the landmark 1930 German film that catapulted Marlene Dietrich to international stardom. The film was directed by Josef Von Sternberg and contained the classic song "Falling in Love Again" (which would have been a *great* number for MM), in addition to the lesser-known "They Call Me Wicked Lola."

*The Blue Angel was* eventually remade by Fox, though Marilyn (who, by then, had story approval) rejected the project. Released in 1959, it was directed by Edward Dmytryk and photographed by Leon Shamroy. It starred May Britt in the Dietrich role that Fox had intended for MM. The reviews were disastrous. Leslie Halliwell (*Film Guide*) called it an

> ill advised attempt at a "realistic" updated remake . . . the result is a total travesty, with the actors aware that stylized melodrama is turning before their eyes into unintentional farce.

**THE BLUE BOOK MODEL AGENCY**

The first agency that Marilyn Monroe ever belonged to and the agency that launched nineteen-year-old Norma Jeane Dougherty's modeling career, which subsequently launched Marilyn Monroe's film career. It was on August 2, 1945, that Norma Jeane filled out the application card to sign with the agency in LA. At that time, Blue Book was located in the Ambassador Hotel and was operated by Miss Emmeline Snively.

COURTESY OF DICK BIEGERT

Blue Book's best models, circa 1946.

**JOSE BOLANOS**

Mexican film writer/producer who met Marilyn on her 1962 furniture-buying expedition in Mexico City. They had a brief affair, and, according to Lena Pepitone, MM's New York personal maid/wardrobe mistress, Marilyn referred to Bolanos as "the greatest lover in the whole wide world."

**IDA BOLENDER**

On June 12, 1926, twelve-day-old Norma Jeane Mortenson (aka Norma Jeane Baker) was taken by her mother to live with a foster couple, Ida and Wayne Bolender. For the next several years, Ida served as Norma Jeane's "aunt," foster guardian, and substitute mother. The devoutly religious Bolenders raised Norma Jeane at their modest home at 459 East Rhode Island Street in Hawthorne, California. In return for raising Norma Jeane, the Bolenders were paid $5 a week by Gladys Baker.

**LESTER BOLENDER**

Lester was Norma Jeane's first playmate in life. He was legally adopted by Ida and Wayne Bolender, and he and Norma Jean (who was two months his senior) were referred to by everyone as "the twins."

**WAYNE BOLENDER**

Albert Wayne Bolender was Norma Jeane's foster father for the first several years of her life. Wayne, originally from the farmlands of Brown County, Ohio, was a mail carrier by profession. As a hobby, he printed religious pamphlets. And although his wife, Ida, objected to Norma Jeane's calling her "Mommy," Wayne had no such objections to NJ's calling him "Daddy"—thus, he was the first in a long string of father figures that NJ/MM would have.

After she left the Bolender home in Hawthorne, Norma Jeane lost contact with Ida and Wayne—except for a few occasions. In 1942, Norma Jeane invited her former foster parents (they accepted) to her wedding ceremony. And years later, after she had established her celebrity, "Marilyn" once telephoned Wayne. He ended the strained conversation by telling Marilyn, "You come see us, Norma Jeane." Marilyn never did go to see the Bolenders—nor did she ever phone them again.

**BOOKS ABOUT MARILYN MONROE**

It's no secret that more books have been written and published about Marilyn Monroe and Elvis Presley than about *any* other show business personalities (Garbo probably places a distant second). Sometimes, it seems as though everyone who ever knew Marilyn (or who just happened to brush past Marilyn on the street or in the supermarket) has written a book, or at least a reflective article, about MM. The single obvious exception, of course, remains Joe DiMaggio.

The following is a chronological list (as well as could be determined) of every nonfiction book ever published about MM. It does *not* include foreign-language titles or books in which Marilyn is only featured—there are too many to mention. Those titles marked with an asterisk (*) are actually cover-to-cover magazines about Marilyn. They are included because they have been incorrectly listed as "books" elsewhere; now the distinction can be made. Some of the books listed are out of print, and some are not. Some of them are awful, most are only fair, and some are mouth-dropping, oh-my-gosh great.

1. *The Marilyn Monroe Story* by Joe Franklin and Laurie Palmer (1953)
2. *Marilyn* by Sidney Skolsky (1954)*
3. *Marilyn Monroe as the Girl: The Making of "The Seven Year Itch"* by Sam Shaw (1955)
4. *Will Acting Spoil Marilyn Monroe?* by Pete Martin (1956)
5. *Marilyn Monroe* by Maurice Zolotow (1960)
6. *Marilyn Monroe: Her Own Story* by George Carpozi, Jr. (1961)
7. *Violations of the Child Marilyn Monroe* by Her Psychiatrist Friend (1962)
8. *The Films of Marilyn Monroe* by Michael Conway and Mark Ricci (1964)
9. *The Strange Death of Marilyn Monroe* by Frank Capell (1964)*
10. *Marilyn, the Tragic Venus* by Edwin P. Hoyt (1965)
11. *Who Killed Marilyn Monroe?* by Charles Hamblett (1966)
12. *The Mysterious Death of Marilyn Monroe* by James A. Hudson (1968)
13. *Marilyn Monroe: A Composite View* by Edward Wagenknecht (1969)
14. *Norma Jean: The Life of Marilyn Monroe* by Fred Lawrence Guiles (1969)
15. *Marilyn, Barven Screen Greats No. 4* by Milburn Smith (1971)*
16. *Marilyn* by Norman Mailer (1973)
17. *Marilyn: An Untold Story* by Norman Rosten (1973)
18. *Marilyn Monroe* by Joan Mellen (1973)
19. *The Life and Curious Death of Marilyn Monroe* by Robert Slatzer (1974)
20. *Marilyn Monroe: A Life on Film* by John Kobal (1974)
21. *My Story* by Marilyn Monroe (1974)
22. *Marilyn: The Last Months* by Eunice Murray (1975)
23. *Conversations with Marilyn* by W. J. Weatherby (1976)
24. *The Secret Happiness of Marilyn Monroe* by James E. Dougherty (1976)
25. *Who Killed Marilyn?* by Anthony Scaduto (aka Tony Sciacca) (1976)
26. *Marilyn & Joe DiMaggio* by Robin Moore and Gene Schoor (1977)
27. *Diary of a Lover of Marilyn Monroe* by Hans Jorgen Lembourn (1979)
28. *The Joy of Marilyn in the Camera Eye* by Sam Shaw (1979)
29. *Marilyn Monroe Confidential* by Lena Pepitone and William Stadiem (1979)
30. *Marilyn, Screen Greats Volume II* by Bob Patrick (1980)*
31. *Of Women and Their Elegance* by Norman Mailer (1980)
32. *Finding Marilyn: A Romance* by David Conover (1981)
33. *Marilyn Lives!* by Joel Oppenheimer (1981)
34. *The Last Sitting* by Bert Stern (1982)
35. *Marilyn Monroe: Murder Cover-Up* by Milo Speriglio (1982)
36. *Monroe: Her Life in Pictures* by James Spada and George Zeno (1982)
37. *The Screen Greats: Marilyn Monroe* by Tom Hutchinson (1982)
38. *Marilyn Monroe* by Janice Anderson (1983)
39. *Marilyn Monroe: In Her Own Words* by Roger Taylor (1983)
40. *Legend: The Life and Death of Marilyn Monroe* by Fred Lawrence Guiles (1984)
41. *Marilyn in Art* by Roger Taylor (1984)
42. *Goddess: The Secret Lives of Marilyn Monroe* by Anthony Summers (1985)
43. *The Marilyn Conspiracy* by Milo Speriglio (1986)
44. *Marilyn Mon Amour* by Andre de Dienes (1986)
45. *Marilyn* by Gloria Steinem (1986)
46. *Joe and Marilyn: A Memory of Love* by Roger Kahn (1986)
47. *Marilyn Monroe: A Life of the Actress* by Carl E. Rollyson, Jr. (1986)
48. *The Unabridged Marilyn: Her Life From A–Z* by Randall Riese and Neal Hitchens (1987)
49. *Marilyn Monroe: An Appreciation* by Eve Arnold (1987)
50. *Marilyn: Among Friends* by Sam Shaw and Norman Rosten (1987)
51. *Marilyn: At Twentieth Century Fox* by Lawrence Crown (1987)
52. *Marilyn Monroe: A Never Ending Dream* by Guus Luijters (1987)

Note: Over the years, *Who Killed Marilyn Monroe?* by Charles Hamblett has been referred to as a book about Marilyn Monroe. In actuality, however, and despite its title, only one chapter of this book is devoted to MM. It is included here for clarification.

**BOOKS THAT MARILYN READ**

During her reign as Hollywood's smartest dumb blonde, Marilyn was often ridiculed by the cynics who refused to believe that she could spell, much less read. And yet she did read. Friends frequently lent her books, which she would later discuss with them at length. Reporters and other visitors to her homes would commonly take mental note of the impressive array of books that were lying about or stacked on the shelves. Still, some critics continued to doubt her reading capability and disregarded it as one of the newly acquired pretensions she picked up when she moved to New York, hobnobbed with the intellectuals, and married Arthur Miller.

But the facts prove otherwise. As early as 1945, Norma Jeane became a member of the Westwood Public Library. In 1946-47, after she began making money, she opened her first charge account—it was, significantly, at a book store. (How many "dumb" blonde starlets do you know who would favor B. Dalton over I. Magnin?) And in 1951 (four years before her sojourn to New York), Marilyn took an evening course at UCLA called "Backgrounds in Literature."

That point proven, the following is an alphabetized, selected compilation of the books that Marilyn read (or "allegedly" read—for the adamant disbelievers) over the years:

*An Actor Prepares* by Kostantin Stanislavsky
*The Autobiography of Lincoln Steffens*
The Bible
*The Biography of Eleanora Duse* by William Weaver

THE RAY VAN GOEYE COLLECTION

In real life MM wouldn't have been caught dead reading material like this!

*The Course of My Life* by Rudolph Steiner
*De Humani Corporis Fabrica (the study of bone structure)* by Andreas Vesalius
*Essays* by Ralph Waldo Emerson
*Gertrude Lawrence as Mrs. A* by Richard Aldrich
*Goodnight Sweet Prince* by Gene Fowler
*Greek Mythology* by Edith Hamilton
*Green Mansions* by W. H. Hudson
*How Stanislavsky Directs* by Michael Gorchakov
*I Married Adventure* by Olso Johnson
*The Importance of Living* by Lin Yutang
*Letters to a Young Poet* by Rainer Maria Rilke
*Life Among the Savages* by Shirley Jackson
*The Little Prince* by Antoine de Saint Exupéry
*Look Homeward Angel* by Thomas Wolfe
*Lust for Life* by Irving Stone
*Magnificent Obsession* by Lloyd Douglas
*The Old Man and the Sea* by Ernest Hemingway
*The Postman Always Rings Twice* by James M. Caine
*The Prophet* by Kahlil Gibran
*Psychology of Everyday Life* by Sigmund Freud
*The Rains Came* by Louis Bromfield
*The Rebel* by Albert Camus
*The Rights of Man* by Thomas Paine
*Science and Health with Key to the Scriptures* by Mary Baker Eddy
*Swann's Way* by Marcel Proust
*To the Actor* by Michael Chekhov
*The Trial* by Franz Kafka
*Ulysses* by James Joyce
*War and Peace* by Leo Tolstoy
*The Web and the Rock* by Thomas Wolfe
*The Works of Edgar Allan Poe*
*Your Key to Happiness* by Harold Sherman

### *BORN YESTERDAY*

Successful 1950 Columbia movie that won an Oscar for Judy Holliday (against the unbelievably formidable competition of both Bette Davis in *All About Eve* and Gloria Swanson in *Sunset Boulevard*). *Born Yesterday* was written by Garson Kanin, from his equally successful Broadway play, and was directed by George Cukor. It costarred William Holden and Broderick Crawford.

Reportedly, while she was at Columbia in 1948, Marilyn screen-tested for the role of Billie Dawn, the part that would make a star out of the superb Judy Holliday. At any rate, the alleged test was ignored by Harry Cohn, and Marilyn was dropped by Columbia.

Interestingly, notable critic Pauline Kael once suggested that MM would have been "right" in a remake of *Born Yesterday*—had she lived.

### TOM BOSLEY

Best known for his long-running stint as "Howard Cunningham" on television's "Happy Days," Tom Bosley narrated a "That's Hollywood" documentary segment about Marilyn Monroe. The segment, entitled "Marvelous Marilyn," initially aired on January 8, 1979, in Los Angeles.

**WALTER BOUILLET**
Walter Bouillet (also spelled *Buillet* according to some sources) was the U.S. Army's chief of entertainment in the Far East during 1954. Accordingly, Bouillet accompanied MM on her tour of Korea in February of that year.

**ELGEE BOVE**
An American fashion designer, Elgee Bove created Marilyn Monroe's purple cocktail dress, which she wore to entertain the troops in Korea (1954). Bove also designed Judy Garland's wardrobe for her Palace engagement and the dress that Eva Peron wore for her audience with the Pope.

**CLARA BOW**
MM once tried to obtain the rights to film actress Clara Bow's life story. However, Bow reportedly declined at that time because she didn't want the movie made while she was still alive. Born in 1905, Bow died of a heart attack in 1965.

Nonetheless, MM got her chance to portray the former "It Girl" in Richard Avedon's photo series for *LIFE*, December 22, 1958.

> "Being a sex symbol is a heavy load to carry, especially when one is tired, hurt and bewildered."
>
> Clara Bow

**JOHN BOWEN**
Bowen was an antiques dealer in Beverly Hills whose client, Doug Villiers, once offered $150,000 for Marilyn Monroe's alleged red diary. However, the financial bait proved to be useless, as the diary has never been located.

**BOX OFFICE**
According to the Quigley Poll, a respected motion picture industry survey, Marilyn Monroe was the top female box office attraction from 1953 until 1956. Moreover, MM's *Some Like It Hot* (1959) was the most financially successful comedy of its time. The following is a closer look at Marilyn Monroe's impressive statistics—box office statistics, that is:

**The 1952 "Stars of Tomorrow" Poll**

1. Marilyn Monroe
2. Debbie Reynolds
3. Marge and Gower Champion
5. Mitzi Gaynor
6. Kim Hunter
7. Rock Hudson
8. Audie Murphy
9. Forrest Tucker
10. Danny Thomas

**The 1953 Top Ten Box Office Stars:**

1. Gary Cooper
2. Dean Martin and Jerry Lewis
3. John Wayne
4. Alan Ladd
5. Bing Crosby
6. Marilyn Monroe
7. James Stewart
8. Bob Hope
9. Susan Hayward
10. Randolph Scott

**The 1954 Top Ten Box Office Stars:**

1. John Wayne
2. Dean Martin and Jerry Lewis
3. Gary Cooper
4. James Stewart
5. Marilyn Monroe
6. Alan Ladd
7. William Holden
8. Bing Crosby
9. Jane Wyman
10. Marlon Brando

**The 1956 Top Ten Box Office Stars:**

1. William Holden
2. John Wayne
3. James Stewart
4. Burt Lancaster
5. Glenn Ford
6. Dean Martin and Jerry Lewis
7. Gary Cooper
8. Marilyn Monroe
9. Kim Novak
10. Frank Sinatra

☆ *Niagara* cost $1,250,000 and grossed $6,000,000.

☆ *How to Marry a Millionaire* cost $2,500,000 and grossed a reported $12,000,000.

☆ *The Seven Year Itch* cost $1,800,000 and grossed an initial $8,000,000.

☆ Marilyn's movies grossed anywhere from $43,000,000 to $250,000,000—depending on whom you believe. It should be noted, though, that $43,000,000 in 1962 would equate to hundreds and hundreds of millions by 1986 standards.

☆ Marilyn's most successful movie at the box-office was *Some Like It Hot.*

☆ *Note:* These figures do *not* include subsequent revival showings, television sales, or home video rentals and sales.

**CHARLES BRACKETT**

Born in 1892, Charles Brackett was a novelist/film critic who became a highly successful screenwriter/producer. In 1953, Brackett produced and cowrote Marilyn's showcase vehicle, *Niagara*. Brackett also enjoyed a long, profitable collaboration with director Billy Wilder. Among their films were *The Lost Weekend* (1945) and *Sunset Boulevard* (1950), both of which won Academy Awards (for producing and writing, respectively) for Brackett. Brackett's final film, before his death in 1969, was the 1962 remake of *State Fair* starring Ann-Margret.

**HARRY BRAND**

Harry Brand was the director of publicity at 20th Century-Fox during Marilyn's rise to stardom. It was Brand, in tandem with Roy Craft, who spearheaded the promotional campaign to put MM "over the top." When the Fox executives panicked after word of MM's nude calendar "leaked," it was Brand who spoke up in her defense. "This isn't going to kill her. It's going to make her," Brand contended. And, of course, he was right.

Just before marrying Joe DiMaggio in San Francisco, Marilyn telephoned Brand—as she had once promised she would—to let him know of her plans. He, in turn, notified the world, as he did nine months later, when Marilyn decided to divorce DiMaggio.

**PHOEBE BRAND**

Brand was an acting instructor who coached MM in the late 1940s at the Actors Lab, which was operated by Brand and her husband, Morris Carnovsky. Years later, Brand was quoted as saying about her former student:

> "What I failed to see in her acting was her wit, her acting sense of humor. It was there all the time—this lovely comedic style she has, but I was blind to it."

**ROBERT BRANDFIELD**

Dr. Robert Brandfield was one of the company doctors during the 1960 shooting of *The Misfits.*

**MARLON BRANDO**

> "I read recently that, before I met Joe, I had had a secret romance with Marlon Brando. That's not true either. I have met Marlon and I like him both as a person and as an actor. I think he is one of the finest actors on the screen. I have been receiving letters from teen-agers who adore Marlon, suggesting that I play in a picture with him. Maybe I'll forward these to Mr. Zanuck."
>
> Marilyn, in her own inimitable way, dually suggesting (1) to Darryl Zanuck that she would like to make a movie with Brando and (2) to Brando that she would like to make a movie with Brando, in addition to having a "secret romance" with him.
>
> *The American Weekly,* 11/23/52

COURTESY OF CINEMA COLLECTORS

Marlon Brando was considered the best and most famous actor of his generation. Marilyn Monroe was the most famous actress of her generation. It seems only appropriate that the two had formed a "mutual admiration society."

Marilyn met Marlon Brando on the 20th Century-Fox set of *Desiree* in 1954. According to several sources, the famous Method acting twosome had an affair in 1955, following Marilyn's divorce from Joe DiMaggio, and before her marriage to Arthur Miller. In December of that year, Brando accompanied Monroe to the world premiere of *The Rose Tattoo*. Following the screening, they went to the Sheraton Astor Hotel for a benefit champagne dinner. Reportedly, MM confided to Milton Greene, the morning after going to bed with Brando, "I don't know if I do it the right way." Anthony Summers's 1985 book, *Goddess: The Secret Lives of Marilyn Monroe* (Macmillan), also attests to a secret Brando/Monroe affair:

> Marilyn spoke of him to Amy Greene as "sweet, tender." She referred to him by the code-name "Carlo."

Marilyn herself was quoted, at various times, as saying the following: "Personally, I react to Marlon Brando. He's a favorite of mine," and "[He is] one of the most attractive men I've ever met."

The alleged affair with Brando reportedly ended when Marilyn's romance with Arthur Miller became public; however, the two maintained a friendship that lasted until Marilyn's death. As for Brando, he refuses to discuss MM.

**MORTIMER BRAUS**
Braus wrote the story on which *Let's Make It Legal* (1951) was based.

***BREAKFAST AT TIFFANY'S***
Movie that was reportedly written for Marilyn (and which she would have been *perfect* in). Scripted by George Axelrod, the film was based on a novel by Truman Capote. The coveted role of Holly Golightly eventually went to Audrey Hepburn, who subsequently won an Oscar nomination for her performance. *Breakfast* was directed by Blake Edwards and was released by Paramount in 1961.

**RICHARD BREEN**
Former president of the Screenwriters Guild and cowriter of *Niagara* (1953). Breen's most notable film was *Titanic* (1953), which he cowrote and won an Oscar for.

**ROBERT BRENNAN**
Robert Brennan wrote the 1983 "Matt Houston" television segment that involved a Marilyn Monroe-based character.

**WALTER BRENNAN**
One of the most popular character actors of all time, the three-time Oscar-winning Brennan costarred in *A Ticket to Tomahawk* (1950) and *Scudda Hoo! Scudda Hay!* (1948), both of which featured MM in a bit part. Brennan's Oscar-winning performances were in *Come and Get It* (1936), *Kentucky* (1938), and *The Westerner* (1948). Among his many other standout films are *To Have and Have Not* (1944) and *Red River* (1948).

**ALFRED BRENNER**
Alfred Brenner scripted "The Eleventh Hour" segment about Marilyn Monroe entitled "Like a Diamond in the Sky." The segment aired on NBC-TV on February 13, 1963.

**BRENTWOOD, CALIFORNIA**

In September 1952, MM moved out of the Bel Air Hotel and into a rented house in Brentwood, where she lived for a couple of months. Nearly ten years later, she returned to Brentwood and purchased a house at 12305 Fifth Helena Drive. It was the only home she ever bought as well as her final residence.

**BRIGGS DELI**

Between July 11 and August 3, 1962, Briggs Deli in Brentwood (address: 13038 San Vicente Boulevard) delivered $215.41 worth of deli and liquor items to Marilyn's Fifth Helena Drive home. MM had a charge account with the deli, which was owned at that time by Don J. Briggs. Today, the deli is known as Briggs Wine and Spirits.

**NORBERT BRODINE**

Productive American cinematographer who worked in Hollywood nonstop from 1919 to 1952. In 1950, Brodine shot MGM's *Right Cross,* which featured MM in a bit part.

**BROOKLYN, NEW YORK**

> "I want to retire to Brooklyn."
>
> MM, following her split from DiMaggio, to radio interviewer Dave Garroway

Marilyn never did retire to Brooklyn. In fact, she never even lived there for any extended period of time. What Marilyn seemed to mean was that she wanted to marry Arthur Miller, who at that time resided in Brooklyn Heights with his wife, Mary Slattery Miller.

**BROTHERS**

**Half-Brother**
Hermitt Jack Baker

**Foster Brother**
Lester Bolender

**Brothers-In-Law**
Marion Dougherty
Tom Dougherty
Thomas DiMaggio
Michael DiMaggio
Vincent DiMaggio
Dominic DiMaggio
Kermit Miller

***THE BROTHERS KARAMAZOV***

> Reporter: Do you want to play *The Brothers Karamazov*?
> MM: I don't want to play the brothers. I want to play Grushenka. She's a girl.

As far back as 1950, Johnny Hyde suggested to Marilyn that she one day play the role of Grushenka in a film based on Fyodor Dostoyevsky's *The Brothers Karamazov*. When Marilyn went public with her ambitions to play the role, she was ridiculed by the press and by the Hollywood community. Director Billy Wilder once said that he would be pleased to direct MM not only in *The Brothers Karamazov* but also in a series of *Karamazov* sequels, such as *The Brothers Karamazov Meet Abbott and Costello.* Twentieth Century-Fox announced that it had no intention of permitting MM to play the role.

*The Brothers Karamazov* was eventually made in 1958 by MGM. The film starred Maria Schell as Grushenka, in addition to a cast that included Yul Brynner, Richard Basehart, Claire Bloom, Lee J. Cobb, Albert Salmi, and William Shatner.

**BROWN AND BIGELOW**

During the late 1940s, artist Earl Moran did "photo illustrations" of MM for the Brown and Bigelow Calendar Company. These calendars (not to be confused with *the* calendar) were distributed in the United States and Mexico.

**JOE E. BROWN**

American comedy star (1892–1973) who has become immortalized due to his delivery of the last line in *Some Like It Hot* (1959): "Nobody's perfect!"

**KAY BROWN**

Arthur Miller's literary agent, who lent her Katonah, New York, home to Miller and MM for their July 1, 1956, wedding ceremony.

**MORRIS BROWN**

MM fan from Champaign, Illinois, who, in 1954, sent $100 to the Beverly Hills Courthouse to pay the bail for MM's traffic violation.

**BRUCE WONG'S**

Chinese Restaurant located on La Cienega Boulevard in Hollywood where MM and Joe would sometimes go for Chinese food.

**JOHN BRYSON**

During 1960, photographer Bryson took thousands of shots of MM on the set of *Let's Make Love*. The photos were for a pictorial in *Paris-Match* magazine and for an eleven-page cover feature in *LIFE*. As always, MM insisted on photo approval; however, according to Bryson, she waived this demand for him. Said Bryson:

> There were, and there are, actresses with greater beauty, more sex appeal and perhaps greater talent, but few of them had that mysterious, magic electricity that bewitches the camera.

**LARRY BUCHANAN**

Larry Buchanan produced and directed the 1976 motion picture *Goodbye Norma Jean*, which starred Misty Rowe as Marilyn Monroe.

**JULES BUCK**

American producer who gained some distinction with his later, British-produced films such as *Becket* (1964) and *The Ruling Class* (1971). In 1951, Buck produced *Love Nest*, which costarred MM.

### THE BUCKET OF BLOOD SALOON

The Bucket of Blood Saloon (address: 3 South C Street) was a bar in Virginia City, Nevada, where MM and Fred Karger would sometimes go, circa 1948. And, in 1960, Clark Gable, Montgomery Clift, and MM frequented The Bucket of Blood during their free time from *The Misfits* shooting.

### BUFFALO, NEW YORK

Where MM and company shot *Niagara* on location during June 1952.

### BULLOCKS

In the early 1940s, teenaged housewife Norma Jeane Dougherty used to spend her husband Jim's salary on shopping sprees at the Bullocks department store.

### BURBANK, CALIFORNIA

During the summer of 1947, Marilyn moved into a house in Burbank, California, to house-sit while the owners were away on vacation. It was while living at this Burbank home that Marilyn was nearly raped (according to MM) by an off-duty policeman. The house was located at 131 South Avon Street.

### BILL BURNSIDE

When Marilyn was dropped by 20th Century-Fox in 1947, Bill Burnside was one of the people present for her to lean on. Burnside once took her to pose for commercial photographer Paul Hesse, who reportedly told her, simply, "Darling, you're too fat." To get Marilyn to stop crying, Burnside reportedly took the photos himself.

According to Anthony Summers's *Goddess: The Secret Lives of Marilyn Monroe* (Macmillan, 1985), Burnside and MM were lovers for a brief period. The alleged affair ended when Burnside departed on an extended trip to Latin America. Upon his return to Hollywood, Marilyn gave him a poem that read:

> I could have loved you once
> and even said it
> But you went away,
> A long way away.
> When you came back it was too late
> And love was a forgotten word.
> Remember?

Also in *Goddess*, Burnside had this to say about MM at twenty-one:

> She was very aware of how she affected men. If I took her to a restaurant, however elegant, the waiters were ready to jump at her bidding. She had it there all right, that star quality. . . .

***BUS STOP* ★★★★**

1956 96 minutes Color
20th Century-Fox
Directed by: Joshua Logan
Produced by: Buddy Adler
Screenplay by: George Axelrod, from the play by William Inge
Photographed by: Milton Krasner
Cast: Marilyn Monroe, Don Murray, Betty Field, Arthur O'Connell, Eileen Heckart, Hope Lange

THE AUTHOR'S COLLECTION

Film adaptation of William Inge's 1955 Broadway play tells the slight but often poignant story of a simple-minded, naive rodeo cowboy (Murray) who goes to the big city in pursuit of an angelic wife to haul back to his ranch.

*Bus Stop* was a pivotal film in the career of Marilyn Monroe. First of all, it contains what is arguably her finest performance. As Murray's would-be angel, a second-rate saloon singer with first-rate aspirations, Marilyn is superb. It was this film, her first after going on "strike" in 1954, that validated Marilyn's value in Hollywood. After *Bus Stop,* the movie colony began to reconsider MM and listen to her plea to be taken seriously. This was also the first film that Marilyn made *without* the services of Natasha Lytess since she had become a star, the first film *with* the guidance of Paula Strasberg, and the first film following her training in "The Method" style of acting.

Marilyn had made a triumphant return to Hollywood in February 1956 to shoot *Bus Stop* after having won her lengthy and crucial dispute with 20th Century-Fox. She was also the president of what promised to be a lucrative venture, Marilyn Monroe Productions, Inc. and she was in the planning stages of becoming Mrs. Arthur Miller. During the shooting itself, Marilyn found herself working with the director she had chosen, the cinematographer she had chosen, and, most significantly, the *material* she had chosen. Marilyn's partner and friend, Milton H. Greene, designed her makeup for the film, and Marilyn picked out her own costumes.

*Bus Stop* completed shooting in May 1956 and was released in the late summer of that year.

**BUS STOP**
Los Angeles diner which serves as a memorial, of sorts, to MM. It is named after one of Marilyn's biggest film hits, and is decorated with Marilyn memorabilia. Bus Stop is located at 5515 Wilshire Blvd.

**FLORENCE BUSH**
According to Fred Lawrence Guiles's 1984 book, *Legend: The Life and Death of Marilyn Monroe* (Stein and Day), it was Fox hairdresser Florence Bush who did Norma Jeane's hair for her 1946 screen test at 20th Century-Fox.

**DAVID BUTLER**
David Butler wrote the 1974 British stage play about Marilyn Monroe entitled *Legend.*

**ROBERT E. BYRON**
Detective Sergeant R. E. Byron is the police officer who arrived at Marilyn's Brentwood home at 5:00 A.M. on August 5, 1962. It was Byron who took over the investigation from Sergeant Jack Clemmons, who had arrived earlier.

# C

### ROBERT CAHN

Cahn was one of the first writers, in what became a series of thousands, to write a feature story on Marilyn Monroe. Cahn's article was published in the September 8, 1951, issue of *Collier's* magazine. Showing adept perception, Cahn wrote:

> Marilyn Monroe is not a girl anyone quickly forgets. While Hollywood Blondes are generally considered the industry's most expendable item, Miss Monroe's value during the past year has risen faster than the cost of living.

### CAL-NEVA LODGE

In the latter part of her life, Marilyn Monroe was a frequent guest at the Cal-Neva Lodge at Lake Tahoe, a casino resort reportedly owned by Frank Sinatra and Sam Giancana. While at the Cal-Neva, Marilyn stayed in cottage #50. In February 1986, the hotel reopened and is located at #2 State Line in the Crystal Bay area of Lake Tahoe, Nevada.

### CALENDAR

In May 1949, Marilyn Monroe was just another blonde Hollywood starlet without a studio. In the preceding three-year period, she had been dropped by both 20th Century–Fox and Columbia. She didn't have a job. She was broke. Photographer Tom Kelley had once asked Marilyn to pose in the nude and she had declined. But in May of 1949, MM could not afford to be so selective. She telephoned Kelley and asked if the offer was still good, which, of course, it was. On the 27th of that month, Marilyn arrived at Kelley's studio, which was located at 736 N. Seward Street in Los Angeles. Also present at the studio was Tom's wife at that time, Natalie, who worked as his assistant. Kelley loaded his eight-by-ten Deardorff View Camera. He draped a sheet of red velvet across the floor. He put an Artie Shaw record on the turntable. And Marilyn took off her clothes. They worked for two hours. Following the session, Marilyn signed the release form and used the half-hearted alias "Mona Monroe." Then she and Kelley, and perhaps his wife, went out and ate chili.

During their session, Tom Kelley shot twenty-four nude poses of Marilyn Monroe. He sold only two of them, one of which became known worldwide as the "Golden Dreams" calendar. A second, less popular calendar, titled "A New Wrinkle," was also issued. The remaining twenty-two poses were later mysteriously stolen from Tom Kelley's file cabinet. In addition to the twenty-four poses, Kelley also shot an additional roll of nudes, which he presented to MM. It has been speculated that MM, in turn, presented these nudes to Joe DiMaggio as a wedding gift.

In February 1952, wire service reporter Aline Mosby learned that the

"Golden Dreams" calendar girl was none other than rising star Marilyn Monroe. Allegedly, it was RKO's *Clash by Night* producers, Jerry Wald and Norman Krasna, who tipped Mosby so that their film (which was slated for release later that year) would benefit from the publicity. At any rate, Mosby contacted the Publicity Department at Fox, where Marilyn was shooting *Don't Bother to Knock,* and asked for a confirmation or a denial. In a state of panic, Fox executives confronted Marilyn, who admitted that she was indeed the red velvet calendar girl. She was promptly instructed to lie, to deny that she had committed the unforgivable sin of posing in the nude. However, Marilyn saw no reason to lie. Thankfully, she was supported in her stand by Fox publicity director Harry Brand. Thus, Marilyn met with Ms. Mosby, and, on March 13, 1952, she issued to the nation's newspapers the "confession" that appears below.

**MARILYN MONROE ADMITS SHE'S NUDE BLONDE OF CALENDAR**
**By Aline Mosby**

A photograph of a beautiful nude blonde on a 1952 calendar is hanging in garages and barbershops all over the nation today.

Marilyn Monroe admitted today that the beauty is she.

She posed, stretched out on rumpled red velvet, for the artistic photo three years ago because "I was broke and needed the money.

"Oh, the calendar's hanging in garages all over town," said Marilyn. "Why deny it? You can get one any place.

"Besides, I'm not ashamed of it. I've done nothing wrong."

The beautiful blonde now gets a fat paycheck every week from an excited 20th Century-Fox Studio. She's rated the most sensational sweater girl since Lana Turner . . . she lives in an expensive hotel room. . . . She dines at Romanoff's.

**LIVED IN ORPHANAGE**

But in 1949 she was just another scared young blonde, struggling to find fame in the magic city, and all alone. As a child she lived in a Hollywood orphanage. She was pushed around among 12 sets of foster parents before she turned an insecure 16.

After an unsuccessful marriage, she moved into Hollywood's famed Studio Club, home of hopeful actresses.

"I was a week behind on my rent," she explained. "I had to have the money. A photographer, Tom Kelley, had asked me before to pose but I'd never do it. This time I called him and said I would as soon as possible, to get it over with.

"His wife was there. They're both very nice. We did two poses, one standing up with my head turned profile, and another lying on some red velvet."

Marilyn speaks in a breathless, soft voice, and she's always very serious about every word she says.

"Tom didn't think anyone would recognize me," she said. "My hair was long then. But when the picture came out, everybody knew me. I'd never have done it if I'd known things would happen in Hollywood so fast for me."

Marilyn's bosses at plushy Fox Studio reached for the ulcer tablets when the calendar blossomed out in January.

"I was told I should deny I'd posed . . . but I'd rather be honest about it. I've gotten a lot of fan letters on it. The men like the picture and want copies. The women, well. . . .

"One gossip columnist said I autographed the pictures and handed them out and said 'Art for Art's sake.' I never said that.

"Why, I only gave two away," said Marilyn, and blinked those big, blue eyes.

With the news of her nude calendar, Marilyn unintentionally perpetrated the single most effective publicity feat in show business history. *Clash by Night* opened to big business. MM's fan mail at 20th Century-Fox multiplied. And the "Golden Dreams" calendar—as well as the subsequent multitude of mass-marketed products bearing MM nude (ashtrays, cocktail glasses, etc.) went on to earn, cumulatively, somewhere near a million dollars. What really *does* seem obscene is that, for the entire photo session, Marilyn Monroe was paid a mere $50 for her work.

**LOUIS CALHERN**

Born Carl Vogt in 1895, Louis Calhern appeared in many films during his thirty-five-year career. In 1950, Calhern portrayed MM's "uncle" in John Huston's *The Asphalt Jungle.* Calhern then proceeded to appear in such films as *We're Not Married* (1952), *Executive Suite* (1954), *The Blackboard Jungle* (1955), and his final film before his death, *High Society* (1956).

**RORY CALHOUN**

Rory Calhoun, formerly known as Francis Timothy Durgin, born in 1922, was the star of mostly mediocre films from the forties through the sixties. In 1953, he made what was probably his best film, *How to Marry a Millionaire,* which starred MM. Calhoun also appeared in two other MM movies: *A Ticket to Tomahawk* (1950) and *River of No Return* (1954).

**CAMP PENDLETON**

Following the shooting of *Monkey Business* in 1952, Marilyn performed before ten thousand Marines at Camp Pendleton. At the time, MM was actively campaigning at Fox to win the coveted role of Lorelei Lee in *Gentlemen Prefer Blondes* (1953). It has been speculated that MM performed at Camp Pendleton to prove to Fox boss Darryl Zanuck that she could sing. On that day, MM performed "Somebody Loves You" and "Do It Again" for the cheering Marines. She also won their hearts with provocative lines like: "I don't know why you boys are always getting so excited about sweater girls. Take away their sweaters—and what have they got?"

Interestingly, the night that Marilyn died she received a phone call from her former son-in-law, Joe DiMaggio, Jr. At that time, young DiMaggio was a Marine, stationed at Camp Pendleton.

**BILLIE CAMPBELL**

*See* ELYDA NELSON.

**CANADA**
Toward the end of 1953, Marilyn went to Banff, in Alberta, Canada, to shoot the location work for *River of No Return.* At one point, Joe DiMaggio and his friend George Solotaire flew to Banff to join MM.

**FRANK A. CAPELL**
Writer of the 1964 book *The Strange Death of Marilyn Monroe.* Capell began his career as an undercover criminal investigator and eventually became the editor of the *Herald of Freedom,* which was termed a "national Anti-Communist educational bi-weekly."

**THE CAPITOL THEATRE**
Broadway theatre (located at Broadway and 51st Street) where the premiere of *The Misfits* was held on January 31, 1961.

**TRUMAN CAPOTE**
Born on September 30, 1924, Truman Capote was a successful novelist of disputed repute. Among his works that have been adapted for the screen are *Breakfast at Tiffany's* (1961) and *In Cold Blood* (1967).

In 1979, Capote published a book titled *Music for Chameleons* (Random House). In it, he included a chapter on his experiences with Marilyn Monroe. The chapter was named "A Beautiful Child." Capote had met MM in Hollywood during the shooting of *The Asphalt Jungle* (1950). According to Capote, they quickly became friends and once danced nude in Cecil Beaton's New York hotel suite. Said Capote on MM:

> There was something exceptional about Marilyn Monroe. Sometimes she could be ethereal and sometimes like a waitress in a coffee shop.

**JACK CARDIFF**

> There's no doubt she had a genius. She wasn't a great actress, she was a genius. She had a talent that in most cases was not seen until it was on the screen. She had this extraordinary magic that came over on camera. Not once did I ever hear her say anything really bitchy, or use a four-letter word. However, she had this double side. Larry [Laurence Olivier] called her schizoid, and she was.
>
> Jack Cardiff on Marilyn Monroe, 1986

> Then she appeared. A door opened behind me; there was a blur of soft material as Marilyn sped swiftly into [Arthur] Miller's arms, not looking at me until she was hugged in his bearlike embrace. Then she slanted a shy, sleepy smile at me. I had never seen this Marilyn before, in any film or photo. This was no hot sex symbol of Hollywood; this was a little girl, with her face pressed into Daddy's chest, shyly curious at a visitor.
>
> Jack Cardiff on MM,
> from his forthcoming autobiography

Born in 1914, Jack Cardiff is the excellent British cinematographer who shot Marilyn Monroe in *The Prince and the Showgirl* (1957). His other films as a

COURTESY OF JACK CARDIFF

COURTESY OF JACK CARDIFF

COURTESY OF JACK CARDIFF

COURTESY OF JACK CARDIFF

COURTESY OF JACK CARDIFF

COURTESY OF JACK CARDIFF

COURTESY OF JACK CARDIFF

THE RAY VAN GOEYE COLLECTION

With Jack Cardiff, on location of *The Prince and the Showgirl*, 1957.

cinematographer have included: *Wings of the Morning* (1937), *Caesar and Cleopatra* (1945), *Black Narcissus* (for which he won a 1946 Oscar), *The Red Shoes* (1948), *War and Peace* (1956), *Death on the Nile* (1978), and *Rambo: First Blood Part II* (1985). Following his work on *The Prince and the Showgirl*, Mr. Cardiff directed such films as *Sons and Lovers* (1960), *My Geisha* (1962), and *Young Cassidy* (1965).

During a break from shooting *The Prince and the Showgirl* in England, Jack Cardiff had a private photo session with Marilyn Monroe. And, in a strike of creative inspiration, Cardiff shot Marilyn as a Renoir girl. The results stand among the most beautiful still photographs ever taken of Marilyn Monroe.

**MACDONALD CAREY**

In 1951, Carey costarred with MM in *Let's Make It Legal*. From the forties on, Carey appeared in nearly twenty mostly nondescript films and on daytime soaps.

**THE CARLYLE HOTEL**

New York hotel that President John F. Kennedy used as his base. It has been speculated that Kennedy conducted his "affair" with MM in his suite at the Carlyle. Carlyle neighbor Jane Shalam told writer Anthony Summers:

> "I saw Marilyn coming and going at that time, and she was certainly in and out enough to notice her."
>
> *Goddess: The Secret Lives of Marilyn Monroe*
> (Macmillan, 1985)

**JEANNE CARMEN**
Marilyn met actress Jeanne Carmen (aka Saber Dareaux) at the Actors Studio in New York in the mid-fifties. Coincidentally, when MM moved back to her Doheny apartment in 1961, Jeanne was her neighbor. According to Carmen, as told by Anthony Summers in his book, *Goddess: The Secret Lives of Marilyn Monroe,* the two became friends and confidantes. They drank together, took pills together, and went to nude beaches together. Carmen also confirmed, as have many sources, MM's alleged romance with Robert Kennedy.

**HOAGY CARMICHAEL**
Actor/composer/lyricist (1899-1981) who was commissioned to write additional songs for Fox's film version of *Gentlemen Prefer Blondes* in 1952. Carmichael partnered with Harold Adamson and came up with "When Love Goes Wrong" and "Ain't There Anyone Here for Love?" Carmichael is best known for his songs "Stardust" and "In the Cool, Cool, Cool of the Evening."

**MORRIS CARNOVSKY**
Stage and film actor, born 1897, who—with his wife, Phoebe Brand—operated the Actors Lab, where starlet MM studied during 1947.

**JOSEPH CAROL**
Coscreenwriter of *Ladies of the Chorus* (1948).

**CAROLWOOD DRIVE**
For a period in 1949, starlet Marilyn Monroe lived in a cottage on the estate owned by Fox magnate Joseph Schenck. It was located at 141 South Carolwood Drive, in the Holmby Hills section of Beverly Hills, California.

**GEORGE CARPOZI, JR.**
Biographer who wrote *Marilyn Monroe: Her Own Story* for Belmont Books in 1961.

**HOWARD CARRINGTON**
Former Olympic weightlifting champion and instructor at the maritime service training base who taught Norma Jean Dougherty how to lift weights during her 1943 residence on Catalina Island.

**BOB CARROLL, JR.**
One of the three writers involved with the 1954 "I Love Lucy" segment, "Ricky's Movie Offer," in which Lucille Ball parodied Marilyn Monroe.

**JOHN CARROLL**
Born Julian La Faye (1906-1979), Carroll somewhat resembled Clark Gable and had a long acting career in mostly dubious productions. In 1947, Carroll, along with his wife, Lucille Ryman, invited hungry starlet MM to live with

them in their "El Palaccio" apartment located in what is now called West Hollywood. According to Fred Lawrence Guiles, Carroll became Marilyn's lover. Reportedly, MM once asked her friend and benefactor Lucille Ryman to divorce Carroll so that she could marry him. Said MM:

> Lucille, I want to have a little talk with you. You don't love John. If you did, you wouldn't be off working all the time. I think I'm in love with him. . . . No one who is that good to me, could *not* be in love with me.
>
> *Norma Jean: The Life of Marilyn Monroe*
> (McGraw-Hill, 1969)

However, Carroll apparently did not want to marry MM. But on December 4, 1947, Carroll did sign MM to a personal management contract—a contract that was later voluntarily withdrawn.

As for their alleged affair, Carroll once told writer Bob Slatzer: "The only thing I ever did with Marilyn was to try to teach her how to sing."

But, Marilyn herself reportedly told Slatzer: "Mmm, what girl *wasn't* in love with him?"

**CARS**

The following is a chronological list of the cars that Marilyn Monroe owned, as well as the cars that she frequently drove or was driven in.

1. The Bolenders' Model-T Ford—Hawthorne, circa 1926–32
2. Jim Dougherty's blue 1940 coupe
3. Jim Dougherty's 1935 Ford sports car—which Norma Jeane retained when the couple divorced
4. A 1948 Ford convertible—which MM purchased when she began to make money and which was soon repossessed
5. A 1950 Pontiac convertible
6. A black Cadillac convertible (license #2T66185)—probably the Cadillac that MM received for appearing on "The Jack Benny Show," circa 1953–54
7. Joe DiMaggio's black Cadillac (license "Joe D")—the car that the DiMaggios hopped into immediately following their 1954 wedding ceremony
8. A black Thunderbird sports car—the car MM drove when she moved to New York in 1956. It may have been purchased for her by Milton H. Greene.
9. Arthur Miller's Jaguar—New York, circa 1957
10. A white Cadillac—the car MM drove (and was driven in) during the 1960 location shooting of *The Misfits*. It was probably rented.
11. A chauffeur-driven black limousine—Upon her return to Los Angeles in 1961, MM did not purchase another car. For certain occasions, she was driven about in this limo.
12. Mrs. Eunice Murray's modest green Dodge—For everyday, noneventful occasions, MM would be driven about Los Angeles by Mrs. Murray, circa 1961–62.

**MM Trivia Quiz #7**

What is the first film in which MM is seen in a car? (Answer on page 577.)

**BONNIE CASHIN**

Miss Cashin was credited as the costume designer on *Scudda Hoo! Scudda Hay!* (1948).

**CASTILIAN DRIVE**

According to Bob Slatzer, MM once lived at 2393 Castilian Drive in the Outpost Estates area of Los Angeles.

**CATALINA ISLAND**

California island where Jim and Norma Jeane Dougherty moved in 1943. Jim spent his days working at the maritime service training base, while Norma Jeane attempted to play housewife but caused havoc instead. Apparently, NJ paraded about the island in an array of tight-fitting fashions from swimsuits to sweaters and aroused, in Jim Dougherty's eyes, far too much admiration from the other uniformed men on the island.

**GILBERT CATES**

Born Gilbert Katz in 1934, Gilbert Cates directed the 1974 television adaptation of Arthur Miller's *After the Fall,* which starred Faye Dunaway in a Marilyn Monroe–based role. Cates has also directed such motion pictures as *I Never Sang for My Father* (1969) and *Summer Wishes, Winter Dreams* (1973). His other television films include *The Affair* (1973) and *Johnny We Hardly Knew Ye* (1977).

**JOHN LEON CAVALLO**

John Cavallo owned the property that was used as the apartment building in *The Seven Year Itch* (1955). The building was located at 164 East 61st Street in New York City. Cavallo was paid the token gift of $200 worth of whiskey for the use of his location.

**CEDARS OF LEBANON HOSPITAL**

If the Beverly Hills Hotel was MM's favorite hotel, then Cedars of Lebanon was certainly her favorite hospital. Over the years, MM checked into this Los Angeles hospital on a regular basis. Here is a list of her visits to Cedars.

- ☆ JOHNNY HYDE: MM was a frequent visitor when Hyde was hospitalized at Cedars following his heart attack; he died there in December 1950.
- ☆ APPENDECTOMY: On March 5, 1952, MM was X-rayed at Cedars, and it was decided that her appendix operation would be postponed until she finished *Monkey Business*. MM eventually had the surgery on April 28, 1952.
- ☆ BRONCHITIS: April 1953
- ☆ "MINOR GYNECOLOGICAL SURGERY": On November 6, 1954, MM entered Cedars again. On November 8, MM had surgery of a "corrective female nature." She left the hospital on November 12. Her room number was 506.
- ☆ BRONCHITIS: During the *Bus Stop* shoot, April 1956.
- ☆ "MINOR GYNECOLOGICAL SURGERY": MM checked into Cedars on either the 24th or 25th of May, 1961. She had what was again dubbed by reporters as "minor gynecological surgery." Lawrence Guiles states that on May 26 MM had part of her pancreas removed.
- ☆ ???: On the weekend of July 20, 1962, two weeks before her death, MM told friends that she was going to Lake Tahoe for a long weekend. However, there has been much speculation that she secretly checked into Cedars and either aborted or miscarried John F. Kennedy's child.

Today, Cedars of Lebanon Hospital is known as the Cedars-Sinai Medical Center and is located at 8700 Beverly Boulevard in Los Angeles.

COURTESY OF MARK GOINS

**CEMETERY**
Marilyn's body remains in a crypt at Westwood Memorial cemetery.

**CENSORSHIP**

> "The Johnston Office spends a lot of time worrying whether a girl has cleavage or not. They ought to worry if she doesn't have any."
> MM to Pete Martin, *The Saturday Evening Post,* May 1956

During her career, Marilyn was actually censored very few times. It seems that she knew just how much she could get away with. The following is a list of those few known exceptions:

☆ The U.S. Army—The Army tried, unsuccessfully, to ban a 1952 photo that pictured MM with a representative WAC, WAVE, and SPAR. The Army felt that MM's decollete dress bared a little too much bosom.

☆ Iraq—In February 1957, *Bus Stop* was banned by the government of Iraq because, they felt, it was "dangerous to boys and young men."

☆ Kansas—In 1959, the Kansas Board of Review (who else?) banned a portion of MM's seduction of Tony Curtis in the yacht scene in *Some Like It Hot.*

☆ The United Arab Republic of Egypt and Syria—In 1959, when they learned that she had converted to Judaism, they banned all of Marilyn Monroe's films.

**CENTRAL PARK WEST**
In 1955, Marilyn began taking acting lessons from Lee Strasberg at his apartment located near Central Park West in Manhattan. In the succeeding years, MM frequently visited the Strasberg apartment for comfort and consultation.

***THE CHALLENGE***
*See THE FIREBALL.*

### GEORGE AGNEW CHAMBERLAIN

Writer whose novel was turned into 20th Century-Fox's 1948 film *Scudda Hoo! Scudda Hay!*—which is generally considered MM's first film.

### CAROL CHANNING

Carol Channing, born in 1921, originally played Lorelei Lee in the Broadway production of *Gentlemen Prefer Blondes.* Reportedly, Miss Channing tested for the film version and was rejected in favor of MM.

### CHARLIE CHAPLIN

It was Milton H. Greene's dream to star Marilyn Monroe in a movie with Charlie Chaplin. Unfortunately for all concerned, MM and Greene split up, and the "dream" pairing never materialized.

### CHARLES CHAPLIN, JR.

According to Anthony Summers's *Goddess: The Secret Lives of Marilyn Monroe* (Macmillan, 1985), MM had an affair with the legendary comedian's son, Charlie Jr., in 1947. The "romance" allegedly ended when Charlie caught MM in bed with his brother, Sydney. Also according to the Summers book, MM had one of her early abortions during this period.

### CEIL CHAPMAN

Ceil Chapman was one of Marilyn Monroe's New York fashion designers.

### CYD CHARISSE

Born Tulla Ellice Finklea in 1921, Charisse was, in her prime, one of the great female dancers in the history of the movies. She has appeared in such films as *Singin' in the Rain* (1952), *The Band Wagon* (1953), and *Silk Stockings* (1957). In 1962, Charisse was slated to costar in *Something's Got to Give,* which was subsequently shelved when Fox fired MM.

### CHARITIES

During her career, MM publicly donated either time or money to the following charities.

- ☆ In 1953, Marilyn Monroe and Jane Russell sang a song at the Hollywood Bowl in a benefit for underprivileged children, sponsored by St. Jude's Hospital of Memphis, Tennessee. The event was coordinated by actor Danny Thomas.
- ☆ Circa 1954–55, MM aided WAIF, an organization that found homes for unwanted children. It was Jane Russell who solicited MM's interest in the project.
- ☆ In 1955, during her hiatus from filmmaking, MM rode atop a pink elephant at Mike Todd's benefit circus for the Arthritis and Rheumatism Foundation. The event was held at Madison Square Garden in New York.
- ☆ MM actively participated in the Milk Fund for Babies. The first independent film MM made under the Marilyn Monroe Productions banner, *The Prince and the Showgirl*, held its world premiere in 1957 to benefit the fund.
- ☆ MM participated in the March of Dimes fashion show held at the Waldorf-Astoria Hotel on January 28, 1958.

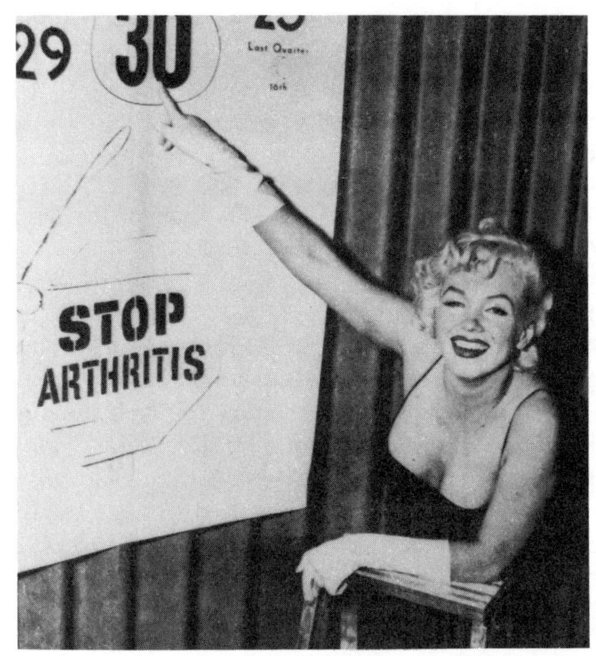


COURTESY OF CINEMA COLLECTORS

☆ MM donated $1,000 to a children's welfare institute that provided free breakfasts to needy youngsters.

☆ On June 1, 1962, MM made an appearance at Chavez Ravine's Dodger Stadium in Los Angeles to benefit muscular dystrophy. It was MM's thirty-sixth birthday and ultimately her final public appearance.

**SYLVIA CHASE**
Television investigative journalist who was to be the correspondent for the "20/20" Marilyn Monroe segment that was abruptly yanked off the air by ABC news chief Roone Arledge, in October 1985. Miss Chase has since left ABC, in favor of a San Francisco television news affiliate.

**CHASEN'S**
Popular Hollywood restaurant (address: 9039 Beverly Boulevard) where Johnny Hyde used to take Starlet MM "to be seen." In the years that followed, MM continued to frequent Chasen's, and in August 1961 she was seen dining there with none other than Joe DiMaggio.

**GEORGE CHASIN**
Chasin was Marilyn's agent at MCA at the time she made *The Misfits* in 1960. At that time, Chasin also represented Clark Gable and Montgomery Clift. Chasin proved to be MM's final agent.

**CHATEAU MARMONT HOTEL**
Popular hotel among the rock and film stars. In 1956, during the *Bus Stop* shoot, reporter Brad Darrach interviewed MM in a suite at the Chateau

Marmont for a *Time* magazine article. The Chateau Marmont (address: 8221 West Sunset Boulevard) later gained notoriety as the hotel in which comedian John Belushi was found dead of a drug overdose.

**CHAUFFEURS**

1. Fred Waldemar—Johnny Hyde's chauffeur, circa 1950
2. "Johnnie"—MM's New York chauffeur, whom MM nicknamed "The Sheik"
3. Rudi Kautzsky—MM's longtime Los Angeles chauffeur

**PADDY CHAYEFSKY**

Born Sidney Stuchevsky, Chayefsky (1923-1981) was the acclaimed television writer who also found success in films. One of MM's early films, *As Young As You Feel* (1951), was the first Chayefsky story to reach the big screen. In the late fifties, Chayefsky wrote a screenplay called *The Goddess* that was a transparent attempt to fictionalize Marilyn Monroe's life story. At one point, Arthur Miller approached Chayefsky and tried to dissuade him from doing the film—without success. *The Goddess* was released in 1958. Other notable Chayefsky films include *Marty* (1955), *The Catered Affair* (1956), *The Bachelor Party* (1957), *The Hospital* (1971), and *Network* (1976).

**MICHAEL CHEKHOV**

Chekhov (1891-1955) was a Russian character actor who became Marilyn's drama coach in the fall of 1951. By July 1952, MM was studying with him twice a week—in addition to studying simultaneously with Natasha Lytess. In class, MM once portrayed Cordelia to Chekhov's King Lear. Chekhov reportedly was blown away by Marilyn's depth and angered by Hollywood's waste of her talents.

As for MM, she religiously studied Chekhov's book, *To the Actor*, and soon came to regard Chekhov as her idol. In 1952, she presented him with an engraving of Abraham Lincoln, with an attached note that read:

> Lincoln was the man I admired most all through school. Now that man is you.

Sometime later, MM sent Chekhov the following note:

> Dear Mr. Chekhov:
>
> Please don't give me up yet—I know (painfully so) that I try your patience. I need the work and your friendship desperately. I shall call you soon.
>
> Love, Marilyn Monroe

By 1954, MM acknowledged Chekhov as the most brilliant man she had ever met. And when he died the following year, MM fought to preserve his name and his work.

**XENIA CHEKHOV**

Following Michael Chekhov's death, MM kept in close contact with his widow, Xenia Julia Chekhov. MM telephoned her frequently, and Mrs.

Chekhov presented MM with nightgowns—she was concerned that MM slept in the nude. Before Marilyn's death, she made Mrs. Chekhov a beneficiary in her will. Unfortunately, Mrs. Chekhov did not receive a payment from the Marilyn Monroe estate until 1976—six years after her own death.

**CHEVIOT HILLS**
Location where MM reportedly met Lucille Ryman and John Carroll at a celebrity golf tournament in 1947. That day, MM was working as a starlet caddie.

THE RAY VAN GOEYE COLLECTION

Starlet Caddy, 1947.

### THE *CHICAGO SUNDAY TRIBUNE MAGAZINE*

Newspaper that featured a lengthy article on MM, written by Hedda Hopper and titled "The Blowtorch Blonde." It was published in the *Tribune*'s May 4, 1952, issue. Another article, also by Hopper, was published on July 16, 1961, titled "Can Marilyn Ever Be Happy?"

### THE CHICAGO WHITE SOX

While still a starlet posing for cheesecake photos, MM posed with ball players Joe Dobson and Gus Zernial of the Chicago White Sox. The photo ran in newspapers throughout the country in 1951, and prompted Joe DiMaggio to ask Zernial, "Who's the blonde?"

### CHILDBIRTH

> "I feel different about a child now. It's one of the things I dream of."
>
> Marilyn Monroe, circa 1954

Early in her career, Marilyn Monroe had no time and no desire to have children. Allegedly, she had as many as twelve abortions during those early struggling years. But by 1956, and following her marriage to Arthur Miller, MM seemed to want children—almost to the point of desperation. She even underwent "corrective female surgery" to increase the odds of her having a successful pregnancy. However, Marilyn reportedly had three miscarriages during her marriage to Miller. Two of them have been documented:

MM became pregnant following the shooting of *The Prince and the Showgirl* (1957), while the Millers were living on Amagansett, Long Island. By the sixth week of the pregnancy, however, Marilyn was rushed to Doctor's Hospital in New York. Subsequently, on August 1, 1957, the pregnancy, which was tubular, was surgically terminated.

MM learned that she was again pregnant while shooting *Some Like It Hot* in September 1958. Consequently, she was extremely cautious during the remainder of the shooting. Reportedly, she showed considerable concern over her health and limited her intake of drugs and alcohol. Nonetheless, on December 17, 1958, following the shooting, Marilyn lost her second child (with Miller) at Polyclinic Hospital in New York.

It has also been speculated that in July 1962 MM was again pregnant—this time with John F. Kennedy's child. Allegedly, MM checked into Cedars of Lebanon Hospital on the weekend of July 20, where the pregnancy was either aborted or miscarried.

### CHILDREN

There has also been a good deal of speculation that Marilyn Monroe actually *did* have a child. Over the years, some individuals (who were blanketly dismissed) stepped forward and purported to be Marilyn Monroe's "long-lost" child. It would sound like a poor, overdone "Dynasty" plot, if Marilyn herself hadn't confessed her "motherhood" to the following people.

- ☆ Amy Greene, with whom MM lived during 1955. MM told Amy that she gave birth while still in her teens and that the child was subsequently adopted.

- ☆ Lena Pepitone, MM's New York maid. According to Pepitone, MM told her that she was raped by a "foster parent" and that the rape resulted in a pregnancy. MM also told Pepitone that the child was adopted after birth.
- ☆ Jeanne Carmen, MM's Los Angeles neighbor, circa 1961. MM told Carmen that she gave birth *after* her marriage to Dougherty and before her initial success in the movies. MM also told Carmen that the child was later adopted.

**MM's Stepchildren**

> "I take a lot of pride in them. Because they're from broken homes. . . . I can't explain it, but I think I love them more than I love anyone."
>
> Marilyn Monroe,
> *Redbook* magazine, 1962

1. Joe DiMaggio, Jr. 2. Jane Miller 3. Robert Miller

**MM Trivia Quiz #8**

What was the first film in which MM has a child? (Answer on page 577.)

## NOBLE "KID" CHISSELL

Former Navy boxing champion turned Hollywood stuntman, Chissell was the purported best man/witness at the 1952 Mexican wedding of Robert Slatzer and Marilyn Monroe. Years later, writer Anthony Summers contacted Chissell, who told Summers the following:

> "It was pure chance. I was down in Tijuana looking up an old Navy buddy, and I saw Bob and Marilyn coming out of a shop . . . and they said, would I be their witness? I said, 'Yes,' I thought it was about time . . . we went to see the lawyer, and his wife gave Marilyn a flower, and they filled out the forms, and he married them. . . ."
>
> *Goddess: The Secret Lives of Marilyn Monroe* (Macmillan, 1985)

Chissell died in November 1987 at the age of 82.

## CHOREOGRAPHER

*See* JACK COLE.

## GENERAL CHRISTENBERRY

Army officer who approached Marilyn and Joe on the airplane enroute to Japan, in 1954, to ask MM if she was interested in entertaining the troops in Korea. She was and she did.

## CHRISTMAS

The following is a compilation of MM's Christmases over the years.

- ☆ *Christmas 1935.* RKO Studios invited the children from the nearby orphanage to visit the studio, where they were presented with ice cream, candy, and a movie.
- ☆ One Christmas, Norma Jeane was given a part in the class play. However, NJ's foster mother asked the teacher to give the role to another child, as she feared that Norma Jeane would forget her lines and embarrass the family.

☆ "When Christmas came, it was always different for me. The families would buy us all dresses, maybe, but I'd get the brown one or the cheapest one. And one year all the other kids in the family I lived with got wonderful presents and I got a ten-cent manicure outfit. And while the rest of the kids sat around the floor and admired their loot, I sat in a corner pushing back my cuticle. Yes, the Christmases were the hardest."—MM to Hedda Hopper, May 4, 1952.

☆ *Christmas 1941.* Norma Jeane went out on her first date with Jim Dougherty. He escorted her to the company Christmas dance held at Adel Precision Products.

☆ *Christmas 1945.* Norma Jeane spent this Christmas with photographer Andre de Dienes following a shooting in the state of Washington. According to Jim Dougherty, Norma Jeane called him, crying, to say that she wished she were home.

☆ According to Bob Slatzer, MM spent one Christmas with him in the late forties. To celebrate, they pooled their limited funds and bought presents for the orphans from Norma Jeane's former orphanage.

☆ *Christmas 1952.* MM attended a studio party at Fox. She then returned to her hotel room—alone. Joe DiMaggio was back home in San Francisco, spending the holidays with his family. Or so she thought. As she flicked on the light switch of her living room, MM was shocked to find a decorated Christmas tree in one corner. Then DiMaggio himself appeared from behind a closet door. It was their first Christmas together. It was also a gesture that MM would later recall as the kindest thing that anyone had ever done for her.

☆ *Christmas 1961.* MM's final Christmas was also spent with DiMaggio. They bought a tree for MM's Doheny apartment and decorated it with Mexican tree ornaments that they had found on Olvera Street in downtown Los Angeles. They spent Christmas day at the home of Marilyn's psychiatrist, Dr. Ralph Greenson. MM told Mrs. Eunice Murray about the saddest of all her childhood Christmases—"the Christmas all the kids in the house got presents but me. One of the other kids gave me an orange."

## THE CHRISTMAS TREE INN

Reno restaurant where *The Misfits* company held a joint birthday party for Arthur Miller and Montgomery Clift on October 17, 1960. The Christmas Tree Inn is located at 23900 Mount Rose Highway.

## JOYCE CHRISTOPHER

In 1982, artist Joyce Christopher sculpted a Marilyn Monroe doll out of clay. The doll was subsequently manufactured in vinyl ($80) and procelain ($400) by the World Doll Company in Brooklyn, New York.

## CHURCH

"Aunt" Ana Lower introduced Norma Jeane to the Christian Science Church, which proved to be the only solid religious affiliation of Marilyn Monroe's life. After she married Jim Dougherty, NJ continued to study the Christian Science principles. She attended the Sherman Oaks Christian Science Church for Sunday services. Norma Jeane remained faithful to this church for a cumulative eight-year period.

## CIGARETTES

Marilyn smoked periodically from the late forties to the mid-fifties. In 1955, she was seen smoking at a Chinese restaurant on Second Avenue in New York

THE SABIN GRAY COLLECTION

MM shares a smoke with Edward R. Murrow, 1955.

while she was dining with Truman Capote. MM also smoked Marlboros at her February 1956 press conference at the Plaza Hotel in New York.

**MM Trivia Quiz #9**
What was the first film in which MM was seen smoking cigarettes? (Answer on page 577.)

**CINEMA COLLECTORS**
Quite possibly the finest store of its kind in the world, Cinema Collectors (1507 Wilcox Avenue, Hollywood, California) houses a vast and impressive collection of motion picture photographs and posters. Most outstanding is its supply of Marilyn Monroe material: at last count, they had over 1,000 different photos. Of Marilyn Monroe, easily their biggest selling star, Cinema Collectors has said:

> Her popularity and admiration from people who love movies is unchallenged in our experience, and in our opinion is likely to remain so even after the name "Hollywood" itself becomes just a dusty memory.

**CINEMATOGRAPHERS**
Even more than other actors, Marilyn understood the importance of the man behind the camera. When her 1955 contract with Fox was being negotiated, she insisted on not only director approval but also approval of the cinematographer. The men in this category who were in Marilyn's favor at that time were Harry Stradling, Harold Rosson, James Wong Howe, and Milton Krasner.

### CINEMATOGRAPHERS WHOM MM WORKED WITH:

| | |
|---|---|
| Lloyd Ahern | *Love Nest* (1951) |
| | *O. Henry's Full House* (1952) |
| Lucien Andriot | *Hometown Story* (1951) |
| Lucien Ballard | *Let's Make It Legal* (1951) |
| | *Don't Bother to Knock* (1952) |
| Norbert Brodine | *Right Cross* (1950) |
| Jack Cardiff | *The Prince and the Showgirl* (1957) |
| William Daniels | *Something's Got to Give* (1962) |
| Daniel L. Fapp | *Let's Make Love* (1960) |
| Harry Jackson | *A Ticket to Tomahawk* (1950) |
| Benjamin Kline | *Dangerous Years* (1947) |
| Milton Krasner | *All About Eve* (1950) |
| | *Monkey Business* (1952) |
| | *The Seven Year Itch* (1955) |
| | *Bus Stop* (1956) |
| Charles Lang, Jr. | *Some Like It Hot* (1959) |
| | *Something's Got to Give* (1962) |
| Joseph La Shelle | *River of No Return* (1954) |
| Joe MacDonald | *As Young as You Feel* (1951) |
| | *Niagara* (1953) |
| | *How to Marry a Millionaire* (1953) |
| William C. Mellor | *Love Happy* (1950) |
| Russell Metty | *The Misfits* (1961) |
| Nicholas Musuraca | *Clash by Night* (1952) |
| Ernest Palmer | *Scudda Hoo! Scudda Hay!* (1948) |
| Franz Planer | *Something's Got to Give* (1962) |
| Frank Redman | *Ladies of the Chorus* (1948) |
| Harold Rosson | *The Asphalt Jungle* (1950) |
| Leon Shamroy | *There's No Business Like Show Business* (1954) |
| Leo Tover | *We're Not Married* (1952) |
| | *Something's Got to Give* (1962) |
| Lester White | *The Fireball* (1950) |
| Harry J. Wild | *Gentlemen Prefer Blondes* (1953) |

### CIRO'S

Marilyn Monroe attended a party in honor of Walter Winchell at Ciro's restaurant in 1953. MM attended with her *How to Marry a Millionaire* costar, Betty Grable. Today, Ciro's is no longer in existence. It has been replaced by the equally famous Comedy Store (address: 8433 Sunset Boulevard).

### CITY NATIONAL BANK

MM's Los Angeles bank at the time of her death was City National Bank in Beverly Hills. She had $2,200 in her checking account at that time.

### JOHN CLARK III

Some of *The Seven Year Itch* (1955) was shot in the apartment of New York attorney John Clark III. Mr. Clark's apartment was located on East 61st Street in New York City.

### *CLASH BY NIGHT* ★★★

1952 105 minutes Black and white
RKO
Directed by: Fritz Lang
Produced by: Harriet Parsons
(A Jerry Wald–Norman Krasna Production)
Screenplay by: Alfred Hayes, based on the play by Clifford Odets
Photographed by: Nicholas Musuraca
Cast: Barbara Stanwyck, Paul Douglas, Robert Ryan, Marilyn Monroe, J. Carrol Naish, Keith Andes

Based on a story by Clifford Odets, this melodrama concerns a hardened city woman (Stanwyck—who else?) who returns to the small fishing village where she was brought up. It's a variation on the old story about the good woman who is repeatedly attracted to the wrong kind of guy.

*Clash by Night*, released nationally on June 18, 1952, offered Marilyn her most significant role to date. Playing somewhat against type, as the not-so-ordinary ordinary girl, who wears blue jeans and works in a fish cannery, Marilyn received costar billing despite the fact that her role was essentially a small one. She also received what were, up to that time, the best reviews of her career.

But even more importantly, MM proved her marquee voltage at the box office. *Clash* was her first film released *after* the nude-calendar news became public. Consequently, the initial theatre grosses were superb. Everyone, it seemed, wanted to see more of the nude, new blonde. Subsequently, the front office executives at Fox *must* have paid particularly close attention to Marilyn's success in another studio's picture. Not to be outdone by RKO, Fox went ahead with plans to cast MM in a couple of costarring roles before showcasing her in a full-blown, star-making vehicle *(Niagara)*.

Marilyn Monroe's imminent popularity (though not the extent of it) was apparent even before the release of *Clash*. During the shooting, MM's costars began to resent her because she was—naturally—stirring up most of the publicity. One of her costars, Paul Douglas, was once quoted as saying: "Why the hell don't these goddamn photographers ever take any pictures of us? It's only that goddamn blonde bitch!"

*Clash* is also significant for two other reasons: First, it was produced by Harriet Parsons, sister of the all-powerful Hollywood columnist, Louella Parsons; this bond must have served to strengthen Marilyn's important relationship with Louella. Second, *Clash* was the first film in which Natasha Lytess coached MM *on* the set. Up until then, Natasha had guided MM from behind the scenes. Beginning with *Clash*, MM refused to shoot a scene unless Natasha was allowed on the set.

### TOM CLAY

In September 1961, Tom Clay was a radio disc jockey for KDAY radio station in Los Angeles. According to Anthony Summers's *Goddess: The Secret Lives of Marilyn Monroe* (Macmillan, 1985), Marilyn repeatedly called the station for about a week. Clay asked for her name, and MM replied, "I'm Marilyn Monroe." Clay, disbelieving, hung up on her. Several days later, MM phoned Clay once again and invited him over to her Doheny apartment to talk. For about three weeks, Clay went to MM's apartment every other day. He once asked MM, "How can you be so lonely?" Marilyn replied, "Have you ever been in a house with forty rooms? Well, multiply my loneliness by forty."

**JACK CLEMMONS**

Sergeant Jack Clemmons was the first police officer to arrive at the scene of Marilyn's death in the early morning of August 5, 1962. It was Clemmons who took the phone call from MM's doctor, Dr. Hyman Engelberg, at 4:35 A.M. Clemmons received the phone call at the West Los Angeles branch of the LAPD. He arrived at MM's Brentwood home a short time thereafter. Upon seeing her body, Clemmons estimated that Marilyn had been dead for at least eight hours, which would have put her death at approximately 9:00 P.M. on August 4, 1962—*not* in the early morning of August 5, which is and was generally accepted. Clemmons later said:

> "It looked like the whole thing had been staged. She couldn't have died in that position. To me, it was an out-and-out case of murder!"

After sticking to his contention that Marilyn was murdered, Clemmons was eventually "let go" by the Los Angeles Police Department. Undaunted, he refused to accept the popular suicide theory, and on April 8, 1986, Clemmons called a press conference to ask for a thorough, official investigation into the "murder" of Marilyn Monroe. His efforts, however, have been, for the most part, ignored.

**MONTGOMERY CLIFT**

> "Monty and Marilyn were psychic twins. They recognized disaster in each other's faces and giggled about it."
>
> Frank Taylor,
> producer of *The Misfits*

Generally considered to be one of the best and most attractive actors of his generation, Montgomery Clift (1920–1966) was one of the few Hollywood actors with whom Marilyn maintained a friendship. As early as 1949, starlet MM told columnist Earl Wilson that she was "starry-eyed" over Clift. Gushed Marilyn, "He's got tremendous talent!" And, in 1955, when she moved east, Montgomery Clift was the one New York-based actor that she wanted to meet.

In 1956, Clift visited the Actors Studio to see Marilyn's performance of *Anna Christie*. Marilyn, in turn, invited Clift over to her apartment for vodka and caviar. According to Lena Pepitone, MM was jealous of Clift's widely reported, close relationship with Elizabeth Taylor. Not be outdone, MM once tried unsuccessfully, to seduce Clift at her East 57th Street apartment. Nonetheless, the two remained friends, and in 1959 they attended Yves Montand's one-man show on Broadway.

The following year, Clift and Monroe leaned on one another during the grueling shooting of *The Misfits*. Except for Marilyn the only person Clift

THE AUTHOR'S COLLECTION

talked to on the set was his makeup man/companion, Frank La Rue. Clift drank an excessive amount of whiskey sours. He also drank vodka and grapefruit juice from a thermos. Marilyn felt protective about Clift. He became a brother to her. Marilyn said to W. J. Weatherby (who wrote *Conversations with Marilyn,* Ballantine, 1976):

> "I [just] saw Monty Clift. That man is beautiful, but he's killing himself slowly. Or, not so slowly."
>
> to W. J. Weatherby

And at another time, she commented: "He's the only person I know who's in worse shape than I am."

In 1961, Clift escorted Marilyn to the New York premiere of *The Misfits.* It was the last time they were seen out together in public. Clift followed *The Misfits* with performances in *Judgment at Nuremberg* (1961), *Freud* (1963), and *The Defector* (1966). His earlier films include *The Search* (1948), *Red River* (1948), *A Place in the Sun* (1951), *From Here to Eternity* (1953), *Raintree County* (1957—the first film he did after his tragic 1956 car accident), and *Suddenly Last Summer* (1959).

On July 23, 1966, at the age of forty-five, Montgomery Clift died of an occlusive coronary artery disease. However, as elaborated in Patricia Bosworth's excellent biography, *Montgomery Clift* (Harcourt Brace, 1978), his death was far more complex than that:

> All of his life he fought his sexual attraction to men. Then, after a car crash that paralyzed the left side of his face, Monty began the longest suicide in Hollywood history, crushing both life and career under an avalanche of pills, booze and inexplicable anguish.

**THE CLIFTON MOTEL**

In January 1954, Joe and Marilyn DiMaggio spent the first two days of their honeymoon at the Clifton Motel in Paso Robles in California. DiMaggio paid $6.50 a night for Room 15. Reportedly, the couple stayed in their room for fifteen hours straight. And, according to *The Los Angeles Times,* the room did have a television set.

**CAREY CLINE**

Cline designed the costumes for the 1952 film, *O. Henry's Full House.*

**COACHES**

**Drama**
Phoebe Brand
Morris Carnovsky
Michael Chekhov
Constance Collier
Natasha Lytess
Helena Sorrell
Lee Strasberg
Paula Strasberg

**Vocal**
Billie Daniels
Fred Karger
Hal Schaefer
Phil Moore
Ken Darby

**Speech**
Margaret McLean

**Dance**
Jack Cole
Mara Lynn
Charles Henderson
Mildred Ann Mauldin

**Mime**
Lotte Gosler

**Piano**
Miss Marion Miller

**CHARLES COBURN**

Charles Coburn had a long, productive career in Hollywood before his death in 1961 at the age of eighty-four. Coburn costarred in two successful films with MM, *Monkey Business* (1952) and *Gentlemen Prefer Blondes* (1953). Coburn won an Oscar for his work in *The More the Merrier* (1943).

**HARRY COHN**

"You had to stand in line to hate him."

Hedda Hopper

Born in 1891, Harry "King" Cohn cofounded Columbia Pictures in 1924 with his brother, Jack. He built Columbia into a major film production force and himself into one of the most powerful men in Hollywood, which he remained for many, many years.

Among his many other accomplishments, Cohn was responsible for making movie stars out of Margarita Carment Cansino and Marilyn Novak—Rita Hayworth and Kim Novak, respectively, However, Cohn committed one of the major blunders of his career, one that he was never permitted to forget, when he dropped starlet Marilyn Monroe's six-month option in 1948.

Earlier that year, Cohn had been persuaded to sign MM to a studio contract as a favor to Joseph Schenck, one of Marilyn's early benefactors. According to several reports, Schenck discussed Marilyn with Cohn over a Saturday night poker game.

At any rate, Cohn did sign Marilyn. However, before he allowed her to appear in Columbia's 1948 production, *Ladies of the Chorus,* Cohn made

Marilyn sing for him in his office. Fred Karger accompanied MM on the piano. Cohn subsequently gave MM the part *not* because of her singing talent, not even because of her good looks. Cohn gave her the part, reportedly, because of her religious affiliation with the Christian Science Church. It seems that Cohn's wife was also an adamant follower of the Christian Science religion.

Nonetheless, after viewing footage of MM in *Chorus*, Cohn reportedly bellowed: "What did you put that fat pig in the picture for? What are you doing, f---ing her?"

He added: "The girl can't act!"

However, Marilyn had a different version of her dismissal from Columbia. Marilyn claimed that Cohn called her and invited her into his office. He then showed her a picture of his yacht and invited her to spend the weekend with him aboard the boat. Marilyn thanked him and added that she had never been to a yachting party before. Cohn explained that it wasn't to be a party. MM then replied by saying, "I'd love to join you and your wife on the yacht, Mr. Cohn," to which Cohn reportedly retorted, "Leave my wife out of this!" He then went on to say, "I know you're Joe Schenck's girl. . . ." Marilyn then stood up to leave. Before she left Cohn's office, though, MM tried to end the fiasco graciously by saying, "Thanks for the invitation. It just happens I have a previous date this weekend. Maybe some other time I might be able to accept." As she left, Cohn barked out, in his inimitable fashion, "This is your last chance, baby."

Unfortunately for Cohn, it ultimately proved to be *his* last chance. After Marilyn Monroe attained worldwide stardom, Cohn tried to lick his wounds by grooming a replacement for Marilyn. He eventually settled on Kim Novak, and though Novak enjoyed a good deal of success, she fell far short of MM's lofty level.

Years after she was dropped by Cohn in 1948, Marilyn sent him an autographed photo of herself from *Gentlemen Prefer Blondes* (1953). The short inscription that she included read, sarcastically: "To My Great Benefactor, Harry Cohn."

Cohn, who once said, "I don't have ulcers. I give them," died in 1958, the year that Columbia's savage, Marilyn Monroe-based film, *The Goddess*, was released to poor reviews.

**CLAUDETTE COLBERT**

Born in 1905, Lily Claudette Chauchoin became one of the most popular actresses in America during the twenties, thirties, and forties. In 1951, Colbert starred in *Let's Make It Legal*, which featured MM in a small part. Among Colbert's many films are *It Happened One Night* (for which she won the 1934 Oscar), *Imitation of Life* (1934), *Cleopatra* (1934), *The Palm Beach Story* (1942), and *Since You Went Away* (1944).

***COLD SHOULDER***

In 1950, shortly after *All About Eve*, MM tested for this Fox movie, which was set to star Richard Conte. She didn't get the part.

**JACK COLE**

Jack Cole (1914–1974) was the dancer/choreographer who choreographed Marilyn's numbers for *Gentlemen Prefer Blondes* (1953), *River of No Return* (1954), *There's No Business Like Show Business* (1954), and *Let's Make Love* (1960). Following *Blondes,* MM would not do a dance number in a movie without Cole. He was her favorite choreographer, as well as her friend. Cole's non-Marilyn movies include *Moon over Miami* (1941) and *Kismet* (1944) as a dancer and *Designing Woman* (1955) as a dancer and choreographer.

**CONSTANCE COLLIER**

Constance Collier, formerly Laura Constance Hardie, was a British stage actress before making a slew of Hollywood films from 1916 to 1950. Collier then became a drama coach and worked with such actresses as Katharine Hepburn, Audrey Hepburn, and Vivien Leigh. Marilyn took lessons from Collier in early 1955, before Collier's death in April of that year. MM attended her funeral, held at the Universal Funeral Home in New York, with Truman Capote.

Among Collier's acting credits are *Anna Karenina* (1935) and *Stage Door* (1937).

***COLLIER'S* MAGAZINE**

*Collier's* had the distinction of being the first national magazine to publish a major feature article on Marilyn Monroe. The article, titled " 'Hollywoods' 1951 Model Blonde," appeared in the *Collier's* September 8, 1951, issue. The article began,

> She's filmdom's Marilyn Monroe; Miss Cheesecake to GIs, whistle-bait in the studios—and, an actress on her way up.

*Collier's* later published the following articles about MM:

☆ 6/27/53: "Gentlemen Prefer Monroe"
☆ 10/16/53: "Marilyn on the Rocks"
☆ 7/9/54: "Marilyn Monroe Hits a New High"
☆ 8/3/56: "That Old Monroe Magic"

**CHARLES COLLINGWOOD**

Charles Collingwood anchored the "Eyewitness" documentary segment about Marilyn Monroe, which was entitled "Marilyn Monroe, Why?" The segment aired on CBS on August 10, 1962, less than a week after Marilyn's death.

**COLLINS COURT**

Before her death in 1984, Marilyn's mother, Gladys Baker, was an in-patient at the Collins Court living facility (address: 4201 S.W. 21st Place, Gainesville, Florida) for the elderly. When asked about Mrs. Baker (then known as Gladys Eley) the Collins Court administrator, Mark Glaeser, had "no comment."

**JOAN COLLINS**

After Marilyn completed *The Seven Year Itch* in 1954, 20th Century-Fox planned to star her in its production of *The Girl in the Red Velvet Swing*. However, MM walked out on Fox and refused to play the girl in the red velvet anything. In February 1955, Fox retaliated by casting relatively unknown British bombshell Joan Collins. However, Collins was not entirely convincing in the film and, in the succeeding thirty years, has not been able to achieve success in American feature films. At the time of *The Girl in the Red Velvet Swing*, the critics wrote:

> Miss Collins has the looks. She's an exquisite, well-endowed beauty. But her performance is vacuous and fails to suggest inner emotion, if any . . .
>
> Joan Collins plays the young Miss Nesbit with ingratiating charm but unconvincing naiveté. . . .

Collins, born in 1933, achieved the biggest success of her career when she joined the cast of ABC-TV's "Dynasty" in 1981.

*The Girl in The Red Velvet Swing*, 1955.

COURTESY OF CINEMA COLLECTORS

**MM Trivia Quiz #10**

In what stage production did Joan Collins almost portray MM? (Answer on page 577.)

**HORTENSIA COLORADO**

Actress Hortensia Colorado portrayed one half of the Marilyn Monroe character in the 1973 New York stage play, *The White Whore and the Bit Player*. The other half of MM's split personality was portrayed by female impersonator, Candy Darling.

**COLUMBIA PICTURES**

Columbia Pictures was founded by, run by, and, made successful by the sheer tenacity of one man—Harry Cohn. By "King" Cohn's death in 1958, Columbia was one of *the* potent production forces in Hollywood.

Columbia signed starlet Marilyn Monroe to its studio on March 9, 1948. She was paid the standard $125-a-week salary. While at Columbia, Marilyn made only one picture, *Ladies of the Chorus*, a grade-B musical. Her only other appearance in a Columbia film was in a photograph on the wall of a Western set, which was serenaded by the film's star, Gene Autry. When her six-month contract lapsed, Marilyn's option was dropped and she was put out of work.

Despite her short term there, Columbia Pictures is significant in the career of Marilyn Monroe for two simple reasons: Natasha Lytess and Fred Karger, who became her drama and vocal coaches.

Incidentally, it is also interesting to note that both mother and daughter, Gladys Baker and Marilyn Monroe, worked under the strict rule of "mogul" Harry Cohn, Gladys in the early 1930s as a Columbia film cutter and Marilyn in 1948 as a studio contract player.

**COLUMBIA PRESBYTERIAN HOSPITAL**

In February 1961, Joe DiMaggio had Marilyn transferred from the ward for the mentally ill of the Payne Whitney Clinic to Columbia Presbyterian Hospital in New York (address: 622 West 168th Street). Marilyn was admitted to the hospital on February 11, 1961 occupying Room 719. She was released three weeks later on March 5, 1961. Marilyn was suffering from (according to her publicists, naturally) "physical and emotional exhaustion."

***COME ON STRONG***

Nineteen-sixty-two Garson Kanin play that opened at the Morosco Theatre in New York, that was reportedly based, in part, on the life of Marilyn Monroe. Carroll Baker was cast as the MM-like blonde actress, Virginia Karger. At the opening of the play, Virginia weds an aging millionaire who subsequently dies on their honeymoon. But, instead of simply inheriting her new husband's millions, Virginia opts to make it the "hard way" in Hollywood.

The play costarred Van Johnson, and opened to mostly poor reviews.

**COMMERCIALS**

In the late 1970s, producer Marty Ingels purchased United Artists' clips of Marilyn Monroe wearing blue jeans from the 1961 film, *The Misfits*. Ingels used them in a special Japanese ad campaign for Levi-Strauss. A brief clip of MM was also used in a 1987 TV commercial for Coors "originals" series.

The only known television commercial that MM ever made was for Royal Triton Oil in 1950. Marilyn's pitch (better if done in a breathy, sexy, Marilynesque fashion) went like this:

> This is the first car I ever owned. I call it Cynthia. She's going to have the best care a car ever had. Put Royal Triton in Cynthia's little tummy . . . Cynthia will just love that Royal Triton.

**COMPTON, CALIFORNIA**

Reportedly, after her two-year residence at the Los Angeles Orphans Home Society, Norma Jeane lived, for a brief period, with a foster family from Compton, California.

**RICHARD CONDON**

Born on March 18, 1915, in New York City, Richard Condon is the popular novelist of such books as *The Oldest Profession, The Manchurian Candidate,* and *Prizzi's Honor.* He also wrote the book *Winter Kills,* a fictionalized account of the Kennedy family, that was later adapted into a 1979 movie of the same name. Both the book and film include a character named "Yvette Malone," who was obviously based on Marilyn Monroe.

**JOHN CONLEY**

Mrs. Anne Karger's brother, and Fred Karger's uncle, who became a friend of Marilyn.

**LESLIE CONN**

London nightclub owner and Marilyn Monroe collector who attended the MM auction held at Christie's in London in 1975. Conn purchased the sequined green satin costume, as well as the black fishnet stockings that Marilyn wore in *Bus Stop* (1956). The price? Seven hundred ninety-eight dollars.

**HAL CONNERS**

Hal Conners is the helicopter pilot who allegedly flew Robert Kennedy from Peter Lawford's beach house to the TWA departure gate at LAX during the early morning of August, 5, 1962—the morning that Marilyn Monroe was officially pronounced dead. According to Jim Zonlick, Conners's former partner, Conners picked Kennedy up sometime between midnight and 2:00 A.M.

**DAVID CONOVER**

In 1945, David Conover was an Army photographer for the Hal Roach Studios in Culver City, California. As fate would have it, Conover was assigned to shoot photographs of women working to aid the war effort. Accordingly, Conover went to the Radio Plane Company, where he spotted eighteen-year-old Norma Jeane Dougherty, who amply filled out her tight overalls. Conover reportedly asked NJ if she had a sweater that she could put on. She did, and unbeknownst to him, he took what were to become the first professional photos ever taken of Marilyn Monroe. Conover's photos of Norma Jeane eventually landed her her first magazine cover. It was on *Yank* magazine. He was also indirectly responsible for NJ's getting her first modeling agency job.

In 1981, Conover published a book about his "discovery" of, and his relationship with, Marilyn Monroe. According to Conover, they became lovers for a brief period (*she* seduced *him*, of course). The book was entitled *Finding Marilyn: A Romance* (Grosset & Dunlap).

**CONSOLIDATED FILM INDUSTRIES**

During the 1920s, Gladys Baker worked as a film cutter at this processing lab, which was located on Melrose Avenue in Hollywood. It was here that Gladys met fellow employee C. Stanley Gifford, who is speculated as being Marilyn Monroe's father.

**RICHARD CONTE**

Richard Conte (1911–1975) was an actor who appeared in many, mostly mediocre, films from the forties to the seventies. In 1950, Conte played opposite starlet Marilyn Monroe in one of her screen tests for a film called *Cold Shoulder* to be made by 20th Century–Fox.

**THE CONTINENTAL HILTON HOTEL IN MEXICO CITY**

During her 1962 furniture buying expedition in Mexico City, Marilyn Monroe stayed at the Continental Hilton Hotel, which was located at Paseo de la Reforma. It was destroyed by the tragic earthquake that devastated Mexico City in 1985.

***CONVERSATIONS WITH MARILYN***

Author: W. J. Weatherby
Publisher: Mason/Charter Books
Year: 1976 (Out of print)

Interesting, though ultimately disappointing, book of recorded conversations that took place between MM and Weatherby in the 1961 period before Marilyn returned to Los Angeles to live. Most of the meetings between the two took place at a typical, unnamed New York bar, and while the concept is fascinating (MM sitting in a New York bar, baring her soul?), not much is ever really said.

Nonetheless, there is very little firsthand material available on MM; thus, *Conversations* is valuable in that respect.

**MICHAEL CONWAY**

Conway is the cowriter of the career compilation book, *The Films of Marilyn Monroe* (Citadel, 1964).

**COOK**

"Hattie" was MM's cook at her East 57th Street apartment in New York.

**ALTON COOK**

Alton Cook was one of the first critics to herald MM as the superstar she had yet to become. In his 1952 review of *Clash by Night,* Cook wrote:

> She is a forceful actress . . . a gifted new star, worthy of all that fantastic press agentry.
>
> *The New York World Telegram & Sun*

**COOKING**

Norma Jeane was not a cook. According to Jim Dougherty, cooking (or, more precisely, *not* cooking) was her biggest flaw. What she *did* "cook" for Jim was her favorite dish of peas and carrots (she liked the combination of colors—they decorated even the drabbest of dining tables!)

Years later, while dating Joe DiMaggio, Marilyn sharpened her culinary skills well enough to prepare a hearty spaghetti dinner (with the combination of peas and carrots on the side, no doubt). She also learned how to broil a steak.

THE RAY VAN GOEYE COLLECTION

When she became Mrs. Arthur Miller, Marilyn was more determined than ever to become a good cook. And, according to various reports, she succeeded—at least to an extent. In a 1960 interview with reporter/artist Jon Whitcomb, MM said the following.

> ***On baking bread:*** "I started from scratch. In fact, from below scratch. I bought a book called *The Joy of Cooking*. Maybe it's joyous, but I notice that some people seem to find cooking quite tedious. . . . My favorite cooking is baking. I'm very good at baking bread."

> ***On noodle soup:*** "For homemade noodles, I roll the dough out very thin, then I slice it into narrow strips . . . then, the book says, 'Wait till they dry.' We were expecting guests for dinner. I waited and waited. The noodles didn't dry. The guests arrived; I gave them a drink; I said, 'You have to wait for dinner until the noodles dry. Then we'll eat.' I had to give them another drink. In desperation, I went and got my little portable hair dryer and turned it on. It blew the noodles off the counter, and I had to gather them all up and try again. This time I put my hand over the strips, with my fingers outspread, and aimed the dryer through them. Well . . . the noodles finally dried. So they *do* leave out a few instructions. I've wanted to write in and ask, 'Please, let people know how long it takes to dry noodles.' But I never did."
>
> *Cosmopolitan*, December 1960

Also for Arthur Miller, Marilyn not only converted to Judaism; she also learned how to prepare such Jewish dishes as borshcht, chicken soup, and matzoh balls.

**JOAN COPELAND**
Actress Joan Copeland was Marilyn Monroe's former sister-in-law, by way of Arthur Miller. Miss Copeland was a student of the Actors Studio, and had appeared in the 1958 Paddy Chayefsky feature about MM, *The Goddess*. In the film, she portrayed Marilyn's Natasha Lytess-like secretary/companion.

***COP-OUT***
*Cop-Out* was a one-act play by John Guare that opened at the Cort Theatre in New York on April 7, 1969. It featured actress Linda Lavin (TV's "Alice") doing a parody of Marilyn Monroe. The comedy was directed by Melvin Bernhardt, and costarred Ron Leibman. Unfortunately for all, though, it opened to mostly poor reviews, and closed a week later.

**LEONORA CORBETT**
In 1955, Milton H. Greene subleased Leonora Corbett's suite at the Waldorf-Astoria Towers in New York for Marilyn to live in.

**SCOTT CORBETT**
Corbett wrote the novel on which *Love Nest* (1951) was based.

**ELLIOTT CORDAY**
Corday was MM's physician from 1948 until the mid-fifties. Years later, Corday told investigative writer Anthony Summers:

> I eventually withdrew from the case because she would not employ a decent psychiatrist. People would understand her death better had they been listening to her in my office back then. There had been many suicide attempts, more than were known. And by 1954 she was using drugs—I think the hard stuff as well as the sleeping pills. In the end I told her I was not going to be around to witness what was going to happen.
> from *Goddess: The Secret Lives of Marilyn Monroe* (Macmillan, 1985)

**SAM CORDOVA**

Cordova was the foreman of the Los Angeles grand jury in 1985. Cordova was replaced after he erroneously reported to the press that the Marilyn Monroe case was being opened for investigation. Apparently, Cordova released the information *before* the grand jury had even voted. When the jury eventually did vote, the verdict was *not* to reopen the Marilyn Monroe case.

**CORONADO BEACH, CALIFORNIA**

The exterior shots of *Some Like It Hot* were filmed at Coronado Beach (substituting for Miami Beach in the 1920s) in September 1958. The *Hot* company spent seven days shooting there. Surprisingly, MM had a relatively easy time shooting these beach scenes.

**CORONERS**

The following information pertains to Marilyn Monroe's death on August 5, 1962, and her subsequent autopsy:

Head Coroner of LA County—Theodore J. Curphey
Deputy Medical Examiner—Thomas Noguchi
Suicide Investigation Team—Dr. Robert Littman, Dr. Norman Farberow
Noguchi's Assistant—Eddy Day
Coroner's Aide—Lionel Grandison
Coroner's Case Number—81128
Coroner's Crypt Number—33

***CORONET* MAGAZINE**

*Coronet* published the following articles on MM:

☆ 10/52: "The Story Behind Marilyn Monroe"
☆ 1/57: "Waif to Woman"
☆ 2/61: "Mosaic of Marilyn"
☆ 1/66: "Marilyn, the Tragic Venus" (serialization of Edwin P. Hoyt's book of the same name, in three parts)

**COSMETIC SURGERY**

☆ Prior to the shooting of *Ladies of the Chorus* in 1948, Fred Karger referred Marilyn to Dr. Walter Taylor, an orthodontist who specialized in cosmetic dentistry. Taylor fixed MM's front teeth, which protruded slightly.
☆ In 1950, Johnny Hyde arranged for Marilyn to have her nose and chin surgically perfected. The specific details are unknown. Some sources claim that MM had a bump at the tip of her nose removed. Other sources claim that it was not a bump removal, but a tip lift.

***COSMOPOLITAN* MAGAZINE**

*Cosmopolitan* published the following articles on MM:

☆ 5/53: "Marilyn Monroe" (she appeared on the cover)
☆ 3/59: "The New Marilyn Monroe"
☆ 12/60: "Marilyn Monroe: The Sex Symbol vs. The Good Wife"

### JOSEPH COTTEN

Born in 1905, Joseph Cotten made his film debut in the 1941 classic *Citizen Kane*. Over the next four decades, Cotten went on to make a multitude of films, including *Niagara* in 1953. Said Cotten of his costar, MM:

> Everything that girl does is sexy. A lot of people—the ones who haven't met Marilyn—will tell you it's all publicity. That's malarkey. They've tried to give a hundred girls the same publicity build-up. It didn't take with them. This girl's really got it!

### RICHARD COTTRELL

Dr. Richard Cottrell was the physician who handled Marilyn's gallbladder operation at the Polyclinic Hospital in New York in June 1961.

### THE COUNTRY INN RESTAURANT

During the shooting of *The Misfits* in 1960, MM often went to this restaurant, located on South B Street in Virginia City, Nevada. At that time, the restaurant was owned by Edith Palmer. Also, as its name implies, the Country Inn Restaurant was also a motel. And, according to present owner Norm Brown, Marilyn Monroe once stayed at the Inn. Thus, today, there is a "Marilyn Monroe Suite" named in her honor.

### COURT

Outside of her marriages and divorces, Marilyn was known to be in court twice.

1. On June 26, 1952, MM was called in to testify in the trial against defendants Jerry Karpman and Morrie Kaplan, who were charged with violations of conducting a nude photos mail order business. Karpman and Kaplan had used the name "Marilyn Monroe" in their advertising. The presiding judge was Kenneth Holaday.
2. On February 28, 1956, MM appeared in court—finally—for a 1954 traffic violation of driving without a license. She was fined $55 by Judge Charles Griffin.

### LESTER COWAN

Lester Cowan was the producer of *Love Happy* (1950) who promised to make Marilyn a star. He ran an item in Louella Parsons's *Los Angeles Examiner* column that he had signed MM to a personal contract and planned to star her in a forthcoming picture. Instead, he sent MM on the cross-country publicity tour to hype *Love Happy*. However, with several weeks and even more cities behind her, the Cowan-dubbed "Mmmmmm Girl" abruptly quit the tour and returned home. Once back in Los Angeles, MM tried to contact the presumably irate Cowan. However, he refused to return her calls and eventually joined the ranks of the men who rejected MM and never lived to forget it.

### WALLY COX

When 20th Century-Fox was casting *Something's Got to Give* in 1962, the producers wanted to hire Don Knotts for one of the supporting roles. However, Marilyn objected. She wanted her friend, Wally Cox, (1924–1973), who was best known for his television series "Mr. Peepers" (1952–1954). Naturally, MM won out, and Knotts was out and Cox was in.

**ROY CRAFT**

When MM was signed to Fox in 1946, studio publicist Roy Craft became one of her earliest allies in the motion picture business. Craft was assigned to write her first studio bio, and in 1951 Craft worked to launch MM as a pinup girl in a massive publicity campaign. It was also Craft who set up the MM-Chicago White Sox photo session that directly resulted in MM and Joe DiMaggio's first date. And, in 1952, when the news of her nude calendar broke, Craft was once again at Marilyn's defense. Knowing a good publicity gimmick when he saw it, Craft distributed a hundred of the infamous calendars to the eager press.

Craft is one of those people (along with his then-boss, Harry Brand) whose contribution to the launching of MM has been unjustly slighted over the years.

**CHERYL CRAWFORD**

Producer/director and one of the founding members of the Actors Studio. In early 1955, Crawford met MM in New York at a dinner party. At that time, Marilyn told Crawford about her intention of becoming a Serious Actress. Crawford responded by telling MM that, if she wanted to be a Serious Actress, she would first have to meet a man named Lee Strasberg. The following afternoon, Crawford took MM to the Strasberg apartment, where she introduced Marilyn to the man who would become her teacher.

**JOAN CRAWFORD**

Marilyn Monroe first met Joan Crawford at the home of Joseph Schenck. Marilyn had not yet attained major stardom. Crawford, on the other hand, was one of the biggest movie stars of all time. In fact, Crawford had been one of the top female actresses as far back as 1926, the year that MM was born.

Reportedly, at that first meeting, Crawford told Marilyn:

> "I think I could help you a great deal if you would let me. For instance, that white knitted dress you're wearing is utterly incorrect for a dinner of this kind."
>
> *My Story,* Marilyn Monroe (Stein and Day, 1974)

Crawford, who belonged to the same church as MM, then proceeded to invite Marilyn to her home. Naturally, Marilyn accepted. Then, according to MM, Crawford dictated (as opposed to suggested) to Marilyn what she should and should not wear.

The next time Marilyn heard from Joan Crawford was under indirect and less pleasant circumstances.

It was after the March 9, 1953, *Photoplay* magazine awards ceremony. Marilyn, of course, stole the spotlight from Hollywood's reigning queens by wearing a strikingly tight gold lamé gown that she had to be literally sewn into. The "scandalous" gown, coupled with the wavy walk, had MM's intended effect on the men in attendance, but what Marilyn *wasn't* prepared for was the onslaught of public condemnation that ensued.

The anti-MM "movement" was spearheaded by none other than Hollywood's matriarch of deceny, "Mommie Dearest" herself, Lucille Fay Le Sueur, aka Billie Cassin, aka Joan Crawford.

In Bob Thomas's syndicated column, Crawford lambasted Marilyn in the following high-browed manner:

> It was like a burlesque show. The audience yelled and shouted, and Jerry Lewis got up on the table and whistled. But those of us in the industry just shuddered. . . . Sex plays a tremendously important part in every person's life. People are interested in it, intrigued with it. But they don't like to see it flaunted in their faces. . . . The publicity has gone too far. She is making the mistake of believing her publicity. Someone should make her see the light. She should be told that the public likes provocative feminine personalities; but it also likes to know that underneath it all, the actresses are ladies.

That's none other than Hollywood's Matriarch of Decency, Joan Crawford, flaunting sex in the public's face, circa 1929.

COURTESY OF CINEMA COLLECTORS

As she frequently did when she was in trouble, Marilyn turned to Louella Parsons's column. In response to Joan Crawford's "statement," MM issued a statement of her own. It read:

> Although I don't know Miss Crawford very well, she was a symbol to me of kindness and understanding to those who need help. At first, all I could think of was WHY should she select me to blast? She is a great star. I'm just starting. And then, when the first hurt began to die down, I told myself she must have spoken to Mr. Thomas impulsively, without thinking. . . .

The MM/Joan Crawford feud was still brewing in November 1954, when all of Hollywood turned out at Romanoff's to welcome Marilyn Monroe with open arms (and clenched fists), to the Hollywood elite. Joan Crawford was glaringly omitted from the guest list.

But, in 1962, after Marilyn Monroe's death, Joan Crawford was still a movie star of considerable power. She had been a star when MM was born, and she was a star when MM died. That year, Crawford enjoyed one of the biggest successes of her career, *What Ever Happened to Baby Jane?* In 1977, Joan Crawford died of a heart attack. She was one of the most durable film stars in movie history. Among her most famous films were *Rain* (1932), *The Women* (1939), *Mildred Pierce* (for which she won a 1945 Oscar), and *Sudden Fear* (1952).

**CRESCENT DRIVE, BEVERLY HILLS, CALIFORNIA**

Reportedly, Marilyn Monroe lived for a period with her drama coach, Natasha Lytess, at 611 N. Crescent Dr. in Beverly Hills, California, circa 1951–52. During this period, MM was sued by the phone company for not paying her phone bills while living at a separate, nearby residence, 618 N. Crescent Dr.

**BING CROSBY**

In 1960, Bing Crosby (1901–1977) "guested" in MM's *Let's Make Love*. And it was at Crosby's Palm Springs home that MM and John Kennedy allegedly spend a weekend together in March 1962.

**IRENE CROSBY**

Irene Crosby was Marilyn Monroe's stand-in during *Gentlemen Prefer Blondes* (1953).

**LAWRENCE CROWN**

Hollywood journalist Lawrence Crown authored the exemplary 1987 book, *Marilyn: At Twentieth Century Fox* published by Planet Books.

**BOSLEY CROWTHER**

Crowther was the powerful critic of *The New York Times* who was, to be kind, "mixed" in his critical evaluation of MM's film performances over the years. At any rate, it was Crowther who summed up the general consensus after the 1956 release of *Bus Stop*. Wrote Crowther:

> Hold onto your chairs, everybody, and get set for a rattling surprise. MM has finally proved herself an actress in *Bus Stop*.

**THE CRYSTAL STAR AWARD**

In 1959, Marilyn Monroe was presented with the Crystal Star Award—the highest movie-acting honor in France—as the "Best Foreign Actress." The award was presented at the French Film Institute and recognized MM's work in *The Prince and the Showgirl* (1957).

**GEORGE CUKOR**

George Cukor (1899-1983) is considered to be one of the most prolific American film directors of all time.

In 1956, Cukor was named to a list of "approved" directors that MM wanted to work with. At that time, Cukor was tentatively scheduled to direct MM in the upcoming production of *The Prince and the Showgirl.* However, for whatever reasons, those plans fell through (unfortunately), and MM did not work with Cukor until the 1960 film *Let's Make Love.* Despite that film's failure, MM again chose Cukor for the 1962 comedy *Something's Got to Give.*

THE RAY VAN GOEYE COLLECTION

With George Cukor on set of *Something's Got to Give*, 1962.

During the shooting, Cukor was generally sympathetic to MM when she was present, and he tried to shoot around her when she was not. He was not responsible for her being fired from the film.

Cukor's personal feelings about Marilyn were mixed, as evidenced by the following:

> "I liked her very much. I found her extremely intelligent—inarticulate, but extremely intelligent. And driven. She was a very peculiar girl. . . ."
>
> And . . .
>
> "There may be an exact psychiatric term for what was wrong with her, I don't know—but truth to tell, I think she was quite mad. The mother was mad, and poor Marilyn was mad. . . ."

Following the uncompleted *Something's Got to Give,* Cukor directed *My Fair Lady* (1964) for which he won an Oscar. During his fifty-year film career,

Cukor was responsible for such classics as *Dinner at Eight* (1933), *Little Women* (1933), *Camille* (1936), *Holiday* (1938), *The Philadelphia Story* (1940), *Adam's Rib* (1949), *Born Yesterday* (1950), and *A Star Is Born* (1954).

**J. CUNNINGHAM**

J. Cunningham wrote and sang the 1974 song, "Norma Jean Wants to Be a Movie Star." The song was recorded on Capitol Records.

**THEODORE CURPHEY**

Theodore J. Curphey was the Los Angeles County coroner at the time of Marilyn Monroe's death in 1962. It was Curphey who released the following statement on August 18, 1962:

> It is my conclusion that the death of Marilyn Monroe was caused by self-administered sedative drugs, that the mode of death is "probable suicide."

**TONY CURTIS**

Born Bernard Schwartz in 1925, Tony Curtis is the *Some Like It Hot* costar who initiated what was probably the most famous feud with Marilyn Monroe.

Initially, MM was excited about the prospect of working with Curtis. She thought he was handsome. However, their relationship soon deteriorated after Curtis publicly denounced Marilyn for her blatant unprofessionalism.

It's easy not to blame Curtis. Marilyn was constantly late, hours late, on the set. This kept Curtis and costar Jack Lemmon waiting endlessly in limbo while standing around in complete female drag. On top of that, when Marilyn *did* show up, she flubbed her lines repeatedly. And according to director Billy Wilder, Curtis was better in his earlier takes, while MM got better as she progressed (reportedly, Curtis once had to endure forty-two takes of eating chicken!). As a result, in the eventual "used" takes, MM appeared fresh, while Curtis was often stale.

THE RAY VAN GOEYE COLLECTION

Thus, it is easy to understand why Tony Curtis did not like Marilyn Monroe. It's also understandable that he would refuse ever to work with Marilyn again. What is not understandable, though, was the snide, bitchy, (and often repeated) comment that Curtis made in public: "Kissing her is like kissing Hitler."

Curtis was also quoted as saying: "I think Marilyn was as mad as a hatter."

For her part in the feud, Marilyn was never known to say anything cruel about Curtis. What she did say, shortly before her death, was:

> "You've read there was some actor that once said about me that kissing me was like kissing Hitler. Well, I think that's his problem. If I have to do intimate love scenes with somebody who really has these kinds of feelings toward me, then my fantasy can come into play. In other words, out with him, in with my fantasy. He was never there."
>
> MM to Richard Meryman,
> *LIFE,* 8/3/62

At any rate, *Some Like It Hot* today probably stands as the finest film ever made starring either Tony Curtis or Marilyn Monroe.

Interestingly, in 1985, Curtis costarred in Nicolas Roeg's film *Insignificance,* in which he portrayed a Joseph McCarthy-based senator who seduces an MM-based character.

**JONAS CURTISS**

In 1985, Curtiss purchased Marilyn's Fifth Helena Drive home in Brentwood. At that time, he announced that a Marilyn Monroe museum would be built into a portion of the house. However, the Monroe Museum never materialized.

**CHRISTIE'S**

Twenty-five photos of MM, circa 1945, shot by David Conover at the Radio Plane Company were auctioned off at Christie's in London for $23,000 in 1987. Ten of the photos had previously been published in Conover's book, *Finding Marilyn.*

## DAN DAILEY

Dan Dailey (1914–1978) was the star of *You Were Meant for Me* (1948) and *A Ticket to Tomahawk* (1950) in which Marilyn Monroe was an extra and bit player, respectively. Several years later, Dailey costarred in *There's No Business Like Show Business* (1954) in which Marilyn also costarred.

## DALLAS LOVE FIELD AIRPORT

On January 20, 1961, enroute to Juarez, Mexico, to obtain her divorce from Arthur Miller, Marilyn Monroe had a two-hour layover at the Dallas Love Field Airport. Reportedly, Marilyn sat alone in an airport cocktail lounge, watching John F. Kennedy's presidential inauguration.

## FRANK DAMBACHER

Dambacher was the deputy coroner's associate who reportedly drove Marilyn's body from the Westwood Mortuary to the County Morgue on August 5, 1962.

## BEVERLY D'ANGELO

Born in 1954, D'Angelo is the excellent, underrated actress who appeared in such films as *Hair* (1979), *Coal Miner's Daughter* (1980), and the TV film version of *A Streetcar Named Desire* (1984). In 1974, Miss D'Angelo portrayed MM in a Canadian radio play entitled "Hey Marilyn!" Among the songs she sang in that production were: "I Can Do More," "Hi 'Ya Joe," and "Do It to Me Daddy."

Of Marilyn Monroe, Beverly D'Angelo has said:

> Her life has become a roadmap, a study for other actresses. She has made every actress since her time aware of her. She's a light that can't be denied. She's a kind of unidentifiable artist. She's not just a sex symbol but a symbol for every actor to follow because she never gave up, nothing was enough, she had to go on to be the best. She has become a kind of buoy to remind us of the dangerous rocks in the water.

## *DANGEROUS YEARS* ★½

1947 62 minutes Black and White
20th Century-Fox
Directed by: Arthur Pierson
Produced by: Sol M. Wurtzel
Screenplay by: Arnold Belgard
Photographed by: Benjamin Kline
Cast: Ann E. Todd, William Halop, Anabel Shaw, Jerome Cowan, Darryl Hickman, Scotty Beckett, Harry Shannon, Richard Gaines, Dickie

Moore, Gil Stratton, Jr., Donald Curtis, Harry Harvey, Jr., Marilyn Monroe, Nana Bryant

Little-seen grade-B film about juvenile delinquency. *Dangerous Years,* released on December 8, 1947, is notable for one reason—it gave twenty-one-year-old Marilyn Monroe her first speaking part in the movies. MM played the bit role of Eve, a waitress at the local hangout frequented by the neighborhood delinquents.

**BILLIE DANIELS**
Singer who coached MM on the "That Old Black Magic" number from *Bus Stop* (1956).

**WILLIAM DANIELS**
William Daniels (1895–1970) was an American cinematographer who shot well over a hundred films during his fifty-year film career. Included in Daniels's credits are *Greed* (shared credit, 1925), *Anna Karenina* (1935), *Camille* (1936), *Pat and Mike* (1952), and *Cat on a Hot Tin Roof* (1958). In 1962, Garbo's former cinematographer was one of four cinematographers to work on Marilyn Monroe's uncompleted *Something's Got to Give* (1962).

**HENRY D'ANTONIO**
Auto mechanic who was hired by Mrs. Eunice Murray, Marilyn's housekeeper, to fix Murray's car. On August 4, 1962, the day of MM's death, D'Antonio arrived at Marilyn's Brentwood home between 2:00 and 4:00 P.M. to deliver Mrs. Murray's car.

**GLEN DANZIA**
Glen Danzia wrote and recorded the song "Who Killed Marilyn?" on the Plan 9 record label. The flip side was something entitled "Spook City."

**KEN DARBY**
Born in 1909, Ken Darby is the composer/arranger who served as the vocal coach at 20th Century-Fox in the 1950s, during Marilyn Monroe's reign. Among the Fox films that Darby was associated with are *Gentlemen Prefer Blondes* (1953), *River of No Return* (1954), *There's No Business Like Show Business* (1954), and *Bus Stop* (1956). Reportedly, Darby also used to escort MM on her shopping excursions in Beverly Hills during the production of *There's No Business Like Show Business.*

**CANDY DARLING**
Female impersonator Candy Darling performed the Marilyn Monroe-based role of the whore in the 1973 New York stage play, *The White Whore and the Bit Player.* Darling died in 1974.

**BRAD DARRACH**
In 1956, during the shooting of *Bus Stop,* Brad Darrach interviewed MM at the Chateau Marmont Hotel for *Time* magazine. According to Anthony

Summers's *Goddess: The Secret Lives of Marilyn Monroe* (Macmillan, 1985), Darrach picked Marilyn up at Fox and drove her to the hotel. Once in the suite, MM reclined in bed, where the interview was conducted. Said Darrach to Summers:

> She was Marilyn, and reasonably pretty. And of course there were those extraordinary jutting breasts and jutting behind. I've never seen a behind like hers; it was really remarkable, it was a very subtly composed ass. Yet I never felt for a moment any sexual temptation. There was nothing about her skin that made me want to touch it. She looked strained and a little unhealthy, as though there was some nervous inner heat that dried the skin. But there was no sexual feeling emanating from her. I am sure that was something that she put on for the camera.

**DATES: THE 100 IMPORTANT MM DAYS**

1. 6/1/26: Birth date
2. 9/13/35: Entered orphanage
3. 6/26/37: Left orphanage
4. 6/19/42: Married James E. Dougherty
5. 6/26/45: Photographed by David Conover for *Yank* magazine
6. 8/2/45: Filled out an application for the Blue Book Modeling Agency (as Norma Jean Dougherty)
7. 7/17/46: First interview at Fox with Ben Lyon
8. 7/19/46: First screen test, for Fox
9. 7/29/46: First time mentioned in a Hollywood gossip column
10. 8/24/46: First studio contract, with Fox
11. 9/13/46: Divorce granted from James E. Dougherty
12. 8/25/47: Dropped by Fox
13. 3/9/48: Contract with Columbia Studios
14. 9/8/48: Dropped by Columbia Studios
15. 5/27/49: Posed for nude calendar
16. 7/24/49: First interview with Earl Wilson
17. 8/15/49: Started *A Ticket to Tomahawk*
18. 1/5/50: Started *The Fireball*
19. 12/10/50: Gets a new Fox contract
20. 12/18/50: Johnny Hyde dies
21. 3/29/51: Presenter at the Academy Awards ceremony
22. 4/18/51: Started *Love Nest*
23. 9/8/51: First full-length national magazine feature (*Colliers*)
24. 3/13/52: Nude calendar story broken to the public
25. 4/7/52: First *LIFE* cover
26. 6/1/52: Found out she had the part of Lorelei Lee in *Gentlemen Prefer Blondes*
27. 9/2/52: Grand marshal at the Miss America pageant
28. 10/4/52: Supposedly married Robert Slatzer
29. 6/26/53: Placed footprints in cement at Grauman's Chinese Theater
30. 9/13/53: First TV appearance on "The Jack Benny Show"
31. 10/53: Met Milton Greene at a party given by Gene Kelly and signed a recording contract with RCA
32. 11/4/53: Premiere of *How to Marry a Millionaire*
33. 12/15/53: *Girl in Pink Tights* scheduled to begin shooting; MM didn't show up

34. 1/4/54: Suspended by Fox
35. 1/14/54: Married Joseph Paul DiMaggio
36. 2/16/54: Went to entertain troops in Korea
37. 9/15/54: Shot famous skirt-blowing scene from *The Seven Year Itch*
38. 10/5/54: Officially left Joe DiMaggio
39. 10/27/54: Divorce granted from Joe DiMaggio
40. 11/5/54: "Wrong Door Raid" took place
41. 11/6/54: Hollywood's royalty honored MM at Romanoff's party
42. 12/31/54: Formed Marilyn Monroe Productions with Milton Greene
43. 1/15/55: Fox suspended MM again
44. 3/31/55: Rode atop a pink elephant at Madison Square Garden for arthritis benefit
45. 4/8/55: Appeared on Edward R. Murrow's "Person to Person"
46. 6/1/55: Premiere of *The Seven Year Itch*
47. 11/1/55: Granted final divorce decree from Joe DiMaggio
48. 12/31/55: The **big** new Fox contract
49. 1/4/56: Announced that MM and Fox had reached a signed agreement over contractual disputes
50. 2/56: Performed a scene from *Anna Christie* at the Actors Studio in New York
51. 2/9/56: Press conference with Olivier to announce their joint project, *The Prince and the Showgirl*
52. 2/25/56: Returned to Hollywood after her exile in New York
53. 5/3/56: Started *Bus Stop*
54. 3/22/56: Darryl Zanuck left Fox
55. 6/3/56: MM returned to New York after finishing *Bus Stop*
56. 6/29/56: Married Arthur Miller in a civil ceremony
57. 7/1/56: Married Arthur Miller in a Jewish ceremony
58. 7/14/56: Landed in London and held a press conference with Olivier to announce their joint project, *The Prince and the Showgirl*
59. 10/29/56: Met Queen Elizabeth at the royal command film performance
60. 11/20/56: Left England
61. 12/18/56: Radio Show from the Waldorf-Astoria
62. 6/13/57: Premiere of *The Prince and the Showgirl*
63. 8/1/57: Miscarriage
64. 8/4/58: Started *Some Like It Hot*
65. 11/6/58: Finished *Some Like It Hot*
66. 12/17/58: Second miscarriage
67. 3/29/59: Premiere of *Some Like It Hot*
68. 3/8//60: Received Golden Globe Award for "Best Actress in a Comedy" for her performance in *Some Like It Hot*
69. 7/18/60: Started *The Misfits*
70. 8/26/60: Flew to LA because of nervous breakdown while shooting *The Misfits*
71. 9/5/60: Returned to the production of *The Misfits*
72. 11/4/60: Finished *the Misfits*
73. 11/11/60: Announced to the press that her marriage to Miller was over
74. 11/16/60: Clark Gable died
75. 1/20/61: Divorce granted from Arthur Miller
76. 1/31/61: Premiere of *The Misfits*
77. 2/7/61: Entered Payne Whitney Psychiatric Clinic at New York Hospital
78. 2/11/61: Left Payne Whitney Psychiatric Clinic and entered Columbia Presbyterian Hospital

| | | |
|---|---|---|
| 79. | 3/5/61: | Released from Columbia Presbyterian Hospital |
| 80. | 11/19/61: | Went to Peter Lawford's beach house to be with President Kennedy |
| 81. | 2/62: | Moved into Brentwood home |
| 82. | 2/1/62: | Dinner in honor of Robert F. Kennedy |
| 83. | 3/62: | Golden Globe Awards: MM presented with the "World's Film Favorite" award |
| 84. | 4/23/62: | Started *Something's Got to Give* |
| 85. | 5/19/62: | Sang "Happy Birthday" and "Thanks for the Memory" to President Kennedy at Madison Square Garden |
| 86. | 5/28/62: | Nude pool sequence shot for *Something's Got to Give* |
| 87. | 6/1/62: | Last day at Fox and last public appearance |
| 88. | 6/8/62: | Fired by Fox |
| 89. | 6/23/62: | Bert Stern shot the sequence called "The Last Sitting" |
| 90. | 6/28/62: | Met with Fox heads regarding *Something's Got to Give* |
| 91. | 7/6/62: | Did Allan Grant shoot for *LIFE* |
| 92. | 7/12/62: | Met with Fox heads at the studio |
| 93. | 7/20/62: | MM allegedly entered Cedars of Lebanon Hospital for an abortion |
| 94. | 7/30/62: | Paula Strasberg returned to New York |
| 95. | 8/3/62: | Appeared on the cover of *LIFE* for the last time before her death |
| 96. | 8/4/62: | MM's last day |
| 97. | 8/5/62: | Death; Autopsy performed |
| 98. | 8/8/62: | MM's funeral |
| 99. | 8/18/62: | Announcement that MM died from a drug overdose by the Suicide Investigation Team |
| 100. | 8/28/62: | MM's death certificate signed |

**CLIFFORD DAVID**

David was an actor at the Actors Studio who once performed a scene in class opposite MM. Reportedly, the scene was specially written for them by Arthur Miller.

**THE DAVID DI DONATELLO AWARD**

In 1959, Marilyn was presented with the highest, most prestigious acting award in Italy—the David Di Donatello Award. It was presented to MM by the Italian Cultural Institute and was given in recognition of her performance in *The Prince and the Showgirl* (1957). MM won in the "Best Actress in a Foreign Film" category.

**THE DAVID STUART GALLERIES**

Art gallery on La Cienega Boulevard in Los Angeles, where Larry Schiller unveiled his August 1972 exhibition, comprised of 185 Marilyn Monroe photographs from fifteen top photographers. The exhibition, entitled "Marilyn Monroe, the Legend and the Truth," was coordinated to commemorate the tenth anniversary of Marilyn's death. The event was a huge success—so much so that it was taken on a nationwide tour. At the David Stuart Galleries, a gold-framed Tom Kelley nude was stolen, as were a half dozen other Marilyn photos. There is no record of these photos ever being recovered.

**BRUCE DAVIDSON**

Davidson is the photographer who took the often-seen shots of MM relaxing with the Montands at the time of the 1960 *Let's Make Love* shooting. He was also assigned by Magnum to shoot location photos on the set of *The Misfits* later that same year.

**BETTE DAVIS**

Born Ruth Elizabeth Davis in 1908, Bette Davis is, of course, one of the most acclaimed American actresses in cinema history. In 1950, Davis had one of her many milestone roles in *All About Eve.* In it, she played a couple of scenes with young starlet Marilyn Monroe.

Among Davis's films are *Of Human Bondage* (1934), *Dangerous* (for which she won a 1935 Oscar), *Jezebel* (1938 Oscar), *Dark Victory* (1939), *The Great Lie* (1941), *The Little Foxes* (1941), *Now Voyager* (1942), *Mr. Skeffington* (1944), *The Corn Is Green* (1945), and *What Ever Happened to Baby Jane?* (1962).

**JUDY DAVIS**

Judy Davis portrayed Marilyn Monroe in the 1982 British stage play *Insignificance.* Born in 1956, Miss Davis has since gained acclaim for her performances in such Australian films as *My Brilliant Career* (1979) and *Winter of Our Dreams* (1981), as well as for the British *A Passage to India* (1984).

**SAMMY DAVIS, JR.**

Entertainer, born in 1925, with whom Marilyn allegedly had an affair circa 1954–55.

**JACK DAWN**

The head of makeup at MGM at the time Marilyn made *The Asphalt Jungle* (1950) and *Right Cross* (1950), both MGM productions.

**BEATRICE DAWSON**

Miss Dawson designed the costumes for *The Prince and the Showgirl* (1957).

**DORIS DAY**

Doris Kappelhoff, aka Doris Day, aka "The Professional Virgin," was born in 1924. It was Day who dominated the box office in the 1960s, following Marilyn's death.

Back in February 1955, according to Hedda Hopper, Day and her then husband, Marty Melcher, planned to adapt *The Sleeping Prince* into a Doris Day vehicle to be shot in England. A year later, Marilyn Monroe held a press conference to announce that *The Sleeping Prince* would be adapted into a Marilyn Monroe vehicle, to be shot in England. The film, of course, became *The Prince and the Showgirl* (1957) with MM and Laurence Olivier.

Then, in 1963, after Marilyn had died, 20th Century-Fox took her last, uncompleted film, *Something's Got to Give,* and revised it into a vehicle for Doris Day, which was then retitled *Move Over Darling.* The critics were less than kind. For example:

> There is so much of Miss Day in this film that one has seen before: the shocked Miss Day, eyes and mouth in fierce contention to see which can open the widest; the righteously affronted Miss Day, enraged to the point of screaming inarticulateness; the teary-eyed Miss Day gallantly blinking back her tears; the scheming Miss Day, darting guilty glances to right and left while forging vehemently ahead with her scheme.
>
> By now, for all of Miss Day's blonde prettiness, I tend to think of her as the perfect den-mother, industrious and highly non-inflammable. . . .
>
> Brendan Gill,
> the *New Yorker*, 1/11/64

Interestingly, Doris Day's best film is the 1959 film that Marilyn wanted for herself, *Pillow Talk*. Other mostly antiseptic Day films: *On Moonlight Bay* (1951), *Calamity Jane* (1953), *The Pajama Game* (1957), *That Touch of Mink* (1962), and *The Thrill of It All* (1963).

**ALBERT DEKKER**
Actor (1905–1968) who appeared in many films from 1937 until his death. In 1951, Dekker costarred in *As Young as You Feel*, which featured MM.

**FRANK DELANEY**
Delaney is the New York attorney who, along with Milton H. Greene, encouraged MM to sever her bond with 20th Century-Fox and form her own Marilyn Monroe Productions. It was at Delaney's Manhattan apartment that MM held a press conference in which she announced the formation of MM Productions, Inc., in January 1955.

**DeLONGPRE AVENUE**
After splitting up with Joe DiMaggio, toward the end of 1954, Marilyn moved out of the Palm Drive home she had shared with DiMaggio and into a duplex at 8336 DeLongpre Avenue in Hollywood.

**REBECCA de MORNAY**
Actress Rebecca de Mornay starred in the 1987 remake of *And God Created Woman*, which was originally intended as a homage to Marilyn Monroe. Miss de Mornay has also starred in such films as *Risky Business* (1983), *The Trip to Bountiful* (1985), and *Runaway Train* (1985).

**HENRY DENKER**
Henry Denker wrote the 1962 New York stage comedy *Venus at Large*, which featured actress Joyce Jameson in a Marilyn Monroe-based role.

**VIRGINIA DENNISON**
In 1962, Virginia Dennison gave Marilyn lessons in yoga.

**REGINALD DENNY**
Denny, born Reginald Leigh Daymore (1891–1967) is the British actor who owned the Radio Plane Company where Norma Jeane Dougherty worked

before becoming a model. Among Denny's films were *Rebecca* (1940) and *Cat Ballou* (1965).

**ARMAND DEUTSCH**

The producer of *Right Cross* (1950), in which MM had a bit part.

**I. A. L. DIAMOND**

Born Itek Dommnici, aka Isadore Diamond, in 1915, Diamond is the superlative screenwriter who became best known for his comedy collaborations with director Billy Wilder. Diamond wrote or cowrote *Love Nest* (1951), *Let's Make It Legal* (1951), *Monkey Business* (1952), and *Some Like It Hot* (1959)—all of which starred or costarred Marilyn Monroe. Among Diamond's other collaborations with Wilder: *The Apartment* (1960) and *Irma La Douce* (1963).

**DIARY**

In the summer of 1962, Marilyn Monroe reportedly purchased a red diary to write about her dates with Robert Kennedy. Supposedly, Marilyn wrote about important political issues that RFK had discussed with her. This diary was shown by MM to Bob Slatzer before her death. It was also seen in the coroner's room by coroner's aide Lionel Grandison before it mysteriously disappeared. As of August 19, 1982, Doug Villiers of the Antiquarius Antique Market made an offer of $150,000 to the person who turned in the missing diary.

Over the years, several people have claimed to possess the potentially explosive diary, but no one has actually produced it.

***DIARY OF A LOVER OF MARILYN MONROE***

Author: Hans Jorgen Lembourn
Publisher: Arbor House Publishing
Year: 1979
$8.95 (ISBN 0-87795-216-7)

Writer Hans Jorgen Lembourn's autobiographical account of his alleged forty-night affair with Marilyn Monroe, which supposedly took place in the late 1950s. Outside of the exploitative title, *Diary* is not offensive reading, but it is not altogether believable, either. Lembourn fails to provide dates, names, places, or photos to validate the book. Thus, it is virtually worthless to any serious student of MM.

**SONDRA DICKENSON**

After actress Joan Collins backed out of the 1974 British stage play about Marilyn Monroe, *Legend*, the role was assumed by relatively unknown Sondra Dickenson.

**ANDRE DE DIENES**

> When I arrived in Hollywood I called a special agency. I wanted a model who would be prepared to pose in the nude if necessary. Yes, they did have a young girl on their books who had no experience

> but was eager to start. She might accept my conditions. An hour later she was at my door: she was wearing a skimpy pink sweater, her curly hair tied with a ribbon to match, and (she) carried a hat box. With child-like smile and clear gaze, she was absolutely enchanting.
>
> Andre de Dienes,
> *Marilyn Mon Amour* (Sidgwick and Jackson, 1986)

Andre de Dienes is, unquestionably, one of the best still photographers that Marilyn Monroe ever worked with. His many, many shots, circa 1945–1949, are the most exquisite documentation of early Marilyn Monroe.

Born in Transylvania in 1913, de Dienes met Norma Jeane Dougherty in 1945. After their successful initial shoot, de Dienes took Norma Jeane on an extended photo expedition that took them to Las Vegas, Oregon, the Mojave, and Yosemite. And, according to de Dienes, two significant things happened during the location shooting. First, he took Norma Jeane to Portland, Oregon, to be reunited with her mother, Gladys Baker:

> Norma Jeane's mother lived in an old hotel in the center of Portland, in a depressing bedroom on the top floor. The reunion between mother and daughter lacked warmth. They had nothing to say to each other. Mrs. Baker was a woman of uncertain age, emaciated and apathetic, making no effort to put us at our ease. Norma Jeane put on a cheerful front. She had unpacked the presents we had brought: a scarf, scent, chocolates. They stayed where they were on the table. A silence ensued. Then Mrs. Baker buried her face in her hands and seemed to forget all about us. It was distressing.
>
> Andre de Dienes,
> *Marilyn Mon Amour* (Sidgwick and Jackson, 1986)

The second thing that happened during the shoot was that Andre de Dienes, the photographer, fell in love with Norma Jeane Dougherty, the model:

> She slipped into the big bed, where I joined her. It seemed the most natural thing in the world. The night was ours. Everything she felt for me, trust, gratitude, even admiration, was fused in her surrender. Everything was so simple, so wonderful. Why had we hesitated, waited, denied ourselves so long? Our bodies were so well matched, made for each other. I could not get enough of that silky skin, of her supple body both docile and demanding, of our shared, repeated pleasure and, suddenly, as my cheek brushed hers, I realized she was crying.
>
> Andre de Dienes,
> *Marilyn Mon Amour* (Sidgwick and Jackson, 1986)

According to de Dienes, the couple planned to get married. And, in order to be with him in New York, Norma Jeane planned to move east to study law at Columbia University. However, once back in Hollywood, Norma Jeane broke off the engagement. De Dienes, understandably, was furious. Nonetheless, when "Marilyn" was in New York in 1949 to promote *Love Happy* the couple rekindled their relationship. Well, at least their professional relationship. At that time, de Dienes shot a photo series of MM romping on Tobey

Beach, outside of New York City. Today, the photographs are classic MM.

The last time de Dienes saw Marilyn Monroe was at the Beverly Hills Hotel on June 1, 1961—Marilyn's thirty-fifth birthday. She had recently had surgery, and was alone. Said de Dienes:

> I took her in my arms, searching for her lips. I lost my head. She cried out, protesting: "Oh please, don't! I'm tired of all that. Don't ask anything of me, you of all people." Her eyes were full of tears. I felt I had been a brute. I was ashamed of myself. I said goodbye and left her in peace.
>
> Andre de Dienes,
> *Marilyn Mon Amour* (Sidgwick and Jackson, 1986)

Andre de Dienes died on April 11, 1985. The following year, his book *Marilyn Mon Amour* was published in Great Britain by Sidgwick and Jackson Limited. It is simply the most stunning, sumptuous photo book available on Marilyn Monroe.

**MARLENE DIETRICH**

Born Maria Magdalena von Losch in 1901, Marlene Dietrich is the legendary German actress who starred in such films as *The Blue Angel* (1930), *Shanghai Express* (1932), *Blonde Venus* (1932), *Desire* (1936), and *Destry Rides Again* (1939). In 1978, Dietrich made an appearance in the David Bowie film, *Just a Gigolo*.

In 1958, Marilyn portrayed Marlene Dietrich in Richard Avedon's photo series for *LIFE* magazine's Christmas issue.

**GIUSEPPE DIMAGGIO**

Joe DiMaggio's father, aka Zio Pepe DiMaggio.

**JOE DIMAGGIO**

> "It's like a good double-play combination. It's just a matter of two people meeting and something clicks."
>
> Joe DiMaggio on dating MM

By the time Joe DiMaggio met Marilyn Monroe, he was a living legend, and she was an actress on the rise.

Joseph Paul DiMaggio was born in Martinez, California, on November 25, 1914. He was the eighth of nine children born to Giuseppe and Rosalie DiMaggio. In 1936, DiMaggio began his career with the New York Yankees. In 1941, he slugged his way into immortality by hitting in fifty-six consecutive games. He led his team into ten World Series championships and was the first ball player in history to receive a salary of $100,000 a year. For fifteen years, Joe DiMaggio was the biggest star in baseball. By the time he retired from playing ball in 1951, Joltin' Joe, the Yankee Clipper, had gone into the annals as one of the greatest, if not *the* greatest ball player the game had ever seen. Subsequently, DiMaggio was elected to the Baseball Hall of Fame in 1955.

Before he officially retired from baseball, DiMaggio (divorced from actress Dorothy Arnold) saw a photograph in the newspaper that aroused his—uh—interest. The photo showed Chicago White Sox players Joe Dobson and Gus Zernial mock-posing with a beautiful blonde movie actress whom Joe had never seen. Reportedly, DiMaggio contacted Zernial, who was his friend, and asked, "Who's the blonde?" And, when Joe discovered that his old pal from Toots Shor's, David March, actually *knew* this blonde, he promptly asked March to set up a date.

In March 1952, David March complied. Initially, Marilyn tried to fend off March's request. She didn't like baseball, and she liked baseball players even less. She actually didn't know who Joe DiMaggio was. She expected him to have slicked-back black hair and flashy clothes to match his equally flashy conversation. Nonetheless, Marilyn agreed to meet DiMaggio at the Villa Nova Restaurant in Hollywood. Also present were March and his date, actress Peggy Rabe.

THE CHRIS BASINGER COLLECTION

In Canada with Joe during *River of No Return* shoot.

The following day, March reportedly telephoned Marilyn to ask her how she had liked DiMaggio. MM was said to have responded, "He struck out."

Apparently, after dinner, Marilyn agreed to drive DiMaggio back to the Knickerbocker Hotel in Hollywood, where he was staying at the time. Reportedly, DiMaggio commenced to make an unsuccessful pass at Marilyn.

Undaunted, DiMaggio telephoned MM every day for two weeks, before he finally gave up in exasperation. However, by that time, Marilyn had learned enough about DiMaggio to be sufficiently impressed to see him again. This time, *she* called *him* for a date.

For the next year and a half, Marilyn Monroe and Joe DiMaggio were an "item"—the hottest item in Hollywood. Their courtship, through the public's eye, was a storybook romance—Cinderella meets Gary Cooper. However, behind the facade, things were not anywhere near that idyllic. There were several obstacles to overcome.

First of all, it's important to see the beginning of their relationship in context. In 1952, and, especially in 1953, Marilyn Monroe shot to worldwide stardom. Everyone wanted to photograph her. Everyone wanted to meet or date her. Everyone *wanted* her, period. Joe DiMaggio, despite all of his personal celebrity, was basically a shy man, leery of cameras, publicity, and anything that glittered. Marilyn's career was built on glitz, glamour, and public spectacle. In addition, Joe DiMaggio was not used to *not* being the center of attention. When he first started dating Marilyn, *he* was still the more popular public personality. However, by the end of 1953, there was no one—man or woman—who was more popular than Marilyn Monroe. Joe DiMaggio's former glory, great as it was, paled beside Marilyn's luminous glow.

And then there was the less than critical problem of the plunging necklines. MM's typically revealing necklines were a few inches too low for DiMaggio's conservative sense of decency. MM conceded for a time by toning down her wardrobe. However, what she *wouldn't* do was get rid of her coach, Natasha Lytess. Natasha and DiMaggio shared a mutual distaste for one another.

Nevertheless, despite their glaring differences, Joe DiMaggio was her "Slugger," her "Giuseppe," her protector against the sometimes brutal Hollywood machinery, and in September 1953 Marilyn agreed to give marriage another attempt. If her decision waivered during the next few months, it was cemented in January 1954, when she was suspended for the first time by 20th Century-Fox. Marilyn and Joe were married on January 14, 1954, in a modest ceremony in San Francisco. The marriage lasted nine months.

There has been a good deal of speculation that the notorious "Skirt Scene" from *The Seven Year Itch* (1955) triggered the MM-DiMaggio split. The scene was shot on the streets of New York City in September 1954. Joe DiMaggio, unfortunately, was among the thousands of cheering, flesh-thirsty spectators who watched as Marilyn Monroe stood over a subway grating while an unseen fan blew her skirt over her ears. At their hotel, following the shoot, MM and Joe had a fight. It has been rumored, over the years, that DiMaggio, on occasion, hit Marilyn. This, reportedly, was one of those occasions. Following the New York shoot, Marilyn returned to Los Angeles and filed for divorce. The marriage was over.

Almost. It was apparent from the start that Joe DiMaggio hadn't yet given up on his love for Marilyn. It may not have been a perfect marriage, but no one could accuse it of being a loveless one. DiMaggio, for whatever reason, hired a private detective to follow Marilyn. This resulted in the somewhat notorious mishap, "The Wrong Door Raid," which took place on November 5, 1954. Months later, in another attempt to reconcile, DiMaggio conceded by escorting MM to the world premiere of *The Seven Year Itch* in New York on June 1, 1955. It was to be the first and only time DiMaggio escorted her to one of her Hollywood-related appearances. Following the screening, DiMaggio took MM to his hangout, Toots Shor's, where he had planned a surprise birthday party for her. For whatever reason, the couple ended up in a fight. The attempted reconciliation failed. A year later, Marilyn married Arthur Miller.

In 1960-61, Marilyn and Joe renewed their relationship. There was

THE AUTHOR'S COLLECTION

considerable interest by the public, perhaps even hope, in what appeared to be a reconciliation. Marilyn went to St. Petersburg, Florida to be with Joe. He took her to see a play (*Hostage*) in New York. Back in Hollywood, Marilyn brewed tea for Joe, because, as she explained to Eunice Murray, "Tea is all he drinks." When giving an interview, or while talking to friends, Marilyn sometimes affectionately referred to Joe, as "Mr. D" or "my ex-ex." And, in the final month of her life, Joe DiMaggio mailed her a pair of his pajamas—so that she would have something to wear to bed.

There is something innately touching about the Joe DiMaggio-Marilyn Monroe love affair. It has been perpetuated, over the years, as an impossible fantasy love. When Marilyn was found dead on August 5, 1962, it was Joe DiMaggio who was there to take care of her. It was DiMaggio who handled the funeral arrangements and who refused to allow it to become another Hollywood circus. It was DiMaggio who broke down at the funeral, as he told Marilyn, one last time, "I love you. I love you. I love you." And it was Joe DiMaggio who ordered that a black vase filled with fresh roses "twice a week—forever" be placed at Marilyn's crypt.

But Joe DiMaggio's biggest testament to Marilyn is the fact that, in the twenty-five years since her death and the thirty-three years since their divorce, he has *not* remarried. Moreover, he has refused to discuss Marilyn or exploit her in any manner. He is also her only husband *not* to have written an autobiographical book or play about their relationship.

**A Relationship in Quotes**

> "I had thought I was going to meet a loud sporty fellow. Instead I found myself smiling at a reserved gentleman in a gray suit, with a gray tie and a sprinkle of gray in his hair. There were a few blue polka dots in his tie. If I hadn't been told he was some sort of ball player, I would have guessed he was either a steel magnate or a congressman."
>
> MM on meeting Joe DiMaggio

> "His hair had a touch of gray in it. I like that."
>
> MM on meeting DiMaggio

> "People are always asking if DiMaggio got to first base."
>
> MM on dating DiMaggio

> "True love is visible not to the eyes, but to the hearts, for eyes may be deceived."
>
> what MM inscribed on a present, from *The Little Prince*

> "What the hell does that mean?"
>
> Joe DiMaggio's response to the above

> "I couldn't be happier. I'm looking forward to being a housewife, too. . . . I want six babies."
>
> MM on her wedding day

> "We decided to go through with it about two days ago. It isn't snap judgment, you know. It's been talked about for some time. Sure, there is going to be a family. Well, at least one."
>
> Joe DiMaggio on his wedding day

"I don't mind playing second fiddle to Marilyn. She's my wife."

Joe DiMaggio in Tokyo

"He's the head of our household, and I'll live wherever he decides."

MM, March 6, 1954

"I'm really a very happy wife. I even like the cooking part of it."

MM, April 15, 1954

"The husband should be the head man, and the wife should always remember that she's a woman. I am certainly no authority on the subject, but when someone asks me how to hold a husband, I tell them this: 'Be yourself, but don't let down.' "

MM, June 6, 1954

"Everything's fine with us. A person's life is more important that any career. A happy marriage comes before everything."

MM, September 1954

"I call him Joe and Giuseppe and some pet names I want to keep secret, but when I refer to him, I say . . . 'my husband.' "

MM, September 1954

"What the hell is going on here?"

Joe DiMaggio, watching MM's
skirt blow over her head, September 1954

"He didn't talk to me. He was cold. He was indifferent to me as a human being and an artist. He didn't want me to have friends of my own. He didn't want me to do my work. He watched television instead of talking to me."

MM, in divorce court, October 1954

"Joe's not bad. He can hit home runs. If that's all it takes, we'd still be married. I still love him, though. He's genuine."

MM to Truman Capote on
(1) DiMaggio's sexual prowess,
(2) her undying love for DiMaggio

"Thank God for Joe, thank God."

MM circa 1961-62

"It was Hollywood that destroyed her—she was a victim of her friends."

Joe DiMaggio

**JOE DiMAGGIO, JR.**

DiMaggio's son by actress Dorothy Arnold. The night of Marilyn's death, Joe Jr. telephoned her to tell her that he had broken off his engagement to his fiancée. According to Mrs. Eunice Murray, the phone call put Marilyn in a great mood.

**MARIE DiMAGGIO**

Joe DiMaggio's sister. It was Marie who maintained the family home in the Marina District of San Francisco, where MM and Joe lived following their marriage.

**ROSALIE DiMAGGIO**

Joe DiMaggio's mother.

**DIMAGGIO'S**

Joe and Dominic DiMaggio owned DiMaggio's restaurant (address: 245 Jefferson Street) on Fisherman's Wharf in San Francisco. During her courtship and marriage to Joe DiMaggio, Marilyn Monroe frequented DiMaggio's. In 1985, the restaurant closed down, and the DiMaggios leased out their location. Today, DiMaggio's is known as Bobby Rubino's: A Place For Ribs.

**DIRECTORS**

> "I worked in some pictures where I was directed by men who never directed before or didn't know a thing about character motivation or how to speak lines. Do you ever see on the screen 'this picture was directed by an ignorant director with no taste'? No, the public always blames the star. Me. I had directors so stupid all they can do is repeat the lines of the script to me like they're reading a timetable. So I didn't get help from them. I had to find it elsewhere."

**The Approved List**

At the end of 1955, when 20th Century-Fox granted MM director approval, Marilyn submitted a list of the sixteen directors that she would agree to work with. They were:

George Cukor
Vittorio De Sica
John Ford
Alfred Hitchcock
John Huston
Elia Kazan
David Lean
Joshua Logan
Joseph L. Mankiewicz
Vincente Minnelli (musicals only)
Carol Reed
George Stevens
Lee Strasberg
Billy Wilder
William Wyler
Fred Zinnemann

**Directors MM Worked With**

| | |
|---|---|
| Roy Baker | *Don't Bother to Knock (1952)* |
| George Cukor | *Let's Make Love (1960)* |
| | *Something's Got to Give* (1962) |
| Tay Garnett | *The Fireball* (1950) |
| Edmund Goulding | *We're Not Married* (1952) |
| Henry Hathaway | *Niagara* (1953) |
| Howard Hawks | *Monkey Business* (1952) |
| | *Gentlemen Prefer Blondes* (1953) |
| F. Hugh Herbert | *Scudda Hoo! Scudda Hay!* (1948) |
| John Huston | *The Asphalt Jungle* (1950) |
| | *The Misfits* (1961) |
| Harmon Jones | *As Young As You Feel* (1951) |
| Phil Karlson | *Ladies of the Chorus* (1948) |
| Henry Koster | *O. Henry's Full House* (1952) |
| Fritz Lang | *Clash By Night* (1952) |
| Walter Lang | *There's No Business Like Show Business* (1954) |

| | |
|---|---|
| Joshua Logan | *Bus Stop* (1956) |
| Joseph L. Mankiewicz | *All About Eve* (1950) |
| David Miller | *Love Happy* (1950) |
| Jean Negulesco | *How to Marry a Millionaire* (1953) |
| Joseph Newman | *Love Nest* (1951) |
| Laurence Olivier | *The Prince and the Showgirl* (1957) |
| Arthur Pierson | *Dangerous Years* (1947) |
| | *Hometown Story* (1951) |
| Otto Preminger | *River of No Return* (1954) |
| Richard Sale | *A Ticket to Tomahawk* (1950) |
| | *Let's Make it Legal* (1951) |
| John Sturges | *Right Cross* (1950) |
| Billy Wilder | *The Seven Year Itch* (1955) |
| | *Some Like it Hot* (1959) |

**WALT DISNEY**

Marilyn Monroe inspired the final image of Walt Disney's animated character Tinker Bell.

**THE DIVORCES**

**Jim Dougherty**

A month before she was signed to her first studio contract, Norma Jeane Dougherty went to Nevada to file for a divorce from her husband, Jim. Jim was subsequently notified of this in a letter from a Las Vegas attorney.

☆ 7/5/46: Norma Jeane files for divorce.

☆ 9/13/46: Divorce is granted in Clark County, Nevada. (Note: some sources give the date as 10/2/46.)

**Joe DiMaggio**

> "I realize a lot of women when they get divorced, they put out all kinds of reasons which aren't the true reasons. But I said the truth. This is what I said. 'Your honor, my husband would get in moods where he wouldn't speak to me for five to seven days at a time. Sometimes longer. . . . I would ask him what was wrong. He wouldn't answer, or he would say, 'Stop nagging me.' I was permitted to have no visitors, no more than three times in the nine months we were married. On one occasion it was when I was sick. Then he did allow someone to come and see me. I offered to give up my work in hopes that would solve our problems, but even this didn't help. I hoped to have out of my marriage love, warmth, affection and understanding. But the relationship was mostly one of coldness and indifference."
>
> MM to Maurice Zolotow,
> *Marilyn Monroe* (Harcourt Brace, 1960)

☆ 10/4/54: The divorce is announced.

☆ 10/5/54: MM officially leaves her Beverly Hills home; the divorce is filed.

☆ 10/27/54: Interlocutory divorce is granted on charges of "mental cruelty" at the Santa Monica Courthouse by Judge Orlando Rhodes.

☆ 10/31/55: Final decree is granted by Judge Elmer Doyle.

**Arthur Miller**

Following the difficult shooting of *The Misfits* (1961), Marilyn officially announced her separation from Miller on Armistice Day. She also chose the day of President Kennedy's inauguration to file for the actual divorce.

☆ 11/11/60: MM announces her separation from Miller.
☆ 1/20/61: Divorce is granted on charges of "incompatibility of character" by Judge Miguel Gomez Guerra in Juarez, Mexico.

**MM Trivia Quiz #11**

In what film(s) did MM portray a divorcee? (Answer on page 577.)

## THE DOCTORS

> "The goddamn doctors killed her. They knew the girl was a pill addict. It's a hell of a tragedy."
>
> John Huston

**Gynecologists**

Dr. Bernard Berglass
Dr. Hilliard Dubrow
Dr. Milton Gottlieb
Dr. Leon Krohn
Dr. Mortimer Rodgers

**Psychiatrists**

Dr. Ralph Greenson
Dr. Hohenberg
Dr. Marianne Kris
Dr. Wexler (when Dr. Greenson was "out of town" in 1962)

**Physicians**

Dr. Elliot Corday
Dr. Hyman Engelberg
Dr. Nathan Headley
Dr. Verne Mason
Dr. Myron Prinzmetal
Dr. Mark Rabwin
Dr. Robert Rosenfeld
Dr. Phillip Rubin
Dr. Phillip Shapiro
Dr. Lee Siegel

## DOCTOR'S HOSPITAL IN NEW YORK

On August 1, 1957, MM was rushed to Doctor's Hospital in New York, where she had her first miscarriage while with Arthur Miller. Doctor's Hospital is located at 170 East End Avenue.

## DOHENY DRIVE

By early 1953, Marilyn was living at 882 N. Doheny Dr., between Sunset and Santa Monica boulevards in Beverly Hills. The three-room modern apartment featured a white-carpeted living room and the white piano that Marilyn once owned as a child. MM was still living at this Doheny apartment when she married Joe DiMaggio in January 1954. By the end of 1961, after returning to Los Angeles, MM was again living at the very same first-floor apartment. At that time, the decor featured heavy blue draperies, a fireplace, a dull blue bedspread, a dressing room with huge floor-to-ceiling mirrors, a green velvet settee, and, a black-enameled front door. The name on the mailbox, under Apartment 3, was Marjorie Stengel, MM's one-time secretary.

**HULDA DOMBEK**

Although MM rarely wore a bra, she did commission—in the latter part of her life—Hulda Dombek to make customized bras for her.

**CLIVE DONNER**

Clive Donner directed the 1975 New York stage production *Kennedy's Children* in which the Marilyn Monroe-based role was portrayed by actress Shirley Knight.

***DON'T BOTHER TO KNOCK*** ★★

1952 76 minutes Black and White
20th Century-Fox
Directed by: Roy Baker
Produced by: Julian Blaustein
Screenplay by: Daniel Taradash, from the novel by Charlotte Armstrong
Photographed by: Lucien Ballard
Cast: Marilyn Monroe, Richard Widmark, Anne Bancroft, Donna Corcoran, Jeanne Cagney, Jim Backus

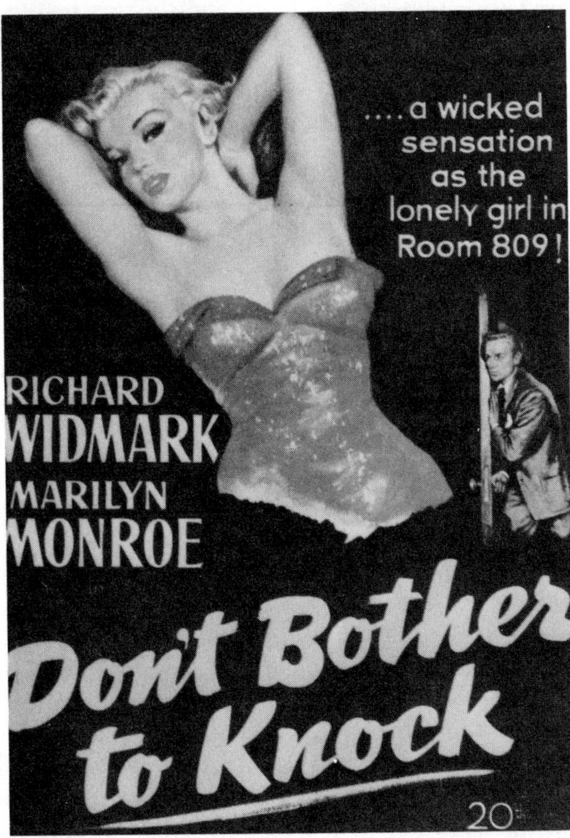


THE AUTHOR'S COLLECTION

Mediocre film about a psychotic babysitter who threatens to kill her bratty charge at a downtown New York City hotel.

One of the biggest mysteries of Marilyn Monroe's career is why 20th Century-Fox chose this slow-moving, melodramatic bore to showcase MM in her first starring role for the studio. If ever there was an inappropriate vehicle for a potentially explosive (and funny) blonde bombshell, this was it. It was almost as if Darryl Zanuck *wanted* MM to flop in her first starring role. *Don't Bother to Knock* was released in the summer of 1952, and, if MM's nude-calendar confessional (made a few months before) hadn't made her the hottest young property in films, *Don't Bother to Knock* might have killed her emerging career. However, despite receiving mostly poor reviews, Marilyn herself felt that this film contained some of her finest dramatic acting. It is also significant in her filmography because Marilyn reportedly did not require a single retake.

Interestingly, Anne Bancroft—who made her film debut in *Don't Bother to Knock*—had the following to say about working with MM:

> It was a remarkable experience. Because it was one of those very few times in all my experiences in Hollywood, when I felt that give and take—that can only happen when you are working with good actors. There was just this scene of one woman seeing another woman who was helpless and in pain, and she was helpless and in pain. It was so real, I responded. I really reacted to her. She moved me so that tears came into my eyes.

**DIANA DORS**

Diana Dors, born Diana Fluck in 1931, was actually making films in the mid-to-late 1940s, before she became known as Britain's "answer" to Marilyn Monroe in the 1950s.

**FYODOR DOSTOYEVSKY**

Russian writer who was one of Marilyn's favorites. Dostoyevsky wrote such classic works as *The Brothers Karamazov, The Idiot, Crime and Punishment,* and *Possessed.*

**BILLIE DOUGHERTY**

Jim Dougherty's sister. *See* ELYDA NELSON.

**EDWARD DOUGHERTY**

Jim Dougherty's father, neighbor of the Goddard's. Originally from Silverton, Colorado.

**ETHEL MARY DOUGHERTY**

Jim Dougherty's mother. Mrs. Dougherty was a good friend of Grace Goddard. Together they plotted for Norma Jeane to marry Jim. While Jim was away in the Merchant Marines during World War II, Mrs. Dougherty taught Norma Jeane how to drive a stick shift, and got her a job at the Radio Plane Company.

When Norma Jeane began to model in 1945, Mrs. Dougherty expressed her disapproval, and Norma Jeane moved out of the Dougherty family home and in with Ana Lower.

## JIM DOUGHERTY

"If I hadn't gone into the Merchant Marine during World War II, she would still be Mrs. Dougherty today."

Jim Dougherty on Marilyn Monroe,
*People* magazine, 5/31/76

By 1942, young Jim Dougherty showed promise of becoming prime husband material. Born in Torrance, California, some twenty-one years before, Dougherty was five feet ten inches tall, with blue eyes and light brown hair. He had a good job at Lockheed Aviation and had been a "big wheel" at Van Nuys High School a few years earlier. Not only was he the student body president; he was also a football star and a member of the Maskers Drama Club. Besides, he owned a car—a blue Ford coupe.

He also had his pick of the girls. In 1941–42, Dougherty's favorite date was Santa Barbara beauty queen Doris Ingram (aka Doris Drennan). However, by the fall of 1941, Jim began to drive his neighbors, Beebe Goddard and Norma Jeane Baker, to and from Van Nuys High School. Both girls had a crush on Jimmy. In December 1941, Grace Goddard asked Jim to escort Norma Jeane to a company Christmas dance. By March 1942, Jim and Norma Jeane were going steady. By May they were engaged.

"Our marriage was a good marriage . . . it's seldom a man gets a bride like Marilyn. . . . I wonder if she's forgotten how much in love we really were."

Jim Dougherty, *Photoplay*, 1953

THE AUTHOR'S COLLECTION

With first groom, Jim Dougherty, June 19, 1942.

Despite Marilyn's later claim that her marriage to Jim was loveless and one of convenience (so she wouldn't have to go back to the orphanage), Jim Dougherty has repeatedly asserted just the opposite. He also dispelled, somewhat, Marilyn's own often-quoted contention that she was raped as a youth. According to Dougherty, Norma Jeane was still a virgin at the time they met.

Despite Norma Jeane's limited culinary skills, Jim Dougherty was, undeniably, a happy husband. He and his young, pretty wife went fishing together at Sherwood Lake. They went skiing at the Big Bear Lodge. They went to the movies at Grauman's Chinese Theatre. And they had sex on the side streets and back roads of the San Fernando Valley.

And then Jim Dougherty made the mistake of joining the Merchant Marine. And while he was away, NJ began to model. She started to meet photographers, agents, would-be-agents, advertising executives, and a whole cast of Hollywood types who were an entirely different breed from the people she had met as Mrs. Jim Dougherty. It was an expansive, exciting world, waiting outside of her domestic doorstep. The die, as they say, was cast.

In 1950, in a sad, almost poignant stroke of fate, Jim Dougherty (by then a policeman) was assigned by the Los Angeles Police Department to protect the glittering assemblage of stars attending the premiere of *The Asphalt Jungle*. Dougherty's task was to hold off the barricaded fans who had crowded the entrance of Grauman's Egyptian Theatre. Mercifully, Marilyn did not show up.

In 1953, Dougherty wrote an article for *Photoplay* magazine titled, somewhat moronically, "Marilyn Monroe Was My Wife." Wrote Dougherty:

> Marilyn Monroe and I were married four years, and if we had stayed married, it's a cinch that today I'd be Mr. Monroe. I like it better the way it is. I'm married again and have three tow-headed daughters. I have a good job with the patrol division of the Van Nuys Police Force and all four females in my house are content to stay on board and let me steer their ship. I'm the captain and my wife is first mate, and I have a crew any man would be proud of.

By 1972, Dougherty's "first mate" had either jumped ship or was thrown overboard. In 1976, thirty years after his split from Norma Jeane, Dougherty published a book titled *The Secret Happiness of Marilyn Monroe* (Playboy). Also in 1976, Dougherty moved to Arizona, where he lived with his third wife, Rita. By 1984, Dougherty was retired and living in Maine.

Jim Dougherty learned about Marilyn's death from his friend, Sergeant Jack Clemmons. Clemmons telephoned Jim from MM's Brentwood home early in the morning of August 5, 1962. Upon hearing the news, Dougherty reportedly put down the phone receiver and said to his wife, "Say a prayer for Norma Jeane."

**MARION DOUGHERTY**

Marion Dougherty was Jim's older brother, who served as best man at Jim and Norma Jeane's wedding in 1942. Marion died in 1973 of a stroke.

**PATRICIA SCOMAN DOUGHERTY**
After his wife, Norma Jeane, left him, Jim Dougherty married Patricia Scoman in 1947. Coincidentally she also worked at the Radio Plane Company. Together, they had three daughters. Reportedly, Patricia was extremely jealous of Jim's former relationship with Marilyn Monroe. MM's name was not allowed to be mentioned. In 1972, Patricia and Jim were divorced.

**TOM DOUGHERTY**
Tom was another Dougherty brother who got on well with Norma Jeane. In 1961, Tom, by chance, ran into Marilyn in Malibu. Reportedly, Tom asked MM to visit him sometime. Marilyn was said to have replied, "How much is it going to cost me?" The Doughertys never heard from Norma Jeane/ Marilyn again.

**PAUL DOUGLAS**
Actor Paul Douglas (1907–1959) costarred opposite Barbara Stanwyck, Robert Ryan, and Marilyn Monroe in the 1952 RKO film *Clash by Night.* The same year, Douglas appeared in another MM-costarring vehicle, *We're Not Married.* Douglas's other credits include *A Letter to Three Wives* (1948) and *The Solid Gold Cadillac* (1956).

**HUGH DOWNS**
Regarding ABC-TV's decision to shelve the "20/20" segment on Marilyn Monroe, correspondent Hugh Downs said he would "not be involved in a cover-up for the company," and despite opinions to the contrary, that the proposed segment on Marilyn "was a superb job of reporting."

**ERVIN DRAKE**
Ervin Drake cowrote the 1952 song about MM, "Marilyn," that was recorded by Ray Anthony.

**THE DRAKE HOTEL**
In 1952, following the location shooting of *Niagara,* MM took a week off in New York to be with Joe DiMaggio. She stayed at the Drake Hotel. Today, the Drake Hotel is known as The Drake Swissotel (address: 440 Park Avenue).

**JAY DRATLER**
Dratler coauthored a story on which *We're Not Married* (1952) was based.

**MARIE DRESSLER**
MM would often cite this character actress of the early 1930s as the actress she most admired. Born Leila Von Koerber, Dressler (1869–1934) appeared in such films as *Anna Christie* (1930), *Min and Bill* (for which she won a 1930 Oscar), *Tugboat Annie* (1933), and *Dinner at Eight* (1933).

**DRUGS**

> In those days, pills were seen as another tool to keep stars working. The doctors were caught in the middle. If one doctor would not prescribe, there was always another who would. When I first treated Marilyn, back in the early fifties, everyone was using pills.
>
> Dr. Lee Siegel to Anthony Summers

> She told me she'd always used drugs. She was a baby when she started taking pills, just seventeen or eighteen years old.
>
> Amy Greene to Anthony Summers

> She used to come to the dressing room and put down a plastic bag; and you never saw so many pills in one bag. There would be uppers, downers, vitamins, and God knows what in the bag.
>
> Bunny Gardel to Anthony Summers
>
> All three quotes from *Goddess: The Secret Lives of Marilyn Monroe* (Macmillan, 1985)

> You've got to get Marilyn off the drugs. You're her husband. And the only one who can do it. If you don't you'll feel guilty as long as you live. If she doesn't stop now, she'll be in an institution in two or three years—or (she'll be) dead.
>
> John Huston to Arthur Miller
> *An Open Book* by John Huston
> (Knopf, 1980)

At the time of Marilyn Monroe's death, fifteen pill bottles were found in her bedroom by the coroner's representative, Guy Hockett. Hockett subsequently turned over all these bottles to the coroner's office. However, curiously, only eight have been itemized on the coroner's toxicology report. They were listed as follows:

1. 27 (out of a container of 50) LIBRIUM CAPSULES 5 milligrams; Prescription #19295; Dated 6/7/62
2. 17 (out of a container of 100) LIBRIUM CAPSULES 10 milligrams; Prescription #20201; Dated 6/10/62
3. 26 (out of a container of 36) SULFATHALLIDINE TABLETS Prescription #205469; Dated 7/25/62
4. Empty container (out of a container of 25) NEMBUTAL CAPSULES Prescription #20858; Dated 8/3/62
5. 10 (out of a container of 50) CHLORAL HYDRATE CAPSULES Prescription #20570; Dated 7/31/62
6. Empty Container (out of a container of 50) NODULAR CAPSULES Prescription #456099; Dated 11/4/61
7. 32 pink/peach-colored tablets named MSD, without label
8. 24 (out of a container of 25) PHENERGAN 25 milligrams; Prescription #20857; Dated 8/3/62

### The Drugs Found in Marilyn's Body

1. Barbiturates: 4.5 mg percent
2. Chloral hydrate: 8 mg percent
3. Pentobarbital: 13 mg percent

### Famous Movie Personalities Who Have Died From a Drug Overdose

Pier Angeli
John Belushi
Charles Boyer
Dorothy Dandridge
Judy Garland
Alan Ladd
Carole Landis
Marilyn Monroe
Mabel Normand
Gail Russell
George Sanders
Jean Seberg
Inger Stevens
Margaret Sullivan
Lupe Velez

**HILLIARD DUBROW**

Dr. Hilliard Dubrow was the gynecologist who operated on Marilyn at the time of her August 1, 1957, miscarriage at Doctor's Hospital in New York.

**PATTY DUKE**

In 1958, twelve-year-old Patty Duke portrayed Marilyn Monroe as a child in the Columbia feature *The Goddess.* The film featured Kim Stanley as the adult MM. Patty Duke has also appeared in such films as *The Miracle Worker* (for which she won a 1962 Supporting Actress Oscar), *Valley of the Dolls* (1967), and *You'll Like My Mother* (1972). She also starred (as twin sisters) in her own television series, "The Patty Duke Show, from 1963–65.

**FAYE DUNAWAY**

Faye Dunaway, born in 1941, is the sometimes excellent, but erratic, actress who portrayed the MM-based Maggie in Arthur Miller's television version of his 1964 play, *After the Fall.* Said Morton Moss of the Los Angeles Herald Examiner:

> Dunaway's is an engrossing Maggie. Her past has left her a time-bomb of dreads and self-loathings. She's malleable, unable to rebuff a man. She can burble and twitter naively. She strangely combines an innocence and a commonness. And she's unnervingly beautiful. Fear causes her debacle. She deteriorates—analysis, drink, pills, recriminations.

Dunaway's feature films have included *Bonnie and Clyde* (1967), *Chinatown* (1974), *Network* (for which she won a 1976 Oscar), *The Eyes of Laura Mars* (1978), and the camp classic *Mommie Dearest* (1981). Dunaway's other TV films include *The Disappearance of Aimee* (1976) and *Evita Peron* (1982).

**DAVID DUNN**

David Dunn is the deputy county clerk who typed MM and Joe DiMaggio's marriage certificate in 1954.

**"THE DuPONT SHOW OF THE WEEK"**

*See* USO WHEREVER THEY GO!

**DURANGO, COLORADO**

Where starlet MM shot location work for *A Ticket to Tomahawk* in 1949.

**ELEANORA DUSE**

Eleanora Duse (1858–1924) was the Italian tragedienne who became one of Marilyn Monroe's few female idols. Marilyn read about her, identified with her, and admired her. At several of her many residences, MM was known to keep a photograph of Duse in prominent display.

## *EAST OF EDEN*

Marilyn was an usherette for the March 9, 1955, premiere of *East of Eden,* which was held at the Astor Theater in New York. The premiere was a benefit for the Actors Studio.

The film was directed by Elia Kazan and starred James Dean, Raymond Massey, Julie Harris, Dick Davalos, and Jo Van Fleet.

## EBBETS FIELD

MM opened a soccer match that took place at Ebbets Field in New York, circa 1957.

COURTESY OF CINEMA COLLECTORS

Opened soccer game, Ebbets Field, NY, 1957.

## BARBARA EDEN

Born Barbara Huffman in 1934, Eden has two known connections to Marilyn Monroe. First of all, in the 1958 television series *How to Marry a Millionaire,* Eden played the role of Pola, the part that MM had played in the 1953 film version. Secondly, after MM's death, Eden sometimes used Marilyn's former stand-in, Evelyn Moriarty.

Barbara Eden is best known, of course, for her role as Jeannie in the 1965–1970 television series "I Dream of Jeannie."

**EGHAM, ENGLAND**

Arthur and Marilyn Miller lived in Egham during the 1956 shooting of *The Prince and the Showgirl.*

***THE EGYPTIAN***

Following the successful premiere of *How to Marry a Millionaire* (1953), MM began to recognize what she thought was her newfound power at 20th Century-Fox. Thus, she requested permission to star in the studio's upcoming film version of *The Egyptian,* which was a dramatic epic adapted from a best-selling novel. Marilyn wanted the role of Nefer-Nefer. However, Darryl Zanuck, who was producing the picture, refused even to test MM for the part. The movie was subsequently made without Marilyn in 1954. It was directed by Michael Curtiz and photographed by Leon Shamroy. The cast included Edmund Purdom, Victor Mature, Peter Ustinov, Bella Darvi, Gene Tierney, Michael Wilding, and Jean Simmons.

**ALBERT EINSTEIN**

According to Shelley Winters, MM once included Albert Einstein on a list of the men she would most like to sleep with. It is not known whether MM fulfilled this fantasy. What *is* known is that she possessed a photograph of Einstein that was inscribed, "To Marilyn, with respect and love and thanks, Albert Einstein." The authenticity of the photo and autograph has never been proven.

Interestingly, the MM-Einstein "relationship" was fictionalized in the Nicolas Roeg 1985 film *Insignificance,* which was based on a stage play of the same name.

**EL CENTRO AVENUE**

From 1935 to 1937, Norma Jean Mortenson lived at the Los Angeles Orphans Home Society, which was located at 815 El Centro Avenue in Hollywood.

**THE EL MOROCCO**

New York restaurant/club (address: 154 East 54th Street) that MM would sometimes visit when she was in town. Marilyn was seen here in 1949, during the *Love Happy* publicity tour; in 1954, during the location shooting of *The Seven Year Itch* (with DiMaggio); and in 1955, with Truman Capote, during her strike against Hollywood.

Today, the El Morocco has been relocated to 307 East 54th Street in New York.

**EL PALACCIO APARTMENTS**

El Palaccio is the name of Lucille Ryman and John Carroll's Hollywood residence, where MM lived for a period in 1947. It was located at La Cienega Boulevard and Fountain Avenue (8491–8499 Fountain Apartment F).

**EL TORO AIR BASE**
*See* MARINE CORPS AIR STATION EL TORO.

**"THE ELEVENTH HOUR"**
*See* "LIKE A DIAMOND IN THE SKY."

**GLADYS ELEY (also spelled *Gladys Ely*)**
*See* GLADYS BAKER.

**BOBBY ELLIS**
Bobby Ellis was an actor who had a minor part in the 1953 film *Niagara.* In one sequence in the film, Ellis danced the jitterbug with Marilyn Monroe. However, for whatever reasons, the scene was cut, and Ellis's shot at stardom was thwarted. He was quoted as saying: "I was disappointed, but I still have my memories."

**EMERSON JUNIOR HIGH SCHOOL**
Norma Jeane Baker attended grades seven through nine at Emerson Junior High school (address: 1650 Selby Avenue) in West Los Angeles. She graduated on June 27, 1941.

**HYMAN ENGELBERG**
Dr. Hyman Engelberg was Marilyn's Hollywood internist at the time of her death in 1962. It was Engelberg who recommended that MM be hospitalized during the 1960 shooting of *The Misfits.* It was Engelberg who prepared Marilyn for her 1961 New York gallbladder operation. And, it was Engelberg who treated MM at the start of *Something's Got to Give* (1962) for a viral infection. Engelberg was also the man who prescribed Marilyn's pills. On August 3, 1962, Dr. Engelberg prescribed twenty-five Nembutal capsules for MM at the San Vicente Pharmacy in Brentwood. Reportedly, these were the drugs that led to MM's death less than two days later.

It was also Dr. Engelberg who officially pronounced Marilyn Monroe dead at 3:40 A.M. on August 5, 1962.

In the period between June 28 and August 3, 1962, Marilyn saw Dr. Engelberg *twenty-nine times—almost once a day.* Controversially, Engelberg reportedly gave MM injections on August 1 and August 3, 1962. However, these needle marks (which should have still been apparent) were *not* included on the official autopsy report. On the September 24, 1982, television talk show "Open Line," Engelberg reportedly refused to answer questions about MM or about the alleged injections.

As of 1986, the seventy-five-year-old Dr. Hyman Engelberg was still practicing medicine in his Beverly Hills offices.

**ENGLEFIELD GREEN**
Located in Egham, England, Englefield Green is the estate where Arthur and Marilyn Miller lived during their 1956 business trip to England.

**"ENTERTAINMENT TONIGHT"**
Vintage black-and-white footage of early Marilyn Monroe was used in a television commercial for "Entertainment Tonight." It aired during the Fall of 1986.

**HENRY EPHRON**
Screenwriter, born in 1912, who cowrote *There's No Business Like Show Business* (1954), which costarred MM. Ephron was also involved with such other films as *Daddy Long Legs* (1955), *Carousel* (1956), and *Desk Set* (1957).

**PHOEBE EPHRON**
Screenwriter (1914–1971) who invariably worked with her husband, Henry. Among their collaborations was *There's No Business Like Show Business* 1954).

**ELLIOTT ERWITT**

> "What impressed me was that in spite of the fact that though she wasn't terribly attractive to look at, she usually came out extremely well in photographs . . . very often, people who look attractive in person look like hell in pictures, but she was the opposite."
> Elliott Erwitt on Marilyn Monroe

Elliott Erwitt was among the large assemblage of photographers hired to shoot on location stills of *The Misfits* (1960) shooting. Erwitt's color group shot of the company's principals is probably the best-known still from that film. It shows MM seated in between Clark Gable and Montgomery Clift. Behind her are John Huston, Eli Wallach, Frank Taylor, and Arthur Miller.

***ESQUIRE* MAGAZINE**
In its March 1961 issue, *Esquire* published an article on MM by A. T. McIntyre entitled "Making *The Misfits* or Waiting for Monroe or Notes from Olympus." The article began:

> What is Marilyn really like? She is like nothing human you have ever seen or dreamed, and nothing on the screen can prepare you for her. It is not special lighting which brings out Monroe and leaves her supporting actors to fade into the woodwork—she is astonishingly white, so radically pale that in her presence you can look at others about as easily as you can explore the darkness around the moon.

Twenty-five years later, *Esquire* put Marilyn on its March 1986 cover and asked the pointed question "Why is Madonna [the virginal, material girl] pretending she's Marilyn?"

*Esquire* published the following other articles on MM:

☆ 11/62: "Big Bite," by Norman Mailer
☆ 7/66: " 'Joe,' said Marilyn Monroe, just back from Korea, 'You never heard such cheering.' 'Yes I have,' Joe DiMaggio answered," by G. Talese
☆ 7/73: "Marilyn Monroe's Last Picture Show," by Walter Bernstein
☆ 11/74: Reprint from the July 1966 issue

**THE ESTATE**

At the time of her death, the Marilyn Monroe estate was estimated at $1,000,000. This included $65,400 worth of real and personal property in Los Angeles, according to attorney Aaron R. Frosch, executor of the estate. It also included Marilyn's interest in Marilyn Monroe Productions and her shares in *Some Like It Hot* (1959), *The Prince and the Showgirl* (1957), and *The Misfits* (1961). However, by June 1965, newspaper reporters and columnists were calling the Marilyn Monroe estate "the one-million-dollar myth." One article read:

> Although Marilyn, in death, still earns about $150,000.00 a year in deferred salaries, and while her total earnings, including movie sales to TV, have come to over $800,000.00, virtually all is going to taxes.

At that time, attorney Elliott Lefkowitz, an associate of Frosch, informed the beneficiaries of Marilyn's will (*see* WILL) that they would *not* be receiving any monies, as there were no funds to be drawn from. In other words, the Marilyn Monroe estate was broke. Dry. According to Lefkowitz, there was not even any money to pay for Gladys Baker's $5,000-a-year care at Rockhaven Sanitarium.

As far back as December 1964, columnist Sheila Graham put it this way:

> Do you remember that half million dollars in the Marilyn Monroe Estate? Well, it isn't there anymore . . . the only asset left, and that still could bring in some money, is the late sex symbol's percentage in *Some Like It Hot*. All that insecurity and agony, for what?

In March 1981, Aaron Frosch was sued for "plundering" MM's estate by $200,000. The case was subsequently settled out of court for an undisclosed amount. As of 1986, Frosch was still the executor of MM's estate. However, in August 1982, attorney Roger Richman was appointed as the new licensing agent of the estate.

**ETHNIC HERITAGE**

According to MM, she was part Irish, Scottish, and Norwegian.

**THE EULOGY**

The eulogy was delivered by Lee Strasberg at Marilyn Monroe's funeral, August 8, 1962.

> Despite the heights and brilliance she attained on the screen, she was planning for the future: she was looking forward to participating in the many exciting things which she planned. In her eyes and in mine, her career was just beginning. The dream of her

> talent, which she had nurtured as a child, was not a mirage. When she first came to me I was amazed at the startling sensitivity which she possessed and which had remained fresh and undimmed, struggling to express itself despite the life to which she had been subjected. Others were as physically beautiful as she was, but there was obviously something more in her, something that people saw and recognized in her performances and with which they identified. She had a luminous quality—a combination of wistfulness, radiance, yearning—to set her apart and yet made everyone wish to be part of it, to share in the childish naiveté which was at once so shy and yet so vibrant. This quality was even more evident when she was on the stage. I am truly sorry that the public who loved her did not have the opportunity to see her as we did, in many of the roles that foreshadowed what she would have become. Without a doubt she would have been one of the really great actresses on the stage.

**DALE EUNSON**

Eunson wrote one of the plays that *How to Marry a Millionaire* (1953) was based on.

**CLARICE EVANS**

> "Marilyn probably got more phone calls than any girl at the Hollywood Studio Club—but she almost never got any mail."
>
> Clarice Evans on MM

Clarice Evans was Marilyn Monroe's one-time roommate at the Studio Club in the mid- to late 1940s. On November 28, 1954, the *Los Angeles Times* printed a two-part article on MM written bv Clarice Evans. The article was far from insightful, but it did include the following information:

1. MM was just as interested in the capacity of the bookshelves as she was in the size of the closets.
2. MM was quiet.
3. MM talked about one day having four children—two of which she planned to adopt.

**TOM EWELL**

Tom Ewell, paired with Marilyn in *The Seven Year Itch* (1955), was one of the

COURTESY OF CINEMA COLLECTORS

very few costars MM ever had who was *not* blown off the screen by her. The handful of others include Jack Lemmon and Jane Russell. Ewell, born S. Yewell Tompkins in 1909, has had a sporadic film career that included *Adam's Rib* (1949), *The Girl Can't Help It* (with Jayne Mansfield, 1957) and *State Fair* (1962). He was also a successful stage actor and had a television series in 1960 titled "The Tom Ewell Show."

**"EYEWITNESS"**
*See* "MARILYN MONROE, WHY?"

### *FADE TO BLACK*
Vernon Zimmerman's mediocre 1980 ode to the movies, *Fade to Black* featured Dennis Christopher as a mentally disturbed, overzealous movie fan who idolized Marilyn Monroe, played by Linda Kerridge.

### FALSIES
Earl Wilson: True or falsie?
MM: Everything I have is mine.

Pete Martin: Has anyone ever accused you of wearing falsies?
MM: Yes. Naturally, it was another actress who accused me. My answer to that is, quote: Those who know me better know better. That's all. Unquote.

### *FAME*
*Fame* was a 1974 Broadway play based on the life of MM that was trashed by certain critics as the worst play of the season. Wrote critic Clive Barnes in the November 19, 1974, issue of *The New York Times*:

> It was *Fame* but not fortune that gratuitously opened at the John Golden Theatre last night. The best part of this limp rag of a comedy, based on the life and times of Marilyn Monroe, came at the intermission.

This debacle was written and directed by Anthony J. Ingrasia and starred Ellen Barber as MM.

### *FAMILY CIRCLE* MAGAZINE
Ironically, considering the notorious reputation that she would later gain, *Family Circle* was one of the very first magazine covers that Norma Jeane/Marilyn appeared on. The issue was dated August 1946.

### FAMOUS ARTISTS AGENCY
Well-established Hollywood agency that Marilyn signed with in 1953, following her dissatisfaction with the William Morris Agency.

### FANS
> "[Homosexuals] have such good taste! That's why they like me, they like Marilyn Monroe, and they love Barbra Streisand."
>
> Bette Davis

> "A bunch of us fellows went down to see *Asphalt Jungle* and when you came on the screen we almost lost our eyeballs. We didn't even know who you were."
>
> an early fan letter

THE ROBERT SLATZER COLLECTION

"The 'public' scares me, but people I trust."

Marilyn Monroe

**The Fan Clubs**

Over the years, an abundant supply of Marilyn Monroe fan clubs have popped up all over the world. Listed below are two of the current, more successful organizations. Write to the Marilyn Forever Fan Club at the following address:

Wendy Beeby, President
P.O. Box 2451
Northridge, CA 91323

Write to the Los Angeles-based Marilyn Remembered Fan Club at the following address:

Greg Schreiner, President
1237 Carmona Avenue
Los Angeles, CA 90019

***FANFAREN DAS LIEBE***

German film that the smash comedy hit, *Some Like It Hot* (1959) was based upon.

**DANIEL L. FAPP**

Cinematographer, born in 1901, who shot MM in *Let's Make Love* (1960). A year later, Fapp would attain his greatest success, *West Side Story,* for which he won a cinematography Oscar.

**FASHIONS**

"Putting a girl in overalls is like having her work in tights, particularly if a girl knows how to wear them."

MM on her uniform at the Radio Plane Company

"When she wiggled through the audience to come up to the podium, her derriere looked like two puppies fighting under a silk sheet."

James Bacon on MM's gown at the 1953 *Photoplay* Awards

"I wasn't aware of any objectionable décolletage on my part—I'd noticed people looking at me all day, but I thought they were looking at my Grand Marshal's badge."

MM on the gown she wore to the 1952 Miss America Parade

"I like to be really dressed up, or really undressed. I don't bother with anything in between."

MM to Jon Whitcomb, 1960 *Cosmopolitan*

When Marilyn Monroe *was* dressed, or more precisely, *almost* dressed, she wore—in her own inimitable style—the following fashions.

1. Her first date: Norma Jeane wore a red silk party dress that she borrowed from Beebe Goddard.
2. Catalina Island: Norma Jeane enticed the uniformed men with a daily parade featuring tight sweaters, tight skirts, white shorts, white blouses, and decorative ribbons in her hair.
3. The first meeting with Emmeline Snively: In 1945, Norma Jeane put on her finest dress for her interview at the Blue Book Model Agency. It was a white sharkskin dress with an orange yoke. She also wore a pair of white suede shoes.
4. The first advertising assignment: A sheer black negligee.
5. The first meeting with Natasha Lytess: White tailored slacks and a white shirt tied at the waist.
6. The first publicity tour: In 1949, MM purchased three wool suits to wear during the *Love Happy* publicity tour. Upon arrival at Grand Central Station in New York, MM was dressed in a navy blue suit with a blue blouse, a beret, a choker of pearls, and three white orchids. Later due to the intense summer heat, MM purchased a blue polka-dotted cotton dress with a low-cut neck and a decorative red velvet belt.
7. The baseball publicity shot: In 1951, MM posed for a publicity photo with two players from the Chicago White Sox. It was this photo that aroused the interest of Joe DiMaggio. MM was dressed in a pair of tight white shorts, a tight jersey blouse, and a baseball player's cap.
8. The meeting with *Clash By Night* producer Jerry Wald: MM wore a low-cut blouse with tight plaid pedal pushers and a pair of loafers to this luncheon interview that resulted in her being hired for *Clash By Night*. To accessorize her outfit, MM strategically placed a decorative red rose in her cleavage.
9. The first date with Joe DiMaggio: MM wore a blue tailored suit with a low-cut white shantung blouse.
10. The Miss America Parade: Marilyn created a mild scandal by appearing at the 1952 Miss America parade wearing a low-cut black dress.
11. The 1953 *Photoplay* Awards: MM caused a sensation, a furor in the movie industry, for the dress she wore to this prestigious (at that time) event. The dress itself would be considered tame by today's post-Cher standards. It was a gold lamé gown, one size too

COURTESY OF CINEMA COLLECTORS

Wardrobe test, *There's No Business Like Show Business*, 1954.

small, that MM had to be literally sewn into. Reportedly, the seams burst open at the awards event, and MM had to be restitched on site. MM actually borrowed the dress, designed by Travilla, from 20th Century-Fox. The dress was used briefly for a scene in *Gentlemen Prefer Blondes*. In 1955, Mrs. Edgar Bergen wore the very same gown to a costume party at Ciro's nightclub; Jayne Mansfield tried it on for size for the 1957 premiere of *The Spirit of St. Louis*. In the 1970s, Sophia Loren once wore it for a European photo session. Jeanne Crain, Marilyn Maxwell, and Gene Tierney have all worn variations of the dress, and Victoria Principal and Priscilla Presley have worn updated versions, designed by Travilla himself.

12. The potato sack: In the early 1950s, the 20th Century-Fox publicity machinery issued a press release claiming that its latest, newest, blondest box-office bait could look sexy in *anything*. To prove the point, they cut all the right holes in all the right places and gussied MM up in actual Idaho burlap, giving new meaning to the terms *potato* and *old bag*.
13. The 1952 Golden Globe Awards: MM attended the 1952 Golden Globe Awards to accept her prize as the "Best Newcomer" of the year. She wore a red velvet evening gown.
14. In Korea: MM sported an Army shirt, Army pants, Army combat boots, and a leather jacket.
15. Performing for the troops in Korea: MM wore a low-cut, plum-colored, sequined gown.
16. Deplaning in New York: In 1954, MM arrived in New York to shoot exterior scenes for *The Seven Year Itch*. She wore a beige-colored wool dress with a white fox fur stole.
17. The DiMaggio Separation: Following the announcement to the press that she and Joe were separating, MM stepped outside of her Beverly Hills home wearing all black—a black wool jersey dress with a black wool coat.
18. The DiMaggio Divorce: MM appeared in court wearing a black silk two-piece suit with a black tilted straw hat and white gloves.
19. The Romanoff's party: To the 1954 Romanoff's party, thrown in her honor, MM wore a black tulle gown with her neckline conspicuously *not* low.
20. Leaving Cedars of Lebanon Hospital: On November 12, 1954, MM left Cedars wearing a man's shirt, a pair of slacks, a mink coat, and no makeup.
21. To classes at the Actors Studio: During 1955, MM would often wear a baggy sweater and jeans to her acting classes in New York.
22. Fur coats: While she was married to Joe DiMaggio, MM owned a full-length black natural mink worth $12,500. She also sported a $15,000 blue sapphire mink, which she either purchased or rented. And, at the time of her death, a $25,000 white ermine coat was retrieved from her New York apartment.
23. First interview with biographer Maurice Zolotow: MM wore a white terry cloth robe with nothing underneath.
24. Second interview with biographer Maurice Zolotow: Black velvet toreador pants and a white blouse.
25. Triumphant return to Hollywood: Following her successful strike against 20th Century-Fox, MM returned to Hollywood on February 25, 1956, to shoot *Bus Stop*. Deplaning at LAX, MM wore a tailored brown two-piece suit with a high neck black blouse. She had won the right to cover up her bosom—if she so desired.

    REPORTER: Marilyn, when we last saw you, you were wearing a low-cut gown. Now you're wearing a high-necked suit. Is this the "New Marilyn?"

    MM: Well, I'm the same person—it's just a different suit.
26. In court for a traffic violation: For her 1956 court appearance, MM wore a somber black chiffon dress, black stockings, black gloves, and black high-heeled pumps.
27. Joshua Logan's party for President Sukarno: a tight-fitting black wool dress.
28. To meet Arthur Miller's parents: A gray skirt, a black blouse, and a scarf wrapped around her hair.
29. The London premiere of *A View from the Bridge*: MM wore a tight red strapless satin

THE RAY VAN GOEYE COLLECTION

This costume was cut because it was too revealing—*Gentlemen Prefer Blondes*, 1953.

gown that stole the spotlight from Arthur Miller. AP said, "Marilyn Monroe's close-fitting dress turned the London opening of her husband's latest play into a near riot."

30. What MM's 1957 closet consisted of: At her New York apartment, circa 1957, MM's closet contained mostly black and brown velvet pants, black and white checked pants, beige and white cotton and silk blouses, flat Ferragamo shoes, four mink coats, and a lot of scarves.
31. What MM wore out in public when she didn't want to be recognized: A black fur coat over a blouse, a pair of slacks, a scarf wrapped around her hair, dark glasses, and no makeup. When she was extremely concerned about not being recognized, MM would don a black wig.
32. What MM wore to pick up her award from the Italian Consulate: A black cocktail dress with a matching black jacket, and black patent leather heels.
33. What MM wore to the 1959 Khrushchev luncheon: A black net dress with a translucent bosom.

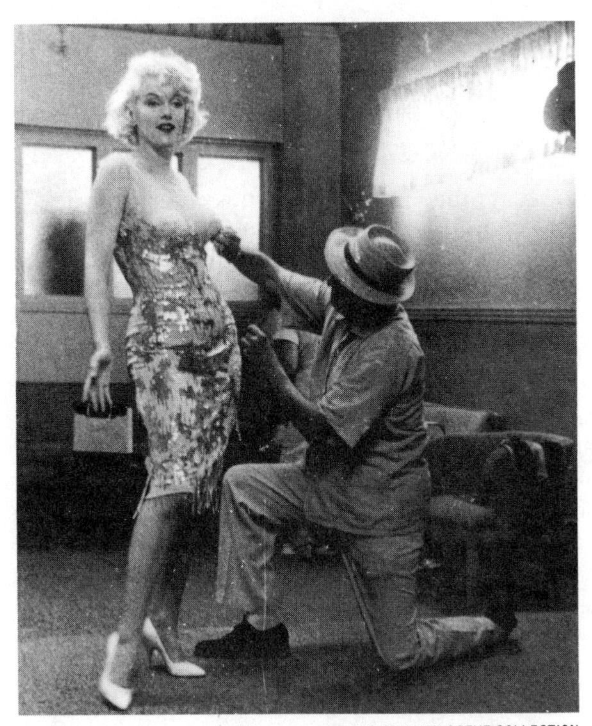

THE RAY VAN GOEYE COLLECTION
Making adjustments to tight-fitting costume, *Some Like It Hot*, 1959.

34. What MM wore to the 20th Century-Fox party honoring Frankie Vaughan and Yves Montand: a champagne-colored chiffon cocktail dress.
35. MM's favorite loafing attire: a sweater and/or blouse, a pair of slacks, and loafers without socks.
36. What MM wore to camouflage aging: Gloves.
37. What MM wore around the house: A terry cloth robe or a red Chinese kimono.
38. What MM wore to a dinner party at Peter Lawford's house: MM wore one of her favorite dresses—a black Norman Norell dress with a matching black broadcloth jacket.
39. What MM wore to be interviewed by Margaret Parton: A sleeveless beige blouse with a high neckline and a tight beige skirt.

40. What MM wore to sing "Happy Birthday" to John F. Kennedy: A sheer, clinging, flesh-colored gown that glittered with hand-sewn rhinestones, designed by Jean-Louis.
41. What MM wore to be interviewed by Alan Levy: A purple dress with a matching purple scarf. MM called it her "Purple People-Eater Wardrobe."
42. What MM wore to meet Bert Stern: Pale green Jax slacks, a cashmere sweater, a scarf around her head, and no makeup.
43. What MM wore under whatever MM wore: Nothing.
44. What MM wore to bed:
    REPORTER: Is it true you only wear one thing to bed—Chanel No. 5?
    MM: I like to wear something different once in a while. Now and then I switch to Arpege.
45. What MM wore on her final day: A white terry cloth robe.
46. What MM was buried in: One of her favorite dresses: a pale green Pucci dress. Marilyn was also buried wearing a slip and a bra. Eunice Murray reportedly objected to putting underpants on MM.

### *Niagara* (1953)

☆ The red dress: Tight, low-cut, and tied at the bust, this was the infamous dress MM "performed" her historical *Niagara* walk in. According to one critic,

> Miss Monroe plays the kind of wife whose dress, in the words of the script, is cut so low you can see her knees.
>
> Otis Guernsey, Jr.,
> *The New York Herald Times*

### *Gentlemen Prefer Blondes* (1953)

☆ The sequined "Little Rock" dress: Tight, red sequined gown, slit up to MM's upper left thigh. It had flesh-colored material covering the low-cut V neckline and a rhinestone necklace collar. MM also wore a red hat with white feathers curving around the right side of her face.

☆ The dinner gown: Tight orange gown outlined in sequins and featuring spaghetti straps and a chiffon scarf that was draped around MM's neck.

☆ The "Diamonds Are a Girl's Best Friend" dress: Tight pink satinlike strapless form-fitting gown. It featured a pink belt, in addition to a big pink bow in the back, and was accessorized with pink evening gloves.

### *How to Marry a Millionaire* (1953)

☆ The mirror dress: Tight, wine-colored, and satin, this fabulous fashion featured a sash that hung down MM's back and a one-shouldered sequined strap.

### *There's No Business Like Show Business* (1954)

☆ The "Heat Wave" outfit: Black and white on the outside and red on the inside, this spicy two-piece number featured a full open skirt that revealed black bikini panties. The top was a strapless black bikini top. MM wore a black scarf tied around her head that was topped by a big floppy white straw hat. The hat was tilted to one side and had big red flowers hanging from it.

☆ The white sequined dress: Tight form-fitting gown that featured white and silver sequins over a flesh-color stocking. It was slit up to MM's upper thigh and featured, at the top of the slit, a huge array of silver and white flowers. MM also wore a small headpiece made out of the same silver and white floral design.

THE RAY VAN GOEYE COLLECTION

*How To Marry a Millionaire*, 1953.

### *The Seven Year Itch* (1955)

☆ The fan-caught-in-the-door-dress: Tight, white, low-cut, and form-fitting, this dress was most identifiable by the straps that crisscrossed at the neck.

☆ The Rachmaninoff dress: Tight, strapless, sequined orange and black tiger gown.

☆ The "Skirt Scene" dress: White halter dress that featured a full pleated skirt. It's best known as the dress that was blown over MM's head on a New York City street.

### *Bus Stop* (1956)

☆ The "Ole Black Magic" dress: Black-and-green satin, sequined outfit that featured spaghetti straps, ratty fishnet stockings, a black sequined tail, a sheer green scarf, and copper-colored heels.

### *The Misfits* (1961)

☆ The cherry dress: a high-waisted, low-cut white dress that featured red stemmed cherries.

### *Something's Got to Give* (1962, uncompleted)

☆ The Jackie Kennedy outfit: Two-piece suit that featured three-quarter-length sleeves, trimmed in fur. The outfit was accessorized with a fur pillbox hat and long white gloves.

### The MM Movie Fashion Designers

1. Bonnie Cashin — *Scudda Hoo! Scudda Hay!* (1948)
2. Carey Cline — *O. Henry's Full House* (1952)

COURTESY OF TRAVILLA

With William Travilla.

| | |
|---|---|
| 3. Beatrice Dawson | *The Prince and the Showgirl* (1957) |
| 4. Edith Head | *All About Eve* (1950) |
| 5. Grace Houston | *Love Happy* (1950) |
| 6. Rene Hubert | *A Ticket to Tomahawk* (1950) |
| 7. Dorothy Jeakins | *Niagara* (1953) |
| | *Let's Make Love"* (1960) |
| 8. Elois Jenssen | *We're Not Married* (1952) |
| 9. Orry-Kelly | *Some Like It Hot* (1959) |
| 10. Charles LeMaire* | *Dangerous Years* (1947) |
| | *The Fireball* (1950) |
| 11. Jean-Louis | *Ladies of the Chorus* (1948) |
| | *The Misfits* (1961) |
| | *Something's Got to Give* (1962) (Incomplete) |
| 12. Renie | *As Young as You Feel* (1951) |
| | *Love Nest* (1951) |
| | *Let's Make It Legal* (1951) |
| 13. Helen Rose | *The Asphalt Jungle* (1950) |
| | *Right Cross* (1950) |
| | *Hometown Story* (1950) |
| 14. Billy Travilla | *Don't Bother to Knock* (1952) |
| | *Monkey Business* (1952) |
| | *Gentlemen Prefer Blondes* (1953) |
| | *How to Marry a Millionaire* (1953) |
| | *River of No Return* (1954) |
| | *There's No Business Like Show Business* (1954) |
| | *The Seven Year Itch* (1955) |
| | *Bus Stop* (1956) |
| 15. Michael Woulfe | *Clash By Night* (1952) |

*For *Dangerous Years* (1948) and *The Fireball* (1950), no costume designer was credited. However, Charles LeMaire was head of the Wardrobe Department at Fox at that time.

**The Personal Fashion Designers**

1. Ceil Chapman
2. Jean-Louis
3. Don Loper
4. John Moore
5. George Nardiello
6. Norman Norell
7. Emilio Pucci
8. Billy Travilla

**MM Trivia Quiz #12**

In what film(s) did MM portray a fashion model? (Answer on page 577.)

## FATHER

Take your pick: Martin Edward Mortenson or C. Stanley Gifford.

**Foster Fathers:**

Albert Wayne Bolender
Erwin "Doc" Goddard
Harvey Giffen
Sam Knebelcamp

**Fathers-in-Law:**

Edward Dougherty
Giuseppe DiMaggio
Isidore Miller

## FAVORITES OF MM

**Favorite Actors:**

1. Marlon Brando
2. Clark Gable
3. Charles Chaplin
4. Charles Laughton
5. Will Rogers
6. Cary Grant
7. John Barrymore
8. Tyrone Power
9. Richard Widmark

**Favorite Actresses:**

1. Greta Garbo
2. Jean Harlow
3. Ginger Rogers
4. Marie Dressler
5. Joan Crawford
6. Olivia de Havilland

**Favorite Airline:**

TWA

**Favorite Artists:**

1. Goya
2. Picasso
3. El Greco
4. Michelangelo
5. Botticelli

**Favorite Beverage:**

Dom Perignon 1953

**Favorite Book:**

*How Stanislavsky Directs*, Michael Gorchakov

**Favorite Colors:**

1. Beige
2. Black
3. White
4. Red

**Favorite Female Singer:**

Ella Fitzgerald

**Favorite Male Singer:**

Frank Sinatra

**Favorite Marilyn Monroe Film Performances:**

1. *The Asphalt Jungle* (1950)
2. *Don't Bother to Knock* (the breakdown scene) (1952)

**Favorite Marilyn Monroe Photograph:**

Cecil Beaton's photo of MM in white dress

**Favorite Musicians:**

1. Louis Armstrong
2. Earl Bostick
3. Ludwig von Beethoven
4. Wolfgang Amadeus Mozart

**Favorite Perfume:**

Chanel No. 5

**Favorite Plays:**
1. *A Streetcar Named Desire*
2. *Death of a Salesman*

**Favorite Playwrights:**
1. Arthur Miller
2. Tennessee Williams

**Favorite Poets:**
1. John Keats
2. Walt Whitman

**Favorite Remembrance:**
Korea

**Favorite Restaurant (Hollywood):**
Romanoff's

**Favorite Store:**
Bloomingdale's

**Favorite Writers:**
1. Fyodor Dostoyevsky
2. J. D. Salinger
3. George Bernard Shaw
4. Thomas Wolfe

**FARRAH FAWCETT**

When Farrah Fawcett abruptly quit the hit television program "Charlie's Angels" in 1977, some industry people equated it to the time when Marilyn Monroe defected from 20th Century-Fox in 1954. They both left at the peak of their popularity. Some newspapers even printed side-by-side photos of MM and FF. It was kind of silly, really, because Marilyn and Farrah had and have very little in common—except for the fact that, for a time, they were both the most popular blonde femme personality in America.

After a handful of mediocre feature films, Fawcett scored a success in the 1985 TV film *The Burning Bed* and the 1986 feature film, *Extremities.*

THE SABIN GRAY COLLECTION
Farrah Fawcett, the 70s MM, circa 1977.

**ED FEINGERSH**

Feingersh was a photographer for the PIX Agency and shot a "Day in the Life of Marilyn Monroe" series for the July 1955 issue of *Redbook* magazine.

**CHARLES FELDMAN**

Charles Feldman (1904–1968) was a noted Hollywood producer/talent agent who signed MM to the Famous Artists Agency in 1953. At the end of 1954, it was Feldman who threw the milestone Romanoff's soiree that initiated MM into the Hollywood elite. Feldman also served as the coproducer of MM's 1955 hit, *The Seven Year Itch*. However, MM dropped Feldman and Famous Artists after the formation of Marilyn Monroe Productions in 1955.

Feldman's impressive non-MM films include *A Streetcar Named Desire* (1951) and *The Big Sleep* (1946).

**GENE FELDMAN**

Gene Feldman cowrote, coproduced, and directed the 1986 cable television documentary about MM entitled "Marilyn Monroe: Beyond the Legend."

**FRANK FENTON**

Fenton adapted the screenplay for *The River of No Return* (1954), which starred MM.

**BETTY FIELD**

Character actress who appeared in *Bus Stop* (1956). Born in 1918, Field also appeared in such films as *Of Mice and Men* (1939), *Picnic* (1956), *Butterfield*

**FRED VANDERBILT FIELD**

A member of the prominent Vanderbilt family. In 1962, Field, along with his wife, Nieves, served as Marilyn's guides on her buying trip in Mexico City.

**JOSEPH FIELDS**

Fields cowrote the musical play *Gentlemen Prefer Blondes,* which was adapted into a 1953 film vehicle for MM.

**SIDNEY FIELDS**

Though it is disputed by Earl Wilson, Sidney Fields is credited as having given MM her first major publicity break by mentioning her in his *New York Daily Mirror* column on June 27, 1949. Fields included a photograph of MM and wrote,

> Marilyn is a very lovely and relatively unknown movie actress. But give her time; you will hear from her.

**W. CLAUDE FIELDS, JR.**

Son of actor W. C. Fields and MM's attorney circa 1954–55. It was Fields who handled MM's driving-without-a-license traffic violation case.

**FIFTH HELENA DRIVE**

Marilyn Monroe's final residence was located off Carmelina Avenue in Brentwood. The address was 12305 Fifth Helena Drive. For a movie star of MM's magnitude, the house was modest. It was a one-story, three-bedroom house that cost less than $90,000. The $37,500 nineteen-year mortgage was held by City National Bank of Beverly Hills. As of March 1, 1962, MM was making payments of $320 a month.

The house itself was Spanish colonial, and, in Marilyn's last months, MM and Mrs. Eunice Murray labored to decorate the house with authentic Mexican furnishings. As a model, they used the home of Marilyn's psychiatrist (and the former home of Mrs. Murray), which they attempted to duplicate. The living room featured white walls, pure white wool carpeting, and a tile fireplace. The kitchen, which MM totally remodeled, featured red brick floors, wooden cabinets, ceramic wall tiles, and a blue refrigerator, stocked with champagne. There was a bedroom for MM, a bedroom for Mrs. Murray (or other guests), and a telephone room. The house had practically no closets; thus, MM's books, magazines, scripts, and records were piled into corners.

The exterior of the house included an oval-shaped pool and a garden that MM became seriously involved in. But, above all, the house at 12305 Fifth Helena Dr. was *private*. It was also sturdy in construction and suggested a permanence that, in 1962, MM was seeking.

**FIFTY-SECOND STREET AND LEXINGTON AVENUE**

The site of MM's famous "Skirt Scene" from *The Seven Year Itch* (1955) was shot at the corner of these New York Streets.

**FIFTY-SEVENTH STREET**

In 1957, Arthur and Marilyn Miller rented an apartment at 444 E. 57th Street in New York City. The apartment, located on the thirteenth floor, overlooked the East River. The large living room featured white walls, white draperies, white wall-to-wall carpeting, white furniture, a beige sofa, and wall-to-ceiling mirrors. MM also displayed the white piano that her mother had once purchased for her.

For the next three years, the Millers divided themselves among this apartment, various hotels, and their getaway homes in Roxbury and Amagansett. Following their separation in 1960, Miller moved out of the 57th Street apartment and into the Roxbury farmhouse. Marilyn retained this apartment as a New York base until her death.

***FILMS IN REVIEW***

In October 1962, this movie magazine—intended mainly for cinema buffs and Hollywood industry types—published a "career article" on MM. It was written by Robert C. Roman and was subtitled "Her Tragedy Was Allowing Herself to Be Misled Intellectually." The article was a biased, slanted piece of journalism that demeaned MM's position in cinema history.

*Films in Review* also put MM on the cover of the following issues: April 1953, October 1956, October 1960, February 1961, October 1962, March 1979.

### *THE FILMS OF MARILYN MONROE*

Authors: Michael Conway and Mark Ricci
Publisher: Citadel Press
Year: 1964
$12.00, hardcover (ISBN 0-8065-0395-5 C265)

Adequate career filmography book that features many photographs and a selection of MM's film reviews.

### *FINDING MARILYN: A ROMANCE*

Author: David Conover
Publisher: Grossett & Dunlap
Year: 1981 (Out of print)

Conover, of course, is the Army photographer who shot the first professional photos of Marilyn Monroe, then known as Norma Jeane Dougherty, at the Radio Plane Company in 1945. In this ludicrously titled book, "the man who discovered Marilyn Monroe?" contends that he and MM were lovers and that they remained close friends until the time of her death.

What this book *does* offer, however, is a great selection of black-and-white photos of pre-MM Norma Jeane. She was budding with youth, vitality, and uninhibited sexuality.

It can be found at collectors' shops and certain libraries.

### FINNOCCHIO'S

Durable, popular San Francisco nightclub (address: 506 Broadway) that features a female impersonator show. During a break from shooting of *The Misfits* in 1960, MM and company drove to SF and went to see the show. Marilyn had heard that one of the men in the show was impersonating her, and she wanted to see his performance. However, before the MM impersonator completed his number, MM and company walked out.

### FIRE ISLAND, NEW YORK

Marilyn Monroe was known to have guested at the Lee Strasberg vacation home on Fire Island in New York.

### *THE FIREBALL* ★★

1950 84 minutes Black and White
20th Century-Fox
Directed by: Tay Garnett
Produced by: Bert Friedlob
Screenplay by: Tay Garnett, Horace McCoy
Photographed by: Lester White
Cast: Mickey Rooney, Pat O'Brien, Beverly Tyler, Glenn Corbett, Marilyn Monroe

Originally titled *The Challenge*, *The Fireball* was a vehicle for the antics of

Mickey Rooney and an unabashed waste of Marilyn Monroe. MM played Polly, one of Rooney's rollerskating groupies. Marilyn started shooting this picture on January 5, 1950 and was finished by February.

**FIRSTS: THE TWENTY-FIVE MM FIRSTS**

1. First home: Hawthorne, California
2. First song: "Jesus Loves Me, This I Know"
3. First slow dance: "Everything Happens to Me"
4. First songs in a movie: "Every Baby Needs a Da Da Daddy," "Anyone Can See I Love You" from *Ladies of the Chorus*
5. First school: Ballona Elementary and Kindergarten school
6. First love: Jim Dougherty
7. First love according to MM: Fred Karger
8. First magazine feature: *Yank*, 1945
9. First *LIFE* cover: 4/52
10. First agent: Emmeline Snively
11. First theatrical agent: Harry Lipton
12. First motion picture screen test: 7/19/46
13. First movie: *Scudda Hoo! Scudda Hay!* (1948)
14. First movie close-up: *Dangerous Years* (1947)
15. First movie review: *Ladies of the Chorus*, 10/23/48
16. First starring role: *Don't Bother to Knock* (1952)
17. First national television appearance: "The Jack Benny Show," 9/13/53
18. First drama coaches: Phoebe Brand, Morris Carnovsky
19. First photograph taken with Joe DiMaggio: on the set of *Monkey Business*, 1952
20. First modeling job: The Holga Steel Company
21. First professional photo session: 6/26/45
22. First date: Jim Dougherty, 12/41
23. First charge account: Marian Hunter's Bookshop
24. First car: a 1948 Ford convertible
25. First studio name: Carole Lind

THE RAY VAN GOEYE COLLECTION

**MM Trivia Quiz #13**

Name the film in which MM got her first screen kiss and who the actor was. (Answer on page 577.)

**ELLA FITZGERALD**

Ella Fitzgerald was Marilyn Monroe's favorite female singer. Born on April 25, 1918, Ella was discovered at the Apollo Theatre's amateur hour by Chick Webb. She was fifteen. In 1958, she won her first of many Grammy Awards. In 1985, she was inducted into the Jazz Hall of Fame.

In the August 1972 issue of *MS* magazine, Ella wrote the following:

> I owe Marilyn Monroe a real debt. It was because of her that I played Mocambo [an important Los Angeles club in the fifties]. She personally called the owner of the Mocambo, and told him she wanted me booked immediately, and if he would do it, she would take a front table every night. She told him—and it was true, due to Marilyn's superstar status—that the press would go wild. The owner said yes, and Marilyn was there, front table, every night. The press went overboard. . . . After that, I never had to play a small jazz club again. She was an unusual woman—a little ahead of her times. And she didn't know it.

**AGNES FLANAGAN**

Agnes Flanagan was Marilyn's longtime personal hairdresser. She was credited as having "dressed" MM's hair for *Bus Stop* (1956) and *The Misfits* (1961). In the year before MM's death, Flanagan was called in to do MM's hair for the following occasions:

8/25/61: *LOOK* magazine shoot
6/26/62: Peter Lawford dinner party
6/28/62: Meeting with Fox executives
6/29/62: *Cosmopolitan* magazine/George Barris shoot
6/30/62: *Cosmopolitan* magazine/George Barris shoot
7/1/62: *Cosmopolitan* magazine/George Barris shoot
7/6/62: *LIFE* magazine/Allan Grant shoot
7/12/62: Meeting with Fox executives

Miss Flanagan also did MM's hair for her funeral.

**JOHN FLOREA**

Photographer who shot the photos used in the *Collier's* September 8, 1951, feature on MM entitled "The 1951 Model Blonde."

**FLORENTINE GARDENS**

Italian restaurant/nightclub where Jim and Norma Jeane Dougherty held their wedding reception in 1942. Norma Jeane upset Jim by drinking too much champagne and joining the festive conga line. Today, the Florentine Gardens is still located at 5951 Hollywood Boulevard in Hollywood.

**FLOWERS**

- ☆ Jim Dougherty gave Norma Jeane her first white orchid.
- ☆ After MM's appendectomy in April 1952, Joe DiMaggio sent two dozen roses to MM's room at Cedars of Lebanon Hospital.
- ☆ Also during the April 1952 hospital stay, actor Dan Dailey sent MM a tulip tree that featured singing toy canaries on every limb.

THE T. R. FOGLI COLLECTION

☆ In 1955, Edward R. Murrow presented MM three dozen red roses for appearing on his television program, "Person to Person."

☆ Joe DiMaggio placed a tiny bouquet of baby pink roses in Marilyn's hands as she was laid to rest.

☆ Following the funeral, DiMaggio ordered six red roses to be placed beside MM's crypt "twice a week—forever." Forever lasted twenty years, as DiMaggio canceled the order on September 1, 1982. It has been estimated that DiMaggio paid between $500 and $850 dollars a year for his floral tribute to MM.

☆ In 1982, Bob Slatzer signed a one-year contract to send yellow or pink roses—once a week—to MM's crypt.

**FOCUS MAGAZINE**

Magazine that put Marilyn Monroe on its December 1951 cover, with an accompanying article titled "Marilyn Monroe: She Breathes Sex Appeal." The article elaborated,

> Her name is Marilyn Monroe, and she's the hottest thing in town. Blonde, blue-eyed and busty (she measures somewhere between Lana Turner's 35″ and Jane Russell's 37½″), she bids fair to outstrip Betty Grable, June Haver and Rita Hayworth as the most sex-citing glamour girl on the 20th Century lot.

**T. R. FOGLI**

T. R. Fogli is a Marilyn Monroe collector, and a member of the Marilyn

Remembered Fan Club in Los Angeles. His collection includes an extensive supply of books, magazines, and MM memorabilia. He also operates a business entitled "Mostly Marilyn," and can be contacted at 4107 Gird Road, Chino Hills, California 91709.

**FONTAINBLEAU HOTEL**
Famed hotel where MM stayed during her February 1962 visit to Florida.

**FOOD**

> "I have grapefruit and coffee for breakfast, and cottage cheese for lunch. Some days I get by with just a little over a dollar a day for food."
>
> MM to Fred Karger, circa 1948

☆ During the lean years: raw hamburgers, peanut butter, hot dogs, chili, crackers
☆ Breakfast, 1951: warm milk, two raw eggs, a dash of sherry
☆ Dinner, 1951: broiled steak, lamb chop or liver, raw carrots
☆ On first DiMaggio date: anchovies on pimento, spaghetti al dente, scallopini of veal
☆ On second DiMaggio date: hamburgers at a drive-in
☆ While dating DiMaggio: spaghetti, steaks
☆ For her 1952 birthday dinner at the Bel-Air Hotel: steak
☆ On the Fox set in 1952: hard-boiled eggs
☆ MM's favorite appetizer circa 1952: tiny tomatoes stuffed with cream cheese and caviar
☆ What MM especially disliked: olives
☆ While filming *River of No Return*: lobster
☆ For her DiMaggio wedding dinner: steak, cooked medium-well
☆ While in Korea: cheese sandwiches
☆ At the Romanoff's party in her honor: chateaubriand
☆ While shooting *Bus Stop*: raw steaks
☆ Breakfast, 1957: three poached eggs, toast, a Bloody Mary
☆ Lunch at the Roxbury farm, 1957: salami and cheese sandwiches
☆ Dinner, 1957: steak or lamb chops, cottage cheese
☆ What Lena Pepitone cooked for MM: spaghetti, lasagne, sausages and peppers
☆ Dinner following her split with Yves Montand: lasagne, hamburger, chocolate pudding
☆ On New Year's Eve, 1960: spaghetti with sweet Italian sausages
☆ MM's favorite snack: caviar
☆ While shooting *The Misfits*: buttermilk and borscht
☆ Breakfast, 1961: egg whites, poached in safflower oil (Note: MM had Eunice Murray save the egg yolks to use in the holiday pound cakes.)
☆ In her refrigerator, 1962: smoked sturgeon, rye bread, bagels and cream cheese, lox, champagne
☆ Breakfast, 1962: hard-boiled eggs, toast
☆ Lunch, 1962: a broiled steak
☆ MM's favorite Italian dinner, 1962: fettuccini Leon and veal piccata
☆ On a 1962 picnic in the backseat of her Cadillac: cold steak sandwiches
☆ The last breakfast, on 8/3/62: a grapefruit

**THE FOREIGN CLUB**

Tijuana nightclub (located at Fourth and Constitution) where MM and Bob Slatzer held their alleged 1952 wedding party. According to Slatzer, MM wanted to dance on the floor where Rita Hayworth had once danced.

**FOREST LAWN**

Cemetery where MM attended Johnny Hyde's December 1950 funeral. It is located at 6300 Forest Lawn Drive in Hollywood Hills.

**CONSTANCE FORSLUND**

Actress who portrayed MM in the 1980 television version of Garson Kanin's *Moviola*.

**FOURSQUARE GOSPEL CHURCH**

Church where Norma Jeane Baker was baptized at the age of six months. After all these years, it is still located at 4503 West Broadway in Hawthorne, California.

**THE FOX-WILSHIRE THEATRE**

Theatre where the November 1953 premiere of *How to Marry a Millionaire* was held. Now called the Wilshire Theatre, it is located at 8440 Wilshire Boulevard in Los Angeles.

**FRAGRANCES**

Much has been written about MM's passion for Chanel No. 5 perfume. Supposedly, Marilyn once had twenty-six bottles of Chanel in her possession at one time. She was also known to have lavishly bathed herself in Chanel. In addition to Chanel, MM would sometimes sprinkle herself with Arpege and Joy fragrances.

**ALAN FRANCE**

Originally from Cleveland, Ohio, Alan France started his Marilyn Monroe collection after he first saw the 1966 television documentary, "The Legend of Marilyn Monroe." Today, Alan is a member of the Marilyn Remembered Fan Club in Los Angeles, and has an extensive MM collection that includes books, magazines, albums, and still photographs.

**JANE FRANCIS**

Actress Jane Francis, aka Jane Millar, portrayed Marilyn Monroe in the stage play *Public Property*, which ran at the Hampstead Theatre in London, circa 1978–1979.

**FRANK AND JOSEPH'S SALON**

Hollywood hair salon that transformed Norma Jeane from a dirty blonde to a bleached blonde in 1945–46. Frank and Joseph's was formerly located at 6513 Hollywood Boulevard in Hollywood.

### FRANKLIN AVENUE

In 1948, during her struggling starlet period, Marilyn Monroe lived in an apartment on Franklin Avenue in Hollywood for a brief period.

### JOE FRANKLIN

Writer who cowrote the first biography written on MM. It was published in 1953 and was titled *The Marilyn Monroe Story.*

### FRANK'S NURSERY

During the week of her death in August 1962, Marilyn ordered citrus trees and flowering plants from this Wilshire Boulevard nursery. They were to be planted in MM's burgeoning garden at her Brentwood home. Ironically, they were delivered to her house on Saturday, August 4, 1962—the eve of her death.

### HUGH FRENCH

MM's agent at the Famous Artists Agency in 1953.

### *FREUD*

Reportedly, director John Huston wanted Marilyn Monroe to costar opposite Montgomery Clift in the 1963 motion picture, *Freud,* based, of course, on the life of Dr. Sigmund Freud. However, Marilyn's analyst advised against the proposal, and the idea was nixed. The role subsequently went to actress Susannah York.

### BERT FRIEDLOB

The producer of *The Fireball* (1950), which featured MM in a small role.

### FRIENDS

Marilyn Monroe made few lasting friendships during her Hollywood career. She made even fewer friendships among the Hollywood community. It's not that she *couldn't* make friends—she made friends easily. However, she tended to sever those friendships almost as easily.

The following is an alphabetized list of Marilyn's friends. Naturally, these friendships varied in intensity. And while some of those listed remained friends with MM until her death, many of them did not.

1. Rupert Allan
2. John Carroll and Lucille Ryman
3. Michael and Xenia Chekhov
4. Montgomery Clift
5. Jack Cole
6. Wally Cox
7. Joe DiMaggio
8. Agnes Flanagan
9. Connie Francis
10. Lotte Goslar
11. Milton and Amy Greene
12. Dr. Ralph Greenson
13. Johnny Hyde
14. Anne Jackson and Eli Wallach
15. Anne Karger
16. Fred Karger
17. Rudy Kautzsky
18. Peter and Patricia Lawford
19. Natasha Lytess
20. Dean and Jeanne Martin
21. Inez Melson
22. Pat Newcomb
23. May Reis
24. Ralph Roberts
25. Norman and Hedda Rosten
26. Jane Russell

27. Carl Sandburg
28. Hal Schaefer
29. Joseph Schenck
30. Mary Karger Short
31. Frank Sinatra
32. Sidney Skolsky
33. Bob Slatzer
34. Allan "Whitey" Snyder
35. Lee and Paula Strasberg
36. Frank and Nan Taylor
37. Clifton Webb

**AARON FROSCH**

Marilyn's New York attorney at the time of her death and the executor of her estate. It was Frosch, representing the law firm of Weissberger and Frosch, who drew up Marilyn's January 1961 will. It was also Frosch who handled the 1962 *Something's Got to Give* negotiations with 20th Century-Fox.

In March 1981, Aaron Frosch was sued for "plundering" Marilyn Monroe's estate by some $200,000. The suit was initiated by the Estate of Dr. Marianne Kris (MM's former NY analyst) and claimed that Frosch had illegally paid himself funds from MM's estate. The case was settled out of court for an undisclosed sum. As of 1986, Frosch was still excutor of MM's estate.

**LARRY FULLER**

Fuller directed and choreographed the 1983 stage musical, *Marilyn,* which featured actress Stephanie Lawrence as MM.

**FUNERAL**

"And, if God choose, I shall but love thee better after death."
Elizabeth Barrett Browning

The arrangements for Marilyn Monroe's funeral were made by Joe DiMaggio, Mrs. Bernice Miracle, and Inez Melson. The funeral took place on August 8, 1962, at the Westwood Memorial Park Chapel. The services were conducted by Reverend A. J. Soldan, a Lutheran minister from the Village Church of Westwood. He read the 23rd Psalm, the 14th chapter of the Book of John, and excerpts from the 46th and 139th Psalms, in addition to reciting the Lord's Prayer. Lee Strasberg delivered the eulogy.

The funeral was very private. The guest list was limited to a select few. Hollywood was conspicuously absent. The Lawfords, the Martins, and Sinatra were all denied invitations. Joe DiMaggio was criticized for refusing to admit MM's "real friends" to the funeral. He responded by saying: "But for those friends she'd be alive."

Marilyn's body was partially exposed in a solid bronze casket that was lined with champagne-colored satin. She was dressed in her green Pucci dress and a green chiffon scarf. Her hair was done in a pageboy.

The music selected for the funeral was Judy Garland's "Over the Rainbow."

**The Pallbearers**

1. Allen Abbott
2. Sidney Guilaroff
3. Ronald Hast
4. Leonard Krisminsky
5. Clarence Pierce
6. Whitey Snyder

**The Invited Guests**

1. Joe DiMaggio
2. Joe DiMaggio, Jr.
3. Agnes Flanagan
4. Aaron Frosch
5. Lotte Goslar
6. Dan and Joan Greenson (Dr. Greenson's children)
7. Dr. Ralph Greenson and his wife Hildi
8. Sidney Guilaroff
9. Anne Karger
10. Mary Karger
11. Rudy Kautzsky
12. Enid and Sam Knebelcamp (former foster parents)
13. Pat and Inez Melson
14. Mrs. Bernice Miracle
15. Mrs. Eunice Murray
16. Pearl Porterfield
17. Pat Newcomb
18. May Reis
19. Ralph Roberts
20. Milton Rudin
21. Sherry Snyder (Whitey's daughter)
22. Whitey and Beverly Snyder
23. George Solotaire
24. Lee and Paula Strasberg
25. Florence Thomas (Mrs. Miracle's friend)

**THE FURNACE CREEK INN**

MM and photographer David Conover stayed at this Death Valley motel while on a photo shoot in the mid-1940s.

### G. RAY HAWKINS GALLERY

In October 1982, the G. Ray Hawkins Gallery featured a Marilyn Monroe photo exhibition entitled "Marilyn Revisited 1982." The exhibit included works by thirteen photographers. The gallery is located at 7224 Melrose Avenue in Hollywood, California.

### CLARK GABLE

> "Last year Clark Gable was sitting next to me in Chasen's, and I asked him to sign my napkin."
>
> MM to Truman Capote

> "I think she's something different to each man, blending somehow the things he seems to require most."
>
> Clark Gable on MM

> "You like me, huh?"
>
> MM to Gable, *The Misfits*

COURTESY OF CINEMA COLLECTORS

> "Christ, I'm glad this picture's finished. She damn near gave me a heart attack."
>
> Gable on MM, at the end of *The Misfits* shooting

> "He never got angry with me once for blowing a line or being late or anything—he was a gentleman. The best."
>
> MM on Gable

> "She's a kind of ultimate, in her way, with a million sides to her, each one of them fascinating. . . . She is completely feminine, and femininity without guile. . . . Everything Marilyn does is different from any other woman, strange and exciting, from the way she talks to the way she uses that magnificent torso."
>
> Gable on MM

> "The place was full of so-called men, but Clark was the one who brought a chair for me between the takes."
>
> MM on Gable

> "She makes a man proud to be a man."
>
> Gable on MM

> MM: Now, there's something a girl could make sacrifices for . . . sable!
> MAN: Sable or Gable?
> MM: Either one!
>
> MM as Miss Caswell, *All About Eve,* 1950

Upon Gable's death, Marilyn Monroe was quoted as saying:

> This is a great shock to me. I'm deeply sorry. Clark Gable was one of the finest men I ever met. He was one of the most decent human beings anyone could have encountered anywhere. He was an excellent guy to work with. Knowing him and working with him was a great personal joy. I send all my love and deepest sympathy to his wife, Kay.
>
> *Marilyn Monroe: Her Own Story* (Belmont Books, 1961)

Marilyn Monroe may have been the uncrowned Queen of Hollywood for a few short years, but Clark Gable was the undisputed King of Hollywood for some thirty years. Born on February 1, 1901, in Cadiz, Ohio, Gable starred in a plethora of films, including such classics as *Red Dust* (1932), *It Happened One Night* (for which he won a 1934 Oscar), *Mutiny on the Bounty* (1935), *San Francisco* (1936), and *Gone with the Wind* (1939).

In the often told story, young Norma Jeane Baker kept a photograph of Gable tacked to her bedroom wall. She fantasized that Gable was her "secret" father. In 1947, MM fell in love with actor John Carroll, who was considered a Gable look-alike. And in 1954, at the Romanoff's party thrown in her honor, MM finally fulfilled her personal dream by meeting Clark Gable. Not only did she meet him, she also danced two dances with him. They got along well together and discussed making a film. By the end of 1954, there were even rumors that an affair had developed between the two of them. While MM was hospitalized at Cedars of Lebanon, a few days after the Romanoff's party, a bushel of red roses was sent to her room. The roses, as the story goes, were sent by Gable.

In 1960, Marilyn Monroe and Clark Gable made *The Misfits* together. It was a grueling location shoot for both of them. It also proved to be the last picture for both of them. The day after *The Misfits* completed shooting, Clark Gable suffered a massive heart attack. Ten days later, on November 16, 1960, he was dead.

**KAY GABLE**

Kay Gable was Clark Gable's fifth and final wife. During the shooting of *The Misfits,* Kay was pregnant with the son Gable would never know. Following Gable's death, Kay publicly suggested that Marilyn Monroe was responsible for her husband's demise. Kay claimed that MM had put Gable under excessive stress during the shooting of *The Misfits.*

Upon hearing this accusation, MM went into severe depression. However, this was relieved when Gable's widow invited MM to the May 1961 christening of John Clark Gable. Naturally, this meant a great deal to MM. It meant that Kay did *not* hold MM responsible for Gable's death.

**ZSA ZSA GABOR**

> [Marilyn Monroe] was a very dull girl. She thought that if a man who takes her out for dinner doesn't sleep with her that night—something's wrong with her. When George [George Sanders, Zsa Zsa Gabor's husband] was making *All About Eve* in San Francisco, we had a suite and next to us Marilyn Monroe had a room. George made a thing out of it and said, "Let's see how many men are going to go into her room tonight!" I'd seen about *four.* That's a terrible thing to say about somebody who the whole country admires.
>
> Zsa Zsa Gabor,
> *Playboy Video* Magazine

Zsa Zsa Gabor did not like Marilyn Monroe. They both "arrived" on the film scene at about the same period. And Marilyn was younger, prettier, and blonder.

While she was still a starlet, MM was invited to a party that was given by photographer Tony Beauchamp and his wife. Zsa Zsa was in attendance with her husband, actor George Sanders. According to Marilyn, Zsa Zsa threw a jealous fit over her very presence and threatened to leave the party.

Also according to MM, Gabor planted "spies" on the set of *All About Eve* (1950) to keep MM away from Sanders, who costarred in the film, and with whom Marilyn reportedly had an affair.

**MARTIN GANG**

Gang was the attorney who, in 1962, negotiated to obtain Marilyn's release from her agency, MCA.

**GRETA GARBO**

Greta Garbo, of course, was the legendary screen presence whom Marilyn Monroe identified with and was frequently compared to.

Born Greta Lovisa Gustafsson on September 18, 1905, Garbo was the number one female movie star in the world when Norma Jeane Baker was growing up. She starred in such films as *Flesh and the Devil* (1927), *Anna Christie* (1930), *Grand Hotel* (1932), *Queen Christina* (1933), *Anna Karenina* (1935), *Camille* (1936), and *Ninotchka* (1939), before retiring—at the peak of her career—in 1941, following her last picture, *Two Faced Woman.*

It is particularly revealing that, in her later years, Marilyn Monroe increasingly identified with Greta Garbo. Not only was MM the most luminous screen personality since Garbo; she was also the most private—and, perhaps, the most alone. Subsequently, MM also "retired" at the peak of her career. It is also not insignificant that MM chose Garbo's vehicle, *Anna Christie* to make her 1956 debut before members of the Actors Studio.

As for Garbo, Truman Capote once reported that she wanted to star in *The Picture of Dorian Gray,* with herself as Dorian and Marilyn Monroe as one of the young girls seduced by Dorian.

**BUNNY GARDEL**

Bunny Gardel did Marilyn Monroe's body makeup for such films as *Bus Stop* (1956) and *The Misfits* (1961).

**GARDENER**

Tataishi was the name of MM's gardener at her Brentwood home in 1962.

**GARDENING**

> "I have a subscription to a horticulture magazine."
>
> "I try to grow things. Flowers and vegetables both. I have a green thumb. I can even plant things without roots. I just transplant them and they grow. I planted some seeds, nasturtiums, I think, when they come up, you're supposed to thin them out. What a pity, I thought, to throw out these little growing things, so I pulled them up and transplanted them very carefully; they had been so close together some didn't even have roots. Arthur said, 'That's impossible, they can't live.' But, all of them did. And it says on the cover of the seed packages that you can't transplant them!"
>
> MM to Jon Whitcomb, *Cosmopolitan,* 12/1960

During the last year of her life, Marilyn became actively involved in the gardening at her Brentwood home. She purchased trees and plants for her yard and took great pride in the flourishing garden, which she personally worked in as a form of therapy.

**JUDY GARLAND**

> "I knew Marilyn and loved her dearly. She asked me for help—ME! I didn't know what to tell her. One night at a party at Clifton Webb's house, Marilyn followed me from room to room. 'I don't want to get too far away from you, I'm scared,' she said. I told her, 'We're all scared. I'm scared too.' "
>
> Judy Garland on MM

If there was a figure in the history of show business more tragic than Marilyn Monroe, it was Judy Garland. Born Frances Gumm in 1922, Garland was the vital, volatile entertainer who starred in such films as *The Wizard of Oz* (1939), *Babes in Arms* (1939), *Meet Me in St. Louis* (1944), and *A Star is Born* (1954).

Marilyn Monroe was a big fan of Garland. Around the house, MM repeatedly played Garland's recording of "Who Cares?" And at MM's funeral it was Garland's classic "Over the Rainbow" that was chosen to be played. Following Marilyn's death, Garland was quoted as saying:

> "I don't think Marilyn really meant to harm herself. It was partly because she had too many pills available, [and] then was deserted by her friends. You shouldn't be told you're completely irresponsible, and [then] be left alone with too much medication."

Seven years later, Judy Garland would be found dead from an accidental overdose of drugs.

**TAY GARNETT**
Garnett (1895-1977) was a director of mostly mediocre productions. In 1950, Garnett directed starlet MM in *The Fireball,* in which she had a small part.

**MORT GARSON**
Garson wrote the music for the 1983 British stage musical, *Marilyn.*

**MITZI GAYNOR**
Born Francesca Mitzi von Gerber in 1930, Mitzi Gaynor was a Vegas-type entertainer who never quite "made it" in films. Among her attempts were *The Joker Is Wild* (1957), *Les Girls* (1957), and *South Pacific* (1958). Gaynor also appeared in *We're Not Married* (1952), in which MM costarred, and *There's No Business Like Show Business* (1954), in which she paled next to MM.

**THE GENERAL BROCK HOTEL**
The hotel where MM stayed during the 1952 shooting of *Niagara.* Today, it is known as the Sheraton Brock Hotel and is located at 5685 Falls in Niagara Falls.

**GENERAL TELEPHONE COMPANY**
MM's telephone records were mysteriously confiscated at GTE's Brentwood office on August 6, 1962, a day and a half after MM's death. Allegedly, the records were taken by the LAPD, for undisclosed reasons. Since the records have never been fully retrieved, it has never been determined who called Marilyn's house the night of her death or whom MM called from the house.

***GENTLEMEN PREFER BLONDES* ★★★½**
1953 91 minutes Technicolor
20th Century-Fox
Directed by: Howard Hawks

Produced by: Sol C. Siegel
Screenplay by: Charles Lederer, from the novel by Anita Loos
Photographed by: Harry J. Wild
Cast: Jane Russell, Marilyn Monroe, Charles Coburn, Tommy Noonan, Norma Varden, Elliott Reid, George Winslow

If *Niagara* was the Big One, then *Gentlemen Prefer Blondes* was the Colossal One. Until this day, *Blondes* is *the* film most associated with Marilyn Monroe. It was not her most popular picture, but it was the one that was indelibly stamped with the Marilyn Monroe persona. It was this film that introduced the singing, dancing, irresistibly and comedically *appealing* Marilyn Monroe. After seeing the initial rushes of *Blondes,* Fox chief Darryl Zanuck enthusiastically released the following statement to the press:

> If anyone has any doubts as to the future of Marilyn Monroe, *Gentlemen Prefer Blondes* is the answer.

THE AUTHOR'S COLLECTION

Originally, *Gentlemen Prefer Blondes* was a novel by Anita Loos that was adapted into a 1928 film starring Ruth Taylor and Alice White. By 1950, it had been readapted into a smash Broadway musical starring Carol Channing. By 1951, the Hollywood studios clamored for the film rights to the *Blondes* diamond mine. Columbia wanted it for Judy Holliday, who had just copped an Oscar for *Born Yesterday.* Fox wanted it for its reigning queen, Betty Grable.

When Holliday refused to do the part, Fox shelled out $500,000 and announced that Grable would topline. And Grable *wanted* the picture. She needed a good film. But, it was already 1952. Marilyn Monroe, by way of the nude-calendar news, *Clash by Night,* and the upcoming *Niagara,* was quickly becoming the hottest personality in films. Grable, on the other hand, was waning. It was time for a younger, blonder, more beautiful, more buxom star—and Marilyn Monroe filled the bodice quite nicely. On June 1, 1952, 20th Century-Fox birthday-presented MM with the news that she would be the movie's Lorelei Lee.

Besides, Marilyn Monroe was cheaper. Betty Grable, reportedly, would have cost $150,000. Jane Russell, the film's costar, wanted (and got) anywhere from $100,000 to $200,000 for the film. Marilyn Monroe on the other hand, was contractually bound to a *maximum* of $1,500 a week (which amounted to $18,000). What she did subsequently insist on, though, was a dressing room. After all, as she objected to the Fox brass: "I *am* the blonde, and it is *Gentlemen Prefer Blondes.*"

Marilyn, of course, got her dressing room. *Gentlemen Prefer Blondes* began shooting in November 1952. And though Marilyn was often characteristically late, everyone was nonetheless impressed by her compulsion for work. She continued to rehearse long after the others had dropped. She demanded one unneccesary retake after another. When director Howard Hawks approved the first take of the "Bye Bye Baby" sequence, MM demanded an additional ten takes. Antagonism developed between MM and Hawks. But this was *her* chance, not his. And she knew it.

*Gentlemen Prefer Blondes* was released in the summer of 1953 to good reviews and better box office. Today, it has endured as an exceptionally entertaining musical comedy. It has a memorable score by Jules Styne and Leo Robin (including the classic, "Diamonds Are a Girl's Best Friend"), additional songs by Hoagy Carmichael, and the striking, incomparable presence of Marilyn Monroe.

**MM Trivia Quiz #14**
What was MM's favorite expression in *Gentlemen Prefer Blondes*? (Answer on page 577.)

**GERMANY**
In 1960, following her split from Arthur Miller, *The National Zeitung,* a newspaper published in East Berlin, condemned MM for being: "a manufactured film star who achieved fame through low-cut gowns and scandal."

**JERRY GIESLER**
In 1954, Marilyn hired attorney Jerry Giesler to handle her divorce case against Joe DiMaggio. Some Hollywood insiders privately criticized MM for hiring a famous criminal lawyer to handle a simple divorce proceeding. The speculation was that MM was trying to milk as much publicity out of the divorce as possible.

**HARVEY GIFFEN**

Harvey Giffen was a neighbor of Gladys Baker when she and Norma Jeane lived off Highland Avenue circa 1933. Approximately one year after Gladys was committed to the Metropolitan State Hospital, Harvey and his wife took Norma Jeane into their home and took care of her. Harvey was a sound engineer at the Radio Corporation of America at that time. And, when the Giffen family prepared to move to Mississippi, they offered to adopt Norma Jeane and take her with them. However, Gladys (from the hospital) would not allow it.

**C. STANLEY GIFFORD**

In 1925–26, C. Stanley Gifford was an employee at Consolidated Film Industries in Hollywood. At about that time, Gifford had an affair with one of his prettier coworkers. Her name was Gladys Baker. The affair reportedly ended when Gladys told him that she was pregnant.

According to Fred Lawrence Guiles, who, out of all MM's biographers, has done the most research on Gifford, Marilyn Monroe believed that C. Stanley Gifford was her father. According to Guiles, in 1945, while still with Jim Dougherty, Norma Jeane telephoned Gifford to say, "This is Norma Jeane. I'm Gladys's daughter." Gifford, reportedly, hung up. By the fall of 1951, Marilyn tried to contact Gifford again. Through a hired private detective, Marilyn tracked Gifford to a farm in the village of Hemet outside of Palm Springs, California. With Natasha Lytess in tow for support, Marilyn drove from Hollywood en route to Hemet, in search of her father. However, in Riverside, she abruptly pulled the car over and called Gifford from a pay phone. Reportedly, Gifford's wife answered the phone and told Marilyn, "He doesn't want to see you. He suggests you see his lawyer in Los Angeles if you have some complaint. Do you have a pencil?"

In 1961, after Marilyn Monroe was an international superstar, Gifford tried to make amends by sending Marilyn the following card:

> Best wishes for your early recovery. From the man you tried to see nearly ten years ago. God forgive me.

However, upon receiving the card, Marilyn confided to a friend, "It's too late."

According to Guiles, Gifford made one last attempt to contact Marilyn. Actually, it was a Palm Springs nurse who telephoned Marilyn at her Brentwood home in 1962. Gifford, the nurse told MM, had had a heart attack and wasn't expected to survive. He wanted to talk to Marilyn before he died. Marilyn responded by saying, "Tell the gentleman I have never met him. But if he has anything specific to tell me, he can contact my lawyer. Would you like his number?"

That was the last time Marilyn heard from Gifford, and vice versa. Gifford survived his heart attack and outlived his daughter—*if* she was indeed his daughter.

**EMIL GILELS**

In 1955, Marilyn Monroe, escorted by Norman Rosten, went to Carnegie Hall to see Russian pianist Emil Gilels in concert. Upon meeting MM, Gilels kissed her hand and told her that she should visit the Soviet Union. Marilyn responded by saying that she was reading Dostoyevsky.

**JOHN GILLAN**

Originally from North Braddock, Pennsylvania, John Gillan began his Marilyn Monroe collection in 1949, after seeing the film *Ladies of the Chorus* (1948). Today, John is a security guard at Sunset Gower Studios in Hollywood (formerly Columbia Studios) and he has approximately *seventy* scrapbooks on MM in his collection, which must stand as one of the most complete records of Marilyn Monroe's career.

***THE GIRL IN PINK TIGHTS***

Marilyn Monroe wanted *The Egyptian.* Darryl Zanuck gave her *The Girl in Pink Tights* instead. Frank Sinatra had signed to play the male lead and was to be paid $5,000 a week. Although Marilyn was to be given top billing and was undisputedly a bigger movie star than Sinatra, she was to be paid only $1,500 a week. Shooting was slated to start on December 15, 1953.

Marilyn, still smarting from Zanuck's refusal to consider her for *The Egyptian,* demanded the right to at least read the *Pink Tights* script before she agreed to do it. Zanuck refused. In Zanuck's eyes, MM was under contract to 20th Century-Fox and was to do as she was told. Thus, December 15 came and went. Marilyn disappeared. Fox responded by suspending its hottest property.

Long after the scheduled shoot date had passed, Marilyn telephoned the studio from San Francisco. This time Fox conceded and sent her the script. The plot, Marilyn learned, revolved around a schoolteacher turned saloon dancer. And, whether it was because of DiMaggio's objections or MM's own repulsion, Marilyn notified Fox that she was outraged by its proposal that she play such a part in such a movie. She refused to return to Hollywood.

Twentieth Century-Fox responded, predictably, by threatening to banish MM. It also dangled a buxom starlet named Sheree North before MM's eyes while publicly announcing that it would be North—and not Monroe—who would be given the prize role in *The Girl in Pink Tights.*

Marilyn responded, of course, by marrying Joe DiMaggio. In doing so, she elicited the cheerleading support of an entire nation. With DiMaggio, Marilyn was bigger than Fox and certainly bigger than anything as minuscule as a starlet named Sheree. Fox, again predictably, withdrew its publicity henchmen and reinstated MM.

*The Girl in Pink Tights* was shelved and lady-in-waiting Sheree North had to wait just a little while longer.

***THE GIRL IN THE RED VELVET SWING***

Another film that Marilyn rejected in the mid-fifties.

As early as January 9, 1954, the *Los Angeles Daily News* printed the following item:

> Now that Fox has obtained clearances from Evelyn Nesbitt and all the still-living dramatis personae involved in the sensational Harry K. Thaw case . . . it looks certain for Marilyn Monroe to play Evelyn in 'The Girl in the Red Swing.' The studio purchased the fictionalized paper-booked biography from Charles Samuels for $3,000.00.

A year later, 20th Century-Fox announced that, following the completion of *The Seven Year Itch* shoot, Marilyn Monroe would indeed begin production on *The Girl in the Red Velvet Swing*.

However, this was about the same time that MM announced her defection from Fox and the formation of her own company, Marilyn Monroe Productions, Inc. Thus, until her old contract was renegotiated, Marilyn refused to make any further pictures for 20th Century-Fox. Fox responded, of course, by suspending MM. And this time, instead of using Sheree North as MM bait, Fox used the little-known British actress Joan Collins.

*The Girl in the Red Velvet Swing* was released by Fox in October 1955, with Joan Collins in the MM-intended lead. Directed by Richard Fleischer, the film opened to mostly mixed reviews. Collins, it was generally agreed, may have been sexy, but she was not Marilyn Monroe. Following *The Girl*, she proceeded to flounder in a series of mostly forgettable features.

It was unfortunate for all that MM did not make *The Girl in the Red Velvet Swing*. The material was potentially explosive and could have been a good vehicle for MM. It was produced by Charles Brackett, who had championed MM a few years before in *Niagara*, and was shot by one of MM's favorite cameramen, Milton Krasner. The Evelyn Nesbitt/Harry K. Thaw case was shot to good advantage in the 1981 film *Ragtime*. Elizabeth McGovern effectively portrayed Nesbitt.

**THE GLADSTONE HOTEL**

After she fled from Hollywood to New York at the end of 1954, MM checked into this East 52nd Street Hotel.

***GLAMOUR PREFERRED***

The first stage play that Marilyn Monroe appeared in before a commercial audience. *Glamour Preferred* opened on October 12, 1947, and was staged at the Bliss-Hayden Miniature Theatre in Beverly Hills. MM auditioned for the play after Fox failed to renew her contract in 1947. She was given the second lead, which she played on alternating nights (actress Jane Weeks played the part on the other nights) *Glamour Preferred* also starred Lee Elson, Christine Larson, Nancy O'Neill, Bill McLean, Charlotte Payne, Trudy Leeds, Jack Hire, Don Hayden, and Owen Tyree. It was written by Florence Ryerson and Colin Clements, and closed on November 2, 1947.

**GERRY GLASKIN**

Gerry Glaskin wrote the 1967 stage play *Turn on the Heat,* which was based on the last hours of Marilyn Monroe's life. It was produced at the Hole in the Wall Theatre in Perth, Australia.

**LEN GLOBUS**

In the early 1950s, Len Globus was a photographer stationed at the Hollywood Roosevelt Hotel in Los Angeles. At that time, Globus photographed Marilyn Monroe for a Tar-Tan Sun Tan Lotion advertisement. The shooting took place at the Roosevelt Hotel. Said Globus of MM: "She came up to my office, I took her down to the pool, shot the picture, gave her the swim suit, and she walked down the street." When asked what he paid Marilyn, Globus replied: "I gave her the swim suit, that was her fee."

**BEEBE GODDARD**

Beebe was Doc Goddard's daughter from a previous marriage. When Norma Jeane moved in with the Goddard family circa the late 1930s, Beebe became her roommate, foster sister, and friend. Beebe was two years younger than Norma Jeane.

**ERWIN "DOC" GODDARD**

Doc Goddard was not a doctor at all. He was an amateur inventor and a research engineer at the Adel Precision Products Company. Around the mid-1930s, Goddard, who had three children from a previous marriage, married Grace McKee. Grace, at that time, was Norma Jeane's legal guardian. Subsequently, Norma Jeane moved into the Goddard family home.

There have been, over the years, many reports of Goddard's drinking problem. Most of these reports contend that, one drunken night, Goddard forcefully kissed Norma Jeane in an "intimate" manner. Subsequently, Norma Jeane moved out of the house, and in with her "aunt," Ana Lower. And, in 1942 when he was transferred to Huntington, West Virginia, Goddard opted not to take Norma Jeane with the rest of the family.

Still, there seemed to be no dissension between Goddard and Norma Jeane. She called him "Daddy," and, when "Marilyn" began to make money, Goddard volunteered to serve as her business manager. However, eventually, Marilyn fazed Goddard out of her life, along with many other remnants of the past.

**GRACE GODDARD**

> "They broke the mold when they made Grace. She was one in a million. She was Gladys' best friend, and she loved and adored Norma Jeane. If it weren't for Grace, there wouldn't be a Marilyn Monroe today."
>
> Mrs. Leila Fields to Maurice Zolotow,
> *Marilyn Monroe* (Harcourt Brace, 1960)

If Marilyn Monroe ever had a mother substitute, Grace McKee was it—though Marilyn herself did not recognize Grace as such.

Grace McKee was Gladys Baker's best friend. Grace worked as a film librarian at Columbia Pictures—the same studio where Gladys worked as a film cutter. The two women became close, although their relationship did not seem to be entirely healthy. Reportedly, Gladys once accused Grace of trying to poison her. In retaliation, Gladys attacked Grace with a butcher knife. The police were called, and Gladys reportedly was taken away.

Nonetheless, it was Grace Goddard who became Norma Jeane's legal guardian when Gladys was institutionalized. Unmarried at that time, Grace placed Norma Jeane into the Los Angeles Orphans Home Society in 1935. Grace paid weekly visits to the orphanage and took Norma Jeane out on frequent outings that typically included a matinee and an ice cream cone.

By 1937, Grace McKee had married "Doc" Goddard and had set up some semblance of a family. Accordingly, Grace took Norma Jeane out of the orphanage. And for the next five years Norma Jeane lived—on and off—at the Goddard home.

But during these years it was not Grace Goddard that Norma Jeane grew to love. It was Grace's aunt, Ana Lower, that Norma Jeane expressed eternal gratitude to. Still, Mrs. Leila Fields, a former coworker of Grace told Maurice Zolotow that Grace had nothing but love for Norma Jeane. According to Mrs. Fields, Grace told Norma Jeane,

> Don't worry, Norma Jeane. You're going to be a beautiful girl. You're going to be an important woman. You're going to be a movie star.
>
> *Marilyn Monroe* by Maurice Zolotow
> (Harcourt Brace, 1960)

Mrs. Fields also claimed that it was Grace who paid for the singing, dancing, and piano lessons that Norma Jeane had when she was a little girl. If true, Norma Jeane/Marilyn Monroe never publicly acknowledged it. Perhaps she resented Grace for accepting county money to raise her. Perhaps she resented Grace for ever putting her in the orphanage in the first place. Or perhaps it was due to some secret, unpublicized reason, known only to Grace and Norma Jeane. One thing does seem certain: Marilyn Monroe, in later years, resented Grace Goddard for taking off to West Virginia and, in effect, deserting her. In Marilyn's eyes, Grace had arranged Norma Jeane's marriage to Jim Dougherty as a convenient way to get rid of her.

At any rate, when Grace died in 1953 from a suicidal overdose of barbiturates, it was Marilyn Monroe who made the funeral arrangements. Grace was buried at Westwood Memorial Park, where Marilyn joined her nine years later. It's interesting to note that Marilyn Monroe did not follow in Gladys Baker's footsteps—she followed in Grace Goddard's.

### *THE GODDESS*

Written by the noted Paddy Chayefsky, *The Goddess* is a rather transparent biography about a troubled girl who becomes a famous movie star and marries a professional athlete (sound familiar?). It was produced by Columbia (Harry Cohn, still trying to lash back at MM) and was directed by John

Cromwell. It starred Kim Stanley and Lloyd Bridges.

It is interesting to note that, upon its release in 1958, everyone concerned emphatically denied that the film was about Marilyn Monroe. Nonetheless, everyone else seemed to know differently.

> . . . a savage attack on the Marilyn Monroe cult, a bit lachrymose and compromised by miscasting.
>
> Leslie Halliwell, *Film Guide* (Granada, 1979)

> By taking advantage of recent headlines, this story of a poor girl who fails to find happiness when she achieves film stardom may gain some topical success. But it is a downbeat movie with very little entertainment in it. And artistically it is labored, stylized and pretentious."
>
> *The Hollywood Reporter* (1958)

### *GODDESS: THE SECRET LIVES OF MARILYN MONROE*

Author: Anthony Summers
Publisher: Macmillan
Year: 1985
$17.95, hardcover, 320 pages (ISBN 0-02-615460-9)

An excellent, exhaustively well-researched biography that brings forth new insight into the life and death of Marilyn Monroe. Particularly of interest is the darker side of Marilyn's life, including her relationship with the Kennedy brothers—all of which is presented here in a well-documented, *believable* manner. The material is fresh, the black and white photographs are evocative and rare, and the tone is unbiased. Anthony Summers claimed to have interviewed six hundred individuals while researching this book. The highest compliment that can be paid is that the work *shows*. *Goddess: The Secret Lives of Marilyn Monroe* must stand as one of the three finest books ever written about Marilyn Monroe.

In 1986, New American Library released a paperback version ($4.95) of *Goddess: The Secret Lives of Marilyn Monroe*. It contains an additional chapter, with updated material (the "20/20" cancellation, et al.) that was not included in the 1985 hardback.

### ROBERT GOLDBERG

Rabbi Goldberg performed the Jewish wedding ceremony between Arthur Miller and MM on July 1, 1956.

### *GOLDEN BOY*

Acclaimed play by Clifford Odets that was adapted as a 1939 movie starring Barbara Stanwyck and William Holden. While studying at the Actors Studio, Marilyn Monroe performed "The Park Bench Scene" from *Golden Boy* before the members of her class.

### GOLDEN DREAMS

*See* CALENDAR.

**THE GOLDEN GLOBE AWARDS**

Unlike the Motion Picture Academy, the Hollywood Foreign Press expressed its appreciation of Marilyn Monroe's talents during MM's lifetime. In 1953, the Foreign Press named MM "The World Film Favorite." In 1961, when others were claiming that she was "all washed up," the Foreign Press presented her with the same award—its highest honor—a second time. And in 1959 it voted her that year's "Best Actress in a Comedy or Musical" for her performance in *Some Like It Hot.*

THE RAY VAN GOEYE COLLECTION

The Golden Globe Awards: *Some Like It Hot*, Best Actress in a Comedy or Musical, 1959.

**AURELIANO GONZALEZ**

Gonzalez was one of the two Mexican attorneys who handled Marilyn's divorce from Arthur Miller in 1961.

***GOODBYE CHARLIE***

> "Fox wanted me for *Goodbye Charlie,* but as far as I'm concerned, it's good-by *Goodbye Charlie,*"
>
> MM to Hedda Hopper, 7/16/61

Another Fox movie that MM rejected. Following her death, it was subsequently produced as a starring vehicle for Debbie Reynolds, in the part that Lauren Bacall had played on Broadway. It costarred Pat Boone, Walter Matthau, and Tony Curtis. It was directed by Vincente Minnelli (one of MM's approved directors), photographed by Milton Krasner (one of MM's approved cinematographers), and written by George Axelrod (the playwright who had written MM's successful *The Seven Year Itch*). The plot revolved around a gangster who is killed and then reincarnated as a dishy blonde.

***GOODBYE NORMA JEAN***

This 1976 feature film claimed, "This is how it happened. Not legend. . . ." An overstatement if there ever was one. Produced, directed, cowritten, and misfired by Larry Buchanan, *Goodbye Norma Jean* failed to capture the essence of Marilyn Monroe. And the film's "star," Misty Rowe, failed to capture MM—period. As Julian Fox wrote in *Films and Filming* magazine,

> . . . Lacking from the film is any sense of narrative cohesion, of reverence for a lost immortal, of any degree of human understanding for the wayward child that was Marilyn Monroe.
>
> When she was alive, she made the world a better place to live in. Now she is dead, her memory seems to bring out the worst in people like Norman Mailer and Larry Buchanan. I'd like to see no more plays, films or conjectures about Marilyn until someone of deep sensitivity and intelligence is prepared to show us *why* she was a star and not concentrate on *how*. . . .

**JAMES GOODE**
Writer of the behind-the-scenes book *The Story of The Misfits* (Bobbs-Merrill), which was published in 1963.

**BENNY GOODMAN**
In 1948, after Columbia Studios dropped her contract, Marilyn Monroe auditioned to be a singer in the Benny Goodman band. Reportedly, Mr. Goodman complimented Marilyn on her singing, but, alas, did *not* give her the job.

**EZRA GOODMAN**
Hollywood columnist whose June 6, 1951, column in the *Los Angeles Daily News* contained the following item:

> Talent will out—I am here today to tell all of you Motion Picture Producers, Heads of Casting Departments and Executives in charge of new faces where there is a vast, new, untapped fund of movie talent. . . .

He went on, of course, to name MM.

**FRANK GOODMAN**
MM's New York publicist in July 1955, during her strike against 20th Century-Fox.

**JACK GORDEEN**
Jack Gordeen was one of Marilyn Monroe's agents at the Famous Artists Agency, circa 1953–55.

**LEE GORDON**
*See* AUSTRALIA.

**LOTTE GOSLAR**
Lotte Goslar was a mime with the Turnabout Theatre in Hollywood. In the spring of 1953, Michael Chekhov took MM to study with Miss Goslar.

Chekhov, who was preparing MM for *How to Marry a Millionaire,* felt that she needed work on her timing. As Miss Goslar told Fred Lawrence Guiles:

> She wanted solo instruction in mime but she needed to be with other people. I placed her in a class with ten pupils. . . . I saw at once how very serious she was about her art. She wore no make-up except for a little lipstick. . . . She was exceptionally talented and one of the best pupils in the group.

Goslar went on to coach and/or advise MM in *River of No Return* (1954) and other subsequent films.

**ANNIE GOTTLIEB**

Gottlieb was given credit for assisting on the text of Bert Stern's 1982 photo book, *The Last Sitting* (William Morrow).

**CAROL GOULD**

Carol Gould directed Roger Newman's stage play about Marilyn Monroe entitled *Public Property.* It was staged at the Hampstead Theatre in London in 1979.

**DEBORAH GOULD**

Gould became Peter Lawford's third wife in 1976 and divorced him shortly thereafter. She claimed in the BBC Documentary "The Last Days of Marilyn Monroe" (1985) that Marilyn had called Peter the night of her death to tell him that she was going to kill herself. Gould also claimed, on camera, that Lawford later went to MM's Brentwood home to "sanitize" it before the reporters arrived.

For her on-camera services, Gould was paid the sum of $5,000 and the promise of an additional $5,000 if the program aired in the United States (it did).

To writer Anthony Summers, Gould repeated the story she had related on the BBC documentary. Gould verified the intimate relationships Marilyn had had with John and Robert Kennedy—in that order. Also, according to Gould, Marilyn left a suicide note that was later secretly destroyed by Peter Lawford.

**EDMUND GOULDING**

Edmund Goulding (1891–1959) was a British director noted as a "woman's director" of the thirties and forties. Among Goulding's films were *Grand Hotel* (1932), *Dark Victory* (1939), *The Old Maid* (1939), *The Great Lie* (1941), and *Razor's Edge* (1946). In 1952, Goulding directed MM et al. in *We're Not Married.*

**GOVERNMENT LODGE**

In 1945, during an extended location shooting, model Norma Jeane Dougherty and photographer Andre de Dienes stayed at the Government Lodge, located near Mount Hood, Oregon. According to de Dienes, it was here where his first tryst with Norma Jeane took place.

**BETTY GRABLE**

"Honey, I've had it. Go get yours. It's your turn now."

Betty Grable to MM, 1953

Betty Grable (1916-1973) was the most famous pinup of World War II. In 1946, she was the highest-paid woman in America, earning a more than respectable $208,000 a year. She remained among the top ten box office stars in America for *thirteen years*—longer than anyone in movie history. In a clever publicity ploy, Grable's legs were insured by Lloyd's of London for one million dollars. And at the time of Norma Jeane Dougherty's first film contract in 1946, Betty Grable was the undisputed Queen of the Fox lot.

Six years later, when Fox purchased the film rights to *Gentlemen Prefer Blondes,* Betty Grable marched into Darryl Zanuck's office and asked him for a favor—one of the few favors that Grable had asked during her long reign as Fox's biggest commodity. She wanted to play the part of Lorelei Lee. Zanuck, of course, assured her that she was already under consideration for the role. Fox even publicly announced that Grable would be playing the part. However, the tide had already changed. There was a new blonde on the lot. And everybody knew it—including Grable.

But if Betty Grable felt any resentment toward Marilyn Monroe, she didn't show it. She was kind to MM—almost impossibly kind. Following the 1953 *Photoplay* Awards, when a faction of Hollywood—led by Joan Crawford—turned their backs on Marilyn, it was Betty Grable who rushed to MM's defense. In Aline Mosby's March 16, 1953, article, Grable commented,

> Why, Marilyn's the biggest thing that's happened in Hollywood in years. The movies were just sort of going along, and all of a sudden, Zowie, there was Marilyn. She's a shot in the arm for Hollywood. . . . I'm not envious of Marilyn. There's room for us all.

When Fox paired Grable and MM in *How to Marry a Millionaire,* everyone anticipated (anxiously?) a bitchy Battle of the Blondes. However, that was not to be the case. In fact, the ever-gracious Grable even gave MM a pedicure during a break from the shooting! Grable's antagonism, if any, was directed at Darryl Zanuck and 20th Century-Fox. As for Marilyn, she admired Grable. Nonetheless, out of nervousness, or perhaps out of latent animosity, Marilyn pushed Grable down one time and stepped on her foot another.

On July 1, 1953, Betty Grable once again marched into Darryl Zanuck's office. This time, it was not to ask a favor; it was to tear up her contract (which still had five years remaining on it). As was characteristic of her, Betty Grable did not show up for the *How to Marry a Millionaire* premiere on November 4, 1953—which was for the best, considering that MM walked off with the film, effortlessly.

After Grable left Fox, Marilyn "inherited" Grable's dressing room, Dressing Room M, which was located in the Star Building at Fox. Marilyn moved into her new dressing room during the production of *There's No Business Like Show Business.*

In an interesting addendum to the Grable/Monroe "rivalry," Grable returned to the Fox lot in 1955 to make *How to Be Very, Very Popular,* which

THE AUTHOR'S COLLECTION

had been written by Nunnally Johnson expressly for Marilyn. However, that was the period of MM's famous walkout, so Zanuck reportedly telephoned Grable's agent and asked if Betty would be interested in *replacing* MM in the movie. Grable eventually agreed, not knowing that she was merely to be a star-billed sidelight to MM's real replacement, Sheree North. The fact that Grable agreed to return to Fox in the first place seems a questionable choice on her part, considering the fact that Fox wanted her to replace MM, just as they wanted MM to replace *her* a few years before. At any rate, the film was released, and it proved to be an embarrassment for all—except, of course, for Marilyn, who had rejected it from the start.

Betty Grable was admirably gracious to Marilyn. But in retrospect, her belief that "there's room for all of us" was incorrect. Grable's career ended with the release of *Gentlemen Prefer Blondes*—the film that Grable had fought for and lost.

**SHEILA GRAHAM**

Hollywood columnist who, in 1963, called for the Motion Picture Academy to bestow a posthumous honorary Oscar on Marilyn Monroe. However, the Academy elected to bypass MM.

THE AUTHOR'S COLLECTION

**DELLA MONROE GRAINGER**

Marilyn's grandmother. Born Della Mae Hogan on July 1, 1876, in Missouri, Della married Otis Elmer Monroe in 1899. The following year, the Monroes had a baby girl. They named her Gladys.

At the time of Norma Jeane's birth, Della lived in Hawthorne, California, across the street from Ida and Wayne Bolender. Della frequently visited Norma Jeane at the Bolenders' house and sometimes took her granddaughter across the street to be with her. Della, who was a devout believer in Sister Aimee Semple McPherson, had Norma Jeane baptized at Sister Aimee's Angelus Temple. In July 1927, Della reportedly attempted to smother Norma Jeane with a pillow. Subsequently, on August 4, 1927, Della was committed to the Metropolitan State Hospital at Norwalk. And, on August 23, Della died from heart failure during a manic seizure.

**GRANDFATHER**
*See* OTIS ELMER MONROE.

**LIONEL GRANDISON**
Grandison was the deputy coroner's aide who later claimed that he was "forced" into signing MM's death certificate as a "probable suicide," even though he personally felt "There were circumstances surrounding her death that should have been investigated."

In an interesting interview with private investigator/writer Milo Speriglio, Grandison claimed that:

☆ there *was* a red diary that mysteriously disappeared
☆ there *was* a note that mysteriously disappeared
☆ there *were* bruises on MM's body that did not show up on the final autopsy report
☆ necrophiliacs had sexually abused MM's body

Grandison's alarming statements were later questioned when it was discovered that he had once served a six-month prison sentence for forgery.

**GRANDMOTHER**
*See* DELLA MONROE GRAINGER.

**ALLAN GRANT**
Although Bert Stern claims to have had "the last sitting" with Marilyn Monroe, many actually credit photographer Allan Grant with having taken the last photos of MM. Grant took several shots of Marilyn casually posing in her new Brentwood home. The photographs appeared in *LIFE* magazine's August 3, 1962, issue.

**CARY GRANT**
The movies most beloved sophisticate, Gary Grant was born Archibald Leach in 1904. His thirty-year film career included such gems as *She Done Him Wrong* (1933), *Bringing Up Baby* (1938), *His Girl Friday* (1940), *The Philadelphia Story* (1940), *Arsenic and Old Lace* (1944), *To Catch a Thief* (1955), and *North by Northwest* (1959).

In 1952, Grant starred in Howard Hawks's *Monkey Business,* which costarred emerging MM. Marilyn reportedly wanted Grant as her costar in the 1960 film *Let's Make Love*; however, he rejected the proposition. It has been printed that Grant spoke with MM over the telephone the night before her death. He later stated that he regretted not having tried harder to help MM.

Cary Grant died on November 29, 1986, at the age of eighty-two.

**MM Trivia Quiz #15**
In what film did MM kiss a Gary Grant impersonator? (Answer on page 577.)

THE RAY VAN GOEYE COLLECTION
With Cary Grant in *Monkey Business*, 1952.

## STEFFI GRANT

Steffi Grant (now Sidney), columnist Sidney Skolsky's daughter, married movie and television business manager Leonard J. Grant on February 14, 1960. As a wedding present, Marilyn and Arthur Miller gave the couple a sterling silver cigarette box with the inscription "For this wonderful day—affectionately, Marilyn and Arthur" engraved atop the box in Marilyn's handwriting. On April 18, 1962, Steffi divorced Grant. Later, after MM's death, a property settlement dispute arose over the ownership of the $85 cigarette box. The case went to court, and Judge Burnett Wolfson awarded the box to Steffi.

## GRAUMAN'S CHINESE THEATRE

> "When I was younger, I used to go to Grauman's Chinese Theatre and try to fit my foot in the prints in the cement there. And I'd say, 'Oh, oh, my foot's too big, I guess that's out.' I did have a funny

feeling later when I finally put my foot down into that wet cement. I sure knew what it really meant to me—anything's possible, almost."

When Norma Jeane Baker was a little girl, she was sometimes treated to a matinee at the famed Grauman's Chinese Theatre, located on Hollywood Boulevard. Norma Jeane saw such films as *Little Women* and *Grand Hotel* at Grauman's. Before and after the films, Norma Jeane used to try to match her feet with the footprints of such stars as Rudolph Valentino. And, during their courtship and marriage, Norma Jeane and Jim Dougherty frequently saw movies at Grauman's Chinese Theatre.

On June 26, 1953, Marilyn Monroe and Jane Russell were invited to place their prints in the Grauman's courtyard. The event was coordinated to promote the opening of *Gentlemen Prefer Blondes.* At that time, MM suggested that Jane Russell bend over and place her bust in the cement. Marilyn also felt that her own buttocks should be cemented for posterity's sake. When that idea was uniformly rejected, Marilyn suggested that a diamond be used to dot her *i*—she eventually settled for a rhinestone, which was later stolen. In the long run, Marilyn had to settle for the traditional hand- and footprints.

THE RAY VAN GOEYE COLLECTION

**GRAUMAN'S EGYPTIAN THEATRE**

As a little girl, Norma Jeane was given a dime on Saturdays, and she would alternate between going to Grauman's Chinese and Grauman's Egyptian theatres—both located on Hollywood Boulevard. NJ especially liked to watch the monkeys, which were caged outside of Grauman's Egyptian.

Nearly twenty years later, *The Asphalt Jungle* (1950) held its world premiere at Grauman's Egyptian Theatre. Marilyn Monroe did *not* attend.

**DOLORES GRAY**

Because MM was contracted to RCA Records in 1953, she was not allowed to sing on the *There's No Business Like Show Business* soundtrack (Decca Records, 1954). Instead, a singer named Dolores Gray was hired to record MM's songs.

**SABIN GRAY**

Originally from Visalia, California, Sabin Gray is a graphic artist and the art director of *Hollywood Studio Magazine*. In 1980, Sabin was hired as the "research consultant" of the made-for-television biopic, "Marilyn: The Untold Story," which starred Catherine Hicks as MM. Today, Sabin is a member of the Marilyn Remembered Fan Club, and is a MM collector. His collection, which began in 1971, features an impressive array of posters, stills, books, and particularly, vintage magazines. He is also an active collector of *all* the 1950s' secondary blondes (Mamie Van Doren, Cleo Moore, Joi Lansing, et al.) and is the president of the Jayne Mansfield Fan Club. He can be contacted at: The Jayne Mansfield Fan Club, 7985 Santa Monica Boulevard, Suite 109, Box 117, West Hollywood, California.

**GREENBLATT'S**

Marilyn Monroe sometimes dined at the famed Greenblatt's Deli on the Sunset Strip in West Hollywood, California. According to Greenblatt's owner, Roy Kavin, Marilyn used to order a hot pastrami with mustard sandwich on rye bread. Today, Greenblatt's is located at 8017 Sunset Boulevard.

**AMY GREENE**

In the mid-1950s, Amy Greene was a New York fashion model and Mrs. Milton Greene. When Marilyn and Milton became friends and formed a partnership, Marilyn and Amy also became friends. Said Amy Greene, "We became close and intimate, like two girls rooming together in a dormitory at college."

In early 1955, Marilyn moved into Amy and Milton's Connecticut home. Amy became Marilyn's friend, confidante, and fashion advisor. Amy took MM shopping at Saks and Bonwit Teller in New York City and selected the "proper clothes" for MM. During MM's 1955 television appearance on "Person to Person," it was Amy Greene who, on camera, guided MM through the interview. Amy did such a fine job on the program that some of MM's wags snickered, "Forget Marilyn. Who's Amy?"

When Marilyn married Arthur Miller in a formal Jewish wedding, Amy Greene served as one of her matrons of honor. When Marilyn made her triumphant return to Hollywood to shoot *Bus Stop* (1956), Amy Greene was at her side. And when Marilyn flew to London for the 1956 shooting of *The Prince and the Showgirl*, she was, once again, accompanied by Amy Greene.

There seems to be no doubt that, for a brief period, Amy Greene was Marilyn's closest female friend. Their friendship deteriorated when MM severed her professional ties with Amy's husband. Amy later became a fashion editor for *Glamour* magazine.

Of her relationship with Marilyn Monroe, Amy Greene told Anthony Summers, "Never forget, that Marilyn wanted above all to become a *great* movie star. She would do anything, give up anyone, to move up."

**JOSH GREENE**

Marilyn became "Auntie" to Milton and Amy Greene's son, Josh. Marilyn would sometimes feed, bathe, and baby-sit young Josh. She also once bought him a pajama bag called "Ethel" and a huge stuffed bear named "Socko."

**MILTON H. GREENE**

MM: Why, you're just a boy!
MHG: And you're just a girl.

Milton Greene and Marilyn Monroe became instant friends. Toward the latter part of 1953, Greene was in Hollywood to shoot a cover story on MM for *LOOK* magazine. MM had just returned to Hollywood following the location shooting of *River of No Return* and met Greene at a party given by Gene Kelly. They began to discuss a possible partnership.

During the next year, Marilyn married and divorced Joe DiMaggio, and Milton H. Greene plotted to "rescue" MM from Hollywood. On November 16, 1954, ten days after the huge MM bash at Romanoff's, Greene flew to Hollywood to retrieve Marilyn and take her back to New York with him—as they had discussed. It has been speculated that, at this point, following her newfound Hollywood acceptance, Marilyn began to reconsider the gargantuan risk she was about to take and that Greene flew to LA to assuage her fears.

At any rate, at the end of 1954, Marilyn Monroe and Milton H. Greene formed Marilyn Monroe Productions, Inc., while MM hid out in a New York hotel. Soon after, she moved into Milton and Amy Greene's Weston, Connecticut, home, where she reveled in her seclusion.

In the beginning of 1955, Marilyn Monroe Productions went public. At that time, Marilyn gushed, "I feel deeply about him. I'm sincere about his genius. He's a genius."

As for Greene, he resigned from his $50,000-a-year job at *LOOK* magazine to guide Marilyn Monroe's career. And during the remainder of 1955 Greene mortgaged his home and borrowed money to the extent of his credit—all to subsidize Marilyn's life and livelihood while she was out of a job. Among Marilyn's expenses were:

1. $1,000 a week for a Waldorf-Astoria Towers apartment
2. $100 a week for Gladys's care
3. $125 a week for MM's psychoanalyst
4. $500 a week for MM's "beautification"
5. $50 a week for perfume
6. a private secretary
7. a press agent

Milton Greene, circa 1956.

THE SABIN GRAY COLLECTION

Greene also purchased a new black Thunderbird sports car for Marilyn, in addition to a new wardrobe that cost $3,000 (over a two-month span). The overall estimated cost of "maintaining" Marilyn Monroe was $50,000 a year.

Not only did Milton Hawthorne Greene "guide" and "maintain" Marilyn's life and career; he also negotiated a new contract for her with 20th Century-Fox. And, when Marilyn returned to Hollywood in 1956, Milton H. Greene was at her side. Everyone asked, "Who is Milton Greene?" Billy Wilder summed it up with, "I don't know who's to blame. Kazan? Strasberg? Milton Greene? Who is Milton Greene anyway?"

Greene was called MM's "Svengali." Some people felt that he and Marilyn were having an affair. Affair or no affair, Greene was largely responsible for the critical success of *Bus Stop* in 1956. Not only did Greene "develop" the project with Marilyn and Joshua Logan; he also designed MM's makeup and lighting. It was also Greene who obtained *The Prince and the Showgirl* (1957) as a vehicle for MM.

It was during the London shooting of *Prince* that the MM/Milton Greene relationship fell apart. Some people blame Arthur Miller for the rift. At any rate, during the shooting, Greene publicly announced his intention to set up a British subsidiary of Marilyn Monroe Productions, with Jack Cardiff as the firm's first director. Reportedly, Miller became furious and accused Greene of plotting behind Marilyn's back. Marilyn also resented the fact that Greene was friendly with Laurence Olivier, whom Marilyn had come to think of as an enemy. Thus, before he left England, Milton H. Greene was offered $500,000 for his interest in Marilyn Monroe Productions. At that time, Greene declined. In September 1956, Greene told Maurice Zolotow,

> "I'm very happy here, and Marilyn is very happy, and Miller and I are good friends . . . and I will never sell my stock in the corporation."

In the spring of 1957, Milton H. Greene sold his stock for a mere $85,000. At that time, Marilyn commented, "My company was not set up merely to parcel out 49.6% of all my earnings to Mr. Greene for seven years."

The partnership was over, and so was the friendship. Milton H. Greene later said,

> "I thought I'd seen them all; being in the business I'd seen so many models and actresses. But I'd never seen anyone with that tone of voice, that kindness, that real softness. If she saw a dead dog in the road, she'd cry. She was so supersensitive you had to watch your tone of voice all the time. Later I was to find out that she was schizoid—that she could be absolutely brilliant or absolutely kind, then, the total opposite."

In retrospect, whatever Milton Greene was, whatever his intentions were, he was undeniably a *great* photographer. His many photos of Marilyn Monroe stand among the finest ever taken. They are and were unusual and striking and creative. They also reveal a glimpse of the woman behind the MM facade.

On Milton Greene's business acuity, columnist Earl Wilson wrote the following in his August 6, 1965, column:

> "Milton Greene can please stand and take a fast bow. He conceived the project [*The Prince and the Showgirl*]. He was blasted—but the figures show now that he masterminded at least a minor, and perhaps a major, success."

By that time, people had stopped asking, "Who *is* Milton Greene?" On August 5, 1985, Greene, born in 1922, died of cancer.

**DAN GREENSON**

Dan Greenson was the son of Marilyn's Hollywood psychiatrist, Dr. Ralph Greenson. Once, according to Eunice Murray, Dan wrote out a list of political questions for Marilyn to ask Robert Kennedy at one of the Peter Lawford dinner parties.

**JOAN GREENSON**

Joan Greenson, Dr. Ralph Greenson's daughter, was approximately twenty years old at the time of Marilyn's death. In MM's final year, she became quite close to Joan. MM took her under her wing like a younger sister. She taught Joan how to walk sexily, how to apply makeup, and how to perform the strip number from *Pal Joey*.

In July 1962, Marilyn threw a birthday party for Joan at her Brentwood home. It was the only known party that MM gave in that home.

**RALPH GREENSON**

Dr. Greenson, born September 20, 1911, was recommended to Marilyn by her Los Angeles attorney, Milton Rudin. Rudin was Greenson's brother-in-law. The first known time that Dr. Greenson treated MM was in August 1960, when Marilyn was admitted to the Westside Hospital in Los Angeles after suffering from a breakdown on the set of *The Misfits*.

When Marilyn returned to Los Angeles to live in 1961, she began seeing Dr. Greenson three times a week at his Santa Monica home. During the following months, MM became quite friendly with Greenson and with the entire Greenson family. He was her doctor, her friend, and, in Marilyn's eyes, her savior. When Greenson told her to hire his friend, Eunice Murray, as her housekeeper/companion, Marilyn obliged. It seemed to some of her friends that Marilyn's life was being run by Dr. Greenson.

However, if Marilyn heard the objections, she paid them no heed. Greenson became, perhaps, the most influential man in her life during that last year. Marilyn nicknamed him "Romey" (his nickname was Romeo). She spent Christmas Day, 1961, at his home. And she purchased a house and remodeled it as a miniature duplicate of Greenson's home.

Marilyn grew increasingly dependent upon Dr. Greenson. After she was fired from Fox, Marilyn began seeing him once—sometimes twice—a day. On Marilyn's final afternoon, Dr. Greenson paid a visit to her Brentwood home. He arrived at her house at approximately 5:15 P.M.. He aroused suspicion when he took a phone call from MM's friend, Ralph Roberts, at approximately 6:30 P.M. Greenson told Roberts—untruthfully—that Marilyn was not at home. Greenson also reportedly asked Pat Newcomb, who was at Marilyn's home, to leave the house.

Later that evening, Greenson telephoned Marilyn's Brentwood home. Mrs. Eunice Murray answered the call and told Greenson that Marilyn was safely in her room. And then the details get sketchy. Allegedly, Mrs. Murray telephoned Greenson at around 3:00 A.M. Marilyn's door was locked, and a telephone cord was coming out of the crack underneath her door. Greenson told Mrs. Murray to go outside and check Marilyn's window. Then, after seeing Marilyn's body through the window, Mrs. Murray retelephoned Greenson and told him to come over right away. Reportedly, Greenson then arrived, broke the window, and found Marilyn dead.

However, over the years, there have been other accounts of Greenson's involvement that evening. Some reports contend that Greenson was somehow involved in a cover-up plot to keep the true circumstances surrounding Marilyn's death a secret.

At any rate, the whole story may never be told. Dr. Greenson died of heart failure on November 24, 1979. And despite all of the speculation, it is important *not* to dismiss the fact that Marilyn herself *believed* in Dr. Greenson. During her last year, she entrusted her life to him. And that is no small show of faith.

**CHARLES J. GRIFFIN**

Judge Charles J. Griffin issued a warrant for Marilyn Monroe's arrest on February 2, 1955, when she failed to appear in court for driving without a license. Judge Griffin set her bail at $100. When MM failed to show up in court a second time, Judge Griffin, on April 6, 1955, issued a new warrant and increased her bail to $200. When MM finally appeared before him on February 28, 1956, he fined her $55 and told her,

> "Laws are made for all of us, rich or poor, without race or creed or whether your name happens to be Miss Monroe or not, and this kind of acting won't win you an Oscar."

**TERRY GROSSMAN**

Grossman cowrote the 1983 "Benson" segment, "Boys Night Out," which featured an MM-based character.

**JOHN GUARE**

Guare is the excellent stage and film writer who penned the 1969 stage comedy *Cop-Out*, which featured actress Linda Lavin in a parody of MM.

**MIGUEL GOMEZ GUERRA**

Guerra was the Mexican judge who granted MM's 1961 divorce from Arthur Miller.

**ALBERT GUESTAFESTE (also spelled *Guastafeste*)**

The soldier who served as Marilyn's pianist during her 1954 performance tour of Korea. Originally from Uniondale, Long Island, Guestafeste was quoted as saying the following about MM:

> "Someone ought to go up and tell her she's Marilyn Monroe. She doesn't seem to realize it. When you make a goof, she tells you *she's* sorry. When she goofs, she apologizes to me!"

**SIDNEY GUILAROFF (also spelled *Sydney*)**

Born in Montreal in 1910 and discovered by Joan Crawford in 1935, Guilaroff became, over the years, the most famous of all of the "hairdressers to the stars." In his thirty-plus-year film career, Guilaroff styled the hair of such famous women as Crawford, Norma Shearer, Rosalind Russell, Clara Bow, Doris Day, Elizabeth Taylor, Liza Minnelli, Shirley MacLaine, Bette Davis, Ann-Margret, and, of course, Marilyn Monroe.

Guilaroff did MM's hair for the September 1959 Fox luncheon honoring Khrushchev and was credited with having styled MM's hair on *The Misfits* (1961).

The night of Marilyn's death, she reportedly telephoned Guilaroff and told him, "I'm very depressed," before she hung up. Said Guilaroff on MM: "[She] was the sweetest, kindest person, the most underrated person. The saddest person aside from Garbo."

**FRED LAWRENCE GUILES**

Biographer, novelist, and aspiring screenwriter Fred Lawrence Guiles has written two biographies on Marilyn Monroe. The first, published in 1969, was entitled *Norma Jean: The Life of Marilyn Monroe* (McGraw-Hill). The second, published in 1984, was *Legend: The Life and Death of Marilyn Monroe* (Stein and Day). The collected works stand among the finest writing ever done on MM.

Born in Iowa in the 1930s and a graduate of Columbia University, Guiles has also written biographies of Marion Davies, Tyrone Power, Stan Laurel, and Jane Fonda.

***GUYS AND DOLLS***

In 1955, Marilyn told columnist Earl Wilson that the role she most wanted to play was the Vivian Blaine part in *Guys and Dolls*. The film version of the stage hit was released in 1955, and it's no wonder MM wanted to be involved in the production. It was written and directed by Joseph L. Mankiewicz, the man who had guided her in *All About Eve* (1950); it was photographed by Harry Stradling, one of her favorite cinematographers; it was choreographed by Michael Kidd; and it starred two of her favorite actors, Frank Sinatra and Marlon Brando. Nevertheless, the Vivian Blaine stage part went to (who else?) Vivian Blaine.

# H

**JOYCE HABER**

Columnist Joyce Haber conducted a 1970 poll that appeared in the *Los Angeles Times* to determine the best movies and best movie performances of the entire past decade. The poll, voted on by Hollywood industry "insiders," cited Marilyn Monroe in the "Best Female Comedy Performance" category. MM placed third, for her exemplary work in *Some Like It Hot,* which was actually released in 1959. MM was topped only by Shirley MacLaine, who came in second for *The Apartment* (1960), and Barbra Streisand, who came in first for her Oscar-winning performance in *Funny Girl* (1968).

**HAIR**

"I wouldn't ever want to be a bleached blonde."

Norma Jeane Dougherty to Emmeline Snively, 1946

"There are several problems with doing Marilyn's hair. Her hair is very fine and therefore hard to manage. It gets oily if it isn't shampooed every day. And her hair is so curly naturally that to build a coiffure for her I have to first give her a straight permanent. . . . The way we got her shade of platinum is with my own secret blend of sparkling silver bleach plus twenty volume peroxide and a secret formula of silver platinum to take the yellow out."

Gladys Rasmussen

"I toned her down from the Jean Harlow platinum blonde to the Lana Turner white on white look. I worked with her hair until it was perfectly white. She called it 'pillow case' white."

George Masters

"If I had done her hair in a way that would evoke the comment, 'Your hair looks fabulous!' I'm sure I would never have seen her again. She didn't want to hear, 'Your hair looks great,' or 'Your earrings are beautiful.' She only wanted to hear, 'You look fantastic!' "

George Masters

**MM Hair Trivia**

☆ Emmeline Snively sent Norma Jeane Dougherty to Hollywood hairstylists at the Frank and Joseph salon. They cut, straightened, and bleached Norma Jeane's hair.

☆ Before she achieved major stardom with *Niagara* (1953) and *Gentlemen Prefer Blondes* (1953), MM's hair had gone through several subtle and not so subtle transitions. In a period of two years, MM's hair was dyed the following shades of blonde:

*The Asphalt Jungle*: ash blonde
*All About Eve*: golden blonde
*As Young as You Feel*: silver blonde
*Let's Make It Legal*: amber blonde
*Love Nest*: smoky blonde
*O. Henry's Full House*: honey blonde
*We're Not Married*: topaz blonde
*Don't Bother to Knock*: unbleached dark blonde
*Monkey Business*: platinum blonde

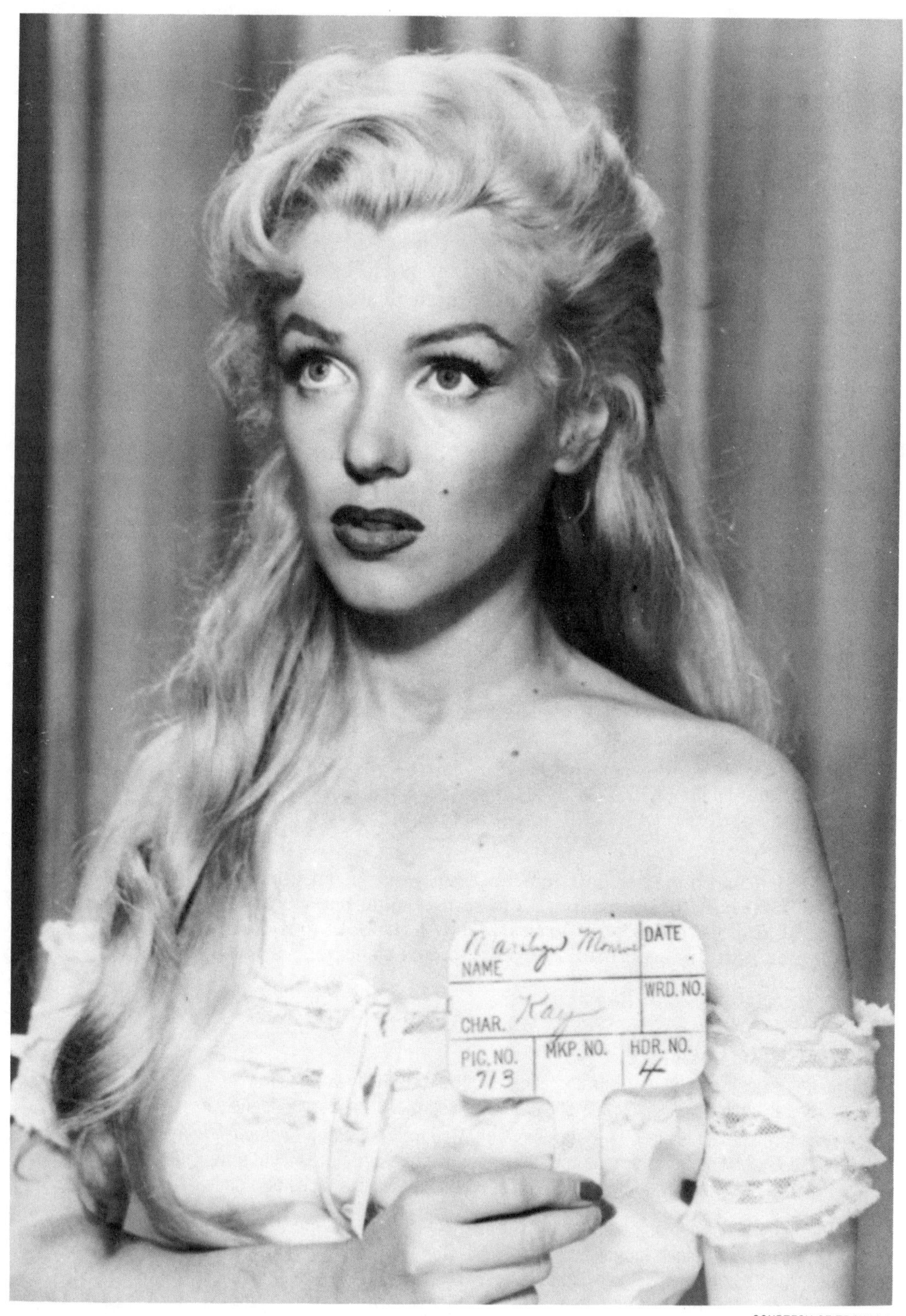


COURTESY OF TRAVILLA

Hair test, *River of No Return*, 1954.

☆ For *Bus Stop*, MM's hair was changed from platinum blonde to a reddish blonde.
☆ When she didn't want to be recognized (such as the time she fled to New York with Milton Greene in 1954), MM donned a black wig and hid behind large dark glasses.
☆ During the production of *Let's Make Love*, Marilyn had her hair colored every Saturday by an old woman from San Diego who claimed that she once colored Jean Harlow's hair.
☆ MM bleached her pubic hair blonde.

**MM Hair Trivia Quiz #16**

After becoming a star, in what film did MM wear a long blonde fall? (Answer on page 577.)

**The Personal Hairstylists**

Kenneth Battelle
Agnes Flanagan
Sidney Guilaroff
Peter Leonardi
George Masters
Gladys Rasmussen

**ANDRE HAKIM**

Born in Egypt in 1915, Hakim produced *O. Henry's Full House* in 1952.

**JAMES E. HALL**

James E. Hall wrote an article for *Hustler* magazine's May 1986 issue entitled "Marilyn Was Murdered: An Eyewitness Account." The witness, of course, was Hall himself.

Back in 1962, James Hall was twenty-two years old and (he claims) an ambulance driver for Schaefer Ambulance. During the early morning hours of August 5, 1962, Hall alleges that he was called to Marilyn's Brentwood home. His story, briefly, went like this:

> Eventually, when we pulled her off the bed and started to do CPR, put the resuscitator on her, her color came back. . . . Normally at this point we'd get out a stretcher and transport the patient to a hospital . . . right then is when a man who said he was Monroe's doctor walked in the door. . . . Then he [the doctor] started pushing on her chest, but he wasn't on the chest. He was way down like on her stomach. I remember noticing then that she had a fairly fresh scar there. Every time he'd push, whatever was in her stomach would come up that airway. It was just gooky-looking. The fluid was dark. Maybe greenish. . . . Then he opened up his doctor's bag and pulled out a hypodermic syringe that already had a hard needle on it. . . . He finally found the place and kind of pushed the breast aside and stuck the needle in. . . . So that needle mark has to be on that rib. . . . Then he put a stethoscope to her chest and said, "I'm going to pronounce her dead. You can leave." If this guy who claimed to be Monroe's doctor had arrived on the scene just a minute later, we would have been at the hospital with her. We would have saved her. I felt sick. . . . When it finally did come out in the paper, it was reported that Monroe had been found in the master bedroom of the main house, reaching out for the telephone. And I said, "Bull!"

Hall later identified the doctor as Dr. Ralph Greenson. He also claimed that Pat Newcomb was present and witness to the alleged scene.

**JAMES M. HALL**
The appraiser of MM's estate.

**PHILIPPE HALSMAN**

> "I remember that one of the girls was an artificial blonde by the name of Marilyn Monroe and that she was not one of the girls who impressed me the most."
>
> Philippe Halsman on MM in 1949

> "Marilyn's very weakness was her great strength. Her inferiority complex, her pathetic, almost childlike need for security are the very things that made her irresistible."

> "Though I have photographed hundreds of actresses, I have never seen one with a greater inferiority complex."

> "I know few actresses who have this incredible talent for communicating with a camera lens. She would try to seduce a camera as if it were a human being."

> "When she faced a man she didn't know, she felt safe and secure only when she knew that the man desired her."

Photographer Phillipe Halsman first met Marilyn Monroe in 1949. He was shooting a photo feature of the new crop of studio actresses. Marilyn was one of the starlets chosen to pose for a variety of dramatic expressions. In 1952, Halsman shot another photo feature of Marilyn. This time, presumably, he was more impressed by her. After seeing his photos (according to Halsman), *LIFE* magazine gave Marilyn Monroe the cover (her first for *LIFE*), along with a substantial story that *must* have made 20th Century-Fox reevaluate MM's worth. The cover photo, of course, featured MM leaning against a wall, exuding a breathless kind of sex and wearing a clinging, white, off-the-shoulders gown that featured a jeweled broach at her cleavage.

In 1959, ten years after first "discovering" her, Halsman shot a series of color shots that featured MM jumping in the air. And while they are certainly different from most typical MM poses, they don't compare favorably to Halsman's earlier MM works. Halsman died in 1979 at the age of 73.

**CHARLES HAMBLETT**
Hamblett wrote the 1966 book, *Who Killed Marilyn Monroe?*, which contained a chapter on MM. He also wrote biographies about Marlon Brando and Paul Newman.

**THE HAMPSHIRE HOUSE HOTEL**
The New York hotel where MM and Joe DiMaggio reportedly stayed during part of the 1954 *The Seven Year Itch* location shooting. It is located at 150 Central Park South.

**VERNON S. HARBIN**
Vernon Harbin is the current archivist for RKO Studios, where he has been an employee since March 1931. Harbin is also the co-author of the book, *The RKO Story*, which was published in 1982. Of Gladys Baker, a former

sometime employee at RKO, Harbin was quoted as saying: "She was known as a bar fly." Gladys, of course, was Marilyn Monroe's mother.

### *THE HARDEST PART OF IT*

*The Hardest Part of It* was a stage play written by Roger Newman, which dealt with the last three years of Marilyn Monroe's life. The play was presented at the Actor's Consort Theatre in New York, circa 1977–78, and, was later produced in England, under the name *Public Property.* Actress Amanda Powers portrayed the MM-based role in the New York production.

### *HARLOW*

Earl Wilson: Have you ever thought of playing the life story of Jean Harlow?

MM: I would like to, providing everything is right for it. It should be done at the highest level. She should be done humanly.

October 6, 1955

Upon his return from Paris over [the] weekend, 20th-Fox exec producer Buddy Adler took the wraps off the studio's long projected plan to bio-pic Jean Harlow with Marilyn Monroe playing the late screen star. . . .

*Variety,* June 4, 1956

"I hope they don't do that to me after I'm gone."

MM after reading the *Harlow* script

Now it can be told. The reason that Marilyn Monroe, for whom Adela Rogers St. John wrote "The Jean Harlow Story," never achieved her own desire to star in it was not because she died too soon but because Arthur Miller, under whose influence she was at the time, wouldn't allow her to appear in it. He didn't think it conformed to her "new image."

*The Hollywood Reporter,* June 18, 1964

THE SABIN GRAY COLLECTION

Jean Harlow, MM's childhood idol, circa 1934.

THE SABIN GRAY COLLECTION

MM, looking like her idol, circa 1952.

Every studio in Hollywood wanted to produce "The Jean Harlow Story." Thus, it was only natural that Buddy Adler and 20th Century-Fox wanted "their" star, Marilyn Monroe, to play the part. After all, who else could have played Jean Harlow? Even Harlow's mother, Mrs. Jean Bello, wanted MM for the role. Buddy Adler purchased the film rights, commissioned Adela Rogers St. John to write the screenplay, and announced that MM would make the picture after she completed *The Prince and the Showgirl* in 1956. Nonetheless, MM stuck to her (or Miller's) objections and refused to do the film, and "The Jean Harlow Story" was shelved.

Paramount eventually filmed *Harlow* nearly ten years later, with Carroll Baker as the legendary star. The film was produced by Joseph E. Levine and directed by Gordon Douglas. The cast included Martin Balsam, Red Buttons, Michael Connors, Angela Lansbury, and Peter Lawford. Interestingly, Sidney Guilaroff, MM's hair stylist, did Miss Baker's hair for the film.

The reviews were fair to horrid.

> Carroll Baker as Harlow is the little engine that couldn't. No matter how hard she huffs and puffs, she cannot conjure up the girl that everyone in the script keeps chattering about—the voluptuous, mercurial creature of fire and ice with the "body of a woman and the emotions of a child." Miss Baker's Harlow displays the body of a Junior Miss and the emotions of a den mother, an insufferable little priss who fails to find love because she makes herself unfailingly unlovely.
>
> *Newsweek*

> Miss Baker's entrapment in this role is more embarrassing than amusing, for it seems to be a personal failure when, in fact, the calamity is collective. She gets no help from any quarter. To begin with—and *why* did Joe Levine begin with—she is patently wrong for the part: attractive but hardly alluring, engaging but not galvanic. Her acting range is limited. Her voice is precarious. She is a perfect setup for a painful knockdown.
>
> *Newsweek*

> Carroll Baker plays Harlow as if she were a saucy puppet, with a straitlaced attitude to men that kept her untouched until she wed. Her performance itself is a travesty. Carroll Baker is to me, coldly pretty but hardly wildly sexy. If, in a few years, they do the same to Marilyn Monroe, I will wash my hands of Hollywood.
>
> a London critic

The same year (1965) a television movie about Jean Harlow was produced. This one starred Carol Lynley, and received generally better reviews than the Carroll Baker feature.

**JEAN HARLOW**

Marilyn Monroe identified with Jean Harlow. When she was a little girl, Jean Harlow was one of her idols. And, although Marilyn never filmed Harlow's life story, she did portray Harlow in Richard Avedon's photo series for *LIFE* magazine, December 22, 1958.

In an insightful article that appeared in *Films in Review* magazine, March 1979, James Haspiel wrote about the Harlow/Monroe Connection:

☆ They both loved champagne.
☆ They both slept in the nude.
☆ They both requested that their personal makeup artist prepare them for their funeral.
☆ They both lived, at one time, on North Palm Drive in Beverly Hills.
☆ They both starred opposite Clark Gable in their final film.
☆ They both preferred not to wear underwear.
☆ They both died at the peak of their careers.

Jean Harlow was born Harlean Carpentier in 1911. In her short but productive film career, the famous wisecracking platinum blonde starred in such movies as *Hell's Angels* (1930), *Public Enemy* (1931), *Red Dust* (1932), *Dinner at Eight* (1933), *Bombshell* (1933), and *China Seas* (1935). She died in 1937, at the age of twenty-six of cerebral edema (swelling of the brain).

**HARPER AVENUE**
Both Natasha Lytess and Mrs. Anne Karger maintained homes on Harper Avenue in West Hollywood. Over the years, Marilyn visited both of them, frequently. And, for a time (circa 1951), MM moved into the Lytess home, which was also occupied by Natasha's daughter, Barbara, and which was located at 1309 Harper.

**FANNY HARRIS**
Mrs. Harris was Marilyn Monroe's maid, circa 1956.

**JAMES HASPIEL**
Born in Brooklyn in 1938, James Robert Haspiel is generally acknowledged as one of the foremost experts on the public Marilyn Monroe. Haspiel is a Monroe student and fan who established a friendly relationship with MM during her "New York period." Since MM's death, Haspiel has worked to preserve MM's name and has written several informative articles on her that have appeared in such publications as *Films in Review, Hollywood Studio Magazine,* and *American Classic Screen.*

**HENRY HATHAWAY**

> "She's the best natural actress I've directed. And I go back. I worked with Barbara LaMar, Jean Harlow, Rene Adoree—right up to today. And she's the greatest natural talent. Wait 'til you see her in this picture. You don't know what she's got."
>
> Henry Hathaway to Sidney Skolsky, July 16, 1952

Hathaway, born in 1898, was a director with more than thirty years of films to his credit, including John Wayne's Oscar-winning *True Grit* in 1969.

In 1952, Hathaway directed MM in *Niagara,* the film that many people believe made her a star. Despite their great success together, Marilyn conspicuously left Hathaway's name *off* her approved list of directors.

**RALPH HATTERSLEY**

Hattersley wrote the insightful 1966 *Popular Photography* article on MM that was entitled "Marilyn Monroe: The Image and Her Photographers." As implied in its title, the article featured interviews with some of MM's best photographers.

**JUNE HAVER**

Born June Stovenour in 1926, June Haver was Betty Grable's "lady-in-waiting" at 20th Century-Fox in 1946, at the time Norma Jeane Dougherty was signed to her first studio contract. Haver was the star of *Scudda Hoo! Scudda Hay!* (1948), which is generally considered MM's first film. She also starred in *Love Nest* (1951), in which MM costarred. In 1953, Haver retired from films and entered a convent. She later left the convent and married actor Fred MacMurray.

Said Miss Haver about her *Love Nest* costar:

> She was so young and pretty, so shy and nervous on that picture, but I remember the scene where she was supposed to be sunning in the back yard of the apartment house we all lived in. When Marilyn walked on the set in her bathing suit and walked to the beach chair, the whole crew gasped, gaped and seemed to turn to stone. They just stopped work and stared; Marilyn had that electric something—and mind you, movie crews are quite used to seeing us in brief costumes. They've worked on so many musicals and beach sequences. But they just gasped and gaped at Marilyn as though they were stunned. In all my years at the studio, I'd never seen that happen before. Sure, the crew gives you the kidding wolf-whistle routine, but this was sheer shock.
>
> *Coronet,* 1/1966

**HAWAII**

En route to Tokyo in 1954, the DiMaggios' airplane stopped off in Hawaii for refueling. At the Honolulu airport, six police officers had to form a human chain around MM and Joe. A frenzied crowd, thousands strong, screamed out Marilyn's name. They swarmed around her and frantically ripped out strands of her hair.

Upon returning to the United States, MM and Joe again stopped off in Hawaii. Marilyn visited a doctor in Hawaii, who diagnosed her as having a slight case of bronchial pneumonia.

**HOWARD HAWKS**

Howard Hawks (1896–1977) was one of the most noted directors in Hollywood history. By the time he made *Monkey Business* (1952) and *Gentlemen Prefer Blondes* (1953), Hawks had helmed such American classics as *Scarface* (1932), *Bringing Up Baby* (1938), *His Girl Friday* (1940), *To Have and Have Not* (1944), *The Big Sleep* (1946), and *Red River* (1948).

Antagonism developed between MM and Hawks on the set of *Gentlemen Prefer Blondes* because Marilyn continuously held up the shooting. When the Fox front office asked Hawks how he could speed up the slowly progressing production, Hawks was quoted as suggesting, "I have three wonderful ideas.

Replace Marilyn, rewrite the script and make it shorter, and get a new director."

On Marilyn, Hawks said,

> Marilyn was just a frightened girl. She never felt that she was good enough to do the things she did. It was hard to get her out of her dressing room. When she got out there, it was easy. We had a lot of fun doing *Gentlemen Prefer Blondes,* but there were a lot of times when I was ready to give up the ghost.

Hawks, sometimes known as "the man who discovered" Lauren Bacall, joined Henry Hathaway by being conspicuously absent from MM's 1955 list of approved directors.

**HAWTHORNE, CALIFORNIA**

Norma Jean's first home was with the Bolender family in Hawthorne, California.

**HAWTHORNE COMMUNITY SUNDAY SCHOOL**

Before she entered kindergarten, Norma Jeane Baker attended the Hawthorne Community Sunday School in Hawthorne, California. Norma Jeane was enrolled in the "Cradle Roll Department" of the school, before she was promoted to the "Beginners Department" on September 28, 1930. The minister of the school at that time was Robert Charles Lewis; the school superintendent was Charles H. Weiskopf.

**STERLING HAYDEN**

Born Sterling Walter Relyea in 1916, Hayden starred in *The Asphalt Jungle* (1950), one of Marilyn's early breakthrough pictures. Later in his career, Hayden appeared in such films as *Dr. Strangelove* (1963), *The Godfather* (1972), and *Nine to Five* (1980).

**ALFRED HAYES**

Alfred Hayes wrote the screenplay for the 1952 picture *Clash by Night* which costarred Marilyn Monroe. The screenplay was adapted from a story by Clifford Odets.

**SUSAN HAYWARD**

Born Edythe Marrener, Susan Hayward (1918–1975) was *the* actress on the Fox lot in 1952. Grable may have been the box office, but Hayward was the prestige. And, although Marilyn Monroe became more popular than Grable and Hayward, it was Susan Hayward who received (from various studios) the powerhouse female roles of the 1950s; e.g., *With a Song in My Heart* (1952), *I'll Cry Tomorrow* (1955), and *I Want to Live* (for which she won a 1958 Oscar).

**RITA HAYWORTH**

Born Margarita Carmen Cansino in 1918 and groomed for stardom by Harry Cohn himself, Rita Hayworth was the undisputed Queen of the Columbia lot in 1948, when Marilyn was signed to her Columbia contract. At that time, Rita was hot off the successes of *Cover Girl* (1944), *Gilda* (1946), and *The Lady from Shanghai* (1948). She had yet to make *Miss Sadie Thompson* (1953), *Pal Joey* (1957), and *Separate Tables* (1958).

THE SABIN GRAY COLLECTION

Rita Hayworth, Columbia's "goddess" when MM was under contract there, circa 1948.

**EDITH HEAD**

In her prime, Edith Head (1907–1981) was generally recognized as *the* Hollywood costume designer. Miss Head won Oscars for her fashions in *The Heiress* (1949), *Samson and Delilah* (1951), *A Place in the Sun* (1951), et al. She also designed the costumes for *All About Eve*, which featured starlet Marilyn Monroe in a small, showcase role.

**NATHAN HEADLEY**

Dr. Headley was Marilyn's personal physician, who treated her for a virus infection and bronchitis in April 1956.

**BEN HECHT**

Ben Hecht (1894–1964) was a noted Oscar-winning screenwriter, responsible (or coresponsible) for such films as *Wuthering Heights* (1939), *Spellbound* (1945), and *Notorious* (1946). Hecht also copenned *Monkey Business* (1952), which costarred MM.

From May 9, 1954, to August 1, 1954, London's *The Empire News* published a series of articles "written" by Marilyn Monroe "as told to" Ben Hecht. Naturally, these articles contained material on the plight of orphan girl Norma Jeane, the rise to stardom, and the marriage to Joe DiMaggio. Much of the material from these articles was compiled into the autobiographical book, *My Story*, which was copyrighted by Milton H. Greene and published by Stein and Day in 1974.

**EILEEN HECKART**
Eileen Heckart, born in 1919, was the only member of the *Bus Stop* (1956) acting company that Marilyn befriended. Perhaps the reason that MM befriended the character actress was that Heckart had just starred, prior to *Bus Stop*, in a stage production of Arthur Miller's *A View from the Bridge.*

**HEIGHT**
Five feet, five and a half inches.

**CHARLES HENDERSON**
Charles Henderson was a dance instructor at 20th Century-Fox who taught starlet Marilyn Monroe a dance routine which she performed at the studio's New Talent Show in 1946.

**AUDREY HEPBURN**
Born Audrey (aka Edda) Hepburn-Ruston in 1929 in Belgium, Hepburn starred in the 1961 film *Breakfast at Tiffany's.* Hepburn portrayed Holly Golightly, a role that was reportedly written for MM. Among Hepburn's other film credits are *Roman Holiday* (for which she won a 1953 Oscar), *Sabrina* (1954), *Funny Face* (1957), *The Nun's Story* (1959), *Wait Until Dark* (1967), and *They All Laughed* (1981).

**"HER PSYCHIATRIST FRIEND"**
"Her Psychiatrist Friend" is the pen name used by Marilyn's friend/lover who authored the mediocre, dubious book *Violations of the Child Marilyn Monroe* (Bridgehead Books, 1962). The real identity of "Her Psychiatrist Friend" is unknown, for understandable reasons.

**F. HUGH HERBERT**
Herbert (1897–1957) wrote and directed the 1948 film *Scudda Hoo! Scudda Hay!*, which is generally considered MM's first film. Herbert was commonly known as the screenwriter of such films as *Margie* (1946), *The Moon Is Blue* (1953), and *Let's Make It Legal* (1951), the latter of which featured MM.

**HERMITAGE STREET**
Norma Jeane Dougherty lived on Hermitage Street in North Hollywood, California, circa 1944–45.

**HEROES AND IDOLS: THE MM LIST**

Michael Chekhov
Eleanora Duse
Albert Einstein
Clark Gable
Abraham Lincoln
Dr. Albert Schweitzer
Lincoln Steffens
Lee Strasberg

**HERSHEY'S CANDY**
A still photograph of Marilyn Monroe from *Some Like it Hot* was used for a Hershey's candy bar television commercial in 1986.

**POTTER HEWETH**
See Potter Hueth.

***HEY, MARILYN!***
Originally a 1974 radio presentation, this Cliff Jones play about Marilyn Monroe was produced at the Citadel Theatre in Canada, circa 1979–80. It starred Lenore Zann and was directed by Peter Coe.

**CATHERINE HICKS**
So far, out of all the actresses to portray Marilyn Monroe in a film biography, Catherine Hicks has come the closest to conveying the MM presence. In the 1980 television film *Marilyn: The Untold Story,* there were a few moments when Hicks *was* Monroe. Deservedly, she won an Emmy nomination for her work but has yet to do anything else of similar value.

**HIGHLAND AVENUE**
In 1934, when she was eight, Norma Jeane moved into a white Arbol Street bungalow adjacent to what is now the Hollywood Bowl. It was at this home that Norma Jeane lived with her mother, Gladys, for the first time.

**HILLDALE AVENUE**
Early in 1952, Marilyn Monroe lived in a small frame house located at 1121 Hilldale Avenue in Hollywood.

**HILTONE HAIR COLORING**
Circa 1953, a photograph of Marilyn Monroe appeared in a print advertisement for Hiltone Hair Coloring. The ad read: "Marilyn Monroe says 'Gentlemen Prefer Blondes and blondes prefer Hiltone.' "

**ALFRED HITCHCOCK**
Truly one of the greatest filmmakers of all time, Alfred Hitchcock (1899–1980) once named three actresses whom he felt were the only genuine female stars in the motion picture industry. They were Elizabeth Taylor, Ingrid Bergman, and Marilyn Monroe.

Hitchcock, of course, directed such classics as *The Lady Vanishes* (1938), *Rebecca* (1940), *Foreign Correspondent* (1940), *Spellbound* (1945), *Notorious* (1946), *Rear Window* (1954), *To Catch A Thief* (1955), *Vertigo* (1958), *North by Northwest* (1959), *Psycho* (1960), and *The Birds* (1963). Although Marilyn included Hitchcock on her 1955 list of approved directors, they never made a film together.

**DON HOCKETT**
Don Hockett accompanied his father, Guy, when Guy picked up Marilyn Monroe's corpse on the morning of August 5, 1962.

**GUY HOCKETT**
In 1962, Guy Hockett was the owner of Westwood Memorial Cemetery and the

coroner's representative who received a 5:25 A.M. call on August 5, 1962, instructing him to go to Marilyn Monroe's Fifth Helena Drive home.

When he arrived at the house, Hockett later claimed that there were three men and three women at the site. He also claimed that advanced rigor mortis had already set in, and he estimated that MM must have been dead for at least eight hours (this would have put MM's death on the evening of August 4, *not* August 5). When Hockett read the newspaper accounts that MM had been dead for less than three hours when she was found, he was shocked.

It was Guy Hockett who carried Marilyn's corpse out of her Brentwood home at 7:30 A.M. on August 5. The body was covered with a pale blue blanket.

In 1984, Guy Hockett died. His body was placed in a crypt at Westwood Memorial Cemetery, not too far from Marilyn's.

**JIMMY HOFFA**

There has been much speculation over the years that Jimmy Hoffa had secret audio tapes of Marilyn Monroe and one of the Kennedy brothers making love. The speculation contends that Hoffa threatened to use the tapes, in addition to other information on the alleged affairs, to blackmail the Kennedy brothers.

**SAMUEL HOFFMAN**

Marilyn Monroe's former Sunday school teacher, who visited her on the set of *The Seven Year Itch* in 1954. At that time, Samuel Hoffman was 77 years old.

**DELLA HOGAN**

*See* DELLA MONROE GRAINGER.

**TILFORD HOGAN**

Marilyn's maternal great-grandfather, who hung himself at the age of eighty-two.

**HOLGA STEEL COMPANY**

The first modeling job MM obtained while with the Blue Book Model Agency was for the Holga Steel Company. MM served as the hostess at an industrial show, which was held at the landmark Pan Pacific Auditorium in Los Angeles. To be available for this job, Norma Jeane called in sick at the Radio Plane Company. She was paid $10 a day for her hostessing.

**BILLIE HOLIDAY**

Born Eleanor Gough, Billie Holiday (1915–1959) was one of the all-time great American blues singers. On one evening in the 1950s, Marilyn, escorted by Bill Travilla, attended a Billie Holiday concert at Tiffany's on Eighth Street in Los Angeles. The story, told by Travilla to Anthony Summers, went something like this: At the concert, Travilla excused himself and went to the men's room. En route, he noticed Marilyn's nude calendar hanging from an office wall. When Travilla told MM of his find, she replied, "Oh, Billy, where? I want to see it." As it turned out, Billie Holiday was using the office as a dressing room. And when she found out that Marilyn Monroe wanted to see a calendar (instead of paying respects to *her*), Holiday crumpled the calendar, threw it in MM's face, and called Marilyn a c—t.

Needless to say, Travilla and MM didn't stay for the performance.

**THE HOLIDAY HOTEL**

Reno hotel (address: 111 Mill Street) that Arthur and Marilyn Miller moved to, following their stay at the Mapes Motel, during the 1960 shooting of *The Misfits.* The Millers occupied suites 846, 848, and 850.

**JUDY HOLLIDAY**

It wasn't enough that Harry Cohn was trying to mold Kim Novak into the next Marilyn Monroe, he also tried to turn one of his most talented actresses, Judy Holliday, into some sort of minor-league Monroe. It didn't work. If anything, it served to damage Holliday's potentially brilliant career.

Born Judith Tuvim, Judy Holliday (1922–1965) burst to fame with the back-to-back successes of *Adam's Rib* (1949) and especially *Born Yesterday* (for which she won a 1950 Oscar). Her later, less appealing films included *The Solid Gold Cadillac* (1956).

**DONA HOLLOWAY**

Dona Holloway was Johnny Hyde's secretary at the William Morris Agency when he met and fell in love with Marilyn Monroe. Hyde's last words to Dona, from his deathbed, were "Be sure that Marilyn is treated as one of the family." However, despite Dona's attempts, the family ostracized MM and silently accused her of being responsible for Johnny's death. It was through Dona's efforts, in tandem with Sam Berke, that Marilyn was allowed to attend Hyde's funeral.

Following Hyde's death, Dona went on to become a Hollywood producer.

***HOLLYWOOD BLUE***

Stag film compilation that included a sequence titled *Apples, Knockers, and the Coke Bottle,* aka *Apples, Knockers and Cokes.* The vintage sequence was heralded as featuring Marilyn Monroe's sexiest film performance. However, *Playboy* later dispelled the speculation by identifying the actress as Arlene Hunter, not MM.

**THE HOLLYWOOD CHRISTIAN GROUP**

Reportedly, during the shooting of *Gentlemen Prefer Blondes* (1953), Jane Russell cajoled Marilyn Monroe into attending a religious gathering of the Hollywood Christian Group. MM attended the meetings just once.

**"HOLLYWOOD CLOSE-UP"**

The "Hollywood Close-Up" television series featured a special documentary on Marilyn Monroe entitled "Marilyn, In Search of a Dream." It aired on ABC on February 19, 1983. Excellently produced, it was narrated by actor

Kevin McCarthy, and included interviews with Terry Moore, Yves Montand, Bob Slatzer, Joseph Jasgur (MM photographer), and Whitey Snyder, MM's make-up artist. The executive producers of this special were David Kellogg and Frank Kelly; the producer was Jonathan Kaplan.

### *HOLLYWOOD . . . HISTORY OF HYSTERICS!*

Early MM posed for a still photograph, shot by cameraman Leo Caloia, which was incorporated into this film.

### *THE HOLLYWOOD REPORTER*

*The Hollywood Reporter* is a popular Hollywood trade daily. Following Marilyn Monroe's withdrawal from 20th Century-Fox and the subsequent formation of Marilyn Monroe Productions in January 1955, *The Hollywood Reporter's* W. R. Wilkerson wrote the following in an editorial: "Marilyn Monroe is a stupid girl and is being fed some stupid advice."

It was a popular (but ultimately incorrect) sentiment in Hollywood at that time.

### THE HOLLYWOOD ROOSEVELT HOTEL

In 1951, rising star Marilyn Monroe had a photo session at the pool of the legendary Hollywood Roosevelt Hotel in Los Angeles (address: 7000 Holly-

COURTESY OF THE HOLLYWOOD ROOSEVELT HOTEL

Hollywood Roosevelt Hotel pool, circa 1952.

wood Boulevard). And, according to Mr. Harold Nay, former general manager of the hotel, Marilyn stayed at the Hollywood Roosevelt in the mid-1950s, and occupied room 1200. Today, the hotel has been completely renovated, and is one of the last vestiges of old-time Hollywood glamour.

**THE HOLLYWOOD STAR PLAYHOUSE**

On Sunday, August 31, 1952, Marilyn Monroe made her live radio dramatic debut on WWJ's Hollywood Star Playhouse. Marilyn's segment was entitled "Statement in Full."

Off the air, NBC Radio, 1952.

**THE HOLLYWOOD WALK OF FAME**

The Hollywood Chamber of Commerce awarded MM her Walk of Fame star in 1960. The exact address of Marilyn's Star is 6774 Hollywood Boulevard.

**CELESTE HOLM**

Born in 1919, Celeste Holm is the fine, agreeable actress who costarred in such films as *Gentlemen's Agreement* (for which she won a 1947 Oscar), *The Snake Pit* (1948), and *High Society* (1956). In 1950, Miss Holm costarred in *All About Eve,* which featured MM.

**HOLMBY HILLS**

MM reportedly lived in Joseph Schenck's guest cottage at his Holmby Hills mansion for a brief period during the late 1940s.

## HOMES

"Someday I want to have a house of my own with trees and grass and hedges all around, but never trim them at all—just let them grow any old the way they want."

MM, 1951

"I thought I could never buy a home alone, but I've done it. It's like being married and not having a husband."

MM, 1962

"I could never imagine buying a home alone. But, I've always been alone, so why couldn't I imagine it?"

MM, 1962

### The Homes that MM Lived In

Listed chronologically, these were Marilyn Monroe's residences.

THE ROBERT SLATZER COLLECTION

595 Beverly Glen Blvd.

| | Address | City | Years |
|---|---|---|---|
| 1. | 5454 Wilshire Blvd. | Los Angeles, CA | 1926 (12 days) |
| 2. | 459 East Rhode Island St. | Hawthorne, CA | 1926–1932 |
| 3. | Unnamed street* | Hollywood, CA | 1932–1934 |
| 4. | Arbol Street | Hollywood, CA | 1934–1935 |
| 5. | Unnamed street** | Hollywood, CA | 1935 |
| 6. | Los Angeles Orphans Home 815 North El Centro Ave. | Hollywood, CA | 1935–1937 |
| 7. | Unnamed street*** | Compton, CA | 1937 |
| 8. | 6707 Odessa Ave. | Van Nuys, CA | 1937 |
| 9. | 14743 Archwood St. | Van Nuys, CA | 1937 |
| 10. | 6707 Odessa Ave. | Van Nuys, CA | 1938 |

*For a brief period in 1933, in Hollywood, Norma Jeane lived with a foster family (an English couple) before moving in with Gladys Baker.

**For a brief period in 1935 after Gladys Baker was admitted to Norwalk State Hospital, Norma Jeane moved in with a neighbor family named Giffen.

***For a brief period in 1937 Norma Jeane lived with a foster family in Compton before moving in with Ana Lower in Van Nuys.

| | | |
|---|---|---|
| 11. 11348 Nebraska Ave. | Sawtelle, CA | 1938–1941 |
| 12. 6707 Odessa Ave. | Van Nuys, CA | 1941–1942 |
| 13. 11348 Nebraska Ave. | Sawtelle, CA | 1942 |
| 14. 4524 Vista Del Monte St. | Sherman Oaks, CA | 1942 |
| 15. Bessemer Street | Van Nuys, CA | 1943 |
| 16. 14747 Archwood St. | Van Nuys, CA | 1943 |
| 17. Unnamed street | Catalina Island, CA | 1943–1944 |
| 18. Hermitage Street | North Hollywood, CA | 1944–1945 |
| 19. 11348 Nebraska Ave. | Sawtelle, CA | 1945–1946 |
| 20. Studio Club<br>1215 North Lodi St. | Hollywood, CA | 1946–1947 |
| 21. 131 South Avon St. | Burbank, CA | 1947 |
| 22. El Palaccio Apts.<br>8491–8499 Fountain Ave. | West Hollywood, CA | 1947–1948 |
| 23. Franklin Avenue | Hollywood, CA | 1948 |
| 24. Bel Air Hotel<br>701 Stone Canyon Rd. | Beverly Hills, CA | 1948 |
| 25. Beverly Carlton Hotel<br>9400 West Olympic Blvd. | Beverly Hills, CA | 1948 |
| 26. Studio Club<br>1215 North Lodi St. | Hollywood, CA | 1948–1949 |
| 27. 141 South Carolwood Dr. | Holmby Hills, CA | 1949 |
| 28. 718 North Palm Dr. | Beverly Hills, CA | 1950 |
| 29. 1309 Harper Ave. | West Hollywood, CA | 1950–1951 |
| 30. Beverly Carlton Hotel<br>9400 West Olympic Blvd. | Beverly Hills, CA | 1951 |
| 31. 3539 Kelton Way | West Los Angeles, CA | 1951 |
| 32. 611 North Crescent Dr. | Beverly Hills, CA | 1951–1952 |
| 33. 1121 Hilldale Ave. | West Hollywood, CA | 1952 |
| 34. Beverly Carlton Hotel<br>9400 West Olympic Blvd. | Beverly Hills, CA | 1952 |
| 35. Bel Air Hotel<br>701 Stone Canyon Rd. | Beverly Hills, CA | 1952 |
| 36. Unnamed street | Brentwood, CA | 1952 |
| 37. Outpost Estates<br>2393 Castilian Dr. | Hollywood Hills, CA | 1952 |
| 38. Beverly Hills Hotel<br>9641 West Sunset Blvd. | Beverly Hills, CA | 1952–1953 |
| 39. 882 North Doheny Dr. | Beverly Hills, CA | 1953–54 |
| 40. 2150 Beach St. | San Francisco, CA | 1954 |
| 41. 508 North Palm Dr. | Beverly Hills, CA | 1954 |
| 42. 8336 Delongpre Ave. | Hollywood, CA | 1954 |
| 43. Voltaire Apartments<br>1424 N. Crescent Heights | West Hollywood, CA | 1954 |
| 44. The Milton Greene Home<br>Fanton Hill Rd. | Weston, CT | 1954–1955 |
| 45. Waldorf Astoria Hotel<br>301 Park Ave. | New York, NY | 1955 |
| 46. Sutton Place Apartment<br>2 Sutton Pl. | New York, NY | 1955–1956 |
| 47. 595 Beverly Glen Blvd. | West Los Angeles, CA | 1956 |
| 48. Roxbury Farm Home | Roxbury, CT | 1956–1960 |
| 49. Parkside House Estate | Egham, England | 1956 |

| | | |
|---|---|---|
| 50. Amagansett Retreat | Amagansett, Long Island, NY | 1957–1958 |
| 51. Fifty Seventh St. Apt.<br>444 East 57th St. | New York, NY | 1957–1962 |
| 52. Beverly Hills Hotel<br>9641 West Sunset Blvd. | Beverly Hills, CA | 1958–1960 |
| 53. The Mapes Hotel<br>30 North Virginia St. | Reno, NV | 1960 |
| 54. The Holiday Hotel<br>111 Mill St. | Reno, NV | 1960 |
| 55. Beverly Hills Hotel<br>9641 West Sunset Blvd. | Beverly Hills, CA | 1961 |
| 56. 882 North Doheny Dr. | Beverly Hills, CA | 1961–1962 |
| 57. 12305 Fifth Helena Dr. | Brentwood, CA | 1962 |

**MM Trivia Quiz #17**
Where was MM's home in *Gentlemen Prefer Blondes*? (Answer on page 577.)

### *HOMETOWN STORY*

1951 61 minutes Black and White
MGM
Directed by: Arthur Pierson
Produced by: Arthur Pierson
Screenplay by: Arthur Pierson
Photographed by: Lucien Andriot
Cast: Jeffrey Lynn, Donald Crisp, Marjorie Reynolds, Alan Hale, Jr., Melinda Plowman, Griff Barnett, Marilyn Monroe

Industrial film that was not released commercially. Produced by General Motors to propagandize American industry, *Hometown Story* featured MM in another one of her secretarial roles. In this one, she was named Miss Martin.

### HOMOSEXUALITY

Marilyn Monroe's expressed feelings about homosexuality seemed to be widely divergent. During her career, she frequently surrounded herself with gay men, known and otherwise. To writer W. J. Weatherby, Marilyn once said the following:

> "I was remembering Monty Clift. People who aren't fit to open the door for him sneer at his homosexuality. What do they know about it? Labels—people love putting labels on each other. Then they feel safe. People tried to make me into a lesbian. I laughed. No sex is wrong if there's love in it."
>
> *Conversations with Marilyn* (Mason/Charter, 1976)

Yet, when *Niagara* (1953) was being cast, MM reportedly objected to a certain good-looking young actor because he was, in her words, "a pansy." The actor, of course, was not hired.

And then there was the matter of Marilyn's own alleged homosexuality . . . Over the years, there have been many rumors that Marilyn had various lesbian affairs. The most frequently reported rumor, of course, was her long and close relationship with her dramatic coach, Natasha Lytess. More than an eyebrow was raised when it was learned that Marilyn was living in Natasha's home. There were, allegedly, other women as well. According to Fred Lawrence Guiles, even Joan Crawford once made a pass at MM.

According to Anthony Summers's *Goddess: The Secret Lives of Marilyn Monroe* (Macmillan, 1985), however, Marilyn "couldn't bear the slightest hint of anything homosexual." Summers contends that Marilyn's psychiatrist, Dr. Ralph Greenson, once wrote that "She [MM] had an outright phobia of homosexuality, and yet unwillingly fell into situations which had homosexual coloring."

But Fred Lawrence Guiles insists otherwise. Said Guiles in *Legend: The Life and Death of Marilyn Monroe* (Stein and Day, 1984):

> Marilyn was never to feel any shame over her warm affection for some women; she always felt especially close to gays of either sex, and they to her. One's sexuality was God-given, she felt; she expressed this to many people at numerous times in her life. Sex was one of the few pure things in life.

**HONEYMOONS**

**With Jim Dougherty**

No real honeymoon.

**With Joe DiMaggio**

MM and Joe spent two weeks alone together at a mountain retreat/lodge near Idyllwild, outside of Palm Springs. They played billiards and *did not* watch television.

MM and Joe took a second honeymoon a month after they were married. On this second trip, they went to Japan and visited Tokyo, Fuji, Osaka, and Yokohama.

**With Arthur Miller**

The Millers had no actual, immediate honeymoon. However, soon after their wedding, they flew to London for the production of *The Prince and the Showgirl.*

The Millers spent a delayed honeymoon in January 1957. They went to Moonpoint, a seaside villa on the island of Jamaica, where they stayed for 16 days beginning on January 3rd.

**J. EDGAR HOOVER**

Despite the fact that Hoover's only close friend in forty years was a *male* colleague, Hoover proudly displayed an original copy of Marilyn Monroe's nude calendar in his home.

**BOB HOPE**

Born Leslie Townes Hope (aka Leslie Towers Hope) on May 29, 1903, Bob Hope is the American comedian known for his string of forties feature comedies, his plethora of television appearances, and his charitable performance shows for the military troops abroad. In 1955, Hope tried, unsuccessfully, to lure Marilyn into performing for the troops in Alaska. He called the Greenes' home in Connecticut, but was falsely told that they didn't know where she was. Said Amy Greene: "Tell me Mr. Hope, is Miss Monroe lost?"

### HEDDA HOPPER

> Blowtorch Blondes are Hollywood's specialty, and Marilyn Monroe who has zoomed to stardom after a three-year stretch as a cheesecake queen is easily the most delectable dish of the day. . . . She is fast supplanting Sam Goldwyn as a source of anecdotes and every producer at Twentieth is bidding for her as box office insurance."
>
> Hedda Hopper, May 4, 1952

> Can Marilyn ever be happy?
>
> Hedda Hopper, July 16, 1961

> In a way we are all guilty. We built her to the skies. We loved her, but left her lonely and afraid when she needed us most.
>
> Hedda Hopper, on MM's death

Born Elda Furry, Hedda Hopper (1890–1966) was an actress who became a powerful Hollywood columnist. Although she was relatively supportive of MM in the early 1950s, Hopper seemed to turn against Marilyn after the release of *There's No Business Like Show Business* (1954). From that point on, MM seemed to find greater favor with Hopper's rival, Louella Parsons.

Nonetheless, it was Hopper's July 19, 1946, column that first attracted Hollywood attention to Norma Jeane Dougherty, the model. The column suggested that Howard Hughes, who had already discovered Jane Russell, wanted to sign Norma Jeane to a film contract.

### ARTHUR HORNBLOW, JR.

Born on March 15, 1893, Hornblow was a writer, attorney, and a Broadway producer before he moved to Hollywood and became a movie producer. Once married to actress Myrna Loy, he produced *The Asphalt Jungle* (1950), in which MM had a part.

### HOSPITALS WHERE MM WAS TREATED

| Hospital | Reason | Date |
|---|---|---|
| 1. Los Angeles General<br>Los Angeles, California | Birth | June 1926 |
| 2. Las Vegas General<br>Las Vegas, Nevada | Trench Mouth | May 1946 |
| 3. Cedars of Lebanon<br>Los Angeles, California | Appendectomy | April 1952 |
| | Bronchitis | April 1953 |
| | Gynecological Surgery | Nov. 1954 |
| | Bronchitis | April 1956 |
| 4. St. Vincent<br>Los Angeles, California | Bronchitis and a Viral Infection | April 1956 |
| 5. Doctors<br>New York, New York | Miscarriage | Aug. 1957 |
| 6. Polyclinic<br>New York, New York | Miscarriage | Dec. 1958 |

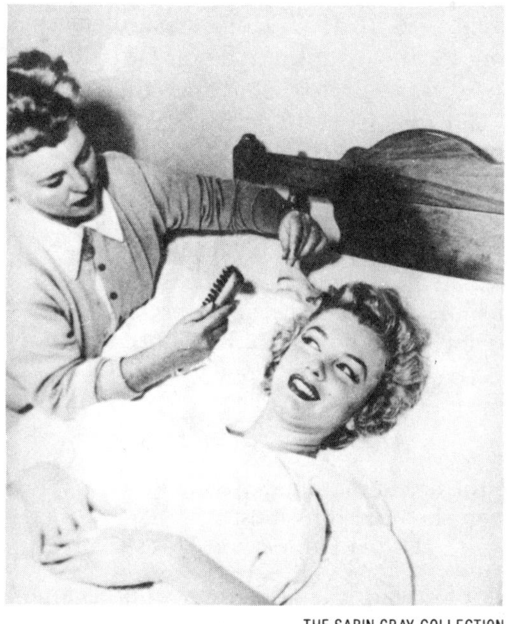

THE SABIN GRAY COLLECTION

In hospital, circa 1952.

| | | | |
|---|---|---|---|
| 7. | Lenox Hill<br>New York, New York | Gynecological Surgery | June 1959 |
| 8. | Westside<br>Los Angeles, California | Emotional Breakdown | Aug. 1960 |
| 9. | Payne Whitney Psychiatric Clinic<br>New York, New York | Mental Health | Feb. 1961 |
| 10. | Columbia Presbyterian<br>New York, New York | Physical and Emotional Exhaustion | Feb.-Mar. 1961 |
| 11. | Cedars of Lebanon<br>Los Angeles, California | Gynecological Surgery | May 1961 |
| 12. | Polyclinic Hospital | Gallbladder | June 1961 |
| 13. | Cedars of Lebanon<br>Los Angeles, California | Alleged Abortion | July 1962 |

**HOT SPRINGS HOTEL**
Hotel, located at 13th and Spring streets in Paso Robles, California, where MM and Joe ate their wedding dinner on January 14, 1954. The hotel was destroyed in a fire in the early 1960s.

**HOTEL DEL CORONADO**
MM stayed at this California hotel (address: 1500 Orange Avenue, Coronado) during the 1958 location shooting of *Some Like It Hot.* While there, she resided in the hotel's "Vista Mar" cottage.

**HOTEL EL RANCHO**
Joe DiMaggio and MM had planned to get married on January 4, 1954, at the Hotel El Rancho in Las Vegas, Nevada. However, for reasons unknown, they canceled their plans at the last minute and waited another ten days before getting married.

## HOTELS WHERE MM STAYED

☆ Banff Springs Hotel, Banff, Canada
☆ Bel Air Hotel, Beverly Hills
☆ Beverly Carlton Hotel, Beverly Hills
☆ Beverly Hills Hotel, Beverly Hills
☆ Cal-Neva Lodge, Lake Tahoe
☆ Chateau Marmont, West Hollywood
☆ Clifton Motel, Paso Robles, California
☆ Continental Hilton Hotel, Mexico City
☆ Country Inn Restaurant, Virginia City, Nevada
☆ Drake Hotel, New York City
☆ Fontainbleau Hotel, Miami
☆ Furnace Creek Inn, Death Valley
☆ Gladstone Hotel, New York City
☆ General Brock Hotel, Niagara Falls
☆ Hampshire House, New York City
☆ Holiday Inn Motel, Reno
☆ Hollywood Roosevelt Hotel, Hollywood
☆ Imperial Hotel, Tokyo
☆ LaFonda Motor Lodge, Van Nuys
☆ Mapes Hotel, Reno
☆ Rosarita Beach Hotel, Baja, Mexico
☆ Sahara Motor Hotel, Phoenix
☆ St. Regis Hotel, New York City
☆ Sherry Netherland Hotel, New York City
☆ Waldorf-Astoria Hotel, New York City

**MM Trivia Quiz #18**
What MM movie is set entirely in a hotel? (Answer on page 577.)

## THE HOUSE UN-AMERICAN ACTIVITIES SUB-COMMITTEE

By the mid-1950s, The House Un-American Activities Sub-Committee had destroyed many Hollywood careers. In 1956, the committee went after Arthur Miller. It has been speculated by many that the committee didn't actually want Miller; it wanted Marilyn—and all of the headlines that she brought along with her.

Miller was subpoenaed. He was asked why he had applied for a passport to go to England. Miller, who had previously been secretive about his marital plans, broke the news, "I will be there to be with the woman who will then be my wife."

When Miller was asked to name names, he refused. He was found in contempt of Congress. During this period, MM remained fiercely loyal to her husband-to-be. Said MM, years later:

> "When Mr. Miller was on trial for contempt of Congress, a certain corporation executive [Spyros Skouras] said either he [Miller] named

names and I got him to name names or I was finished. I said, 'I'm proud of my husband's position and I stand behind him all the way,' and the court did too [Miller was acquitted]. 'Finished,' they said. 'You'll never be heard of.' "

**HOUSEKEEPERS**

☆ May Reis managed Marilyn's East 57th Street apartment in New York while the actual cleaning was done by a girl named Cora.

☆ Mrs. Eunice Murray managed Marilyn's 1962 Brentwood household.

**GRACE HOUSTON**

Miss Houston designed the gowns for *Love Happy* (1950).

***HOW TO BE VERY, VERY POPULAR***

> Marilyn Monroe has been tentatively set to star in *How to Be Very, Very Popular* an original [screenplay] by Nunnally Johnson who will produce and direct the film which rolls at 20th Fox in January.
>
> Item that appeared in Los Angeles papers, 1954

Nunnally Johnson, who had penned the successful *How to Marry a Millionaire* screenplay in 1953, wrote an original screenplay expressly for Marilyn Monroe. Imagine how insulted he must have been when MM walked out on Fox at the end of 1954 and refused to do *How to Be Very, Very Popular* in 1955. Marilyn did not show up on the lot for the January 15, 1955, shooting. In retaliation, Fox suspended MM and replaced her with Sheree North (again).

Fox pulled out all the stops on this one. Not only did it want to prove to the public that it could get along well without Marilyn Monroe, it wanted to prove it to Marilyn Monroe and, to itself! To add to the hyped charms of Sheree North, Fox reenlisted the services of its former Queen, Betty Grable. It also spiked the case with Charles Coburn and Tommy Noonan—both of whom had served MM well just two years before in *Gentlemen Prefer Blondes*. Then Fox hired Milton Krasner, one of Marilyn's favorite cinematographers, to photograph the film. Fox also undoubtedly wielded its mighty power with the press to assure the film good publicity and the best reviews it could muster.

Nonetheless, when *How to be Very, Very Popular* opened at the end of July 1955, the reviews were mixed to poor, and the box office fared no better. For everyone involved with the production, *How to Be Very, Very Popular* should have been retitled *How to Be Very, Very Foolish.* One part Sheree North, one part Betty Grable, one part Nunnally Johnson does *not,* and never could, add up to Marilyn Monroe. According to the critics,

> The much heralded debut of Sheree North may only bring mild response. But then the part she plays is necessarily colorless. . . .
>
> *Los Angeles Times,* 1955

> Miss North wisely submitted this performance to the editors of the *Harvard Lampoon,* asking to be nominated the worst actress of the year. She may have been a little hasty, however, for Betty Grable, also in the picture, manages to outdo Miss North in the same category. . . .
>
> *Saturday Review,* 1955

***HOW TO MARRY A MILLIONAIRE*** ★★★

1953 96 minutes Technicolor
20th Century-Fox
Directed by: Jean Negulesco
Produced by: Nunnally Johnson
Screenplay by: Nunnally Johnson, based on plays by Zoe Akins, Dale Eunson, and Katherine Albert, and a book by Doris Lilly
Photographed by: Joe MacDonald
Cast: Marilyn Monroe, Betty Grable, Lauren Bacall, David Wayne, William Powell, Fred Clark, Rory Calhoun, Cameron Mitchell

THE AUTHOR'S COLLECTION

The second film (*The Robe* was first) and the first comedy released in CinemaScope featured an amiable plot about three women who rent an expensive New York apartment and scheme to trap themselves a trio of millionaires.

Today the film remains enjoyable, though very much dated and slightly offensive—due mainly to the equal rights movement. But, when initially released in November 1953, *How to Marry a Millionaire* did much to cement Marilyn's newfound stardom in Hollywood. It immediately followed the considerable success of *Gentlemen Prefer Blondes* and had most of the critics relenting that MM had some talent as a comedienne. Even more interestingly, the film paired, side by side, Marilyn Monroe and Betty Grable. And anyone who claimed *not* to have compared the two famous Fox blondes probably worked in some publicity department somewhere.

This film was a test of sorts for Monroe. It was also a test for Grable. But just as there was no "backstage" feud, there was no on-screen competition, either. Either Betty Grable handed the film to MM or Marilyn simply walked off with it—or both. During the production, Betty Grable tore up her Fox contract and subsequently was stripped of her top billing—which Marilyn, one presumes, accepted graciously.

Interestingly, MM initially objected to playing the part of Pola because she didn't want to wear glasses in the film. Instead, Marilyn opted for Betty Grable's role of Loco. MM felt that Fox was favoring Grable by giving her the better part. Eventually, though, director Jean Negulesco convinced MM that the part of Pola was a better one for her. Today, after reviewing the film, it is difficult to imagine MM in the Grable role and vice versa.

**MM Trivia Quiz #19**
What was MM's favorite proverb in *How to Marry a Millionaire*? (Answer on page 577.)

**CHESTER HOWELL**
Chester Howell was a friend of the Dougherty family who lent his Westwood home for the 1942 wedding of Norma Jeane and Jim. The Howell home was located at 432 South Bentley Avenue.

**EDWIN P. HOYT**
Hoyt wrote the 1965 book about MM, *Marilyn, the Tragic Venus* (Chilton).

**RENE HUBERT**
Hubert designed the costumes for *A Ticket to Tomahawk* (1950).

**JAMES A. HUDSON**
Hudson wrote the 1968 book about MM, *The Mysterious Death of Marilyn Monroe* (Volitant). Before the Monroe book, Hudson was a journalist for twenty years and had penned two books: *Svetlana Alliluyeva, Flight to Freedom* and *Unsafe at Any Altitude.*

**ROCK HUDSON**
Born Roy Fitzgerald (1925–1985), Rock Hudson epitomized the ideal American male during the 1950s and 1960s. In 1955, when *Bus Stop* was being cast, both Josh Logan and Marilyn Monroe expressed an interest in hiring Hudson for the male lead. Thus Milton Greene began negotiations with Hudson's agent, Henry Willson. However, by the time Greene came to terms with Hudson and Willson, Marilyn's insecurities had begun to take over. She worried that Rock might overshadow her (presumably in the looks department). Consequently, by the time Marilyn agreed to sign Hudson, he had already backed out. Either he had already committed to another project or he was simply upset over Marilyn's indecision. At any rate, Hudson soon scored a personal triumph in *Giant* which was released in 1956. It was probably the greatest film success of Rock Hudson's career and earned him an Oscar nomination.

THE ALAN FRANCE COLLECTION

With Rock Hudson, Golden Globe Awards, 1961.

Then, in 1960, MM and Jerry Wald tried to obtain Hudson from Universal for *Let's Make Love*. Once again, MM was not successful. She seemed destined *not* to make a movie with Rock Hudson. However, if Hudson held any grudges against MM, he didn't show it when he hosted 20th Century-Fox's 1963 posthumous tribute to MM, titled *Marilyn*. On October 2, 1985, Rock Hudson died, tragically, from AIDS. In death, he is on his way to attaining legendary status.

**POTTER HUETH (also spelled *Heweth*)**

Potter Hueth was David Conover's photographer friend, whom Norma Jeane agreed to pose for. Hueth shot MM with a dalmation, in a sweater and a plaid skirt, in a tight sweater and a pair of slacks, and on a bale of hay. Hueth was so impressed by NJ's photographs that he took them to the Blue Book Model Agency, which subsequently launched Norma Jeane Dougherty's modeling career.

**HOWARD HUGHES**

As a publicity ploy, Norma Jeane's modeling agent, Emmeline Snively, sent out a press release to Hedda Hopper. The item subsequently appeared in Hopper's column on July 29, 1946. Over the years, there have been two variations of the item. Nonetheless, they both say essentially the same thing:

> Howard Hughes is on the mend. Picking up a magazine, he was attracted by the cover girl and promptly instructed an aide to sign her for pictures. She is Norma Jean Dougherty.

> Howard Hughes must be on the road to recovery. He turned over in his iron lung and wanted to know more about Jean Norman, this month's covergirl on *Laff* magazine.

According to Fred Lawrence Guiles, during the production of *Clash by Night* (1952), RKO owner Hughes sent word to Marilyn that he wanted to see her. Once airborne, Hughes proceeded to kiss Marilyn. Hughes's wife, Terry Moore, later verified that HH did give MM a jeweled $500 pin. And, reportedly, Marilyn once told her coach, Natasha Lytess, that she and Hughes had a brief affair.

**ROGER HUNT**

Roger Hunt served as Marilyn's bodyguard during her stay in England for the 1956 shooting of *The Prince and the Showgirl*. Hunt had been a former superintendent of Scotland Yard.

**KEN HUNTER**

In another puzzle surrounding the circumstances of MM's death, some sources contend that ambulance attendant Ken Hunter was dispatched to MM's Brentwood home at 2:00 A.M. on August 5, 1962. Hunter reportedly placed Marilyn on a stretcher and drove her to Santa Monica Hospital—*alive but unconscious*. According to the official police report, Marilyn's dead body was found shortly after 3:00 A.M. at her Brentwood home—and no ambulance was required.

### HUSBANDS

1. Jim Dougherty: June 1942–September 1946
2. Bob Slatzer*: October 1952–a few days later
3. Joe DiMaggio: January 1954–October 1954
4. Arthur Miller: June 1956–January 1961

---

*Marilyn's alleged marriage to Bob Slatzer is being included here for the record. However, it should be noted that the Mexican marriage has never been documented by a marriage certificate, nor did MM and Slatzer ever really live together as man and wife.

### *HUSTLER* MAGAZINE

In its May 1986 issue, *Hustler* featured what was called an "eyewitness account" of the murder of Marilyn Monroe. The article was written by the supposed witness, James E. Hall.

### JOHN HUSTON

> "I was far more taken with her in the flesh than on the screen when we first worked together. I had no idea that she would go so far so fast."
>
> John Huston on MM

> "Mr. Huston was an exciting looking man. He was tall, long-faced, and his hair was mussed. He interrupted everybody with outbursts of laughter as if he were drunk. But he wasn't drunk. He was just happy for some mysterious reason, and he was also a genius—the first I had ever met."
>
> MM on John Huston

> "Mr. Huston . . . was interested in the acting I did. He not only watched it, he was part of it. And even though my part was a minor one, I felt as if I were the most important performer in the picture—when I was before the camera. This was because everything I did was important to the director, just as important as everything the stars of the picture did."
>
> MM on Huston and *The Asphalt Jungle*

> "Nobody would have heard of me if it hadn't been for John Huston. [He told me] If you're *not* nervous, you might as well give up. John has meant a great deal in my life. It's sort of a coincidence to be with him ten years later."
>
> MM on Huston and *The Misfits*

> "The picture? The hell with the picture! The girl's whole career was at stake!"
>
> John Huston on the making of *The Misfits*

> "Beauty was part of her fascination. It contributed largely to it because it was unique. But as time went on, her beauty would have coarsened, and that fragile, tremulous, lovely thing that we all witnessed would have been gone and then she would have lost her appeal, because her appeal was largely physical."
>
> John Huston on MM

When John Huston had cast Marilyn Monroe in the 1950 film *The Asphalt Jungle,* he had already seen Marilyn at Columbia a few years before. In fact, at that time Huston wanted to screen test MM for a role in *We Were Strangers*. However, Sam Spiegel (or was it Harry Cohn?) refused to test MM, claiming that it would cost too much.

At any rate, Huston went on to direct Marilyn in her first important picture, *The Asphalt Jungle*. Interestingly, he also directed her in her last completed picture, *The Misfits*, ten years later. And, reportedly, Huston considered casting Marilyn in his 1963 Montgomery Clift film, *Freud*.

John Huston was generally fond of Marilyn, and, following her death, he narrated the 1966 documentary *The Legend of Marilyn Monroe*.

Born in 1906, Huston's non-MM films include such American classics as *The Maltese Falcon* (1941), *The Treasure of the Sierra Madre* (1947), *The African Queen* (1952), and *Prizzi's Honor* (1985). Huston, who died in 1987, also had success as a screenwriter and actor.

Once, during a break from the shooting of *The Misfits*, Marilyn and Huston were entertaining themselves at the crap table . . .

MM: What should I ask the dice for, John?
JH: Don't think, honey. Just throw. That's the story of your life. Don't think, do it.

**TOM HUTCHINSON**
Hutchinson was a film critic and an editor of several books on the cinema. Among his works is *The Screen Greats: Marilyn Monroe* (1982).

**JOE HYAMS**
In 1962, movie reporter Joe Hyams wrote a rather nasty article about MM for *Show Business Illustrated* magazine. The article was titled "Marilyn Monroe: Star at a Turning Point." In the article, Hyams contended that, at 20th Century-Fox,

> Marilyn Monroe used to receive 8,000 letters a week and needed bushel baskets to accommodate the overflow. There are no baskets for Marilyn today. The 50 letters she averages each week barely fill one slot.

True or not, was this fair "reporting" considering it was a well-known fact that MM had recently suffered an emotional breakdown? And what Hyams failed to mention was that, in a six-year period, Marilyn had (voluntarily) made only one film for 20th Century-Fox, which would account for her slowdown of mail at the Fox lot. Nor did he mention that MM was still basking in the biggest box office success of her career, *Some Like It Hot* (1959), which was *not* made for 20th Century-Fox.

Nonetheless, it was Joe Hyams whom photographer Lawrence Schiller called on to break the news of MM's *Something's Got to Give* (1962) nude photos a short time later.

**JOHNNY HYDE**

"You're going to be a great movie star."

Johnny Hyde to Marilyn Monroe

> "Johnny was more than twice my age, a gentle, kind, brilliant man, and I had never known anyone like him. He had great charm and warmth. It was Johnny who inspired me to read good books and enjoy good music."
>
> Marilyn Monroe, 1952

> "It's hard for a star to get an eating job, a star is only good as a star. You don't fit into anything less. Yes, it's there. I can feel it. I see a hundred actresses a week. They haven't got what you have. Do you know what I'm talking about?"
>
> Johnny Hyde to MM

> "Johnny Hyde gave me more than his kindness and love. He was the first man I had ever known who understood me. Most men (and women) thought I was scheming and two-faced. No matter how truthfully I spoke to them or how honestly I behaved, they always believed I was trying to fool them."
>
> MM on Johnny Hyde

The man most credited as having discovered Marilyn Monroe. Marilyn herself had always acknowledged Johnny Hyde. If there had been no Johnny Hyde, one can assuredly contend that there never would have been a Marilyn Monroe.

Hyde was born Johnny Haidabura, the son of a Russian acrobat. By the time he met Marilyn Monroe at the Racquet Club in Palm Springs in 1949, the fifty-three-year-old Hyde had a family of four sons and a wife of long standing, Mozelle Cravens Hyde. He had also established himself as one of the most powerful agents in Hollywood. Among his clients Hyde had counted Rita Hayworth, Betty Hutton, Bob Hope, Esther Williams, and Lana Turner. By the time he met Marilyn, he was vice president of the William Morris Agency, the most powerful such agency in all of Hollywood. He had also developed a "bad" heart. Oh, and one more thing: he had recently seen an advance screening of a Marx Brothers picture, *Love Happy*.

When she met Johnny Hyde, Marilyn Monroe was twenty-two, in budding good health, hungry, and, without a studio. She was also still in love with Fred Karger.

It's no secret that Marilyn Monroe became Johnny Hyde's girl. But to think of the relationship in those terms is to slight and demean it. Johnny Hyde fell wildly, completely in love with Marilyn. He became her agent/manager/advisor/confidant/teacher/mentor/lover/friend and general-purpose companion. Hyde pleaded, repeatedly, for Marilyn to marry him. She declined. She loved him, but she was not "in love" with him. Hyde left his wife, and set up a home on North Palm Drive in Beverly Hills. Marilyn moved in with him, but she continued to resist marriage. Hyde told her that she would inherit his fortune if she married him. Even Joe Schenck reportedly tried talking MM into marrying Hyde. But Marilyn persisted. . . .

As did Johnny Hyde. Hyde had to almost literally shove Marilyn Monroe's footage and photos down the husky-voiced throats of every studio executive in Hollywood. And if they did consider Marilyn, they later rejected her as not having "star quality." Besides, she was, in their eyes, just another blonde, sleeping with just another (powerful) agent.

Finally, in tandem with Metro's Lucille Ryman, Hyde got a break. He got MM in to read for John Huston for a part in *The Asphalt Jungle* (1950). The film became a breakthrough for Marilyn, and things got a little easier for Johnny Hyde. Following *Jungle*, Hyde obtained the heavyweight Joe Mankiewicz picture, *All About Eve* (1950), as MM's follow-up. From the success of these two major films Hyde was able to negotiate a new studio contract for Marilyn at 20th Century-Fox. Thus, though he never lived to enjoy the realization of his prophecy, Johnny Hyde *did* live long enough to secure the future of the woman he loved.

Johnny Hyde died on December 18, 1950. His last known words were about Marilyn Monroe, although the specific words are not known.

**MOZELLE HYDE**

"It's happened, and I can't do anything about it."

Johnny Hyde to his wife, Mozelle

After hearing those words, Mozelle Hyde filed for divorce from her longtime husband. As reported by Fred Lawrence Guiles, Mozelle was later to say,

> "I tried to take it for a long time, but in the end, it was impossible. I'm a tolerant person, but there is always a limit. I remember once Jimmy [her son] was down in the cellar, looking over some old things of his father's and he found Marilyn's nude calendar. He brought it upstairs, but I was so annoyed over that whole business, I made him get rid of it."

# I

## "I LOVE LUCY"

Lucille Ball did a take off on Marilyn Monroe on the November 8, 1954 episode of "I Love Lucy." The segment was entitled "Ricky's Movie Offer."

## I. MAGNIN

Beverly Hills clothing store where starlet Marilyn Monroe opened up one of her first charge accounts.

## ILLNESSES

> "The executives can get colds and stay home forever and phone it in; but, how dare you, the actor, get a cold or virus. . . . I wish they had to act in a comedy with a temperature and a virus infection."
>
> MM to Richard Meryman,
> *LIFE*, 8/3/62

> "Sleep was her demon."
>
> Arthur Miller on MM

1. Whooping Cough: As a child, while still living with the Bolenders, Norma Jeane contracted whooping cough.
2. Rickets: As a child, MM suffered from rickets.
3. Trench mouth: While in Las Vegas, awaiting a divorce from Jim Dougherty, MM contracted trench mouth.
4. Ménierè's syndrome: During 1949, MM developed Ménierè's syndrome, an ailment that caused dizziness and partial loss of hearing in her right ear. She reportedly suffered from this throughout the rest of her life.
5. Endometriosis: During the late forties, MM suffered from painful, abnormal tissue buildup in her uterus, which is progressive, worsening with time.
6. Cold: while filming *A Ticket to Tomahawk* (1950), MM developed a cold.
7. Insomnia: MM suffered from insomnia throughout her adult life.
8. Appendectomy: In April 1952, MM had her appendix removed.
9. The flu: while shooting *Gentlemen Prefer Blondes* in Feburary 1953.
10. Bronchitis: In April 1953, MM suffered from bronchitis.
11. Bronchial pneumonia: Following her trip to Korea (2/54), MM developed bronchial pneumonia.
12. Laryngitis: Following her performance in *Anna Christie* (2/56) at the Actors Studio, MM developed laryngitis.
13. Viral infection and bronchitis: While filming *Bus Stop* (4/56), MM developed a viral infection and bronchitis.
14. Acute exhaustion: During the filming of *The Misfits* (8/60), MM collapsed from acute exhaustion.
15. Exhaustion: Following MM's divorce from Miller (2/61), she again collapsed from exhaustion.
16. Viral infection: In April 1962, MM developed a viral infection.

**MM Trivia Quiz #20**
In what film did MM feign laryngitis? (Answer on page 577.)

**THE IMPERIAL HOTEL**
During their February 1954 visit to Tokyo, Joe and Marilyn DiMaggio stayed at the Imperial Hotel (address: 1-1, Shinkawa 1-Chome, Chuo-Ku).

**"IN SEARCH OF: THE DEATH OF MARILYN MONROE"**
Alan Landsburg's nationally syndicated TV series, "In Search of," featured a special investigatory documentary of MM's death that was written by Abraham Lewenstein, Annette Marie Bettin, and John D. Ackelson. The program aired in Los Angeles on November 18, 1980.

**WILLIAM INGE**
Noted playwright (1913-1973) whose works include *Come Back Little Sheba* (1952), *Picnic* (1956), *The Dark at the Top of the Stairs* (1960), *The Stripper* (1963). (Note: the years given represent the release of the *film* versions of Inge's plays.)

In 1956, Marilyn starred in the film version of Inge's *Bus Stop*.

**MARTY INGELS**
Producer who secured the rights to a clip of MM from *The Misfits* (1961), which was subsequently used in a Japanese Levis commercial.

**ANTHONY J. INGRASIA**
Ingrasia wrote and directed the 1974 stage play about Marilyn Monroe entitled Fame. The play opened to poor reviews at the John Golden Theatre in New York City.

***INSIGNIFICANCE***
Fascinating, original, Nicolas Roeg semifantasy, *Insignificance* is set on an evening in the 1950s, with a cast of characters including Senator Joe McCarthy, Albert Einstein, Joe DiMaggio, and Marilyn Monroe.

Ironically, *Insignificance,* released in 1985, emerges as one of the finest film evocations of Marilyn Monroe—ironic because it really isn't *about* her. Certainly, it includes one of the finest portrayals of MM—with Theresa Russell giving an outstanding performance. Equally fine are Tony Curtis (McCarthy), Michael Emil (Einstein), and Gary Busey (DiMaggio).

The British stage play on which the movie was based, was written by Terry Johnson. It opened at London's Royal Court Theatre on July 8, 1982. The Marilyn Monroe-based character was portrayed by actress Judy Davis.

***IRMA LA DOUCE***
Despite once claiming that he would never work with Marilyn Monroe again, director Billy Wilder reportedly offered MM the title role in *Irma La Douce.* The movie was eventually made with Shirley MacLaine as Irma and was released in 1963. MacLaine was nominated for a "Best Actress" Oscar for her performance.

**IRVING TRUST BANK**
Marilyn's New York bank in 1961. At that time, Marilyn was overdrawn on her account by $5,000. The amount was covered by Joe DiMaggio, who later recouped the sum from the Marilyn Monroe estate.

**PHIL IRWIN**
Private detective who was involved in "The Wrong Door Raid" fiasco in 1954.

**ARATA ISOZAKI**
Isozaki is the talented architect of the Museum of Contemporary Art building in Los Angeles. In the interior of the building are unusually curved chairs, which Isozaki created as a homage to Marilyn Monroe.

**THE ITALIAN CULTURAL INSTITUTE**
Where Marilyn received Italy's David Di Donatello Award as the "Best Actress in a Foreign Film" in 1959. The award was given in recognition of MM's performance in *The Prince and the Showgirl* (1957). The Institute is located at 686 Park Avenue in New York City.

# J

### "THE JACK BENNY SHOW"

Marilyn Monroe made her national television debut on this CBS series. Marilyn appeared on the show on September 13, 1953. The title of her segment was "The Honolulu Trip."

MM: In the picture, all I wanted was money and diamonds. But now, for the first time, I realize that all I really want is you.

JB: Marilyn . . .

Announcer: Dream on, Mr. Benny, dream on.

JB: Marilyn, Marilyn—I'm mad about you.

MM: I'm mad about you, too, Jack. Jack, Jack—will you do something wonderful for me? It would make me very happy.

JB: Well, of course, Marilyn. I'd do anything—anything—for you. What is it?

MM: Well, in my next picture, there's going to be so many love scenes, I want *you* for my leading man!

JB: Oh, Marilyn, I'd, I'd love to be your leading man!

MM: Good! Now, if we can only get permission from Darryl Zanuck.

JB: Why? Who did Mr. Zanuck have in mind?

MM: Himself.

JB: Gee, Marilyn. I, I just can't get over—just the both of us, here, all alone on the Loreline.

MM: Yes, Jack. I never dreamed it could happen to I.

JB: Neither did me.

MM: (sighs)

JB: Marilyn, why, why are you sighing?

MM: I was just thinking, Jack, how generous you are. Just so we can be alone on this trip, you chartered the Loreline for 600,000 dollars!

JB: I did?

Announcer: If that doesn't wake him up, nothing will!

JB: Marilyn. Marilyn—I know this is sudden, but—will you, will you marry me?

MM: Marry? But, look at the difference in our ages!

JB: Well, there isn't much difference Marilyn—you're 25 and I'm 39.

MM: Yes, but what about 25 years from now? When I'm 50 and you're 39?

JB: Gee, I never thought of that—

Announcer: I did!

JB: You shut up!

JB: Marilyn, Marilyn—will you, will you have dinner with me tonight?

MM: I'd love to Jack. Thanks ever so.
JB: At eight o'clock?
MM: All right, but I'd better be going now. (She sings "Bye Bye Baby"; she and Benny kiss.)
MM: My, that's strange.
JB: What's strange?
MM: I'm crazy about you. But that kiss didn't affect me at all!
JB: That's funny, I'm a wreck!
MM: See you later, Jack.
JB: Don't forget. Marilyn, don't forget dinner tonight.
MM. I won't.
JB: At eight o'clock.
MM: I'll remember.
JB: Marilyn—come back here a minute. Please come back. Marilyn—give me one more kiss before you go.

**ANNE JACKSON**
Actress and wife of actor Eli Wallach (*Misfits* costar). During Marilyn's Arthur Miller period, she was friendly with both of the Wallachs.

**HARRY JACKSON**
Cinematographer on the 1950 film *A Ticket to Tomahawk,* which featured MM in a small role.

**ARTHUR JACOBS**
Jacobs's New York publicity firm represented Marilyn from the mid-1950s until the time of her death. Just prior to MM's death, Jacobs was planning to coproduce Marilyn's next proposed feature film.

**JACK JACOBS**
Jack Jacobs was an employee of Malone Studio Service Cleaners and had been picking up Marilyn's laundry for years. Once, according to Eunice Murray, Jacobs found $60 in one of MM's housecoat pockets, which he returned within fifteen minutes.

**NATALIE JACOBS**
On the evening of August 4, 1962, Arthur and Natalie Jacobs attended a Henry Mancini concert at the Hollywood Bowl. According to Natalie, toward the end of the concert, her husband received a message that Marilyn was dead. According to Mrs. Jacobs, her husband received the fatal news *by 11:30 P.M.* According to the police report, Marilyn's body wasn't even found until *after 3:00 A.M., on August 5, 1962.* Said Mrs. Jacobs to Anthony Summers:

> "We got the news long before it broke, we left the concert at once and Arthur left me at our house. He went to Marilyn's house, and I don't think I saw him for two days. He had to fudge [to] the press."

**SAM JAFFE**
Sam Jaffe (1893–1984) was a character actor in many films from 1934 until 1980. In 1950, Jaffe costarred in *The Asphalt Jungle.*

**JAMAICA**

On January 3, 1957, Arthur and Marilyn Miller flew to Jamaica, for their delayed honeymoon. They stayed at Moon Point, a villa that was owned by Lady Pamela Bird. The Millers returned to New York City on January 19, 1957.

**JOYCE JAMESON**

Joyce Jameson built a career out of portraying Marilyn Monroe in various productions. Jameson's MM impersonations were seen in the *Billie Barnes Revue,* in Billy Wilder's *The Apartment* (1960), and in the stage play *Venus at Large* (1962).

**JANTZEN**

In 1947, Norma Jeane posed for the *Jantzen Wholesale Swimwear Catalogue.* The swimsuit NJ wore was called the "Double Dare."

PHOTO COURTESY OF JANTZEN, INC.

The Jantzen "Double Dare," 1947.

**JAPAN**

The DiMaggios' 1954 honeymoon trip to Japan was a long-planned promotional trip, funded by the newspaper *Yomiuri Shimbun* to launch the opening of the Japanese baseball season. The DiMaggios were accompanied on this trip by Joe's friend Frank "Lefty" O'Doul and his wife, Jean.

At Tokyo's Haneda International Airport, 10,000 screaming Oriental fans greeted the DiMaggios. They yelled out "Monchan!" and other Japanese endearments in honor of their favorite blonde goddess. Marilyn actually had to escape through the baggage hatch and hide out in the customs office.

While in Japan, the DiMaggios and the O'Douls visited Toyko, Fuji, Osaka, and Yokohama.

Over the years, Marilyn's extreme popularity in Japan has failed to wane. In 1980, a Japanese department store (Depaato) even featured a power-compressed Marilyn Monroe robot that sang, moved its lips, and strummed a guitar.

**JOSEPH JASGUR**

Jasgur is a photographer who had shot photos of Norma Jeane Dougherty while she was a model with the Blue Book Model Agency in the mid-1940s. According to Jasgur, Norma Jeane once asked him to marry her, an offer he claims to have declined. Also, according to Jasgur, once Marilyn had become famous, she acted as though she didn't know him. In the press, over the years, Jasgur has been less than kind to MM's memory. Nonetheless, he has continued to sell (and presumably profit from) his photographs of Norma Jeane.

**JAX**

> "She used to come in all the time just to say 'hi' to the sales girls, Yuki and Corby. She really liked them. This was before she was famous. She used to play basketball to lose weight. At that time she was going with one of the Schenck brothers, a big shot at one of the studios. She was the kind of kid you just wanted to help."
>
> Jack Hanson, the owner of JAX on early MM

Both before and after she became famous, JAX was one of Marilyn Monroe's favorite clothing stores. MM used to frequent JAX on Wilshire Boulevard in Beverly Hills, and the one on West 57th Street in New York. Today, JAX is located at 324 North Rodeo Drive in Beverly Hills.

**DOROTHY JEAKINS**

The costume designer on both *Niagara* (1953) and *Let's Make Love* (1960).

**JEAN-LOUIS**

Jean-Louis, born October 5, 1907, was the head costume designer at Columbia Pictures for seventeen years. During his reign there, he designed the fashions for such stars as Rita Hayworth, Kim Novak, Lana Turner, Marlene Dietrich, Grace Kelly, Katharine Hepburn, and, in one film (*Ladies of the Chorus*), Marilyn Monroe.

Jean-Louis later designed the costumes for *The Misfits* (1961). And shortly before her death, Marilyn purchased a white sequined evening gown from Jean-Louis at the cost of $1,600. In addition, during the months preceding her death, Marilyn worked closely with Jean-Louis on the costumes for *Something's Got to Give.* Reportedly, Marilyn telephoned Jean-Louis's shop on Friday, August 3, 1962, and made plans to meet with him on the upcoming Monday, August 6.

**NORMAN JEFFRIES II**

Jeffries was Mrs. Eunice Murray's son-in-law, who worked as Marilyn's handyman at her 1962 Brentwood home. Reportedly, Jeffries was paid the sum of $180 a week. Among Jeffries's tasks: he completely tore out the existing kitchen cabinets to make way for new ones, and, on the morning of August 5, 1962, he repaired the broken bedroom window in Marilyn's house *before the police arrived.*

**ELOIS JENSSEN**

The costume designer on *We're Not Married* (1952).

**ADELE JERGENS**

Born in 1922, Adele Jergens was the star of mostly grade-B pictures during the 1940s and 1950s. In 1948, Jergens toplined *Ladies of the Chorus,* which costarred MM.

**JEWELRY**

> "Flashy earrings, necklaces and bracelets detract from a lady's looks. And even if I have to wear that stuff, I don't have to own it. The studio loans it to me whenever they want to show me off."
>
> MM to Bob Slatzer

> "Marilyn never wore jewelry of any kind because she wanted nothing to detract from her. Frank Sinatra gave her a stunning pair of emerald earrings. She wore them once, then gave them away."
>
> George Masters

> "I wish I could wear rings, but I hate people to notice my hands. They're too fat. Elizabeth Taylor has fat hands. But, with those eyes, who's looking at her hands?"
>
> Marilyn Monroe

**MM Trivia Quiz #21**

What kind of jewelry was *not* acceptable to MM in *Gentlemen Prefer Blondes*? (Answer on page 577.)

**JIM DOWNEY'S**

Jim Downey's was a popular restaurant among the New York theatre elite in the mid-1950s. One of the prized features at this hang-out was a wall full of photographs of Broadway actors and actresses. To have one's photograph on the Jim Downey's wall was a coveted distinction, of sorts. Thus, during her "New York Period" Marilyn Monroe was reportedly determined to have her photo put on that wall. However, the criteria for that honor was that one had to have *appeared on the Broadway stage*. Thus, Marilyn Monroe appeared on stage, incognito, at the Martin Beck Theatre during the curtain calls of *The Teahouse of the August Moon*. For her efforts, Marilyn was rewarded with a photograph of herself on the Jim Downey's wall. Today, Jim Downey's has been revamped into The Barking Fish Cafe (address: 705 8th Avenue).

**JOBS**

- ☆ In 1944–45, Norma Jeane Dougherty worked at the Radio Plane Company. Marilyn once told columnist Earl Wilson that she started at Radio Plane as a typist. However, because she could only type 35 wpm, she was transferred to the assembly line, where she inspected parachutes. Bored as a parachute inspector, Norma Jeane was transferred to the "dope room," where she sprayed fuselages.
- ☆ According to Anthony Summers's *Goddess: The Secret Lives of Marilyn Monroe* (Macmillan, 1985), Marilyn worked during her struggling years (and between film roles) as a magician's assistant and as a trick golfer.
- ☆ According to Lena Pepitone, Marilyn's New York maid, MM once told her that, years before, Norma Jeane Dougherty collected pocket change by offering sexual favors.
- ☆ According to writer Richard Lamparski, MM was a stripper at the Mayan Theatre in Los Angeles during September 1948.

**MM Trivia Quiz #22**
What was the name of the cafe where MM worked in *Bus Stop*? (Answer on page 577.)

**JOE AND MARILYN: A MEMORY OF LOVE**
Writer: Roger Kahn
Publisher: William Morrow & Company
Year: 1986
269 pages, $16.95, HC (ISBN 0-688-02517-X)

A dual biography of Joe DiMaggio and Marilyn Monroe, with an emphasis on the former. *Joe and Marilyn: A Memory of Love* features the famous twosome's individual achievements, as well as the courtship, the failed marriage, and the eventual friendship. For the MM student and/or fan who is primarily intrigued in Marilyn's relationship with DiMaggio, this book should be of particular interest. It is certainly of far better quality than the 1977 book, *Marilyn & Joe DiMaggio* by Robin Moore and Gene Schoor.

**ELTON JOHN**
Born Reginald Kenneth Dwight on March 25, 1947, Elton John has had one of the most successful, profitable careers in the entire history of pop/rock music. On John's 1973 mega-selling album, *Goodbye Yellow Brick Road*, he paid tribute to Marilyn Monroe with a song entitled "Candle in the Wind":

> Goodbye Norma Jean
> Though I never knew you at all
> You had the grace to hold yourself
> while those around you crawled
> Goodbye Norma Jean

From the young man in the 22nd row
Who sees you as something more than sexual
More than just Marilyn Monroe.

---



**ERSKINE JOHNSON**

Hollywood correspondent who wrote an August 5, 1952, article titled "Marilyn Inherits Harlow's Mantle," which read:

> Hollywood took fourteen years, three-score screen tests and a couple of million dollars to find a successor to Jean Harlow, who melted movie celluloid from 1927 to 1938 . . .

Several months before that, shortly after the nude-calendar news was released, Johnson broke the following news story in the *Los Angeles Daily News*:

**MARILYN MONROE CONFESSES
MOTHER ALIVE, LIVING HERE
By Erskine Johnson**

Marilyn Monroe—Hollywood's confessin' glamour doll who made recent headlines with the admission that she was a nude calendar cutie—confessed again today.

Highly publicized by Hollywood press agents as an orphan waif who never knew her parents, Marilyn admitted that she's the daughter of a one-time RKO studio film cutter, Gladys Baker, and that "I am helping her and want to continue to help her when she needs me."

Recovering from an appendectomy in a Los Angeles hospital, Marilyn gave me an exclusive statement through the 20th Century-Fox studio following the appearances at the studio of five women claiming Marilyn as their "long-lost daughter."

Said Hollywood's new glamour queen:

"My close friends know that my mother is alive.

"Unbeknown to me as a child, my mother spent many years as an invalid in a state hospital.

"I was raised in a series of foster homes arranged by a guardian through the County of Los Angeles and I spent more than a year in the Los Angeles Orphans Home.

"I haven't known my mother intimately, but since I have become grown and able to help her I have contacted her.

"I am helping her and want to contine to help her when she needs me."

Hollywood friends of her mother supplied the rest of the story.

When Marilyn was a small child her father was killed in an automobile accident and her mother subsequently suffered a nervous breakdown. A friend of her mother was appointed her legal guardian.

Marilyn's mother recovered from her illness in 1945 and lived with her daughter for a short time in 1946. In the same year her mother remarried and became a widow for the second time last week when her husband died following a short illness.

The news that Marilyn's mother is alive and in Hollywood came as an eyebrow-lifting surprise because of extensive studio publicity that Marilyn had never known her mother or her father.

But the new star's confession that her twice-widowed mother is in Hollywood and that "I am helping her" came as a relief to the 20th Century-Fox studio legal department, which has been confronted with wild claims by women insisting that Marilyn is their "daughter."

## NUNNALLY JOHNSON

"Marilyn made me lose all sympathy for actresses. In most of her takes she was either fluffing lines or freezing. I don't think she could act her way out of a paper script. She's just an arrogant little tail switcher who's learned to throw sex in your face."

Nunnally Johnson on MM, following *How to Marry a Millionaire* (1953)

"She was either too fey for me to understand, or too stupid, and certainly too unprofessional for me."

Nunnally Johnson on MM

"[She was] ten feet under water . . . a wall of thick cotton . . . you stick a pin in her and eight days later it says 'ouch.' "

Nunnally Johnson on MM

If Nunnally Johnson disliked Marilyn Monroe so much, as the above statements imply, *why*, in 1955, did he *expressly* write the film *How to Be Very, Very Popular* for her? And *why*, as late as 1962, did he continue to work with MM? (Johnson was the coscreenwriter on *Something's Got to Give.*) Could it be that Nunnally Johnson was simply miffed that MM had turned her nose up at Johnson's *How to Be Very, Very Popular* project? It certainly couldn't have helped matters between MM and Johnson when, without Marilyn's presence, the film, which Johnson wrote, produced, *and* directed, bombed.

Born in 1897, Johnson's other, more respectable, non-MM films include *The Grapes of Wrath* (1940) and *The Three Faces of Eve* (1957). His other MM-related feature was *We're Not Married* (1952), which he wrote and produced.

## TERRY JOHNSON

Terry Johnson wrote the 1982 British stage play *Insignificance,* which featured a Marilyn Monroe-based character. Johnson also wrote the screenplay adaptation for the 1985 movie of the same name.

## CLIFF JONES

Cliff Jones wrote the stage musical *Hey, Marilyn!* which ran at the Citadel Theatre in Canada circa 1979–1980.

## HARMON JONES

Director whose first directorial job was *As Young as You Feel* (1951), which costarred rising starlet MM. Jones went on to direct a string of mostly mediocre productions.

**TED JORDAN**

Actor, once married to striptease artist Lily St. Cyr, who claimed to have had Marilyn's infamous red diary. However, when pressed, Jordan never produced *the* diary. He has also *claimed* to have once been Marilyn's lover (who hasn't?).

**CONNIE JORGENSEN**

Pan American stewardess who cared for Marilyn during MM's 1954 flight from Honolulu to San Francisco. At that time, MM was ill with bronchial pheumonia. Said Miss Jorgensen, "She's the greatest sport I ever saw."

***THE JOY OF MARILYN IN THE CAMERA EYE***

Author: Sam Shaw
Publisher: Exeter Books
Year: 1979 (Out of Print)

Black-and-white photo book, related and presented by photographer Sam Shaw, who was friendly with Marilyn during her New York period. The photos and accompanying text offer an intimate glimpse of Marilyn in her New York and Connecticut settings. Refreshing and worthwhile.

***JULIA S. DUMONT***

The freighter that took Jim Dougherty to Townsville, Australia, and, out of Norma Jeane/Marilyn Monroe's life.

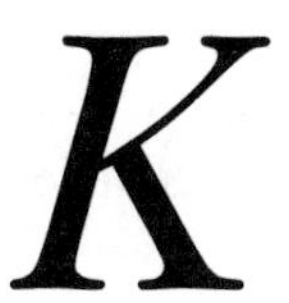

## DEMETRIE KABBAZ

Excellent painter who has devoted much of his work to the memory of Marilyn Monroe. Based in Hollywood, Kabbaz specializes in remarkably accurate, larger-than-life-size "cut-outs" of Marilyn. His collection also includes interpretations of Marlon Brando, James Dean, and others.

## PAULINE KAEL

Noted film critic who was never a big fan of Marilyn Monroe. However, Kael once relented that MM would have been "right" for the following films:

- ☆ *Bombshell* (a remake)
- ☆ *Bonnie and Clyde*
- ☆ *Born Yesterday* (a remake)
- ☆ *Breakfast at Tiffany's* (a remake)
- ☆ *Lord Love a Duck*
- ☆ *A Period of Adjustment*
- ☆ *Red Dust* (a remake)
- ☆ *Sweet Charity*

> Her mixture of wide-eyed wonder and cuddly drugged sexiness seemed to get to just about every male; she turned on even homosexual men.
>
> Pauline Kael on Marilyn Monroe

> Her face looked as if, when nobody was paying attention to her, it would go utterly slack—as if she died between wolf calls.
>
> Pauline Kael on Marilyn Monroe

> She would bat her Bambi eyelashes, lick her messy suggestive open mouth, wiggle that pert and tempting bottom, and use her hushed voice to caress us with dizzying innuendoes. Her extravagantly ripe body bulging and spilling out of her clothes, she threw herself at us with the off-color innocence of a baby whore.
>
> Pauline Kael on Marilyn Monroe

## IVAN KAHN

Reportedly, *before* she met with Ben Lyon at 20th Century-Fox in July 1946, Norma Jeane Dougherty first met with Ivan Kahn, from the Fox talent department, who referred her to Ben Lyon. Lyon, of course, subsequently gave Norma Jeane a screen test, a new name, and a studio contract.

## ROGER KAHN

Roger Kahn is the author of the 1986 dual biography, *Joe and Marilyn: A Memory of Love.* He is also the author of bestselling baseball books such as *The Boys of Summer.*

## GARSON KANIN

Writer/director, born in 1912, who wrote such films as *A Double Life* (1948),

*Adam's Rib* (1949), and *Pat and Mike* (1952). Kanin, formerly known as Gershon Labe, also directed *Funny Girl* on Broadway, won a Pulitzer Prize for *The Diary of Anne Frank*, and married actress Ruth Gordon.

In 1962, Kanin wrote and directed *Come on Strong* at the Morosco Theatre on Broadway. It was based, somewhat, on the life of Marilyn Monroe and proved to be unsuccessful with the critics. Kanin was more successful with his 1979 Hollywood novel, *Moviola*, which chronicled—among other things—Marilyn Monroe's rise to stardom. *Moviola* was later adapted into a series of made-for-television movies.

Like many writers, Garson Kanin has shown a particular interest in Marilyn Monroe. It is interesting to note, then, that as a Columbia starlet, MM reportedly tested for the lead in Kanin's *Born Yesterday* and was rejected.

**JUDY KANTOR**

One of the matrons of honor at the 1956 Jewish wedding between Arthur Miller and Marilyn Monroe.

**JONATHAN KAPLAN**

Jonathan Kaplan was the producer of the 1983 "Hollywood Close-Up" television special about MM entitled "Marilyn, In Search of a Dream."

**ANNE KARGER**

Marilyn Monroe did not marry Fred Karger, but she did establish an important, lifelong bond with Karger's mother, Mrs. Anne Karger.

"Nana" Karger took an immediate liking to Marilyn Monroe. It was 1948, and Marilyn was still a struggling starlet—without a family, without a foundation, without love, and without a good home-cooked meal in her belly. And, although she couldn't force her son to marry Marilyn, Mrs. Karger could (and did) see to it that MM had a home, an advisor, a friend, and a mother figure—if not a mother.

Marilyn responded in kind. When Ana Lower died in 1948, Anne Karger became Marilyn's most beloved female. And, throughout the stardom years, as Marilyn shed most of her old friends, she worked to retain her close relationship with the mother of her first love. Anne Karger became one of the longest personal associations of Marilyn Monroe's life.

**FRED KARGER**

> "A new life began for me. . . . I had always thought of myself as someone unloved. Now I know there had been something worse than that in my life. It had been my own unloving heart. . . . I even forgot Norma Jeane. A new me appeared in my skin—not an actress, not somebody looking for a world of bright colors. When he said 'I love you' to me, it was better than a thousand critics calling me a great star."
>
> Marilyn Monroe to Ben Hecht

When Marilyn Monroe was signed by Columbia Pictures in 1948, she was introduced to the studio's vocal coach, Fred Karger. Karger was talented, good-looking, and an attractive thirty-two. He was also a recently divorced father. Marilyn Monroe, at that point, was just another twenty-one-year-old struggling studio starlet—blonde, beautiful, obviously ambitious, and malleable.

Karger was assigned by the studio honchos to coach the new blonde. Marilyn entered Karger's office and made an attempt at singing "Love Me or Leave Me." Karger, as time would tell, decided to do both.

Over the years, Marilyn frequently referred to Fred Karger (as opposed to Jim Dougherty) as her first love. And it is easy to reason why she fell in love with him. It was Fred Karger who hand-placed her in the safe, pleasant, and inexpensive Hollywood Studio Club. It was Karger who arranged for Marilyn to have the protrusion of her two front teeth cosmetically corrected. It was Karger who introduced Marilyn to fine literature and classical music. It was Karger who took Marilyn to seaside suppers in Malibu, to nightclubs on the Sunset Strip, to the beach in Santa Monica, to the old mining towns in Nevada, and to the concerts at the Hollywood Bowl. And it was Fred Karger who took Marilyn into his mother's home. Moreover, it was Fred Karger who taught Marilyn how to sing—for her Columbia feature *Ladies of the Chorus* (1948).

Marilyn Monroe wanted to marry Fred Karger. However, he did not consider MM to be appropriate wife and/or mother material. He reportedly told MM, "You cry too easily. That's because your mind isn't developed. Compared to your figure, it's embryonic."

But Marilyn was smitten. When she read in Louella Parson's column that producer Lester Cowan planned on signing her to a personal contract, Marilyn went out and purchased a $500 gold watch for Karger—on credit. Two years later, long after the Karger relationship had been severed, MM was still making payments on that watch.

> "[There was] one cloud in my paradise. I know he liked me and was happy to be with me but his love didn't seem anything like mine. Most of his talk to me was a form of criticism. He criticized my mind. He kept pointing out how little I knew and how unaware of life I was. . . ."
>
> MM on Fred Karger

In 1952, Fred Karger married actress Jane Wyman, whom he later divorced and remarried and divorced (the old, typical Liz and Dick syndrome—*before* Liz and Dick). Karger died of leukemia on August 5, 1979—seventeen years *to the day* after Marilyn's death.

**MARY KARGER**
*See* Mary Karger Short.

**PHIL KARLSON**
Born Philip Karlstein in 1908, Karlson directed a slew of mostly Grade-B pictures, including *Ladies of the Chorus* (1948), which costarred Columbia starlet Marilyn Monroe.

**ELLIOTT KASTNER**
Elliott Kastner coproduced the British stage musical, *MARILYN!* which opened at the Adelphi Theatre in London on March 17, 1983.

**KATONAH, NEW YORK**

Location where the July 1, 1956, Jewish wedding ceremony between Arthur Miller and Marilyn Monroe took place.

**GINA KAUS**

Ms. Kaus coauthored a story on which *We're Not Married* (1952) was based.

**RUDI KAUTZSKY (*Also Spelled* Rudy Kadinsky, Rudy Karensky, and Rudy Kautzky)**

Marilyn's longtime friend and chauffeur, whose name no one knows how to spell.

**ELIA KAZAN**

Born Elia Kazanjoglous in 1909, Elia "Gadge" Kazan is one of the most prolific stage and screen directors of all time. Kazan's films include *A Streetcar Named Desire* (1951), *Viva Zapata* (1952), *East of Eden* (1955), *Splendor in the Grass* (1961), *Gentleman's Agreement* (1947), and *On the Waterfront* (1954), the last two of which won Oscars for him.

Elia Kazan met Marilyn Monroe in 1950. Allegedly, they had a brief affair. At that time, Kazan had been married to playwright Molly Thatcher for over eighteen years. He was also a good friend of Arthur Miller.

In 1952, Kazan testified before the House Un-American Activities Subcommittee and informed on his leftist acquaintances. As a result, he and Arthur Miller severed their friendship in 1953. Nonetheless, when MM moved to New York in 1955, Kazan was instrumental in her being introduced to Lee Strasberg. And, by 1964, the rift between Kazan and Miller had apparently mended, as Kazan directed Miller's play *After the Fall,* which, interestingly, starred Kazan's second wife, Barbara Loden, in the MM-based role of Maggie.

**NATALIE KELLEY (aka Natalie Kelley Grasko)**

Tom Kelley's former wife, who was present at the photo studio in 1949, when Marilyn Monroe made history by posing nude on a sheet of red velvet.

**TOM KELLEY**

Photographer who made history by shooting the Marilyn Monroe red velvet nudes in 1949. Kelley—who also used MM for beer ads and various other modeling assignments—paid her $50 for the nude series, which, of course, later spawned the million-dollar "Golden Dreams" calendar.

**DAVID KELLOGG**

David Kellogg was one of the executive producers of the "Hollywood Close-Up" television special about MM entitled "Marilyn, In Search of a Dream." The special aired on ABC on February 19, 1983.

**FRANK KELLY**

Frank Kelly was also one of the executive producers of the "Hollywood Close-Up" television special about MM entitled "Marilyn, In Search of a Dream."

**GENE KELLY**

Born Eugene Curran Kelly in 1912, Gene Kelly is the dancer/choreographer/director who starred in such films as *For Me and My Gal* (1942), *Cover Girl* (1944), *On the Town* (1949), *An American in Paris* (1951), and *Singin' in the Rain* (1952).

On August 5, 1962, Gene Kelly was scheduled to meet with Marilyn Monroe to discuss their upcoming film project, *What a Way to Go*. Previously, Kelly had guested in *Let's Make Love* (1960).

**GRACE KELLY**

Marilyn Monroe was the queen of Hollywood in the mid-1950s, and Grace Kelly (1928–1982) was, appropriately, the princess. Before retiring in 1956, Kelly had starred in such films as *High Noon* (1952), *Rear Window* (1954), *The Country Girl* (for which she won a 1954 Oscar), *To Catch a Thief* (1955), and *High Society* (1956).

Once, on a flight from New York to Los Angeles, the two royal blondes shared the same plane. Grace was seated in economy class, while MM slept in a compartment up front. They never met.

**KELTONWAY AVENUE**

According to Bob Slatzer, MM lived at 3539 Keltonway Avenue in West Los Angeles, for a brief period in 1950–51.

**JOHN F. KENNEDY**

"I think I make his back feel better."

Marilyn Monroe to (1) Earl Wilson; (2) Ralph Roberts

"I made it with the Prez."

Marilyn Monroe to David Conover

In May 1962, the world witnessed as a blonde, breathy, sequined, and champagned Marilyn Monroe sang a sexy-slurred rendering of "Happy Birthday" and "Thanks for the Memory" to President John F. Kennedy at Madison Square Garden.

What isn't generally known is that, as early as the early 1950s, Marilyn was allegedly having an affair with the then-Senator Kennedy—an affair that reportedly lasted through Kennedy's presidency. In October 1954, when JFK was hospitalized, a poster of Marilyn hung over his bed. The poster featured MM in blue shorts, standing with her legs spread apart—Kennedy reportedly hung the poster upside down so that Marilyn's legs stuck up in the air.

Today, over twenty years after his assassination, it has become generally accepted that John Kennedy did more than his share of womanizing—both before and during his marriage and presidency. Reportedly, Kennedy once told Clare Boothe Luce, "Dad told all the boys to get laid as often as possible."

Also, according to Anthony Summers's *Goddess: the Secret Lives of Marilyn Monroe* (Macmillan, 1985):

Nancy Dickerson, a reporter who dated Kennedy, has said, "You couldn't help but be swept over by him. But sex to Jack Kennedy was like another cup of coffee, or maybe dessert." For this Kennedy, evidently, sex was not to be confused with love.

"Happy Birthday, Mr. President," New York, 1962.

THE RAY VAN GOEYE COLLECTION

During the 1960 presidential campaign (which, incidentally, coincided with the breakup of MM's marriage to Arthur Miller), Marilyn allegedly continued her affair with JFK. At Kennedy's July 1960 Romanoff's bash, Marilyn was seen with the president-to-be. She was also seen coming and going—frequently—from Kennedy's penthouse suite at the Carlyle Hotel in New York. There have also been several reports that MM spent the weekend of March 24, 1962, at Bing Crosby's Palm Springs Home with John F. Kennedy. And, in her last years, Marilyn was a frequent visitor to Peter Lawford's Santa Monica beach house, which, in the early 1960s, served as the Los Angeles base for the Kennedy family.

The details surrounding Marilyn's "breakup" with JFK are even sketchier than the details of the affair itself. Reportedly, Robert Kennedy was administered to divert Marilyn's attention away from his brother—or, in other words, to get Marilyn off of the president's bad back. Allegedly, audio tapes were secretly made of MM and JFK in the act of sex—tapes that may or may not have been used to blackmail the Kennedy family. Other reports contend that, shortly before her death, Marilyn was pregnant with Kennedy's child. At any rate, it is presumed that Marilyn Monroe became too much of a risk to the Kennedy name and that she was thus phased out of the president's life.

However, since both Marilyn Monroe and John F. Kennedy are dead, it is impossible to know for a fact exactly what went on behind those closed Presidential doors, regardless of the immense speculation and the years of accumulated tabloid rumors. What *is* known is that on May 19, 1962, at Madison Square Garden, one public figure sang "Happy Birthday" to another public figure. It went something like this:

***Peter Lawford:*** Mr. President—the *late* Marilyn Monroe!

***Marilyn:*** Happy—birthday—to you,
Happy birthday to you,
Happy birthday, Mr. Pres-i-dent,
Happy birthday to you.

Following the applause, MM continued, to the tune of "Thanks for the Memory,"

***Marilyn:*** Thanks, Mr. President,
For all the things you've done,
The battles that you've won,
The way you deal with U.S. Steel,
And our problems by the ton,
We thank you—so much.

Everybody, Happy Birthday!

MM proceeded to lead the audience in a rousing version of "Happy Birthday," which was followed by:

***Announcer:*** Ladies and gentlemen, the president of the United States.
***John Kennedy:*** I can now retire from politics after having had "Happy Birthday" sung to me in such a sweet, wholesome way.

**ROBERT F. KENNEDY**

"Bobby Kennedy promised to marry me."

Marilyn Monroe to Bob Slatzer

"I do not think I have seen anyone so beautiful . . . my encounters, however, were only after breaking through the strong defenses established by Robert Kennedy who was dodging around her like a moth around the flame."

Adlai Stevenson on Marilyn Monroe,
at John Kennedy's 1962 birthday celebration

There has been a plethora of speculation about Marilyn Monroe's alleged affair with Robert Kennedy. The best documentation was provided in Anthony Summers's *Goddess: The Secret Lives of Marilyn Monroe* (Macmillan, 1985). To support his contention, Summers included the following information:

Dr. [Robert] Litman says today that [Dr. Ralph] Greenson spoke to him of a "close relationship [that Marilyn had] with extremely important men in government," that the relationship was sexual, and that the men concerned were "at the highest level."

"It was the day before she died. She said she was very much in love, and was going to marry Bobby Kennedy. But she sounded depressed."

Elizabeth Karger (Fred Karger's final wife)
on Marilyn's conversation with Mrs. Anne Karger

"I was at Marilyn's place one evening [in 1961] when the doorbell rang. She was in the tub, and she called to me to get it. I opened the door, and there was Bobby. . . . Finally I got out of the way, and Marilyn came flying out of the bathroom, and jumped into his arms . . . she kissed him openly, which was out of character for her."

Jeanne Carmen

"Of course there was nothing discreet about either of the Kennedys, Bob or Jack. It was like high-school time, very sophomoric. The things that went on in that beach house were just mind-boggling. Ethel could be in one room and Bobby could be in another with this or that woman."

Jeanne Martin (the former Mrs. Dean Martin)

"There was certainly an affair. She was star-struck over him, staring at him half the time with her eyes fluttering. I hate the word 'macho,' but Kennedy was playing a sort of macho role. He was never animated, never cracked a smile. She was all over him. I think she was turned on by the idea of mental genius. She liked that type, instead of being pushed around like a piece of meat."

Peter Dye, Santa Monica neighbor of Peter Lawford

"She told me that she was seeing somebody, but she didn't want to burden me with the responsibility of knowing who it was, because he was well known. So she was going to call him 'The General.' "

Joan Greenson

According to Fred Lawrence Guiles's *Legend: The Life and Death of Marilyn Monroe* (Stein and Day, 1984), Marilyn met Attorney General Kennedy in 1961 at one of the Peter Lawford Santa Monica dinner parties. Other sources contend that the famous pair did not meet until the May 1962 Madison Square Garden birthday bash for JFK. At any rate, most reports agree that the alleged affair between MM and RFK took place in 1962, in the months before Marilyn's death. On June 26, 1962, Marilyn attended yet another Lawford dinner party honoring RFK. She arrived two-and-a-half hours late. The following day, Kennedy made an appearance at Marilyn's Brentwood home.

During the month of July 1962, Marilyn made repeated phone calls to the Justice Department (phone number: RE7-8200) in Washington, DC, where Attorney General Robert Kennedy worked. It was during this period that Marilyn confided to Bob Slatzer that Bobby Kennedy had refused to accept or return her phone calls.

On August 3, 1962, Robert Kennedy flew into San Francisco. Apparently, Marilyn was finally able to contact him, because, on August 4, Kennedy flew to Los Angeles. According to the October 14, 1985, issue of *Newsweek,* former Los Angeles mayor Sam Yorty said, "[Police Chief] William Parker said Bobby was supposed to be someplace else . . . but he was at The Beverly Hilton."

Also in 1985, Mrs. Eunice Murray, Marilyn's housekeeper, finally admitted that Bobby Kennedy *was* at Marilyn's Brentwood home on the afternoon of her death. In a sworn deposition regarding Marilyn's death, Kennedy allegedly testified that he did indeed go to Marilyn's house on August 4 and that he was escorted by a doctor, who injected MM with a tranquilizer to calm her down.

What happened later is still not clear after all these years. What is known is that Marilyn telephoned the Lawford home later that evening and that a few hours later she was dead. Some people have accused Kennedy of being responsible for Marilyn Monroe's "murder," while others have accused him of a mere cover-up surrounding the circumstances of Marilyn's death. According to Peter Lawford's ex-wife, Deborah Gould, the delay in reporting Marilyn's death was intended to give Kennedy time to get out of town in order to protect the Kennedy name. Gould claimed that he was whisked away via helicopter from Lawford's beach house to the Santa Monica airport, where he then boarded a plane back to San Francisco. This report was embellished by a *Rolling Stone* magazine investigation in December 1985.

In 1965, Joe DiMaggio attended a ceremonial lineup for Mickey Mantle at Yankee Stadium. When Robert Kennedy appeared before the line, DiMaggio reportedly backed away and refused to shake Kennedy's hand. According to DiMaggio friend Harry Hall, as reported by Anthony Summers, DiMaggio held Bobby Kennedy responsible for Marilyn's death.

Nearly six years after MM's death on June 5, 1968, Robert Kennedy was assassinated in the Embassy Room of the Ambassador Hotel in Los Angeles.

***KENNEDY'S CHILDREN***

Robert Patrick's 1975 theatrical dramatization of the 1960s, which was set in a bar and featured five characters who spoke in a series of monologues, directly to the audience. One of Patrick's patrons was a beautiful blonde named Carla (Shirley Knight) whose impossible life quest was to *be* Marilyn Monroe.

Directed by Clive Donner, *Kennedy's Children* opened at the John Golden Theatre (address: 252 West 45th Street) on Broadway to good reviews. The cast featured Barbara Montgomery, Douglas Travis, Don Parker, Michael Sacks, Kaiulani Lee, and Shirley Knight.

**LINDA KERRIDGE**

Over the years, many pretty blondes have attempted to parlay their resemblance to MM into a film career. Very few have been as successful as Linda Kerridge. Born in Wagga Wagga, Australia, Kerridge worked as a model before she landed several French television commercials in which she portrayed MM. In 1978, Kerridge was slated to star as an MM look-alike in a feature film called *Stars*. However, it was in 1980's *Fade to Black* that she obtained a full-blown opportunity to portray Marilyn. Unfortunately for Kerridge, the film was a bust, and her acting career has been somewhat thwarted ever since.

**NIKITA KHRUSHCHEV**

In September 1959, Marilyn was invited to attend (as were Elizabeth Taylor and Debbie Reynolds) a 20th Century–Fox luncheon for Soviet leader Nikita Khrushchev. Prior to the luncheon, MM was given the complete beautification treatment: hair by Sidney Guilaroff, face makeup by Whitey Snyder, massage by Ralph Roberts, and body makeup by Agnes Flanagan. Despite the elaborate and time-consuming preparations, Marilyn shocked everyone by showing up at the luncheon *early.*

About her meeting with Khrushchev, MM reportedly told Lena Pepitone, "[He was] fat and ugly and had warts on his face and growled."

She was also quoted as saying,

> "I could tell Khrushchev liked me. He smiled more when he was introduced to me than for anyone else at the whole banquet. He squeezed my hand so long and hard I thought he would break it. I guess it was better than having to kiss him, though."
>
> *Marilyn Monroe Confidential* (Simon and Schuster, 1979)

**DOROTHY KILGALLEN**

The following is from Dorothy Kilgallen's syndicated column following the release of *Gentlemen Prefer Blondes* in July 1953:

> Dear Dorothy:
>
> I am sending you herewith a little affidavit about Marilyn Monroe's singing as you asked me to tell the truth. If I just wrote you a note there might be reason for a lingering doubt. The affidavit is my solemn oath, so you can be sure, I'm not kidding. Marilyn's voice was a surprise to me, and even more of a surprise to the MGM record company and the musicians and technicians who took part in the recording.
>
> Best personal regards,
> Sincerely, Darryl F. Zanuck.
>
> Dear Darryl:
>
> Of course I DO take your word for it, notarized or otherwise, but you can understand my skepticism, can't you? It just floors me that a girl who can sing as well as Marilyn does on the *Gentlemen Prefer Blondes* soundtrack (okay, it's not Dinah Shore, but it's a competent professional job) just happened to pick up the talent recently. I would have thought that a girl who looked like Marilyn, and could sing like that—or even considerably worse—would have bought herself an $18 black satin dress with a low-cut V neckline and snagged a job as a singer in a grade B nightclub when things got tough for her. I listen to a great many singers in all kinds of cafes in the course of a year, and I guarantee you most of them warble a lot worse than Marilyn and don't come anywhere near her in the appearance department. My question is, if she could sing that well, why did she have to pose in the nude for calendar pictures to get eating money?
>
> D.K.

As for MM's opinion of DK, the following appeared in Truman Capote's book, *Music For Chameleons* (Random House, 1979):

> "[P. J. Clarke's saloon is] full of those advertising creeps. And that bitch Dorothy Kilgallen, she's always in there getting bombed. What is it with these micks? The way they booze, they're worse than Indians . . . she's written some bitchy stuff about me."
>
> MM to Truman Capote

**KENNY KINGSTON**

Marilyn Monroe's private psychic. In August 1972, to commemorate the tenth anniversary of Marilyn's death, Kingston conducted a séance at his home. According to Kingston, MM appeared before him, dressed in white. She was accompanied by actor Clifton Webb, who was dressed in white tie and tails. To Kingston, Marilyn reportedly confided that she would still be alive on earth if she had remained married to Joe DiMaggio. She also claimed that, of the two men responsible for her death, one was still alive on earth (in 1972), and the other was in paradise. To Kingston, Marilyn also "predicted" that one of her former directors, Otto Preminger, would win two Academy Awards by 1977. However, as time proved, Preminger had *not* won a single Oscar by 1986, when he died.

Undaunted, in 1981, Kingston told the *Los Angeles Herald Examiner* that Marilyn had been reincarnated on the island of Capri under the name Luigi.

**DOUGLAS KIRKLAND**

> When we were alone, off came the robe, and there was a very bare Marilyn. . . . I was holding the camera so she had to *get* to me.
>
> Douglas Kirkland, *Popular Photography*, 1966

In 1962, relative newcomer Douglas Kirkland shot a series of photos of Marilyn for *LOOK* magazine. Over the years, one of Kirkland's shots has become one of the most famous of MM's photographs. The photo features Marilyn lying nude under white sheets, clutching a white pillow.

**HELEN KIRKPATRICK**

In 1954, Helen Kirkpatrick was secretary to attorney Jerry Giesler. It was Miss Kirkpatrick who went to the Monroe/DiMaggio North Palm Drive home to obtain both of their signatures on the divorce complaint. Miss Kirkpatrick witnessed Marilyn's signature on the second floor of the home, before she served the papers to DiMaggio on the first floor.

**JOE KIRKWOOD, JR.**

In 1948–49, Joe Kirkwood, Jr., aka actor Joe Palouka, was a trick-shot golfer. At that time, Kirkwood was in need of a decorative, briefly clad, female assistant who could hold a plastic ball in her hand. Reportedly, Fred Karger suggested the out-of-work Marilyn Monroe for the job. Marilyn's first performance was at the Veteran's Hospital in Los Angeles. It also proved to be her last such performance. Apparently, MM was so nervous she was not able to hold the ball steady.

***KISS ME, STUPID***

Nineteen sixty-four Billy Wilder comedy that starred Dean Martin and Kim Novak. Reportedly, Wilder intended Novak's character, Polly, to be a memorial, of sorts, to Marilyn Monroe.

**BENJAMIN KLINE**

Cinematographer on the 1947 film *Dangerous Years*, which featured MM in a small role.

## ENID AND SAM KNEBELCAMP

Reportedly, the Knebelcamps acted as Norma Jeane's foster parents for a short period. They were the only set of "parents" to attend Marilyn's funeral in 1962.

## THE KNICKERBOCKER HOTEL

Hollywood hotel where Joe DiMaggio usually stayed while in Los Angeles. It was at the Knickerbocker (address: 1714 North Ivar) where MM dropped Joe off following their first date in 1952.

The Knickerbocker was sold in 1972 and is currently an apartment building for senior citizens.

## SHIRLEY KNIGHT

Born in 1937, Knight was the film and stage actress who portrayed the Marilyn Monroe-inspired character, Carla, in the 1975 Broadway play *Kennedy's Children.*

## JOHN KOBAL

John Kobal has written, compiled, or edited numerous books on the cinema. He also possesses one of the largest collections of film stills in the world, most of the photos incorporated into the 1974 book *Marilyn Monroe: A Life on Film,* are from Mr. Kobal's personal collection.

## KOREA

> This was the best thing that ever happened to me. . . . Come to see us in San Francisco.
>
> MM to the soldiers in Korea,
> shortly after her marriage to Joe DiMaggio

The Korean War, or, more precisely, the soldiers in Korea, helped to make Marilyn Monroe a star by unofficially crowning her their favorite pinup. Marilyn responded in February 1954 by interrupting her honeymoon with Joe DiMaggio to entertain the troops in Seoul. MM left Japan on February 16 and was accompanied by Jean O'Doul, wife of DiMaggio's friend "Lefty" O'Doul.

Marilyn was flown via helicopter to the First Marine Division. She lay, face down, on the floor of the copter and blew kisses to the thousands of cheering soldiers. For her performance, Marilyn wore a low-cut, plum-colored, sequined gown and sang "Diamonds Are a Girl's Best Friend," "Bye Bye Baby," "Somebody Love Me," and "Do It Again." The lyrics to the last were later changed to "Kiss Me Again" because one of the military officers felt that they were too sexually suggestive.

In a period of four days, Marilyn performed ten shows for over one hundred thousand troops, including the First Marine Division, the Second Infantry Division, the Third Army Division, the Seventh Infantry Division, the Fortieth Infantry Division, and the Forty-Fifth Infantry Division, where a rock-throwing riot took place.

THE T. R. FOGLI COLLECTION

Korea, 1954

Marilyn returned to Japan on February 21, 1954, and to Los Angeles on March 5, 1954. She was later to cite her Korea trip as one of the greatest highlights of her life. Certainly, she had never before experienced such overwhelming adulation. As she reportedly told Amy Greene, "I never felt like a star before in my heart. It was so wonderful to look down and see a fellow smiling at me."

COURTESY OF CINEMA COLLECTORS

**MM Trivia Quiz #23**
Other than Korea, where did MM perform for the American military troops? (Answer on page 577.)

**HENRY KOSTER**
Born Hermann Kosterlitz in 1905, Koster was a German film director who worked in Hollywood from the mid-1930s to the mid-1960s. In 1952, Koster directed MM in *O. Henry's Full House*. His other films included *The Robe* (1953), *Flower Drum Song* (1960), and *The Singing Nun* (1966).

**FLORENCE KOTZ (aka Florence Kotz Ross)**
Florence Kotz was the tenant of the "wrong" apartment who was victimized in the scandalous "Wrong Door Raid" incident that took place in Hollywood on November 5, 1954. Miss Kotz subsequently filed a $200,000 suit against Sinatra, DiMaggio, et al., but accepted a 1957 out-of-court settlement of $7,500. (For more information see "THE WRONG DOOR RAID.")

**NORMAN KRASNA**
Born in 1909, Krasna was a playwright/screenwriter who occasionally produced and directed motion pictures. In 1952, Krasna coproduced *Clash by Night*, a pivotal film for Marilyn Monroe. Eight years later, Krasna wrote the screenplay for *Let's Make Love*.

**MILTON KRASNER**
Milton Krasner, born in 1901, was one of Marilyn Monroe's "approved" cinematographers. Krasner shot a total of four Monroe movies—*All About Eve* (1950), *Monkey Business* (1952), *Bus Stop* (1956), and *The Seven Year Itch* (1955).

Krasner's non-MM movies included *The Farmer's Daughter* (1947), *Love with the Proper Stranger* (1964), and *Three Coins in the Fountain* (1954), for which he won an Academy Award.

**TIBOR KREKES**
Film critic who is generally considered the first man to review a Marilyn Monroe movie performance. In his 1948 review of *Ladies of the Chorus*, Krekes wrote in the *Motion Picture Herald*,

> One of the bright spots is Miss Monroe's singing. She is pretty, and, with her pleasing voice and style, she shows promise.

**MARIANNE KRIS**
Dr. Marianne Kris was Marilyn's New York psychiatrist, who recommended that she check into the Payne Whitney Clinic for "emotional exhaustion" in February 1961. Dr. Kris was later named one of the primary beneficiaries in Marilyn's will. Reportedly, Dr. Kris assigned her inheritance to the Hampstead Child Therapy Clinic in London.

**LEON KROHN**
Dr. Leon "Red" Krohn was MM's Hollywood gynecologist for several years. Dr. Krohn was present at MM's appendectomy in 1952. He also performed Marilyn's "operation of a corrective nature" in November 1954.

**KYRON WAY**
At the time of the *Love Happy* release in 1950, Marilyn appeared in a print advertisement for the Kyron Way diet tablets. In the photograph, MM stood with her legs slightly spread and her hands behind her back. She wore a one-piece bathing suit. The ad itself read, in part:

> **FAMOUS DOCTOR OF MOVIE STARS**
> **REVEALS HOW TO LOSE UGLY FAT SAFELY!**
> "Screen beauties can't be fat—and no one needs to be!" says Dr. Miller, who recommends the KYRON way to reduce. "Amazing KYRON helps you lose ugly fat safely and easily, without drugs, exercise or starvation. You eat 3 delicious meals a day, yet watch your figure grow slimmer, younger-looking day by day!" . . . If you want slim, youthful lines like Miss Monroe and other stars, start the KYRON Way to slenderness—today!"

# FAMOUS DOCTOR OF MOVIE STARS* REVEALS HOW TO LOSE UGLY FAT SAFELY!

MARILYN MONROE, Lovely Screen Star

*Appearing in the latest Marx Brothers smash hit, "Love Happy"—a United Artists release.*

If you want slim, youthful lines like Miss Monroe and other stars, start the KYRON Way to slenderness today!

YOU May Lose up to 7 Lbs. the Very First Week the KYRON Way, says Dr. J. J. Miller, D.C., Consultant to Top Stars of Screen and Radio!

"Screen beauties *can't* be fat—and *no one wants* to be!" says Dr. Miller, who recommends the KYRON way to reduce. "Amazing KYRON helps you lose ugly fat safely and easily, without drugs, exercise or starvation. You eat 3 delicious meals a day, yet watch your figure grow slimmer, younger-looking, *day by day!*"

**Energy UP—Weight DOWN!**

KYRON concentrated food tablets are harmless to take daily, yet work wonders for fat folks! Used with simple KYRON reducing instructions, they help appease hunger, supply valuable nutritive elements that help keep up your "pep"—while *pounds* disappear! Get KYRON today!

**Dr. J. J. Miller, D.C.,***

**Hollywood, California Consultant to Stars of Screen and Stage**

Dr. Miller has been the close personal adviser on health and weight control to outstanding Hollywood personalities for many years. His methods and results are famous wherever stars gather.

*Dr. J. J. Miller, D.C., 942 Crenshaw Bl, Los Angeles, Calif.

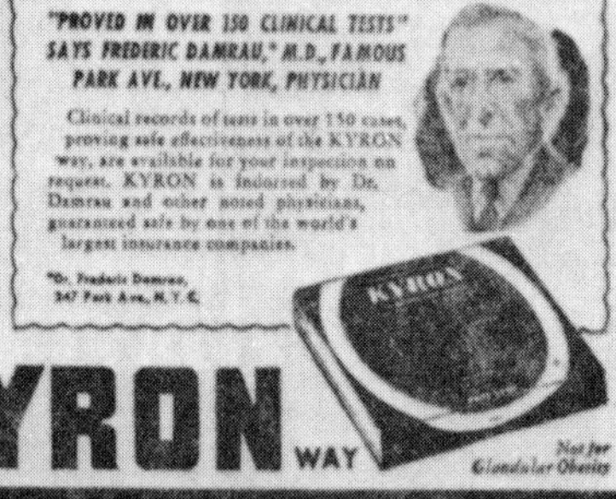

"PROVED IN OVER 150 CLINICAL TESTS" SAYS FREDERIC DAMRAU,* M.D., FAMOUS PARK AVE., NEW YORK, PHYSICIAN

Clinical records of tests in over 150 cases, proving safe effectiveness of the KYRON way, are available for your inspection on request. KYRON is indorsed by Dr. Damrau and other noted physicians, guaranteed safe by one of the world's largest insurance companies.

*Dr. Frederic Damrau, 347 Park Ave., N.Y.C.



**MAKE 7 DAY NO RISK TEST!**

Try the KYRON Way one week on MONEY-BACK GUARANTEE! Get KYRON today—follow reducing instructions. If in 7 days you are dissatisfied, and have not lost up to 7 pounds of excess fat, return empty box for full refund of purchase price. You lose weight—or pay nothing!

REDUCE SAFELY THE **KYRON** WAY

*Not for Glandular Obesity*

**OWL DRUG STORES**

THE ALAN FRANCE COLLECTION

# L

## KATIE LABOURDETTE

Katie Labourdette is an actress who has portrayed Marilyn Monroe on television ("Matt Houston," "Benson"), on-stage ("Movie Star"), and in concert ("Legends in Concert").

## *LADIES HOME JOURNAL* MAGAZINE

Over the years, *Ladies Home Journal* has published the following features on Marilyn Monroe:

- ☆ 11/67: Excerpts from the 1969 Fred Lawrence Guiles book *Norma Jean: The Life of Marilyn Monroe*
- ☆ 7/73: Excerpts from the 1973 book by Norman Mailer, *Marilyn*
- ☆ 8/73: Continued excerpts from the book, *Marilyn*
- ☆ 11/73: "I Was There the Night Marilyn Monroe Died," Eunice Murray interviewed by George Carpozi, Jr.
- ☆ 5/75: "Marilyn Monroe and Joe DiMaggio"—Excerpts from the book, *Where Have You Gone Joe DiMaggio?*
- ☆ 4/76: "Marilyn Monroe"—Excerpts from the 1976 W. J. Weatherby book, *Conversations with Marilyn*
- ☆ 9/80: Excerpts from the 1980 Norman Mailer book, *Of Women and Their Elegance*
- ☆ 8/82: "Remembering Marilyn Monroe"—Excerpts from the 1982 James Spada and George Zeno book, *Monroe: Her Life in Pictures*
- ☆ 8/87: "Marilyn, the Legend Lives On"

## *LADIES OF THE CHORUS* ★★

1948 61 minutes Black and White
Columbia Pictures
Directed by: Phil Karlson
Produced by: Harry A. Romm
Screenplay by: Harry Sauber and Joseph Carol, from a story by Harry Sauber
Photographed by: Frank Redman
Cast: Adele Jergens, Marilyn Monroe, Rand Brooks, Nana Bryant, Marjorie Hoshelle, Eddie Garr

Low-budget musical that gave Marilyn Monroe her first costarring role. The nimble plot was aptly described by the December 3, 1948, edition of *The Hollywoood Reporter*:

> Columbia's *Ladies of the Chorus* sets out to prove that burlesque queens are really quite proper wives for wealthy young members of socially prominent families and does a fairly competent job of making its audience like it.

*Ladies* was Marilyn's only film for Columbia Pictures. It did little to launch her career, but it did introduce her to both Fred Karger and Natasha

Lytess. Also, as the Burlesque star named Peggy, MM was given the opportunity to perform two songs: "Every Baby Needs a Da-Da-Daddy" and "Anyone Can Tell I Love You." It was the first time MM sang on the screen. Moreover, for *Ladies,* MM also received the first film reviews of her fledgling career.

**THE LAFONDA MOTOR LODGE**
In 1945, on Jim Dougherty's leave from the military, he and Norma Jeane checked into the LaFonda Motor Lodge on Ventura Boulevard in the San Fernando Valley. Their stay was, reportedly, a "marathon sexual reunion."

**GAVIN LAMBERT**
Critic turned screenwriter who showed unusual perception in his 1953 review of *Niagara.* Wrote Lambert,

> For all the wolf calls that she gets and deserves, there is something mournful about Miss Monroe. She doesn't look happy. She lacks the pin-up's cheerful grin. She seems to have lost something, or to be waking up from a bad dream.

**RICHARD LAMPARSKI**
Richard Lamparski is the author of the book, *Hidden Hollywood.* According to Lamparski, Marilyn Monroe was once a stripper at a Los Angeles burlesque house named the Mayan Theatre.

**DICK LANE**
Dick Lane was a 20th Century-Fox make-up man who went to Cedars of Lebanon Hospital in April 1952 to make Marilyn's face up, before she was presented to reporters and photographers. At that time, Marilyn had recently undergone an appendectomy.

**THOMAS LANE**
During the 1953 production of *Gentlemen Prefer Blondes,* Marilyn began to furnish her new three-room flat on North Doheny Drive. At the suggestion of her costar, Jane Russell, MM hired Thomas Lane to decorate the interior of her apartment.

**CHARLES LANG, JR.**
Born in 1902, Lang was the notable cinematographer of *Some Like It Hot* (1959)—despite the fact that he was not on MM's list of "approved" cinematographers. Lang was also one of four cinematographers credited with working on the 1962 unfinished film, *Something's Got to Give.*

Lang's non-MM pictures include *A Farewell to Arms* (for which he won a 1933 Oscar), *Desire* (1936), *Sudden Fear* (1952), *Charade* (1963), and *Cactus Flower* (1969).

**FRITZ LANG**
Fritz Lang (1890–1976) was the German maker of such films as *Metropolis*

(1926) and *M* (1931), both of which are generally considered to be among the finest pictures ever made.

In 1952, Lang directed Marilyn Monroe in *Clash by Night*. Tension brewed on the set between the two of them. Lang demanded that MM's coach, Natasha Lytess, be barred from the set. Lang was, in fact, the first of several directors to make this demand. At that time, Lang was quoted as saying,

> I do not want anybody directing behind my back. I want this Lytess woman kept off my set. I am giving orders not to allow her on the set."

However, Marilyn counterobjected, and a compromise was soon negotiated. Later, Lang said the following about MM:

> "She was a very peculiar mixture of shyness and—I wouldn't say 'star allure'—but she knew, exactly, her impact on men."

**WALTER LANG**

Director of MM's first screen test for 20th Century-Fox in July 1946. Eight years later, Lang directed MM in *There's No Business Like Show Business*.

Walter Lang (1896–1972) also directed such other pictures as *With a Song in My Heart* (1952), *Call Me Madam*, (1953), and *The King and I* (1956).

**HOPE LANGE**

Born in 1931, Hope Lange's first film was *Bus Stop* in 1956. Prior to the shooting, MM insisted that Miss Lange's hair be dyed a darker shade of blonde so that it wouldn't look so similar to MM's hair color.

Hope Lange's subsequent films included *Peyton Place* (1957) and *Pocketful of Miracles* (1961). She later found success in television with *The Ghost and Mrs. Muir* (1968) and *The New Dick Van Dyke Show* (1971).

**LANKERSHIM SCHOOL**

In 1938, at the age of eleven, Norma Jeane Baker attended Lankershim School (address: 5250 Bakman Avenue) in North Hollywood, California. While at Lankershim, Norma Jeane won two first-place awards in the jumping and running track and field events. Norma Jeane's teacher at that time was Grace Pettes. Her principal was C. L. Johns.

Today, the Lankershim School is called Lankershim Elementary. It still stands at the Bakman Avenue location.

**LOUIS LANTZ**

*River of No Return* (1954) was based on a story written by Louis Lantz.

**LA SCALA**

Beverly Hills Italian restaurant (address: 9455 Santa Monica Boulevard) that was one of Marilyn's favorite eateries during the summer of 1962. In fact, she had dined there the night of August 3, 1962, with Peter Lawford and Patricia Newcomb.

**JOSEPH LA SHELLE**

Cinematographer, born in 1903, of such films as *Laura* (for which he won a 1944 Oscar), *The Apartment* (1960), and *Irma La Douce* (1963). La Shelle also shot the 1954 western *River of No Return,* which starred MM.

**LAS VEGAS**

In 1946, Norma Jeane Dougherty went to Las Vegas, Nevada, to file for a divorce from her husband, Jim Dougherty.

In the following years, the glitzy entertainment capital beckoned MM to return—to no avail. In March 1955, Sammy Lewis offered Marilyn a mega-dollar deal to perform at the New Frontier Hotel—a deal that never materialized. And, up until the days before her death, Marilyn was discussing the possiblity of headlining a live stage show in Vegas, where she would have joined the ranks of such luminaries as Elvis Presley and Frank Sinatra.

**LAS VEGAS GENERAL HOSPITAL**

During her May 1946 stay in Las Vegas, Norma Jean Dougherty was treated at Las Vegas General Hospital (address: 201 North 8th Street) as an outpatient for a case of trench mouth. The hospital has since been condemned.

***THE LAST DAYS OF MARILYN MONROE***

*See* MARILYN: SAY GOODBYE TO THE PRESIDENT.

**THE LAST FRONTIER HOTEL**

During her May 1946 stay in Las Vegas, Norma Jeane once had dinner with Roy Rogers and his film crew at the restaurant located in this hotel. The hotel has since changed its name to the Frontier Hotel and is located at 3120 South Las Vegas Boulevard.

***THE LAST MAN ON WAGON MOUND***

In the early 1950s 20th Century-Fox proposed that MM make *The Last Man on Wagon Mound,* in which she would've portrayed a frontier widow. The film would have been executive produced by Raymond Klune, and would have costarred Mitzi Gaynor, Debra Paget, and Jean Peters. However, plans to produce the film failed to materialize.

***THE LAST SITTING***

Author/Photographer: Bert Stern, with text by Annie Gottlieb
Publisher: William Morrow & Company
Date: 1982 (Out of print)

In June 1962, shortly before Marilyn's death, Bert Stern shot a series of photographs of MM for *Vogue* magazine. The photos featured MM nude, seminude, and in high fashion. Twenty years later, Stern published his photographs in this attractive, well-produced book. And while the photographs do not stand well among Marilyn's best, they *are* original. MM's body (revealing a scar from her gallbladder operation) is amply displayed through transparent, colored scarves. Stern's photos present a somewhat different

Marilyn, aging and champagned and not exactly beautiful.

The text itself, complete with Stern's own personal sexual desire for MM, is not flattering to Marilyn—or to Stern. *The Last Sitting* provides some interesting photographs of Marilyn Monroe toward the end of her life and little more.

**LATENESS**

Marilyn Monroe was always—well, almost always—late. Her incessant tardiness infuriated her colleagues, her friends, and just about everyone else. She was even two hours late for her own appendectomy!

> "I've been on calendars, but never on time."
>
> MM to photographer Douglas Kirkland
> after being only thirty minutes late

> She's never on time. It's a terrible thing for an acting company, the director, the cameraman. You sit there and wait. You can't start without her. Thousands of dollars you see going into the hole. You can always figure a Monroe picture is going to run an extra few hundred thousand dollars because she's coming late. It demoralized the whole company. It's like trench warfare. . . . I don't think Marilyn is late on purpose. Her idea of time is different, that's all. I think maybe there's a little watchmaker in Zurich, Switzerland, he makes a living producing special watches only for Marilyn Monroe.
>
> Billy Wilder

> "It's not really me that's late. It's the others who are in such a hurry."
>
> Marilyn Monroe

> "The people at Fox who are responsible for seeing that she gets to appointments on time are certain that if each day had 30 hours, Marilyn would use them all in getting ready. No matter how much advance notice she is given, she is always late. Her 'I'll be just a minute' can range anywhere from 20 minutes to two hours."
>
> *Collier's* magazine, 1951

> "Oh, baby, I'm so sorry. But see, I got all made up, and then I decided maybe I shouldn't wear eyelashes or lipstick or anything, so then I had to wash all that off, and I couldn't imagine what to wear. . . ."
>
> MM to Truman Capote, on being late
> for the funeral of Constance Collier
> *Music for Chameleons* (Random House, 1979)

> "Late? Look, if we had a 9:00 A.M. call, she'd make it by eleven. That was on her good days. On her bad days, she didn't show up until after we came back from lunch. She had days when she didn't make it till three."
>
> Tony Curtis, on MM during the shooting of *Some Like It Hot*

> "I feel a queer satisfaction in punishing the people who are wanting me now. But it's not them I'm really punishing. It's the long-ago people who didn't want Norma Jeane . . . the later I am, the happier Norma Jeane grows."
>
> Marilyn Monroe

> "What I tell her is, 'You are the one who gets on the screen, not the others who make the movie. You are the star! Only amateurs watch production costs.' "
>
> Paula Strasberg, *Esquire,* March 1961

> "When I'm late or don't show up, it costs the studio thousands of dollars. . . . How else can I get a fair deal? I'm not unionized, you know."
>
> Marilyn Monroe

> "It's a bad habit, I know, but I believe that you shouldn't do anything in life until you're ready. Half of life's heartaches come from decisions that were made in a hurry. One should make haste slowly."
>
> Marilyn Monroe

> "If she was scheduled for a sitting at 9:00 A.M., I simply put her down in my book for 7:00 P.M.—and went ahead planning the rest of my day."
>
> Richard Avedon

Erskine Johnson, a Hollywood columnist, once devoted an entire newspaper article to Marilyn Monroe's notorious, chronic lateness. The article was titled "Waiting for Marilyn" and included the following:

> "Waiting for Marilyn" I'll never forget, and I doubt if Hollywood ever will. People may admire Marilyn Monroe, envy Marilyn Monroe, dislike Marilyn Monroe—but, most of all, people wait for Marilyn Monroe.
>
> Once I waited for Marilyn in Phoenix. A visit to the set and a chat with her on location for *Bus Stop* had been arranged. I waited all day and Marilyn never came out of her dressing room. Another newsman, who had more time, waited in Phoenix for Marilyn for five days and she never came out of her hotel room. Or invited him in.
>
> Newsmen have waited for Marilyn to come out of airplanes. Airplanes have waited for Marilyn. Newsmen have waited for Marilyn to come out of trains. Trains have waited for Marilyn. Movie producers, husband Arthur Miller, clothes designers have waited for Marilyn. Waiters have waited for Marilyn. . . .

But, of all the commentaries on Marilyn's lateness, it was Billy Wilder who expressed it best with:

> "I would rather have Marilyn Monroe two hours late than another actress an hour early. . . . [But] the question then arises: How do I feel about Marilyn Monroe—*six* hours late?"

**MM Trivia Quiz #24**
In *Clash by Night,* what made MM punctual? (Answer on page 577.)

**CHARLES LAUGHTON**

Charles Laughton (1899-1962) was the well-respected character actor in such films as *The Private Life of Henry VIII* (for which he won a 1933 Oscar),

*Mutiny on the Bounty* (1935), *The Hunchback of Notre Dame* (1939), and many others.

In 1952, Laughton costarred opposite Marilyn Monroe in *O. Henry's Full House.*

**ANTON LAVEY**

According to *The Intimate Sex Lives of Famous People* (Dell, 1982), Marilyn had an affair with LaVey in the late 1940s.

> An intimate glimpse of Marilyn's sexuality in this period is afforded by Anton LaVey, then an 18-year-old accompanist at a strip joint where the 22-year-old actress worked briefly after being fired from Columbia. LaVey, who had a two-week affair with Marilyn in motels (or, when they were broke, in her car), describes her as sexually passive, a tease who enjoyed the ogling admiration of men, but not their more pressing attentions.

**EMILE LA VIGNE**

La Vigne was credited as the makeup artist on *Some Like It Hot* (1959).

**LINDA LAVIN**

Linda Lavin was a noted stage actress in New York, before she gained television fame as Alice Hyatt on the once popular CBS series, "Alice." Miss Lavin made her Broadway musical debut in the 1966 production of *It's a Bird . . . It's a Plane . . . It's Superman.* Three years later, she did a parody of Marilyn Monroe in John Guare's stage comedy, *Cop-Out.* Of her performance, critic Clive Barnes wrote in the April 8, 1969 edition of *The New York Times*:

> Miss Lavin—one minute the slinky Manhattan hostess, next a legless police spy, or an Off-Broadway Monroe—carries versatility almost to the point of paranoia, and camps up a storm.

**PATRICIA LAWFORD**

Reportedly, Patricia Lawford was one of Marilyn Monroe's closest friends in 1962. The sister of John and Robert Kennedy, Pat was at that time the wife of Peter Lawford. Nevertheless, according to the August 8, 1962, *Los Angeles Herald Examiner*, Pat was denied access to Marilyn's funeral—despite the fact that she had flown cross-country to attend.

**PETER LAWFORD**

> "I saw Peter Lawford in the role of pimp for Jack Kennedy."
>
> Jeanne Martin (the former Mrs. Dean Martin), in Anthony Summers's *Goddess: The Secret Lives of Marilyn Monroe* (Macmillan, 1985)

Peter Lawford (1923–1984) was a mediocre actor who gained fame by marrying John F. Kennedy's sister, Patricia. Subsequently, in-law Lawford served as the Kennedy family's Hollywood connection. When John, Robert, or others in the Kennedy clan visited Hollywood, they often guested at the

Lawford beach house in Santa Monica. During these and other trips, Lawford introduced his famous political relatives to his famous Hollywood friends.

Peter Lawford reportedly first met Marilyn Monroe at the William Morris Agency, circa 1950. In November 1952, Marilyn told *American Weekly* magazine,

> "I have been reported as being seen here and there with Peter Lawford. As a matter of fact, I never have had a date with Peter. We were at the same table at a nightclub (one of my few appearances at a nightclub, I don't care for them) and I may have danced with him, but that hardly constitutes a date, and certainly not a romance."

However, years later, Lawford told writer Anthony Summers,

> "I'll never forget going to pick her up on our first date. When I walked into the apartment I had to step around the dogshit. Marilyn just looked and said, 'Oh, he's done it again.' . . . We had a couple of dates, I guess."

Summers himself added, "Lawford . . . fell for Marilyn in a big way, and she failed to respond."

It has been generally accepted that Peter Lawford introduced Marilyn Monroe to the Kennedy brothers, both of whom she *did* respond to. It was Lawford who invited MM to the various dinner parties that were attended by one or the other Kennedy. It was Lawford who invited MM to spend the night at his Santa Monica beach house, which was allegedy used as a "love nest" for the Kennedy brothers. And it was Lawford who invited MM to sing "Happy Birthday" to JFK at Madison Square Garden in 1962.

Reportedly, on the night of Marilyn's death, Lawford telephoned her at approximately 7:00 P.M. According to Lawford, he called to invite MM to dinner, and she declined. According to Fred Lawrence Guiles's *Legend: The Life and Death of Marilyn Monroe* (Stein and Day, 1984), sometime after 8:00 P.M. that evening, Lawford received a disturbing phone call from Marilyn. However, rather than sending direct help, Lawford contacted his manager/agent. It was Lawford's third wife, Deborah Gould, who actually incriminated him in the alleged cover-up of Marilyn's death. In the BBC documentary, "The Last Days of Marilyn Monroe," Gould said,

> "Peter told me that [Robert] Kennedy came to see Marilyn. Marilyn knew then that it [her affair with RFK] was over. She was very distraught and depressed. Marilyn phoned Peter to inform him that she couldn't take any more. She was going to kill herself. Peter had been drinking a great deal; he had a cynical sense of humor. He didn't take her seriously. He said, 'For God's sake, Marilyn, pull yourself together, but my God, whatever you do, don't leave any notes.' "

However, according to Gould, Marilyn *did* leave a note, which was later retrieved and destroyed by Peter Lawford.

Other sources have claimed that Marilyn's last words were to—and about—Peter Lawford. Allegedly, over the telephone, a drowsy, drugged MM told Lawford,

> Say goodbye to Pat, say goodbye to Jack, and say goodbye to yourself, because you're a nice guy.

Nice guy or not, Deborah Gould has claimed that, on the morning of August 5, 1962, Peter Lawford went to Marilyn's Brentwood home to "tidy up the place before the reporters and what-have-you found out about the death."

And, according to Anthony Summers's *Goddess: The Secret Lives of Marilyn Monroe* (Macmillan, 1985), on the morning of August 5, Lawford went to the office of private detective Fred Otash. Also present in the office was a "security man." According to Summers,

> The security man understood that Marilyn had left some sort of note, which had already been removed. His job, he was told, was to check her house, especially for papers or letters that might give away her affairs with the Kennedys. He was also to try to discover potential sources of leaks, and take action to silence them.

Later, when asked about Marilyn's death, Lawford was quoted as saying,

> "Pat and I loved her dearly. She was probably one of the most marvelous and warm human beings I have ever met. Anything else I could say would be superfluous.

And, at another time, "Marilyn found relief in death. It was a sort of liberation for her."

Peter Lawford was not invited to Marilyn's funeral at Westwood Memorial Park. Ironically, today, Peter Lawford's own ashes lie a mere fifty feet away from Marilyn's crypt.

**STEPHANIE LAWRENCE**
Actress who portrayed MM in the 1983 British musical production *Marilyn!*

**TIMOTHY LEARY**
Famous psychologist Dr. Timothy Leary introduced Marilyn—at her request—to LSD in May 1962.

**JOHN LEBOLD**
John Lebold is a member of the Marilyn Remembered Fan Club in Los Angeles, and, an MM collector who specializes in obtaining Marilyn's movie costumes. Lebold is also a film historian, and the founder of the Hollywood Costume Museum which closed down in 1985.

**CHARLES LEDERER**
Charles Lederer (1911-1976) wrote the screenplay for *Gentlemen Prefer Blondes* (1953) and cowrote the screenplay for *Monkey Business* (1952). His non-MM credits include *The Front Page* (1931) and *His Girl Friday* (1940).

**JAMES LEE**
James Lee wrote the teleplay for "Moviola: This Year's Blonde" (1980)—the

segment about MM and Johnny Hyde—which was adapted from Garson Kanin's best-selling novel.

**ELLIOT LEFKOWITZ**

Lefkowitz was one of Marilyn's New York attorneys at the time of her death.

***LEGEND***

1974 British stage play about the last four days of Marilyn Monroe's life. The play was written by David Butler, produced by James Whiteley, and featured actress Sondra Dickenson as MM.

**"THE LEGEND OF MARILYN MONROE"**

One-hour television documentary tribute to MM that was comprised mainly of off-screen footage of Marilyn. Produced by David L. Wolper and narrated by John Huston, this film was completed in August 1964 and aired on ABC-TV on November 30, 1966.

***LEGEND: THE LIFE AND DEATH OF MARILYN MONROE***

Author: Fred Lawrence Guiles
Publisher: Stein and Day
Year: 1984, $17.95, 440 pages (ISBN 0-8128-2983-2)

With Guiles's earlier *Norma Jean: The Life of Marilyn Monroe* as a companion, *Legend* is an exemplary work. While much of the biographical material is necessarily the same as that presented in *Norma Jean, Legend* is a less cautious and, therefore, more complete work than its predecessor. Guiles has included additional interviews with Jim Dougherty, Lee Strasberg, and Arthur Miller, et al. The Miller material is particularly revealing, worthwhile, and rare. There are also a good number of black-and-white photographs, some of which have been seen infrequently, if ever.

*Legend: The Life and Death of Marilyn Monroe* is the definitive biography of a Hollywood star. It is extremely well written and researched and is must reading for any fan and/or student of Marilyn Monroe.

**"LEGENDS IN CONCERT"**

"Legends in Concert" is a Las Vegas-based production show that features impersonations of Marilyn Monroe, Elvis Presley, Judy Garland, et al. The show opened on May 5, 1983 at the Imperial Palace in Las Vegas, and, has been running ever since. MM is impersonated by singer Susan Griffiths, who is one of the original members of the company. Her numbers include: "I Wanna Be Loved By You," "My Heart Belongs to Daddy," and "Diamonds Are a Girl's Best Friend."

**MURRAY LEIBOWITZ**

According to the December 5, 1985, issue of *Rolling Stone* magazine, Leibowitz was an ambulance attendant who rushed Marilyn Monroe to Santa

Monica Hospital at 2:00 A.M., August 5, 1962. This, of course, conflicts with the official police report, which claimed that Marilyn was found—dead—at her Brentwood home just after 3:00 A.M. on August 5.

### JANET LEIGH

Born Jeanette Morrison in 1927, actress Janet Leigh was Marilyn Monroe's contemporary. She was also the wife of actor Tony Curtis during the period in which *Some Like It Hot* (1959) was shot. Years later, Miss Leigh had the following to say about MM:

> Marilyn was tortured by insecurity. This exquisite creature, so talented, so vulnerable, so irretrievable, labored just to come on the set. She was there at the studio, but was hard put to muster the courage to appear. It was not malicious game playing or status tactics, but just plain terror that forced her to retreat. This was very trying, especially for the boys. They would report for make-up and wardrobe, and then wait. And wait. The more intolerable their position, the more intolerant their attitude. Of course they were sympathetic to her plight; it was an unfortunate situation. But, oh boy, when she did make it, when Billy [Wilder] did get it out of her, the screen sizzled. What a high price to pay!

### VIVIEN LEIGH

Born Vivien Hartley, Vivien Leigh (1913-1967) was the superb British actress in such films as *Lady Hamilton* (1941), *A Streetcar Named Desire* (1951), and *Gone with the Wind* (1939), the last two of which won her Academy Awards.

In 1956, at the time of *The Prince and the Showgirl* shooting in London, Miss Leigh was married to Sir Laurence Olivier. Reportedly, Mrs. Olivier and Mrs. Miller did *not* become the best of friends. First of all, it was Vivien Leigh who had originated the role of the showgirl opposite Olivier—the role that Marilyn Monroe bought for herself to play. Second, Lady Olivier was not in good health—she was a manic depressive who had been diagnosed as a schizophrenic. As for the undereducated MM, she was ill at ease among the elegant, more sophisticated Oliviers.

As production of *Prince* started, Vivien Leigh announced to the press that, after sixteen years of marriage and at the age of forty-two, she was pregnant with Sir Laurence's child. With this news, Vivien replaced Marilyn on the front page of every newspaper in the country. At that time, ugly rumors abounded that Lady Olivier was not pregnant at all—that she simply wanted to outdo Marilyn Monroe in attracting publicity. At any rate, a few weeks later, on August 12, 1956, Lady Olivier suffered a miscarriage. Eleven years later, on July 7, 1967, she died following a bout with tuberculosis.

### CHARLES LEMAIRE (also spelled *LeMair*)

In July 1946, Charles LeMaire was the head of Wardrobe at 20th Century-Fox. It was LeMaire who selected the gown that Norma Jeane wore for her first screen test with Fox. LeMaire also worked on MM's wardrobe for her succession of films at 20th Century-Fox.

**HANS JORGEN LEMBOURN**

Danish screenwriter who penned the autobiographical book *Diary of a Lover of Marilyn Monroe* (1979), in which he claimed to have had a forty-night love affair with MM in the late 1950s.

**JACK LEMMON**

Fine actor, born in 1925, known for such films as *Mister Roberts* (for which he won a 1955 Oscar), *The Apartment* (1960), *The Days of Wine and Roses* (1962), *The Odd Couple* (1968), *Save the Tiger* (for which he won a 1973 Oscar), and *The China Syndrome* (1979). In 1959, Lemmon costarred opposite Marilyn Monroe in the classic comedy *Some Like It Hot.*

**LENOX HILL HOSPITAL**

New York hospital (address: 100 East 77th Street) where, in June 1959, Marilyn Monroe underwent what was termed "gynecological surgery of a corrective nature." She entered Lenox Hill on June 22, was operated on on the 23rd, and was released on June 26.

**PETER LEONARDI**

In Marilyn's "New York period" in the mid-1950s, Peter Leonardi served as her secretary/hairdresser/assistant.

***LET'S MAKE IT LEGAL*** **★★**

1951 79 minutes Black and White
20th Century-Fox
Directed by: Richard Sale
Produced by: Robert Bassler
Screenplay by: F. Hugh Herbert and I. A. L. Diamond, from a story by Mortimer Braus
Photographed by: Lucien Ballard
Cast: Claudette Colbert, Macdonald Carey, Zachary Scott, Barbara Bates, Robert Wagner, Marilyn Monroe, Frank Cady, Jim Hayward, Carol Savage, Paul Gerrits

Thinly plotted comedy about Grandma Colbert, about to be divorced, who is courted by a former sweetheart. Originally titled *Don't Call Me Mother, Legal* gave MM another one of her minor roles as a decorative blonde. In this one, she was cast as Joyce, a voluptuous gold digger who husband-hunts at a posh hotel.

During the shooting, Marilyn once clashed with director Richard Sale. It seems that MM (way back in 1951!) kept the film's stars, Colbert and Carey, waiting on the set for forty minutes. Angered, Sale lashed out at MM in front of the entire company and demanded an apology. Marilyn refused and reportedly threatened to telephone her powerful friend, Joe Schenck, who was an executive at 20th Century-Fox. Marilyn stormed off the set but returned a few minutes later and apologized to everyone involved. She also hugged Sale and thanked him for "straightening" her out.

*Let's Make It Legal* was released in November 1951.

***LET'S MAKE LOVE* ★★**
1960 118 minutes Color
20th Century-Fox
Directed by: George Cukor
Produced by: Jerry Wald
Screenplay by: Norman Krasna, with additional material by Hal Kanter
Photographed by: Daniel L. Fapp
Cast: Marilyn Monroe, Yves Montand, Frankie Vaughan, Tony Randall, Wilfrid Hyde-White, David Burns, Mara Lynn, Michael David, Dennis King, Jr.
Guest stars: Milton Berle, Bing Crosby, Gene Kelly

The movie whose title Marilyn Monroe and Yves Montand took too seriously. Originally titled *The Billionaire* and later named *The Millionaire* for French audiences, *Let's Make Love* is generally considered Marilyn's *least* successful starring vehicle.

In 1955–56, MM contracted to do four films in a seven-year period for 20th Century-Fox. However, by the beginning of 1960, Marilyn had only made *one* film for Fox, *Bus Stop*. Thus, in order to recognize her obligation, MM agreed to make *Let's Make Love,* which was, apparently, the best of the scripts that Fox had offered her.

There were problems from the start. First of all, MM was not happy with the completed script as written by Norman Krasna. Thus, she elicited the services of her Pulitzer Prize–winning husband, Arthur Miller, who was busy writing the script for her *next* feature, *The Misfits* (1961). Miller, who went uncredited on the picture, rewrote the script by tailoring it more to MM's talents.

And then there was the dilemma of casting the male lead. Gregory Peck, initially slated to costar opposite MM, balked when he read the Miller rewrite and walked off the production. Cary Grant, Charlton Heston, and Rock Hudson subsequently turned down the Krasna/Miller script. Then, along came Yves Montand. And as is common knowledge, Montand and Monroe had an affair.

Considering the problems and passions involved in the production of *Let's Make Love,* it has surprisingly little to offer. This is especially disconcerting when one considers the talents involved: director Cukor, choreographer Jack Cole, and musical supervisor Lionel Newman. One of the few highlights is a lengthy production of MM singing Cole Porter's "My Heart Belongs to Daddy." Other MM songs featured in this debacle are "Incurably Romantic," "Specialization," and "Let's Make Love."

Following the failure of *Let's Make Love,* critics and other industry insiders began to signal the demise of Marilyn's reign.

**PETER LEVATHES**

"Marilyn Monroe has been removed from the cast of *Something's Got to Give.* This action was made necessary because of Miss Monroe's repeated willful breaches of contract. No justification was

> given by Miss Monroe for her failure to report for photography on many occasions. The studio has suffered losses through these absences."
>
> Peter Levathes

Peter Levathes took control of 20th Century-Fox in 1960, while Marilyn was making *The Misfits* for United Artists. Reportedly, Levathes had more faith in the box-office appeal of Jayne Mansfield than in Marilyn Monroe and wanted to replace Monroe with Mansfield as Queen of the Fox blondes. At any rate, Marilyn's first film for Fox under Levathes's tutelage was the ill-fated *Something's Got to Give* in 1962. In June, following Marilyn's incessant failure to show up on the set, Levathes became the first and only man to fire Marilyn Monroe. As aptly put by Fred Lawrence Guiles, Levathes

> . . . was a former advertising man who felt his big moment had come. World attention was upon him. He had done what no one had ever dared do. He had fired Marilyn Monroe.

At his press conference, Levathes said,

> "Gentlemen, there isn't much I can say. We can't afford to risk millions on unreliable stars. This was behind my decision this week to sue Miss Monroe and her corporation for half a million dollars. We may have to increase that figure to a million."

**ALAN LEVY**
Author of the August 1962 interview of Marilyn that appeared in *Redbook* magazine.

**ABRAHAM LEWENSTEIN**
Abraham Lewenstein cowrote the 1980 "In Search of" television segment about MM entitled "In Search of: The Death of Marilyn Monroe."

**BOB LEWIN**
One of the publicists on *The Misfits* (1961).

**JERRY LEWIS**
Marilyn once included Jerry Lewis on a list of her choice for "The Most Outstanding Men." However, at the 1953 *Photoplay* magazine awards, host Lewis was just another howling male, lost under the mesmerizing Monroe spell.

**PERRY LIEBER**
Head of Publicity at RKO at the time MM made *Clash by Night* (1952).

**ART LIEBERMAN**
Art Lieberman produced the 1962 television documentary about MM entitled, appropriately, "The Marilyn Monroe Story." The special was later marketed as a home video, under the title, "Marilyn Monroe."

***THE LIFE AND CURIOUS DEATH OF MARILYN MONROE***

Author: Robert Slatzer
Publisher: Pinnacle Books
Year: 1974
$3.95, paperback, illustrated, 480 pages (ISBN 0-523-41859-0)

Fascinating and provocative, *The Life and Curious Death of Marilyn Monroe* is an important work because it was largely responsible for igniting public controversy over the circumstances surrounding Marilyn's death.

Well researched and documented, Slatzer's account has become, over the years, a favorite among those who believe that Robert Kennedy and/or Peter Lawford were involved in Marilyn's death. What *is* questionable about this book, though, is Slatzer's liberal use of quotes that he has attributed to Marilyn. In certain cases, the "quotations" are superfluous and somewhat ridiculous. For instance, following the 1950 release of *The Fireball*, Slatzer includes this:

> "I don't think I was even mentioned in the reviews," Marilyn said, still smiling and hoping, "but I learned a lot about roller skating."

Nonetheless, *The Life and Curious Death of Marilyn Monroe* is certainly laudable. Significantly, it was given the stamp of approval by Marilyn's makeup artist of sixteen years, Allan "Whitey" Snyder, who wrote the foreword. And, unlike many of the other exploitative books about Marilyn Monroe, this one was obviously written as a testament, out of affection.

***LIFE* MAGAZINE**

Marilyn Monroe had a long-standing love affair with *LIFE* magazine, and since her death *LIFE* has continued to carry the torch. As of August 1982, Marilyn had appeared on eleven American covers of *LIFE* magazine—more than any other individual in history, save Elizabeth Taylor, who has appeared on a dozen covers.

*LIFE* first featured Marilyn in its October 10, 1949, issue. MM was included in photographer Philippe Halsman's photo roundup of the then-current crop of Hollywood studio starlets. The layout also included aspiring actresses Suzanne Dalbert, Cathy Downs, Dolores Gardner, Laurette Luez, Lois Maxwell, Jane Nigh, and Ricky Soma. Each was photographed in a series of acting poses; e.g., "Seeing a Monster," "Hearing a Joke," "Embracing a Lover," etc. The article read: "*LIFE*'s readers can judge for themselves whether the girls have anything to offer the movies besides their good looks."

In its August 17, 1962, edition, *LIFE* published an eleven-page memorial tribute to Marilyn Monroe. The text read: "Her death has diminished the loveliness of the world in which we live."

In 1972, and again in 1982, *LIFE* put Marilyn on its cover, posthumously, to commemorate the tenth and twentieth anniversaries of her death.

*LIFE* has published the following articles on MM:

☆ 10/10/49: "Eight Girls Try Out Mixed Emotions"
☆ 1/1/51: "Apprentice Goddesses"
☆ 4/7/52*: "Hollywood Topic A-Plus"
☆ 5/25/53*: "Marilyn Takes Over as Lorelei"
☆ 1/25/54: "Merger of Two Worlds"
☆ 3/1/54: "Pin-up Takes Shape"
☆ 9/27/54: "Marilyn on the Town"
☆ 10/18/54: "Last Scene: Exit Unhappily"
☆ 11/29/54: "Life Goes to a Select Supper for Marilyn"
☆ 7/16/56: "Wedding Wine for Marilyn"
☆ 8/27/56: "Unveiling of the New Monroe"
☆ 6/3/57: "Unlikely Pair Make Great Match"
☆ 12/22/58: "Fabled Enchantresses"
☆ 12/22/58: "My Wife Marilyn"
☆ 4/20/59*: "Walk Like This Marilyn"
☆ 11/9/59*: "Marilyn, Part of a Jumping Picture Gallery"
☆ 8/15/60*: "Marilyn's Movie Lover: With Account by David Zeitlin"
☆ 11/21/60: "End of Famous Marriage"
☆ 6/22/62*: "They Fired Marilyn: Her Dip Lives On"
☆ 8/3/62: "Marilyn Let's Her Hair Down About Being Famous"
☆ 8/17/62*: "Last Long Talk with a Lonely Girl"
☆ 8/17/62*: "Remember Marilyn"
☆ 1/25/63: "Growing Cult of Marilyn"
☆ 8/7/64*: "What Really Killed Marilyn?"
☆ 11/4/66: "Behind the Myth the Face of Norma Jean"
☆ 7/23/71: "Gallery: Young Marilyn Monroe Before the Wave"
☆ 9/8/72*: "For Marilyn, a Look Back in Adoration"
☆ 10/81*: "Mania for Marilyn"
☆ 8/82*: "The Last Time I Saw Marilyn"
☆ 7/83: "A Marilyn for All Seasons"

---

**LIFE* covers that MM appeared on.
*Note: LIFE* also published two international editions with Marilyn on the covers. They were the 7/8/57 and 9/7/64 issues.

**MM Trivia Quiz #25**
Who appeared on the cover of *LIFE* first: Marilyn Monroe or Elizabeth Taylor? (Answer on page 577.)

**"LIKE A DIAMOND IN THE SKY"**
A one-hour television drama about an MM-based character that aired on NBC-TV's "The Eleventh Hour" on February 13, 1963. It was written by Alfred Brenner and starred Julie London as an MM-like torch singer/sex symbol named Joan Ashmond who dies suddenly under mysterious circumstances.

**DORIS LILLY**

Society authoress of the best-selling nonfiction book *How to Marry a Millionaire,* the title of which 20th Century-Fox purchased and turned into a 1953 film vehicle starring Monroe, Grable, and Bacall.

**ABRAHAM LINCOLN**

> "My father is Abraham Lincoln—I mean I think of Lincoln as my father. He was wise and kind and good. He is my ideal, Lincoln. I love him."
>
> Marilyn Monroe to Maurice Zolotow

THE RAY VAN GOEYE COLLECTION

"My father is Abraham Lincoln"—circa 1954.

Marilyn Monroe kept a photograph of Abraham Lincoln over her bed at her Doheny Drive apartment in Beverly Hills. She also kept a photo of Lincoln on her nightstand at her East 57th Street apartment in New York. Reportedly, when Marilyn moved from home to home, Lincoln's photograph moved with her. To display her idolatry of Lincoln, MM traveled to Bement, Illinois, in 1955 (during her self-imposed exile from Hollywood) to dedicate a museum in honor of America's sixteenth president.

Interestingly, in the latter part of her life, Marilyn struck up a friendship with Carl Sandburg, who was Abraham Lincoln's biographer.

**BENJAMIN LINGENFELDER**

Reverend Lingenfelder married Jim Dougherty to Norma Jeane Baker on June 19, 1942.

## LINGERIE

> "It was like the Lindbergh homecoming, recalls a studio executive. People were leaning out of every window. And there was Marilyn, naive and completely unperturbed, smiling and waving up at everybody she knew, didn't know or hoped to know."
>
> Robert Cahn, *Collier's* magazine

> "Was she mad, went a query through the studios, or a sexual bomb that Zanuck did not know how to use?"
>
> Norman Mailer

Before stardom, and at a time when she was in danger of falling into the abyss of forgotten bleached blondes, Marilyn single-handedly pulled a publicity stunt that caught the eye and attention of every man on the Fox lot.

On a day when she was scheduled to pose for studio publicity photos, Marilyn changed into a slinky negligee at the Fox wardrobe department and then proceeded to parade across six blocks to the lot's photo studio. Enroute, MM attracted the attention (how could she not?) of the studio messenger boys, who quickly bicycled the "news" throughout the lot. By the time Marilyn had completed her spectacle, the lot was lined with ogling, cheering spectators. The following day, several items appeared in the industry trades, and MM became the talk of Hollywood.

## HARRY LIPTON

Norma Jeane's first theatrical agent. Lipton, representing the National Concert Artists Corporation, was reportedly responsible for Norma Jeane's 1946 interview with Ben Lyon, which resulted in her being signed by 20th Century-Fox.

Lipton has also been credited as being responsible for Marilyn Monroe's interview with producer Lester Cowan for the 1950 Marx Brothers picture, *Love Happy*. And it was Harry Lipton who allowed Marilyn's contract to be purchased by Johnny Hyde, of the powerhouse William Morris agency—although Lipton *did* retain a percentage of MM's future profits for himself.

Of Harry Lipton, Marilyn was once quoted as saying to Robert Slatzer:

> "I never showed him any real appreciation for what he did for me at the beginning. . . . I really owe him so much, and I feel guilty that I didn't give him more credit. He was wonderful. I can't imagine how he put up with me in those days."

## "LITTLE ANNIE FANNY"

As a homage to Marilyn Monroe, the October 1962 edition of *Playboy* magazine introduced a busty, blonde cartoon character by the name of "Little Annie Fanny." The character, created by artists Harvey Kurtzman and Wil Elder, has been a regular feature in *Playboy* ever since.

## THE LITTLE CORNER RESTAURANT

A Connecticut restaurant, managed by Milton H. Greene's brother, that MM frequented circa 1955. Marilyn reportedly indulged in sandwiches and chocolate éclairs.

**ROBERT LITTLEFIELD**

Littlefield did MM's makeup for the MGM industrial film *Hometown Story* (1951).

**BARBARA LODEN**

Actress and wife of director Elia Kazan who initially played the Maggie/Marilyn character in Arthur Miller's 1964 play, *After the Fall.* Said the critics:

> This girl is magnificently played by Barbara Loden. Miss Loden, ash blonde, very beautiful and very sexy, is an astonishing reminder of the late Marilyn Monroe.
>
> *New York Daily News*

> The second most important part, that of the tragic girl celebrity, is movingly and appealingly played by Barbara Loden. . . .
>
> *New York Post*

> Barbara Loden . . . stuns the audience with the bitter, heartbreaking truth of her change from total trust to destructive suspicion.
>
> *New York World-Telegram and Sun*

**LOEW'S CAPITOL THEATRE**

Broadway theatre where *Some Like It Hot* premiered on March 29, 1959.

**LOEW'S STATE THEATRE**

New York theatre where *The Seven Year Itch* premiered on June 1, 1955.

**JOSHUA LOGAN**

> "When I tell people Marilyn Monroe may be one of the very finest dramatic talents of our time, they laugh in my face. But I believe it. I believe it to such an extent that I would like to direct her in every picture she wants me for, every story she can dig up."
>
> Joshua Logan, 1956

Joshua Logan was born in Texarkana, Texas, in 1908. The first film he directed was *I Met My Love Again* in 1938. He then became a noted New York stage director before he trekked back to Hollywood to shoot the film version of *Picnic* (1956).

Following *Picnic,* Logan directed Marilyn Monroe in what became her most acclaimed dramatic performance—the role of Cherie in William Inge's *Bus Stop* (1956). It was an extremely important "comeback" film for Marilyn, and Joshua Logan was the perfect director for the job. Not only had Logan studied under Konstantin Stanislavsky; he was also on friendly terms with Marilyn's drama coach at that time, Lee Strasberg.

Prior to the shooting, Logan contacted Milton H. Greene and requested that MM's coach, Paula Strasberg, stay off the *Bus Stop* set to avoid potential conflicts. Nevertheless, Logan and MM got along well—with one exception. It was while shooting on location in Phoenix. At 6:05 P.M., Logan sent his assistant director, Ben Kadish, to fetch MM. But Marilyn didn't show up.

Logan then administered his script girl to go and retrieve MM and Kadish. When this failed to produce the desired results, Logan himself ran to the Sahara Motor Hotel, where MM was staying, and literally pushed her before the cameras.

Still, Joshua Logan remained Marilyn Monroe's champion—at least until she saw the final cut of *Bus Stop*. Reportedly, Marilyn became furious with Logan because she thought that he had cut her best moments from the picture. However, after *Bus Stop* opened later that year, Marilyn Monroe received the best film reviews of her career. As for Joshua Logan, he is one of the few directors that MM worked with who has remained faithful to her over the years.

Of Marilyn, Logan has been quoted:

> "The second offer from Fox was Marilyn Monroe in *Bus Stop* and that was thrilling because I loved the play. I'd seen it in New York. I loved the idea of doing it right away. They said, 'All right, now we'll find out whether you're on her list of directors.' And I said, 'What do you mean by that?' 'Well,' they said, 'she has a whole new contract. She is now Marilyn Monroe Incorporated.' It had all been arranged by Milton H. Greene, the photographer, who is a terribly bright man and who had more or less taken over the business side of her life because he felt she was getting a raw deal, which indeed she was. They were using her in a shameless way, giving her rotten scripts, the wrong directors, everything."
>
> "I felt very, very close to her. I think it was impossible to work with her without falling for her. She was so darling, cuddly, warm, and she was so sincere. She cared and she was so ambitious. She wanted to be good, she wanted to be great, and everyone began to want her to be."
>
> "I worked with Brando later and there was a similarity; they were both tremendously talented people. But I don't think I ever cared as much for anyone as I did for her. And I don't think I ever did any better work. I was so astounded by her ability to make me cry and at the same time to bring on a laugh."
>
> "She is the most constantly exciting actress I've ever worked with. I don't mean the kind of excitement that is related to her being a celebrity. I mean the kind of excitement that comes from her humanness, from the way she sees life all around her."
>
> "I found her to be one of the greatest talents of all time."
> "[She was] luminous and completely desirable. Yet naive about herself and touching, rather like a little frightened animal, a fawn or a baby chicken."
>
> "Monroe is as near genius as any actress I ever knew. . . . She is the most completely realized actress since Garbo. Watch her work. In any film. How rarely she has to use words. How much she does with her eyes, her lips, with slight, almost accidental gestures. . . . Monroe is pure cinema."
>
> "It is a disease of our profession that we believe a woman with physical appeal has no talent."

### LONDON, ENGLAND

> She walks. She talks. She really is as luscious as strawberries and cream.
>
> *The London Evening News,*
> on Marilyn's arrival, July 1956

The newly wed Mr. and Mrs. Arthur Miller arrived at the London airport on July 14, 1956, to begin preparations for the shooting of *The Prince and the Showgirl*. Accompanying the Millers was an entourage consisting of twenty-seven pieces of luggage, three of which belonged to Arthur. The total cost of the excess baggage was an estimated $1,500. Also accompanying Mr. and Mrs. Miller were Mr. and Mrs. Milton H. Greene, Mr. and Mrs. Lee Strasberg, and Mrs. Hedda Rosten. The Millers were greeted at the London airport by Mr. and Mrs. Laurence Olivier, who then escorted them to a large rented estate at Egham that the Oliviers had selected for them.

Marilyn's visit to London created quite a stir. In anticipation of her arrival, one London newspaper printed a special "Marilyn Monroe Edition" in June 1956. And once, while she was shopping at Harrod's for presents for her stepchildren, Marilyn was mobbed, and the British police had to be called in to empty the store. At least one photographer was crushed and trampled on in a frenzy to get to and at Marilyn Monroe.

But the London public and press did not take well to Marilyn's standoffish persona. They wanted the sexy Marilyn. The witty Marilyn. The dumb blonde Marilyn. Instead, Marilyn served them—or tried to—the English reserve Marilyn. As a result, MM received mostly negative press during her stay. She was labeled pretentious and was criticized for her taste in clothes (or her lack of it, in their eyes) and also for her disrespectful treatment of Lord Olivier.

Nevertheless, on October 29, 1956, Marilyn was presented in a Royal Command Performance before Queen Elizabeth. Following the completion of *The Prince and the Showgirl* shooting, the Millers packed their many bags and left England on November 20, 1956.

### JULIE LONDON

Singer/actress Julie London was born Julie Peck in 1926. In February 1963, Miss London portrayed a Marilyn-based character in an NBC-TV movie entitled *Like a Diamond in the Sky*. London has acted in several motion pictures but is perhaps best known for her stint as a nurse in the television series "Emergency" (1972–77).

### *LOOK* MAGAZINE

*Look* published the following articles on MM:

- ☆ 6/20/50: "The Girls in the Asphalt Jungle—Two New Stars?"
- ☆ 10/23/51:* "Who Says Hollywood is Dying?"
- ☆ 6/3/52:* "The Tragedy of West Point's Class of '50"
- ☆ 9/9/52:* "Yea, Georgia Tech! Marilyn Monroe"
- ☆ 6/30/53:* "Monroe, Bacall, and Grable: Take on a New Dimension"
- ☆ 11/17/53:* "Marilyn Monroe; Photographs"

☆ 5/29/56: "New Marilyn"
☆ 10/30/56: "Olivier and Monroe"
☆ 10/1/57: "Marilyn's New Life"
☆ 7/5/60:* "Marilyn Meets Montand"
☆ 1/31/61:* "Gable's Last Movie: Prelude to Tragedy"
☆ 1/16/62: "Four for Posterity"
☆ 9/11/62: "Tribute to Marilyn from a Friend"
☆ 2/19/79: "A Revealing Last Interview (1962) with Marilyn Monroe"

---

**LOOK* covers that MM appeared on.

**ANITA LOOS**

Anita Loos (1891–1981) is the writer whose novel-turned-play-turned-movie-turned-musical-movie, *Gentlemen Prefer Blondes* (1953), made a superstar out of Marilyn Monroe.

At the time of Marilyn's death in 1962, a typewritten note from a representative of Anita Loos was found in Marilyn's home. It read:

> On behalf of Anita Loos, now in Europe, we would like to know if you would be interested [to] star [in] new musical based on French play *Gogo*. Book by Anita Loos, lyrics by Gladys Shelley, and enchanting music by Claude Leville. [I] can send you script and music if you express interest.
>
> —Natalia Danesi Murray

**MARY LOOS**

Mary Loos cowrote the screenplay for *A Ticket to Tomahawk* (1950), which featured MM in a brief bit as a chorus girl.

**SOPHIA LOREN**

> "We both rose from the same place . . . and she is like a sister to me. And of course I feel like I could've [saved her] if I tried. But it's a full-time job to save someone like that. Maybe if I'd met her I could have. . . . I would've written her things, poems, plays. Sure I could have saved her . . . just to take her to lunch every once in a while. I've known women like that who are still around. Not that I saved them, but they just needed some friends, some encouragement, and no one ever called her."
>
> "She was a marvelous actress with a lively personality. Her life cannot have been very happy, but she always succeeded in appearing happy and serene."
>
> Sophia Loren on Marilyn Monroe

When Arthur Miller's Broadway play *After the Fall* was being adapted into a feature film, it was Sophia Loren who was slated to star in the MM-based role of Maggie. The June 23, 1964, *Hollywood Reporter* ran the following item:

> Arthur Miller's play, *After the Fall,* will be filmed by Carlo Ponti and Ira Steiner, former Ashley-Steiner Famous Artists agency topper,

for MGM release. Screen rights reportedly brought $500,000. Sophia Loren and Paul Newman will star and Fred Zinnemann is sought to direct, subject to Miller's approval. Miller starts work on the screenplay in September.

### *THE LOS ANGELES EXAMINER*

Los Angeles city newspaper that carried many items and feature stories on Marilyn Monroe during her career. Interestingly, the *Examiner* was one of two major Los Angeles newspapers to fold in 1962—the year that Marilyn died.

### LOS ANGELES GENERAL HOSPITAL

Hospital where Norma Jeane Mortenson was born to Gladys Pearl Mortenson on June 1, 1926. Today, Los Angeles General is called the L.A. County U.S.C. Medical Center and is located at 1200 N. State Street.

### *THE LOS ANGELES MIRROR*

The second of two Los Angeles newspapers to fold in 1962. Over the years, the *Mirror* published two important series of articles on Marilyn Monroe. The first was a three-part feature entitled "Wolves I Have Known." It was "written" by Marilyn, "as told to" columnist Florabel Muir, and appeared in 1952. In 1960, the *Mirror* ran *daily* features on MM. The articles featured material from Maurice Zolotow's then recently published biography, *Marilyn Monroe*.

### THE LOS ANGELES ORPHANS HOME SOCIETY

It is no secret to any student of Marilyn Monroe that Norma Jeane Baker was placed in an orphanage when she was a child. Most of Marilyn's biographers have placed Norma Jeane at the Los Angeles Orphans Home Society (address: 815 N. El Centro Avenue) in Hollywood from September 19, 1935, until June 26, 1937—a total of twenty-one months—when Norma Jeane would have been nine, ten, and eleven years old. However, according to at least one administrator of the orphanage, Norma Jeane lived at the home for only a nine-month period.

In 1930, a young Mexican girl named Maria was placed in the orphanage. Several years later, a young girl, the same age as Maria, was brought to live at the orphanage. Some forty-five years later, Maria (then in her fifties) remembered Norma Jeane as "a very quiet, very gentle girl." Recalled Maria:

> "I'll never forget how good and kind she was to me. So even today if I hear people putting her down, it's like a knife in my heart. She was a very generous person who would never say no to you if you asked her for something. I remember her sitting quietly at a piano we had there and playing for us. She always reminded me of a doe. A funny thing: In 1962, I got the feeling that I should write to her. Whether she'd remember me or not, I wanted to let her know she had a friend. I did write the letter and a month later, she passed away."

Norma Jeane was placed in the orphanage by her legal guardian, Grace McKee. She slept in the twenty-seventh bed, and her bedroom window faced the RKO Studios water tower. She carried out her mandatory chores, for which she was paid a token sum. And while at the orphanage she learned how to swim—a skill that Marilyn Monroe chose *not* to use later in life.

Ten years after Norma Jeane left the orphanage, on October 4, 1947, an entry was recorded in Norma Jeane's file at the orphanage. It read:

> Norma Jeane Baker has great success in pictures and promises to be a star. She is a very beautiful woman and is now acting as Marilyn Monroe.

According to Bob Morgan, the current assistant director of the home, The Los Angeles Orphans Home Society was rebuilt in 1956. A year later, it was officially renamed Hollygrove. Today, Hollygrove still stands at 815 N. El Centro Avenue, in the heart of Hollywood, near Paramount Studios.

## THE LOS ANGELES ORTHOPEDIC FOUNDATION

The August 8, 1962, edition of the *Hollywood Reporter* contained the following item:

> Request has been made by the immediate family of Marilyn Monroe that rather than flowers, expressions of sympathy should be in the form of donations to the Los Angeles Orthopedic Foundation, or similar Children's Hospital.

## THE LOS ANGELES POLICE DEPARTMENT

Chief of Police in 1962: William H. Parker
First officer on the scene: Jack Clemmons
Police report filed by: R. E. Byron

### DEATH REPORT OF MARILYN MONROE

> Death was pronounced on 8/5/62 at 3:45 A.M., possible accidental, having taken place between the time of 8/4 and 8/5/62, 3:35 A.M., at residence located at 12305 Fifth Helena Drive, Brentwood, in Rptg. Dist. 814, Report # 62-509-463.
>
> Marilyn Monroe on August 4, 1962 retired to her bedroom at about eight o'clock in the evening; Mrs. Eunice Murray of 933 Ocean Ave., Santa Monica, Calif., 395-7752, CR 61890, noted a light in Miss Monroe's bedroom. Mrs. Murray was not able to arouse Miss Monroe when she went to the door, and when she tried the door again at 3:30 A.M., when she noted the light still on, she found it to be locked. Thereupon Mrs. Murray observed Miss Monroe through the bedroom window and found her lying on her stomach in the bed and the appearance seemed unnatural. Mrs. Murray then called Miss Monroe's psychiatrist, Dr. Ralph Greenson of 436 North Roxbury Drive, Beverly Hills, Calif., CR 14050. Upon entering after breaking the bedroom window, he found Miss Monroe, possibly dead.
>
> Then he telephoned Dr. Hyman Engelberg of 9730 Wilshire Boulevard, also of Beverly Hills, CR 54366, who came over and then

pronounced Miss Monroe dead at 3:35 A.M. Miss Monroe was seen by Dr. Greenson on August 4, 1962 at 5:15 P.M., at her request, because she was not able to sleep. She was being treated by him for about a year. She was nude when Dr. Greenson found her dead with the telephone receiver in one hand and lying on her stomach. The Police Department was called and when they arrived they found Miss Monroe in the condition described above, except for the telephone which was removed by Dr. Greenson. There were found to be 15 bottles of medication on the night table and some were prescription. A bottle marked 1½ grains Nembutal, prescription #20853 and prescribed by Dr. Engelberg, and referring, to this particular bottle, Dr. Engelberg made the statement that he prescribed a refill for this about two days ago and he further stated there probably should have been about 50 capsules at the time this was refilled by the pharmacist.

Description of deceased: Female Caucasian, age 36, height 5′4″, weight 115 pounds, blonde hair, blue eyes, and slender, medium build.

Occupation: Actress. Probable cause of death: overdose of Nembutal, body discovered 8/5/62 at 3:25 A.M. Taken to County Morgue—from there to Westwood Mortuary. Report made by Sgt. R. E. Byron, #2730, W.L.A. Detective Division. Next of kin Gladys Baker (Mother).

Coroner's office notified. The body was removed from premises by Westwood Village Mortuary.
(8/5/62 11:00 A.M., W.L.A. hf—J. R. Brukles 5829)

### DEATH REPORT OF MARILYN MONROE
### Follow-Up

Upon reinterviewing both Dr. Ralph Greenson (Wit #1) and Dr. Hyman Engelberg (Wit #2) they both agree to the following time sequence of their actions.

Dr. Greenson received a phone call from Mrs. Murray (reporting person) at 3:30 A.M., 8-5-62 stating that she was unable to get into Miss Monroe's bedroom and the light was on. He told her to pound on the door and look in the window and call him back. At 3:35 A.M., Mrs. Murray called back and stated Miss Monroe was laying on the bed with the phone in her hand and looked strange. Dr. Greenson was dressed by this time, left for deceased residence which is about one mile away. He also told Mrs. Murray to call Dr. Engelberg.

Dr. Greenson arrived at deceased home at about 3:40 A.M. He broke the window pane and entered through the window and removed the phone from her hand.

Rigor Mortis had set in. At 3:50 A.M., Dr. Engelberg arrived and pronounced Miss Monroe dead. The two doctors talked for a few moments. They both believe that it was about 4:00 A.M. when Dr. Engelberg called the Police Department.

A check with the Complaint Board and WLA Desk, indicates that the call was received at 4:25 A.M. Miss Monroe's phone GR 61890 has been checked and no toll calls were made during the hours of this occurrence. Phone number 472-4830 is being checked at the present time.

R. E. Byron 2730, 8-6-62

### THE LOS ANGELES PRESS CLUB

In 1948, starlet Marilyn Monroe was named the very first "Miss Press Club." Her duty in this position was to act as the hostess at the Los Angeles Press Club's functions and meetings. The Los Angeles Press Club was headquartered at The Ambassador Hotel, where Marilyn's former modeling agency, The Blue Book Model Agency, was also located.

COURTESY OF DICK BIEGERT

First Miss Press Club posing at a club function, circa 1953.

**LOUIS CREATIVE HAIRDRESSERS**
A photograph of Marilyn Monroe appeared in a print advertisement for Louis Creative Hairdressers circa 1952. The ad read:

> The finest permanents regularly $10, $15, $20—now $5, complete.
> No extra charge for haircutting, test curls, shampoo, styling . . .
> includes poodle cuts, too!

***LOVE HAPPY* ★★**
1949 85 minutes Black and White
United Artists (a Mary Pickford presentation)
Directed by: David Miller
Produced by: Lester Cowan
Screenplay by: Frank Tashlin and Mac Benoff, from a story by Harpo Marx
Photographed by: William C. Mellor
Cast: Groucho Marx, Harpo Marx, Chico Marx, Ilona Massey, Vera-Ellen, Marion Hutton, Raymond Burr, Bruce Gordon, Melville Cooper, Leon Belasco, Paul Valentine, Eric Blore, Marilyn Monroe

*Love Happy* was the last of the Marx Brothers' films. It was, by most accounts, a surprising failure.

In early 1949, after being out of movie work for nearly half a year, Marilyn Monroe was cast in a walk-on bit in *Love Happy*. Some sources contend that it was Hollywood agent Louis Shurr who encouraged MM to audition for producer Lester Cowan. Others credit Marilyn's own agent, Harry Lipton. Still others claim that it was Marilyn herself who hustled her own interview with Cowan and Groucho Marx at RKO Studios. At any rate, Marilyn did audition. And, in her words,

THE CHRIS BASINGER COLLECTION

> "There were three girls there and Groucho had us each walk away from him. I was the only one he asked to do it twice. Then he whispered in my ear, 'You have the prettiest ass in the business.' I'm sure he meant it in the nicest way."

Marilyn got the part and was given a couple lines of dialogue as a tip. And although the role was brief and the lines were inconsequential, Marilyn *did* manage to make an impression.

> GROUCHO: Is there anything I can do for you? What a ridiculous statement.
> MARILYN: Mr. Grunion. I want you to help me . . . Some men are following me.
> GROUCHO: Really, I can't understand why.

When *Love Happy* was released in the spring of 1950 Marilyn was given an "Introducing Marilyn Monroe" on-screen credit—despite the fact that she had made three previous films. And though she was only on screen for some ninety seconds, *Love Happy* is important in Marilyn Monroe's filmography for two reasons. First, it introduced "the Marilyn Walk" to screen audiences and Hollywood insiders. Second, it introduced her, indirectly, to Hollywood super-agent Johnny Hyde.

In June 1949, Marilyn Monroe was broke, out of work, and still hopelessly in love with Fred Karger. Thus, when producer Lester Cowan offered her the chance to go on a national tour to promote *Love Happy*, she accepted.

To prepare for her first major trip, Marilyn went to the May Company department store and splurged (with money given to her by Cowan) on three wool suits. She was whisked via limousine to Union Station in Los Angeles, where she boarded a train on the Santa Fe Chief railroad. In Chicago, MM boarded the Twentieth Century Limited, which took her to the tour's first stop: New York City. MM had never been to New York, but she understood that it was colder there than in Los Angeles, so she had packed only warm clothes. What she didn't realize was that New York was in the throes of a summer heat wave. Thus, once in the city, one of the *Love Happy* press agents had the bright idea of shooting a publicity shot of the sweating MM indulging herself with three ice cream cones. The accompanying photo caption read, "Marilyn Monroe: the hottest thing in Hollywood, cooling off." Quite a lot of hype for an unknown starlet with a walk-on bit, no money, and no studio.

While in New York, Marilyn was dubbed, inanely, "the Woo Woo Girl" and "the Mmmm Girl." She interviewed with columnists Sidney Fields and Earl Wilson. She met with reporters at her Sherry Netherland Hotel suite. And she posed for a series of photographs, taken at Tobey Beach, for her old friend and ex-lover, Andre de Dienes.

From New York, MM peddled her "Woo Woo" curves and her "cooling off" ice cream routine in Detroit, Cleveland, Chicago, and Milwaukee. Finally, exasperated, she quit the tour while in Rockford, Illinois (much to the chagrin of Cowan), and returned to Los Angeles in August.

### *LOVE NEST* ★★

1951 84 minutes Black and White
20th Century-Fox
Directed by: Joseph Newman
Produced by: Jules Buck
Screenplay by: I. A. L. Diamond, based on a novel by Scott Corbett
Photographed by: Lloyd Ahern
Cast: William Lundigan, June Haver, Marilyn Monroe, Frank Fay, Leatrice Joy, Jack Paar, Maude Wallace

After the "Negligee Incident," after the 20th Century-Fox exhibitors party, after Fox honcho Spyros Skouras took a personal interest in her, and before the nude-calendar news, Marilyn Monroe was reportedly cast in every/any Fox production that could use a buxom blonde. *Love Nest* was one such production.

*Love Nest* was Marilyn's second film under her new contract with 20th Century-Fox. In it, MM played Roberta Stevens, aka Bobbie, a former WAC who wreaks havoc on the June Haver/Bill Lundigan marriage.

*Love Nest* began shooting on April 18, 1951, and was released on October 10, 1951.

### GLORIA LOVELL

Gloria Lovell was Frank Sinatra's secretary, who lived next door to MM at her Doheny apartment, circa November 1961. It was Miss Lovell who "inherited" Marilyn's dog, Maf, after MM's death.

### THE LOVERS

> She was Johnny Hyde's mistress. She was the mistress of Joseph Schenck, Chairman of the Board of 20th Century-Fox, and she had affairs with many others and slept casually with many, many men. So, by ordinary moral standards, Marilyn's conduct left much to be desired.
>
> Edwin P. Hoyt, *The Tragic Venus* (Chilton, 1965)

> The champagne turned me into Clark Gable, and soon Marilyn and I were lying on the couch passionately kissing each other, touching each other. It was heaven. Soon we were naked in bed. . . . Dom Perignon has to be the greatest aphrodisiac of all time.
>
> James Bacon, *Hollywood Is a Four-Letter Town* (Avon, 1976)

> She broke into laughter and sat on the bed beside me. Shutterbug, you're so funny. When two people are together night after night, no one is doing anybody else a favor. She dropped the big white beach towel around her breasts and put her arms around me and kissed me and whispered, "Let's do what comes naturally." We did.
>
> David Conover, *Finding Marilyn*(Grosset & Dunlap, 1981)

Over the years, an innumerable number of men—and a few women—have been reported to have had a sexual relationship with Marilyn Monroe. In some cases, the claim was made by the individuals themselves. The following is a selective list of Marilyn's lovers—actual and alleged.

THE SABIN GRAY COLLECTION
With some of her alleged lovers, Sammy Davis, Jr., Mel Torme, and Milton Greene, circa 1956.

James Bacon
Milton Berle
Jose Bolanos
Marlon Brando
John Carroll
Charlie Chaplin, Jr.
Sydney Chaplin
David Conover
Sammy Davis, Jr.
Andre de Dienes
Joe DiMaggio
James Dougherty
Charles Feldman
Milton H. Greene
Howard Hughes
Johnny Hyde
Georgie Jessel
Ted Jordan
Fred Karger
Elia Kazan
John F. Kennedy
Robert F. Kennedy
Anton La Vey
Hans Jorgen Lembourn
Ben Lyon
Natasha Lytess
Arthur Miller
Nico Minardos
Yves Montand
Edward G. Robinson, Jr.
Henry Rosenfeld
George Sanders
Hal Schaefer
Joseph Schenck
Frank Sinatra
Robert Slatzer
Spyros Skouras
Franchot Tone
Mel Torme
Billy Travilla
Tommy Zahn

**MM Trivia Quiz #26**
In what film did MM engage in an adulterous affair? (Answer on page 577.)

**ANA LOWER**

Norma dear, read this book. I do not leave you much except my love, but not even death can diminish that; nor will death ever take me far away from you.

Ana Lower, inscribed in the book, *Science and Health with Key to the Scriptures*

"She changed my whole life. She was the first person in the world I ever really loved and she loved me. She was a wonderful human being. I once wrote a poem about her . . . it was called 'I Love Her.' She never hurt me, not once. She couldn't. She was all kindness and all love. She was good to me."

MM to Maurice Zolotow

"There's only one person in the world that I've ever really loved. That was Aunt Ana . . . Aunt Ana was sure—surer than I am now—that I was right in my ambition to be an actress and that I'd be a success. But she'll never know whether she was right or wrong. She died before my first bit part."

MM to Clarice Evans in the late 1940s

"Aunt" Ana Lower was Grace Goddard's aunt, and she adored Norma Jeane. NJ/MM was in close contact with Ana Lower for a period of over ten years, which proved to be one of the longest and happiest personal associations of Marilyn Monroe's life.

Shortly after her release from the orphanage in 1937, Norma Jeane went to live with Aunt Ana for the first time. For the next nine years, Norma Jeane lived—on and off (mostly "off" during NJ's marriage to Jim Dougherty)—with her beloved Aunt Ana. It was Aunt Ana who introduced Norma Jeane to the Christian Science Church. And it was Aunt Ana who "gave the bride away" at Norma Jeane's first wedding on June 19, 1942. It was also Aunt Ana who consoled Norma Jeane following the demise of that marriage.

Ana Lower was born on January 17, 1880. Sadly, she died on March 14, 1948, before Marilyn Monroe had achieved any real celebrity as an actress.

**CLARE BOOTHE LUCE**

Luce penned the ten-page *LIFE* magazine feature "What Really Killed Marilyn?" that appeared in the August 7, 1964, issue.

**LUCEY'S RESTAURANT**

Not to be confused with the popular Mexican restaurant, Lucey's El Adobe, Lucey's Restaurant was located at 5444 Melrose Avenue in Hollywood, across from Paramount Studios. It was here that Marilyn met with producer Jerry Wald to interview for a part in *Clash by Night* (1952).

Lucey's closed in the mid-1960s and has been replaced by Walter's Plant Rentals.

**LUSTRE-CREME SHAMPOO**

Reportedly, Lustre-Creme was the shampoo company that changed Norma Jeane from a dirty blonde to a blonde blonde for a series of print advertisements. And, in 1953, during the run of *Gentlemen Prefer Blondes,* MM appeared in another ad for this same company. In it, Marilyn vouched, "Yes, I use Lustre-Creme Shampoo."

THE ALAN FRANCE COLLECTION

**NED LUTZ**

In 1954, Ned Lutz was the restaurant manager of the Paso Robles Hot Springs Hotel, where Marilyn and Joe DiMaggio ate dinner on their wedding night, January 14, 1954.

**BEN LYON**

> "It's Jean Harlow all over again."
>
> Ben Lyon on first meeting Norma Jeane Dougherty

Ben Lyon (1901–1979) is the man who "discovered" Marilyn Monroe. He named her. He gave her her first motion picture screen test. And he signed her to her first motion picture studio contract.

It was on a day in mid-July 1946 that Norma Jeane Dougherty walked into Lyon's office at 20th Century-Fox. Without proper consent from his boss, Darryl Zanuck, Lyon was sufficiently impressed by MM to arrange a *color* screen test for her. The test, of course, resulted in Norma Jeane's being signed by Fox. Reportedly, Lyon was also responsible for MM's being cast in the Sol Wurtzel picture *Dangerous Years* (1948).

Allegedly, there was more to the Lyon/Monroe relationship than just casting director/contract player. As reported in Anthony Summers's *Goddess: The Secret Lives of Marilyn Monroe* (Macmillan, 1985), "According to writer Sheilah Graham, Lyon had been sleeping with Marilyn and promising to further her career."

By the time Ben Lyon met Norma Jeane Dougherty, he had been a film star in his own right for nearly twenty years. Years later, after Marilyn Monroe had become a full-fledged star, she sent Lyon an autographed photo of herself. The inscription read: "You found me, named me and believed in me when no one else did. My love and thanks forever."

**BARBARA LYTESS**

Natasha Lytess's daughter, who lived on Harper Avenue with her mother—and, for a period in 1951, with Marilyn Monroe.

**NATASHA LYTESS**

> NATASHA: You're wonderful. I love you.
> MARILYN: Don't love me. Teach me.

> "She was a great teacher, but she got really jealous about the men I saw. She thought she was my husband!"
>
> Marilyn Monroe on Natasha Lytess

> "Without Natasha, there would be nothing. . . . To me, Natasha is an ally—not an enemy."
>
> Billy Wilder

> "[Marilyn needed me] like a dead man needs a coffin."
>
> Natasha Lytess, years after her split from Marilyn Monroe

> "I had been her private director for years, working with her day and night. Yet when she was asked to do something for me, she had the feeling that she was being used."
>
> Natasha Lytess on MM

"I taught her how to walk, how to breathe."

Natasha Lytess on MM

Marilyn Monroe was twenty-five minutes late for her first meeting with Natasha Lytess. It was April 1948. Marilyn had recently been signed to a six-month contract with Columbia Pictures. At that time, Natasha was Columbia's head drama coach. Columbia's head of talent, Max Arnow, along with *Ladies of the Chorus* (1948) producer Harry Romm, asked Natasha to work with Marilyn.

Natasha and Marilyn developed an important, intense relationship that lasted seven years, until the completion of *The Seven Year Itch* (1955) shooting. Natasha took Marilyn seriously as an actress at a time when no one else did. As she told the press,

> "There's more to Marilyn than meets the eye. The trouble is that when people look at her they immediately figure her as a typical Hollywood Blonde. It's not their fault though. Marilyn's soul just doesn't fit her body."

So strong was Natasha's belief in her pupil that, when Marilyn was signed for *The Asphalt Jungle* in 1950, Lytess quit her job so that she could coach MM from the sidelines. After 1951, beginning with *Clash by Night* (1952), Marilyn refused to do a scene unless Natasha was present on the set. Marilyn became increasingly dependent on Natasha. Years later, Natasha herself said,

> "Her habit of looking at me the second she finished a scene was to become a joke in projection rooms. . . . The film of the daily rushes was filled with scenes of Marilyn, finishing her dialogue and immediately shading her eyes to find me, to see if she had done well."

To prepare for the shooting of *Don't Bother to Knock* (1952), Marilyn moved in with Natasha at the latter's West Hollywood home on Harper Avenue. Insiders began to question Natasha's influence over Marilyn. Reportedly, MM gave Natasha a car and a fur coat. She also got Natasha on the 20th Century-Fox payroll.

With the exception of Billy Wilder, Natasha was regarded as an obstacle by most of Marilyn's directors. She was barred (and later reinstated) from the set of *River of No Return* (1954). Nonetheless, Marilyn remained adamant and stood by her coach.

Rumors spread in underground Hollywood that Marilyn was involved in a lesbian affair with Natasha. This alleged affair was later "verified" by Marilyn's New York maid, Lena Pepitone, and also by columnist Florabel Muir. And, according to *The Gay Book of Days,* "Is it any wonder that she [MM] once found a rare moment of comfort in an affair with a female drama coach . . . ?"

At any rate, Natasha did *not* approve of Marilyn's personal involvements with men. She certainly did not approve of Joe DiMaggio, nor he of her. It can be deduced, then, that as Marilyn's relationship with DiMaggio intensified, her bond with Lytess deteriorated.

With Natasha Lytess, her drama coach, circa 1952. THE ROBERT SLATZER COLLECTION

In 1956, when Marilyn returned to Hollywood to shoot *Bus Stop,* she was required to confront Natasha—who was still on the Fox payroll—and tell her that her services were no longer required. While in New York, Marilyn had picked up a new, more prestigious acting coach, Mrs. Paula Strasberg. However, instead of personally informing Natasha, Marilyn had an East

Coast law firm send her an impersonal telegram. Marilyn also refused to see or talk to Natasha, who was understandably miffed. Said the ousted coach,

> "With just a motion of her fingers, she could have told them [Fox] she wanted me to stay at the studio, even if she didn't want me herself on this picture."

In 1966, *Coronet* magazine published an article that contained the following explanation:

> Marilyn was terrified after she broke with Miss Lytess; she talked as if she were afraid for her life, but what she was really saying was that she had committed a terrible crime against Miss Lytess and therefore ought to be afraid for her life. She could no more face Miss Lytess and tell her that the "new" Marilyn had a new way of dealing with the matter of acting, than she could work with her old teacher. She felt guilty and angry and ashamed, all at once. Instead of explaining or trying to explain, Marilyn dropped Natasha Lytess cruelly in a way that injured the acting coach as a force in Hollywood.

Before her death in 1964 from cancer, Natasha wrote an autobiographical account entitled "My Years with Marilyn." And, while it *is* true that Marilyn used (and cruelly disposed of) Natasha Lytess, it is undeniable that Natasha *also* used Marilyn Monroe. Through Marilyn, Natasha found acclaim, celebrity, power, and financial compensation.

# M

**JOE MacDONALD**
Joe MacDonald was the cinematographer on three of Marilyn Monroe's movies: *As Young as You Feel* (1951), *Niagara* (1953), and *How to Marry a Millionaire* (1953). His non-MM pictures include *Viva Zapata* (1952) and *A Hatful of Rain* (1957).

**BOB MACKIE**
Famed fashion designer, Bob Mackie, was one of three writers of the 1982 stage play, *Movie Star* which featured a Marilyn Monroe-based character.

**SHIRLEY MacLAINE**
Interestingly, when Marilyn Monroe died in 1962, Shirley MacLaine was one of the actresses who took over some of the projects that had been proposed for MM. Acutally, even before Marilyn died, 20th Century-Fox threatened to replace MM with MacLaine on *Something's Got to Give* (1962). A year later, Miss MacLaine starred in *Irma La Douce*—a film that Billy Wilder reportedly offered to MM as far back as 1960. MacLaine received an Oscar nomination for her performance. Then, in 1964, MacLaine starred in *What a Way to Go.* It was the film that Marilyn had planned to make following *Something's Got to Give.*

Born Shirley Maclean Beaty in 1934, actress/dancer/singer/writer Shirley MacLaine has become one of the most outstanding all-around talents of our time. Her acting career was capped with the "Best Actress" Oscar for her performance in *Terms of Endearment* (1983). Her other films include *The Trouble with Harry* (1955), *Ask Any Girl* (1959), *The Apartment* (1960), *Sweet Charity* (1968), and *The Turning Point* (1977).

**BARBARA MacLEAN**
Barbara MacLean was the owner of the Beverly Hills home on North Palm Drive that Marilyn and Joe DiMaggio rented in 1954. When the couple left later that year, Miss MacLean reported that the home was in "neat as a pin" condition.

**BEN MADDOW**
Ben Maddow was the coscreenwriter of *The Asphalt Jungle* (1950).

**MADISON SQUARE GARDEN**
Marilyn Monroe made two known public appearances at Madison Square Garden (address: 4 Pennsylvania Ave.) in New York City. The first of these was on March 31, 1955. During her self-imposed hiatus from filmmaking, Marilyn appeared atop a 36-year-old pink female elephant named Karnaudi

for Mike Todd's benefit for the Arthritis and Rheumatism Foundation. MM stole the night, naturally.

Then, on May 19, 1962, MM caused quite a sensation when she sang "Happy Birthday" to John F. Kennedy, before seventeen thousand democrats. Also present that night were Jack Benny, Harry Belafonte, Henry Fonda, Ella Fitzgerald, Maria Callas, Peggy Lee, Bobby Darrin, Jimmy Durante, Mike Nichols, and Elaine May, among others. Not only did MM perform; she also paid the stiff admission price of $1,000.

Marilyn's appearance at Madison Square Garden, when she was contracted to be in Hollywood to shoot *Something's Got to Give,* made Fox executives irate. Reportedly Marilyn's widely publicized Garden appearance precipitated her dismissal from Fox.

**MADONNA**

Old legends never die. They just come back as new legends.

*Esquire* magazine
March 1986

If Ann-Margret came the closest to being the Marilyn Monroe of the sixties and early seventies, then it is Madonna who has come the closest to being the Marilyn Monroe of the eighties.

It was *Esquire* magazine, March 1986, that brought the Marilyn/Madonna comparison to the forefront. *Esquire* put both of the "M" ladies on its cover and posed the question, "Why is Madonna pretending she's Marilyn?" The magazine elaborated,

> Give or take a Kennedy or a Penn, the Material Girl is really just "Diamonds Are a Girl's Best Friend," all dressed down with somewhere to go.

THE AUTHOR'S COLLECTION

In July 1986, *The Los Angeles Times* continued the controversial comparison. In its "Letters" section, *The Times* printed the following comment by one of its readers, Kathleen Rogers. Said Miss Rogers,

> "[The comparison is] ludicrous and irritating to those of us who are Marilyn fans. . . . Marilyn was a truly beautiful woman, while Madonna would be hard-pressed to win a beauty contest anywhere in the world, save the Soviet Union, perhaps. . . ."

The following week, also in the "Letters" section of *The Los Angeles Times*, Marilyn's biographer, Maurice Zolotow, wrote in to offer his viewpoint on the "debate":

> ". . . as Monroe's first, and probably best, biographer, and one who knew the lady personally, may I say that I don't find the comparison that awry. Madonna has a similar kind of screen presence as Monroe and, at this point in her career, she is more advanced than Marilyn was at hers. . . ."

Madonna Louise Ciccone is the female pop phenomenon of the 1980s. In her pop music videos, and in her debut film, *Desperately Seeking Susan* (1985), Madonna projected a sexy, funny flirtation with the camera and an unbelievably striking screen *presence,* the likes of which hasn't been seen since the early 1960s. For her "Material Girl" video, and with a predominant sense of humor, Madonna portrayed Marilyn portraying the gold digger in *Gentlemen Prefer Blondes.* And she did an admirable job. Of all the actresses who have attempted to portray MM (in full-blown stage and screen productions), it is Madonna who has come closest to capturing the Monroe magnetism.

There are many other comparisons between Marilyn and Madonna. They both started out as models. They have both been accused of using their men to get to "the top." They both married men preeminent in their respective professions (DiMaggio, baseball; Miller, theatre; Penn, movies). They both posed in the nude when they were struggling and hungry. They both caused a not-so-minor sensation when their nude photos later resurfaced. They both had, and have, a keen, confident awareness of the camera. And, they both had, and have, a geniuslike talent that defies categorization.

Not surprisingly, Madonna grew up idolizing Marilyn Monroe. It shows. She has learned her lessons well. Certainly, Marilyn would be proud.

**MAGNUM PHOTOS**

The photo agency that was hired to cover, in pictures, the making of *The Misfits* in 1960. Reportedly, Magnum photographers shot a total of $36,000 worth of publicity stills for the film.

**MAIDS**

1. Fanny Harris
2. Lena Pepitone
3. Hazel Washington

**KATE MAILER**

Kate Mailer was born in 1962, two weeks after Marilyn Monroe died. Twenty-four years later, in early 1986, Kate portrayed MM in her father, Norman Mailer's, production of *Strawhead,* which ran for two weeks at the Actors Studio in New York.

*Vanity Fair* had the following to say about Kate Mailer's performance:

> [She] amazingly *became* Marilyn. She whimpered and flirted, was seductive and coy; she babbled to herself in a nervous, breathy voice; she emanated sex.

**NORMAN MAILER**

> "He pumps so much wind into his subject that the reader may suspect that he's trying to make Marilyn Monroe worthy of him."
>
> Pauline Kael on Norman Mailer's *Marilyn*

> "He's too impressed by power, in my opinion."
>
> Marilyn Monroe to W. J. Weatherby,
> on Norman Mailer, circa 1960-61,
> *Conversations with Marilyn* (Mason/Charter, 1976)

Norman Mailer never knew Marilyn Monroe, but he cannot seem to get her out of his system. First, there was his 1973 literary opus, *Marilyn.* He followed that up in 1980 with *Of Women and Their Elegance.* Then, in 1986, Mailer produced *Strawhead,* his play about MM, at the Actors Studio in New York—same subject, different medium. And, to top it all off, he cast his own daughter, Kate, in the role of Marilyn!

Norman Mailer was born on January 31, 1923, in Long Branch, New Jersey. His first novel, *The Naked and the Dead,* brought him considerable recognition. He gained additional celebrity when he ran, unsuccessfully, for the office of mayor of New York City and when he stabbed one of his former wives with a pen knife. Today Mailer is considered to be one of America's best and most famous novelists.

In his "novel biography" of Marilyn Monroe, Mailer wrote:

> In later years, when Miller was married to Monroe, the playwright and the movie star lived in a farmhouse in Connecticut not five miles away from the younger author [Mailer himself], who, not yet aware of what his final relation to Marilyn Monroe would be, waited for the call to visit, which of course never came. The playwright and the novelist had never been close. Nor could the novelist in conscience condemn the playwright for such avoidance of drama. The secret ambition, after all, had been to steal Marilyn; in all his vanity he thought no one was so well suited to bring out the best in her as himself, a conceit which fifty million other men may also have held. . . ."

**MAKEUP**

Marilyn Monroe was an expert at doing her own makeup. In fact, for her important 1946 screen test Norma Jeane Dougherty opted to do her own makeup, despite the fact that a professional was on hand to do the job. However, when Norma Jeane stepped onto the set, cameraman Leon Shamroy balked and insisted that her makeup be redone. Norma Jeane relented, and Marilyn's longtime makeup artist, Allan "Whitey" Snyder, made her up for the first time.

Snyder once told MM biographer Maurice Zolotow that it took him one-and-a-half hours to make MM up. Said Snyder,

> "Marilyn has make-up tricks that nobody else has and nobody knows. . . . She has certain ways of lining and shadowing her eyes that no other actress can do. She puts on a special kind of lipstick. It's a secret blend of three different shades. I get that moist look to her lips for when she's going to do a sexy scene by first putting on the lipstick and then putting on a gloss. . . ." [The gloss was a mixture of Vaseline and wax.]

THE AUTHOR'S COLLECTION

**The MM Movie Makeup Artists**

| | |
|---|---|
| Mel Berns | *Clash by Night* (1952) |
| Clay Campbell* | *Ladies of the Chorus* (1948) |
| Jack Dawn | *The Asphalt Jungle* (1950) |
| | *Right Cross* (1950) |
| Bunny Gardel | Did MM's body makeup for various films |
| Milton H. Greene | Designed MM's makeup for |
| | *Bus Stop* (1956) |
| | *The Prince and the Showgirl* (1957) |
| Emile La Vigne | *Some Like It Hot* (1959) |
| Robert Littlefield | *Hometown Story* (1951) |
| Fred Phillips | *Love Happy* (1950) |
| Allan "Whitey" Snyder | *All other films* |
| Roy Stork | *Let's Make It Legal* (1951) |
| | *O. Henry's Full House* (1952) |

*The *Ladies of the Chorus* credits do not list a makeup artist. However, at that time, Clay Campbell was the head of makeup at Columbia Pictures.

**MM Trivia Quiz #27**
What was the first film in which MM was seen applying makeup? (Answer on page 577.)

**The MM Personal Makeup Artists**
George Masters
Allan "Whitey" Snyder

## THE MAKING OF THE MISFITS

Paperback reprint by Limelight of James Goode's book, *The Story of the Misfits* (1963).

## MATTY MALNECK

Malneck was the composer/conductor and music supervisor of *Some Like It Hot* (1959). MM worked with him on such musical numbers as "Runnin' Wild."

## MANAGERS

| Business Managers | Personal Managers |
|---|---|
| Erwin "Doc" Goddard | John Carroll |
| Inez Melson | Johnny Hyde |

## CHARLES MANDELSTAM

Charles Mandelstam was the attorney for Dr. Marianne Kris, who was one of the primary beneficiaries in Marilyn's will. In 1982, Mandelstam conducted an investigation to determine why his client, Kris, had not received any monies from the Marilyn Monroe Estate.

## JOSEPH L. MANKIEWICZ

> "Imagine Marilyn alive today—very fat, boozing it up. I think she'd have been a pitiful, dreadful mess and nobody would be able to remember what they do remember."
>
> Joseph Mankiewicz on Marilyn Monroe

Joseph L. Mankiewicz was the writer/director of the bitingly brilliant classic, *All About Eve* (1950), which featured starlet Marilyn Monroe in a small role. For that film, Mankiewicz was awarded Oscars for both his script and his direction. His other pictures include *A Letter to Three Wives* (1949), *The Barefoot Contessa* (1954), *Cleopatra* (1963), and *Sleuth* (1972).

## MANNY WOLF'S CHOPHOUSE

According to MM's New York maid, Lena Pepitone, Marilyn used to frequent the bar at Manny Wolf's Chophouse (at Third Avenue and 50th Street), to see if men would try to pick her up.

## JAYNE MANSFIELD

> "Marilyn and I are entirely different. We've really never been in competition. I admire Marilyn and she's told me she admires me."
>
> Jayne Mansfield on MM

Mansfield studying Monroe.

THE SABIN GRAY COLLECTION

> "They probably expect me to do that someday, but they don't know me well enough to know it couldn't happen."
>
> Jayne Mansfield on Marilyn's death

Jayne Mansfield was the not-so-dumb blonde who actively campaigned to replace Marilyn Monroe. And although she never even came close to succeeding, she did manage to establish her own niche in the Hollywood annals.

Born Vera Jayne Palmer on April 19, 1932, in Bryn Mawr, Pennsylvania, Jayne Mansfield began her career as a model in Texas. Subsequently, she achieved a good deal of success on Broadway in *Will Success Spoil Rock Hunter?* in which she played a Monroelike movie star. In Hollywood, Miss Mansfield scored with *The Girl Can't Help It* (1957) and the film version of *Will Success Spoil Rock Hunter?* (1957). However, she became better known for her outlandish publicity stunts and for her 40-24-36 superstructure than she did for her film roles. She was killed in an automobile accident on June 29, 1967, in Mississippi.

**CHARLES MAPES**

Charles Mapes built and ran the Mapes Hotel in Reno, Nevada, where *The Misfits* company lived during the 1960 shooting.

**THE MAPES HOTEL**

The Mapes Hotel (address: 30 North Virginia Street, Reno, NV) served as the company residence during the 1960 shooting of *The Misfits*. The cast and crew took up more than half of the hotel, where they stayed beginning in July. Marilyn arrived at the hotel on July 20, 1960, and stayed with Arthur Miller in Room 614. The Millers, who were experiencing severe marital difficulties during this period, left the Mapes on September 21, 1960.

**MARA LYNN**

Mara Lynn was the dance coach that MM hired to teach her the routines for *Let's Make Love* (1960). Mara Lynn was also given a part in the movie.

**DAVID MARCH**

David March was the man who set up the first date between Marilyn Monroe and Joe DiMaggio. Reportedly, DiMaggio contacted his old friend, March, to arrange the meeting. In March 1952, March obliged. The fateful date took place at the Villa Nova Restaurant on Sunset Boulevard in Hollywood.

**FREDRIC MARCH**

When Norma Jeane was a child, her mother presented her with a secondhand grand piano that had once belonged to actor Fredric March. However, the piano was later sold off following Gladys's institutionalization. Years later, Marilyn tracked down the same piano, which she refurbished and displayed in her New York apartment.

**MARIAN HUNTER'S BOOK SHOP**

After she achieved a small amount of success, starlet Marilyn Monroe opened her first charge account. It was at Marian Hunter's Book Shop (address: 352 North Camden Drive) in Beverly Hills.

**"MARILYN"**

Twentieth Century-Fox's hour-and-a-half documentary "tribute" to Marilyn Monroe, released on April 18, 1963, just eight months after MM's death. *Marilyn* contains footage from fifteen Monroe movies. However, there *are* some blatant, non-Fox omissions. Unfortunately excluded are *The Asphalt Jungle* (MGM, 1950), *The Prince and the Showgirl* (Warner Brothers, 1957), *The Misfits* (United Artists, 1961), and *Some Like It Hot* (United Artists, 1959).

Originally titled "The World of Marilyn Monroe," this documentary feature was initially scheduled to be hosted by Frank Sinatra. However, when those plans failed to materialize, Rock Hudson agreed to take over the narrative chores. The script was written by Harold Medford, and the footage was edited by Pepe Torres.

Although *Marilyn* was a transparent attempt by 20th Century-Fox to capitalize on Marilyn's postdeath popularity, it remains, nevertheless, a fascinating account of the on-screen Monroe magic. Particularly rare and worthwhile is the footage from Marilyn's last, and incomplete, picture, *Something's Got to Give*.

***MARILYN***
Author: Norman Mailer
Publisher: Grosset & Dunlap
Year: 1973 (out of print)

> . . . Marilyn Monroe who was blonde and beautiful and had a sweet little rinky-dink of a voice and all the cleanliness of all the clean American backyards. She was our angel, the sweet angel of sex. . . .
>
> *Marilyn* by Norman Mailer

Norman Mailer's *Marilyn* is fascinating reading and even more fascinating writing, but it ultimately reveals more of Mailer's obsession with MM than of Marilyn herself. This is *not* the definitive biography of Marilyn Monroe. In fact, much of it, it is presumed, is one big "factoid," to borrow a word that Mailer himself coined for this "novel biography." Nonetheless, it *is* the most colorful work ever done on Marilyn Monroe. Some readers will be repelled by Mailer's incessant use of sexual references (e.g., "Her breasts popped buds and burgeons on flesh over many a questing sweating moviegoer's face. She was a cornucopia. She excited dreams of honey for the horn."), while other readers will be vicariously entertained.

What Norman Mailer's *Marilyn* does have to offer, hype and controversy aside, is a collection of some of the best photographs ever taken of Marilyn Monroe. The photos originated as an exhibition entitled "Marilyn Monroe: The Legend and The Truth" that was conceived by photographer Lawrence Schiller. Included are the works of twenty-four photographers who have captured, collectively, the many faces of MM. The photos alone make Norman Mailer's *Marilyn* a must. The text itself is optional.

***MARILYN***
Author: Sidney Skolsky
Publisher: Dell Publishing Company
Year: 1954 (Out of print)

Early run-of-the-movie-publicity-mill biography written by columnist and MM acquaintance Sidney Skolsky. It begins, predictably, with Norma Jeane's pitiful childhood years and, ends with Marilyn's return to Hollywood from Korea. Even though this book is considered a rare collector's item, it is disappointingly sophomoric and superficial. Instead of being an intimate portrait of early MM, as told by one of her friends, it reads like contrived studio hype.

*Marilyn* is a magazine-format book (a cover-to-cover *magazine*) that has been identified, over the years, as *The Story of Marilyn Monroe* and *The Marilyn Monroe Story*. And, although it has little to offer—except some interesting black-and-white photos—this *Marilyn* cost only 25¢ at the time of its publication.

***MARILYN***
Author: Gloria Steinem
Publisher: Henry Holt Publishing
Year: 1986
$24.95, 224 pp. (ISBN 0-8050-0060-7)

What would Marilyn Monroe be like if she were living today? Would she have been *saved* by the feminist movement? Would she have become a feminist? Was she actually a feminist, ahead of her time? These and other questions are the basis for Gloria Steinem's *Marilyn*. Ms. Steinem, like many, many prominent figures, has, over the years, taken an inordinate interest in the life and times of Marilyn Monroe. And, although her *Marilyn* is pure conjecture, it is interesting conjecture. As an added feature, the book includes photographs of MM taken by George Barris in the last few months of her life.

***MARILYN!***
*Marilyn!* was a musical stage production that opened at the Adelphi Theatre in London on March 17, 1983. It was written by Americans Jacques Wilson and Mort Garson, directed and choreographed by American Larry Fuller, produced and directed by Americans, and staged in London with an all-British cast.

Produced in the same operatic style as the smash hit *Evita, Marilyn!* opened to mostly poor reviews. Stephanie Lawrence, as MM, was generally praised for her performance; however, the musical score (which contained some twenty-nine numbers) was blanketly panned. Included in the score were such song titles as "Can You Hear Me Mama?," "8x10 Glossies," "Bigger Than Life," "A Girl Like You Needs a Little Protection," "There's So Much to Do in New York," "Dumb Blonde," and "Somewhere a Phone Is Ringing."

***MARILYN: A BALLET***
On February 4, 1975, choreographer Adam Darius presented *Marilyn: A Ballet* at the Arts Theatre Club in London, England. The ballet featured dancer Tessa Bill-Yeald as the adult MM, and Louise Beckett as the child MM.

***MARILYN, BARVEN SCREEN GREATS NO. 4***
Editor: Milburn Smith
Publisher: Barven Publications, Inc.
Year: 1971 (Out of print)

Over the years, *Marilyn, Barven Screen Greats No. 4* has frequently been referred to as a *book* about Marilyn Monroe. In actuality, however, it is a cover-to-cover collector's *magazine* about MM. Essentially, it is standard studio material with standard black-and-white photographs. As an added feature, it has a complete MM filmography, as well as a MM IQ quiz. When it was released in 1971, this publication cost 75 cents. Today, however, that copy price has multiplied several times over.

### *THE MARILYN CONSPIRACY*

Author: Milo Speriglio
Publisher: Pocket Books
Year: 1986
$3.50, 221 pp. (ISBN 0-671-62612-4)

More on the Marilyn Monroe "murder." *The Marilyn Conspiracy* is actually little more than an update of Milo Speriglio's earlier work, *Marilyn Monroe: Murder Cover-Up* (1982). And, although much of the material is provocative (Investigator Speriglio has been working on the case for fifteen years!) very little has yet to be proven. Still, speculation can be entertaining.

### *MARILYN, A FABLE OF THE 20TH CENTURY*

Yet another stage play about Marilyn Monroe. This one was not American or British; it was Australian. Produced in 1982 by Bill May, Malcom Cook, and Dolores Quinton.

### *MARILYN: AN AMERICAN FABLE*

Eight months after *Marilyn!* opened in London, an entirely separate production named *Marilyn: An American Fable* opened at the Minskoff Theatre on Broadway. And, if the London musical was panned, then the Broadway musical was bombed. Said Clive Barnes in the *New York Post,* November 21, 1983:

> There was once a controversy as to whether Marilyn Monroe was, in fact, murdered. Well, she certainly was at the Minskoff Theatre last night when the musical *Marilyn [An American Fable]* opened.

This unequivocal mess had sixteen producers, ten songwriters, and an actress named Alyson Reed doing her best MM impersonation. The production was directed and choreographed by Kenny Ortega, the "libretto" was written by Patricia Michaels, and the songs were credited to Jeanne Napoli, Doug Frank, Gary Portnoy, Beth Lawrence, Norman Thalheimer, "and others."

### *MARILYN: AN UNTOLD STORY*

Author: Norman Rosten
Publisher: Signet/New American Library
Year: 1973 (Out of print)

Affectionate, poetic account of Marilyn Monroe by her friend, Norman Rosten. *Marilyn: An Untold Story* is not really a biography, although it is biographical (and autobiographical) in nature. It is intimate, without being at all personal or offensive. It offers a glimpse of the private Marilyn—the Marilyn who cooked stews, omelettes, roast beef, and bouillabaisse for her friends; the Marilyn who phoned in daily reports on the condition of her pregnant cat; the Marilyn who wrote poetry; and the Marilyn who wrote notes like the following:

> "Dear Norman,
> . . . I'm so glad you were born and I'm living at the same time as you."

***MARILYN & JOE DIMAGGIO***
Authors: Robin Moore and Gene Schoor
Publisher: Manor Books
Year: 1977 (Out of Print)

A superficial, fan magazine-like account of the romance between The Ball Player and The Body. Don't waste your time.

***MARILYN IN ART***
Compiled by: Roger G. Taylor
Publisher: Salem Hse. Ltd., Merrimack Pub. Cir.
Year: 1984
$19.95, 160 pp. (ISBN 0-88162-054-8)

Marilyn Monroe and her image have been interpreted innumerable times by an expansive list of artists. *Marilyn in Art* is a compilation book that contains many of the artworks that have been inspired by MM over the years. Used to good advantage are accompanying quotes.

**"MARILYN, IN SEARCH OF A DREAM"**
*See* "Hollywood Close-up."

***MARILYN LIVES!***
Author: Joel Oppenheimer
Publisher: Delilah Books
Year: 1981
$8.95, paperback, 128 pp. (ISBN 0-933328-02-8)

Inanely titled, *Marilyn Lives!* is not actually about Marilyn's life—or her death, for that matter. Rather, it is about her fans—why and how they were individually affected by MM. The "confessionals" are mildly interesting, though hardly revelatory. What *is* worthwhile about *Marilyn Lives!* is the well-chosen collection of photographs.

***MARILYN MON AMOUR***
Author/Photographer: Andre de Dienes
Publisher: Sidgwick and Jackson, Limited
Year: 1986
$27.95, 155 pp. (ISBN 0-283-99337-5)

Simply *stunning* pictorial tribute to MM by one of her most gifted photographers, Andre de Dienes. Most of the photographs included in this book have never before been published. And, if nothing else, they certainly serve as a testament to early Marilyn's natural beauty and unprecedented "love affair" with the still camera.

The text, also by de Dienes, is telling but hardly scandalous. De Dienes recalls how he met and fell in love with Norma Jeane and includes details of their extended 1945 photo shoot throughout Oregon and the desert.

*Marilyn Mon Amour* was first published in France in 1985 by E. P. Filipacchi. *This* is the ultimate Marilyn Monroe photo book.

**"MARILYN MONROE"**
ABC-TV movie comprised of still photographs and footage of Marilyn that aired on March 24, 1963.

**"MARILYN MONROE"**
Home video that is in actuality a reprise of the 1963 television special "The Marilyn Monroe Story."

***MARILYN MONROE***
Author: Janice Anderson
Publisher: The Hamlyn Publishing Group Limited
Year: 1983 (Out of Print)

Despite some good color and black-and-white photographs, *Marilyn Monroe* by Janice Anderson is just another stock MM bio.

***MARILYN MONROE***
Author: Joan Mellen
Publisher: Pyramid Publications
Year: 1973 (Out of print)

Predictable rehash of old MM information.

***MARILYN MONROE***
Author: Maurice Zolotow
Publisher: Harcourt Brace
Year: 1960 (Out of print)

The first comprehensive biography ever published on Marilyn Monroe. Upon its release in 1960, Zolotow's *Marilyn Monroe* set a standard that all subsequent MM biographies have been compared to—most of them unfavorably.

Unlike Norman Mailer's more conjectural work, Zolotow's biography is a definitive genre item. It is well researched, intricately detailed, unfailingly well written, and, finally, evocative. And, unlike the other biographies that have succeeded it, Zolotow's work contains material derived directly from interviews with Marilyn herself. The interviews, conducted in three "sittings," took place in July 1955, during Marilyn's New York period.

Naturally, due to its early release (it was published while MM was still alive), Zolotow's *Marilyn Monroe* does not include any reference to Marilyn's infamous, alleged relationship with the Kennedy brothers or any material on the controversy surrounding her subsequent death. However, it does provide an illustrative canvas of the Norma Jeane years, the struggle and rise to stardom, and the DiMaggio and Miller marriages.

There have been many unworthy imitators over the years, but Maurice Zolotow's *Marilyn Monroe* has remained the bible for every post-1960 book published on the life and times of Marilyn Monroe.

***MARILYN MONROE: A COMPOSITE VIEW***
Editor: Edward Charles Wagenknecht
Publisher: Chilton Books
Year: 1969 (Out of print)

*Marilyn Monroe: a Composite View* is just that—various writers' different interpretations of Marilyn Monroe. Included are the August 3, 1962, Richard Meryman *Life* interview, the August 1962 Alan Levy *Redbook* interview, and the 1966 Ralph Hattersley *Popular Photography* article. Especially good is the piece by Alexander Walker, "Body and Soul: Harlow and Monroe."

***MARILYN MONROE: A LIFE OF THE ACTRESS***
Author: Carl E. Rollyson, Jr.
Publisher: UMI Research Press
Year: 1986
$29.95, 270 pp. (ISBN 8357-1771-2)

*Marilyn Monroe: A Life of the Actress* is, amazingly, the first book to evaluate Marilyn Monroe as a Serious Actress. Not only does Carl E. Rollyson, Jr., take his subject seriously, he also *dissects* her film performances with a microscopic eye. Conspicuously absent from this work is any trace of sensationalism. Instead, Marilyn is treated here, twenty-four years after her death, as she always wanted to be treated in life: as an artist.

***MARILYN MONROE AS THE GIRL: THE CANDID PICTURE-STORY OF THE MAKING OF* THE SEVEN YEAR ITCH**
Writer: Photographs by Sam Shaw
Publisher: Ballantine Books
Date 1955: (Out of print)

This book features a foreword by George Axelrod, and candid black-and-white shots of Marilyn that were taken in 1954 to promote the movie, *The Seven Year Itch* (1955).

**"MARILYN MONROE: BEYOND THE LEGEND"**
"Marilyn Monroe: Beyond the Legend" was a 1986 Cinemax cable television documentary about MM. It was written and produced by Gene Feldman and Suzette Winter, directed by Feldman, and narrated by actor Richard Widmark (MM's costar in *Don't Bother to Knock* (1952). The film is a compendium of movie clips, newsreels, still photographs, and personal interviews. Among those interviewed for this production were Celeste Holm, Joshua Logan, Robert Mitchum, Don Murray, Sheree North, Susan Strasberg, Laszlo Willinger, and Shelley Winters. MM expert James Haspiel served as a consultant.

***MARILYN MONROE: A LIFE ON FILM***
Author: John Kobal, with an introduction by David Robinson
Publisher: Exeter Books (USA), The Hamlyn Publishing Group (England)
Year: 1974 (Out of Print)

Well-mounted, London-based career book that is notable for some 250 black-and-white photographs and sixteen pages of color photographs. It includes an accessible cast list and discography that should be welcomed by any MM student.

***MARILYN MONROE CONFIDENTIAL***
Authors: Lena Pepitone and William Stadiem
Publisher: Simon and Schuster
Year: 1979
$9.95, 251 pp. (ISBN 0-671-24289-X); paperback $2.50 (ISBN 0-671-83038-4)

*Confidential* was cowritten by Lena Pepitone, who served as Marilyn's maid/wardrobe mistress/sometime cook at the East 57th Street apartment in New York. What has triggered hostility against this book is Pepitone's inclusion of details involving Marilyn's personal hygiene. *Confidential* contends that Marilyn dyed her pubic hair blonde and that she did not always properly dispose of her sanitary napkins. Many readers, critics, and MM aficionados have cited these and other examples as being exploitive and tasteless. It is exactly this type of intimate, trashy, peep-show material that separates *Marilyn Monroe Confidential* from the countless other MM accounts. Repellent as some of the inside information may be, it is not, alas, all that hard to believe. What *is* difficult to stomach is the portrait of an oh-so-close mother/daughter/sister/confidante/best friend relationship that Lena Pepitone claims to have shared with Marilyn Monroe. If such was the case, then *Marilyn Monroe Confidential* is a *violation* of that relationship.

***MARILYN MONROE: HER OWN STORY***
Author: George Carpozi, Jr.
Publisher: Belmont Books
Year: 1961 (Out of print)

Like Maurice Zolotow's earlier book, *Marilyn Monroe: Her Own Story* was written and published while MM was still alive. It also consists of material that came directly from Marilyn herself. George Carpozi, Jr., begins his biography with a January 28, 1955, interview on the way to, from, and in Central Park that he conducted with MM.

Despite his personal (although brief) contact with Marilyn, Carpozi's book is disappointingly standard. There are, however, a few interesting quotes from Marilyn and some rare photographs that were taken expressly for this publication.

***MARILYN MONROE: IN HER OWN WORDS***
Compiled by: Roger G. Taylor
Publisher: Delilah/Putnam
Year: 1983
$6.95, paperback, 128 pages (ISBN 0-399-41014-7)
Straightforward compilation book of inimitable Marilyn Monroe quotations. Included are many black-and-white photographs.

### THE MARILYN FOREVER FAN CLUB

This Los Angeles-based international fan club was founded in 1986, and is seeking new membership. See THE FAN CLUBS.

### THE MARILYN MONROE MAMBA

After he saw Marilyn Monroe's "Heat Wave" number in *There's No Business Like Show Business* (1954), famed dance instructor Arthur Murray created and named a dance after MM. He called it "The Marilyn Monroe Mamba."

### THE MARILYN MONROE MEMORIAL FUND

A man named Bruno Bernard founded this German organization in September 1982 to benefit young, struggling actors.

### *MARILYN MONROE: MURDER COVER-UP*

Author: Milo A Speriglio
Publisher: Seville Publishers
Year: 1982
$7.95, paperback, 276 pp. (ISBN 0-930990-77-3)

Milo A. Speriglio's investigative *Marilyn Monroe: Murder Cover-up* is somewhat of an extension of Bob Slatzer's earlier *The Life and Curious Death of Marilyn Monroe* (1974). Both books more than suggest that Marilyn was murdered. In fact, Slatzer and Speriglio have worked in tandem to prove that MM was, in fact, murdered—or at least to prove that there was a highly suspicious cover-up involved in the circumstances surrounding her death. Both books openly cited Marilyn's relationship with the Kennedy brothers, and both books have demanded an official inquest into her death.

*Murder Cover-up* hits the reader over the head with facts, figures, and eyebrow-raising questions. And it certainly does its job in perpetuating the Monroe murder conspiracy theory. However, its overall tone is dry, technical, and impersonal.

### MARILYN MONROE PRODUCTIONS

> "Well, it will be the first time in history that a vice-president didn't want the president assassinated."
>
> Nunnally Johnson, on the formation of Marilyn Monroe Productions

It was late 1954, early 1955. The Hollywood studio star system was still very much in power. At that time, Marilyn Monroe was the number one female box office star in the world. Nonetheless, she was *told* what movie she would be starring in, who would be starring opposite her, who would be directing her, and when and where her services would be required. Moreover, she was still committed to a contract that had been made *before* she became a star. Thus, she was receiving only that contract's ceiling salary limit of $1,500 a week. To retaliate, Marilyn conducted several secret meetings with her photographer friend/partner Milton H. Greene in September 1954, during the New York location shooting of *The Seven Year Itch*. And by the end of that year the not-so-dumb blonde formed her own independent film production company. It was named Marilyn Monroe Productions.

It was not an easy undertaking. First of all, Marilyn still had four years that she was legally bound to 20th Century-Fox. However, Milton Greene's attorney, Frank Delaney, assured Marilyn that he could invalidate her contract. Delaney claimed that the Fox contract was, basically, a "slave contract" that forced Marilyn to play roles that were essentially immoral. He also pointed out an important legal loophole—Fox had apparently neglected to notify MM that it would be renewing her contract (which, of course, it would have).

THE RAY VAN GOEYE COLLECTION

"I feel wonderful. I'm incorporated!," 1955.

Thus convinced, Marilyn Monroe took the bold step forward and publicly announced the formation of Marilyn Monroe Productions in January 1955. Fox executives, understandably, became livid. They threatened to sue Marilyn and charged that she would never work in Hollywood again. They also, in all probability, manipulated public sentiment to turn against Marilyn. She became the target of cruel jokes. It was as though Cinderella had betrayed her fairy godmother. She was publicly lambasted within the Hollywood community and in the press. *Time* magazine quoted one of Marilyn's former co-workers as sneering: "Act? That blonde can't act her way out of a whirlpool bra!" Others, who felt that Marilyn was taking herself too seriously, laughed and dubbed her "The Bernhardt in a Bikini." Milton Greene, Marilyn's partner and primary perpetrator of Marilyn Monroe Productions, fared no better. Industry insiders were asking one another: "Who the hell is Milton Greene, anyway?"

Marilyn Monroe Productions was established with 101 shares of company stock. Marilyn, as president, controlled 51 of the shares. It was her job to star in movies selected and produced by Marilyn Monroe Productions. One of Marilyn's aspirations at that time was to star as Grushenka in the film version of Dostoyevsky's *The Brothers Karamazov.* Milton H. Greene, the company's vice president, retained the remaining shares of stock. It was his job to conduct all of the business and, significantly, to pay all of the bills.

By June 1955, the bills had mounted, while the company's foremost asset remained out of work. And then something happened that changed the course of events. *The Seven Year Itch,* shot the year before, was released to excellent reviews and even better box-office receipts. Marilyn Monroe had her first bona fide hit in two years. The public demanded more Marilyn. So did Fox stockholders. Thus, begrudgingly, the Fox executives were forced to renegotiate a new contract for Marilyn. And it was a good thing, too. Because by November 1955 Marilyn Monroe Productions had already gone some $20,000 into debt.

On December 31, 1955, Marilyn victoriously signed her new agreement with 20th Century–Fox. The new, nonexclusive contract gave Marilyn Monroe Productions director approval, story approval, cinematographer approval, and a salary hike to $100,000 a picture. It also required Marilyn to make only four pictures for Fox in a seven-year period. Upon signing the agreement, Marilyn received a compensation check in the amount of $142,500. In addition, Marilyn Monroe Productions was paid $200,000 for the rights to a screenplay based on the novel *Horns for the Devil,* which it owned.

Marilyn Monroe's victory was a landmark case. Everyone stopped laughing. And everyone began to take Marilyn Monroe Productions seriously. On January 5, 1956, *The Los Angeles Mirror News* printed the following story:

> **ACTRESS WINS ALL DEMANDS FROM STUDIO**
> Marilyn Monroe, victorious in her year-long sitdown strike against 20th Century–Fox, will return to the studio next month with a reported $8,000,000.00 deal. Veterans on the movie scene said it was one of the greatest single triumphs ever won by an actress.

Without her realizing it, Marilyn's personal strike against 20th Century–Fox and her exertion toward financial and artistic independence signaled the demise of the Hollywood studio star system. Inadvertently, Marilyn helped to break down the same studio system that had made her a mass-marketed movie star.

The first film made in association with Marilyn Monroe Productions was 20th Century–Fox's *Bus Stop* in 1956. The first independent film made under the Marilyn Monroe Productions banner was *The Prince and the Showgirl,* which was released in 1957.

### *THE MARILYN MONROE STORY*

Authors: Joe Franklin and Laurie Palmer
Publisher: Rudolph Field
Year: 1953 (Out of print)

The first book ever written about Marilyn Monroe.

### "THE MARILYN MONROE STORY"

"The Marilyn Monroe Story" (aka *The Story of Marilyn Monroe*) was a thirty-minute 1963 television documentary special about MM. It was produced and directed by Art Lieberman, written by Marvin Wald, and narrated by Mike Wallace. It also contained a photo sequence credited to Andre de Dienes. The October 3, 1963, issue of *Hollywood Reporter* contained the following item:

> "The Marilyn Monroe Story," half-hour TV actuality special, is being produced for December release, according to producer Art Lieberman, following conclusion of a world-wide distribution deal for the special program with Official Films.
>
> Composer Elmer Bernstein has been signed to write and conduct the music. Marvin Wald is scripting the show, and Philip R. Rosenberg is editing. A Hollywood star is expected to narrate.
>
> An objective presentation is planned, Lieberman said after conferences with Official Films president Seymour Reed. Simplicity without sermonizing or editorializing will be the aim of the program, the producer stated.

Whatever aims the producer may have had, he fell short of them. The special is strictly surface and not even entirely accurate. Its only actual value is the incorporation of some rare stills and footage. The documentary aired on ABC on March 24, 1963.

"The Marilyn Monroe Story" has since been recycled into a home video under the name "Marilyn Monroe."

**THE MARILYN MONROE THEATRE**

The Marilyn Monroe Theatre is located at 7932 Santa Monica Blvd., West Hollywood, California. It is a division of the Lee Strasberg Theatre Institute.

**"MARILYN MONROE, WHY?"**

On August 10, 1962, less than one week after Marilyn's death, CBS aired this half-hour documentary on its "Eyewitness" program. Initially titled "Who Killed Marilyn Monroe?" and executive-produced by Les Midgley, this half-hour review featured interviews with Emmeline Snively, Lee Strasberg, George Cukor, Jean Negulesco, and Clifford Odets (who prophesized that MM would be an even bigger legend in death). It also incorporated clips from *The Misfits* (1961) and from Marilyn's 1955 television appearance on Edward R. Murrow's "Person to Person."

"Marilyn Monroe, Why?" was hosted by "Eyewitness" anchor Charles Collingwood.

**"MARILYN REMEMBERED"**

"Marilyn Remembered" is a 1974 television documentary about MM that is, in actuality, an extended (by half an hour) version of the 1966 television documentary "The Legend of Marilyn Monroe." Added to this updated version is commentary by Peter Lawford and Shelley Winters. It aired on ABC on February 27, 1974.

**THE MARILYN REMEMBERED FAN CLUB**

Founded in 1983, this club is limited to MM fans and collectors in the Los Angeles area. The club has thirty members and is intent on promoting a positive image of Marilyn Monroe. The group gets together once a month to listen to guest speakers, and to share and exchange MM photographs, movies, and all other MM memorabilia. For contact information, *see* THE FAN CLUBS.

**"MARILYN, SAY GOODBYE TO THE PRESIDENT"**

"Marilyn, Say Goodbye to the President" is the home video version of the 1985 BBC documentary "The Last Days of Marilyn Monroe." This production, written and directed by Christopher Olgiati, provides one of the most startling investigations into the curious death of Marilyn Monroe. It is a brave, no-holds-barred exploration that seemingly spares nothing, including the Kennedy name.

Author Anthony Summers served as a consultant to "Marilyn, Say Goodbye to the President." His presence and remarkable research are felt throughout.

***MARILYN, SCREEN GREATS VOLUME II***

Editor: Bob Patrick
Publisher: Starlog Press
Year: 1980
$2.95, 82 pages (ISBN 0-931064-32-5)

Although it credits a different editor, this cover-to-cover magazine about Marilyn Monroe is actually a recycled version of *Marilyn, Barven Screen Greats No. 4* (Milburn Smith, editor; 1971). Once again, the material is standard fan magazine fluff.

***MARILYN'S DAUGHTER***

*What if* Marilyn Monroe had a child by either John or Robert Kennedy? That is the basic premise of this 1986 novel by John Rechy. The central figure is a young innocent from Gibson, Texas, named "Normalyn Morgan," who discovers that her mother may have been Marilyn Monroe. Naturally, Normalyn relocates to Los Angeles, where she attempts to determine the origins of her birth. If all this sounds familiar, that's because it is. It's all been seen before on television's "Dynasty." But, then again, there are a lot of "Dynasty" fans out there.

***MARILYN: THE LAST MONTHS***

Author: Eunice Murray, with Rose Shade
Publisher: Pyramid Books
Year: 1975 (Out of print)

One of the most controversial figures to have emerged from Marilyn Monroe's death in 1962 was her housekeeper/chauffeur/interior decorator/companion, Mrs. Eunice Murray. Over the years, Mrs. Murray has changed her "story" and contradicted her own statements about the events that took place before and after Marilyn's demise. *Marilyn: The Last Months* was written, presumably, to set the record straight. However, as late as 1985, ten years after this book was published, Eunice Murray was *still* changing her story. Thus, *Marilyn: The Last Months* seems an incomplete, inconsistent, and unsatisfying work.

### *MARILYN: THE TRAGIC VENUS*

Author: Edwin P. Hoyt
Publisher: Chilton Books
Year: 1965 (Out of Print)

*Marilyn: The Tragic Venus* is certainly not the most factual book ever written about Marilyn Monroe; nevertheless, its tone and its insights have a resounding truth about them. It commences the day that Norma Jeane Dougherty walked into Emmeline Snively's modeling agency, and it ends after MM's death. The Marilyn depicted by author Edwin Hoyt is a smart, manipulative, ambitious, contradictory, and, ultimately, likable Marilyn. It's not a popular view, certainly not to Marilyn's die-hard fans, but it is a poignant one.

The black-and-white photographs are standard and mostly of the mass-marketed studio publicity kind.

### "MARILYN: THE UNTOLD STORY"

Lawrence Schiller produced this admirable made-for-television movie, which aired on ABC on September 28, 1980. It was based on the biography *Marilyn* (1973) by Norman Mailer. The highlight of the production is Catherine Hicks's surprising, Emmy-nominated performance as MM. There are actual *moments* when Miss Hicks comes close to conveying the indescribable Monroe presence.

Interestingly, Sheree North, Marilyn's would-be successor in the 1950s, was cast as MM's mother, Gladys Baker. Miss North was also credited as the film's dialogue coach. Also of interest is the fact that *three* directors were credited with the production—Jack Arnold, John Flynn, and Lawrence Schiller.

### MARINE CORP AIR STATION EL TORO

Marilyn Monroe made a personal appearance at this Santa Ana, California, military base in 1950. Marilyn, who was accompanied by Fred Karger, performed one of her favorite numbers: "Do It Again."

### MARITIME SERVICE TRAINING BASE

Base located on Catalina Island in California where Jim and Norma Jeane Dougherty lived in a two-bedroom apartment during 1943.

### MARRIAGES

> "Actually our marriage was a sort of friendship with sexual privileges. I found out later that marriages are often no more than that. And that husbands are chiefly good as lovers when they are betraying their wives."
> Marilyn Monroe, on her marriage to James Dougherty

Jim Dougherty: June 19, 1942

Bob Slatzer: October 4, 1952*
Joe DiMaggio: January 14, 1954
Arthur Miller: June 29, 1956 (civil ceremony); July 1, 1956 (Jewish ceremony)

---

*Marilyn's alleged marriage to Bob Slatzer is being included here for the record. However, it should be noted that the Mexican marriage has never been documented with a marriage certificate—nor did MM and Slatzer ever actually live together as "man and wife."

**MM Trivia Quiz #28**
Name the film(s) in which MM got married at the finale. (Answer on page 577.)

**DEAN MARTIN**

> "I have the greatest respect for Miss Remick and her talent and for all other actresses who were considered for the role, but I signed to do the picture with Marilyn Monroe, and I will do it with no one else."
>
> Dean Martin

Singer/actor/personality Dean Martin was born Dino Crocetti in 1917. In the early to mid-1950s, Martin partnered with comedian Jerry Lewis and enjoyed spectacular box-office success in such vehicles as *The Stooge* (1952), *The Caddy* (1955), and *Pardners* (1956). He also, ultimately, proved to be Marilyn Monroe's last leading man.

Reportedly, Marilyn Monroe hand-picked Dean Martin to costar opposite her in the 1962 film *Something's Got to Give.* When Marilyn was abruptly fired from that film, Martin called a press conference to announce that he would not complete the film without MM. In retaliation, 20th Century-Fox filed a lawsuit against Martin, who responded by filing a countersuit. Marilyn was, by all accounts, touched by Martin's display of loyalty. Following Marilyn's death, all lawsuits were dropped. At about that time, Dean Martin was quoted as saying:

> "I'm sure it was an accident. Marilyn was at my home just a few days ago. She was happy, in excellent spirits, and we were making plans to resume the picture early next year."
>
> "She was a wonderful person and a wonderful talent. I was anxiously looking forward to finishing our film later this year."

**PETE MARTIN**
Pete Martin wrote a series of articles on Marilyn Monroe that appeared in the *Saturday Evening Post* in three parts during May 1956. Much of the same material, which included interviews with Marilyn herself, was used in Martin's book, *Will Acting Spoil Marilyn Monroe?* (Doubleday, 1956).

**"MARVELOUS MARILYN"**
*See* "That's Hollywood!"

**GROUCHO MARX**

As a member of the famed Marx Brothers zany comedy team, the wise-cracking, cigar-chomping, mustachioed Groucho Marx (Julius Marx, 1890–1977) starred in such romping nonepics as *Animal Crackers* (1930), *Monkey Business* (1931), *Duck Soup* (1933), *A Night at the Opera* (1935), and *A Day at the Races* (1937).

In 1949, Groucho, along with producer Lester Cowan, was casting a bit part for his latest film, *Love Happy*. The bit called for, in Groucho's words:

> ". . . a young lady who can walk by me in such a manner as to arouse my elderly libido and cause smoke to issue from my ears."

One of the young ladies who was tested for the walk-on was starlet Marilyn Monroe. After she completed her walking audition, Groucho (presumably still fanning the fumes) commented that Marilyn was: ". . . Mae West, Theda Bara and Bo Peep all rolled into one." Not only did Groucho give Marilyn the part; he was also sufficiently impressed to write a couple lines of dialogue for MM.

Of her film performance in *Love Happy*, Marilyn was later quoted as saying:

> "No acting, just sex again. I had to wiggle across a room. I practiced jiggling my backside for a week. Groucho loved it.

**HARPO MARX**

*Love Happy* (1950) was based on a story written by Harpo (Adolph Marx, 1888–1964).

**"M*A*S*H"**

This popular CBS television series (1972–1982) featured a fictional story about Marilyn Monroe during its eleventh season. The segment was entitled

"Bombshells," and it was set in 1952; it aired on November 29, 1982. The plot concerned an appearance in Korea that MM had planned but was unable to fulfill (Marilyn did not appear in Korea until 1954). The segment ended with Marilyn sending the "M*A*S*H" outfit the following telegram:

> Dear MASH 4077:
> Unavoidably detained in rushes—Stop. Filming schedule changed—Stop. Am unable to get away—Stop. Feel heart sick—Stop. Please give big wet kiss to doctors—Stop. Kiss, kiss—Stop. Love, love—Stop.
>
> Marilyn

**VIC MASI**

Vic Masi was an old friend of Joe DiMaggio who lived in the San Fernando Valley in California. To get away from the Hollywood scene, Joe and Marilyn spent many evenings with Masi and his wife.

**VERNE MASON**

Reportedly, Dr. Verne Mason was one of Marilyn Monroe's Hollywood doctors, circa 1954.

**MASSEUR**

Marilyn's masseur was Ralph Roberts.

**GEORGE MASTERS**

> "My first meeting with Marilyn Monroe is etched in my memory. She was a mess. She was waiting for me in her suite at the Beverly Hills Hotel, the world's greatest sex symbol, in a terry cloth robe, one shoulder torn, her yellow hair hanging down around her neck, no make-up, and champagne and caviar everywhere. . . . Thus began my adventures with the world's greatest sex symbol, who was, in fact, about as passionate as a calculating machine. She was two personalities inhabiting the same body."

It has been said before (most likely prior to the feminist movement) that no one knows a woman better than her hairdresser. If that is indeed true, then very few people knew Marilyn Monroe better than George Masters.

George Masters, born in 1939, is the renowned hairstylist/makeup artist of the stars. In 1966, Masters opened his own salon in Beverly Hills. He has worked on such women as Bo Derek, Lynda Bird Johnson, Rita Hayworth, and Ann-Margret (whom he has cited as his favorite client). In the early 1960s, "Killer George," as Marilyn referred to him, began working on La Monroe. It is George Masters who is generally credited with giving Marilyn her white-on-white look.

> "I toned her down from the Jean Harlow platinum blonde to the Lana Turner white-on-white look. I worked with her hair until it was perfectly white. She called it 'pillow case' white. And I lightened her skin tone to look like alabaster. . . . She wore false eyelashes, eye shadow, eyeliner, mascara, very little foundation, very little rouge, powder, and lipstick, and that was it . . . her eyelashes

THE SYLVIA BARNHART COLLECTION

Publicity still, circa 1947.

were a pain in the neck to me. She liked to wear loads of them. I had to hand-trim them for her because there were no ready-trimmed eyelashes then. Marilyn knew how I hated this chore so when she was mad at me she always gave me several extra pairs of eyelashes to trim as my punishment."

George Masters on MM's hair and makeup

"In her own peculiar way, Marilyn was very outgoing and generous. There was never any haggle about fees or tips. . . . She was most generous in bestowing financial—not sexual—favors. I once flew to New York, at her request and expense, to do her for an important event . . . she greeted me at the door of her suite with, 'Oh, George, I don't feel like it now. Come back next week.' And she put a crumpled two thousand dollar check in my shirt pocket."

George Masters on MM's generosity

"My eyes were the same color as hers and my hair the same shade as hers at the time. There wasn't much she could do about my eyes. I could have darkened my hair for her but I wouldn't. She never forgave me."

George Masters on his relationship with MM

"My basic beauty routine with Marilyn never varied too much. I would arrive at her place about eight hours early to get her started. I worked with her first in her suite at the Beverly Hills Hotel, then at her small apartment on Doheny . . . then at her new house in Brentwood where she died. . . . As a general rule Marilyn would begin turning on about eight hours after I had started with her, while I was applying her lipstick or adjusting her dress . . . until then she was a girl you wouldn't look at twice. When she became secure enough to turn into this other person named Marilyn Monroe, then all of a sudden something happened. That's when it was goose bump time. You could really see it with your own eyes, you could feel it in the room—the complete transformation, like Dr. Jekyll and Mr. Hyde. Her mannerisms, her gestures, everything was changed, not only her dress and make-up. She was a totally different person, an exploding image, a projection of sexuality and magnetism beyond belief. Even remembering it now I get goose bumps. She was phenomenal to watch."

George Masters on Marilyn's beauty transformation

George Masters's impressions of MM, and of his other clients as well, were included in his 1977 book, *The Masters Way to Beauty* (E. P. Dutton).

**"MATT HOUSTON"**

In 1983, the television program "Matt Houston" featured a storyline about a gangster who forces an innocent woman to look, act, and *be* Marilyn Monroe. When she refuses, the gangster murders her boyfriend and then threatens to kill her. Naturally, Matt Houston himself arrives just in the nick of time and rescues the fair would-be MM.

Marilyn was portrayed by actress Katie Labourdette. The segment aired on October 21, 1983.

**MRS. ESTHER MATTHEWS**

Mrs. Matthews was the secretary to the principal at Van Nuys High School who once told MM biographer Maurice Zolotow:

"We are proud to claim Jane Russell, but we do not claim Marilyn Monroe. She didn't learn anything about acting while she was at Van Nuys High."

**GEORGE MATTSON**

Mattson was one of the photographers who was present at, and got shots of, Marilyn's February 9, 1956, press conference in which she announced the intended production of *The Prince and the Showgirl* (1957).

**MILDRED ANN MAULDIN**

Miss Mauldin was Marilyn's dance coach for the "Lazy" number that was performed in *There's No Business Like Show Business* (1954).

**PHIL MAX**

Phil Max was a camera shop owner who, in the 1950s, was thrown into jail on an obscenity charge for displaying Marilyn's nude calendar in the window of his store.

**MAX FACTOR**

In 1985, a photograph of Marilyn Monroe appeared in a print advertisement for the Max Factor cosmetics company. The ad read:

His passion for rich color helped create the red-hot glamour of Marilyn Monroe. He was Max Factor. The man who made generations of moviegoers see red.

**MAXELL TAPES**

In 1986, an illustration of Marilyn Monroe appeared in a print advertisement for the Maxell Corporation of America. The ad read:

> "Wow!" the world said, from the very first time she stepped onto the big screen. And through 29 films she remained the delicious dessert of movie goers everywhere, and the very best part of every man's fantasy. Today Maxell helps you preserve her films, with tapes that are manufactured up to 60% above industry standards. So even after 500 plays her sensual beauty will light up your consciousness, just as it did in the early fifties, when the world first discovered the magic of Marilyn Monroe.

**THE MAYAN THEATRE**

According to writer Richard Lamparski, Marilyn Monroe was a stripper at the Mayan Theatre (address: 1044 South Hill Street) in downtown Los Angeles, during September 1948. Lamparski contends that, following her dismissal from Columbia, Marilyn stripped at the Mayan for two weeks, under the names of Marilyn Monroe, then Marilyn Marlowe, and then, Mona Monroe.

**MCA**

Marilyn Monroe's final theatrical agency. Not long before Marilyn's death, she reportedly hired the services of an attorney to negotiate her release from MCA. Following MM's death, MCA filed a request in the amount of $80,168, which it claimed was owed to them by the Marilyn Monroe Estate.

***McCALLS* MAGAZINE**

*McCalls* has published the following articles on MM:

- ☆ 4/60: "Marilyn Monroe: Condensation"
- ☆ 8/67: "Dear Marilyn"
- ☆ 8/72: "About Marilyn" (Norman Rosten)
- ☆ 7/74: "My Story" (Excerpts from *My Story*)
- ☆ 2/76: "Marilyn Nobody Knew" (Excerpts from *The Secret Happiness of Marilyn Monroe* by Jim Dougherty)
- ☆ 7/82: "Marilyn Monroe: The Meaning of Her Life and Death" (Diana Trilling); MM appeared on cover, also

**JOHN McCARTEN**

John McCarten of *The New Yorker* was the critic who showed the least amount of appreciation for Marilyn Monroe over the years. For example, of *Niagara* (1953) McCarten wrote:

> Marilyn Monroe, whom Hollywood has been ballyhooing as a new-day Lillian Russell, takes a fling at big-league melodrama in *Niagara* and demonstrates a wide assortment of curves and a tendency to read her lines as if they were in a tongue she is not entirely familiar with . . . however admirably constructed Miss Monroe may be, she is hardly up to competing with one of the wonders of this continent.

**HORACE McCOY**
McCoy cowrote the screenplay for *The Fireball* (1950), which featured MM in a small role.

**ALICE T. McINTYRE**
Miss McIntyre penned the article "Making 'The Misfits' or Waiting for Monroe or Notes from Olympus" on Marilyn Monroe that appeared in *Esquire* magazine, March 1961.

**GRACE McKEE**
*See* GRACE GODDARD.

**MARIAN McKNIGHT**
In 1957, the year after Marilyn Monroe married Arthur Miller, Joe DiMaggio began dating MM look-alike Marian McKnight. However, the romance fizzled when Miss McKnight was crowned "Miss America" of 1957.

**BILL McLEAN**
In 1947, actor Bill McLean was cast in the Bliss Hayden Miniature Theatre's production of *Glamour Preferred.* Also in the cast was a young, unknown actress named Marilyn Monroe. Nearly forty years later, Mr. McLean had the following to say about working with MM:

> "She was so very, very sweet and nice. Very inexperienced on stage. However, when she walked on stage, she stood out so much that nobody looked at anybody else."

**MARGARET McLEAN**
Margaret McLean was starlet Marilyn Monroe's speech coach at the Actors Lab in Hollywood, circa 1947.

**ALBERT McCLEERY**
Producer Albert McCleery offered Marilyn Monroe the opportunity to star in a television production of *The Brothers Karamozov.* However, for whatever reason, the deal failed to materialize. The dramatic presentation would have aired in three parts, in the fall of 1956.

**SISTER AIMEE SEMPLE McPHERSON**
Della Monroe Grainger, Marilyn's grandmother, was a devout follower of Sister Aimee Semple McPherson. It was Della who arranged for Norma Jeane Baker to be baptized in Sister Aimee's Angelus Temple.

**THE MEASUREMENTS**
Dress size: 12
Pant size: 8

As for her bust-waist-hips measurements, Marilyn Monroe either fluctuated *daily* or else she simply screwed up her numbers and/or tape measure and gave out a different figure to each person she spoke with. The following, then, is a compilation of the various accounts of Marilyn's ultimately unaccountable figure:

☆ The Blue Book Model Agency, circa 1945 .......... 36-24-34
☆ Robert Slatzer, circa 1946 .......... 36-24-36
☆ *Collier's* magazine, circa 1951 .......... 37-23-34
☆ Sidney Skolsky, 1952 .......... 36½-23-34
☆ *The Los Angeles Mirror*, 1954 .......... 37-24-35
☆ 20th Century–Fox, circa early 1950s .......... 36½-23-34
☆ 20th Century–Fox, 1955 .......... 38-23-36
☆ Billy Travilla (Marilyn's designer), 1955 .......... 38-23-36
☆ Billy Travilla, circa 1980s .......... 35-22-35
☆ *Time* magazine, 1956 .......... 37-23-37
☆ Maurice Zolotow .......... 38-26-37
☆ *Good Housekeeping* magazine, 1980 .......... 37-23-37
☆ *The Los Angeles Herald Examiner* .......... 36D bra size

Marilyn herself once told a reporter that she would like her epitaph to read: "Here lies Marilyn Monroe, 38-23-36."

**HAROLD MEDFORD**
Harold Medford wrote the narration of the 1963 20th Century–Fox documentary tribute to MM entitled *Marilyn*. The narration was read by actor Rock Hudson.

**JOAN MELLEN**
Joan Mellen is a writer and a professor of literature and film at Temple University in Philadelphia. Among Mellen's books are *The Battle of Algiers, Women and Sex in the Cinema,* and *Politics and Film.* In 1973, Mellen's *Marilyn Monroe* was published by Pyramid Books.

**WILLIAM C. MELLOR**
William Mellor is the cinematographer of such films as *A Place in the Sun* (for which he won a 1951 Oscar), *Giant* (1956), and the remake of *State Fair* (1962). In 1949, Mellor shot the Marx Brothers picture *Love Happy,* which featured unknown starlet Marilyn Monroe in a walk-on bit.

**INEZ MELSON**
When Marilyn Monroe's career began to soar in the early 1950s, it was Inez Melson who replaced "Doc" Goddard as Marilyn's business manager. In 1952, it was Melson who convinced Marilyn to appoint her as Gladys Baker's guardian. It was Melson who arranged for Gladys to be transported from a state hospital to a private nursing home. It was also Melson who testified, in Marilyn's behalf, at the Joe DiMaggio divorce proceedings in 1954. It was also Melson who was one of the first persons to arrive at Marilyn's Brentwood home on the morning of August 5, 1962. And it was Inez Melson who claimed Marilyn Monroe's body at the county morgue later that day.

At the end of October 1962, Inez Melson contested Marilyn's will. She claimed that the will had been made under the undue influence of either Lee Strasberg or Marianne Kris—both primary beneficiaries in the will. However, Melson's claim was denied, and the will was admitted into probate.

Nevertheless, Inez Melson continued to visit Gladys Baker once a month at the Rockhaven private sanitarium. It was one of Marilyn's last wishes to see that her mother was well taken care of. And it was Inez Melson who saw to it that that wish was carried out. Miss Melson died on July 6, 1986, in Los Angeles.

**MEN**

> "There's another guy in the room . . . way over in the corner . . . maybe he's kind of nervous and shy and perspiring a little. . . . First you look past him, but then you sort of sense that he is gentle, and kind and worried and that he'll be tender with you and nice and sweet and that's what's really exciting!"
>
> MM to Tom Ewell, *The Seven Year Itch*, 1955

> "I don't know why, but I had always been attracted to men who wore glasses. Now when he [Fred Karger] put them on, I felt suddenly overwhelmed."
>
> Marilyn Monroe

> "I'm not going to date any jerks the studio tells me to date. There isn't a decent man in Hollywood. They're all out for one thing. They don't even bother romancing you. Some of them are good looking and they think that's enough. To hell with that. I don't care for a man who's good looking."
>
> Marilyn Monroe to David March

> "Men are like wine—they improve with age. But I don't have nothing against younger men."
>
> Marilyn Monroe

> "A woman can bring a new love to each man she loves . . . providing there are not too many."
>
> Marilyn Monroe

> "We have a mutual appreciation of being male and female."
>
> Marilyn Monroe on men

Marilyn Monroe was not especially attracted to what would be termed the traditional good-looking man. Just take a look at her marital track record. Arthur Miller and Joe DiMaggio were not ugly, but they were *not* Rock Hudson (or even Robert Wagner!) either. Instead, Marilyn preferred her men to be older, wearing glasses, and without perfect teeth (she once rationalized that men who had perfect teeth were not so perfect in some other department). She also liked her men to be straightforward, the type who was not afraid of insulting her, and the type who did not talk too much about himself.

In 1954, Marilyn was queried as to whom she considered to be the most outstanding men of that period. MM responded by citing Marlon Brando, Michael Chekhov, John Huston, Arthur Miller, Jerry Lewis, and Jawaharlal Nehru. Also, according to actress Shelley Winters, Marilyn once composed a list of all the men that she'd like to "sleep" with. The alleged list included

Zero Mostel, Eli Wallach, Charles Boyer, Jean Renoir, Lee Strasberg, Nick Ray, John Huston, Elia Kazan, Harry Belafonte, Yves Montand, Charles Bickford, Ernest Hemingway, Charles Laughton, Clifford Odets, Dean Jagger, Albert Einstein, and, of course, Arthur Miller.

**MM Trivia Quiz #29**
Who was MM's first onscreen date? (Answer on page 577.)

**ETHEL MERMAN**
Brassy, bossy, booming Ethel Merman (Ethel Zimmermann, 1908-1984) belted her way to Broadway legendry. However, she was far less successful in motion pictures. Among her film credits were *Alexander's Ragtime Band* (1938) and *Call Me Madam* (1953). In 1954, Miss Merman costarred with Marilyn Monroe in 20th Century-Fox's tribute to Irving Berlin, *There's No Business Like Show Business.*

**GARY MERRILL**
Born in 1914, actor Gary Merrill costarred in Joseph L. Mankiewicz's classic *All About Eve* (1950).

**VIOLET MERTZ**
Miss Mertz was Marilyn's landlady at the Doheny apartment in Beverly Hills, where MM had lived in the early 1950s, pre-DiMaggio. In 1961, it was Miss Mertz who permitted MM to move back into the very same Doheny apartment.

**RICHARD MERYMAN**

> "I really felt that she needed to control the interview—that she wanted to be in control of it—you know, on top of the situation. And she was!"
>
> Richard Meryman, former *LIFE* writer, on his 1962 interview with MM

In 1962, Richard Meryman was a relatively unestablished writer for *LIFE* magazine. At that time, he sought out a famous personality to interview for that publication. He chose Cary Grant. When Mr. Grant refused, Meryman set his sights on Marilyn Monroe. The subsequent interview was set up through Pat Newcomb. It was to be Marilyn Monroe's final interview.

> "She did something that no one had ever done before or since with me—she asked for the questions in advance. She was really prepared, yet spontaneous. Either she was a good actress or very well rehearsed. Let me say that she handled the interview in a very business-like manner. Very business-like."
>
> Richard Meryman on MM, 1986

> "I was very impressed by her, she was much smarter than I had expected. I liked her very much. I only think that she did the piece to get her voice out in the world. You know, she had just been fired from Fox, and she wanted her side told. I've often thought what a sad person Marilyn Monroe would be if she were alive today. I always privately believed that she only intended to scare people with

the pills. There was no sign to me that this woman was on the way to suicide."

Richard Meryman's article on Marilyn appeared in the August 3, 1962, edition of *LIFE* magazine—the week of Marilyn's death. Reportedly, MM was very proud of this interview, as well she should've been. It remains, today, one of the finest pieces ever done on her. As for Richard Meryman, his story on Marilyn launched a series of articles on the famous for him. He left *LIFE* in 1972 and has since written several books. His most recent work was a collaboration with Joan Rivers on her bestseller, *Enter Talking* (1986).

**METAPHYSICS**

Marilyn was introduced to many books on the subject of metaphysics by Dr. G. W. Campbell, the man who gave MM her specialized facial treatments at Renna's Salon in Beverly Hills.

**METHOD ACTING**

The Method style of acting was employed by Lee Strasberg and the Actors Studio in New York, where Marilyn Monroe took drama classes beginning in 1955. The style itself requires an actor to draw from his or her own personal experience. It was once a controversial style that has been dubbed the "total immersion system." Lee Strasberg himself defined the Method in the following manner:

> The sum total of the experience of the great actors throughout all ages and countries. The best things in it come from Stanislavsky. The rest comes from me. It sets no rules. It points a path that leads to control rather than hit or miss inspiration.It fosters fusion of the actor with the character. It is now represented in universities, and with workshops, dramatic schools, and little theatre groups in every corner of every hamlet.

**METRO-GOLDWYN-MAYER**

Even though it had the opportunity in the early 1950s, Metro-Goldwyn-Mayer, aka MGM, aka Leo the Lion, never did sign Marilyn Monroe to a studio contract. However, it did hire her for her very first pivotal film role—the role of Angela Phinlay in *The Asphalt Jungle* in 1950. Following MM's success in that film, Metro cast Marilyn in two other pictures, *Right Cross* (1950) and *Hometown Story* (1951).

**THE METROPOLITAN STATE HOSPITAL IN NORWALK**

Formerly named the Norwalk State Hospital, this California asylum is where Marilyn's grandmother, Della Monroe Grainger, was committed on August 4, 1927, and, where she succumbed less than three weeks later. It is also where Marilyn's mother, Gladys Baker, was institutionalized in 1934. The Metropolitan State Hospital is located in Norwalk at 11400 S. Norwalk Boulevard.

**RUSSELL METTY**

Russell Metty (1906–1978) was the fine cinematographer of such pictures as

*Bringing Up Baby* (1938), *All My Sons* (1948), *Magnificent Obsession* (1954), and *Spartacus* (for which he won a 1960 Oscar).

Metty was also the cinematographer of Marilyn Monroe's last completed film, *The Misfits* (1961).

**MEXICO**

In 1952, Marilyn Monroe allegedly married Robert Slatzer in Tijuana, Mexico. More than eight years later, Marilyn returned to Mexico—specifically, to Juarez—to obtain a divorce from Arthur Miller. And in February of the final year of her life, MM trekked back to Mexico on a shopping spree to furnish her new home in Brentwood. While in Mexico City, Marilyn was feted by actor Cantiflas and by the entire Mexican movie colony. It was during this Mexican buying trip that Marilyn met one of her last lovers, Jose Bolanos.

**PATRICIA MICHAELS**

Patricia Michaels wrote the "libretto" for the Broadway musical *Marilyn: An American Fable* that was staged in 1983.

***MIDDLE OF THE NIGHT***

A 1959 film written by Paddy Chayefsky, adapted from one of his earlier television plays. The film was produced by Columbia Pictures and was directed by Delbert Mann. It starred Fredric March and Kim Novak, the latter in a role that Marilyn had wanted.

**LES MIDGLEY**

Les Midgley was the executive producer of the 1962 television documentary on Marilyn Monroe, "Marilyn Monroe, Why?"

**ARTHUR MILLER**

> "We're so congenial. This is the first time I've been really in love. Arthur is a serious man, but he has a wonderful sense of humour. We laugh and joke a lot. I'm mad about him."
>
> Marilyn Monroe, circa 1956

> "He is a wonderful writer, a brilliant man. But I think he is a better writer than a husband."
>
> Marilyn Monroe, circa 1962

By the time Marilyn Monroe met playwright Arthur Miller, he had already won the New York Drama Critics Circle Award for *All My Sons* (1947), as well as the Pulitzer Prize for *Death of a Salesman* (1949). He was considered, at the time, to be America's premier (living) dramatist—a title that he shared with Tennessee Williams. At age thirty-five, Miller had talent, success, respect, and the promise of future greatness—attributes that Marilyn wanted, with a vengeance, for herself.

It was December 1950. The location was the 20th Century-Fox lot, where Marilyn was shooting her bit as a secretary in *As Young as You Feel*. Johnny Hyde had just died. And starlet MM was distraught, alone, and still

COURTESY OF CINEMA COLLECTORS

struggling. As fate would have it, while Marilyn was walking toward the studio commissary, she spotted two men. Her companion, actor Cameron Mitchell, proceeded to introduce Marilyn to the two distinguished observers. One of them was director Elia Kazan. The other one, "the tall one," was Arthur Miller. Reportedly, for Marilyn, it was love at first sight.

The odd coupling of The Beauty and The Brain met again, later the same week. It was at a party given by Famous Artists agent Charlie Feldman. Later, soon after he had returned back east, Miller wrote Marilyn a letter that read:

> "Bewitch them [the public] with this image they ask for, but I hope and almost pray you won't be hurt in this game, nor ever change. . .

Judging by the tone of this early correspondence, Arthur Miller took a protective, good-Samaritan-like stance toward Marilyn Monroe from the start. As for MM, she once said, in retrospect, "He [Miller] was going to make my life different—better—a lot better."

However, there were obstacles to the burgeoning Miller/Monroe relationship. Foremost was Miller's marriage to the former Mary Slattery, his girlfriend from the University of Michigan. By the time Miller met Marilyn, he had been married for ten years. He had also fathered two children, Jane and Robert Miller, who at that time were five and three years old, respectively.

Six years later, Marilyn Monroe fulfilled her long-standing quest: she married Arthur Miller. In the explosive intervening years, Marilyn had married and divorced the legendary Joe DiMaggio and had become the most celebrated movie star, blonde or otherwise, in the world. Miller and Marilyn were reunited in May 1955, after MM moved to New York, in her sojourn away from Hollywood and after her divorce from DiMaggio. When Miller learned that she was in town, he obtained her phone number from Paula Strasberg. For the next year, the couple "secretly" dated. When they were queried as to the nature of their relationship, the famous twosome contended that they were "just good friends." After all, at that time, it was Mary Slattery, not Marilyn Monroe, who was wearing Arthur Miller's wedding band.

But that was soon to change. In February 1956, Marilyn returned to Hollywood, victoriously, with a new studio contract and a new marriage looming on the horizon. During the shooting of *Bus Stop* Arthur Miller reportedly telephoned her long-distance, nightly. When she spoke of him, Marilyn referred to Arthur cautiously, as "Mr. A." And a few months later, in April, "Mr. A" flew to Reno to obtain a divorce. Following the separation from his wife, Miller publicly stated:

> "I met Marilyn in 1951 in Hollywood. I often see her at the home of friends. But we've never been alone and there is definitely no romance."

Arthur Miller's divorce from Mary Slattery was granted on June 11, 1956. He then returned to New York, where he was reunited with Marilyn, who had completed work on *Bus Stop*. Then, several days later, on June 20, *The New York Post* broke the news that Marilyn and Arthur would be married before July 16—when Marilyn was scheduled to fly to London for the filming of *The Prince and the Showgirl*. The following day, while in Washington, D.C., Miller was forced to admit that he and MM would indeed become man and wife. Said Miller: "When she [Marilyn] goes to London she will go as Mrs. Miller."

As could be expected, the worldwide press was agog. They dubbed the unlikely pair "The Egghead and The Hourglass." Miller and Monroe were barraged. In an attempt to sate public curiosity, the soon-to-be Millers held a press conference in New York City to announce their intentions. However, the rather sketchy conference did little to quiet the public furor, and the couple was besieged. Miller was quoted as saying to a reporter: "It's your job versus my privacy. That's a remorseless conflict."

Finally, after a female reporter had been accidentally killed while in pursuit of them, the Millers decided to put the spectacle to rest. They were married in two ceremonies, one civil and one Jewish, on June 29 and July 1, respectively.

> "If I were nothing but a dumb blonde, he wouldn't have married me."
>
> Marilyn Monroe, on her marriage to Arthur Miller

Then it was on to England. It was during the production of *The Prince and the Showgirl* that Arthur Miller began to manage Marilyn's affairs. This pitted him in direct conflict with Milton H. Greene, who was at that time vice president of Marilyn Monroe Productions. Miller even assumed the not-so-lofty responsibility of approving or rejecting his wife's still photographs. It was also at about this time that Marilyn discovered an unflattering journal entry that Miller had written about her. Reportedly, the general tone of the entry was that Miller was disappointed in his new wife. Marilyn, perhaps overreacting, felt betrayed by Miller's words. Years later, she confided to her housekeeper/companion, Mrs. Eunice Murray:

> "One day I found a diary he was keeping about me. He had written down everything about our personal life. How could a man who said he loved me do a thing like that!"

THE ALAN FRANCE COLLECTION

Some associates of Marilyn, including the Strasbergs, reportedly felt that the discovery of this journal entry signalled the beginning of the end for the newlywed Millers.

Shortly after they returned to the United States, Marilyn learned that she was pregnant. However, while at their rented retreat at Amagansett, Long Island, Marilyn suffered from complications and was rushed to Doctor's Hospital in New York City, where she had a miscarriage. It was this tragedy that prompted Arthur Miller to begin writing *The Misfits* as a tribute to and for his beloved wife. Previously, Miller had written a short story titled "Please Don't Kill Anything" in which the heroine was based on MM. It was also at about this time that Miller dedicated his collected edition of plays to MM. The dedication read, simply, "To Marilyn."

In the succeeding months, the Millers divided their time between their East 57th Street apartment in New York City and their summer farm retreat in Roxbury, Connecticut. In 1958, and again in 1960, the Millers flew to Hollywood, where Marilyn filmed *Some Like It Hot* and *Let's Make Love,* respectively. It was for *Love* that the Pulitzer Prize-winning Miller reduced himself to write script revisions—at the request of his wife.

> "I've promised myself never to let Marilyn Monroe get in the way of Mr. and Mrs. Arthur Miller."
>
> Marilyn Monroe

It was during the 1960 shooting of *Let's Make Love* that the marriage between The Movie Star and The Intellectual fell irrevocably apart. Marilyn still referred to her husband, affectionately, as "Art," "Arturo," "Papa," and "Popsie," but they were mere surface endearments. Miller, one of the most respected artists of his time, had made the fatal mistake of devoting not only his craft, but also his *existence,* in a sacrificial homage, to his blonde and beautiful wife. But Miller was destined to fall from Marilyn's grace when it became apparent to her that he was just a man and not a savior at all.

Subsequently, Marilyn sought out other fantasies and found comfort in an affair with her *Let's Make Love* costar Yves Montand.

By the time *The Misfits*—Miller's ultimate testimonial to his wife—was finally ready to shoot in July 1960, the Miller-Monroe marriage was a formality, at best. And when the bedraggled production was completed in November, Marilyn and Arthur flew back to New York—on separate airplanes. Said Miller:

> "I still don't understand it. We got through it [the movie]. I made a present of this to her, and I left it without her. I didn't even ride home with her on the last day."

On November 11, 1960, Marilyn officially announced her separation from Arthur Miller. Several days later, *Time* magazine quoted Miller as saying, in response:

> "She has more guts than a slaughterhouse. Being with her, people want not to die. She's all woman, the most womanly woman in the world."

Nevertheless, two months later, the couple was divorced. The same year, Arthur Miller married photographer Inge Morath. A year later Marilyn was dead. Arthur Miller did not attend her funeral. What he did do was write *After the Fall* (1964). The Marilyn Monroe presented in *After the Fall* was the flip side of the Marilyn he had presented in *The Misfits* (1961). It was a dark, ugly, and desperate portrait of Hollywood's beloved goddess, and Miller was publicly condemned for his unmistakably autobiographical depiction.

Nevertheless, despite *After the Fall*, there can be no doubt that an intense love was shared by Marilyn Monroe and Arthur Miller. Paula Strasberg, who presumably knew the couple well, once commented that:

> "I have never seen such tenderness and love as Arthur and Marilyn feel for each other. How he values her. I don't think any woman I've ever known has been so valued by a man."

Marilyn herself doomed the relationship from the start. She placed Arthur Miller on a pedestal—between Abraham Lincoln and Albert Einstein, no less. She made Miller into her idol/husband/father/lover/friend/teacher/manager/publicist/screenwriter/nurse/protector and savior. It must have been an impossible situation, one that very few men could have lived up to. It was a storybook romance that could not weather the realities of day-to-day living. Miller wrote extensively about their relationship in his 1987 autobiography, *Timebends: A Life* published by Grove Press.

For Arthur Miller, there has been an undistinguished creative life since *After the Fall*. His *The American Clock*, which faltered on Broadway in 1980, was given a new mounting in England in 1986 and achieved some critical success. However, he has had no major work to compare with his earlier successes. Perhaps his relationship with Marilyn Monroe was more devastating than anyone realizes. Or perhaps, like his Willy Loman in *Death of a Salesman*, Arthur Miller just grew tired of peddling his trade.

**AUGUSTA MILLER**

"She opened her heart to me"

Mrs. Augusta Miller on Marilyn Monroe

Augusta Miller was Arthur's mother and Marilyn's mother-in-law. She taught MM how to cook borscht, chicken soup, matzoh balls, and other Jewish delicacies. Marilyn attended Mrs. Miller's funeral on March 8, 1961.

**DAVID MILLER**

Born in 1909, David Miller was the editor-turned-director who guided MM in her walk-on bit in *Love Happy* (1950). Miller's other directorial efforts include *Sudden Fear* (1952), which starred Joan Crawford.

**FLORENCE J. MILLER**

Florence Miller, the wife of Arthur's cousin Morton, was one of two witnesses who signed the June 29, 1956, marriage certificate of Arthur and Marilyn Miller.

**GEORGE MILLER**

George Miller is the photographer who took the shots of the Marilyn Monroe/George Carpozi, Jr. interviews that took place at Marilyn's Sutton Place apartment and in Central Park, during January 1955.

**ISIDORE MILLER**

"Dad, I feel fine"

Marilyn Monroe to Isidore Miller, ten days before her death

Long after her split from Arthur Miller, Marilyn kept in close contact with his father, Isidore Miller. Reportedly, they spoke on the telephone, long-distance, at least once a week. And it was Mr. Miller whom Marilyn chose to take to the historic Madison Square Garden birthday bash for President John Kennedy in May 1962.

On August 4, 1962, the day of Marilyn's death, Mr. Miller telephoned his former daughter-in-law at approximately noon. According to Mr. Miller, he was told, by "the housekeeper," that Marilyn was dressing and that she would return his call—which she never did.

**JANE MILLER**

Arthur and Mary Miller's daughter, and Marilyn's stepdaughter, who was fifteen years old in 1960, when Arthur and MM split.

**MARILYN MILLER**

The original Marilyn Miller (1898–1936) was Mary Pickford's sister-in-law and the Broadway star of such 1920s musicals as *Ziegfeld Follies, Sally, Sunny, Rosalie,* and *As Thousands Cheer*. And it was *this* Marilyn Miller whom 20th Century-Fox casting director, Ben Lyon, named Norma Jeane Dougherty after in 1946.

Miss Miller's life story has been told in two motion pictures: *Till the Clouds Roll By* (1946) with Judy Garland, and *Look for the Silver Lining* (1949) with June Haver.

**MARION MILLER**
Yet another MM, Miss Marion Miller was little Norma Jeane Baker's piano teacher at Ida and Wayne Bolender's home in Hawthorne, California, circa 1932.

**MARY SLATTERY MILLER**
Arthur Miller's first wife and the mother of Jane and Robert Miller. Arthur was married to the former Mary Slattery for some fifteen years before he divorced her in 1956 to marry Marilyn Monroe.

**MORTON MILLER**
On June 27, 1956, Morton Miller, Arthur's cousin, rushed Arthur's and Marilyn's blood to the State Bureau of Laboratories for the premarriage tests. Two days later, Morton served as a witness at the civil wedding ceremony of the famous couple.

**REBECCA MILLER**
On September 15, 1962, just over a month after Marilyn's death, Rebecca Miller was born to Arthur and Inge Morath Miller.

**ROBERT MILLER**
Arthur Miller's son by Mary Slattery, who was thirteen years old at the time of the Miller/Monroe separation in 1960.

***THE MILLIONAIRE***
*See LET'S MAKE LOVE.*

**HARRY MINES**
One of the publicists involved in *The Misfits* (1961).

**BERNICE MIRACLE**

> "I have never seen my half-sister. We have nothing in common. She is married to an airplane engineer. I am not sure where he lives. It's in Florida, Clearwater or St. Petersburg."
>
> Marilyn Monroe to Maurice Zolotow

Sometime after Marilyn Monroe made the above denouncement, she was reunited with her half-sister, Bernice (also spelled *Berneice*) Miracle, the former Bernice Baker.

Bernice Inez Gladys Baker was born to Jack and Gladys Baker on July 30, 1919—seven years before the birth of Norma Jeane Mortenson. While Norma Jeane was brought up in a series of foster homes and an orphanage, Bernice was being raised by her father in Kentucky. Thus, Norma Jeane never had the opportunity to get to know her half-sister, but Marilyn Monroe did.

In 1961, after her split from Arthur Miller, Marilyn invited Bernice to come and visit her in New York. Reportedly, the two sisters got on quite well, and, when Marilyn visited Joe DiMaggio in Florida, she also stopped by to see Bernice, who was living in Gainesville, Florida.

Following Marilyn's death, Bernice worked in tandem with DiMaggio in making the burial arrangements for MM's funeral. Somewhat surprisingly, Bernice was named as a primary beneficiary in Marilyn's will. In 1967, Bernice became the legal guardian of her mother, Gladys Baker.

***MISCHIEF***

*Don't Bother to Knock* (1952) was based on a suspense serial that was published in *Good Housekeeping* magazine. The serial was written by Charlotte Armstrong.

***THE MISFITS*** ★★½

1961 124 minutes Black and White
United Artists
Directed by: John Huston
Produced by: Frank Taylor
Screenplay by: Arthur Miller, from his own short story
Photographed by: Russell Metty
Cast: Clark Gable, Marilyn Monroe, Montgomery Clift, Eli Wallach, Thelma Ritter, James Barton, Estelle Winwood, Kevin McCarthy

To Marilyn Monroe, *The Misfits* must have seemed, at first, the consummate career move. The script was to be written by her then (1957) beloved husband, Arthur Miller, as a tribute to *her*. It would be produced by a trusted friend of the Millers, Frank Taylor. It would costar one of her lifelong idols, Clark Gable, and would boast a supporting cast that included her friends Montgomery Clift and Eli Wallach. Moreover, it would be directed by another one of her

THE ALAN FRANCE COLLECTION

*The Misfits* cast attempting to confuse identities: from left, Eli Wallach, Clark Gable, MM, and Montgomery Clift, 1961.

idols, John Huston, who was one of the men responsible for her early success. It would also give Marilyn a dramatic part, tailored to her talents, in which she could flaunt her Strasbergian skills. If nothing else, *The Misfits* would prove to skeptics that Marilyn Monroe the Bombshell was serious about Marilyn Monroe the Serious Actress.

> "Husbands and wives are killing each other."
> Marilyn Monroe, in *The Misfits,* written by Arthur Miller

But it didn't work out that way. Perhaps the timing was just wrong. Who knows? If *The Misfits* had been made in 1958, or maybe even in 1959, it might have been the artistic, creative success that it was designed to be. On the other hand, there couldn't have been a *worse* time to shoot this picture than July 1960. First of all, there was the heat factor. The summer temperature in Reno, Nevada, blazed to and past an excruciating 110 degrees, which was devastating to even the most seasoned crew hand. And then, in contrast, was the anything-but-warm marital relationship between Arthur Miller and Marilyn Monroe. Not only was it over; it was hostile.

*The Misfits* was actually scheduled to begin shooting on March 3, 1960. However, an unexpected actors' strike delayed the production of *Let's Make Love* for five weeks, which, in turn, pushed back the start date of *The Misfits.* Because of this delay, Marilyn was rushed directly from *Let's Make Love* (and a broken "romance" with Yves Montand) into *The Misfits*—without a break. Not surprisingly, MM was less than thrilled when she arrived at the sweltering Reno location in the third week of July.

> "It's their movie. It's really about the cowboys and the horses. That's all they need. They don't need me at all. Not to act—just for the money. To put my name on the marquee."
> Marilyn Monroe, during production of *The Misfits*

The production, which was shot in sequence, was problematic from the start. On July 30 and, again on August 1, shooting was postponed because Marilyn was "indisposed." In the following weeks, *The Misfits* cast and crew split into two camps: Miller vs. Monroe. During this period, Marilyn suffered from insomnia and consumed an unknown quantity of Nembutal. As the temperature continued to blister, Marilyn suffered an emotional and physical breakdown and on August 27 she was flown to the Westside Hospital in Los Angeles. John Huston, forced into an impossible situation, shut down the production. One week later, on September 5, a seemingly revitalized MM returned to the Reno location, and shooting resumed the following day. However, within one week—on September 12, September 13, and September 19—the production was again postponed due to Marilyn.

In retrospect, it seems a minor miracle that *The Misfits* got finished at all. One must credit John Huston for remaining intact and pulling the film together. The shooting was completed, finally, on Stage 2 at Paramount Studios in Hollywood. However, after United Artists executive Max Youngstein saw a rough-cut version of the film and was displeased, Huston, Miller, and Taylor decided to reshoot several scenes. This decision was vetoed by Clark Gable, who had script approval. Thus, on November 4, 1960, *The*

*Misfits* had its last day of shooting. By then, the film had gone some forty days over budget. Its final cost was $3,955,000. It was, up until that time, the most expensive black-and-white motion picture ever made.

After postproduction was completed, the film's producers attempted to rush *The Misfits* into release to qualify for the 1960 Academy Award nominations. The consensus, at that time, was that Clark Gable would get a posthumous Oscar nod (which he did not). When the film failed to qualify in time, it was rushed out in February 1961 as a tribute to Gable, who had died on November 16, 1960—less than two weeks following the completion of the grueling shoot.

*The Misfits* started out as a testimonial of love and ended up as a bleak reminder of a failed marriage. The making of *The Misfits* was an emotionally depleting, painfully desperate, all-consuming, and ultimately tragic experience for the principals involved. However, very little of the pathos or passion was translated to the screen. As drama, it is a rather dull, pretentious failure, albeit a curious and fascinating failure. Today, when reviewing the film, one *can* find a doomed sense of tragedy in *The Misfits*; however, that evocation is due more to the ill-fated stars—Gable, Clift, and Monroe—than to the film itself.

> "He could have written me anything, and he comes up with this. If that's what he thinks of me, well, then, I'm not for him and he's not for me."
>
> Marilyn Monroe, on Arthur Miller and *The Misfits*

As Roslyn, the fragile figurine of *The Misfits,* Marilyn Monroe succeeded in shedding the delectable dish image, but in the transition she also lost that indescribable MM glow, vitality, and *presence* that had catapulted off the screen in her earlier films. She walks through most of *The Misfits* in a somnambulistic trance that seems to be the result of a drug-induced stupor. Her eyes are glazed, and her whole appearance in this film is tired and fuzzy—as if the camera lens were soft-focused throughout her entire performance.

Upon its release, *The Misfits,* a work of collective genius, was greeted with, at best, mixed reviews. Over the years, however, it has enjoyed numerous revivals and has garnered somewhat of a following of admirers. Nonetheless, it remains notable for the drama that transpired behind its dusty scenes, rather than for what actually appears on the screen. It is also a landmark motion picture because it proved to be the final completed film for both the King and Queen of Hollywood—Clark Gable and Marilyn Monroe.

Of what *does* appear in *The Misfits,* one of the most striking images is the sight of Marilyn Monroe, *the* Marilyn Monroe, blonde, colorful, glamorous MM, walking about in the dirt, wearing tight blue denim, in a black-and-white cowboy movie. No wonder she looks lost.

**MISS AMERICA**

Marilyn Monroe never entered the Miss America pageant (she was a *Mrs.* at the age of sixteen!), but she did serve as the grand marshal at the September 2, 1952, Miss America Parade, which was held in Atlantic City, New Jersey.

Marilyn was, in fact, the first woman ever to be named the grand marshal of that particular parade.

Marilyn's appearance at the parade was arranged by 20th Century-Fox in conjunction with the promoters of the Miss America pageant. It was considered a promotional event to publicize Marilyn's latest film at that time, *Monkey Business.* Not only did she ride in the parade; she also posed with each of the forty-eight beauty queen aspirants.

COURTESY OF CINEMA COLLECTORS

Grand Marshall, Miss America Parade, Atlantic City, NJ, 1952.

**MM Trivia Quiz #30**

As Annabel Norris in the 1952 film *We're Not Married,* Marilyn Monroe won the state competition of the Miss America program. Which state title did MM win? (Answer on page 577.)

**MISS GOLDEN DREAMS**

*See* CALENDAR.

**MISS WESTERN FASHION**

Miss Western Fashion was a beauty contest that starlet Marilyn Monroe was determined to win. Apparently, she was under the impression that a beauty title would be her entree through the big studio gates. Thus, Marilyn reportedly entered the pageant twice a year, during her struggling years, and was defeated each time.

### THE MISSION INN

En route to their honeymoon hideaway in Paso Robles, Marilyn and Joe DiMaggio stopped at the Mission Inn, which was located in Old Monterey, California.

### CAMERON MITCHELL

> "Then, as you know her, you find out she's no goddamn gold-plated birdbrain. She's a serious dame. At the time I first met her, she was on a big psychiatry kick. She was studying Freud, Menninger, that kind of thing."
>
> Cameron Mitchell, on early Marilyn Monroe

Actor Cameron Mitchell was the man who, on the 20th Century-Fox lot, first introduced Marilyn Monroe to Arthur Miller. Mitchell and Monroe were en route to the Fox commissary when they "ran into" Miller, who was with director Elia Kazan. It was December 1950.

Born in 1918, Cameron Mitchell appeared in Arthur Miller's Broadway production of *Death of a Salesman* (1949) before appearing in the film version of that play in 1952. A year later, Mitchell was featured in one of Marilyn's vehicles, *How to Marry a Millionaire*. Mitchell subsequently appeared in the television series *High Chaparral* (1967-71) as well as the motion picture *My Favorite Year* (1982).

### JIMMY MITCHELL

Jimmy Mitchell was a 20th Century-Fox photographer who shot photos of Marilyn's nude swimming sequence on the set of *Something's Got to Give* in 1962. However, for the tidy sum of $10,000, Mitchell sold the rights to his photos to the enterprising Lawrence Schiller.

### ROBERT MITCHUM

In the 1940s, an unknown actor named Robert Mitchum worked at the Lockheed Plant alongside Marilyn Monroe's first husband, Jim Dougherty. Reportedly, young Dougherty once showed Mitchum a photograph of Norma Jeane nude.

Years later, Mitchum, who was born in 1917, costarred opposite Marilyn Monroe in Otto Preminger's *River of No Return* (1954). Among Mitchum's numerous other films are *The Sundowners* (1960), *Ryan's Daughter* (1971), and *Farewell My Lovely* (1975).

### JOHN J. MITTY

Reportedly, in 1954, Joe DiMaggio wanted a church wedding. However, his request was turned down by the archbishop of San Francisco, John J. Mitty. Apparently, the church refused to recognize DiMaggio's divorce from former actress Dorothy Arnold. Subsequently, when DiMaggio married Marilyn Monroe in a civil service, he was automatically excommunicated from the Roman Catholic Church.

**CYRIL MOCKRIDGE**

Cyril Mockridge (1896–1979) composed the musical scores for the following Marilyn Monroe movies: *A Ticket to Tomahawk* (1950), *As Young as You Feel* (1951), *Love Nest* (1951), *Let's Make It Legal* (1951), *We're Not Married* (1952), *How to Marry a Millionaire* (1953), *River of No Return* (1954), and *Bus Stop* (1956).

**THE MOJAVE DESERT**

Location used by photographer David Conover in July 1945 for his photo session with model Norma Jeane Dougherty. Later that year, in December, another photographer, Andre de Dienes, also chose the Mojave as the location for a photo session with Norma Jeane.

***MONKEY BUSINESS*** ★★

1952 97 minutes Black and White
20th Century-Fox
Directed by: Howard Hawks
Produced by: Sol C. Siegel
Screenplay by: Ben Hecht, Charles Lederer, I. A. L. Diamond, from a story by Harry Segall
Photographed by: Milton Krasner
Cast: Cary Grant, Ginger Rogers, Charles Coburn, Marilyn Monroe, Hugh Marlowe

Originally titled *Darling, I Am Growing Younger, Monkey Business* signaled Marilyn's return to comedy, following her not altogether successful dramatic turn in *Don't Bother to Knock* (1952). It also signaled the end of Marilyn's long string of supporting roles (excluding her appearance in *O. Henry's Full House*. After *Monkey Business,* 20th Century-Fox showcased Marilyn Monroe in starring or costarring vehicles only.

*Monkey Business* went into production on February 26, 1952, and was released later that September. The plot, intended as madcap comedy, featured a chimpanzee, a magical potion of youth, and Marilyn Monroe as "Lois Laurel," a secretary whose assets did not include typing or dictation.

Although *Monkey Business* did fairly well at the box office, it is a surprisingly dull film—especially when one considers the calibre of talents involved in the production. Surely, Howard Hawks, Ben Hecht, Charles Lederer, I. A. L. Diamond, Cary Grant, Ginger Rogers, et al., could have collectively concocted something better than this.

**DELLA MONROE**

*See* DELLA MONROE GRAINGER.

***MONROE: HER LIFE IN PICTURES***

Authors: James Spada and George Zeno
Publisher: Doubleday
Year: 1982
$14.95, paperback, 208 pp. (ISBN 0-385-17940-5, DOLP); $24.95, hardcover (ISBN 0-385-17940-5 DOLP)

Sumptuously mounted photo book with an accompanying text. The collection of photographs alone, many of them quite rare, makes this a worthwhile effort.

**JAMES MONROE**

Marilyn Monroe claimed that she was a descendant of James Monroe, who served as the fifth president of the United States.

**MARILYN MONROE: ALL ABOUT MARILYN**

Marilyn Monroe was an extremely difficult person to analyze or categorize. She was, by most reports, a highly complex and confused woman, tainted by scars from her past and overloaded with contradictions. She, like Rock Hudson, had a chameleonlike charm (or flaw), in which she adapted to her surroundings and company. Over the years, she told many stories to many different people—some of them fabricated, some of them exaggerated, and some of them true. Also over the years, many, many people have had quite a few stories to tell about Marilyn Monroe. The following, then, is a selective composite view of Marilyn, through the words of some of those who knew her and some who did not.

> "There isn't enough upper lip between the end of your nose and your mouth."
>
> Emmeline Snively to Norma Jeane Dougherty

> "I got a cold chill. This girl had something I hadn't seen since silent pictures. She had a kind of fantastic beauty like Gloria Swanson, when a movie star had to look beautiful, and she got sex on a piece of film like Jean Harlow."
>
> Leon Shamroy, on MM's 1946 screen test

> "When you look at Marilyn on the screen, you don't want anything bad to happen to her. You really care that she should be all right . . . happy."
>
> Natalie Wood

> "Marilyn's insecurities nearly screamed out of her. If she had an eight o'clock date, I had to be there at noon to start on her. If I was two minutes late she was furious, though she thought nothing of keeping others waiting for hours or days."
>
> George Masters

> "This is a little kid who wants to be with the other little kids sucking lollipops and watching the rollercoaster, but she can't because they won't let her. She's frightened to death of that public which thinks she is so sexy. My God, if they only knew."
>
> Allan "Whitey" Snyder

> "She was not the usual movie idol. There was something democratic about her. She was the type who would join in and wash up the supper dishes even if you didn't ask her."
>
> Carl Sandburg

> "We were in mid-flight, and there was a nut on the plane."
>
> Billy Wilder on MM and the shooting of *Some Like It Hot*

THE SABIN GRAY COLLECTION

"Miss Monroe has just about worn the Welcome off this observer's mat. . . . 'Heat Wave' [Marilyn's production number in *There's No Business Like Show Business*] is easily one of the most flagrant violations of good taste this observer has ever witnessed."

Ed Sullivan

"A great force of nature, she was becoming a victim of the propaganda machine, of her own struggle to build herself up. About her swirled a hurricane, and she was its eye. She longed for privacy, but she had murdered privacy, as Macbeth had murdered sleep. Her time was not hers. And her personality was not hers."

Maurice Zolotow

"I took her as a serious actress before I ever met her. I think she's an adroit comedienne, but I also think that she might turn into the greatest tragic actress that can be imagined."

Arthur Miller

". . . She was chewed and spat out by a long line of grinning men! Her name floating in the stench of locker rooms and parlor-car cigar smoke!"

Quentin on Maggie in Arthur Miller's *After the Fall*

"Marilyn was an incredible person to act with . . . the most marvelous I ever worked with, and I have been working for 29 years."

Montgomery Clift

"When you speak of the American way of life, everybody thinks of chewing gum, Coca-Cola and Marilyn Monroe."

the Russian magazine *Nedyela*

"This whole thing about her feeling she has to get married and have children and be normal and well adjusted—I blame it on psychoanalysis."

Norman Mailer

"She walks like a young antelope, and when she stands up it's like a snake uncoiling."

Jerry Wald on early MM

"She comes out of the dressing room Norma Jeane. When she stepped in front of the camera, she was Marilyn."

Lawrence Schiller

"A lady from way back . . . quiet, gentle, gracious, and the sort of girl you'd like to bring home and say, 'Mama, this is Marilyn.'

Columnist Henry McLemore, 1953

"Marilyn played the best game with the worst hand of anybody I know."

Edward Wagenknecht

"Marilyn Monroe is not a raving beauty, and her legs are too short for the rest of her."

Laurence Willinger

"She was among the least 'naturally' sexy or beautiful women I've ever worked on. Ann-Margret, Jennifer Jones, Cyd Charisse, Audrey Hepburn, Rita Hayworth, without make-up—I could name dozens who are more naturally sexy and beautiful than Marilyn Monroe was."

George Masters

"Marilyn is a dreamy girl. She's the kind who's liable to show up with one red shoe and one black shoe."

Jane Russell

"That girl really has something. She looks like a new, model Lana Turner."

Producer Frank King to Sidney Skolsky, 1951

"Miss Monroe is one of the greatest comedy actresses of our time. She is simply superb. Miss Mansfield I've never seen."

Vladimir Nabokov, when asked his opinion of America's sex symbols

"It was impossible to think of Marilyn Monroe except as Cinderella."

Diana Trilling

"One of the most unappreciated people in the world."

Joshua Logan

"The trouble with Marilyn was she didn't trust her own judgment, always had someone around to depend on. Coaches, so-called friends. Even me."

Allan "Whitey" Snyder

"Marilyn was so bright about acting. Her trouble was only that she'd get so scared she wasn't going to be able to do it, and so tied up in knots, that then everyone thought she was dumb."

Peggy Feury

"She's scared and unsure of herself. I found myself wishing that I were a psychoanalyst and she were my patient. It might be that I couldn't have helped her, but she would have looked lovely on a couch."

Billy Wilder

"When she's there, she's there. All of her is there! She's there to work."

Clark Gable

"It was like being sucked into a vacuum."

Tommy Noonan on kissing MM in *Gentlemen Prefer Blondes*

"She looked like, if you bit her, milk and honey would flow from her."

Artist Franz Kline

"Still she hangs like a bat in the heads of the men who met her, and none of us will ever forget her."

Sammy Davis, Jr.

"Marilyn's need to be desired was so great that she could make love to a camera. Because of this, her lust aroused lust in audiences, sometimes even among women. There was nothing subtle about it. She was no tease. She was prepared, and even eager, to give what she offered."

William Manchester

"There's a broad with her future behind her."

Constance Bennett

THE T. R. FOGLI COLLECTION

"There's a broad with her future behind her."—Constance Bennett

"She would have been a very unfortunate woman, because she would have had to get a face lift and she'd have lost most of her beauty, I'm afraid. She would have continued to drink and would probably have not been very attractive anymore and trying to get character parts and not have been able to get them."

Earl Wilson on MM, if she had lived to grow old

"Miss Marilyn Monroe calls to mind the bouquet of a fireworks display."

Cecil Beaton

"I had always thought that all those amusing remarks she was supposed to have made for the press had probably been manufactured and mimeographed by her press agent, but they weren't. She was a very bright person, an instinctive type."

Photographer Elliott Erwitt

"On the surface, she was still a happy girl. But those who criticized her never saw her as I did, crying like a baby because she often felt herself so inadequate."

Bill Travilla

"Look at that face—she could be five years old."

Laurence Olivier

"I did know her, and out of that sentiment for her, I could never talk about her for publication."

Marlon Brando

"Do you remember when Marilyn Monroe died? Everybody stopped work, and you could see all that day the same expressions on their faces, the same thought: 'How can a girl with success, fame, youth, money, beauty . . . how could she kill herself?' Nobody could understand it because those are the things that everybody wants, and they can't believe that life wasn't important to Marilyn Monroe, or that her life was elsewhere."

Marlon Brando

"She had such magnetism that if 15 men were in a room with her, each man would be convinced he was the one she'd be waiting for after the others left."

Publicist Roy Craft

"It's difficult to say what Marilyn's future would have been, but I believe her career would have continued, and she would have been an important actress. I never worked with her, but I think some of the people who did failed to give her the patience and consideration she needed. She had her problems. She was disturbed in many areas, and those who weren't close friends of hers may not have realized how grave some of her personal problems were."

Peter Lawford

"She's worth all the trouble."

Joshua Logan to Laurence Olivier

"You say hello to her or it's a nice day today, and she answers with a line from the script. She forgets everything but the work."

Jean Negulesco

"Hollywood, Broadway, the night clubs all produce their quota of sex queens, but the public takes them or leaves them; the world is not as enslaved by them as it was by Marilyn Monroe, because none but she could suggest such a purity of sexual delight."

Diana Trilling

"I asked her where she lived, and when she said at the Studio Club, I was impressed because I knew that a girl who looked like that could have the biggest house in Beverly Hills, she could have whatever she wanted because men would give it to her. Therefore, if she lived at the Studio Club it was because she had character."

Ben Lyon on his 1946 meeting with
Norma Jeane Dougherty

"I have great faith that her career would have continued. She was one of the greatest draws in the history of motion pictures, and today I think she would have been tops. Marilyn had a childlike quality which made men adore her. Yet women weren't jealous. Like John Wayne and a few other giants, she had a star quality that had nothing to do with acting. . . . What women in pictures can compare with her today? Nobody."

Ben Lyon

"Marilyn is a moonwalker. When she used to live in my house, I often felt like she was a somnambulist walking around."

Natasha Lytess

"She'd come out of our apartment in a shleppy old coat, looking like my maid, and all the people would push her aside to get *my* autograph. She loved it."

Shelley Winters

"Marilyn Monroe had the most beautiful mouth ever. No one has ever been able to convey so much sex appeal with just one feature."

George Masters

COURTESY OF CINEMA COLLECTORS

"It may sound peculiar to say so, because she is no longer with us, but we were very close. Once when we were doing that picture together, I got a call on the set: my younger daughter had had a fall. I ran home and the one person to call was Marilyn. She did an awful lot to boost things up for movies when everything was at a low state; there'll never be anyone like her for looks, for attitude, for all of it."

Betty Grable

"She once got her life so balled up that the studio hired a full-time secretary maid for her. So Marilyn soon got the secretary as balled up as she was, and she ended up waiting on the secretary, instead of vice-versa."

Jane Russell

"She can make any move, any gesture, almost insufferably suggestive."

Henry Hathaway

"It's no fun being married to an electric light."

Joe DiMaggio

"Joe DiMaggio may not have made a good husband for Marilyn, but no one cared more for her. He was always, before the divorce, and after the divorce, her best friend."

Allan "Whitey" Snyder

"Marilyn wanted only herself to look like Marilyn Monroe. She wanted no one else to look anything like her and nothing or nobody to detract from her."

George Masters

"I never worked with Marilyn Monroe, but if she'd lived, I think she would have been all right. She would have been President of the United States."

Walter Matthau

"Dietrich made sex remote, Garbo made it mysterious, Crawford made it agonizing, but Monroe makes it amusing. Whenever a man thinks of Marilyn, he smiles at his own thoughts."

Milton Shulman

"She represents to man something we all want in our unfulfilled dreams. She's the girl you'd like to double-cross your wife with. A man, he's got to be dead not to be excited by her."

Jean Negulesco

"This [*The Seven Year Itch*] will be her last picture for anyone but 20th Century-Fox for three years and four months. She's under contract to this studio, and she'll fulfill it."

Darryl F. Zanuck on the formation of
Marilyn Monroe Productions

"Gone was the shy, tense little girl voice, the slow groping for just the right word, the hesitation in answering a question . . . she came up, in a few minutes, with sprightlier conversation than most stars can manage in hours."

Dorothy Manning on the "new" Marilyn, circa 1956

"[She was] so terrified she couldn't speak a word, just stood there mute but refusing to engage in the vacuous small talk."

Arthur Miller on early Marilyn Monroe

"I don't think I ever saw two people so dizzy with love for each other. Having known Arthur a long time as an introspective guy, it was, well, like a miracle to see him so outgoing."

Jim Proctor

"Since her divorce from Arthur Miller, she's been in her best condition for a long time. She's happy!"

Allan "Whitey" Snyder, shortly before Marilyn's death

Marilyn Monroe's unique charisma was the force that caused distant men to think that if only a well-intentioned, understanding person like me could have known her, she would have been all right. In death, it has caused women who before resented her frolicsome sexuality to join in the unspoken plea she leaves behind—the simple, noble wish to be taken seriously.

*Time* magazine

"Is not Monroe the image par excellence of this New Woman? She is voluptuous, but she admires Dostoyevsky."

Maurice Zolotow

"She was a difficult woman, you know. We liked her and we said the nicest things about her and she deserved them; but, she was trouble and she brought that whole baggage of emotional difficulties of her childhood with her."

Norman Rosten

"Marilyn didn't use expressions like, 'being made love to,' she used a shorter, stronger word."

Earl Wilson

"She knows the world, but this knowledge has not lowered her great and benevolent dignity, its darkness has not dimmed her goodness."

Edith Sitwell

"She's one of the few stars who don't act as if she's made it. She does not coast. She worked harder in *Let's Make Love* than she did in *Clash by Night*. She's still the same person."

Jerry Wald

"She could let herself look like an old bag for two weeks. She'd smell sometimes, and never comb her hair for weeks. That's why it would take nine hours to get her ready to re-create Marilyn Monroe."

George Masters

"She had one long blonde hair on her chest that she wouldn't let me cut off. She liked to play and fondle it. It was her security blanket."

George Masters

"She is a beautiful child. I don't think she's an actress at all, not in any traditional sense. What she has—this presence, this luminosity, this flickering intelligence—could never surface on the stage. It's so fragile and subtle, it can only be caught by the camera. . . . But anyone who thinks this girl is simply another Harlow or harlot or whatever, is mad. I hope, I really pray, that she survives long enough to free the strange lovely talent that's wandering through her like a jailed spirit."

Constance Collier

"I sat near her. She gulped wine by the glassful. When her name was called, she had to be helped out of her chair onto the stage. She accepted the award almost in a caricature of herself."

James Bacon on Marilyn Monroe at the
1962 Golden Globe Awards

"I have the same problem as Marilyn. We attract people the way honey does bees, but they're generally the wrong kind of people. People who want something from us—if only our energy. We need a period of being alone to become ourselves."

Montgomery Clift

"She seemed to have a kind of unconscious glow about her physical self that was innocent, like a child. When she posed nude, it was . . . 'Gee, I am kind of, you know, sort of dishy,' like she enjoyed it without being egotistical."

Elizabeth Taylor

"She's really got an infection. It can't be psychological. It's a germ."

Peter Levathes to George Cukor, after MM failed to show
up for the shooting of *Something's Got to Give*

"She was pure of heart. She was free of guile. She never understood either the adoration or the antagonism which she awakened."

Edward Wagenknecht

"She stood for life. She radiated life. In her smile hope was always present. She glorified in life, and her death did not mar this final image. She had become a legend in her own time, and in her death, took her place among the myths of our century."

John Kobal

"The girl was an addict of sleeping tablets and she was made so by the goddam doctors."

John Huston

Blonde and beautiful Marilyn Monroe, a glamorous symbol of the gay, exciting life of Hollywood, died tragically Sunday. Her body was found nude in bed, a probable suicide. She was 36. The long-troubled star clutched a telephone in one hand. An empty bottle of sleeping pills was nearby.

The Associated Press, August 6, 1962

"I'm just as sorry as the next fellow about Marilyn Monroe. But as long as she had to do it, what a break that she did it in August."

a newspaper official

"She was a fool to kill herself. She could have been the first great woman director because she understood how to make movies."

Andy Warhol

"It is my feeling that Marilyn looked forward to her tomorrows."

Mrs. Eunice Murray

"It can't be, it can't be, she couldn't have killed herself, she had three deals going."

a Hollywood agent

"This atrocious death will be a terrible lesson for those whose principal occupation consists in spying on and tormenting the film stars."

Jean Cocteau

"Anyone who has ever felt resentment against the good for being the good, and has given voice to it, is the murderer of Marilyn Monroe."

Ayn Rand

"It had to happen. I didn't know when or how, but it was inevitable."

Arthur Miller

COURTESY OF CINEMA COLLECTORS

"A lady from way back . . . quiet, gracious, and the sort of girl you'd like to bring home and say, 'Mama, this is Marilyn.' "—Columnist Henry McLemore

"She will go on eternally."

Jackie Kennedy Onassis

"In one sense, then, her life is completed, because her spirit is formed and has achieved itself. No matter what unpredictable events may be in her future, they cannot change who she is and what she has become."

Maurice Zolotow, 1960

"She could have made it with a little luck."

Arthur Miller

"But you're a victory, Maggie, you're like a flag to me, a kind of proof, somehow, that people can win."

Quentin to Maggie in Arthur Miller's *After the Fall*

**MARION MONROE**

Marion Monroe was Della Monroe Grainger's first child, Gladys Baker's brother, and Norma Jeane Baker's uncle, who was destroyed by paranoid schizophrenia.

**MONROE, NEW YORK**

A town in the state of New York that changed its name—for one day in 1953—to Marilyn Monroe, New York in tribute to MM and to commemorate the opening of *How to Marry a Millionaire.*

**OTIS ELMER MONROE**

Otis Elmer Monroe was Della Monroe Grainger's husband, Gladys Baker's father, and Norma Jeane Baker's grandfather. Born in Scotland, Monroe was a house painter who was committed to a mental institution. He subsequently died of general paresis, a form of insanity provoked by syphilis.

**RICARDO MONTALBAN**

Born in 1920, Ricardo Montalban has appeared in such films as *Sayonara* (1957), *Sweet Charity* (1968), and *Star Trek II: The Wrath of Khan* (1982). In 1977, Montalban began a successful run of the television series "Fantasy Island." When that program was finally cut, Montalban joined the cast of ABC's "The Colby's."

In 1950, Montalban costarred in MGM's *Right Cross,* which featured starlet Marilyn Monroe in a bit part.

**YVES MONTAND**

> "With a married man, it's all so simple. I mean, it can't possibly ever get drastic."
>
> MM to Tom Ewell in *The Seven Year Itch* (1955)

> "Next to my husband [Miller], and along with Marlon Brando, I think Yves Montand is the most attractive man I've ever met."
>
> Marilyn Monroe

Yves Montand was born Ivo Livi on October 13, 1921, in Monsummano, Italy. At the age of eighteen he was "discovered" by legendary singer Edith Piaf, with whom he subsequently had an affair. In 1949, Montand married actress Simone Signoret. Six years later, the Montands starred in the French film version of Arthur Miller's *The Crucible.* It was entitled *The Witches of Salem.* Then, in 1959, Montand took his one-man stage show to Broadway.

In 1959, Arthur Miller and Marilyn Monroe were having an exceptionally difficult time casting the male lead in MM's upcoming film comedy, *Let's Make Love.* Gregory Peck, Cary Grant, Charlton Heston, Rock Hudson, James Stewart, and Yul Brynner had already nixed the project. And then Marilyn went to see Yves Montand's one-man show on Broadway.

At that time in his career, Yves Montand was an established actor in France. However, he was still unknown in America and was looking for an introductory vehicle. What could've been more promising than the romantic lead opposite Marilyn Monroe in a George Cukor comedy?

THE RAY VAN GOEYE COLLECTION

During the production of *Let's Make Love,* the Montands took up residence at the Beverly Hills Hotel, adjacent to the suite occupied by the Millers. As fate would have it, Arthur Miller and Simone Signoret were soon required elsewhere, and Montand and Monroe were left alone. Montand, of course, has claimed that it was Marilyn who threw herself at him. At one point, he was quoted as saying to friends, "She's got so she'll do whatever I ask her to do on the set." Publicly, Montand stated:

> "She has been so kind to me, but she is a simple girl without any guile. Perhaps I was too tender and thought that maybe she was as sophisticated as some of the other ladies I have known. . . . Had Marilyn been sophisticated, none of this ever would have happened. . . . Perhaps she had a schoolgirl crush. If she did, I'm sorry. But, nothing will break up my marriage."

Immediately following the November 1960 completion of *The Misfits,* Marilyn met Montand at Idlewild Airport in New York. There, in the backseat of her limousine, Marilyn and Montand drank champagne and said their goodbyes. The widely reported affair was over.

And so, apparently, was Montand's acting career in America. Instead of *Let's Make Love* bolstering his career, the scandal attached to it seemed to hurt him.

**MONTEREY, CALIFORNIA**
*Clash by Night* (1952) was shot on location in Monterey, California.

**ROBERT MONTGOMERY**

Montgomery was Arthur Miller's New York attorney, whom Marilyn consulted regarding the termination of her contract with Milton H. Greene, in early 1957.

**MONTGOMERY WARD**

Norma Jeane Dougherty's second assignment with the Blue Book Agency was modeling fashions for the Montgomery Ward department store catalogue. However, after just two days of work, Norma Jeane was sent home. Apparently, she was displaying *herself* better than she was the clothes.

**JOHN MOORE**

John Moore, a designer for Talmack, was one of Marilyn Monroe's personal fashion designers.

**PHIL MOORE**

Reportedly, in 1941, Phil Moore became the first black musician hired by a Hollywood studio music department. In 1952-53, Moore served as Marilyn Monroe's vocal coach on 20th Century-Fox's *Gentlemen Prefer Blondes*. Of MM, Moore has been quoted as saying: "She always sounds as if she's just waking up. You'd be surprised what kind of effect that has on male listeners." In addition to tutoring MM, Phil Moore had worked with Lena Horne, Ava Gardner, and Dorothy Dandrige. Moore died in May 1987.

**ROBIN MOORE**

Robin Moore was the cowriter of the book *Marilyn & Joe DiMaggio*, which was published in 1977.

**TERRY MOORE**

According to the RKO Archives, actress Terry Moore was initially slated for the role of "Peggy" in *Clash by Night*. However, the film eventually went to Marilyn Monroe, who was given costar billing. A few years later, Miss Moore was considered by 20th Century-Fox to replace MM in *The Girl in Pink Tights*, a film project that was subsequently shelved. As for Terry Moore (born Helen Koford in 1929), she was banished forever to mostly forgettable films, and had to settle for being married to Howard Hughes.

**WILLIAM MOORE**

William Moore is, quite simply, one of the finest celebrity illustrators in the business. His "Moore Legends" is a series of realistic, intricately detailed pencil graphic of such stars as Marilyn Monroe, Elizabeth Taylor, Judy Garland, Sophia Loren, James Dean, Barbra Streisand, Ann-Margret, and many, many more. His original artworks are usually 15″ × 20″, and are estimated at $1,200 each. Reportedly, Joe DiMaggio owns a few of Moore's lithographs of Marilyn Monroe. Moore Legends is located at 8621 Wilshire Boulevard, Suite 125, in Beverly Hills, California.

**EARL MORAN**

In 1946, calendar and magazine illustrator Earl Moran hired the Blue Book Agency's Norma Jeane Dougherty to model for him. He paid her $10 an hour. For the next four years, Moran hired Marilyn on and off and was a fairly steady source of income for her during those erratic, hungry years. MM was once quoted as saying, "Earl saved my life many a time."

Of Marilyn, Moran has said:

> "She knew exactly what to do, her movements, her hands, her body were just perfect. She was the sexiest. Better than anyone else. Emotionally, she did everything right. She expressed just what I wanted."

With Earl Moran, circa 1947.

COURTESY OF CINEMA COLLECTORS

*Forty years* after Earl Moran first began working with Norma Jeane Dougherty, *Playboy* magazine (January 1987) unearthed a series of early Marilyn Monroe nudes, photographed and illustrated by Earl Moran.

**INGE MORATH**

European, dark, and slender, Inge Morath was the photographer who replaced Marilyn Monroe in Arthur Miller's affections. Miss Morath was a Magnum agency photographer who met Miller on the turbulent set of *The Misfits* in 1960. After Marilyn filed for a divorce in January 1961, Inge Morath became Arthur Miller's third wife. Several years later, Miller dedicated his *After the Fall* (1964) "to my wife Ingeborg Morath."

**FRED MORGAN**

Fred Morgan was a photographer who was present at the January 1955 press conference at which the formation of Marilyn Monroe Productions was announced.

**EVELYN MORIARTY**

> "Any little thing I did for her, she was so appreciative. She treated me more like a friend than a studio associate. Before I would go into a scene to stand in for her, she would come over and fix my hair and my clothes and she'd give me the motivation for the scene, so I would know what I was doing. She was my Paula Strasberg."
>
> Evelyn Moriarty on Marilyn Monroe

Evelyn Moriarty was Marilyn Monroe's stand-in on *The Misfits*. Following Marilyn's death, Miss Moriarty became Barbara Eden's stand-in on *The New Interns* television program. Her services were later requested by Ann-Margret.

**WALTER MOROSCO**

Walter Morosco was the producer of *Scudda Hoo! Scudda Hay!* (1948), which is generally credited as Marilyn Monroe's first motion picture.

**EDWARD MORTENSON**

Until this day, there is confusion about Martin Edward Mortenson (also spelled *Mortensen*), who was Gladys Baker's second husband. Mortenson is, of course, one of the men suggested as being the father of Norma Jeane Mortenson.

Mortenson was born in Haugesund, Norway, in 1897. He was a baker by trade, and by 1923 he had a wife and three children—all of whom he deserted when he moved to the United States. Shortly afterward (on October 11, 1924), Mortenson met and married Gladys Baker. However, when that relationship soured, Mortenson fled town and was later killed in a motorcycle accident on June 18, 1929, in Ohio.

However, to compound the confusion, a *second* Martin Edward Mortensen died of a heart attack in Riverside, California, in 1981. This Mortensen was eighty-three years old and had claimed to have been the forgotten father of Marilyn Monroe. In his possession, at the time of his death, was a copy of Norma Jeane's birth certificate.

Now that Mortenson and Mortensen are both dead, it is probable that it will never be known which of them—if either—was Marilyn Monroe's real father. However, it should be noted that on her birth certificate, Norma Jeane's father is listed as "Edward Mortenson." On her DiMaggio and Miller marriage certificates, Marilyn's father is also listed as "Edward Mortenson."

**GLADYS MORTENSON**
*See* GLADYS BAKER.

**ALINE MOSBY**
Aline Mosby was the UPI wire-service reporter who broke the news about Marilyn Monroe's red velvet nude calendar. Miss Mosby's story, which was printed on March 13, 1952, was sympathetic in tone and actually furthered Marilyn's career instead of hindering it. (*See* CALENDAR for more detailed information.)

**GLORIA MOSOLINO**
Amply dimensioned Gloria Mosolino (37-24-36) was Marilyn Monroe's stand-in on *The Seven Year Itch* (1955). Miss Mosolino, who hailed from Pottsville, Pennsylvania, and was a graduate of Syracuse University, was paid $20 a day for her stint on *Itch*. Previously, she had served as Eva Marie Saint's stand-in on *On the Waterfront* (1954).

**MOTHER**
*See* GLADYS BAKER.

**MOTHERS-IN-LAW**
1. Ethel Mary Dougherty
2. Rosalie DiMaggio
3. Augusta Miller

**THOMAS F. MOULTON**
At the Academy Awards ceremony in 1951, starlet Marilyn Monroe presented the Oscar for "Best Sound Recording." The winner was Thomas F. Moulton, for his work on *All About Eve*.

***MOVE OVER DARLING***
Approximately one year after Marilyn's death, 20th Century-Fox retailored *Something's Got to Give* into a vehicle for Doris Day, which eventually evolved into *Move Over Darling* (1963). *Darling* is, in actuality, a remake of the 1940 Cary Grant/Irene Dunn romp, *My Favorite Wife*. The plot revolves around wife Doris, who returns home to hubby, James Garner, after being shipwrecked on a desert island for five years. This latest incarnation was directed by Michael Gordon, written by Hal Kanter and Jack Sher, and costarred Polly Bergen, Thelma Ritter, and Chuck Connors.

## THE MOVIES

1. *Scudda Hoo! Scudda Hay!* (1948)
2. *Dangerous Years** (1947)
3. *Ladies of the Chorus* (1948)
4. *Love Happy* (1950)
5. *A Ticket to Tomahawk* (1950)
6. *The Asphalt Jungle* (1950)
7. *All About Eve* (1950)
8. *The Fireball* (1950)
9. *Right Cross* (1950)
10. *Hometown Story* (1951)
11. *As Young as You Feel* (1951)
12. *Love Nest* (1951)
13. *Let's Make It Legal* (1951)
14. *Clash by Night* (1952)
15. *We're Not Married* (1952)
16. *Don't Bother to Knock* (1952)
17. *Monkey Business* (1952)
18. *O. Henry's Full House* (1952)
19. *Niagara* (1953)
20. *Gentlemen Prefer Blondes* (1953)
21. *How to Marry a Millionaire* (1953)
22. *River of No Return* (1954)
23. *There's No Business Like Show Business* (1954)
24. *The Seven Year Itch* (1955)
25. *Bus Stop* (1956)
26. *The Prince and the Showgirl* (1957)
27. *Some Like It Hot* (1959)
28. *Let's Make Love* (1960)
29. *The Misfits* (1961)
30. *Something's Got to Give* (uncompleted) (1962)

"Diamonds" number, 1953.

**Dangerous Years* was made after *Scudda Hoo! Scudda Hay!*, but was released first.

### The Most Memorable MM Movie Moments

1. *Love Happy*: The Walk scene
2. *The Asphalt Jungle*: The Couch scene
3. *All About Eve*: The Staircase scene
4. *Niagara*: The "Kiss" number
5. *Niagara*: The Walk scene
6. *Gentlemen Prefer Blondes*: The "Two Little Girls from Little Rock" number
7. *Gentlemen Prefer Blondes*: The stuck in port hole scene
8. *Gentlemen Prefer Blondes*: The "Diamonds Are a Girl's Best Friend" number
9. *How to Marry a Millionaire*: The Dressing Room scene
10. *River of No Return*: The "I'm Gonna File My Claim" number
11. *There's No Business Like Show Business*: The "Heat Wave" number
12. *The Seven Year Itch*: The Skirt scene

13. *Bus Stop*: The "That Old Black Magic" number
14. *Bus Stop*: The On-the-bus scene (with Hope Lange)
15. *Some Like It Hot*: The Train scene (MM's introduction)
16. *Some Like It Hot*: The "Runnin' Wild" number
17. *Some Like It Hot*: The Yacht Seduction scene
18. *Let's Make Love*: The "My Heart Belongs to Daddy" number
19. *The Misfits*: The Paddle Ball scene
20. *Something's Got to Give*: The Pool scene

THE RAY VAN GOEYE COLLECTION

*The Seven Year Itch*, dress, 1955.

### The Movies That MM Refused to Do

"What's the use of being a star if you have to play something you're ashamed of?"

Marilyn Monroe

*The Blue Angel*
*Can-Can*
*The Girl in Pink Tights*
*The Girl in the Red Velvet Swing*
*Goodbye Charlie*
*Harlow*
*How to Be Very, Very Popular*
*The Revolt of Mamie Stover*
*Size 12*

### The Movies That MM Wanted to Do but Didn't

*Baby Doll*
*Breakfast at Tiffany's*
*The Brothers Karamazov*
*The Egyptian*
*Irma La Douce*
*Middle of the Night*
*Paris Blues*
*Pillow Talk*
*A Tree Grows in Brooklyn* (a musical remake)

### The Movies about MM or That Featured an MM-Based *Major* Character (English language only)

1. *Will Success Spoil Rock Hunter?* (1957)
2. *The Goddess* (1958)
3. *The Misfits* (1961)
4. *Marilyn* (1963)
5. *Goodbye Norma Jean* (1976)
6. *Fade to Black* (1980)
7. *Insignificance* (1985)

### The Television Movies about MM or That Featured an MM-Based *Major* Character

1. "Marilyn Monroe, Why?" (from the series "Eyewitness," 1962)
2. "The Marilyn Monroe Story" (1963)
3. "Like a Diamond in the Sky" (from "The Eleventh Hour," 1963)
4. "Marilyn Monroe" (1963)
5. "The Legend of Marilyn Monroe" (1966)
6. "The Sex Symbol" (1974)
7. "Marilyn Remembered" (1974)
8. "After the Fall" (1974)
9. "Moviola: This Year's Blonde" (1980)
10. "Marilyn: The Untold Story" (1980)
11. "The Last Days of Marilyn Monroe" (1985)
12. "Marilyn Monroe: Beyond the Legend" (1986)
13. "Hoover vs. The Kennedys" (1987)
14. "Remembering Marilyn" (1988)

### MM Trivia Quiz #31

In one of her films, MM played the piano. First, name the film, then name the composition she tried to play. (Answer on page 577.)

## *MOVIE STAR*

*Movie Star* was a stage play that opened at the Westwood Playhouse in Los Angeles on April 12, 1982. In the play, a Marilyn Monroe character, portrayed by actress Katie LaBourdette, sings a song called "Does Anybody Here Love Me?" The show was created and written by Ray Aghayan, Billy Barnes, and

Bob Mackie, and received generally favorable reviews. Wrote Dan Sullivan in the *Los Angeles Times*:

> The most memorable performer is Katie LaBourdette in a number called "Does Anybody Here Love Me?" Barnes's song is mawkish—to the effect that poor Marilyn Monroe died of trying to please—but the image of Monroe posing for that famous nude photograph is striking, and the actress delicately evokes the woman without doing an impression of her.

### *MOVIOLA*

*Moviola* was a clever, best-selling Hollywood novel written by Garson Kanin and published by Simon and Schuster in 1979. Among other things, *Moviola* essayed the cliched story of Marilyn Monroe's rise and fall in cinema Babylon. Kanin loosely and plausibly interwove fact and fiction to optimum effect. Said *The Boston Globe*:

> "Go make yourself some popcorn before digging into this gossipy, glitzy, glamorous novel. The last sixty years of the movie business come alive, and then some."

### "MOVIOLA: THIS YEAR'S BLONDE"

The first installment of a three-part series (which aired on consecutive nights) based on Garson Kanin's novel *Moviola.* "This Year's Blonde" aired on NBC on May 18, 1980. It was executive-produced by David L. Wolper, produced by Stan Margulies, and directed by John Erman. Unlike the book, this film version only chronicled Marilyn's life through her relationship with Johnny Hyde and ended with her at the brink of stardom. The cast was toplined by Lloyd Bridges as Hyde and Constance Forslund as MM.

Even though the facts of Marilyn's life have been altered, "Moviola: This Year's Blonde" is a highly entertaining Hollywood bio, extremely well mounted by John Erman. What is unfortunate, though, is that its title was later changed, moronically, to "The Secret Love of Marilyn Monroe."

### *MS.* MAGAZINE

Gloria Steinem's feminist publication, *Ms.* magazine, has published the following articles on Marilyn Monroe:

☆ 8/72: "Growing Up with Marilyn"
☆ 8/72: "The Real Marilyn"
☆ 8/83: "The Time Marilyn Monroe Hid Out at Our House"
☆ 8/86: "If Marilyn Had Lived . . . Who Would She Be Today?"
—Excerpts from the book, *Marilyn*, by Gloria Steinem

### MS. MONROE'S

Ms. Monroe's was the name of two Illinois restaurants in Worth and St. Charles that were dedicated to the memory of Marilyn Monroe. The menu items were named after Marilyn's movie titles, and the house burger was named "The Monroe Burger."

**FLORABEL MUIR**

Florabel Muir was a syndicated columnist who collaborated with MM on Marilyn's autobiographical "Wolves I have Known" article, which appeared in *The Los Angeles Mirror* during September, 1952. "Wolves" is one of three essays "authored" by Marilyn.

**MARTIN MULL**

Actor/singer Martin Mull recorded a 1974 song about MM entitled, appropriately, "Marilyn." The song was featured on Mull's album *In the Soop,* which was recorded on Vanguard Records.

**THAD MUMFORD**

Thad Mumford cowrote the 1982 "M*A*S*H" segment that involved Marilyn Monroe. The segment was entitled "Bombshells."

**ARTHUR MURRAY**

*See* THE MARILYN MONROE MAMBA.

**DON MURRAY**

> DON MURRAY (to MM): C'mon. No wonder you're so pale and scaly.
> JOSHUA LOGAN: Cut! You said scaly, Don, instead of white.
> DON MURRAY: Oh, I'm sorry.
> MARILYN MONROE: Don, do you realize what you just did? You made a Freudian slip. You see, you were in the mood of the scene, you were in the proper mood because it's a sexual scene, and you said, "scaly," which means that you were thinking of a snake. A snake is a phallic symbol. Do you know what a phallic symbol is?
> DON MURRAY (angered): Know what it is? I've got one!

Marilyn Monroe and Don Murray did *not* get along well during the 1956 shooting of *Bus Stop.* Marilyn was fresh from her victorious strike against 20th Century-Fox and was beginning to exert her newfound power and independence at the studio. Don Murray, on the other hand, was a novice. *Bus Stop* was his first motion picture.

Don Murray was born in 1929. He studied at the American Academy of Dramatic Arts in New York and made his theatrical debut in *An Ant, the Insect Comedy* (1948). He was cast in *Bus Stop* after Joshua Logan had seen him in a stage production of *The Skin of Our Teeth.* Marilyn, reportedly, was not particularly enthusiastic about Murray in the role of her leading man. Not only was he inexperienced; he was also twenty-seven—three years younger than MM. Marilyn was used to, and preferred, having her leading men older and less attractive than herself. She did not want anyone—male or female—to detract from her. Moreover, during the production of *Bus Stop* Don Murray romanced and married Hope Lange, one of the supporting players in the film. It is quite likely that Marilyn resented Murray's attentions to the younger (twenty-five) Miss Lange.

The undertone of tension between Murray and Monroe seemed to peak during one scene, in which Marilyn whipped her sequined tail across Murray's face—so hard, in fact, that he suffered several cuts. Nonetheless, the "New" Marilyn refused to apologize.

Following *Bus Stop*, Don Murray appeared in such films as *The Bachelor Party* (1957), *A Hatful of Rain* (1957), *Advise and Consent* (1962), and, ironically, the made-for-television movie *The Sex Symbol* (1974).

**EUNICE MURRAY**

> "She was drawn to psychology, feeling a need to work with people and their problems. Eunice read and studied, and when an opportunity came to care for a psychiatric case in the patient's home, Eunice was prepared with enough knowledge and understanding to work under the guidance of a psychiatrist as his aide, helping in any kind of therapy that seemed indicated. She worked with many kinds of patients."
>
> Rose Shade on Eunice Murray
> from *Marilyn: The Last Months* (Pyramid, 1975)

> "I don't think we'll take that drive after all, Mrs. Murray."
>
> Marilyn Monroe to Eunice Murray, August 4, 1962

There are many contradictions involving Mrs. Eunice Murray, who served as Marilyn Monroe's "housekeeper" from November 1961 through August 5, 1962. First of all, Mrs. Murray was *not* Marilyn's housekeeper at all—at least, not in the traditional sense. In the past, Mrs. Murray has described her relationship with Marilyn as having been that of chauffeur/advisor/interior decorator/social secretary and companion. Yet, in her book, *Marilyn: The Last Months* (cowritten by Rose Shade), Eunice Murray states that, prior to working with MM, she had spent ten years caring for psychiatric patients. And just over a week after Marilyn's death, Mrs. Murray told the *Los Angeles Herald Examiner*, in her typically vague manner:

> "Dr. Greenson [Marilyn's psychiatrist] gave me certain instructions about Marilyn, but I can't say what they were."

What is known is that, on February 2, 1902, the former Elaine Joerndt was born in Chicago and that, in 1948, Mrs. Eunice Murray sold her Mexican-style house to a Dr. Ralph Greenson. Thirteen years later, Dr. Greenson encouraged his patient, Marilyn Monroe, to hire Mrs. Murray as a companion/nurse/"housekeeper." Mrs. Murray, who, coincidentally, had an adult daughter named Marilyn, was initially paid $60 a week for her services. However, that fee was soon multiplied to $200 a week, when it became apparent that more of Mrs. Murray's on-the-job time would be required.

In February 1962, through the efforts of Eunice Murray, Marilyn "found" her dream house—a private, modest, stable one-story home in Brentwood. For the next five months, these oddly-coupled women busied themselves decorating the new house with authentic Mexican furnishings.

On August 4, 1962, Eunice arrived at Marilyn's Brentwood home at 8:00 A.M. That night, Mrs. Murray stayed at the house at the request of Dr. Greenson. The remainder of the story, though, has been altered so many times over the years that it is difficult to determine what to believe.

According to the first *and second* police report, Mrs. Murray became alarmed in the middle of the night when she spotted a light on in Marilyn's bedroom. Later, at 3:30 A.M., Mrs. Murray noticed that the light was still on. She thus proceeded to go outside, where, through the bedroom window, she saw Marilyn's body lying on the bed in an "unnatural" position. Mrs. Murray then telephoned Dr. Greenson, who promptly rushed to the scene.

However, according to Jack Clemmons, the first police officer on the scene, Mrs. Murray initially told him that she had discovered Marilyn's body shortly after midnight and that Drs. Greenson and Engelberg (Marilyn's internist) had been at the Brentwood home since 12:30 A.M.! This information is even more interesting when it is coupled with the fact that the police were not notified until 4:25 A.M.

Years later, Mrs. Murray confirmed to Bob Slatzer that she had discovered Marilyn's body at around *midnight* and that rigor mortis had already set in—meaning, of course, that Marilyn had died the night of August 4, *not* the morning of August 5, 1962, which is generally accepted as Marilyn's death date. What compounds the confusion further is that, according to Jack Clemmons, Mrs. Murray was washing clothes, cleaning out the refrigerator, and packing away items when he arrived at the death scene at 4:40 A.M.

The following day, August 6, Eunice Murray held a press conference at her Santa Monica apartment. At that time, Mrs. Murray told the press the story that, on the night of August 4, Marilyn had received a mysterious, disturbing phone call. But, she said: ". . . in the past few weeks, Marilyn had everything to live for. The plans we made were so wonderful."

Following Marilyn's death, Eunice Murray went away to Europe. It has been reported that she remained abroad for six months. However, Mrs. Murray has claimed that she was away for only six weeks.

Over the years, one question has been brought up repeatedly: How could Eunice Murray have seen an alarming light on in Marilyn's bedroom when there was *no* space between the door and the carpeting for the light to escape? In her 1975 book, Mrs. Murray attempted to silence those questions by claiming it was not a light at all that had initially alarmed her—it was a telephone cord that ran under Marilyn's door.

Then, in 1985, Eunice Murray continued to draw controversy to herself by changing her story once again. Up until that time, Mrs. Murray had steadfastly contended that Robert Kennedy had been nowhere near Marilyn's Brentwood home on August 4. Then, in the BBC documentary, "The Last Days of Marilyn Monroe," Mrs. Murray confessed, on camera, that Kennedy was indeed at Marilyn's home the afternoon of her death. However, Mrs. Murray later refused to repeat that story. Instead, she said: "I'm in my 82nd year. Once in awhile, everything becomes confused."

For the past twenty-five years, the death of Marilyn Monroe has been shrouded in confusion, due, in part, to the conflicting stories of Mrs. Eunice Murray. Mrs. Murray, of course, has never been called in actually to testify under oath, because there has never been an official inquest into the death of Marilyn Monroe.

In an interesting addendum, in his 1984 book, *Legend: The Life and Death of Marilyn Monroe* (Stein and Day), Fred Lawrence Guiles contended that:

> By the end of July, Marilyn was taking tentative steps toward replacing Mrs. Murray. She had gone to the home of her former black housekeeper, Florence Thomas, and asked her to come back to work for her. Florence believed that she was to take Mrs. Murray's place.

Also of interest is the 1962 police report made by Sgt. Robert E. Byron. Byron's report read, in part:

> It is this officer's opinion that Mrs. Murray was vague and possibly evasive in answering questions pertaining to the activities of Miss Monroe during this time. It is not known whether this is or is not intentional.

**MUSCULAR DYSTROPHY**

On the evening of June 1, 1962, her thirty-sixth birthday, Marilyn Monroe made an appearance in behalf of muscular dystrophy at the Chavez Ravine baseball park.

**MUSIC**

> I like, well, jazz, like Louis Armstrong, you know, and Beethoven.
>
> MM

When queried as to what Beethoven numbers in particular, Marilyn responded, "I have a terrible time with numbers. But I know it when I hear it."

☆ Marilyn loved Frank Sinatra, Ella Fitzgerald, and Judy Garland.

☆ MM liked an instrumental recording of "I Cover the Waterfront."

☆ According to Lena Pepitone, MM loved such recordings as "Every Day I Have the Blues," "The Man I Love," and Sinatra's "All of Me."

☆ According to Eunice Murray, Marilyn repeatedly listened to Judy Garland's recording of "Who Cares?" to prepare herself for a public appearance.

☆ At her Brentwood home, at the time of her death, MM's record collection included Bach, Vivaldi, Beethoven, and Jelly Roll Morton.

☆ In 1955, Earl Wilson reported that Marilyn's musical favorites were Louis Armstrong, Earl Bostick, Mozart, and Beethoven.

☆ On the night of her death, Marilyn listened to Frank Sinatra records.

**MUSSO AND FRANK GRILL**

During her starlet period, Marilyn was sometimes taken to the Musso and Frank Grill (address: 6667 Hollywood Boulevard), which has been a popular movie industry eatery since 1919. In the mid-1950s, Marilyn was seen dining with Joe DiMaggio at this restaurant. However, according to a Mrs. Keegel, the current co-owner of the Musso and Frank Grill, the restaurant never became one of Marilyn's favorites because,

> "This wasn't the type of restaurant that she would come to, because she couldn't make a very big entrance from the back door."

**NICHOLAS MUSURACA**

Born in 1895, Nicholas Musuraca is the cinematographer of such pictures as *Cat People* (1942), *The Spiral Staircase* (1945), and *Out of the Past* (1947). In 1952, Musuraca shot *Clash by Night,* which was one of Marilyn Monroe's most important early films.

***MY STORY***

Author: "Marilyn Monroe"
Publisher: Stein and Day
Year: 1974 (Out of print)

Marilyn's "autobiographical" book that was, in actuality, probably penned by Ben Hecht from a series of articles that he did on Marilyn for London's *The Empire News* in 1954. The material was copyrighted, questionably, by Milton H. Greene in 1974 and was subsequently published in this form with Marilyn as its author.

The material itself is hardly shocking or revelatory. The writing is simple, direct, and anything *but* the gospel truth. It was written at a time when Marilyn was atop a crest of popularity, and most everything has been glazed over with romanticism and sweetness. It opens, predictably, with the poor unwanted orphan waif who is never kissed by her foster parents and ends after Marilyn's triumphant tour of Korea and before her split with Joe DiMaggio. Of DiMaggio, the "author" Marilyn wrote:

> And so we were married and took off for Japan on our honeymoon. That was something I had never planned on or dreamed about—becoming the wife of a great man. Any more than Joe had ever thought of marrying a woman who seemed eighty percent publicity . . . what I seem to Joe I haven't heard yet. He's a slow talker. What Joe is to me is a man whose looks, and character, I love with all my heart.

*My Story* is a storybook Cinderella fantasy. It resembles a studio-issued biography on the life of Marilyn Monroe—without the pain, poetry, or grit. And while it is not altogether believable, it *does* serve the image.

**JOHN MYERS**

In 1960, Marilyn Monroe posed for a portrait by oral surgeon/artist Dr. John Myers. Myers depicted MM as a "modern Mona Lisa." Following Marilyn's death and the opening of *After the Fall* (1964), Dr. Myers attacked Arthur Miller in the press, stating that:

> "Arthur Miller's conscience will plague him for the rest of his days. No writer has so fully and completely violated the rules of fair play and decency."

***MYRA BRECKINRIDGE***

*Myra Breckinridge* was a 1970 20th Century-Fox film starring Mae West and Raquel Welch that incorporated a clip of Marilyn's bathing suit scene from *Something's Got to Give* (1962).

***THE MYSTERIOUS DEATH OF MARILYN MONROE***

Author: James A. Hudson
Publisher: Volitant Books
Year: 1968 (Out of print)

*The Mysterious Death of Marilyn Monroe* was one of the pioneers in investigating the Marilyn Monroe/Kennedy family connection. It was also one of the first books to identify Marilyn's death as a potential murder rather than a probable suicide. And, although Hudson failed to provide any conclusive answers, he did succeed in raising several unanswered questions.

Today, in retrospect, *The Mysterious Death of Marilyn Monroe* is rather tame and dated. However, at the time of its release, it did create something of a stir.

***MARILYN: AMONG FRIENDS***

Photographer/Author: Sam Shaw/Norman Rosten
Publisher: Bloomsbury Publishing, Ltd.
Year: 1987
$45.00, 192 pp. (ISBN 0747500126)

Between photographer Sam Shaw and poet Norman Rosten, this is their fourth book about their friend. This book features photographs taken during Marilyn's New York period, circa 1954–59, with text and poetry by Rosten.

***MARILYN: AT TWENTIETH CENTURY FOX***

Author: Lawrence Crown
Publisher: Planet Books
Year: 1987
$31.00, 215 pp. (ISBN 1-85227-025-X)

Obviously developed with the cooperation of Twentieth Century Fox, this book features an interesting combination of publicity stills, advertisements, off-guard production shots, and interviews. Much of the material is rare, indicating that Fox may have unlocked its MM vaults to Crown.

***MARILYN MONROE: AN APPRECIATION***

Author/Photographer: Eve Arnold
Publisher: Alfred A. Knopf
Year: 1987
$30.00, 141 pp. (ISBN 0-394-55672-0)

Primarily a photo book featuring shots of MM during the shooting of *The Misfits* (1961). The text is not particularly revealing and the photos are not particularly flattering.

***MARILYN MONROE: A NEVER ENDING DREAM***

Compiled and Edited by: Guus Luijters
Publisher: St. Martin's Press
Year: 1987
$22.95, 176 pp (ISBN 0-312-01148-2)

This book promises a complete filmography, discography, and bibliography, however, there is nothing complete about it. Additionally, the photographs are decidedly more routine than rare.

## *THE NAKED TRUTH*

*The Naked Truth* was a proposed film project that Marilyn had discussed with producer Harold Mirisch in 1961 that failed to materialize before Marilyn's death.

## NAMES

> "I've never liked the name Marilyn. I've often wished that I had held out that day for Jean Monroe. But I guess it's too late to do anything about it now."
>
> Marilyn Monroe, 1952

***Born:*** Norma Jeane Mortenson
***Baptized:*** Norma Jeane Baker
***School names:*** Norma Jeane Baker, Norma Jean Baker, Norma Baker
***Name on marriage certificate, 1946:*** Norma Jeane Mortensen
***Married name, 1946:*** Norma Jeane Dougherty
***Modeling names:*** Norma Jeane Dougherty, Norma Dougherty, Jean Norman
***The first mention in Hedda Hopper's column, 1946:*** Norma Jean Dougherty
***First studio name:*** Carole Lind
***Studio names considered:*** Marilyn Miller, Jean Monroe
***Name on marriage certificate, 1954:*** Norma Jeane Dougherty
***Maiden name on marriage certificate, 1954:*** Norma Jean Mortenson
***Married name, 1954:*** Marilyn DiMaggio
***Name on marriage certificate, 1956:*** Marilyn Monroe
***Married Name, 1956:*** Marilyn Miller
***Name on death certificate, 1962:*** Marilyn Monroe

### The Aliases

***Name used to sign the nude-calendar release:*** Mona Monroe
***Name used to check into a Westwood motel, 1954:*** Norma Baker
***Name used en route to New York, 1954:*** Zelda Zonk
***Name used when publicly paging Sidney Skolsky:*** Miss Caswell
***Name used when calling Arthur Miller (before his divorce):*** Mrs. Leslie
***Name used to check into the Payne-Whitney Clinic, 1961:*** Miss Faye Miller
***Names used when working at a strip joint:*** Marilyn Monroe, Marilyn Marlowe, Mona Monroe
***Name used when traveling to Palm Springs, 1962:*** Tony Roberts

### The Nicknames

***What her classmates called her:*** Norma Jeane, The Human Bean, String Bean
***What Grace Goddard called her:*** The Mouse

***What the Karger family called her:*** Maril
***What Earl Wilson called her:*** The Mmmmmmm Girl
***What a* Love Happy *press agent called her:*** The Woo Woo Girl
***What the soldiers called her:*** Miss Flamethrower, Miss Cheesecake, Miss Morale, The Girl We'd Rather Have Come Between Us and Our Wives
***What Jane Russell called her:*** Baby Doll, The Round One
***What Pete Martin called her:*** The Girl with the Horizontal Walk
***What Hedda Hopper called her:*** The Blowtorch Blonde
***What Arthur Miller called her:*** Penny Dreadful, Sugar Finney, Gramercy 5
***A Few Other Nicknames:*** The Atomic Blonde, Miss Bountiful, The Nation's #1 Sex Thrill

**GEORGE NARDIELLO**
Fashion designer Nardiello created a new wardrobe for MM in the mid-1950s, during her New York period.

**NATIONAL CONCERT ARTISTS CORPORATION**
National Concert Artists Corporation was Norma Jeane Dougherty's first theatrical agency. In 1946, when Norma Jeane was signed, the agency was headed by Helen Ainsworth. Norma Jeane's personal agent was Harry Lipton. In 1946, the agency was at 9059 Sunset Blvd. in Los Angeles.

**FRANK NEAL**
Frank Neal was a press agent who served as the unit publicist on several of Marilyn's films.

**NEBRASKA AVENUE**
In the late 1930s, young Norma Jeane Baker moved out of the Goddard family home and went to live with her beloved "Aunt" Ana Lower in West Los Angeles. Aunt Ana's two-story home was located at 11348 Nebraska Ave. Years later, in 1945, the married Norma Jeane asserted her independence from her Dougherty in-laws by returning to this Nebraska Avenue home. It was also at this address that Norma Jeane lived, for a period, with her mother, Gladys Baker—Norma Jeane and Gladys shared the bottom floor of the house, while Ana Lower lived on the top floor.

**JEAN NEGULESCO**
In 1953, filmmaker Jean Negulesco had somewhat of a reputation as a "woman's director" within the motion picture industry. Thus, it must have seemed appropriate to the front office at 20th Century-Fox that Negulesco helm Fox's major 1953 Cinemascope production of *How to Marry a Millionaire.* Not only was that film set to star the then-slipping-queen of the Fox lot, Betty Grable, as well as the almost regal presence of Lauren Bacall; it was also set to trumpet the arrival of the *new* queen of the lot—and a temperamental one at that—Marilyn Monroe. But all concerned, including the three women, must have felt secure under the directorial wand of Negulesco. Prior to *Millionaire,* Negulesco, born in Romania in 1900, had elicited Jane Wyman's

Oscar-winning performance in *Johnny Belinda* (1948), as well as Joan Crawford's acclaimed performance in *Humoresque* (1947).

Jean Negulesco was the first director, since John Huston, that Marilyn Monroe got along well with. During the production of *How to Marry a Millionaire,* Negulesco the artist painted an oil portrait of Marilyn. He also lent her books, which they discussed. But, despite the fact the film was a major success for Marilyn, Negulesco *was not* included on Marilyn's 1956 list of "approved" directors.

Negulesco's others credits include *Three Coins in the Fountain* (1954), *Woman's World* (1954), and *Daddy Longlegs* (1955).

**ELYDA NELSON**

Elyda Nelson (aka Billie Dougherty, aka Billie Campbell) was Marilyn's former sister-in-law, by way of James Dougherty, who wrote an article about MM after she had become famous. The article was entitled "The True Life Story of Marilyn Monroe," and it appeared in the December 1952 issue of *Modern Screen* magazine.

**"THE NEW MARILYN"**

> Unique is an overworked word, but in her case it applies. There will never be another like her, and Lord knows, there have been plenty of imitations.
>
> Billy Wilder on Marilyn Monroe

As early as February 1953—*before* Marilyn Monroe had even reached her peak in popularity—the Hollywood studios were searching (in vain, as time would prove) for "The New Marilyn." This was illustrated in *The Los Angeles Herald and Express* newspaper. The article, dated February 5, 1953, was titled "Studios Push Beauties in Glamor Derby" and, was subtitled "All Want Queen Marilyn's Crown." The article read, in part:

> Filmtown's top studios are drum-beating today to promote their most dangerously curved beauties in a stampede to compete with 20th Century-Fox's M-bomb—Marilyn Monroe.

In the 1950s, there was an overabundance of big-bosomed blondes waiting in the proverbial wings, clamoring to oust Marilyn Monroe from her throne. Some of them were sexier, blonder, and bustier than MM—but those were surface effects, at best. Some of them had talent, but most just had ambition and a bottle of hair dye. Some of them even gussied themselves up in their best MM drag and pouted and slinked their way into near obscurity. The one thing that they all had in common was that they all tried—and failed—to replace the irreplaceable.

As early as December 1962, the media and the world resumed a search for "The New Marilyn"—just as they had done when Jean Harlow died decades before. In a *New York Times* article dated December 14, 1962, writer Larry Glenn wrote "Hollywood Lacks a New Goddess: Industry Fails to Provide Successor to Marilyn". The article read, in part:

> It will soon be a half year since the passing of Marilyn Monroe, the

> latest—and perhaps the last—of a long dynasty of actresses unchallenged as paragons of feminine appeal: or, in cinematic and sociological lore, "goddesses" of a) love or b) sex. A war of succession normally should have developed by now, with heiresses presumptive clawing for the diadem, honors, and riches of the fallen champion. The steps to the throne, however, are curiously quiet. . . .

Over the years, an endless parade of actresses and *actors* have been compared to Marilyn Monroe—everyone from Diane Keaton to Mick Jagger to Mia Farrow to John Travolta to Holly Woodlawn, et al. Marilyn Monroe has become a standard, an icon, that all others are held up to. Some twenty-five years have passed, and it is glaringly obvious that the Hollywood machinery has failed to replace Marilyn Monroe. Nevertheless, over the sixties, seventies, and eighties, there *have* been a handful of actresses who have "inherited" mixed and varying portions of Marilyn's beauty, sex appeal, talent, comedic timing, vulnerability, and presence. Some of these actresses have merely traded on their sculpted bodies (Welch, Andress), while others have actually shown *moments* of possessing that flickering Monroe magic and luminosity (A-M, Streep, Madonna).

The following, then, is a selective compilation of the actresses who attempted to oust MM in the 1950s, as well as the actresses who have followed—either innocently or by design—the Marilyn Monroe legacy.

**The 1950s: The Would-Be Threats**

1. Kim Novak
2. Doris Day
3. Brigitte Bardot
4. Jayne Mansfield
5. Carroll Baker
6. Sheree North
7. Mamie Van Doren
8. Diana Dors
9. Anita Ekberg
10. Barbara Nichols
11. Monique Van Vooren
12. Joi Lansing
13. Terry Moore
14. Zsa Zsa Gabor
15. Roberta Haynes
16. Ursula Theiss
17. Elaine Stewart
18. Mary Murphy
19. Beverly Michaels
20. Cleo Moore
21. Virginia Mayo
22. Laurette Luez
23. Joan Olander
24. Lily St. Cyr
25. Sally Forrest
26. Vanessa Brown
27. Joanne Dru
28. Leigh Snowden

THE SABIN GRAY COLLECTION

Cleo Moore, Columbia's MM, circa 1954.

THE SABIN GRAY COLLECTION

Sheree North, Fox's MM threat, circa 1955.

THE SABIN GRAY COLLECTION

Diana Dors, Britain's MM, circa 1955.

THE SABIN GRAY COLLECTION

Joi Lansing, MGM's MM, circa 1958.

THE SABIN GRAY COLLECTION
Mamie Van Doren, Universal's MM circa 1955.

THE SABIN GRAY COLLECTION
Barbara Nichols, RKO's MM, circa 1958.

29. Rosalina Neri
30. Carla Blake
31. Maria Stinger
32. Ruth Muller
33. Liz O'Leyar
34. Eleanor Todd
35. Jan Sterling
36. Nadine Fitzpatrick
37. Mara Lane
38. Kathleen Hughes

THE SABIN GRAY COLLECTION
Beverly Michaels, Columbia's MM, circa 1955.

**The 1960s: The Heiresses**

1. Ann-Margret
2. Doris Day
3. Carroll Baker
4. Shirley MacLaine
5. Joanne Woodward
6. Raquel Welch
7. Ursula Andress
8. Yvette Mimieux
9. Stella Stevens
10. Ruta Lee

**The 1970s: The Heiresses**

1. Ann-Margret
2. Farrah Fawcett

**The 1980s: The Heiresses**

1. Madonna
2. Meryl Streep

**MM Trivia Quiz #32**

In the mid 1980s a male British pop personality named "Marilyn" received considerable press because of his relationship with what famous singer? (Answer on page 577.)

**"A NEW WRINKLE"**

*See* Calendar.

**PATRICIA NEWCOMB**

> "If you want to know who knew more about Marilyn than anyone, it's Pat Newcomb. But you could never get anything out of her."
>
> Jeanne Martin to Anthony Summers
> *Goddess: The Secret Lives of Marilyn Monroe* (Macmillan, 1985)

Margot Patricia Newcomb was born July 9, 1930, in Washington, D.C. A graduate of Mills College, Pat was hired by the Arthur Jacobs Public Relations agency in New York—the agency that represented Marilyn Monroe. In 1956, when Marilyn returned to Hollywood to shoot *Bus Stop,* it was Pat Newcomb who was chosen to accompany her. However, during the production of that film, the two women clashed, becoming sexual rivals, and Marilyn had Newcomb replaced.

Then, toward the completion of the harrowing production of *The Misfits* some four years later, Marilyn's press representative, Rupert Allan, quit. Once again, Pat Newcomb was chosen to be Marilyn's personal press rep, and this time, somehow, the two women jelled. It was Pat Newcomb who accompanied Marilyn to Juarez, Mexico, where Marilyn obtained her divorce from Arthur Miller. A few months later, it was Pat Newcomb who escorted Marilyn out of Columbia Presbyterian Hospital. And it was Pat Newcomb who went with Marilyn to Mexico City on MM's 1962 furniture-buying trip. The two women reportedly became very close. Newcomb became very protective of Marilyn. She even began answering all of Marilyn's phone calls. She stepped far beyond the traditional boundaries of a press agent.

On the evening of August 3, 1962, Pat Newcomb had dinner with Peter Lawford and MM at La Scala restaurant in Beverly Hills. That night, Newcomb slept over at Marilyn's Bentwood home. The following day, Saturday, Newcomb was stricken with bronchitis. For theraputic purposes, Pat spent most of the day lounging at Marilyn's pool, basking in the sun.

Later, that afternoon, Dr. Ralph Greenson arrived at Marilyn's house. He then asked Pat Newcomb to leave the house. Reportedly, Marilyn was, for some reason, upset with Pat. According to Anthony Summers's *Goddess,* it was because Pat had taken a more than casual interest in Robert Kennedy. It was that old *Bus Stop* sexual rivalry all over again.

At any rate, Newcomb left the house and reportedly never saw Marilyn Monroe alive again. In the early morning hours of August 5, Pat was awakened by a telephone call from Marilyn's attorney, Mickey Rudin. Immediately, she drove back to the Brentwood home. Then, according to Mrs. Eunice Murray, Pat Newcomb became hysterical. She screamed and shouted and refused to leave the house. After Marilyn's body was taken away, Mrs. Murray was finally able to get Pat out of the house. When she was questioned, at the site, by reporters, Pat retorted: "When *your* best friend kills herself, how do *you* feel? What do *you* do?"

Following the death of her "best friend," Pat Newcomb was flown to the Kennedy compound in Hyannisport. Newcomb then went away, for six months, to Europe. Upon her return to the United States, Pat was hired by the U.S. government and worked in an office adjacent to that of the U.S. Attorney General, Robert Kennedy. Later, when Kennedy ran for the position of New York State Senator, Pat Newcomb joined his staff.

In 1982, Patricia Newcomb was back in New York City, with the powerhouse Rogers and Cowan Public Relations agency. Three years later, Pat had worked her way into becoming a vice-president at MGM Studios in Culver City, California.

**ROY NEWELL**

Roy Newell was a plumber who, in 1962, was hired by Marilyn Monroe to install the appliances and equipment in MM's Brentwood home. According to Mrs. Eunice Murray, Newell was so devoted to Marilyn that he overexerted himself and suffered a mild heart attack.

**ALFRED NEWMAN**

Alfred Newman (1901-1970) was a musician who composed several hundred film scores and collected more than several Academy Awards in the process. Among his works are such Marilyn Monroe films as *All About Eve* (1950), *O. Henry's Full House* (1952), *How to Marry a Millionaire* (1953, musical director only), *There's No Business Like Show Business* (1954, musical director credit shared with Lionel Newman), *The Seven Year Itch* (1955), and *Bus Stop* (1956, musical score credit shared with Cyril Mockridge).

Among Mr. Newman's non-MM pictures were *Alexander's Ragtime Band* (1938), *Tin Pan Alley* (1940), *The Song of Bernadette* (1943), *Mother Wore Tights* (1947), *With A Song in My Heart* (1952), *Call Me Madam* (1953), *Love Is a Many Splendored Thing* (1955), and *The King and I* (1956)—all of which he won Oscars for.

**JOSEPH NEWMAN**

Born in 1909, Joseph Newman directed a slew of forgettable films, including *Tarzan the Ape Man* (1959) and *The George Raft Story* (1962). In 1951, Newman directed *Love Nest* which featured Marilyn Monroe in a supporting role.

**LIONEL NEWMAN**

> I think she was a better singer than most people who were professional singers. She worked hard and was always on time. She was one of the best to work with—whether she was late for other portions of the movie [*Gentlemen Prefer Blondes*]—I can't say. But, for the musical portion, she was always on time. She was very easy to work with. I can't say enough about her.
>
> Lionel Newman, 1986

Lionel Newman, born in 1916, was the younger brother of Alfred Newman. Lionel was a good luck charm, of sorts, to Marilyn Monroe. First of all, he served as the musical director of *You Were Meant for Me* (1948), in which unknown starlet MM worked as an extra. He was also the musical director of *Scudda Hoo! Scudda Hay!* (1948), which is generally acknowledged as Marilyn's first film. Lionel also composed the score of *Don't Bother to Knock* (1952), which was Marilyn's first starring vehicle. Then, in 1953, it was Lionel Newman who conducted the orchestra for *Gentlemen Prefer Blondes*—which of course, was the film that catapulted Marilyn Monroe over the top.

A year later, producer Sol Siegel hired *Alfred* Newman to conduct the music for *There's No Business Like Show Business.* When Marilyn balked, Siegel was pressured into hiring Lionel to work on Marilyn's numbers. Six years later, Lionel Newman worked with Marilyn Monroe on one last picture, *Let's Make Love* (1960).

Newman's non–MM credits are less interesting, but they do include *How to Be Very, Very Popular* (1955) and *Move Over Darling* (1963)—both of which were intended as Monroe pictures.

**ROGER NEWMAN**

Roger Newman wrote the play *The Hardest Part of It* aka *Public Property* (1979), about Marilyn Monroe, that was staged in New York and London, under those respective titles.

***NEWSWEEK* MAGAZINE**

*Newsweek* has published the following articles on MM:

☆ 1/25/54: "Mr. and Mrs. Joe DiMaggio
☆ 3/1/54: "This is Competition"
☆ 10/18/54: "Parting"
☆ 7/2/56: "Engagement Party"
☆ 11/19/56: "For Art's Sake"
☆ 6/17/57: "Talk with a Showgirl"
☆ 9/12/60: "Who's a Misfit?"
☆ 10/31/60: "Constellation Is Born"
☆ 11/21/60: "Out of the Fishbowl"
☆ 8/13/62: "Early, too Early, for Once"
☆ 8/20/62: "I Love You . . . I Love You; Funeral Arrangements"
☆ 11/19/62: "End as a Woman?"
☆ 7/10/63: "Exploiters"
☆ 12/2/63: "Mythraker"
☆ 7/5/65: "Losers"
☆ 11/28/66: "Homebody"
☆ 7/14/69: "American Dream"
☆ 10/16/72: "Taking a New Look at MM"*
☆ 7/30/73: "Double Monroe"
☆ 8/2/82: "Keeping the Monroe Memories Aglow"
☆ 10/14/85: "The Star-Crossed Kennedys"

---

**NEWSWEEK* cover that MM appeared on.

**NEW YORK CITY**

For Marilyn Monroe, New York City represented another world, a second chance at a new career and, more importantly, a new life.

It was 1954. Twenty-eight-year-old MM had already conquered Hollywood. She had attained everything she could have ever wanted. Except, of course, for two things: love and respect. Her marriage to Joe DiMaggio had been a storybook disaster; and Hollywood was smugly content to use her in a series of second-rate productions that emphasized cleavage over talent.

New York City promised to be different. Marilyn's newfound friend,

Milton H. Greene, along with his attorneys, had set up Marilyn Monroe Productions, Inc., which was designed to give her artistic control and the opportunity to showcase her dramatic skills. New York also offered the services of the Actors Studio, which came to embody Marilyn's hopes for acting greatness. Moreover, for Marilyn, New York presented an overture of romance, in the form of playwright Arthur Miller, whom she had set her sights on years before.

Marilyn Monroe moved to New York at the end of 1954. In less than two years, she fulfilled both of her primary goals. She won her independence from 20th Century-Fox and received newfound acclaim as an actress; she also married Arthur Miller.

Marilyn remained in New York, off and on, until after her 1961 divorce from Miller. Nonetheless, even after she moved back to Hollywood, she retained her New York City apartment as a second home, which she visited for the last time in May 1962.

***NIAGARA* ★★★**
1953 89 minutes Technicolor
20th Century-Fox
Directed by: Henry Hathaway
Produced by: Charles Brackett
Screenplay by: Charles Brackett, Walter Reisch, Richard Breen
Photographed by: Joe MacDonald
Cast: Marilyn Monroe, Joseph Cotten, Jean Peters, Casey Adams, Richard Allen, Don Wilson

Marilyn Monroe owes a debt of gratitude to Henry Hathaway and Joe MacDonald, the director and cinematographer, respectively, of *Niagara.* Rarely in the history of motion pictures has an actress been photographed so *lovingly* or more flatteringly or showcased to better advantage. Charles Vidor did it with Rita Hayworth in *Gilda* (1946), George Sidney did it with Ann-Margret in *Bye Bye Birdie* (1963), and Henry Hathaway did it with Marilyn Monroe in *Niagara.*

*Niagara,* of course, is the film that launched Marilyn Monroe into that fickle and potentially dangerous vehicle to stardom. In this film, she is unearthly *striking,* more of an apparition than a scheming blonde at a honeymoon vacation lodge. Everyone and *everything,* including the falls, is secondary to Marilyn Monroe's presence. It is as if everything she had done prior to 1952 had been done in preparation for *Niagara.* The half-lidded gaze; the moist, painted, parted lips; the artificially blonde hair; and the low, husky, breathy voice—it's all here. Moreover, it all works. And then there was the matter of *that* walk.

It has often been remarked, sometimes flippantly, that Marilyn's walk in *Niagara* is what made her a star—that she turned her back on the camera and walked her way toward immortality. And that is not altogether untrue. Marilyn's 116-foot walk in *Niagara* was, up until that time, the longest, most luxuriated walk in cinema history. Clad in a tightly sewn black skirt and blazing red top, Marilyn simply walked—in her distinctly exaggerated style—while Henry Hathaway's camera remained transfixed on Marilyn's bottom. It was a daring scene for the early 1950s, and Hathaway must be credited for his audacity. Today the scene serves as vintage Monroe, which, surprisingly, has retained much of its original impact.

*Niagara* was initially set to star Anne Baxter, then one of Fox's biggest stars, in the Jean Peters role. However, after Marilyn's notoriety began to explode in early 1952, the film was retailored to showcase MM. Anne Baxter, understandably, withdrew from the picture, and by its January 1953 release *Niagara* was, without question, Marilyn Monroe's picture.

Although Marilyn's reviews were extremely varied, *Niagara* clearly signaled her arrival. In retrospect, her dramatic performance as Rose Loomis is sometimes overstated—but, highly effective, nonetheless. It's a difficult role. Still, Marilyn manages to be vulnerable, and even likable, as the murderous, adulterous wife of Joseph Cotten. Also in this film, Marilyn was given the all-too-brief opportunity to sing. Marilyn's sexy, sultry rendering of the song "Kiss" has remained, over the years, yet another classic MM movie moment.

*Niagara,* as a whole, is an entertaining though wildly uneven Hitchcockian suspenser. The reason for its imbalance is glaringly obvious: Marilyn Monroe. She simply blows everyone off of the screen and throws the entire movie out of whack.

**MM Trivia Quiz #33**

What was the name of the cabin in which MM stayed in *Niagara*? (Answer on page 577.)

**MALENE NIELSEN**

Malene Nielsen was a Danish housewife who claimed to be the daughter of Edward Mortenson and the half-sister of Marilyn Monroe. Mortenson is one of the men who is purported to have fathered MM.

***NIGHT WITHOUT SLEEP***

*Night Without Sleep* was the original title of *Don't Bother to Knock* (1952), which starred Marilyn Monroe. The title was changed because there was another movie on the Fox schedule with that same title. Interestingly, *both* *Don't Bother to Knock* and *Night Without Sleep* were directed by Roy Baker. *Night Without Sleep* starred Linda Darnell and Gary Merrill.

**RICHARD NIXON**

In 1962, the City News Service Editors of Los Angeles voted Richard Nixon's electorial defeat by Edmund Brown for the office of governor of the state of California the number two news story of the year. They called it, at that time, Nixon's "bitter farewell to politics." The number one news story of 1962, according to the editors, was the death of Marilyn Monroe.

**THOMAS NOGUCHI**

Thomas Noguchi is, in all probability (and for what it's worth), the most famous coroner of our time. In 1962, at the time of Marilyn Monroe's death, Noguchi was an autopsy surgeon for Los Angeles County. On August 5, 1962, at 10:30 A.M. Thomas Noguchi conducted the autopsy on Marilyn Monroe. The procedure took approximately five hours.

Noguchi's findings were that *no* trace of barbiturates showed up in Marilyn's stomach or digestive tract. He also failed to report any evidence of needle marks (despite the fact that Marilyn's internist, Dr. Engelberg, had given her injections on August 1 and August 3). What Noguchi *did* find, though, that he was unable to explain, was a fresh bruise on Marilyn's lower back.

Over the years, Noguchi has been highly criticized for his allegedly incomplete and inconclusive autopsy of Marilyn Monroe. Specifically, Noguchi has been lambasted for *not* testing Marilyn's small intestine to determine whether or not any trace of the barbiturates were located there.

Since his autopsy of Marilyn Monroe, Thomas Noguchi, the Coroner of the (dead) Stars has conducted the operations on Sharon Tate, William Holden, Natalie Wood, John Belushi, and Robert Kennedy. Ultimately, he was promoted to and demoted from the prestigious office of the chief medical examiner.

In November 1985, after twenty-three years, Thomas Noguchi finally stepped forward and announced that the Marilyn Monroe case should be reopened.

**TOMMY NOONAN**

Born Thomas Noon in 1921, Tommy Noonan was Marilyn's costar in *Gentlemen Prefer Blondes* (1953). Noonan also appeared in such films as *A*

*Star Is Born* (1954) and *How to Be Very, Very Popular* (1955) before his death in 1968.

**NORMAN NORELL**

In 1955, Amy Greene asked Norman Norell, the famous fashion designer of that era, to construct a more elegant wardrobe for the "new" New York Marilyn. Norell, of course, complied.

***NORMA JEAN: THE LIFE OF MARILYN MONROE***

Author: Fred Lawrence Guiles
Publisher: McGraw-Hill
Year: 1969

Maurice Zolotow's *Marilyn Monroe* was published nine years earlier than *Norma Jean: The Life of Marilyn Monroe.* Nonetheless, when it arrived in 1969, *Norma Jean* stood on its own as a remarkably refreshing and original work. Although it covers much of the same territory as explored by Zolotow, *Norma Jean* was written *after* Marilyn's death and therefore encompassed a broader scope. Included is a fairly in-depth account of Marilyn's final years—the turbulent shooting of *The Misfits,* the return to Hollywood and the purchase of a new home and the crushing defeat at the hands of her "makers," 20th Century-Fox. *Norma Jean* also probes delicately into the curious circumstances surrounding Marilyn's death. However, three other subsequent books have handled this last and highly controversial area in far more comprehensive detail: Bob Slatzer's *The Life and Curious Death of Marilyn Monroe* (1974), Anthony Summers's *Goddess: The Secret Lives of Marilyn Monroe* (1985), and Guiles's own follow-up/extension of *Norma Jean, Legend: the Life and Death of Marilyn Monroe* (1984).

Nonetheless, *Norma Jean* is an impressive achievement. It is extremely perceptive, laced with color, and written by a man who obviously admired, without bias, his subject. Along with his companion book, *Legend,* Fred Lawrence Guiles's *Norma Jean* is *the* consummate cradle-to-career-to-tomb biography of Marilyn Monroe.

**SHEREE NORTH**

> "The times you need to have privacy, you can find an excuse. Sometimes I kid the fans. They say, 'Oh, you're Marilyn Monroe! I say, 'Oh, no, I'm Mamie Van Doren' or, 'Sheree North'—if I'm in a real hurry."
>
> Marilyn Monroe to Earl Wilson, 10/6/55

> "[Sheree] will not use the Monroe technique, however. She will play the entire role with her mouth closed."
>
> Nunnally Johnson, on the replacement casting of Sheree North in *How to Be Very, Very Popular,* 1955

In the 1950s, Sheree North—born Dawn Bethel in 1933—obtained a reputation as being the girl who would *not* replace Marilyn Monroe. Actually, it was the front office at 20th Century-Fox that used Sheree as a pawn to threaten the misbehaving moneymaker, MM. In 1954, when Marilyn refused to do *There's No Business Like Show Business,* Fox dangled the younger Sheree in front of Marilyn's ego. Convinced, Marilyn agreed to do the picture—a decision she later regretted. Shortly after, Marilyn rejected *The Girl in Pink Tights* and *How to Be Very, Very Popular.* Fox responded, predictably, by publicly announcing that Sheree North would replace Marilyn in both productions. This time, Marilyn did not bite.

There was a good deal of anticipation surrounding the release of *How to Be Very, Very Popular* (1955). *LIFE* magazine, perhaps due to "encouragement" by Fox, even put the unknown, untested Sheree on its cover. *The Los Angeles Times* also jumped on the "Sheree is *in,* Marilyn is *out*" bandwagon by exclaiming that the only difference between the two actresses was that: "Sheree's working."

*How to Be Very, Very Popular* began production in February 1955. When it was released later that year, it proved to be anything but popular. As for Miss North, plans for her to film *The Girl in Pink Tights* were shelved. All industry speculation that she would replace MM ended. The talent simply did not measure up to the hype. And when Marilyn triumphantly returned to Fox in 1956, Sheree North was banished forever to the land of lesser film productions.

Interestingly, in 1980, Sheree portrayed Marilyn's mother in the telefilm, "Marilyn, The Untold Story." She also served as that film's dialogue coach.

**NORWALK STATE HOSPITAL**

*See* METROPOLITAN STATE HOSPITAL IN NORWALK.

**KIM NOVAK**

"I want a young girl—another Monroe."

Harry Cohn to Max Arnow

In 1953, after Marilyn Monroe's star soared into the stratosphere, Harry Cohn, the head of Columbia, began an active campaign to replace her. What Cohn's head of talent, Max Arnow, produced *was* another Marilyn—but, alas, *not* another Monroe. Her name was Marilyn Novak. And her claim to fame at that point was the beauty title, "Miss Deepfreeze." The first order of business, under King Cohn's tutelage, was to change Miss Novak's name. Cohn wanted another Marilyn, but he did *not* want another Marilyn *named* Marilyn. Thus, Marilyn Novak, with the wave of the Cohn wand, became "Kim."

Although Kim Novak never accomplished her assigned task of replacing Marilyn Monroe, she did manage to carve out a respectable and profitable niche of her own. In the 1950s, Miss Novak scored in such productions as *Pushover* (1954), *Phffft* (1954), *Picnic* (1956), *Jeanne Eagels* (1957), *Pal Joey* (1958), and *Vertigo* (1958). In 1959, Kim was cast in Paddy Chayefsky's *Middle of the Night* in a role that Marilyn, Monroe that is, had wanted for herself.

In 1962, 20th Century-Fox threatened to replace MM in *Something's Got to Give* with Kim Novak. In fact, after firing Marilyn, Fox offered the picture to Miss Novak, who admirably (and wisely) declined.

Kim Novak, who was born in 1933 in Chicago, succeeded in becoming a major star, but she was never quite acknowledged as an actress. There was something artificial about her performances and about her appearance. However, she has managed to survive, over the years, as a remnant of the old Hollywood studio star system and, the glamour that it evokes.

In 1986, Miss Novak joined the cast of the television series "Falcon Crest."

**NUDITY**

"Nobody ever objected to Botticelli's Venus, so why should they object to my posing in the nude?"

Marilyn Monroe

"The wish for attention had something to do, I think, with my trouble in church on Sundays. No sooner was I in the pew with the organ playing and everybody singing a hymn than the impulse would come to me to take off all my clothes. I wanted desperately to stand up naked for God and everyone to see. I had to clench my teeth and sit on my hands to keep myself from undressing. . . . I even had dreams about it. In the dreams I entered the church wearing a hoop skirt with nothing under it. The people would be lying on their backs in the church aisle, and I would step over them, and they would look up at me."

MM on Norma Jeane

"People have curious attitudes about nudity, just as they have about sex. Nudity and sex are the most commonplace things in the world. Yet people often act as if they were things that existed only on Mars."

Marilyn Monroe

"It was just like celebrating my birthday in my birthday suit."

MM on her nude swim, 1962

"A perfect body like Marilyn's looks beautiful nude, and beauty is never vulgar."

Agnes Flanagan

"My impulse to appear naked and my dreams about it had no shame or sense of sin in them. Dreaming of people looking at me made me feel less lonely. I think I wanted them to see me naked because I was ashamed of the clothes I wore—the never-changing faded blue dress of poverty. Naked, I was like the other girls and not someone in an orphan's uniform."

Marilyn Monroe

"We did some test scenes of me in a pool, sort of nude. I hope they give me some good nude lines to go with it."

Marilyn Monroe

"She had lost the contours of a young woman by then, but she refused to acknowledge her body was becoming mature. She insisted that she could measure up to the kind of nudity or semi-nudity that was being printed in *Playboy* and similar magazines. Her blindness to her physical change was almost tragic."

Photographer Eve Arnold on MM in 1961

"She usually draped herself in a bath towel. If it slid off, okay. She didn't care if she had anything on or not and this was before nudity was in. She was ahead of her time."

George Masters

"Marilyn was so cute when she did that swimming sequence for *Something's Got to Give*. Director George Cukor asked her if she would do it nude, and told her he'd watch the camera angles so that there'd be nothing indelicate about the scene, in which she was supposed to playfully take a midnight swim in the pool, aware that her husband, Dean Martin, was peeking at her. She said yes, without being coy about it. When she saw the rushes later she roared at herself and said 'I actually look like a good swimmer. Who'd guess that I'm just a dog paddler?' "

Marjorie Plecher

Marilyn appeared nude (although she was covered up by a bedsheet or some other such nuisance) in the following films:

*Niagara* (1953): Marilyn's first nude scenes in a movie took place, sensibly, in a bed and in a shower. At that time, Marilyn called her nudity "realism."
*Bus Stop* (1956): Marilyn, as Cherie, appeared nude in a morning bed scene.
*The Misfits* (1961): In the "morning after" bed scene between Clark Gable and MM, Marilyn lay nude in bed while Gable stood hovering over her. During the shooting of the scene, on take seven, Marilyn dropped the "protective" sheet and revealed one of her breasts. Later, director John Huston decided against using *that* take, despite Marilyn's immodest protests.
*Something's Got to Give* (1962): On May 28, 1962, on Stage 14 at 20th Century-Fox, Marilyn shot her final nude movie scene. It was a swimming pool sequence, and, reportedly, Marilyn's flesh-colored swimsuit was too tight. Thus, Marilyn pulled off the suit and dog-paddled in the buff. Later, Marilyn posed for Lawrence Schiller and two other photographers outside of the pool. Of the photos, Marilyn approved forty of the black-and-white shots and twelve of the color. The photos were subsequently published in thirty-two countries. They served as Marilyn Monroe's last hurrah. They also made a good deal of money for Lawrence Schiller.

**More MM Nudity**

☆ According to Bob Slatzer, the narcissistic MM used to stand naked, for hours, in front of a full-length mirror.

☆ According to Lena Pepitone, Marilyn rarely wore clothes around the East 57th Street apartment in New York—even when guests were around.

☆ According to Eunice Murray and others, Marilyn slept in the nude—despite Norman Mailer's claim that she slept wearing a bra.

☆ Sometime between 1946–50, Norma Jeane Dougherty/Marilyn Monroe posed nude for illustrator Earl Moran. However the nudes were forgotten and went undiscovered until *Playboy* magazine published them in its January 1987 issue.

☆ In 1949, Marilyn posed horizontally nude, on a sheet of red velvet, for photographer Tom Kelley.

☆ In 1960, and again in 1961, Marilyn posed seminude for photographer Eve Arnold.

☆ In 1962, Marilyn posed nude and seminude for photographer Bert Stern.

**GILBERT NUNEZ**

Dr. Gilbert Nunez is the man who purchased Marilyn's Brentwood house following her death in 1962. Dr. Nunez purchased the home at an auction.

**BEN NYE**

Before and during Marilyn's reign at 20th Century-Fox, Ben Nye was the head of the Fox makeup department. Thus, Nye was credited as the makeup artist on most of Marilyn's movies. He has also been sometimes cited as the man who did Marilyn's makeup for her crucial 1946 screen test. However, in actuality, it was Allan "Whitey" Snyder who did Marilyn's makeup for that screen test and for most of her other Fox-related projects. According to Snyder, Ben Nye "never *once* touched her face."

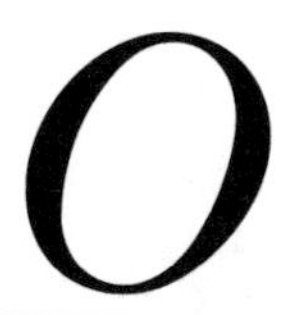

### PAT O'BRIEN

Pat O'Brien (1899–1983) starred in such popular 1930s pictures as *The Front Page* (1931), *Bombshell* (1933), *Boy Meets Girl* (1938), and *Angels with Dirty Faces* (1938). In 1959, O'Brien was featured in Billy Wilder's *Some Like It Hot*, which starred Marilyn Monroe.

### ARTHUR O'CONNELL

Arthur O'Connell (1908–1981) was a stage actor who also appeared in such films as *Picnic* (1956), *The Solid Gold Cadillac* (1956), *The Man in the Grey Flannel Suit* (1956), *Anatomy of a Murder* (1959), and *The Poseidon Adventure* (1972). In 1956, O'Connell costarred as Virgil in *Bus Stop*, which starred Marilyn Monroe.

### DONALD O'CONNOR

In 1954, Marilyn Monroe balked at the casting of Donald O'Connor as her love interest in *There's No Business Like Show Business*. First of all, according to MM, O'Connor *looked* too young for the part (in actuality, he was a year older than Marilyn); secondly, MM complained that O'Connor was three inches too short for her. Nevertheless, the brass at Fox paid Marilyn no heed, and the film was made as planned. Today, in retrospect, it is obvious that Marilyn *was* right about her instincts. The Monroe-O'Connor love pairing is never quite believable.

Donald O'Connor was the popular, perennially teenaged, musical star of the forties and fifties. Among his films are *Patrick the Great* (1945), *Francis* (1949), *Singin' in the Rain* (1952), *Call Me Madam* (1953), and *I Love Melvin* (1953).

Of working with Marilyn Monroe, Donald O'Connor once said: "I thought she was going to throw her weight around [but she didn't]. She's subtle. She's an ingenious actress."

### ODESSA AVENUE

Shortly after her release from the orphanage, Norma Jeane Baker went to live at "Aunt" Ana Lower's house on 6707 Odessa Avenue in Van Nuys, California. Several years later, Norma Jeane, accompanied by the "Doc" Goddard family, returned to live at the same Odessa Avenue home.

### CLIFFORD ODETS

Clifford Odets (1903–1963) was the renowned playwright of such works as *Golden Boy* and *The Country Girl*, both of which were later filmed successfully. In 1952, Odets's *Clash by Night* was produced for the screen with rising star Marilyn Monroe in one of its supporting leads. It became one of Marilyn's most important early films.

**JEAN AND "LEFTY" O'DOUL**

When Marilyn and Joe DiMaggio took their honeymoon trip to Japan, they were accompanied by DiMaggio's baseball buddy, "Lefty" O'Doul, and his wife, Jean. During the same trip, when Marilyn went to Korea to entertain the troops, she was flanked by Jean O'Doul.

***OF HUMAN BONDAGE***

*Of Human Bondage* is the W. Somerset Maugham story that brought fame to Bette Davis in 1934. It was refilmed in 1946 and again in the early 1960s. For that latter production, director Henry Hathaway wanted Marilyn Monroe for the female lead. His second choice at that time was Elizabeth Taylor, and his third choice was Natalie Wood. However, when the film went into production for Seven Arts/MGM, Marilyn had already died, and it was Kim Novak who was chosen to play the part, opposite Laurence Harvey. Upon its release, the movie proved to be a dismal failure, with most of the critics in agreement that Miss Novak was miscast.

***OF WOMEN AND THEIR ELEGANCE***

Writer: Norman Mailer
Photographer: Milton H. Greene
Publisher: Simon and Schuster
Year: 1980 (Out of print)

*Great* black-and-white photographs by Milton H. Greene, and excessive, wet-dream prose by Norman Mailer are the features of this slick, well-produced book about MM. And while some of the material was based on Marilyn's relationships with Amy and Milton Greene, most of it is rooted in Mailer's obsession with MM. The book itself offers the disclaimer: "[*Of Women and Their Elegance*] does not pretend to offer factual representations and in no way wishes to suggest that these are the actual thoughts of Miss Monroe or of anyone else who appears in these pages." A good disclaimer but, photos aside, *not* a very good book.

***O. HENRY'S FULL HOUSE*** ★★

1952 117 minutes Black and White
20th Century-Fox
Directed by: Henry Koster
Produced by: Andre Hakim
Screenplay by: Lamar Trotti, based on a story by O. Henry
Photographed by: Lloyd Ahern
Cast: Charles Laughton, Marilyn Monroe, David Wayne

*O. Henry's Full House* was the filmed version of five short stories by O. Henry. The segments each featured a different cast and a different director and were introduced by writer John Steinbeck. The segment that featured Marilyn Monroe was entitled "The Cop and the Anthem." Chronologically, it was the first of the five.

Why 20th Century-Fox put Marilyn in this bit part (playing a prostitue, yet!) remains questionable. At the time this film was made, Marilyn was at the doorstep of major stardom. It would seem that Fox was more interested in Marilyn's marquee value than in showcasing her star potential. Nevertheless, within a year of the release of *O. Henry's Full House,* Marilyn Monroe would be a movie star of explosive stature.

### *OKINAWA*

Columbia compilation war film (1952) that included Marilyn's song and dance routine, "Every Baby Needs a Da-Da-Daddy" from *Ladies of the Chorus* (1948).

### CHRISTOPHER OLGIATI

Christopher Olgiati wrote and directed the BBC television documentary *The Last Days of Marilyn Monroe* (1985), which is now known as the home video *Marilyn, Say Goodbye to the President.*

### LAURENCE OLIVIER

> "It's the best combination since black and white."
>
> Joshua Logan on the pairing of Olivier and Monroe
>
> "Okay, Marilyn, be sexy."
>
> Olivier directing Monroe during the shooting of *The Prince and the Showgirl*
>
> "You never told me what to do when I'm explaining a scene to her and she walks away from me in mid-sentence."
>
> Olivier to Joshua Logan
>
> "He gave me the dirtiest looks, even when he was smiling."
>
> Monroe on Olivier

Sir Laurence Olivier is commonly acknowledged as the finest actor—stage or screen—of our time. He was born in 1907 and knighted forty years later. He has appeared in a plethora of film classics, among them *Wuthering Heights*

THE RAY VAN GOEYE COLLECTION

(1939), *Rebecca* (1940), *Henry V* (for which he won a 1944 Oscar), *Hamlet* (for which he won a 1948 Oscar), *Richard III* (1956), *The Entertainer* (1960), *Sleuth* (1972), and *The Marathon Man* (1976).

When Marilyn Monroe announced to the world in 1956 that she would team with Laurence Olivier to produce *The Prince and the Showgirl,* she was ridiculed for what was termed her pretensions. Nevertheless, Marilyn did produce *Prince.* Moreover, she starred in it and even had the audacity to give herself top billing over Lord Olivier, who, by the way, directed.

Following the February 1956 announcement of the joint production, Olivier returned to England, where he promptly received a cable from Marilyn. It read, simply, "Missing You Already." It was to be one of the few endearments exchanged between America's queen and England's knight.

After seeing the early rushes of *Prince,* Olivier told Marilyn that her teeth were too yellow. He suggested that she brush them with lemon and baking soda to brighten them. Marilyn, Olivier's *boss,* was reportedly insulted and furious. As for Olivier, he detested the Method style of acting that Marilyn employed; he objected to the presence of Paula Strasberg, who "coached" Marilyn on the set; and he was appalled by Marilyn's incessant tardiness and lack of professionalism. Olivier once referred to Marilyn as "a professional amateur." Meanwhile, behind his back, Marilyn mockingly referred to Olivier as "Sir Olivier" or, worse, "Mr. Sir."

Nonetheless, despite his obvious distaste for Marilyn Monroe, Laurence Olivier was later quoted as saying, regarding the outcome of *The Prince and the Showgirl*: "I was as good as could be; and, Marilyn! Marilyn was quite wonderful, the best of all. So. What do you know?"

**ARISTOTLE ONASSIS**

Reportedly, it was Aristotle Onassis who, in 1955, encouraged Prince Rainier of Monaco to marry a glamorous American movie star. To carry out his plan, Onassis had George Schlee scout for a suitable marital prospect. Schlee, in turn, contacted Gardner Cowles, the publisher of *LOOK* magazine, who approached none other than Marilyn Monroe with the royal proposition.

However, at that time, the would-be princess MM had already locked her gaze on Arthur Miller.

**JESS OPPENHEIMER**

Jess Oppenheimer was one of three writers who scripted the 1954 "I Love Lucy" segment in which Lucille Ball portrayed Marilyn Monroe. The segment was entitled "Ricky's Movie Offer."

**JOEL OPPENHEIMER**

Poet and *Village Voice* columnist Joel Oppenheimer wrote the 1981 book *Marilyn Lives!* He was born and raised in Yonkers, New York, and attended Cornell University, the University of Chicago, and Black Mountain College.

**ORPHANAGE**

*See* LOS ANGELES ORPHANS HOME SOCIETY.

**MARY ORR**
*All About Eve* (1950) was based on the story "The Wisdom Of Eve," which was written by Mary Orr.

**ORRY-KELLY**
Orry-Kelly (1897–1964) was the Australian fashion designer who won an Academy Award for the costumes in *Some Like It Hot* (1959).

**KENNY ORTEGA**
Kenny Ortega directed and choreographed *Marilyn: An American Fable,* the 1983 Broadway musical about MM.

**THE OSCARS**

> "[Marilyn's] performance that year was better than any other. It was a classical film performance."
>
> Joshua Logan after MM was not nominated for a 1956 Oscar for *Bus Stop*

Marilyn Monroe never won an Oscar. She was never even nominated. In 1951, she *was* invited to be a presenter at the awards ceremony. Starlet MM presented the "Best Sound Recording" award to Thomas Moulton for *All About Eve.*

In 1956–57, there was a good deal of speculation that Marilyn would be nominated as "Best Actress" for her startling work in *Bus Stop.* The winner that year was Ingrid Bergman for *Anastasia.* Then, in 1959–60, Marilyn was again a serious contender in the same category for her contributions to the smash hit, *Some Like It Hot.* The winner that year, interestingly, was Simone Signoret, Yves Montand's wife, for *Room at the Top.*

In her March 8, 1963 column, Sheila Graham publicly proposed that the Motion Picture Academy honor Marilyn with a special, lifetime Oscar at that year's upcoming awards ceremony. However, Miss Graham's suggestion went unrecognized by the academy. Then, ten years later, columnist Dorothy Manners reproposed the idea. Charlie Chaplin had been awarded a special Oscar the year before; thus, Miss Manners felt it was appropriate to bestow a similar award to MM in 1973. However, once again, the Motion Picture Academy snubbed its gold-plated nose at Marilyn Monroe.

**MM Trivia Quiz #34**
When the Best Actress nominees of 1956 were announced, MM's name was glaringly omitted. Name the five actresses who *did* make the list. (Answer on page 577.)

**FRED OTASH**
According to Anthony Summers's *Goddess* (Macmillan, 1985), Fred Otash was a private detective who was allegedly involved in the wire-tapping surveillance of Marilyn Monroe in 1961.

***OUI* MAGAZINE**
Adult "men's magazine" that published an article entitled "Who Killed

Marilyn Monroe?" in its October 1975 issue. The article, written by Anthony Scaduto, examined the inaccuracies, controversies, and contradictions of Marilyn's death.

Some three years later, *Oui* continued its coverage on Marilyn with a photo feature entitled "Marilyn's Back and Front." The "spread" featured an MM look-alike, proudly flaunting—what else?—her back and front.

**OUTPOST ESTATES**

In 1952, Marilyn lived for a period in the Hollywood Hills. In the November 16, 1952, issue of *The American Weekly* magazine, MM said the following:

> "I am living at present in a one-bedroom house in the Outpost section of Hollywood. I have a six-months lease on it, the first lease I have ever signed. I have a horror of signing leases. I live alone."

Marilyn's address in the Outpost Estates was 2393 Castilian Drive.

# P

**JACK PAAR**

"Looking back, I guess I should have been excited, but I found her pretty tiresome. She used to carry around books by Marcel Proust with their titles facing out; but I never saw her read one. She was always holding up shooting by talking on the phone. Judging from what's happened, though, I guess she had the right number."

Jack Paar on early MM

"I fear that beneath the facade of Marilyn there was only a frightened waitress in a diner."

Jack Paar on early MM

Before he became a major television personality, Jack Paar appeared in the 1951 comedy *Love Nest,* which also featured Marilyn Monroe.

Born in Canton, Ohio, on May 1, 1918, Paar subsequently gained fame with his television shows, "The Jack Paar Show" (1953–1956), "The Tonight Show" (1957–1962), and "The Jack Paar Show" (1962–1965).

**CHARLES PACE**

Charles Pace is the deputy coroner who picked up Marilyn's body at 8:15 A.M. on August 5, 1962, and deposited it at the Los Angeles County Morgue.

**PACIFIC TELEPHONE AND TELEGRAPH CO.**

On June 12, 1952, Marilyn Monroe was sued by the Pacific Telephone and Telegraph Co. for unpaid telephone bills that totaled $168. The bills were from the period between October 1951 and June 1952.

**JACK PALANCE**

Jack Palance, born Walter Palanuik in 1920, was the New York stage actor who, in the fall of 1951, introduced Marilyn Monroe to drama coach Michael Chekhov.

Among Palance's films are *Panic in the Streets* (1950), *Shane* (1953), and *The Big Knife* (1955).

**PALM DRIVE**

Circa 1950, after he separated from his wife Mozelle, Johnny Hyde moved into a home at 718 North Palm Drive in Beverly Hills. Soon after, struggling starlet Marilyn Monroe moved in with him. In the dining room of the house, Hyde installed four white leather booths and a dance floor to resemble Marilyn's favorite restaurant at that time, Romanoff's.

Some four years later, in April 1954, Marilyn and Joe DiMaggio rented an Elizabethan cottage on Palm Drive, not far from the old Johnny Hyde residence. The DiMaggio home was located at 508 North Palm Drive, three blocks away from Santa Monica Boulevard. The owner of the house was Barbara Maclean. The rent was a then stiff $700 a month.

**PALM SPRINGS**

- ☆ In 1949, Marilyn Monroe met agent Johnny Hyde at the Racquet Club in the resort area of Palm Springs, California. The meeting changed the course of Marilyn's life.
- ☆ Nearly five years later, in January 1954, the newlywed Marilyn and Joe DiMaggio spent two weeks honeymooning in a cabin located near Palm Springs.
- ☆ On March 24, 1962, Marilyn Monroe allegedly went to Bing Crosby's Palm Springs home to be with President John F. Kennedy.

**ERNEST PALMER**

Ernest Palmer (1885–1978) was the longtime cinematographer who shot Marilyn Monroe's first motion picture, *Scudda Hoo! Scudda Hay!* (1948). Palmer's other credits include 1941's *Blood and Sand,* for which he won an Academy Award.

**LAURIE PALMER**

Laurie Palmer was the coauthor of *The Marilyn Monroe Story* (1953), which was the first book ever published about MM.

**THE PAN PACIFIC AUDITORIUM**

The Pan Pacific Auditorium is a Los Angeles landmark where, for ten days in 1945, Norma Jeane Dougherty worked as a hostess at the Los Angeles Home Show. She was paid $10 a day.

**KORLA PANDIT**

Pandit is a hypnotist who has claimed that one of his subjects, a Las Vegas cocktail waitress, transformed into Marilyn Monroe when she was induced into hypnosis.

**PARAMOUNT STUDIOS**

Marilyn Monroe never made a movie for Paramount, but she did shoot her final scenes of *The Misfits* on the Paramount lot (address: 5555 Melrose Avenue, Hollywood) in 1960.

**THE PARAMOUNT THEATRE BUILDING**

The New York location of the Actors Studio, where MM attended classes twice a week in the mid 1950s.

***PARIS-MATCH* MAGAZINE**

*Paris-Match* is the magazine for which reporter Mara Scherbatoff was covering the impending 1956 marriage between Arthur Miller and Marilyn Monroe when she was tragically killed.

Upon Marilyn's own death, six years later, *Paris-Match* paid a lavish thirty-six-page memorial tribute to her in its August 18, 1962, issue.

**PARISIAN FLORISTS**

Parisian Florists was the Hollywood florist that, for twenty years, between August 1962 and September 1982, delivered Joe DiMaggio's red roses to Marilyn's gravesite twice a week.

Following the cancellation of DiMaggio's order, Bob Slatzer contracted Parisian Florists to continue a weekly Westwood floral delivery. Parisian Florists is still located at 7528 Sunset Boulevard.

**DOROTHY PARKER**

When Marilyn lived on Doheny Drive in the early fifties, she befriended Dorothy Parker and her husband, Alan Campbell, who lived nearby.

**WILLIAM H. PARKER**

William H. Parker was the chief of police in Los Angeles at the time of Marilyn Monroe's death. Over the years, there has been speculation that Parker was involved in a cover-up regarding the circumstances of Marilyn's death. Some reports have contended that it was Parker who seized MM's telephone records in 1962, which he allegedly planned to use to obtain J. Edgar Hoover's FBI post—after Bobby Kennedy was elected president.

However, on July 16, 1966—four years after MM and two years before RFK—Chief Parker died, suddenly, at the age of sixty-four. While receiving a standing ovation from a thousand marine veterans at a Hilton Hotel, Parker leaned back in his chair and began gasping. Half an hour later, William Parker was dead.

**PARKSIDE HOUSE**

Estate located at Egham, England, where Marilyn and Arthur Miller lived during the 1956 shooting of *The Prince and the Showgirl.*

**PAUL PARRY**

> "I was sitting in my office chinning with a couple of other fellows one day, when this girl—her name was Norma Jeane Dougherty then—came in and asked if I thought she could be a model. I'll never forget it, because she was wearing a pink sweater—and the other two fellows just fell right off their chairs. *Could she!*"
>
> Paul Parry to Hedda Hopper, 5/4/52

Paul Parry was one of Norma Jeane's earliest photographers. He paid her $15 for her modeling services.

**HARRIET PARSONS**

Harriet Parsons (1906–1983) was a film producer and the daughter of powerful Hollywood columnist Louella Parsons. In 1952, Harriet produced *Clash by Night,* which gave MM one of her most important early roles.

**LOUELLA PARSONS**

> "You and Mr. Schenck were my first friends in Hollywood, and I've never forgotten."
>
> Marilyn Monroe to Louella Parsons

COURTESY OF CINEMA COLLECTORS

With Louella Parsons, circa 1953.

Hollywood matriarch Louella Parsons was born Louella Oettinger on August 6, 1881, in Freeport, Illinois. Along with her bickering rival, Hedda Hopper, Miss Parsons became the most powerful movie columnist/observer in the history of the industry.

Louella Parsons was also the one columnist who was most instrumental in Marilyn Monroe's success and popularity. Miss Parsons was always sympathetic to MM, and over the years she repeatedly and publicly justified Marilyn's actions in her daily *Herald Examiner* gossip column. Even before *Gentlemen Prefer Blondes* (1953), Miss Parsons heralded MM as "the number one movie glamour girl." It was a claim that no one dared to dispute.

In the years that followed, it was to Louella Parsons that Marilyn turned when she was in trouble. In 1953, MM used the Parsons column to respond to the attack made on her by Little Miss Morality, Joan Crawford. Two years later, when she created controversy by leaving Fox, Marilyn again solicited the help of Louella Parsons. In an attempt to elicit sympathy and regain public support, MM humbly pleaded:

> "I've never said I won't make pictures for 20th Century-Fox. I think *The Seven Year Itch* is the best picture I've ever made. I loved working with Billy Wilder and I learned a lot from him. I need somebody to help me and he gave me great help. I *want* to make musicals, good comedies and drama—not [just] heavy drama as everyone says."

When Louella Parsons died on December 9, 1972, a Hollywood era died along with her.

**MARGARET PARTON**

Margaret Parton was a writer who interviewed MM in New York, circa 1961-62. However, Miss Parton's article was not published until seventeen years later, when it appeared in the February 19, 1979, issue of *LOOK* magazine.

**PASO ROBLES, CALIFORNIA**
Marilyn and Joe DiMaggio spent the first two weeks of their 1954 honeymoon in Paso Robles, California.

**PASSPORT**
Reportedly, and believe it or not, Marilyn Monroe had difficulty in obtaining her passport for her 1954 Japan trip because—she did not have a photograph of herself. Thus, Joe DiMaggio rushed her out to the nearest coin-operated arcade, where they got one.

**ROBERT PATRICK**
Robert Patrick wrote the 1975 stage play *Kennedy's Children,* which featured actress Shirley Knight in a major MM-based role.

**THE PAYNE WHITNEY CLINIC**
On February 7, 1961, under the alias "Miss Faye Miller," Marilyn Monroe voluntarily checked into the Payne Whitney Psychiatric Clinic in New York City. It was after the extremely difficult shooting of *The Misfits* (1960), the death of Clark Gable, the final split from Yves Montand, and the divorce from Arthur Miller.

Marilyn was, reportedly, severely distraught. She was placed in the ward for the mentally ill. Vague and conflicting reports about MM's disturbed mental health appeared in the nation's newspapers. Then, four days later, Marilyn mysteriously checked out of the clinic. She had been allowed one phone call, and she telephoned Joe DiMaggio, long-distance, who promptly flew to New York to "rescue" his ex-wife. With DiMaggio at her side, Marilyn secretly left Payne Whitney and entered the less intense, more comfortable Columbia Presbyterian Hospital.

Today, Payne Whitney is known as the Cornel Medical-Payne Whitney Clinic and is located at 525 East 68th Street.

**UNA PEARL**
Una Pearl, of Croydon, Surrey, England, was Marilyn Monroe's stand-in during the 1956 shotting of *The Prince and the Showgirl* (1957).

**GREGORY PECK**
Gregory Peck was initially slated to costar opposite Marilyn Monroe in the 1960 film *Let's Make Love,* aka *The Billionaire.* However, after Arthur Miller rewrote the film's script to enlarge Marilyn's part, Peck walked out on the production. At that time, Peck was quoted as saying:

> "I am genuinely sorry not to be able to work with Miss Monroe. I am mercenary enough to know that with her in a picture, the chances of success are improved."

Gregory Peck, born in 1916, *did* appear in the following films: *Spellbound* (1945), *Duel in the Sun* (1946), *Gentleman's Agreement* (1947), *Roman Holiday* (1953), *The Man in the Grey Flannel Suit* (1956), *To Kill a Mockingbird* (for which he won a 1963 Oscar), and *The Omen* (1976).

## *PENTHOUSE* MAGAZINE

In its October 1980 issue, *Penthouse* featured an article entitled "The Bluest Marilyn" that included still photographs from a stag film that Marilyn Monroe allegedly "performed" in prior to being signed by 20th Century-Fox in 1946. *Penthouse* touted the article and accompanying photos by claiming to have "overwhelming evidence" that the girl in the photos was MM. However, neither the article nor the photos fulfilled that promise.

## *PEOPLE* MAGAZINE

*People* magazine put Marilyn Monroe on the cover of its October 21, 1985, issue. The inside story dealt with ABC-TV's "cover-up" decision to axe the "20/20" investigative segment on Marilyn's death and her association with John and Robert Kennedy.

*People* has published the following articles on MM:

☆ 4/29/74: "The Unquiet Ghost of Marilyn Monroe"
☆ 10/21/80: "Abbess in High-heeled Shoes"—excerpts from the book *Music for Chameleons*
☆ 3/9/81: "Do a Dead Man's Files Finally End Marilyn Monroe's Search for Her Dad?"
☆ 8/9/82: "He Makes Sure DiMaggio's Roses are There"
☆ 8/9/82: "20 Years After Her Suicide, the Magic of Monroe Survives in Rarely Seen Photos:—excerpts from the book *Monroe: Her Life in Pictures*
☆ 2/21/83; "MM-Mania Hits the Stores and a New Generation Discovers Wearing Marilyn's Dress is a Breeze"
☆ 8/8/83: "The Time Marilyn Monroe Hid Out at Our House"
☆ 7/2/84: "My Romance with Marilyn Monroe"
☆ 10/21/85*: "The Monroe Report: ABC-TV'S Cancelled Report on Marilyn Monroe"
☆ 4/7/86: "Anecdotes, Facetial, Satire, Etc."

---

**People* cover that MM appeared on.

## LENA PEPITONE

From October 1957 through the next five years, Lena Pepitone served as Marilyn Monroe's New York maid and wardrobe mistress at the East 57th Street apartment. Mrs. Pepitone, who was born in Italy in 1928, has also claimed (and who *hasn't*?) to have had a very close friendship with MM.

In 1979, Lena Pepitone published her "autobiographical" account of life with Marilyn. It was titled *Marilyn Monroe Confidential*. The book, which can fairly be described as tabloid trashy, has been lambasted by Marilyn's fans as being exploitative and vulgar.

## "PERSON TO PERSON"

In 1955, while she was living with Milton and Amy Greene at their Connecticut home, Marilyn Monroe made a rare television appearance on Edward R. Murrow's interview program, "Person to Person." The show aired on CBS on April 8, 1955.

## JEAN PETERS

Actress Jean Peters costarred with MM in *As Young as You Feel* (1951) and *Niagara* (1953). She also appeared, though not in the same segment as MM, in *O. Henry's Full House* (1952).

Among Miss Peters's other films were *Viva Zapata* (1952) and *Three Coins in the Fountain* (1954). In the mid-fifties, Jean Peters retired from the movies to marry Howard Hughes.

## "PETRONELLA"

Norma Jeane, in one of her earliest acting roles, portrayed a boy in the Emerson Junior High School production of *Petronella.*

## PETS

> "I like animals. If you talk to a dog or a cat it doesn't tell you to shut up."
>
> Marilyn Monroe

Marilyn Monroe loved animals. During her lifetime, she had the following pets:

1. Tippy: Tippy was a black-and-white dog given to Norma Jeane by her foster father, Albert Wayne Bolender. Every day, Tippy accompanied Norma Jeane to school. He even used to wait for her to play with him at recess. Circa 1932, Tippy was shot dead by a neighbor who claimed that Tippy had been rolling around in his garden.
2. A Spaniel: When Norma Jeane lived with the Goddard family, she and her "sister," Beebe, shared a pet spaniel, circa 1940.
3. Muggsie: Jim Dougherty bought his wife a pet collie named Muggsie. However, after she began her modeling career, Norma Jeane had less time for her dog. Subsequently, Muggsie died of a "broken heart."
4. A Chihuahua: At the time she was signed by Columbia Pictures in 1948, Marilyn Monroe owned a pet Chihuahua.
5. Mitsou: Mitsou was a white Persian cat that Marilyn Monroe owned in New York in the mid 1950s.
6. Hugo: A basset hound who lived with MM and Arthur Miller at their East 57th Street apartment in New York. Once, Norman Rosten and Marilyn spoon-fed straight scotch to Hugo to cheer him up. When Marilyn and Arthur split up, Arthur retained possession of Hugo.
7. Butch was a parakeet owned by the Millers. Butch also resided at the East 57th Street apartment.
8. Ebony: A riding horse that the Millers purchased from Frank and Nan Taylor for their Connecticut farm. MM rode Ebony only a few times.
9. Maf: Maf was a little white French poodle who was given to MM in New York by Frank Sinatra. Sinatra had purchased the dog from Natalie Wood's mother. As has been widely reported, Marilyn named the dog "Maf" because of Frank Sinatra's alleged mafia connections. Interestingly, to spite Arthur Miller, Marilyn used to let Maf sleep on an expensive white beaver coat that Miller had presented her. When Marilyn returned to live in Hollywood, she had Maf flown back to be with her. Following her death, Maf was inherited by Frank Sinatra's secretary, Gloria Lovell.

**FRED PHILLIPS**

Fred Phillips is the man who did Marilyn's makeup for the 1950 Marx Brothers movie *Love Happy.*

**PHOENIX, ARIZONA**

The rodeo scenes in *Bus Stop* were shot on location in Phoenix, Arizona, in March 1956.

**PHOTOGRAPHERS**

> "She understood photography and she also understood what makes a great photograph. Not the technique, but the content."
>
> Richard Avedon

During her reign as the Queen of Hollywood, Marilyn Monroe was the most photographed woman in the world. She has been photographed by thousands of photographers in millions of photographs. The following is a selective, alphabetized list of some of Marilyn's best and best-known photographers:

THE SABIN GRAY COLLECTION

1. Eve Arnold
2. Zinn Arthur
3. Richard Avedon
4. George Barris
5. Cecil Beaton
6. Anthony Beauchamp
7. Hal Berg
8. Bernard of Hollywood
9. John Bryson
10. Bill Burnside
11. Cornell Capa
12. Jack Cardiff
13. David Conover
14. Ed Coonenwerth
15. Henri Dauman
16. Bruce Davidson
17. Andre de Dienes
18. Alfred Eisenstaedt
19. Elliott Erwitt
20. Ed Feingersh
21. John Florea
22. Len Globus
23. Allan Grant
24. Milton H. Greene
25. Ernst Haas
26. Philippe Halsman
27. Potter Hueth
28. Joseph Jasgur
29. Tom Kelley
30. Douglas Kirkland
31. Hans Knopf
32. Lee Lockwood
33. Joshua Logan
34. George Miller
35. Inge Morath
36. Nikolas Muray
37. Arnold Newman
38. Lawrence Schiller
39. Sam Shaw
40. George Silk
41. Bert Stern
42. Phil Stern
43. Earl Theisen
44. John Vachon
45. Seymour Wally
46. Laszlo Willinger
47. Bob Willoughby
48. Gary Winogrand
49. Raphael Wolff
50. William Read Woodfield

**The Great MM Poses**

1. The red velvet calendar nudes, Tom Kelley, 1949
2. The Jones Beach/Tobey Beach series, Andre de Dienes, 1949
3. The first *LIFE* cover, Philippe Halsman, 1952

4. The potato sack, Earl Theisen, 1952
5. Sitting on a chair, Phil Stern, 1953
6. *Seven Year Itch* skirt scene, Sam Shaw, 1954
7. The black hat and fishnet series, Milton H. Greene, 1956
8. Lying in bed with a flower, Cecil Beaton, 1956
9. The hair-swept goddess, Jack Cardiff, 1956
10. The leg out of the pool, Lawrence Schiller and William Read Woodfield, 1962
11. Clutching a white pillow, Douglas Kirkland, 1962
12. The head and shoulders shot (with white eyeshadow), Bert Stern, 1962

**MM Trivia Quiz #35**
Which of MM's photographers later produced a film about her life? (Answer on page 577.)

### *PHOTOPLAY* MAGAZINE

Over the years, industry powerhouse *Photoplay* magazine was generally supportive of Marilyn Monroe and published a myriad of articles about her—far too many to index here. Among the "more important" *Photoplay* articles on MM were the March 1953 piece by Jim Dougherty titled "Marilyn Monroe Was My Wife" and the September 1965 tribute written by *Photoplay* editor Adele Whitely Fletcher.

Marilyn's first affiliation with *Photoplay* was a 1949 publicity stint that she did to promote the movie *Love Happy.* Still unknown at that time, MM participated in *Photoplay*'s "Dream House" caper, which took place near Albany, New York. For the event, Marilyn pushed a vacuum cleaner around the house and posed for photographers.

#### *Photoplay* Magazine Awards

*Photoplay* awarded MM its prestigious "Fastest Rising Star of 1952" award on March 9, 1953. The presentations were held at the Beverly Hills Hotel. As was characteristic of him, Joe DiMaggio declined to be Marilyn's escort. Thus, she attended on the arm of early confidant Sidney Skolsky. She arrived two hours late. But, as she walked to and from the stage to accept her award, MM easily snatched the evening away from even the most bespangled matrons of Hollywood glamour. She performed the famed Marilyn walk with such efficacy that the male members of the star-studded audience began to howl, and host Jerry Lewis began to jump up and down on a table. It was hardly behavior befitting one of Hollywood's most distinguished and traditional social gatherings.

And then there was the matter of *that dress.* Against protestation from all sides, Marilyn showed up wearing a gold lamé gown, one size too small, that she literally had to be sewn into. The gown was designed by MM's favorite at the time, Billy Travilla, for the movie *Gentlemen Prefer Blondes* (1953). Thus, Marilyn rationalized that if the dress was good enough to wear publicly in a movie, then it was good enough to wear publicly—period. In the days that followed the *Photoplay* awards, a Hollywood furor brewed over MM and *that dress.*

The following year, in March 1954, *Photoplay* honored Marilyn with its

"Best Actress" award for her performances in *Gentlemen Prefer Blondes* (1953) and *How to Marry a Millionaire* (1953).

**JIM PIERCE**

Jim Pierce was the man who used to deliver Joe DiMaggio's roses to Marilyn Monroe's gravesite in Westwood.

**ARTHUR PIERSON**

Arthur Pierson was the first man to direct Marilyn Monroe twice—in the 1947 film *Dangerous Years* and again in the 1951 film *Hometown Story*, the latter of which he also wrote and produced.

***PILLOW TALK***

*Pillow Talk* (1959) is the movie that Marilyn Monroe wanted but couldn't get. It became, of course, one of Doris Day's most successful film vehicles. *Pillow Talk* costarred Rock Hudson, was directed by Michael Gordon, and was produced by Ross Hunter and Martin Melcher.

**PINEWOOD STUDIOS**

Pinewood Studios is the location where *The Prince and the Showgirl* was shot in 1956. Pinewood was located at Iver, Buckinghamshire, London.

**FRANZ PLANER**

Franz Planer (1894–1963) was one of four cinematographers who worked on the unfinished *Something's Got to Give* (1962). Among Planer's credits are *Death of a Salesman* (1952) and *The Nun's Story* (1959).

***PLAYBOY* MAGAZINE**

Marilyn Monroe was *Playboy* magazine's first playmate. In December 1953, MM appeared on the cover of *Playboy*'s very first issue. Displayed prominently within that first issue was Marilyn's nude calendar shot, which *Playboy*'s enterprising mastermind, Hugh Hefner, had purchased for a mere $500. With MM's incomparable copy appeal, *Playboy* quickly sold out, Hefner began his bunny empire, and history was made.

Shortly before her death in 1962, *Playboy* shelled out $25,000 for photographer Lawrence Schiller's *Something's Got to Give* nude pool shots of MM. At the time, that figure was the highest ever paid by a magazine for a single pictorial. The nudes were scheduled to run in the December 1962 issue. In addition to the nudes, Marilyn had agreed to pose for a front and back cover. The front cover was to have been MM wearing just a white stole, and the back cover was to have been the same pose, shot simultaneously from the rear. However, the Thursday prior to the scheduled shoot, Pat Newcomb telephoned Hefner himself to cancel the proposed covers. Marilyn had changed her mind. That Sunday, MM was found dead in her Brentwood home.

*Playboy* waited a respectable period before publishing the Schiller nudes. In its January 1964 issue, *Playboy* printed a fourteen-page tribute to MM, in which the nude shots were presented in their full flesh-colored splendor.

Over the years, *Playboy* continued to carry the torch for MM, its first love. And, in its January 1987 issue, *Playboy* published a revelatory series of MM nudes, shot circa 1946. The nudes were photographed by illustrator Earl Moran and had gone undiscovered for over forty years.

## PLAYS

Excluding her brief, incognito appearance in *Teahouse of the August Moon* (1955) on Broadway and an alleged performance in the Bliss Hayden's production of *Stage Door* (1948), Marilyn Monroe appeared in just one stage play before a commercial audience. The play was *Glamour Preferred,* and it was performed at the Bliss Hayden Playhouse in Beverly Hills. Marilyn auditioned for the play after being dropped by 20th Century-Fox in 1947. She was given the second lead, which she alternated playing with actress Jane Weeks.

### Plays About MM or Featuring an MM-Based Major Character

The following is a selective, chronological list of English-language plays.

1. *Will Success Spoil Rock Hunter?* (USA, 1955)
2. *Venus at Large* (USA, 1962)
3. *Come on Strong* (USA, 1962)
4. *After the Fall* (USA, 1964)
5. *Turn on the Heat* (Australia, 1967)
6. *Cop Out* (USA, 1969)
7. *The White Whore and the Bit Player* (USA, 1973)
8. *Legend* (England, 1974)
9. *Fame* (USA, 1974)
10. *Kennedy's Children* (USA, 1975)
11. *The Hardest Part of It* (USA, 1978) aka *Public Property* (England, 1979)
12. *Hey, Marilyn* (Canada, 1979)
13. *Marilyn, A Fable of the 20th Century* (Australia, 1982)
14. *Marilyn!* (England, 1983)
15. *Marilyn: An American Fable* (USA, 1983)
16. *Insignificance* (England, 1982)
17. *Strawhead* (USA, 1986)

### MM Trivia Quiz #36

What was the name of the play that MM auditioned for in *All About Eve*? (Answer on page 577.)

## THE PLAZA HOTEL

On February 9, 1956, Marilyn Monroe gave a press conference in the Terrace Room of the Plaza Hotel (address: Fifth Ave. and 59th St., New York) to announce the production of *The Sleeping Prince,* aka *The Prince and the Showgirl.*

## MARJORIE PLECHER

Marjorie Plecher was Marilyn Monroe's longtime movie wardrobe girl/ costumer, who also dressed MM for her 1962 burial. Miss Plecher was also the wife of Marilyn's friend and makeup man, Whitey Snyder.

**PLUMBER**
*See* ROY NEWELL.

**POETRY**

> Help Help
> Help I feel life coming closer
> when all I want is to die.
>
> Marilyn Monroe

Marilyn Monroe may not have been a poet of professional caliber, but, she was a poet of the heart. Over the years, she wrote a good deal of poetry—from the "I Miss Her" (aka "I Love Her")tribute to Ana Lower in the late forties to the verses she shared with her poet friend, Norman Rosten, years later. Said Rosten of MM's poetic prowess:

> "She liked poetry. It was a shortcut for her. She understood with the instinct of a poet, that it led directly into the heart of experience."

One of Marilyn Monroe's most revealing poems included the following:

> Life—I am of both your directions
> Somehow remaining
> Hanging downward the most
> Strong as a cobweb in the wind. . . .

**POISON**
Less than a week after Marilyn's death, the *Chicago Tribune* reported that the cause of her death may have been cyanide poisoning. According to that newspaper, red blotches had been found on Marilyn's body and such discoloration was symptomatic of cyanide poisoning. The *Chicago Tribune* further commented that the corrosion found on Marilyn's lips, tongue, and internal organs was also consistent with a cyanide dose.

**HAL POLAIRE**
Hal Polaire was Billy Wilder's assistant director on *Some Like It Hot* (1959). Reportedly, one day on the set, Polaire knocked on Marilyn's dressing room door to notify her that the crew was ready for her. Allegedly, Marilyn snapped back at Polaire, "Go fuck yourself." This story, true or not, did not add to Marilyn's personal popularity with Billy Wilder or with the other members of the cast and crew.

**POLITICS**
In 1960, Marilyn Monroe was a registered Democrat. In that election year, she was named an alternate delegate to the national convention, representing the Roxbury, Connecticut, community where she and Arthur Miller had a farm home.

**THE POLYCLINIC HOSPITAL**
Following the shooting of *Some Like It Hot* (1959), on December 17, 1958, Marilyn suffered a miscarriage at the Polyclinic Hospital (on West 50th Street) in New York. The following year, MM reentered Polyclinic and

underwent an operation to increase her chances of a successful pregnancy.

On June 29, 1961, Marilyn was rushed back to Polyclinic, where she underwent a major, two-hour surgery to remove an inflamed gallbladder. The operation took place on June 30, and Marilyn was released from the hospital on July 11, 1961. Today, the French and Polyclinic Medical School and Hospital has been relocated to 330 West 30th Street in New York City.

**WILLIAM SIDNEY PORTER**

William Sidney Porter, alias O. Henry, wrote the original stories on which the movie *O. Henry's Full House* (1952) was based.

**PEARL PORTERFIELD**

The day before Marilyn Monroe had her hair styled for an important engagement, she would have it bleached the "pillow white" shade that she favored during the latter part of her life. This task, an integral part of the intricate MM beautification process, was performed by Pearl Porterfield, better known as "Porter," who was in her sixties at that time.

**PORTLAND, OREGON**

After she was released from the mental institution in 1945, Gladys Baker moved to Portland, Oregon, where she resided in an old hotel. During their December 1945 photo shoot, Andre de Dienes escorted Norma Jeane Dougherty to Portland to visit her mother.

**DICK POWELL**

Dick Powell (1904–1963) was a Hollywood star in the 1930s and 1940s. In 1950, Powell starred in MGM's production of *Right Cross,* in which starlet Marilyn Monroe had a bit part.

**AMANDA POWERS**

Amanda Powers portrayed MM in the stage play by Roger Newman, *The Hardest Part of It,* which was presented at the Actor's Consort in New York, circa 1977–78.

**PREMIERES**

***All About Eve***

Despite the "requests" made by Darryl Zanuck and Joe Mankiewicz, Marilyn Monroe opted to forgo the 1950 star-studded premiere of *All About Eve.* Marilyn's excuse was that she had to study her lines for a screen test that she had the following morning.

***How to Marry a Millionaire***

The premiere of *How to Marry a Millionaire* took place on November 4, 1953, at the Fox Wilshire Theatre in Beverly Hills. Marilyn attended the event with Humphrey Bogart, Lauren Bacall, and Mr. and Mrs. Nunnally Johnson. Joe DiMaggio opted not to attend.

For Marilyn Monroe, the *Millionaire* premiere was a major event. Just after noon that day, Marilyn drove to the 20th Century-Fox studio. For the next six hours and twenty minutes, Marilyn underwent her beautification transformation. She was sewn into the studio dress that she herself had chosen to wear. It was made of flesh-colored crepe de chine, and embroidered with thousands of sequins. The dress had a long velvet train and a gold belt. Marilyn accessorized her outfit with a white fox fur stole and a pair of long white evening gloves. Marilyn's hair was done by Gladys Rasmussen, and her makeup was done by Whitey Snyder.

After the studio limousine picked her up, Marilyn was taken to the home of the Nunnally Johnsons. Even though Johnson was not terribly fond of MM, it was The Big Night, and all grievances were shelved—temporarily. Upon arriving at the Johnson home, Marilyn quickly downed two bourbon and sodas before sitting down to dinner. Also present were Johnson's wife, Dorris, Humphrey Bogart, and Lauren Bacall. After dinner, Marilyn had another bourbon and was quite intoxicated before arriving at the theatre. Nunnally Johnson was later quoted as saying, "Women who have been sewn into their clothes should never drink to excess."

Nevertheless, *Hollywood Reporter* columnist Mike Connolly had the following to say about MM's entrance:

> "Nothing like it since Gloria Swanson at her most glittering . . .
> Lauren Bacall was there too. Pic's third star, Betty Grable,
> wasn't. . . ."

Following the successful screening of the movie, Marilyn declined to attend the post-theatre parties. Instead, she limo'ed back to the studio, where she shed her borrowed sequins and changed into a shirt, a pair of slacks, and a pair of loafers. She then climbed back into her car and drove herself back home to her apartment. Alone.

***The Seven Year Itch***

The widely ballyhooed premiere of *The Seven Year Itch* took place on June 1, 1955, at Loew's State Theatre in New York City. Marilyn arrived at the theatre some twenty minutes after the movie had begun. And, for the first (and only) time in their relationship, Joe DiMaggio escorted his recently divorced wife, MM, to a premiere of one of her films. Following the victorious screening, MM and Joe went to Toots Shor's restaurant, where Joe had arranged a surprise birthday party for Marilyn. However, as the evening progressed, MM and Joe had an argument, and Marilyn asked her friend, Sam Shaw, to drive her home.

***The Prince and the Showgirl***

*The Prince and the Showgirl* was premiered at Radio City Music Hall in New York City on June 13, 1957. Marilyn attended the event with her husband, Arthur Miller.

***Some Like It Hot***

*Some Like It Hot* had its world premiere at Loew's Capitol Theatre in New York City, on March 29, 1959. MM wore a silver lamé gown.

***Let's Make Love***
The planned Reno premiere of *Let's Make Love* (1960) was canceled due to an unexpected power failure.

***The Misfits***
*The Misfits* was premiered at the Capitol Theatre on Broadway on January 31, 1961. The very recently divorced MM was escorted by Montgomery Clift and Lee Strasberg. Marilyn wore a low-cut, black gown with a black fur wrap.

## OTTO PREMINGER

> "Directing her was like directing Lassie. You need fourteen takes to get each one of them right."
>
> Otto Preminger on Marilyn Monroe

Marilyn Monroe did not like Otto Preminger, and the sentiment was more than reciprocated.

Otto Preminger (1906-1986) was the Austrian director of such notable American films as *Laura* (1944), *The Moon Is Blue* (1953), *Carmen Jones* (1954), *The Man with the Golden Arm* (1956), and *Anatomy of a Murder* (1959).

In 1953, Preminger directed the hottest new star in Hollywood, Marilyn Monroe, in a contrived, mediocre western, *River of No Return*. During the shooting, there was a considerable amount of tension between MM and Preminger, particularly due to the presence of Natasha Lytess, whom Preminger had tried, unsuccessfully, to ban from the set. During the production, Marilyn was said to have referred to Preminger as that "pompous ass." In 1960, Preminger was asked whether or not he would ever make another film with MM. He stated, predictably, that he would not—not for a million dollars.

## PRESS CONFERENCES

The following is a selective, chronological compilation of the Marilyn Monroe press conferences:

☆ Upon arrival at Tokyo's Haneda Airport at the end of January 1954, MM held a press conference for the Japanese press.

Press: Do you wear underwear?
MM: I'm buying a kimono.

Press: How long have you been walking that way?
MM: I started when I was six months old and haven't stopped yet.

Press: What kind of fur are you wearing?
MM: Fox. And not the 20th Century kind.

☆ On January 7, 1955, Marilyn held a press conference/cocktail party at the home of attorney Frank Delaney at 59 East 64th Street in Manhattan. The purpose of the conference was to announce the formation of Marilyn Monroe Productions, Inc., and to introduce the "new," more sophisticated MM to the press. The event was scheduled for 6:00 P.M. However, the "new" Marilyn resorted to her old bad habits when she did not

THE SABIN GRAY COLLECTION

arrive until 7:00 P.M. This led some wary members of the press to wag that she was just "the same old Marilyn." Nevertheless, she *did* look stunning in a skin-tight, white satin sheath gown, an ermine coat, and a pair of rhinestone earrings. Also in attendance that evening were such celebrities as Richard Rogers, Janet Leigh, Tony Curtis, and Marlene Dietrich.

Press: Marilyn, we heard there's something new about you. What is it?

MM: Well, my hair is new. I used to be platinum, but I dyed it. Now I'm a subdued platinum. Not as loud as the other. My career is going to be different. I'm going to broaden my scope. You know, people have scope, you know, they really do.

MM: I formed my own corporation so I can play the better kind of roles I want to play. I didn't like a lot of my pictures. I'm tired of sex roles. I don't want to play sex roles anymore.

Press: What role would you like to play?

MM: I don't know. I'd like to play one of the parts in *The Brothers Karamazov* by Dostoyevsky.

Press: Do you want to play the Brothers Karamazov?

MM: I don't want to play the brothers. I want to play Grushenka. She's a girl.

MM: I want to produce, such as television and all kinds of things.

☆ At noon on February 9, 1956, in the Terrace Room of the Plaza Hotel in New York City, Marilyn Monroe and Laurence Olivier teamed up to announce the planned production of Terence Rattigan's play, *The Sleeping Prince*. It was to be the first independent production under the Marilyn Monroe Productions banner and would feature Olivier as director/costar and Marilyn as *producer*/costar. Some two hundred reporters and photographers showed up to cover the event. It was a mostly hostile press, a rare occurrence for MM. The press, perhaps partially due to the influence of 20th Century-Fox, had turned against MM. They also had not warmed to the prospect of Marilyn's new role as producer. For the event, Marilyn wore a black velvet sheath. During the press conference, either by accident or by design, one of her shoulder straps broke, which—as can be imagined—created quite a sensation. Film critic Judith Crist, then of the *New York Herald Tribune*, gave Marilyn a safety pin and assisted her in pinning the strap. It has often been suggested that Marilyn purposely broke the strap to divert attention away from Laurence Olivier. However, when one bold reporter intimated this, Marilyn angrily retorted: "How would *you* feel if something of *yours* broke in front of a whole room full of strangers?!" Marilyn then stomped out of the room and ended the press conference. Years later, Laurence Olivier contended that "It was fixed that Marilyn's shoulder strap should break as she made her first curtsey." At any rate, planned or not, Marilyn's broken strap proved to be the highlight of the event.

☆ On March 1, 1956, Jack Warner held a press conference to welcome Marilyn Monroe to the Warner Brother's "family" by announcing that WB would distribute the Marilyn Monroe Productions presentation of *The Prince and the Showgirl*. Marilyn, who was accompanied by Milton H. Greene, surprised reporters by wearing the same outfit that she had worn (and was photographed in) at a court appearance the day before.

☆ Due to overwhelming public pressure, MM and Arthur Miller held a hasty press conference on June 22, 1956, to announce their marriage plans (although they did not give away the exact wedding date). The conference was attended by a hundred newspapermen and was held outside of Marilyn's Sutton Place apartment building in New York City. Marilyn wore a cream-colored man's shirt, a black skirt, and a pair of gloves.

☆ Following the Sutton Place announcement, MM and Miller were required to hold another, larger press conference to sate the almost blood-thirsty press. This second event took place in Roxbury, Connecticut, and was attended by some four hundred photographers and reporters. Marilyn wore a gold blouse with a black skirt.

☆ MM held her first British press conference on July 14, 1956, after arriving at the London airport. The purpose of the event was to announce to the London press the British production of *The Prince and the Showgirl*. Marilyn held her second British press conference at the Savoy Hotel in London. For Marilyn, it was not a successful appearance. The press was turned off by her pretentiousness and reserve. However, she did manage one witty moment:

Press: What inspired you to study acting?
MM: Seeing my own pictures.

☆ In February 1962, during her Mexican shopping trip, Marilyn held a press conference at the Continental Hilton Hotel in Mexico City. Marilyn wore a pale sea-green Pucci dress—the dress she was later buried in.

☆ According to Bob Slatzer, Marilyn had planned to schedule a press conference for Monday, August 6, 1962. The purpose of the event, according to Slatzer, was Marilyn's intention to "go public" about her relationships with John and Robert Kennedy.

### *THE PRINCE AND THE SHOWGIRL* ★★★

1957 117 minutes Technicolor
Warner Brothers/Marilyn Monroe Productions
Directed by: Laurence Olivier
Produced by: Laurence Olivier
Screenplay by: Terence Rattigan, from his play *The Sleeping Prince*
Photographed by: Jack Cardiff
Cast: Marilyn Monroe, Laurence Olivier, Sybil Thorndike, Richard Wattis, Jeremy Spenser, Esmond Knight, Rosamund Greenwood, Maxine Audley, Aubrey Dexter, Paul Hardwick, Andrea Malandrinos

Upon its American release in 1957, *The Prince and the Showgirl* received mixed reviews and only tepid box office. However, over the years, American audiences have taken a second, more favorable view of this British production.

In 1956, Milton H. Greene purchased Terence Rattigan's play *The Sleeping Prince* as a starring vehicle for Marilyn Monroe. The material had already proven itself to be a stage success in England with Laurence Olivier and Vivien Leigh in the primary roles. The film version of *Prince* was to be the first production independently produced under the Marilyn Monroe Productions banner.

Initially, the worldwide press laughed at the Monroe/Olivier *Prince* proposition. Marilyn, it was generally felt, was eons out of her thespian league and was expected to be blown off the screen by the acting genius of Lord Olivier, and by the rest of the British-dominated cast as well. However, by the time of the film's release, Marilyn had won newfound respect in Hollywood (by way of *Bus Stop*), and expectations were raised somewhat.

At the outset of the production, Olivier referred to Marilyn as "Sweetie," while she acknowleged him, appropriately, as "Larry." However, by the end of the production on November 17, 1956, the prince and the showgirl were barely speaking.

There were problems, mostly ego-related, from the start. First of all, executive producer Milton H. Greene signed Olivier to direct *before* obtaining the approval of Marilyn's coach/mentor, Lee Strasberg. Not far into the production, Marilyn began causing costly delays with her characteristic tardiness and absenteeism. Moreover, when Marilyn *did* appear on the set, she brought coach Paula Strasberg with her, much to the chagrin of Olivier. Finally, midway through the production, presumably with Olivier's blessing, Paula flew back to New York, and Marilyn's New York analyst was flown in to England to replace her. And then there was the problem of the growing rift between Marilyn's business and marital partners, Milton Greene and Arthur Miller, respectively. By the time the production of *Prince* was over, so was Marilyn's once loving relationship with Milton Greene.

The plot of *The Prince and the Showgirl* matched the wiles of an American chorus girl, Elsie Marina (MM), with the stuffy regality of a Prince Regent (Olivier) and concerned their quest for romance and/or mutual respect. Interestingly, prior to the film's production, Milton Greene fought to have musical numbers for MM incorporated into the scenario (after all, she *was* playing a chorus girl). However, Arthur Miller objected to the proposition, and the idea, unfortunately, was dropped.

*The Prince and the Showgirl* could have used some of Marilyn's musical magic. Nonetheless, it still emerges as an impeccably crafted, beautifully photographed, affecting movie. It is not one of her most entertaining films, but it is an admirable work and boasts one of Marilyn's finer performances. It was for this film that MM received several prestigious European film acting honors. As for the improbable teaming of Marilyn Monroe and Laurence Olivier, Marilyn more than held her own.

## MYRON PRINZMETAL

Dr. Myron Prinzmetal was one of Marilyn Monroe's physicians circa April 1952.

## PRODUCERS WITH WHOM MM WORKED

| | |
|---|---|
| 1. Buddy Adler | *Bus Stop* (1956) |
| 2. Robert Bassler* | *A Ticket to Tomahawk* (1950) |
| | *Let's Make It Legal* (1951) |
| 3. Julian Blaustein | *Don't Bother to Knock* (1952) |
| 4. Charles Brackett | *Niagara* (1953) |
| 5. Jules Buck | *Love Nest* (1951) |
| 6. Lester Cowan | *Love Happy* (1950) |
| 7. Armand Deutsch | *Right Cross* (1950) |
| 8. Charles Feldman | *The Seven Year Itch* (1955) |
| 9. Bert Friedlob | *The Fireball* (1950) |
| 10. Andre Hakim | *O. Henry's Full House* (1952) |
| 11. Arthur Hornblow, Jr. | *The Asphalt Jungle* (1950) |
| 12. Nunnally Johnson* | *We're Not Married* (1952) |
| | *How to Marry a Millionaire* (1953) |
| 13. Walter Morosco | *Scudda Hoo! Scudda Hay!* (1948) |
| 14. Laurence Olivier | *The Prince and the Showgirl* (1957) |
| 15. Harriet Parsons | *Clash by Night* (1952) |
| 16. Arthur Pierson | *Hometown Story* (1951) |
| 17. Harry A. Romm | *Ladies of the Chorus* (1948) |
| 18. Stanley Rubin | *River of No Return* (1954) |
| 19. Sol C. Siegel | *Monkey Business* (1952) |
| | *Gentlemen Prefer Blondes* (1953) |
| | *There's No Business Like Show Business* (1954) |
| 20. Frank Taylor | *The Misfits* (1961) |
| 21. Lamar Trotti | *As Young as You Feel* (1951) |
| 22. Jerry Wald | *Let's Make Love* (1960) |
| 23. Henry Weinstein** | *Something's Got to Give* (1962) |
| 24. Billy Wilder* | *The Seven Year Itch* (1955) |
| | *Some Like It Hot* (1959) |
| 25. Sol Wurtzel | *Dangerous Years* (1947) |
| 26. Darryl F. Zanuck | *All About Eve* (1950) |

*Produced more than one movie with Marilyn Monroe
**Produced Marilyn's last, incomplete film, *Something's Got to Give* (1962)

## ROGER L. PROVOST

On February 6, 1953, Marilyn Monroe selected Roger L. Provost as "The Boy with Whom She Would Most Like To Be Cast Adrift." At the time, Provost was an eighteen-year-old seaman aboard the U.S.S. *Taconic*.

## JULIET PROWSE

Born in South Africa in 1937, Juliet Prowse was a Hollywood actress/dancer who went on to become a headliner in Las Vegas. In the early 1960s, it was Juliet Prowse whom Frank Sinatra had "left" Marilyn Monroe for.

### *PUBLIC PROPERTY*

Written by Roger Newman and presented by Carol Gould, *Public Property* was a play about the last three years in the life of Marilyn Monroe. The play was staged at the Young Vic Theatre and the Hampstead Theatre in London, circa 1978–79. The part of MM was played by Jane Francis.

*Public Property* was formerly known under the title *The Hardest Part of It*, which had been staged in New York, circa 1977–78.

### PUBLICISTS: THE PRESS AGENTS WHO REPRESENTED MM

**The Personal Publicists**

Rupert Allan
Frank Goodman
Patricia Newcomb
John Springer
Lois Weber

**The Studio/Movie Publicists**

Ernest Anderson
Harry Brand
Roy Craft
Bob Lewin
Perry Lieber
Harry Mines
Frank Neill
Sheldon Roskin
Sonia Wolfson

### AL PUCCI

Al Pucci was a photographer who was present at the press conference in which Marilyn Monroe and Arthur Miller announced their plans to marry.

### EMILIO PUCCI

In the latter part of her life, one of Marilyn's favorite fashion designers was Emilio Pucci. In fact, she was buried in her favorite Pucci dress.

### MADELYN PUGH

Madelyn Pugh was one of the three writers responsible for the "Ricky's Movie Offer" segment of "I Love Lucy," in which Lucille Ball impersonated Marilyn Monroe.

## *QUICK* MAGAZINE

As early as November 19, 1951, the *Quick* magazine news weekly put Marilyn Monroe on its cover and lauded her as "the new Jean Harlow." The accompanying article went on to call MM "the most striking new property in Hollywood."

## JACK QUINN

"Jack Quinn" (an alias) was an alleged, mysterious informant who contacted Bob Slatzer in August 1972 and revealed what could be pertinent information regarding the cover-up of the death of Marilyn Monroe. According to Quinn, the original police report contained 723 pages of documentation—which was subsequently edited down to a mere 54 pages. The complete report, according to Quinn, contained testimony by Robert Kennedy in which Kennedy admitted to having been at Marilyn's Brentwood home on the afternoon of her death. The alleged deposition also contended that an argument had ensued between Kennedy and Marilyn and that Marilyn was sedated with an injection of phenobarbital. Quinn also told Slatzer that Peter Lawford, in his deposition, had "lied through his teeth," as had Mrs. Eunice Murray.

Unfortunately, however, after his meeting with Bob Slatzer, the mysterious Jack Quinn mysteriously disappeared. He hasn't been heard from since.

## QUOTING MARILYN

> "My arrival in school, with painted lips and darkened brows, started everybody buzzing. Why I was a siren, I hadn't the faintest idea. I didn't want to be kissed, and I didn't dream of being seduced by a duke or a movie star. The truth was that with all my lipstick and mascara and precocious curves, I was as unresponsive as a fossil. But I seemed to affect people quite otherwise."
>
> MM to Ben Hecht
> on the student Norma Jeane

> "Jim's such a wonderful person. I want to marry him, but I don't know anything about sex. Can we get married without having sex?"
>
> Norma Jeane to Grace Goddard
> on Jim Dougherty

> "I used to think as I looked out on the Hollywood night—there must be thousands of girls sitting alone like me, dreaming of becoming a movie star. But I'm not going to worry about them. I'm dreaming the hardest."
>
> MM on her early aspirations

> "My marriage brought me neither happiness nor pain. My husband and I hardly spoke to each other. This wasn't because we were angry. We had nothing to say."
>
> MM on her marriage to Jim Dougherty

"To me, she was just that red-haired woman."

MM on her mother

"You sit alone. It's night outside. Automobiles roll down Sunset Boulevard like an endless string of beetles. Their rubber tires make a purring high-class noise. You're hungry, and you say, 'It's not good for my waistline to eat.' There's nothing finer than a washboard belly."

MM on her struggling years

COURTESY OF LEO AND FRANCES CALOIA

"When you're a failure in Hollywood, that's like starving to death outside a banquet hall, with smells of filet mignon driving you crazy."

"I was never used to being happy, so that wasn't something I ever took for granted. You see, I was brought up differently from the average American child because the average child is brought up expecting to be happy."

"No one ever told me I was pretty when I was a little girl. All little girls should be told they're pretty, even if they aren't."

"I think if other girls know how bad I was when I started they'll be encouraged. I finally made up my mind I wanted to be an actress and I was not going to let my lack of confidence ruin my chances."

"There were dozens of us on the set, bit players, with a gesture to make and a line or two to recite. A few were young and had nice bosoms; but I knew they were different from me. They didn't have my illusions. My illusions didn't have anything to do with being a fine actress. I knew how third-rate I was. I could actually feel my lack of talent, as if it were cheap clothes I was wearing inside. But, my God, how I wanted to learn, to change, to improve! I didn't want anything else. Not men, not money, not love, but the ability to act."

"I strove to look like Betty Grable, but I thought Alice Faye had more class to her looks."

"My first contract with 20th Century-Fox was like my first vaccination. It didn't take."

QUESTION: If 50 percent of the experts in Hollywood said you had no talent and should give up, what would you do?

MM: Look, if 100 percent told me that, all 100 percent would be wrong.

MM to a friend, circa late 1940s

"I will do whatever you tell me."

MM to Natasha Lytess, upon their first meeting, 1948

"I kept driving past the theatre with my name on the marquee. Was I excited. I wished they were using 'Norma Jeane' so that all the kids at the home and schools who never noticed me could see it."

MM on the release of *Ladies of the Chorus,* 1948

"In Hollywood a girl's virtue is much less important than her hairdo. You're judged by how you look, not by what you are. Hollywood's a place where they'll pay you a thousand dollars for a kiss, and fifty cents for your soul. I know, because I turned down the first offer often enough and held out for the fifty cents."

"I hear you're looking for a sexy blonde to play with the Marx Brothers. Would you like to see me? I'm blonde and I'm sexy."

MM to Lester Cowan on the casting of *Love Happy,* 1949

THE T. R. FOGLI COLLECTION

"I think cheesecake helps call attention to you. Then you can follow through and prove yourself."

"I think cheesecake helps call attention to you. Then you can follow through and prove yourself."

MM to Bob Thomas, 1951

"People ask me if I am going on making cheesecake pictures now that I'm a star. My answer is that as long as there is a boy in Korea who wants a pinup of me, I'll go on posing for them."

MM to Hedda Hopper, 1952

Reporter: Didn't you have anything on?
MM: Oh yes. I had the radio on.

MM, when asked about posing for her nude calendar

"Wouldn't it be nice to be like men, just getting notches in your belt, having affairs with the most atttractive men . . . and not getting emotionally involved?"

MM to Shelley Winters

"You would think all other women kept their bodies in vaults."

MM, after causing a scandal
for wearing a low-cut dress, 1952

"I always thought that movie stars were exciting and talented people, full of special personality. Meeting one of them at a party I discover usually that he (or she) is colorless and even frightened. I've often stood silent at a party for hours listening to my movie idols turn into dull and little people."

"It isn't necessary to use your voice in any special way [to sound sexy]. If you think something sexy the voice just naturally goes along."

"I've given pure sex appeal very little thought. If I had to think about it, I'm sure it would frighten me."

"What do I wear in bed? Why, Chanel No. 5, of course."

MM to Sidney Skolsky, 1952

"It's like salt on a steak. All you need is a little bit of it."

MM on jealousy, 1952

"If I am a star, the people made me a star. No studio, no person, but the people did."

"A photographer once told me that my two best points are between my waist and my neck."

"I feel wonderful. I'm incorporated!"

MM, 1955

"My fan is caught in the door."

MM, *The Seven Year Itch*, 1955

"I think you're just elegant."

MM to Tom Ewell, *The Seven Year Itch*, 1955

"I've fallen in love with Brooklyn. I'm going to buy a little house in Brooklyn and live there. I'll go to the coast only when I have to make a picture."

MM, July 1955

"I am not interested in money. I just want to be wonderful."

"I want to continue my growth in every way."

"I used to get the feeling, and sometimes I still get it, that I was fooling somebody—I don't know who or what—maybe myself. I have feelings some days when there are scenes with a lot of responsiblity, and I'll wish, gee, if only I would have been a cleaning woman."

"Even though I was born there, I still can't think of one good thing to say about it. If I close my eyes, and picture LA, all I see is one big varicose vein."

MM to Truman Capote
on Los Angeles, 1955

"Everybody says I can't act. They said the same thing about Elizabeth Taylor. And they were wrong. She was great in *A Place in the Sun*. I'll never get the right part, anything I really want. My looks are against me. They're too specific."

MM to Truman Capote

"I've always known Errol [Flynn] zigzagged. I have a masseur, he's practically my sister, and he was Tyrone Power's masseur, and he told me all about the thing Errol and Ty Power had going."

MM to Truman Capote

"Dogs never bite me. Just humans."

MM to Truman Capote

"They've said I want to direct pictures. I couldn't direct traffic."

MM to Earl Wilson, 1955

"I don't mind this being a man's world—as long as I can be a woman in it."

"I wanna guy I can look up to . . . I just gotta feel that whoever I marry has some real regard for me, aside from all that loving stuff."

MM in *Bus Stop,* 1956

"I like actors very much, but to marry one would be like marrying your brother. You look too much alike in the mirror."

"I don't consider myself an intellectual. And this is not one of my aims. But I admire intellectual people."

"A woman can't be alone. She needs a man. A man and a woman support and strengthen each other. She just can't do it by herself."

"A career is wonderful, but you can't curl up with it on a cold night."

"The most unsatisfactory men are those who pride themselves on their virility and regard sex as if it were some form of athletics at which you win cups. It is a woman's spirit and mood a man has to stimulate in order to make sex interesting. The real lover is the man who can thrill you just by touching your head or smiling into your eyes or by just staring into space."

"Johnny Hyde was wonderful, but he was not my Svengali. Milton Greene was not my Svengali . . . I'm nobody's slave and never have been . . . Now they write that Lee Strasberg is my Svengali . . . and Arthur Miller isn't my Svengali."

THE RAY VAN GOEYE COLLECTION
"A photographer once told me that my two best points are between my waist and my neck."

"Why haven't I the right to grow and expand like everybody else?"

"I hope you will all forgive me. It wasn't my fault. I've been sick all through the picture. Please, please, don't hold it against me."
MM, to the cast and crew of *The Prince and the Showgirl,* 1956

"I'm not going back into that film until Wilder reshoots my opening. When Marilyn Monroe comes into a room, nobody's going to be looking at Tony Curtis playing Joan Crawford. They're going to be looking at Marilyn Monroe."
MM, after walking off the set of *Some Like It Hot,* 1958

"Some of those bastards in Hollywood wanted me to drop Arthur. Said it would ruin my career. They're born cowards and want you to be like them. One reason I want to see Kennedy win is that Nixon's associated with that whole scene."
MM to W. J. Weatherby, circa 1960

"I want him to direct me again. But he's doing the Lindbergh story next. And he won't let me play Lindbergh."
MM, following her "feud" with Billy Wilder, 1960

"What am I afraid of? Do I think I can't act? I know I can act, but I am afraid. I am afraid and I should not be and I must not be."
a notation made in MM's notebook while making *Let's Make Love, 1960*

"Doesn't he look like Joe?"

MM to Lena Pepitone on Yves Montand, 1960

"No, I'm Mitzi Gaynor."

MM to an extra on the set of *The Misfits* who asked her, "Are you Marilyn Monroe?", 1960

"Remember now, cheers, no tears. . . ."

MM to the cast at the completion of *The Misfits* shooting, 1960

"As of today, I have absolutely no regrets. I think I am a mature person now who can take things in stride. I'm grateful for people in my past. They helped me get to where I am, wherever that is. But now, I'm thinking for myself and sitting in on all business transactions."

MM, 1961

"The reality is very different—it's better to be unhappy alone than unhappy with someone—so far."

"Arthur [Miller] and I are finished. Arthur saw the demon in me . . . a lot of people like to think of me as innocent, so that's the way I behave to them . . . if they saw the demon in me they would hate me . . . I'm more than one person, and I act differently each time . . . most of the time I'm not the person I'd like to be—certainly *not* a dumb blonde like they say I am; a sex freak with big boobs."

MM to Jack Cardiff

"I'm looking forward to eventually becoming a marvelous—excuse the word *marvelous*—character actress. Like Marie Dressler, like Will Rogers."

"I don't know if high society is different in other cities, but in Hollywood important people can't stand to be invited someplace that isn't full of other important people. They don't mind a few unfamous people being present because they make good listeners. But if a star or studio chief or any other great movie personages find themselves sitting among a lot of nobodies, they get frightened—as if somebody was trying to demote them."

"An actor is supposed to be a sensitive instrument. Isaac Stern takes good care of his violin. What if everybody jumped on his violin?"

"It seems to me it's time they stopped knocking their assets around."

MM, upon being fired from Fox, 1962

"I've never been in a Hollywood fight or feud. I have the most wonderful memory for forgetting things."

MM to Sidney Skolsky

"I am trying to prove to myself that I am a person. Then maybe I'll convince myself that I am an actress."

MM, 1962

"I have a very big head, you know. Nothing in it, of course, but a big head."

MM, joking to a hat maker, 1962

THE T. R. FOGLI COLLECTION

"Payne Whitney gives me a pain. It was obviously an error in judgment to place me in Payne Whitney. The doctor who recommended it realized it and tried to rectify it."

MM, on committing herself
to the Payne Whitney Clinic

"My travels have always been of the same kind. No matter where I've gone or why I've gone there it ends up that I never see anything. Becoming a movie star is living on a merry-go-round. When you travel you take the merry-go-round with you. You don't see natives or new scenery. You see chiefly the same press agents, the same sort of interviewers, and the same picture layouts of yourself."

"I always sleep with my mouth open. I know because it's open when I wake up."

"I never quite understood it—this sex symbol—I always thought symbols were those things you clash together! That's the trouble, a sex symbol is a thing. But if I'm going to be the symbol of something, I'd rather have it sex than some other things they've got symbols of!"

"It's nice to be included in people's fantasies, but you also like to be accepted for your own sake."

MM, 1962

"Please believe me, it was not my doing . . . I so looked forward to working with you."

MM to the cast and crew of *Something's Got to Give*, 1962

"Can you imagine me as first lady?"

MM to Bob Slatzer, 1962

"How can I learn something about the most famous philosophers in a few hours? I'm going to a party tonight and I want to be able to hold my own."

MM to Dr. G. W. Campbell, circa 1962

"I have never been very good at being a member of any group—more than a group of two, that is."

MM, 1962

"I never intentionally mean to hurt anyone, but you can't be too nice to people you work with, else they will trample you to death."

MM to James Bacon

"I used to say to myself, 'What the devil have you got to be proud about, Marilyn Monroe?' And I'd answer, 'Everything, everything,' and I'd walk slowly and turn my head slowly as if I were a queen."

"I don't mind being burdened with being glamorous and sexual. But what goes with it can be a burden. We are all born sexual creatures, thank God, but it's a pity so many people despise and crush this natural gift."

"Fame will go by and, so long, I've had you, fame. If it goes by, I've always known it was fickle."

MM, 1962

"I feel as though it's all happening to someone right next to me. I'm close, I can feel it, I can hear it, but it isn't really me."

MM on her fame, 1962

COURTESY OF CINEMA COLLECTORS

"But fame is not really for a daily diet, that's not what fulfills you. It warms you a bit, but the warming is temporary."

"I think that when you are famous every weakness is exaggerated."

"I don't look at myself as a commodity, but I'm sure a lot of people have. Including, well, one corporation in particular, which shall be nameless."

"I think I have one talent. I think it's observing. I hope that it adds up to acting. I hope to put it to good use."

"My work is the only ground I've ever had to stand on. To put it bluntly, I seem to have a whole superstructure with no foundation. But I'm working on the foundation."

"Thirty six is great when kids twelve to seventeen still whistle."
MM, when asked about her age, 1962

"I'm a failure as a woman. My men expect so much of me because of the image they've made of me and that I've made of myself, as a sex symbol. Men expect so much, and I can't live up to it. They expect bells to ring and whistles to whistle, but my anatomy is the same as any other woman's. I can't live up to it."
MM to Peter Levathes, 1962

"If I'd observed all the rules, I'd never have got anywhere."

"It might be kind of a relief to be finished."

"Please don't make me a joke. End the interview with what I believe. I don't mind making jokes, but I don't want to look like one. I want to be an artist, an actress with integrity."

Interviewer: Are you happy?
MM: Let's put it this way. I'm slim."

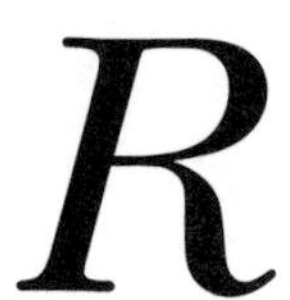

### PEGGY RABE

In March 1952, Joe DiMaggio and David March double-dated at the Villa Nova Restaurant on Sunset Boulevard in Hollywood. DiMaggio's date, of course, was Marilyn Monroe. It was their first meeting. March's date was actress Peggy Rabe.

### MARK RABWIN

On April 28, 1952, Dr. Mark Rabwin, a Beverly Hills surgeon, removed Marilyn Monroe's appendix at Cedars of Lebanon Hospital in Los Angeles.

### THE RACQUET CLUB

In 1949, the Racquet Club was an elite Palm Springs, California, gathering site, which was managed by silent film idol Charlie Farrell. It was here that Marilyn Monroe first met agent Johnny Hyde. It was also here that Hyde suffered his fatal heart attack, on December 17, 1950.

### RADIO

☆ Marilyn Monroe made her first radio broadcast in 1946 on an interview program for KFI radio station in Los Angeles. Marilyn was a model at that time and was known as Norma Jeane Dougherty. Present on that day was photographer/cinematographer Leo Caloia, who had the eye to recognize Norma Jeane's blossoming beauty and potential. Over *forty* years later some of his very rare photographs have been reprinted here, with his permission.

COURTESY OF LEO AND FRANCES CALOIA

Leo Caloia photographing model Norma Jeane.

ALL PHOTOS COURTESY OF LEO AND FRANCES CALOIA

☆ Marilyn made her radio dramatic debut on NBC Radio's "Hollywood Star Playhouse" on August 31, 1952. Marilyn's segment was entitled "Statement in Full."

☆ In November 1952, Marilyn guested on the Edgar Bergen–Charlie McCarthy radio program.

☆ On December 18, 1956, following her return from the overseas shooting of *The Prince and the Showgirl*, Marilyn did a radio broadcast from the Waldorf-Astoria Hotel in New York.

**RADIO CITY MUSIC HALL**
New York City landmark where the premiere of *The Prince and the Showgirl* was held on June 13, 1957.

**THE RADIO PLANE COMPANY**
Circa 1943–44, young Norma Jeane Dougherty got a job at the Radio Plane Company defense plant in Burbank, California. The company was owned by actor Reginald Denny. Norma Jeane got the job through the influence of her mother-in-law, Ethel Dougherty, who worked at Radio Plane as a nurse. It was Norma Jeane's first job.

Norma Jeane proved to be such a hard worker that she was awarded with an "E" certificate from her employers—for excellence on the job. It was also at Radio Plane that Norma Jeane received an award of another kind. It was here that she was "discovered" by army photographer David Conover, who had been assigned to shoot photos of women at work for *Yank* magazine. Conover, naturally, selected Norma Jeane as his model and set her on the road to future fame.

Interestingly, after Norma Jeane quit Radio Plane and divorced Jim Dougherty, Jim took himself a second bride. Her name was Pat, and she was also an employee of the Radio Plane Company.

Years later, Marilyn Monroe had the following to say about her tenure at Radio Plane:

> "It was the Radio Plane Company, and I first had a job inspecting parachutes—not the kind of parachutes a life depends on, the little parachutes they use to float down the targets after the gunners are through with them. That was before I worked in the 'dope' room, the hardest work I've ever done. The fuselage and various parts of the ship were made of cloth at that time—they use metal now—and we used to paint the cloth with a stiffening preparation. It wasn't sprayed on; it was worked in with brushes, and it was very tiring and difficult. We used a quick-drying preparation—a type of lacquer, I guess, but heavier—the smell was overpowering, very hard to take for eight hours a day. It was actually a twelve-hour day for the other workers, but I only did eight because I was underage. After the cloth dried, we sanded it down to glossy smoothness."

**GEORGE RAFT**
George Raft (1895–1980), born George Ranft, was more famous for his alleged connections to the underworld than for his rather dubious skills as an actor. Among Raft's pictures were *Scarface* (1932), *Bolero* (1934), *The Glass Key* (1935), and *Each Dawn I Die* (1939). In 1959, Raft appeared in the Billy Wilder smash comedy, *Some Like It Hot*, which starred Marilyn Monroe.

### *RAIN*

Marilyn Monroe planned to make her television dramatic debut in W. Somerset Maugham's *Rain*. She was expected to tape the special in the spring of 1961. Fredric March and Florence Eldredge were tentatively set to play the Reverend Davidson and his wife.

However, complications arose when NBC refused to grant Marilyn's request that it hire Lee Strasberg to direct. When Marilyn remained adamant that Lee Strasberg, and only Lee Strasberg, be hired to direct the production, NBC shelved the project. Marilyn turned down the then astronomical sum of $125,000 and remained loyal to her teacher.

If Marilyn Monroe *had* made the film, it would have been the fourth time that the W. Somerset Maugham story had been produced by Hollywood. It was made initially as *Sadie Thompson* in 1928, with Gloria Swanson; four years later, Joan Crawford played the same role in *Rain*; and then, in 1953, Rita Hayworth played it as *Miss Sadie Thompson*.

### PRINCE RAINIER

Princess Marilyn instead of Princess Grace? It could have been. Reportedly, it was Aristotle Onassis, part owner of the principality of Monaco, who encouraged Prince Rainier III to marry a Hollywood movie star to lend Monaco some added glamour. The rather amazing story contends that Onassis consulted George Schlee, who approached Gardner Cowles, the publisher of *LOOK* magazine. According to Cowles (who knew Marilyn), Schlee approached him with the proposition that Marilyn Monroe marry Prince Rainier. When Cowles told Marilyn of this royal request, he asked her if she thought that the prince would want to marry her. Said MM, "Give me two days alone with him, and of course he'll want to marry me."

However, at that time, Marilyn was intent on marrying Arthur Miller. And, as history would have it, Marilyn never met Rainier, who, of course, went on to marry Grace Kelly.

Interestingly, shortly after this proposition, Marilyn Monroe formed her own production company. The first film made by Marilyn Monroe Productions was *The Prince and the Showgirl*.

### WALTER RAMAGE

In 1960, Walter Ramage was the manager of the Mapes Hotel in Reno, where the company of *The Misfits* resided. It was Ramage who saw to the needs of Marilyn Monroe, Arthur Miller, Clark Gable, Montgomery Clift, John Huston, et al.

### TONY RANDALL

Born Leonard Rosenberg on February 26, 1920, actor Tony Randall is best known for his light film comedies from the late 1950s to the mid-1960s, as well as for his successful television ventures, "Mr. Peepers" (1952–1955) and "The Odd Couple" (1970–1974).

In 1960, Randall appeared in *Let's Make Love*, which starred Marilyn Monroe. Randall's other films include *Will Success Spoil Rock Hunter?* (1957), *Pillow Talk* (1959), and *Send Me No Flowers* (1964).

**RAPE**

As she rose to stardom, Marilyn Monroe told many people, including several reporters, that she had been raped as a child. As was customary for her, Marilyn told varying stories to different people. Thus, it is impossible to ascertain when, where, how, and by whom she was raped—if indeed she was raped at all. Nevertheless, some of the accounts are as follows:

☆ At age six, she was raped by a friend of the family.
☆ At age seven, a Mr. Litman penetrated Norma Jeane with his finger. Litman was a boarder at one of the foster homes Norma Jeane lived at.
☆ At age eight, she was molested by a boarder at one of the foster homes.
☆ At age eight, she was molested by a Mr. Kimmel, a boarder at one of the foster homes.
☆ At age eight, she was raped by a Mr. K. It was because of this violation that she began to stammer.
☆ Before moving in with Grace Goddard, Norma Jeane was raped by a foster parent. She became pregnant.
☆ At age eleven, she was raped by a boarder at one of the foster homes.
☆ After being caught stealing fruit, a grocery store manager forced her to give him oral sex.
☆ At age twelve, she was beaten and raped by an artist.

Also, in the summer of 1947, while living with a family in Burbank, Marilyn claimed that an off-duty policeman attempted to rape her. The attempted rape was subsequently reported in *The Hollywood Citizen-News*.

**GLADYS RASMUSSEN**

Gladys Rasmussen was Marilyn Monroe's longtime hairdresser at 20th Century-Fox.

**TERENCE RATTIGAN**

Sir Terence Rattigan (1912–1977) was the British playwright of *The Sleeping Prince*, which he adapted into *The Prince and the Showgirl* (1957) as a film vehicle for Laurence Olivier and Marilyn Monroe.

**OLLIE AND JOE RAUH**

From May 13 to May 24, 1957, Arthur and Marilyn Miller lived in the Washington, D.C., home of Ollie and Joe Rauh. It was during the difficult period when Arthur Miller was being tried by the House Un-American Activities Sub-Committee.

**JOHNNIE RAY**

John Alvin Ray was born January 10, 1927, in Dallas, Oregon. In 1951, he attained fame with a song called "Cry," which showcased his unique singing style. Three years later, Ray made an appearance in the film *There's No Business Like Show Business*, which costarred Marilyn Monroe.

**JANET RAYMOND**

Marilyn Monroe collector Janet Raymond gained some notoriety in the press when she professed to be the long-lost daughter of MM. According to Miss Raymond, who is an orphan, she was born while Marilyn Monroe was at Cedars of Lebanon Hospital in 1952, when Marilyn was supposedly having an appendectomy. However, Miss Raymond has not been able to substantiate her claim.

**RAYVE SHAMPOO**

During the release of *Love Nest* in 1951, Marilyn Monroe appeared in a print advertisement for Rayve Shampoo. The ad read:

> Charming blonde Marilyn Monroe keeps her hair bright and beautiful with Rayve Shampoo. "Such a wonderful shampoo! It leaves my hair so shining soft, so easy to curl! My hair just sparkles with life and light after a Rayve shampoo!" says lovely Marilyn Monroe. "That creamy-rich Rayve lather is so gentle, so wonderfully cleansing, that my hair falls right into the softest, prettiest waves! This limp-wave test proves it!" Marilyn Monroe says, "Shampoo with Rayve at the very tag-end of your permanent, when your wave's at its lowest ebb! See how Rayve revives even a limp wave—washes new sparkle into your hair!" Get a tube or jar of Rayve Creme Shampoo today . . . see how it makes even a tired wave *want* to curl!

**RCA RECORDS**

In October 1953, Marilyn Monroe signed a recording contract with RCA Records. It was because of this contract that Marilyn's voice was *not* recorded on the soundtrack of *There's No Business Like Show Business* (Decca Records, 1954). And, although MM never recorded an album for RCA, she did cut three singles in 1954. They were:

1. "I'm Going to File My Claim"
   "River of No Return"
   April 9, 1954
2. "You'd be Surprised"
   "Heat Wave"

THE SABIN GRAY COLLECTION

MM signs RCA recording contract, 1953.

"Lazy"
"After You Get What You Want You Don't Want It"
December 10, 1954

3. "A Fine Romance"
"She Acts Like a Woman Should"
September 3, 1954 (not released)

**RONALD REAGAN**

Indirectly, President Ronald Reagan was responsible for the "discovery" of Marilyn Monroe. It was 1945. At that time, Reagan was photographer David Conover's commanding officer. Thus, it was Reagan who instructed Conover to shoot photos of women working to aid the war effort at the Radio Plane Company in California.

THE RAY VAN GOEYE COLLECTION

Ronald Reagan, circa 1954.

**JOHN RECHY**

John Rechy penned the 1987 novel about Marilyn Monroe's would-be daughter entitled, appropriately, *Marilyn's Daughter.* Rechy is the former Times Square hustler turned author, whose best-selling books include *City of Night* (1963), *The Sexual Outlaw* (1977), and *Bodies and Souls* (1983).

**THE RECORDS: A MM DISCOGRAPHY**

**Albums**

1. *Marilyn Monroe*
Label: ASCOT
Date: 1962
Songs included:
"I Wanna Be Loved by You"
"River of No Return"
"I'm Through with Love"
"Running Wild"
Other Instrumental Selections from MM's Movies

2. *Marilyn*
   Label: 20th Century-Fox Records
   Date: 1963
   Songs included:
   "Heat Wave"
   "Lazy"
   "After You Get What You Want You Don't Want It"
   "One Silver Dollar"
   "I'm Going To File My Claim"
   "River of No Return"
   "A Little Girl from Little Rock"
   "When Love Goes Wrong"
   "Diamonds Are a Girl's Best Friend"
   "Bye Bye Baby"

3. *Marilyn*
   Label: 20th Century-Fox Records
   Date: 1964 Reissue of Album #2

4. *The Unforgettable Marilyn Monroe*
   Label: Movietone Records (A Division of 20th Century-Fox Records)
   Date: 1967 Reissue of Album #2

5. *Remember Marilyn*
   Label: 20th Century-Fox Records
   Date: 1972 Reissue of Album #2

6. *La Voce, Le Musiche e i Films of Marilyn Monroe*
   Label: RCA (Italian)
   Date: 1974
   Songs included:
   "You'd Be Surprised"
   "A Fine Romance"
   "Bye Bye Baby"
   "I'm Going to File My Claim"
   "My Heart Belongs to Daddy"
   "Heat Wave"
   "River of No Return"
   "She Acts Like a Woman Should"
   "Kiss"
   "After You Get What You Want You Don't Want It"
   "Diamonds Are a Girl's Best Friend"
   "Lazy"

7. *The Voice, Songs and Films of Marilyn Monroe*
   Label: RCA
   Date: 1976 Reissue of Album #6

8. *The Story of Marilyn Monroe*
   Label: Oxford Records (Italy)
   Date: 1976
   Songs included: Same as Album #2
   "Heat Wave"
   "Lazy"
   "After You Get What You Want You Don't Want It"
   "One Silver Dollar"
   "I'm Going To File My Claim"
   "River of No Return"
   "A Little Girl from Little Rock"

"When Love Goes Wrong"
"Diamonds Are a Girl's Best Friend"
"Bye Bye Baby"

9. *Marilyn Monroe: Never Before and Never Again*
   Label: Stet Records
   Date: 1978

   Songs included:
   "Do It Again"
   "Kiss"
   "This Is a Fine Romance"
   "You'd Be Surprised"
   "She Acts Like a Woman Should"
   "Heat Wave"
   "Happy Birthday, Mr. President"
   "Diamonds Are a Girl's Best Friend"
   "A Little Girl from Little Rock"
   "Bye Bye Baby"
   "A Little Girl from Little Rock" Reprise
   "When Love Goes Wrong"

10. *Marilyn Monroe: Rare Recordings 1948–1962*
   Label: Sandy Hook Records
   Date: 1979

   Songs included:
   "A Fine Romance"
   "She Acts Like a Woman Should"
   "You'd Be Surprised"
   "That Old Black Magic"
   "Down in the Meadow"
   "I Found a Dream"
   "Anyone Can See I Love You"
   "Every Baby Needs a Da-Da-Daddy"
   "Some Like It Hot"
   "Kiss"
   Scene from *Love Happy* with Groucho Marx
   Royal Triton commercial for Union Oil (1950)
   "River of No Return"
   "The Jack Benny Show" ("Bye Bye Baby"), Sept. 13, 1953
   Korea ("Diamonds Are a Girl's Best Friend")
   Scenes from *How to Marry a Millionaire*
   Scenes from *The Seven Year Itch*
   "A Man Chases a Girl" (with Donald O'Connor)
   Accepting 1952 Photoplay Award from Lauren Bacall
   Scenes from *Something's Got to Give*
   Press conference for *Bus Stop* on her return to Hollywood
   "You'd Be Surprised" (Another recorded version)
   "Happy Birthday, Mr. President"
   "A Little Girl from Little Rock"

11. *The Voice, Songs, and Films of Marilyn Monroe*
   Label: RCA
   Date: 1984 Reissue of Album #6.

12. *Marilyn Monroe: Diamonds Are a Girl's Best Friend*
   Label: NCB Records (Denmark)
   Date: 1985

Songs included:
"Heat Wave"
"Lazy"
"After You Get Want You Want You Don't Want It"
"You'd Be Surprised"
"A Fine Romance"
"One Silver Dollar"
"River of No Return"
"I'm Going To File My Claim"
"A Little Girl from Little Rock"
"When Love Goes Wrong"
"Diamonds Are a Girl's Best Friend"
"Bye Bye Baby"

13. *Marilyn Monroe: Greatest Hits*
Label: Neon Records (Belgium)
Date: 1986
Songs included:
"My Heart Belongs to Daddy"
"Diamonds Are a Girl's Best Friend"
"River of No Return"
"I'm Going To File My Claim"
"Bye Bye Baby"
"After You Get What You Want You Don't Want It"
"One Silver Dollar"
"Heat Wave"
"When I Fall in Love"
"Specialization"

14. *Marilyn Monroe: The Best from Her Movies*
Label: Lotus Records (Italy)
Date: 1986
Songs included:
"Bye Bye Baby"
"Diamonds Are a Girl's Best Friend"
"When Love Goes Wrong"
"A Fine Romance"
"She Acts Like a Woman Should"
"Specialization"
"When I Fall in Love"
"Heat Wave"
"River of No Return"
"After You Get What You Want You Don't Want It"
"I'm Going To File My Claim"
"You'd Be Surprised"
"Lazy"
"My Heart Belongs to Daddy"
"A Little Girl from Little Rock"
"Kiss"

15. *Marilyn Monroe: The Legend Lives On*
Label: Picture Disc
Date: 1986
Songs included:
"Diamonds Are a Girl's Best Friend"
"Bye Bye Baby"
"River of No Return"
"Heat Wave"

"After You Get What You Want You Don't Want It"
"I'm Going To File My Claim"
"One Silver Dollar"
"My Heart Belongs to Daddy"
"Specialization"
"When I Fall in Love"

16. *The Marilyn Monroe Collection: 20 Golden Hits*
Label: Deja Vu Records (Italy)
Date: 1986
Songs included:
"Diamonds Are a Girl's Best Friend"
"River of No Return"
"Heat Wave"
"Do It Again"
"Kiss"
"My Heart Belongs to Daddy"
"I'm Going To File My Claim"
"A Fine Romance"
"A Little Girl from Little Rock"
"Happy Birthday, Mr. President"
"After You Get What You Want You Don't Want It"
"You'd Be Surprised"
"She Acts Like a Woman Should"
"Lazy"
"When Love Goes Wrong"
"One Silver Dollar"
"Things"
"Bye Bye Baby" (duet)
"Bye Bye Baby"
"When I Fall in Love"

17. *For the First Time*
Label: Legends 1000/1
Date: No Date Available
Songs included:
"A Fine Romance"
"She Acts Like a Woman Should"
"You'd Be Surprised"
"That Old Black Magic"
"Down in the Meadow"
"I Found a Dream"
"Anyone Can See I Love You"
"Every Baby Needs a Da-Da-Daddy"
"Some Like It Hot"
"Kiss"
Scene from *Love Happy* with Groucho Marx
Royal Triton Commercial for Union Oil (1950)
"River of No Return"
"The Jack Benny Show" ("Bye Bye Baby"), Sept. 13, 1953
Korea ("Diamonds Are a Girl's Best Friend")
Scenes from *How to Marry a Millionaire*
Scenes from *The Seven Year Itch*
"A Man Chases a Girl" (with Donald O'Connor)
Accepting a *Photoplay* Award from Lauren Bacall
Scenes from *Something's Got to Give*
Press conference for *Bus Stop* on MM's return to Hollywood
"You'd Be Surprised" (another recorded version)

### Extended-Play Albums

1. *Recorded from the Soundtrack of* Gentlemen Prefer Blondes
   Label: MGM Records
   Date: 1953
   Songs included:
   "A Little Girl from Little Rock"
   "Diamonds Are a Girl's Best Friend"
   "Ain't There Anyone Here for Love?" (Jane Russell)
   "When Love Goes Wrong"
2. *Songs from* There's No Business Like Show Business
   Label: RCA Records
   Date: 1954
   Songs included:
   "You'd Be Surprised"
   "Heat Wave"
   "Lazy"
   "After You Get What You Want You Don't Want It"
3. *From the Soundtrack of* Some Like It Hot
   Label: United Artists
   Date: 1959
   Songs included:
   "Some Like It Hot"
   "Running Wild"
   "I'm Through with Love"
   "I Wanna Be Loved by You"
4. *Marilyn, Poo Poo Pa Doop*
   Label: United Artists
   Date: 1978
   Songs included:
   "I Wanna Be Loved by You"
   "Running Wild"
   "I'm Through with Love"

### Soundtrack Albums

1. *Gentlemen Prefer Blondes*
   Label: MGM Records
   Date: 1953 Reissued 1957
   Songs included:
   "Bye Bye Baby"
   "A Little Girl from Little Rock"
   "Diamonds Are a Girl's Best Friend"
   "When Love Goes Wrong"
   Other musical numbers from the show
2. *Some Like It Hot*
   Label: ASCOT (United Artists)
   Date: 1959, Reissued 1964
   Songs included:
   "Running Wild"
   "Some Like It Hot"
   "I'm Through with Love"
   "I Wanna Be Loved by You"
   Other musical numbers from the show

3. *Let's Make Love*
   Label: Columbia
   Date: 1960
   Songs included:
      "My Heart Belongs to Daddy"
      "Incurably Romantic"
      "Let's Make Love"
      "Specialization"
      Other musical numbers from the show

**Compilation Albums**

1. *Til the Clouds Roll By/Gentlemen Prefer Blondes*
   Label: MGM Records
   Date: 1957, Reissued 1972
   Songs included:
      "Bye Bye Baby"
      "A Little Girl from Little Rock"
      "Diamonds Are a Girl's Best Friend"
      "When Love Goes Wrong"
2. *More Original Soundtracks and Hit Music from Great Motion Picture Themes*
   Label: United Artists
   Date: 1961
   Songs included:
      "I Wanna Be Loved by You"
3. *Superalbum: Selections from Original Soundtracks and Scores*
   Label: ASCOT (United Artists)
   Date: 1963
   Songs included:
      "I Wanna Be Loved by You"
      "I'm Through with Love"
      "Running Wild"
4. *Hear Them Again*
   Label: Readers Digest (RCA-A 10 Album Collection)
   Date: 1968
   Songs included:
      "You'd Be Surprised"
5. *Hooray for Hollywood*
   Label: RCA
   Date: 1972
   Songs included:
      "I'm Going To File My Claim"
6. *The Edgar Bergen Show with Charlie McCarthy: With Special Guest: Marilyn Monroe (Comedy Series #13 Release #34)*
   Label: Radiola
   Date: 1974
   Included:
      Comedy Skit featuring MM
7. *Va-Va-Voom*
   Label: Rhino Records
   Date: 1985
   Songs included:
      "You'd Be Surprised"
      "Lazy"

"River of No Return"
"She Acts Like a Woman Should"
"Heat Wave"

8. *Hollywood on the Air Presents: The Feminine Touch*
   Label: Star-Tone Records
   Date: No Date Available
   Included:
   Comedy skit featuring MM, Edgar Bergen, and Charlie McCarthy

**Singles**

1. Recorded from the soundtrack of *Gentlemen Prefer Blondes*
   Label: MGM Records
   Date: 1953
   Songs:
   "Bye Bye Baby" (MM)
   "Bye Bye Baby" (Jane Russell)
2. Recorded from the Soundtrack of *River of No Return*
   Label: RCA
   Date: 1954
   Songs:
   "I'm Going To File My Claim"
   "River of No Return"
3. *Marilyn Monroe Sings*
   Label: 20th Century-Fox Records (Promotional for the album "MARILYN")
   Date: 1963
   Songs:
   "River of No Return"
   "One Silver Dollar"

**MM Trivia Quiz #37**

In what film was MM's favorite record destroyed? (Answer on page 577.)

## RECREATION

Marilyn Monroe was *not* a sports enthusiast. There were very few recreational activities that she participated in. Among the exceptions:

☆ Canoeing, with Jim Dougherty, at Pop's Willow Lake
☆ Hiking, with Jim Dougherty, in the Hollywood Hills
☆ Skiing, with Jim Dougherty, at Big Bear, circa 1942
☆ Fishing, with Jim Dougherty, at Sherwood Lake in Ventura County
☆ Horseback riding, with Jim Dougherty, in the San Fernando Valley and on Catalina Island
☆ Billiards, with Joe DiMaggio, circa 1954
☆ Golf, with Joe DiMaggio
☆ Badminton, with the Rosten family, in Long Island
☆ Bicycling, with Arthur Miller, in Central Park and on Ocean Parkway in Brooklyn

*Note:* Although she took great pride in the pool at her Brentwood home, Marilyn Monroe never swam in it.

## *THE RED HOUSE*

Before she signed her first studio contract with 20th Century-Fox in August

1946, Norma Jeane Dougherty auditioned for a film entitled *The Red House,* which was to star actor Lon McCallister. However, upon seeing Norma Jeane, the film's director rejected her by commenting: "No. Your head and Lon's head wouldn't be right together."

**THE RED ROCK DAIRY**
Dairy farm that was owned by C. Stanley Gifford, the man who was thought, by some, to be Marilyn Monroe's father. The Red Rock Dairy was located in the town of Hemet, near Palm Springs, California.

***REDBOOK* MAGAZINE**
*Redbook* was a women's magazine that was generally favorable to Marilyn Monroe. In *Redbook*'s July 1952 issue, Marilyn wrote a letter to the editor, courting the magazine's favor. The following spring, *Redbook* honored MM with its "Best Young Box Office Personality" award.

*Redbook* has published the following articles on MM:

☆ 6/52: "So Far To Go Alone"
☆ 7/55: "The Marilyn Monroe You've Never Seen"
☆ 2/58: "Marilyn Monroe's Marriage"
☆ 8/62: "Marilyn Monroe: A Good Long Look at Myself"
☆ 2/63: "Marilyn Monroe"

**FRANK REDMAN**
Frank Redman was the cinematographer of *Ladies of the Chorus* (1948), which costarred starlet Marilyn Monroe in her first movie musical.

**ALYSON REED**
Alyson Reed is the actress who portrayed MM on Broadway in the ill-fated 1983 production, *Marilyn, An American Fable.* Miss Reed later landed the coveted role of Cassie in the film version of *A Chorus Line* (1985).

Of her performance as MM, the critics said the following:

> Alyson Reed, the professional and hardworking performer cast in the title role, has precious little to do under the circumstances. In Act I, she must deliver most of her characterization with her chest and derriere. Monroe she's not, but, when she's stuffed into the famous costumes, you can squint your eyes and accept her as a Madame Tussaud's replica. Miss Reed also mimics Monroe's voice effectively—until she takes to delivering her Act II songs in a standard Broadway belt.
>
> Frank Rich, *The New York Times*

> The transformation is sensational, and Alyson Reed, playing Marilyn complete with kiss curl, pout and breathy voice, handles it with enviable aplomb. The famous still poses are almost all there, and Miss Reed freezes into them with commanding authority. This act of impersonation is almost the show's solitary virtue.
>
> Clive Barnes, *The New York Post*

**IRA REINER**

In November 1985, despite a spate of public curiosity, Ira Reiner, the LA County District Attorney, issued the following statement to the press:

> "No evidence, new or old, has been brought to our attention which would support a reasonable belief or even a bare suspicion that Ms. Monroe was murdered."

Due to Reiner's stance on the matter, the LA County Grand Jury opted not to further investigate Marilyn's death.

**MAX REINHARDT**

It was a Saturday in December 1952. The location was the Roy Goldenburg Auction Galleries in Beverly Hills. One hundred seventy-eight books, plays, and scripts, which had been annotated by the late great theatrical producer Max Reinhardt (1873–1943), were being auctioned off. There to bid for the revered manuscripts were representatives from the top universities and museums from around the country. Jake Zeitlin, a rare-book dealer, was hired by USC to purchase the books. His "opponent" in the final bidding was none other than Marilyn Monroe.

Apparently, Marilyn had been encouraged to purchase the collection by Natasha Lytess, who had once been a member of the Reinhardt acting ensemble. Marilyn prevailed in the bidding, of course, for the sum of $1,335. However, that was not to be the end of the matter. Following her "victory," Marilyn was ridiculed in the press for her "pretensions," as well as for her audacity in depriving the nation's best schools of the Reinhardt works.

The debacle finally ended when Reinhardt's son, Gottfried, contacted MM and asked if he could purchase the collection. Out of sentiment, Marilyn agreed and sold it for the price that she had paid. Much to Marilyn's chagrin, however, Gottfried turned around and sold the collection to a university for a considerable profit.

**MAY REIS**

Initially, May Reis was hired to handle the multitude of scripts that had piled up in Marilyn's East 57th Street apartment in New York City. She became Marilyn's private secretary, the manager of Marilyn's household, and Marilyn's friend. When Marilyn labored through the 1960 shooting of *The Misfits,* May Reis was at her side. And two months after Marilyn's divorce from Arthur Miller it was May Reis who accompanied MM from Columbia Presbyterian Hospital.

May Reis was also one of the few beneficiaries in Marilyn's will. She was left $10,000. However, Miss Reis did not even begin to receive her bequest until the end of 1971.

Interestingly, following her tenure with Marilyn Monroe, May Reis went on to become the secretary of Barbra Streisand. She also became politically active in demonstrating against American intervention in Vietnam.

**WALTER REISCH**

Walter Reisch (1900–1983) was the cowriter of *Niagara* (1953), which toplined Marilyn Monroe. Among Reisch's other works were *Ninotchka* (1939), *Titanic* (for which he won a 1952 Oscar), and *The Girl in the Red Velvet Swing* (1955).

**RELIGION**

- ☆ Marilyn Monroe's only solid religious affiliation was with the Christian Science Church, which she was introduced to by her Aunt Ana Lower. Norma Jeane/Marilyn was a member of this church for an eight-year period.
- ☆ Upon marrying Arthur Miller in 1956, MM converted from Protestantism to Judaism.
- ☆ By late 1961, following her divorce from Miller, Marilyn referred to her religion as "atheist Jew."

**LEE REMICK**

> "I feel Marilyn should have been replaced. I don't believe actors should be allowed to get away with that type of behavior."
>
> Lee Remick on MM's dismissal from Fox, 1962

> "I don't know whether to feel sorry for her or not. I feel she should have been replaced. The movie business is crumbling down around our ears because of that kind of behavior. Actors shouldn't be allowed to get away with that kind of thing."
>
> Lee Remick

> "It's a business anyway, despite all the glamour. Other people get fired from their jobs for behaving the way she did."
>
> Lee Remick

Lee Remick is, of course, the actress who tried—and failed—to replace Marilyn Monroe. When the front office at 20th Century-Fox fired Marilyn Monroe from *Something's Got to Give* in 1962, it was Lee Remick who took over Marilyn's role. However, Miss Remick herself was later dropped from the project when the film's costar, Dean Martin, refused to work with her. Ironically, it was Lee Remick who hosted the 1988 documentary tribute to MM entitled "Remembering Marilyn."

Remick made her film debut in the 1957 film *A Face in the Crowd* and most recently appeared in the 1987 television mini-series, "Nutcracker: Money, Madness, Murder."

**RENIE**

Renie was the costume designer on three of Marilyn Monroe's movies: *As Young as You Feel* (1951), *Love Nest* (1951), and *Let's Make It Legal* (1951).

**RENNA'S SALON**

As a part of her beautification treatment, Marilyn Monroe used to frequent Renna's Salon in Beverly Hills, where she received specialized facial treatments from a Dr. G. W. Campbell. Reportedly, Dr. Campbell had founded a system of keeping faces young and firm. Marilyn had a particular problem with a small pad of fat under her chin, which Dr. Campbell reduced through his treatments.

Because of her infamous tendency for lateness, Marilyn used to make (and pay for) a two-hour appointment to guarantee herself a one-hour treatment.

**RENO, NEVADA**
Location where *The Misfits* was shot in 1960.

THE SABIN GRAY COLLECTION
Arriving in Reno for shooting *The Misfits*, 1960.

**RESTAURANTS**
Marilyn Monroe's favorite Hollywood restaurants were:

☆ Chasen's
☆ La Scala
☆ Romanoff's
☆ Trader Vic's
☆ Villa Capri

Over the years, Marilyn was also seen dining at a number of restaurants located around the country, including:

Barney's Beanery, Hollywood
Bruce Wongs, Hollywood
The Christmas Tree Inn, Nevada
Club Gigi, Miami
Costello's, New York
The Country Inn, Virginia City, Nevada
DiMaggio's, San Francisco
The El Morocco, New York
The Four Seasons, New York
Googie's Beanery, Hollywood
Greenblatt's Deli, Hollywood
Jim Downey's, New York
Lawry's, Hollywood
Lucey's, Hollywood
Malibu Lodge, Los Angeles
Musso and Frank, Hollywood
Petite Couvee Restaurant, New York
The Pump Room, Chicago
Saratoga, Hollywood
Schwab's Coffee Shop, Hollywood
The Stork Club, New York
Toots Shor's, New York
The Villa Nova Restaurant, Hollywood

**MM Trivia Quiz #38**
The night before her death, MM was seen dining at what restaurant? (Answer on page 578.)

**THE RETAKE ROOM**
After she met with John Huston to discuss *The Asphalt Jungle* (1950), Marilyn went to the Retake Room Bar on Washington Boulevard in Los Angeles. She was escorted by Johnny Hyde.

**TOMMY RETTIG**
Tommy Rettig was Marilyn Monroe's twelve-year-old costar in *River of No Return* (1954). For the first three days of shooting, Tommy blatantly ignored Marilyn. This was because, as Tommy later explained, his priest had told him not to socialize with a woman like MM. Nevertheless, in time, Marilyn won Tommy over. In fact, during a break from shooting, MM and the visiting Joe DiMaggio treated the young Rettig to a fishing expedition.

Indirectly (and innocently), Rettig was partially responsible for the onset of tension between MM and Otto Preminger, the film's director. Apparently, Marilyn's coach, Natasha Lytess, had warned Tommy that he would lose his talent by the age of fourteen if he did not begin to take acting lessons to polish his "instrument." Frightened, Tommy broke out crying. When Preminger learned why Tommy was crying, he ordered Natasha off the set. Marilyn retaliated by contacting Darryl Zanuck in Hollywood, who cajoled Preminger into readmitting Natasha.

It is not known whether Tommy Rettig ever did take drama lessons, but it is known that his movie career proved to be shortlived. He did, however, star for a season or more on the TV series, "Lassie."

**THE REVIEWS**
The following is a selective collection of the movie reviews that Marilyn Monroe received during her career.

***Ladies of the Chorus* (1948)**

> One of the bright spots is Miss Monroe's singing. She is pretty and, with her pleasing voice and style, she shows promise.
>
> Tibor Krekes, *The Motion Picture Herald*

> Enough musical numbers are inserted, topped with nifty warbling of Marilyn Monroe. . . . Miss Monroe presents a nice personality in her portrayal of the burley singer.
>
> *Variety*

> Marilyn Monroe is cute and properly naive.
>
> *The Hollywood Reporter*

> Pretty girls, good songs here and there, with adequate performances, should make this lively entertainment about burlesque stand up in the dual market. There is nothing new about the story, but acting lifts it out of the mediocre class. [Note: this review referred to MM as "Merilyn Monroe."]
>
> *The Los Angeles Mirror*

***The Asphalt Jungle* (1950)**

Marilyn Monroe would fetch the wolves out of any jungle, asphalt or otherwise.

*The People*

There's a beautiful blonde, too, name of Marilyn Monroe, who plays Calhern's girlfriend, and makes the most of her footage.

Liza Wilson, *Photoplay*

Performances in this Arthur Hornblow, Jr., production are all uniformly good, render the proper color variations and other requirements. Sterling Hayden registers strongly as the hoodlum who has a rendezvous with fate. James Whitmore has another meaty role to further bolster his upcoming string. Louis Calhern is a convincing two-timing lawyer. Jean Hagen, Teresa Celli and Marilyn Monroe capably play wives, mistresses and molls.

*Film Daily*

It has taut direction, jolting pace, top acting by Louis Calhern and Marilyn Monroe.

*Quick*

***Hometown Story* (1951)**

Marilyn Monroe, Barbara Brown and Griff Barnett are up to script demands.

*Variety*

***As Young as You Feel* (1951)**

Albert Dekker is mighty amusing as a fat-headed small-business boss, Marilyn Monroe is superb as his secretary and Constance Bennett does grandly as his neglected wife.

Bosley Crowther, *The New York Times*

Curvy Marilyn Monroe is a secretary.

Frank Quinn, *The New York Daily Mirror*

***Love Nest* (1951)**

A mild variety of comedy which gets a considerable boost from the expert talents—in that line—of Frank Fay. Rarely seen, he registers here as a smoothie, glib and ultrasophisticated, handy with the correct word on the correct occasion. Leatrice Joy is also present in this number. She gives mature warmth to the proceedings. Marilyn Monroe has that other quality.

*Variety*

***Let's Make It Legal* (1951)**

Marilyn Monroe parades her shapely chassis for incidental excitement.

Frank Quinn, *The New York Daily Mirror*

An inconsistent farce that luckily has sufficient saving graces, the predominating benefit being performances by the popular and comedy-wise costars, Claudette Colbert and Macdonald Carey. . . . Marilyn Monroe is amusing in a brief role as a beautiful shapely blonde who has her eye on Zachary Scott and his millions.

Wanda Hale, *The New York Daily News*

Marilyn Monroe is voluptuously amusing as a girl on a husband hunt.

*The Hollywood Reporter*

Gorgeous Marilyn Monroe's in, flittingly. First time I've noticed her diction. It's execrable.

Philip K. Scheuer, *The Los Angeles Times*

**_Clash by Night_ (1952)**

That gorgeous example of bathing beauty art (in denim), Marilyn Monroe, is a real acting threat to the season's screen blondes. Miss Stanwyck looks remarkably youthful—though not when she's face to face with Miss Monroe, a real charmer.

Irene Thirer, *The New York Post*

While Marilyn Monroe is reduced to what is tantamount to a bit role, despite her star billing, she does manage to get over her blonde sexiness in one or two scenes, and the film could have used more of her.

*Variety*

Also on hand, in a minor role, shapely Marilyn Monroe as a fish-cannery employee who bounces around in a succession of slacks, bathing suits and sweaters.

*Time*

Before going on any further with a report on *Clash by Night,* perhaps we should mention the first full-length glimpse the picture gives us of Marilyn Monroe as an actress. The verdict is gratifyingly good. The girl has a refreshing exuberance, an abundance of girlish high spirits. She is a forceful actress, too, when crisis comes along. She has definitely stamped herself as a gifted new star, worthy of all that fantastic press ageantry. Her role here is not very big, but she makes it dominant.

Alton Cook, *The New York World Telegram & Sun*

*Clash by Night* also gives us a glimpse of Marilyn Monroe and Keith Andes, who play a pair of lovers. Both are quite handsome, but neither can act.

John McCarten, *The New Yorker*

Marilyn Monroe, who is the new blonde bombshell of Hollywood, manages to look alluring in blue jeans. She plays the secondary role of the cannery worker, Peggy, with complete assurance, and she and young Andes make their marks on the screen against the stiff competition given them by the three principals.

Kate Cameron, *The New York Daily News*

**_We're Not Married_ (1952)**

Marilyn Monroe . . . looks as though she had been carved out of cake by Michelangelo.

Otis L. Guernsey, Jr., *The New York Herald Tribune*

**_Don't Bother to Knock_ (1952)**

In *Don't Bother to Knock* at the Globe, they've thrown Marilyn Monroe into the deep dramatic waters, sink or swim, and while she doesn't really do either, you might say that she floats. With that figure, what else can she do . . . but I thought she was surprisingly good, considering her lack of dramatic seasoning and her abundance of showgirl attributes. I could be prejudiced, though.

Archer Winsten, *The New York Post*

It proves conclusively that she is the kind of big new star for which exhibitors are always asking.

Vincent Conley, *Motion Picture Herald*

All the equipment that Miss Monroe has to handle the job are a childishly blank expression and a provokingly feeble, hollow voice.

Bosley Crowther, *The New York Times*

Marilyn Monroe, whose screen roles have had little import except to show her natural physical attributes, now emerges in *Don't Bother to Knock* at the Globe as more than a sexy dame. She has good dramatic promise. Richard Widmark shares star billing . . . but fizzles in the light of the new beauty. . . . Miss Monroe's delineation of the deranged beauty is a surprise. She is completely in charge of her role, the direction of which merits praise for young Britisher Roy Baker. . . . *Don't Bother to Knock* has good pace, intriguing story and many assets—of which Marilyn Monroe is the most important.

Frank Quinn, *The New York Daily Mirror*

Miss Monroe, as the pivotal figure, only increases the uncertainty. She is supposed to be a "sick girl" and she plays the part like a sick girl. This may have the sound of praise; but when you see her you will be uneasily aware that her portrayal is reinforced by virtually no acting resources whatsoever. The paradox is that here is a woman of sensuous physical beauty who, although she arrays herself briefly in finery, conveys the overall impression of being lackluster and drab. Her voice seems as dead as her spirit.

Philip K. Scheuer, *The Los Angeles Times*

***Monkey Business* (1952)**

Marilyn Monroe garners laughs and whistles, bouncing in and out as a secretary who can't type. Typing skill, however, is the only attribute which the lady appears to be lacking in.

Janet Graves, *Photoplay*

Marilyn Monroe can look and act dumber than any of the screen's current blondes.

*The New York Daily News*

Not having seen Miss Monroe before, I know now what that's all about, and I've no dissenting opinions to offer. She disproves more than adequately the efficacy of the old stage rule about not turning one's back to the audience.

Paul V. Beckley, *The New York Herald Tribune*

***O. Henry's Full House* (1952)**

Marilyn Monroe, again as sleek as she was in *The Asphalt Jungle,* is a streetwalker of stunning proportions.

Archer Winsten, *The New York Post*

***Niagara* (1953)**

Seen from any angle, the Falls and Miss Monroe leave little to be desired by any reasonably attentive audience.

A. H. Weiler, *The New York Times*

Miss Monroe plays the kind of wife whose dress, in the words of the script, "is cut so low you can see her knees." The dress is red—the actress has very pretty knees, and she gives the kind of serpentine performance that makes the audience hate her while admiring her.

Otis Guernsey, Jr., *The New York Herald Tribune*

What lifts the film above the commonplace is its star, Marilyn Monroe.

*Time*

When she is not ridiculous, she is a tiresome bore.

*The Daily Worker*

For all the wolf calls that she gets and deserves, there is something mournful about Miss Monroe. She doesn't look happy. She lacks the pinup's cheerful grin. She seems to have lost something or to be waking up from a bad dream.

Gavin Lambert

The producers are making full use of both the grandeur of the Falls and its adjacent areas as well as the grandeur that is Marilyn Monroe. The scenic effects in both cases are superb. . . . Perhaps Miss Monroe is not the perfect actress at this point. But neither the director nor the gentlemen who handled the cameras appeared to be concerned with this. . . . They have illustrated pretty concretely that she can be seductive—even when she walks. . . . As has been noted, *Niagara* may not be the place to visit under these circumstances, but the Falls and Miss Monroe are something to see.

A. H. Weiler, *The New York Times*

Two of nature's greatest phenomena, Niagara Falls and Marilyn Monroe, get together in *Niagara* and the result is the sexiest, tingling-est, suspenseful-est film in lo, these many months. . . . Here is the greatest natural star since Jean Harlow. She has more intelligence than Harlow. She out-lures Lana. She makes any other glamour girl you care to name look house-wifely.

Ruth Waterbury, *The Los Angeles Examiner*

All the performances are competent, but Marilyn Monroe—hitherto typed as a glamour girl—easily comes off best with a surprisingly effective impersonation of a mousy maniac.

*Newsweek*

Marilyn Monroe is vulgar and faintly repulsive.

*The Monthly Film Bulletin*

***Gentlemen Prefer Blondes* (1953)**

And there is Marilyn Monroe! Zounds, boys, what a personality this one is! Send up a happy flare. At last, she is beautifully gowned, beautifully coiffed, and a wonderful crazy humor flashes from those sleepy eyes of hers.

Ruth Waterbury, *The Los Angeles Examiner*

As Lorelei Lee, Marilyn looks as delectable as a ripe peach. She also surprises with a remarkably stylish voice piping "Diamonds Are a Girl's Best Friend" in a lavish production number.

Margaret Harford, *The Los Angeles Citizen News*

As usual, Miss Monroe looks as though she would glow in the dark, and her version of the baby-faced blonde whose eyes open for diamonds and close for kisses is always amusing as well as alluring.

Otis Guernsey, Jr., *The New York Herald Tribune*

The pneumatic aspects of Marilyn Monroe and Jane Russell are examined extensively in *Gentlemen Prefer Blondes,* and while it is plain that both ladies are most pleasantly configured, it is also apparent that neither of them have more than a glancing acquaintance with the business of acting.

John McCarten, *The New Yorker*

It is an empty and graceless remake of a fair to middling musical that only comes alive when Marilyn Monroe and Jane Russell stop talking and start wiggling.

Hollis Alpert, *Saturday Review*

***How to Marry a Millionaire* (1953)**

Certain for audience favor is Miss Monroe's stock delivery of the blond stigmatism who almost goes through life bumping into things, including men, because she thinks glasses would detract.

*Variety*

It is particularly noteworthy that Miss Monroe has developed more than a small amount of comedy polish of the foot-in-mouth type.

Archer Winsten, *The New York Post*

The big question, "How does Marilyn Monroe look stretched across a broad screen?" is easily answered. If you insisted on sitting in the front row, you would probably feel as though you were being smothered in baked Alaska. From any normal vantage point, though, her magnificent proportions are as appealing as ever, and her stint as a deadpan comedienne is as nifty as her looks. Playing a nearsighted charmer who won't wear glasses when men are around, she bumps into the furniture and reads books upside down with a limpid guile that nearly melts the screen. . . . *How to Marry a Millionaire* is measured, not in square feet, but in the size of the Johnson-Negulesco comic invention and the shape of Marilyn Monroe—and that is about as sizable and shapely as you can get.

Otis Guernsey, Jr., *The New York Herald Tribune*

***River of No Return* (1954)**

There's no doubt that Miss Monroe means every bit of business that she's required to do in the adventure yarn, but the heavily dramatic elements of the film are just a little too much for her at this point in her acting career.

Lynn Bowers, *The Los Angeles Examiner*

It's a toss-up whether the scenery or the adornment of Marilyn Monroe is the feature of greater attraction in *River of No Return.* The mountainous scenery is spectacular, but so, in her own way, is

Miss Monroe. The patron's preferences, if any, probably will depend upon which he's interested in.

Bosley Crowther, *The New York Times*

There is something at once incongruous and strangely stimulating in Miss Monroe's dazzled and dazzling antics in the surroundings of nature. She herself is a leading representative of the natural instinct mentioned previously, and she is also, by reason of the artificial aspect of her coloring and makeup, in opposition to nature. This creates a kind of tension, not too easily defined, but very easily translated into publicity, popularity, and public interest.

Archer Winsten, *The New York Post*

***There's No Business Like Show Business* (1954)**

Miss Monroe's s.a. treatment of her vocal must be seen to be appreciated. It's not going to chase 'em away from the box office, on the other hand, as a song salesgirl, per se, she'll never worry Miss Merman. She's more competitive to Mae West in her delineations.

*Variety*

When it comes to spreading talent, Miss Gaynor has the jump on Miss Monroe, whose wriggling and squirming in "Heat Wave" and "Lazy" are embarrassing to behold.

Bosley Crowther, *The New York Times*

***The Seven Year Itch* (1955)**

Tom Ewell and La Monroe deserve most of the credit for carrying off the comedy coup. As for Monroe, a fine comedienne, her pouting delivery, puckered lips . . . make her one of Hollywood's top attractions, which she again proves here.

*The New York Daily Mirror*

Marilyn is just about perfect in the role of the pleasantly vacuous and even more pleasantly curved heroine.

*The Hollywood Reporter*

Marilyn Monroe's eye-catching gait is more tortile and wambling than ever. She also displays a nice comedy touch, reminiscent of a baby-talk Judy Holliday.

*Time*

From the moment she steps into the picture, in a garment that drapes her shapely form as though she had been skillfully poured into it, the famous screen star with the silver-blonde tresses and the ingeniously wide-eyed stare emanates one suggestion. . . . Mr. Wilder has permitted Miss Monroe, in her skin-fitting dresses and her frank gyrations, to overpower Mr. Ewell. She, without any real dimensions, is the focus of attention in the film.

Bosley Crowther, *The New York Times*

[It] offered stimulating views of Marilyn Monroe as a substitute for the comedy George Axelrod got into the original version of this trifle. There are occasions when Tom Ewell evokes a laugh or two, but when Miss Monroe turns up as a young lady too substantial for dreams, the picture is reduced to the level of a burlesque show.

John McCarten, *The New Yorker*

***Bus Stop* (1956)**

Speaking of artists, it is beginning to appear that we have a very real one right in our midst . . . in *Bus Stop* Marilyn Monroe effectively dispels once and for all the notion that she is merely a glamour personality, a shapely body with tremulous lips and come-hither blue eyes.

Arthur Knight, *The Saturday Review*

Playing opposite Mr. Murray is Marilyn Monroe, equipped with a rich southern accent and a nice sense of the humorous possibilities for her role.

John McCarten, *The New Yorker*

This is Marilyn's show, and, my friend, she shows plenty in figure, beauty and talent. The girl is a terrific comedienne as the bewildered little "chantoose" of the honky-tonk circuit. Her stint at the Actor's Studio in New York certainly didn't hurt our girl.

Dorothy Manners, *The Los Angeles Examiner*

We told you so: she had the skills, all she needed was a role with some depth, but for most, her performance was a revelation. In *Bus Stop* she has a wonderful role, and she plays it with a mixture of humor and pain that is very touching. This is also the special genius of the movie. One minute it is uproariously funny, the next minute tender and fragile, and somehow director Josh Logan preserves the delicate balance.

William K. Zinsser, *The New York Herald Tribune*

Hold onto your chairs, everybody, and get set for a rattling surprise. Marilyn Monroe has finally proved herself an actress in *Bus Stop*. She and the picture are swell! For the striking fact is that Mr. Logan has got her to do a great deal more than wiggle and pout and pop her big eyes and play the synthetic vamp in this film. He has got her to be the beat-up B-girl of Mr. Inge's play, even down to the Ozark accent and the look of pellagra about her skin. . . . Fortunately for her and for the tradition of diligence leading to success, she gives a performance in this picture that marks her as a genuine acting star, not just a plushy personality and a sex symbol, as she has previously been.

Bosley Crowther, *The New York Times*

***The Prince and the Showgirl* (1957)**

The unpredictable waverings of Marilyn Monroe's acting promise soar to a triumphant peak in *The Prince and the Showgirl*. . . . As her costar and director, Laurence Olivier brings out qualities none of her films ever summoned. She is captivatingly kittenish in her infectious mirth. Her love scenes are played as a girlish game. She romps through slapstick and turns solemn moments into part of her fun.

Alton Cook, *The New York World Telegram & Sun*

The film emerges as the season's sparkling comedy surprise.

Justin Gilbert, *The New York Mirror*

Apart from the whimsicality of teaming up England's leading actor with a young lady whose dramatic experience has been largely confined to wiggling about in Technicolor pastries cooked up in Hollywood, it offers little in the way of diversion.

John McCarten, *The New Yorker*

As for Marilyn Monroe, she has never seemed more in command of herself as person and as comedienne. She manages to make her laughs without sacrificing the real Marilyn to playacting. This, of course, is something one can expect from great, talented, practiced performers. It comes as a most pleasant surprise from Marilyn Monroe, who has been half-actress, half-sensation.

Archer Winsten, *The New York Post*

Marilyn's role has no such fine shadings. This is a dumb, affable showgirl and nothing more, and Miss Monroe goes through the motions of pleasure, pouts of annoyance, eyes big as golf balls, and many a delighted toss of her rounded surfaces.

William K. Zinsser, *New York Herald Tribune*

This, I am sure, is Miss Monroe's best cinema effort. Under Olivier's direction, she reveals a real sense of comedy. Miss Monroe also proves that she can command attention now by other means than her famous hip-swinging walk.

John Scott, *The Los Angeles Times*

***Some Like It Hot* (1959)**

To coin a phrase, Marilyn has never looked better. She's a comedienne with that combination of sex appeal and timing that just can't be beat.

*Variety*

To get down to cases, Marilyn does herself proud, giving a performance of such intrinsic quality that you begin to believe she's only being herself and it is herself who fits into that distant period and this picture so well.

Archer Winsten, *The New York Post*

Mr. Curtis is trying to impress a dipsomaniacal singer played in sprightly style by Marilyn Monroe.

John McCarten, *The New Yorker*

As the band's somewhat simple singer-ukulele player, Miss Monroe, whose figure simply cannot be ignored, contributes more assets than the obvious ones to this madcap romp . . . and proves to be the epitome of a dumb blonde and a talented comedienne.

A. H. Weiler, *The New York Times*

***Let's Make Love* (1960)**

Miss Monroe, basically a first-rate comedienne, doesn't have a single bright line. Of course, the famous charms are in evidence.

Justin Gilbert, *The New York Daily Mirror*

Marilyn Monroe is geared for some of the loudest laughter of her life in *Let's Make Love*, a gay, preposterous and completely delightful romp. . . . Marilyn actually dares comparison with Mary Martin by

> singing "My Heart Belongs to Daddy" in her first scene. The night I saw it, the audience broke into the picture with applause.
>
> Alton Cook, *The New York World Telegram & Sun*

> The old Monroe dynamism is lacking in the things she is given to do by the cliché-clogged script of Norman Krasna and by George Cukor, who directed the film. It doesn't seem very important that she is finally brought together with Mr. Montand.
>
> Bosley Crowther, *The New York Times*

> In the acting department, Miss Monroe is not impressive as in comedy-type roles. She plays a straight part here and does little that is effective. Visually? Marilyn offers her famous curves, not a little on the fleshy side. Diet, anyone?
>
> Lowell E. Redelings, *Hollywood Citizen News*

### *The Misfits* (1961)

> Miss Monroe has seldom looked worse; the camera is unfailingly unflattering. But there is a delicacy about her playing, and a tenderness that is affecting.
>
> *The Hollywood Reporter*

> Gable has never done anything better on the screen, nor has Miss Monroe. Gable's acting is vibrant and lusty, hers true to the character as written by Miller.
>
> Kate Cameron, *The New York Daily News*

> Here Miss Monroe is magic, but not a living pinup dangled in skin-tight satin before our eyes. . . . And can anyone deny that in this film these performers are at their best?
>
> Paul V. Beckley, *New York Herald Tribune*

## *THE REVOLT OF MAMIE STOVER*

Following the completion of *The Seven Year Itch* (1955), Buddy Adler and 20th Century-Fox wanted Marilyn Monroe to star in *The Revolt of Mamie Stover,* a film about a dance hall girl who fled San Francisco and moved to Hawaii. However, Marilyn refused to do the film. Apparently, her instinctive judgment about the picture was correct. Leslie Halliwell's *Film Guide* had the following to say:

> Absolutely bowdlerized and boring film version of a novel about a sleazy prostitute; hardly worth making at all in this form, especially as the cast seems well capable of a raunchier version.

*The Revolt of Mamie Stover* was released by 20th Century-Fox in 1956, with none other than Jane Russell in the lead role. It was directed by Raoul Walsh.

## DEBBIE REYNOLDS

After Marilyn Monroe rejected George Axelrod's *Goodbye Charlie,* 20th Century-Fox cast Debbie Reynolds in the starring role. The film was released, to lukewarm reaction in 1964.

Interestingly, it was Debbie Reynolds who purchased (and who currently owns) what is probably Marilyn Monroe's most famous movie costume—the white, "skirt scene" dress that was blown over Marilyn's ears in *The Seven Year Itch*. The dress was designed by Billy Travilla.

**RHODE ISLAND STREET, HAWTHORNE, CALIFORNIA**

In June 1926, twelve-day-old infant Norma Jeane Mortenson was sent to live with Wayne and Ida Bolender at their home in Hawthorne, California. The modest house was located at 459 East Rhode Island Street, and it served as Norma Jeane's home until 1932.

**ORLANDO H. RHODES**

Rhodes was the superior court judge who, in October 1954, granted Marilyn Monroe her interlocutory divorce from Joe DiMaggio. For the record, MM *was* present in court that day. Joe DiMaggio was not.

**MARK RICCI**

Mark Ricci was the cowriter of the career book *The Films of Marilyn Monroe*, which was published in 1964.

**DAVID LOWELL RICH**

Born in 1923, David Lowell Rich directed the 1974 made-for-television biopic *The Sex Symbol*. Rich has also directed such feature films as *Madame X* (1966), *Rosie* (1967), *Eye of the Cat* (1969), and *The Concorde—Airport 1979*.

**MIRANDA RICHARDSON**

Miranda Richardson is the British actress who made her film debut in 1985's *Dance with a Stranger*. Upon the release of that film, Miss Richardson was repeatedly compared, favorably, with Marilyn Monroe.

Miranda Richardson, *Dance With a Stranger*, 1985, was compared to MM.

THE SABIN GRAY COLLECTION

**WILLIAM RICHERT**

William Richert directed the 1979 film *Winter Kills*, which included a Marilyn Monroe-based character. Mr. Richert also adapted the screenplay from the book by Richard Condon.

**ROGER RICHMAN**

In August 1982, the Marilyn Monroe estate hired Roger Richman as the "duly appointed licensing agent" of the estate. Since that time, Richman has overseen all advertising and/or merchandising that has been done in connection with Marilyn Monroe. According to Richman, as of January 1987, at least 49 companies had purchased licenses to use the MM name and/or image.

***RIDERS OF THE WHISTLING PINES***

In the film *Riders of the Whistling Pines* (1949, Columbia), Gene Autry serenaded a photograph of a rancher's dead wife. The photograph was of Marilyn Monroe, who, at that time, was an unknown contract player at Columbia.

**PAMELA RIES**

Pamela Ries was the former fiancée of Joe DiMaggio, Jr. When young DiMaggio telephoned Marilyn Monroe on the evening of August 4, 1962, it was to tell her that his engagement to Miss Ries had been called off.

At the time of her courtship with Joe, Jr., Pamela Ries worked in Kansas City, Missouri, for a trading stamp company.

***RIGHT CROSS*** **★½**

1950 90 minutes Black and White
MGM
Directed by: John Sturges
Produced by: Armand Deutsch
Screenplay by: Charles Schnee
Photographed by: Norbert Brodine
Cast: Dick Powell, June Allyson, Lionel Barrymore, Ricardo Montalban, John Gallaudet, Barry Kelley, Marianne Stewart, Mimi Aguglia, Teresa Celli

*Right Cross* was Marilyn's second of three movies made in conjunction with MGM. The first, of course, was *The Asphalt Jungle* (1950), in which she had made a stellar impact. *Right Cross,* comparatively, is a major disappointment—as a film and as a vehicle for early MM. She has a mere bit part, in which she appears as Dick Powell's girlfriend. Marilyn was not even billed in the cast credits. A waste.

**CARROLL RIGHTER**

Famed astrologer Carroll Righter once asked MM if she knew that she was born under the same astrological sign (Gemini) as Rosalind Russell, Judy Garland, and Rosemary Clooney. Marilyn was said to have responded:

> "I know nothing of these people. I was born under the same sign as Ralph Waldo Emerson, Queen Victoria, and Walt Whitman."

**THELMA RITTER**

It is somewhat amazing that Thelma Ritter (1905–1969), one of the finest character actresses in the history of motion pictures, never received an Academy Award. Nevertheless, she did leave behind a legacy of some excellent motion picture performances, including *A Letter to Three Wives* (1949), *With a Song in My Heart* (1952), *Rear Window* (1954), *Pillow Talk* (1959), and *Birdman of Alcatraz* (1962).

Miss Ritter also appeared in three movies that featured Marilyn Monroe: *All About Eve* (1950), *As Young as You Feel* (1951), and *The Misfits* (1961).

***RIVER OF NO RETURN*** ★½

1954 91 minutes Technicolor
20th Century-Fox
Directed by: Otto Preminger
Produced by: Stanley Rubin
Screenplay by: Frank Fenton, based on a story by Louis Lantz
Photographed by: Joseph LaShelle
Cast: Robert Mitchum, Marilyn Monroe, Rory Calhoun, Tommy Rettig, Murvyn Vye, Douglas Spencer, Ed Winton, Don Beddoe, Claire Andre. Jack Mather

THE RAY VAN GOEYE COLLECTION

With Robert Mitchum, *River of No Return*, 1954.

Not only is *River of No Return* a lousy movie; Marilyn Monroe is lousy in it. With the exception of her musical numbers, particularly "I'm Gonna File My Claim," Marilyn is hardly believable (though highly *watchable*). She tends to overplay everything with her exaggerated, husky-voiced, half-lidded style—which is in direct contrast to Robert Mitchum's slow, drowsy, beagle-eye style.

Why 20th Century-Fox chose *River of No Return* for Marilyn is a mystery. Perhaps, after her great successes of 1953 (*Niagara, Gentlemen Prefer Blondes, How to Marry a Millionaire*), MM began to wield her newfound power at the studio; perhaps she began to demand more money and the other amenities that go along with being a movie star. And perhaps 20th Century-Fox responded by banishing MM to this watered-down, washed-up, waste-of-time western.

Surely, the Fox front office could have come up with a more appropriate starring vehicle for its biggest box office commodity. Not long after the 1954 release of *River of No Return,* Marilyn plotted to defect from Fox. It's easy to see why. She was once quoted as saying, about *River*:

> "Knowing what I know now, I wouldn't accept *River of No Return.* I think I deserve a better deal than a 'Z' cowboy movie, in which the acting finishes third to the scenery and Cinemascope."

**GERALDO RIVERA**

Geraldo Rivera, born July 4, 1943, is the investigative television journalist who stirred up controversy when ABC-TV mysteriously decided to shelve a "20/20" magazine segment that explored the circumstances surrounding Marilyn's death. At that time, Rivera commented:

> I'm appalled. I think that story was a solid piece of TV reporting. They are not going to get away with this. It's going to be a major controversy. . . . The decision smacks of cronyism, though I can't prove that. If a politician did this, we'd do an exposé. But it happened within our own ranks.

Following his public remarks, Rivera's contract was not renewed by ABC executive Roone Arledge. The 1985 segment, which reportedly included revealing material on Marilyn's relationships with John and Robert Kennedy, has never been aired. As for the multi-award-winning Rivera, he was later quoted, understandably, as saying: "I wish I'd never heard of Marilyn Monroe." He has since gone on to host several successful investigative television documentaries.

**RKO**

> At nights when all the kids were asleep, I'd perch on the dormitory window sill and look across at the RKO water tank, with RKO in big letters, and light shining like a Hollywood premiere. "My mother used to work there," I'd whisper. "Someday I'd like to be a star there."
>
> Marilyn Monroe, 1952,
> on her childhood dreams

The Radio Keith Orpheum, more commonly known as RKO Radio Pictures

Incorporated, was founded in 1921. In 1948, Howard Hughes acquired a hefty percentage of the company stock, before the studio was sold to Desilu Productions in the 1950s.

At one point, Gladys Baker, Marilyn's mother, worked at the RKO Studios (address: 780 Gower St., Hollywood) as a negative cutter. Years later, also at RKO, unknown starlet Marilyn Monroe auditioned for—and got—her brief but important role in *Love Happy* (1950). A few years after that, 20th Century-Fox loaned its budding star, MM, to RKO for the prestige picture *Clash by Night* (1952), which proved to be a pivotal success for MM.

Reportedly, RKO also attempted to obtain Marilyn's services for two other pictures, both of which 20th Century-Fox rejected. One was entitled *High Heels,* which was, predictably, the story of a dance hall hostess. The other was entitled *Big Heat.*

**MM Trivia Quiz #39**
Who was RKO's first choice for MM's part in *Clash by Night*? (Answer on page 578.)

**RALPH ROBERTS**
Ralph Roberts was Marilyn Monroe's masseur, confidant, and friend. They met through the Strasberg family while Marilyn was still living in New York. During the production of *The Misfits* in 1960, Roberts was hired as the company masseur. He was also given a small role in the film as an ambulance attendant.

On the afternoon of August 4, 1962, Ralph Roberts telephoned Marilyn at her Brentwood home. He and MM had tentatively scheduled a dinner engagement for that evening, and Roberts had called to confirm. However, Marilyn did not answer the phone. Instead, it was answered by Dr. Ralph Greenson, who promptly told Roberts that Marilyn was not at home. Roberts, reportedly, was curious about why Dr. Greenson would be at Marilyn's house if she was not at home. Later that night, Roberts's telephone answering service received a message from a woman thought to be Marilyn, before she slipped into unconsciousness.

**LEO ROBIN**
Born in 1899, Leo Robin is the lyricist who wrote "Diamonds Are a Girl's Best Friend," "Bye Bye Baby," and "We're Just Two Little Girls from Little Rock"—all of which are from the smash 1953 hit *Gentlemen Prefer Blondes.*

Mr. Robin is also responsible for the song "Thanks for the Memory," which won him a 1938 Oscar (from the movie *Big Broadcast of 1938*) and which has since become Bob Hope's theme song.

**SEYMOUR ROBINOWITZ**
Judge Seymour Robinowitz performed the civil wedding ceremony between Arthur Miller and Marilyn Monroe on June 29, 1956 in White Plains, New York.

**DAVID ROBINSON**
David Robinson is a well-respected writer on film. His books include a Buster Keaton biography and *World Cinema*. He was also a film critic and an associate editor of *Sight and Sound* magazine. He also wrote the lengthy introduction to the book *Marilyn Monroe: A Life on Film* (1974).

**ROBOTS: THE MARILYN MONROE ROBOT**
In 1980, a department store in Japan constructed and promoted a Marilyn Monroe robot that sang, strummed a guitar, and moved its lips (of course!). The robot, which was designed to attract customers into the store, was powered by compressed air.

**THE ROCKHAVEN SANITARIUM**
In 1953, as her star began its rise, Marilyn Monroe had her mother, Gladys Baker, transferred from a state mental institution into the Rockhaven private nursing home. At that time, Rockhaven was managed by a woman named Agnes Richards. It was located at 2713 Honolulu Avenue, in the Verdugo section of Glendale, California.

Following Marilyn's death in 1962, the Marilyn Monroe estate continued to pay for Gladys's care at Rockhaven. Gladys lived there until 1967, when she moved to Florida to live with her other daughter, Bernice.

**DICK RODGERS**
According to Fred Lawrence Guiles, Dick Rodgers was Gladys's coworker at Consolidated Film Industries, who took up a collection to pay for Gladys's maternity bills in 1926.

**MORTIMER RODGERS**
On June 23, 1959, Marilyn underwent an operation of a "corrective nature" at Lenox Hill Hospital in New York. The surgery was conducted by Dr. Mortimer Rodgers.

**NICOLAS ROEG**
Nicolas Roeg is the acclaimed British director of such films as *Don't Look Now* (1973), *The Man Who Fell to Earth* (1976), and *Bad Timing* (1979). In 1985, Roeg directed the excellent *Insignificance,* which featured a Marilyn Monroe-based character.

**GINGER ROGERS**
Born Virginia McMath on July 16, 1911, Ginger Rogers is the multimarried, durable actress/dancer of such films as *Flying Down to Rio* (1933), *The Gay Divorcee* (1934), *Top Hat* (1935), *Swing Time* (1936), and *Kitty Foyle* (for which she won a 1940 Oscar).

While Norma Jeane Baker was growing up, Ginger Rogers was one of her favorite actresses. Years later, Marilyn Monroe appeared in two films that costarred her former idol: *We're Not Married* (1952) and *Monkey Business* (1952).

**ROY ROGERS**

Born Leonard Slye in 1911, Roy Rogers is the cowboy singing star who became famous for his partnerships with his horse, Trigger, and his wife, Dale Evans.

Norma Jeane Dougherty first met Roy Rogers at a sporting goods store in Van Nuys, California. They met again in Las Vegas, in May 1946, while he was making a movie and she was getting a divorce. Reportedly, Norma Jeane had dinner with Rogers at the Last Frontier Hotel in Vegas.

**ROI-TAN CIGARS**

In 1980–1981, a Bert Stern photograph of Marilyn Monroe was used in a print advertisement for Roi-Tan Cigars. The ad copy read: "While you're watching an old flame . . . Start up a new one: Roi-Tan little cigars."

**THE ROLES**

The following is a chronological breakdown and description of the roles that Marilyn Monroe portrayed during her film career:

| MOVIE | ROLE | DESCRIPTION |
|---|---|---|
| 1. *Scudda Hoo! Scudda Hay!* (1948) | no name | a boat rower |
| 2. *Dangerous Years* (1947) | Eve | a waitress |
| 3. *Ladies of the Chorus* (1948) | Peggy Martin | a burlesque queen |
| 4. *Love Happy* (1950) | Grunion's client | a girl in trouble |
| 5. *A Ticket to Tomahawk* (1950) | Clara | a chorus girl |
| 6. *The Asphalt Jungle* (1950) | Angela Phinlay | the mistress |
| 7. *All About Eve* (1950) | Miss Caswell | an aspiring actress |
| 8. *The Fireball* (1950) | Polly | a rollerskating groupie |
| 9. *Right Cross* (1950) | no name | Dick Powell's girlfriend |
| 10. *Hometown Story* (1951) | Miss Martin | a secretary |
| 11. *As Young as You Feel* (1951) | Harriet | a secretary |
| 12. *Love Nest* (1951) | Roberta Stevens | an ex-WAC |
| 13. *Let's Make It Legal* (1951) | Joyce | the gold-digging "other woman" |
| 14. *Clash by Night* (1952) | Peggy | a fish cannery worker |
| 15. *We're Not Married* (1952) | Annabel Norris | a beauty queen contestant |
| 16. *Don't Bother to Knock* (1952) | Nell | a psychotic babysitter |
| 17. *Monkey Business* (1952) | Lois Laurel | a secretary |

| | | |
|---|---|---|
| 18. *O. Henry's Full House* (1952) | no name | a streetwalker |
| 19. *Niagara* (1953) | Rose Loomis | an adulterous, murderous wife |
| 20. *Gentlemen Prefer Blondes (1953)* | Lorelei Lee | a gold digger |
| 21. *How to Marry a Millionaire* (1953) | Pola Debevoise | a nearsighted gold digger |
| 22. *River of No Return* (1954) | Kay Weston | a hardened saloon singer |
| 23. *There's No Business Like Show Business* (1954) | Vicky | a hardened nightclub singer |
| 24. *The Seven Year Itch* (1955) | The girl upstairs | a sexy neighbor/model/actress |
| 25. *Bus Stop* (1956) | Cherie | an abducted, would-be chanteuse |
| 26. *The Prince and the Showgirl* (1957) | Elsie Marina | the showgirl |
| 27. *Some Like It Hot* (1959) | Sugar Kane | an alcoholic singer/ukulele player of an all-girl band |
| 28. *Let's Make Love* (1960) | Amanda Dell | a Broadway actress |
| 29. *The Misfits* (1960) | Roslyn Tabor | a vulnerable divorcee |

**The Roles that Marilyn Wanted to Play (but Didn't)**
Grushenka, *The Brothers Karamazov* (on film)
Blanche DuBois, *A Streetcar Named Desire* (on Broadway)
Julie, *Bury the Dead* (on stage)
Gretchen, *Faust* (on stage)
Teresa, *Cradle Song* (on stage)
Sadie Thompson, *Rain* (on television)
Lady Macbeth, opposite Marlon Brando's Macbeth

**MM Trivia Quiz #40**
Which one of MM's characters was described as a graduate of the Copacabana School of Dramatic Arts? (Answer on page 578.)

**CARL E. ROLLYSON, JR.**
An assistant dean at Wayne State University in Detroit, Carl E. Rollyson, Jr., is the author of the 1986 career book on MM entitled *Marilyn Monroe: A Life of the Actress*. Rollyson's other works include a book on William Faulkner's novels and a biography of playwright Lillian Hellman.

**ROBERT C. ROMAN**
Robert Roman wrote a "career article" on MM for *Films in Review*'s October 1962 issue. The article was entitled "Marilyn Monroe: Her Tragedy Was

Allowing Herself to be Misled Intellectually." It was a biased, slanted article that demeaned Marilyn Monroe's talent and her position in film history. Wrote Roman:

> She was an example, more than any screen "image" of comparable notoriety, of how fatal ignorance can be. She was shrewd enough to exploit her body, her "deprived" childhood, her mother's insanity, and, to a certain extent, the resources of 20th Century-Fox's publicity department. But apparently she was not shrewd enough to learn about the even shrewder people with whom she had to deal as her fame increased.

Granted, that particular commentary may not be altogether untrue. What was untrue, and *offensive,* was Roman's scathing evaluation of Marilyn's film performances:

On *Gentlemen Prefer Blondes*:

> Jane Russell, as Dorothy, walked off with the film. "Diamonds Are a Girl's Best Friend" was not effectively sung by a dead-pan Monroe.

On *Bus Stop*:

> Marilyn Monroe was often downright ridiculous.

On *Some Like It Hot*:

> It proved to be a rather vulgar film revolving around female impersonation.
>
> Her "flesh-impact" was clearly diminishing.

On Marilyn's career, if she had lived:

> It was practically a certainty she would never work in Hollywood again. And 20th's [law]suit, which was almost sure to be won, would bankrupt her.

Why a respectable publication such as *Films in Review* would devote *twenty-one pages* to such a slanderous attack on Marilyn Monroe, shortly after her death, is beyond comprehension. Robert Roman's article is perhaps the best illustration of Hollywood's smug, complacent disregard for Marilyn Monroe. However, some twenty-five years have elapsed since that article was published, and it is glaringly obvious that Marilyn Monroe has survived such outlandish attacks. Not only has she survived; she has also been recognized as one of the most original talents of our time.

**GLORIA AND MIKE ROMANOFF**

Gloria Romanoff and her husband, "Prince" Mike, were the co-owners of Romanoff's restaurant in Los Angeles, which was one of Marilyn Monroe's favorite eateries.

**ROMANOFF'S**

At the time when Marilyn Monroe was attempting to launch her career, Romanoff's was *the* restaurant in Beverly Hills. Thus, it was here that Johnny

Hyde and others escorted Marilyn "to be seen." In fact, it was at Romanoff's that MM and Hyde had their first luncheon date.

Even after stardom, Marilyn continued to frequent Romanoff's. As a gesture to welcome her to the Hollywood inner circle, the movie industry elite honored MM at a party held at Romanoff's on November 6, 1954. In attendance that evening was a select group of eighty invited guests. The Hollywood Royal Guard included Samuel Goldwyn, Leland Hayward, Jack Warner, Darryl Zanuck, Claudette Colbert, Doris Day, Susan Hayward, William Holden, Jimmy Stewart, Gary Cooper, Humphrey Bogart, Clark Gable, Billy Wilder, Lauren Bacall, Irving Lazar, et al. Marilyn drank champagne, danced with Clark Gable, and sang a duet with Mrs. Billy Wilder. The highly successful party was organized by Marilyn's agent at that time, Charles Feldman, who also served as the coproducer of *The Seven Year Itch* (1955).

In 1960, another Hollywood party was thrown at Romanoff's. However, this one was not for Marilyn. Instead, it was for director Billy Wilder and the well-received screening of *The Apartment.* Marilyn attended the party despite the fact that she and Wilder had been feuding.

Romanoff's, which is no longer in existence, was located at 326 North Rodeo Drive, Beverly Hills. It was owned by Gloria and Mike Romanoff. The Maitre d', during Marilyn's Hollywood heyday, was Kurt Niklas.

**HARRY ROMM**

Harry Romm was the Columbia Pictures producer who helmed *Ladies of the Chorus,* which provided MM with her first costarring vehicle in 1948. It was Romm, in tandem with Max Arnow (the head of talent at Columbia), who teamed Marilyn with drama coach Natasha Lytess.

**MICKEY ROONEY**

The durable, multimarried Mickey Rooney was born Joe Yule, Jr., in 1920. His career as an entertainer has spanned some sixty years. Among his films: *Boys Town* (for which he won a special 1938 Oscar), *Babes in Arms* (1939), *Breakfast at Tiffany's* (1961), and *The Black Stallion* (1979). Rooney has also achieved major success with *Bill,* a 1981 TV movie, and *Sugar Babies,* the long-running stage musical.

In 1950, Mickey Rooney starred in a Fox rollerskating flick, *The Fireball.* The film featured, in a brief role, starlet Marilyn Monroe. Marilyn and Mickey crossed paths again in March 1952, at the Villa Nova Restaurant in Hollywood. Marilyn was engaged in her first date with Joe DiMaggio when Rooney sauntered over to their table—not to see her, but to talk to DiMaggio, instead. Rooney, it seems, was a baseball enthusiast. Little did he know that he was interrupting the romantic flow of what was to become one of Hollywood's most talked-about relationships.

**THE ROSARITA BEACH HOTEL**

According to Robert Slatzer, he and Marilyn Monroe spent their secret October 4, 1952, wedding night at the Rosarita Beach Hotel in Baja, Mexico.

**THE ROSE PARADE**

While under her first contract to 20th Century-Fox, in 1947, starlet Marilyn Monroe rode in the world-famous Tournament of Roses Parade, which takes place annually in Pasadena, California.

**HELEN ROSE**

Helen Rose was credited with doing the costumes for the movies that Marilyn made for MGM: *The Asphalt Jungle* (1950), *Right Cross* (1950), and *Hometown Story* (1951).

**HENRY ROSENFELD**

Henry Rosenfeld was a wealthy New York dress manufacturer whom Marilyn allegedly had an affair with. They first met in 1949, when Marilyn was in New York to promote *Love Happy.*

**ROBERT ROSENFELD**

Dr. Robert Rosenfeld treated Marilyn Monroe during her illness while shooting *There's No Business Like Show Business* in 1954.

**JAIK ROSENSTEIN**

Reportedly, two years before her death, Marilyn told writer Jaik Rosenstein that she had, in fact, used sex to "get ahead" in Hollywood. As recorded in Anthony Summers's *Goddess* (Macmillan, 1985), Marilyn is said to have told Rosenstein:

> "When I started modeling, it was like part of the job. All the girls did. They [the photographers] weren't shooting all those sexy pictures just to sell peanut butter in an ad, or get a layout in some picture magazine. They wanted to sample the merchandise, and if you didn't go along, there were twenty-five girls who would. It wasn't any big dramatic tragedy. Nobody ever got cancer from sex."

**SHELDON ROSKIN**

Sheldon Roskin was one of the publicists on *The Misfits* (1961). He later became co-owner of the successful entertainment public relations firm Solters & Roskin.

**FLORENCE KOTZ ROSS**

*See* FLORENCE KOTZ.

**HAROLD ROSSON**

Harold Rosson (1895–1960) was the acclaimed cinematographer of such films as *Tarzan and the Apes* (1932), *The Garden of Allah* (for which he won a 1936 Oscar), *The Wizard of Oz* (1939), *On the Town* (1949), and *Singin' in the Rain* (1952).

In 1950, Rosson lensed *The Asphalt Jungle,* which featured Marilyn Monroe in her first *major* movie. Five years later, after she had attained superstar status, Marilyn included Harold Rosson on her list of "approved" cinematographers.

superstar status, Marilyn included Harold Rosson on her list of "approved" cinematographers.

Interestingly, Rosson photographed the original film version of *Gentlemen Prefer Blondes* in 1928.

**HEDDA ROSTEN**

Hedda Rosten, Norman Rosten's wife, served as Marilyn's secretary/companion/friend during the 1956 shooting of *The Prince and the Showgirl* in England. However, Hedda and the film's director, Laurence Olivier, reportedly clashed; thus she returned to the United States in September, before the shooting was completed.

**NORMAN ROSTEN**

Poet Norman Rosten was one of Marilyn Monroe's closest friends—from her New York period, circa 1945, until her death.

It was photographer Sam Shaw who introduced Marilyn to Norman and Hedda Rosten in the spring of 1955. At that time, the Rostens were also good friends with Arthur Miller, whom Marilyn was "secretly" dating. In fact, it was at the Rostens' Brooklyn home that Miller and Marilyn would frequently meet. For further privacy, they would also occasionally visit the Rosten summer home in Port Jefferson, Long Island. And, after Arthur and Marilyn married, in 1956, the Rostens were frequent visitors to their famous friends' East 57th Street apartment in New York City.

Norman Rosten, whom Marilyn referred to as "Claude" (because he resembled actor Claude Rains), was exposed to a particularly vulnerable and intimate side of Marilyn Monroe. It was to Rosten that Marilyn shared her poetry, which contained, presumably, her innermost thoughts. And, in a mutual admiration society of sorts, he, in turn, shared his poetry with her.

Norman Rosten also wrote plays and novels. Among his works are *Under the Boardwalk, Over and Out,* and the adapted screenplay of Arthur Miller's *A View from the Bridge* (1962). In 1973, Signet Books published Rosten's literary tribute to his famous friend, *Marilyn: An Untold Story. Marilyn: Among Friends,* featuring photographs by Sam Shaw and Ian Woodner with poetry and text by Rosten was published in 1987.

**PATRICIA ROSTEN**

Patricia Rosten was the daughter of Norman and Hedda Rosten. Marilyn had a special affinity for Pat, and Marilyn once presented her with a dog named Cindy as a birthday present. Once, when Pat was ten or eleven, Marilyn gave her a complete hair and cosmetic make-over. However, most telling is the fact that, in her will, Marilyn left Patricia $5,000 to be used for her education. Unfortunately, however, Patricia did not receive her total bequest until 1975—seven years after she had graduated from college.

**HEND ROSTOM**

Actress, considered to be "The Egyptian Marilyn Monroe."

**PHIL ROTH**

Phil Roth was a young actor and student at the Actors Studio in New York who was assigned to rehearse and perform a scene with fellow student Marilyn Monroe. One day, MM showed up at Roth's apartment, but before they rehearsed their scene, Marilyn insisted on cleaning his apartment for him.

**MISTY ROWE**

Misty Rowe is the actress who portrayed MM in the 1976 feature film *Goodbye Norma Jean*. After her work in this picture, it was "Goodbye, Misty Rowe"—at least as far as a movie career was concerned.

**ROXBURY, CONNECTICUT**

To avoid the sweltering New York City heat in the summertime, Arthur and Marilyn Miller annually retreated to their Roxbury, Connecticut, farm home. Originally a 1783 colonial house, the two-story structure was situated on 325 acres.

Upon their separation in 1960, Marilyn resided in New York, while Miller chose to live at and retain the Roxbury country home.

**THE ROXY THEATRE**

*Monkey Business* opened at the Roxy Theatre in New York City during September 1952.

**THE ROYAL COMMAND PERFORMANCE**

> "Look her [the queen] straight in the eye and say to yourself, 'I'm just as pretty as you are.' "
>
> Anne Karger's advice to MM, 1956

Before the completion of *The Prince and the Showgirl* shooting in England, Marilyn Monroe was requested to appear at a Royal Command Film Performance before Queen Elizabeth. The event took place at the Empire Theatre in London on October 29, 1956. The film screened that evening was *The Battle of the River Plate*. Other luminaries invited to appear that night were Anita Ekberg, Belinda Lee, Victor Mature, Arlene Dahl, Maureen Swanson, Brigitte Bardot, Vera-Ellen, Dana Andrews, and Joan Crawford. Reportedly, Marilyn was the highlight of the evening.

As instructed, when Marilyn was presented to the queen, she curtsied, to which the queen of England responded: "That's a very proper curtsy." Answered MM: "Curtsying isn't difficult for me now. I learned how to do it. For this picture, I have to do it three or four times."

That night, Marilyn was also presented to Princess Margaret, who discussed bicycling with MM.

**ROYAL TRITON OIL**

In 1950, before attaining major stardom, Marilyn Monroe appeared in a television commercial for the Royal Triton Oil Company. (*See* COMMERCIALS.)

**PHILLIP RUBIN**

Phillip Rubin is the doctor who gave Marilyn Monroe instructions *not* to appear on the 1962 set of *Something's Got to Give* because of a virus that she had contracted. It was Marilyn's repeated absences from the set of that film that provoked 20th Century-Fox to fire her.

**STANLEY RUBIN**

Stanley Rubin was the producer of the 1954 debacle *River of No Return*, which starred Robert Mitchum and Marilyn Monroe.

**MICKEY RUDIN (aka Milton Rudin)**

Mickey Rudin was one of Marilyn Monroe's attorneys at the time of her death. Reportedly, Rudin spoke with MM on the day of her death and said that "she appeared to be happy—she was in perfect physical condition, was feeling great, and we made plans for her to talk with me in my office today [Monday, August 6, 1962]." The meeting was called because Marilyn allegedly wanted to change her will.

At approximately 9:00 or 10:00 P.M. on August 4, 1962, Mickey Rudin telephoned Marilyn's Brentwood house to find out if MM was all right. Over the years, it has been speculated that Rudin had just received a telephone call from Peter Lawford, who had just spoken with Marilyn and was concerned about MM's mental and physical condition. However, Mrs. Eunice Murray answered Rudin's phone call and, without investigating, reported that Marilyn was fine.

Early the next morning, Mickey Rudin arrived at Marilyn's home and began to make the arrangements for her burial.

Mickey Rudin is also the attorney/manager of Frank Sinatra.

**BARNEY RUDITSKY**

Barney Ruditsky was a private detective (using the operating license of Deputy Marshal Jack Stambler) who was hired by Frank Sinatra (for Joe DiMaggio) to lead what became the infamous "Wrong Door Raid" in November 1954. (*See* "WRONG DOOR RAID.")

**JANICE RULE**

Marilyn Monroe may have been the standout pin-up of 1952, but she was *not* the standout body—at least not according to the Artists Institute of America, which claimed that Marilyn's legs were too short and her derriere was too sloped. The winner of the institute's "standout body" designation was actress Janice Rule.

Janice Rule, born in 1931, has appeared in such films as *Holiday for Sinners* (1952), *Bell, Book, and Candle* (1958), *The Chase* (1966), and *Missing* (1982).

**JANE RUSSELL**

"There are two good reasons why men will go to see her."

Howard Hughes on Jane Russell

> "We got along nicely—Jane called me the 'round one'—I don't know what she means by that, but I assume she means it to be friendly."
>
> Marilyn Monroe on Jane Russell

When it was announced that Russell would star opposite Monroe in *Gentlemen Prefer Blondes* (1953), the press braced themselves for a bitchy cat fight of mammoth proportions, if not an all-out war. Columnist Earl Wilson described it, gleefully, as "the battle of the bulges"; Sidney Skolsky called it the "bout for the glamour championship of the world." Perhaps to spite the press, or perhaps out of genuine affection, Russell and Monroe became friends. After all, Jane Russell may have gotten top billing in the film, but Marilyn Monroe was *the blonde,* and gentlemen *did* prefer blondes!

Ernestine Jane Russell was born on June 21, 1921, in Bemidji, Minnesota. She attended Van Nuys High in California, which Norma Jeane Baker would also attend a few years later. One of Jane's costudents at Van Nuys was none other than Jim Dougherty, Norma Jeane's husband-to-be. Both Jane and Jim were members of the Van Nuys Maskers Drama Group. In fact, she once portrayed his daughter in a school play entitled *Shirtsleeves.* On another occasion, Jane and Jim competed opposite one another in a vocal talent contest. Jim won.

Following her graduation from school, Jane Russell began to model while she studied acting at Max Reinhardt's Theatrical Workshop. As is well known, Jane was "discovered" by Howard Hughes, who cast her in his western picture, *The Outlaw.* However, because of Jane's prominently displayed bosom, *The Outlaw* was censored and had to wait several years before it was released. Jane Russell remained under contract to Hughes for twenty-seven years. During that period, she appeared in such productions as *The Paleface* (1948), *Gentlemen Prefer Blondes* (1953), *Gentlemen Marry Brunettes* (1955), and *The Revolt of Mamie Stover* (1957).

It is easy to see why and how Jane Russell and Marilyn Monroe became friendly acquaintances. After all, they had a lot in common—namely, Van Nuys High School, Jim Dougherty, Max Reinhardt, and Howard Hughes. Moreover, at that time, Jane was married to ex-pro-football-player Bob Waterfield while Marilyn was considering marriage to Joe DiMaggio. And, as many people seemed to do, Jane Russell took a protective, almost maternal attitude toward Marilyn Monroe. She helped Marilyn sort out her life, deal with her newfound stardom, and decorate her Doheny Drive apartment.

As is often the case in Hollywood, the friendship between The Bust and The Bottom diminished following the completion of the film's shooting. Nevertheless, when Jane telephoned MM in 1955 to ask for her assistance in WAIF—an organization dedicated to finding homes for unwanted children—Marilyn readily agreed. And this was during her reclusive New York period, in which she had shunned most of Hollywood.

Today, in re-viewing *Gentlemen Prefer Blondes,* it is obvious that one of the reasons the film worked so well was that there was no animosity or competition between the two female costars. In fact, it almost seems as though Jane Russell consciously took a step backward and *handed* the film to MM. If so, it was a wise and generous gesture—and certainly one uncommon in the Hollywood jungle.

**LEON RUSSELL**

Rock and roll star Leon Russell wrote and sang a 1978 song entitled "Elvis and Marilyn." The Paradise Records single also featured a flip-side recording called "Anita Bryant."

**LILLIAN RUSSELL**

Born Helen Louise Leonard, Lillian Russell (1861-1922) was a popular lecturer/singer around the turn of the century. Miss Russell has been portrayed in films by Alice Faye in *Lillian Russell* (1940), Ruth Gillette in *The Great Ziegfeld* (1936), Andrea King in *My Wild Irish Rose* (1947), and Binnie Barnes in *Diamond Jim* (1935).

Marilyn Monroe also portrayed Lillian Russell, but not in a motion picture. It was in Richard Avedon's photo series that appeared in *LIFE* magazine on December 22, 1958.

**THERESA RUSSELL**

Theresa Russell is the excellent actress who portrayed MM in Nicolas Roeg's fascinating 1985 film *Insignificance.*

Born Theresa Papp in San Diego in 1957, Miss Russell has also appeared in such films as *The Last Tycoon* (1976), *Straight Time* (1978), and Nicolas Roeg's *Bad Timing* (1980). She also won NATO's "New Star of the Year" award in 1986 for her performance in *Black Widow.*

**RUSSIA**

According to old reliable, Louella Parsons, Marilyn Monroe applied for a visa to visit Moscow in August 1955, during her sojourn away from Hollywood. However, Marilyn never did make the trip, although she did meet Soviet leader Nikita Khrushchev in Hollywood in 1959.

In 1960, after Marilyn's announced split from Arthur Miller, the Russian youth magazine *Nedyela,* which was edited by Khrushchev's son-in-law, attacked MM. The article read, in part:

> . . . She found in Miller what she lacked. She exploited him without pity. He wrote scripts for her films and made her a real actress. Marilyn paid him back—she left him.

Following Marilyn's death, the Moscow paper *Izvestia* commented: "Hollywood gave birth to her and it killed her."

In 1987, during the 25th anniversary of Marilyn's death, the official Soviet news agency reactivated the theory that Marilyn may have been murdered. The news agency repeated the report that two doctors (Greenson and Engelberg) alerted the police a half hour after having found Marilyn's body and questioned, "Why the delay? What did those people do in the house of the film actress before the arrival of the police?"

**ROBERT RYAN**

During his lengthy career in Hollywood, actor Robert Ryan (1909-1973) appeared in such films as *Gangway for Tomorrow* (1943), *Crossfire* (1947), *Bad*

*Day at Black Rock* (1944), *God's Little Acre* (1958), *Billy Budd* (1962), and *The Wild Bunch* (1969).

In 1952, Ryan costarred with an increasingly popular Marilyn Monroe in Fritz Lang's *Clash by Night*.

**LUCILLE RYMAN**

MGM talent scout Lucille Ryman was one of the individuals instrumental in the early success of Marilyn Monroe. It was Lucille Ryman who initially interested director John Huston in casting Marilyn for his prestigious 1950 picture *The Asphalt Jungle*.

There is some confusion as to where and how Lucille Ryman first became aware of Marilyn Monroe. Some reports have contended that Ryman met Marilyn in 1947 at a celebrity golf tournament in which MM served as a "starlet caddy." However, other accounts have claimed that Ryman inadvertently came across Marilyn's 1946 Fox screen test and was sufficiently impressed to request a meeting.

At any rate, Lucille Ryman became one of Marilyn's earliest and staunchest supporters. She welcomed the financially struggling MM into the home that she shared with her husband, actor John Carroll. She also gave Marilyn an allowance of $25 a week (for "walking around money") and generally created an environment in which Marilyn was able to concentrate on her acting career. Moreover, following Marilyn's impressive registering in *The Asphalt Jungle*, Lucille Ryman campaigned, albeit unsuccessfully, to obtain a contract for MM at MGM.

Later, as she began her ascent at 20th Century-Fox, Marilyn contacted Lucille and attempted to repay her early benefactor. Ryman was later quoted as telling Hedda Hopper (May 4, 1952):

> "I was stunned. It was the first time anyone had ever offered to pay me back. I told her to forget it, and to pass the money along to some other kid someday—some kid who needed a helping hand."

# S

### THE SAHARA MOTOR HOTEL

During the 1956 location shooting of *Bus Stop*, Marilyn Monroe stayed at the Sahara Motor Hotel (address: 401 N. 1st Street) in Phoenix, Arizona.

### THE ST. REGIS HOTEL

During the 1954 location shooting of *The Seven Year Itch*, Marilyn and Joe DiMaggio stayed at the St. Regis Hotel in New York City (address: Fifth Avenue and 55th Street). The DiMaggios occupied Suites 1105 and 1106. Today the hotel is still in business, operating as the St. Regis-Sheraton.

### ST. VINCENT HOSPITAL

In April 1956, Marilyn Monroe was hospitalized at St. Vincent Hospital in Los Angeles. She was suffering from bronchitis and a viral infection. The hospital, still in existence, is located at 2131 W. 3rd Street and is known as the St. Vincent Medical Center.

### MRS. M. SAKAKEENY

Mrs. Sakakeeny was a Massachusetts woman who was undoubtedly one of the first people to recognize Marilyn Monroe's "star quality." In the October 31, 1949, "Letters" section of *LIFE* magazine, Mrs. Sakakeeny wrote:

> Marilyn Monroe is not only the most beautiful, but the one who will no doubt make a name for herself in Hollywood.

Mrs. Sakakeeny's comments were made in response to a *LIFE* feature on the new crop of Hollywood starlets.

### SAKS FIFTH AVENUE

Not surprisingly, one of Marilyn Monroe's favorite clothing stores in New York was the legendary Saks Fifth Avenue (address: 12 E. 49th Street).

### SALARY

In all probability, Marilyn Monroe was the worst-paid major movie star in Hollywood history. For example, for her work in *Gentlemen Prefer Blondes* (1953), one of her most successful pictures, Marilyn was paid the estimated, paltry sum of $18,000. This pales even further when compared to the $100,000 (or $200,000—depending on your source) that Jane Russell earned for the same film.

It was not until after her 1955 strike that Marilyn Monroe began to earn a respectable salary worthy of her stardom. The following is a selective breakdown of Marilyn's earnings over the years.

1. Starting salary at the Radio Plane Company, circa 1943–44: $20 a week
2. Ending salary at Radio Plane, 1945: $50 a week

3. Early modeling assignments, 1945: $5 an hour
4. As a hostess/model for the Holga Steel Company, 1945: $10 a day
5. For an extended photo shoot with Andre de Dienes, Christmas 1945: $200 flat fee
6. Posing for illustrator Earl Moran, 1946–1950: $10 an hour
7. First contract with 20th Century-Fox, 1946: $75 a week
8. Fox contract renewal, 1947: $150 a week
9. Columbia contract, 1948: $125 a week
10. Posing for nude calendar, 1949: $50 flat fee
11. Promoting *Love Happy*, 1949: $100 a week
12. For *The Asphalt Jungle*, 1950: $350 a week (MM received a total of $1,050 for her work)
13. Second Fox contract, with semiannual increases until a $1,500 ceiling limit was reached, 1951: $500 a week
14. *Clash by Night* (RKO), 1952: $500 a week
15. *We're Not Married*, 1952: $750 a week
16. By the end of 1952: $1,000 a week
17. *Gentlemen Prefer Blondes*, 1953: $1,250 a week
18. May 11, 1953: $1,500 a week (contractual ceiling limit)
19. For appearing on "The Jack Benny Show," September 1953: a new black Cadillac
20. For *River of No Return* (1954), *There's No Business Like Show Business* (1954), and *The Seven Year Itch* (1955): $1,500 a week
21. New Fox contract, 1956: $100,000 a film flat fee, plus $500 a week for expenses
22. *Some Like It Hot*, 1959: $100,000 flat fee, plus 10% of the profits
23. *The Misfits*, 1961: $300,000 flat fee, plus 10% of the profits
24. What MM would have received for *Something's Got to Give*, 1962: $100,000 flat fee

**RICHARD SALE**

Richard Sale directed Marilyn Monroe twice, in the films *A Ticket to Tomahawk* (1950), which he also cowrote, and *Let's Make It Legal* (1951).

Sale, born in 1911, also cowrote and directed *Gentlemen Marry Brunettes*, the 1955 sequel to *Gentlemen Prefer Blondes* (1953).

**SAMUEL GOLDWYN STUDIOS**

Location where much of the *Some Like It Hot* production was shot in 1958. Goldwyn Studios, presently named the Warner Hollywood Studios, was situated at 1041 N. Formosa Avenue in Hollywood.

**SAN FRANCISCO**

Following her January 1954 marriage to Joe DiMaggio, Marilyn Monroe considered San Francisco as her new home—at least temporarily. Marilyn escorted Joe DiMaggio, Jr., to such famous San Francisco sites as Seal Point and the Cliff House. Marilyn was also a frequent patron of her husband's restaurant on Fisherman's Wharf.

However, as much as Marilyn may have been enamored of the City by the Bay, she was even more anxious to return to Hollywood. Thus, in April 1954, the newlywed DiMaggios packed up their belongings and bade farewell to their home, which was located at 2150 Beach St.

**CARL SANDBURG**

"She told him, 'Let me hold your hand,' and they sat and talked for an hour. The friendship was a good one after that."

Harry Golden, on the friendship between MM and Carl Sandburg

"She was a good talker. There were realms of science, politics and economics in which she wasn't at home, but she spoke well on the national scene, the Hollywood scene, and on people who are good to know and people who ain't. We agreed on a number of things. She sometimes threw her arms around me like people do who like each other very much. Too bad I was forty-eight years older—I couldn't play her leading man."

Carl Sandburg on Marilyn Monroe

Poet/biographer Carl Sandburg was born on January 6, 1878, in Galesburg, Illinois. He became well known for his exhaustive biography of Abraham Lincoln and received many prestigious awards for his poetry. He died in July 1967, at the age of 89.

Long before she ever met Carl Sandburg, Marilyn Monroe had been encouraged, by Arthur Miller, to read the Lincoln biography. Then, in 1959–1960, when Sandburg was in Hollywood to script *The Greatest Story Ever Told,* Marilyn sought his friendship. The odd couple met again in New York shortly thereafter and cemented their bond. The friendship lasted until Marilyn's death in 1962.

Initially, Joe DiMaggio invited Carl Sandburg to give the eulogy at Marilyn's funeral. However, his health would not permit it; thus, Lee Strasberg was called in. Nevertheless, before his own death, Sandburg sermonized about Marilyn:

"She never fully realized herself.
The best years for her were ahead of her,
the best years were the years to come."

**GEORGE SANDERS**

Actor George Sanders was born July 3, 1906, in St. Petersburg, Russia. Over a Hollywood career that spanned nearly forty years, Sanders gained a reputation for his adept portrayals of scoundrels and cads. Sanders's filmography includes *Strange Cargo* (1936), *Rebecca* (1940), *Foreign Correspondent* (1940), *The Picture of Dorian Gray* (1944), and *Village of the Damned* (1960).

In 1950, Sanders costarred in *All About Eve,* for which he won a "Best Supporting Actor" Oscar. Also in that film, as Sanders's protege, was starlet Marilyn Monroe. Reportedly, Marilyn and Sanders had an off-screen affair as well, much to the chagrin of Zsa Zsa Gabor, Sanders's wife at the time.

In 1960, George Sanders published his autobiography, which was entitled *Memoirs of a Professional Cad.* He died on April 25, 1972.

**TERRY SANDERS**

Terry Sanders produced, directed, edited, and cowrote the 1964 one-hour television documentary, "The Legend of Marilyn Monroe."

**SANTA BARBARA AVENUE**

Nineteen twenties Hollywood location of the residence of Gladys Baker and Edward Mortenson.

**THE SANTA FE CHIEF**

Locomotive that took MM from Los Angeles's Union Station to Chicago during the 1949 *Love Happy* tour.

**SANTA MONICA HOSPITAL**

Over the years, a plot involving Santa Monica Hospital has been added to the controversy surrounding Marilyn's death. Reportedly, at approximately 2:30 A.M. on August 5, 1962, the Schaefer Ambulance Company rushed Marilyn's alive but unconscious body to the Santa Monica Hospital (address: 1225 15th Street). However, the official police report contends that Marilyn's body was not found until approximately 3:30 A.M. and that no ambulance or hospital was involved.

***SATURDAY EVENING POST***

The *Saturday Evening Post* has published the following articles on MM:

☆ 5/5/56: "The New Marilyn Monroe" (first of three articles by Pete Martin)
☆ 5/12/56: "The New Marilyn Monroe: Here She Talks About Herself"
☆ 5/19/56: "The New Marilyn Monroe: Blonde, Incorporated"
☆ 8/18/56: "Will Acting Spoil Mrs. Miller?"
☆ 7/31/65: "Marilyn Monroe"
☆ 7/76: "I Call on Marilyn Monroe"
☆ 8/85: "Legends That Will"

**HARRY SAUBER**

Harry Sauber cowrote *Ladies of the Chorus* (1948), which featured Marilyn Monroe in her first costarring role.

**PHIL SAVENICK**

Phil Savenick wrote and produced "Marvelous Marilyn," a special segment of "That's Hollywood" that aired on ABC-TV on January 8, 1979.

**THE SAVOY HOTEL**

Following her July 1956 arrival in London, Marilyn Monroe held a press conference at the Savoy Hotel (address: 1, Savoy, HI WC2) to announce the shooting of *The Prince and the Showgirl* (1957).

## SAWTELLE, CALIFORNIA

Shortly after her release from the orphanage in 1937, Norma Jeane Baker went to live with her "Aunt" Ana Lower in the West Los Angeles district of Sawtelle.

## SAWTELLE BOULEVARD SCHOOL

While living with Ana Lower, Norma Jeane attended the Sawtelle Boulevard School. Her principal was Nora Sterry. Norma Jeane was a member of the School Safety Committee. On January 31, 1939, Norma Jeane was presented with a certificate "in recognition of the personal service rendered by her as a member of the School Safety Committee."

In 1941, the Sawtelle Boulevard School changed its name to the Nora Sterry School. It is located at 1730 Corinth Avenue in West Los Angeles.

## ANTHONY SCADUTO

Anthony Scaduto, *aka* Tony Sciacca, is the author of the book *Who Killed Marilyn?* (1976). Material from that book also appeared in the October 1975 edition of *Oui* magazine. Of MM, Scaduto had the following to say: "She was a cunning, ambitious woman who exploited people and situations . . . to get what she wanted; she used others at least as often as she herself was used."

## HAL SCHAEFER

When Marilyn Monroe separated from Joe DiMaggio in the fall of 1954, it was widely speculated that it was because of Marilyn's "affair" with her vocal coach, Hal Schaefer.

In July 1954, Schaefer reportedly attempted to commit suicide by drinking a poisonous solution that contained typewriter-cleaning fluid. Rumors of his alleged adulterous involvement with Marilyn Monroe went public after she visited his Santa Monica Hospital bedside following his unsuccessful suicide attempt. Of his relationship with MM, Schaefer was quoted as saying at that time:

> "Joe DiMaggio jealous of me? That's kind of silly. Why, it's ridiculous! I'm embarrassed about the whole thing. Marilyn's one of my pupils and I coached her for singing in *Gentlemen Prefer Blondes, River of No Return* and *There's No Business Like Show Business.*"

Recently, from his home in Port Washington, New York, Schaefer opted not to discuss his personal involvement with MM. However, he did offer the following insights on his business relationship with her:

> Jack Cole was working with her and I had worked with him on other productions, and he introduced us during the movie *Gentlemen Prefer Blondes.* I don't know if it was Ken Darby, who was head of the vocal department at Fox at that time, or Cole who actually got me the [vocal coach] job, or if Marilyn herself did. It

> *was* Marilyn who got me my first screen credit for *There's No Business Like Show Business.* I'd worked on a lot of pictures, but had never gotten a screen credit. Marilyn pushed and pushed until they gave me a credit.

And, on her talent:

> I always felt she never really achieved her potential as a singer—I felt she could have been a really good singer. I gave her Ella Fitzgerald albums to listen to for homework, and she fell in love with Ella. She had great potential and never realized it.

**WALTER SCHAEFER**

Walter Schaefer was the owner of the Schaefer Ambulance Service in Hollywood. In 1985, Schaefer appeared in the BBC documentary "The Last Days of Marilyn Monroe" and claimed that, on the night of Marilyn's death, his drivers had taken a comatose MM to Santa Monica Hospital. This is in direct conflict with the official police report, which contended that Marilyn's body was found dead at her Brentwood home and that there was never a need for an ambulance. Mr. Schaefer died on January 23, 1986.

**DORE SCHARY**

Despite Marilyn Monroe's considerable success in Metro's *The Asphalt Jungle* (1950), MGM chief Dore Schary (1905-1980) refused to sign her to a studio contract. He didn't think that Marilyn was photogenic or that she had star quality. He also commented that she didn't have the looks to become a movie star.

Years later, Schary conceded that not signing MM was not the only blunder of his career. Apparently, he had also declined to invest in *A Streetcar Named Desire—before* it became one of the most successful Broadway plays of all time.

**MARIA SCHELL**

One of the film roles that MM most desired was the part of Grushenka in Dostoyevsky's *The Brothers Karamazov.* The film was eventually made in 1958, with Maria Schell in the role that Marilyn had coveted. Nonetheless, when MM was asked her opinion of the movie, Marilyn responded: "I thought Maria was wonderful in it."

**JOSEPH SCHENCK**

> "Get this straight: Mr. Schenck and I were good friends. I know the word around Hollywood was [that] I was Joe Schenck's girlfriend, but that's a lie."
>
> MM to Maurice Zolotow

> "I went to his house because I liked Mr. Schenck and I liked his food and it was better than the Studio Club food. I don't mean to imply the Studio Club had bad food. I mean, let's say that Mr. Schenck's cook was just better than their cook."
>
> MM to Maurice Zolotow

Joe Schenck was born on December 25, 1878, in Rybinski, Russia. In 1933, he established 20th Century Productions. By 1935, he was the head of 20th Century-Fox. However, Schenck's momentum was interrupted in 1941, when he was imprisoned for perjury after bribing a labor racketeer. In 1943, Schenck was reappointed the head of production at 20th Century-Fox.

By the time he met contract player Marilyn Monroe, Joe Schenck was nearly seventy years old. She was twenty-one. It was 1947, on the lot of 20th Century-Fox. Schenck was in his limousine when he spotted Marilyn. He had his chauffeur stop the car. He called Marilyn over to the car and asked her name, then invited her to his house for dinner.

Marilyn Monroe had many, many dinners with Joe Schenck at his Holmby Hills mansion (address: 141 S. Carolwood Drive). And, although she repeatedly denied it, it is generally accepted in Hollywood that Marilyn Monroe *was* "Joe Schenck's girl." Jim Bacon, in his book, *Hollywood Is a Four Letter Town* (Avon, 1976), contended that he once visited MM when she lived at Schenck's guest house and that Marilyn admitted to having occasional sex with her elderly benefactor.

Reportedly, it was Joe Schenck who obtained Marilyn's 1948 Columbia contract from Harry Cohn, which led to her first costarring role, in *Ladies of the Chorus*. And, in the succeeding years, after MM re-signed with Fox, Joe Schenck kept a protective, powerful eye on his blonde discovery.

Considering all of the available "evidence," it seems that the Schenck-Monroe pairing can best be described as a friendship with sexual favors.

**MARA SCHERBATOFF**

Mara Scherbatoff was a forty-eight-year-old New York bureau chief for *Paris-Match* magazine when she was tragically killed in a car accident. It was June 1956, at a time when the worldwide press was frantically hounding Marilyn Monroe and Arthur Miller for news on their imminent marriage. Miss

THE CHRIS BASINGER COLLECTION

MM runs from press after accident that killed Scherbatoff, Roxbury, 1956.

Scherbatoff was a passenger in a car that was following a green Oldsmobile in which Miller and MM were passengers. The location was a winding country road, named Goldmine Road, not far from Miller's farmhouse in Roxbury, Connecticut. The accident occurred when the car containing Miss Scherbatoff struck a tree, hurling her fatally through the windshield. She was rushed to New Milford Hospital in Connecticut, where she died.

The driver of the Scherbatoff car was eighteen-year-old Ira Slade, who was injured. The driver of the Miller car was Arthur's cousin, Morton Miller.

**PHILIP K. SCHEUER**

On August 27, 1950, a full-length feature article appeared in *The Los Angeles Times* about starlet Marilyn Monroe. Written by Philip K. Scheuer, the article was one of the very first important features ever written about MM.

**LAWRENCE SCHILLER**

> "She loved it, when I photographed her in the nude. She loved it. You know, she wasn't that busty and she had a little heavy hips. And she had freckles all over. And there were some varicose veins in there. She was just like the girl next door."
>
> Lawrence Schiller on MM

> "You're already famous, Marilyn. Now you can make me famous."
>
> Schiller to MM, 1962

In May 1962, photographer Lawrence Schiller was assigned by *Paris-Match* magazine to do a shooting of Marilyn Monroe at work on *Something's Got to Give*. The shooting, as fate would have it, changed Schiller's life.

On Monday, May 28, Schiller shot director George Cukor shooting Marilyn's swimming pool sequence. What wasn't expected was that—while in the pool—Marilyn would pull off her flesh-colored swimsuit. It is not certain whether the decision was Cukor's or Marilyn's, but it is known that MM reveled in the idea of dog-paddling in the buff. And very fortunate Larry Schiller was there to capture it all in black and white and in color. Moreover, not only did Marilyn pose in the pool; she also posed out of the pool. These photographs were to become known worldwide as "the nude session."

Three days later, Schiller was present at Marilyn's casual thirty-sixth birthday celebration at 20th Century-Fox. At that time, Schiller asked Marilyn's permission to reproduce the daring photographs in the worldwide press. He also asked her what she wanted in return for the valuable nudes. Marilyn replied, perhaps carelessly, that all she wanted was a slide projector to display the photos.

Following the swimming pool event, Larry Schiller was in contact with MM on a daily basis until the time of her death. Shrewdly, Schiller shelled out $10,000 to photographer Jimmy Mitchell—who was also present for the impromptu nude session—for the rights to *his* photographs of MM. Meanwhile, Schiller was making a small fortune by selling his photos to magazines from around the world. In addition, Schiller arranged for Marilyn to do a special cover sitting for *Playboy*—a session that was later canceled at Marilyn's request.

The last time Larry Schiller saw Marilyn Monroe alive was on August 4,

1962, between 9:00 and 10:00 A.M. at her Brentwood home.

Nonetheless, over the next two decades, Marilyn Monroe would remain an integral part of Lawrence Schiller's life. In the early 1970s, Schiller produced an exhibition of MM photographs entitled "Marilyn Monroe: The Legend and The Truth." The exhibition, which toured the country, was so successful that a book was planned. The photo book evolved into Norman Mailer's *Marilyn: A Biography* (Grosset and Dunlap, 1973). The book was produced and designed by Lawrence Schiller.

Then, in 1980, Schiller produced the fine telefilm *Marilyn: The Untold Story* for ABC. It was based, predictably, on the Norman Mailer book.

Today, several years later, it is not yet certain whether or not Lawrence Schiller has gotten Marilyn Monroe out of his system. Surely, his life would have been different without her. Regardless, Schiller has gone on to produce such television projects as *The Executioner's Song* (1981), which was based, of course, on Normal Mailer's award-winning book.

**GEORGE SCHLEE**

In 1955, Aristotle Onassis reportedly approached George Schlee with the proposition that Marilyn Monroe marry Prince Rainier of Monaco. Schlee, in turn, contacted Gardner Cowles, who discussed the possibility with MM.

**CHARLES SCHNEE**

Charles Schnee wrote the screenplay for the 1950 film *Right Cross,* which featured Marilyn Monroe in a small part. Among Schnee's other credits are *I Walk Alone* (1947), *The Bad and the Beautiful* (for which he won a 1952 Oscar), and *Butterfield 8* (1960).

**SCHOOLS**

The following is a chronological listing of the Los Angeles-area schools that Norma Jeane/Marilyn Monroe attended:

| *SCHOOL* | *YEAR* | *GRADE* | *AGE* |
|---|---|---|---|
| 1. Ballona Elementary and Kindergarten | Sept. 1931-June 1932 | Kindergarten | 5-6 |
| 2. Vine Street | Sept. 1932-June 1934 | 1st Grade | 6-7 |
| | | 2nd Grade | 7-8 |
| 3. Selma Street | Sept. 1934-June 1935 | 3rd Grade | 8-9 |
| 4. Vine Street | Sept. 1935-June 1937 | 4th Grade | 9-10 |
| | | 5th Grade | 10-11 |
| 5. Lankershim | Sept. 1937-June 1938 | 6th Grade | 11-12 |
| 6. Sawtelle Blvd. | Sept. 1938-June 1939 | 7th Grade | 12-13 |
| 7. Emerson Jr. High | Sept. 1939-June 1941 | 8th Grade | 13-14 |
| | | 9th Grade | 14-15 |
| 8. Van Nuys High | Sept. 1941-Feb. 1942 | 10th Grade | 15 |
| 9. University High* | Feb. 1942 | 10th Grade | 15 |
| 10. University of Cal. at Los Angeles (UCLA)** | Feb. 1951 | Extension | 24 |

*Norma Jeane Baker dropped out of University High in the spring of 1942 to marry Jim Dougherty.

**Marilyn Monroe took extension evening courses in Art Appreciation and Literature in February 1951.

**GENE SCHOOR**

Gene Schoor was the cowriter of the book *Marilyn & Joe DiMaggio,* which was published in 1977.

**FLORA RHETA SCHREIBER**

Flora Rheta Schreiber penned an article about Marilyn Monroe that appeared in the January 1963 edition of *Good Housekeeping* magazine.

**LEW SCHREIBER**

Schreiber was 20th Century-Fox executive Darryl Zanuck's first assistant, who, in 1955, negotiated with Milton H. Greene and Frank Delaney to reobtain the services of the on-strike Marilyn Monroe.

**GREG SCHREINER**

Greg Schreiner has been the president of the Marilyn Remembered Fan Club since its inception in 1983. A pianist by profession, Greg hails from Orangeville, Illinois. He was twelve years old when his parents took him to see *Some Like It Hot* (1959), and he has been hooked on Marilyn Monroe ever since. Greg's MM collection includes two of her personal gowns, stills, thirty books, an extensive record collection, and two of her personal scripts.

**SCHWAB'S**

Schwab's was a famed Hollywood pharmacy/coffee shop (address: 8024 Sunset Boulevard) where aspiring actors and actresses used to drink coffee and hang out in the hope of being "discovered." Marilyn Monroe was one of those struggling starlets. After she starred in *Ladies of the Chorus* in 1948, Marilyn returned to Schwab's but was disappointed to find that no one recognized her.

In 1949, while having lunch at Schwab's, MM learned that a sexy blonde was needed for a bit part in the new Marx Brothers picture, *Love Happy.* She promptly landed herself an audition at RKO, which, of course, she won.

**TONY SCIACCA**

"Tony Sciacca" is the pen-name of writer Anthony Scaduto, who authored the 1976 book about MM entitled *Who Killed Marilyn?* Reportedly, Scaduto used the alias because of the book's controversial contents.

**MARK SCOTT**

Mark Scott was a radio and television broadcaster who was a friend of Joe DiMaggio. Following the DiMaggio-Monroe separation, Scott told reporters: "They're still in love with each other. Their marriage can be saved."

**ZACHARY SCOTT**

In 1951, actor Zachary Scott (1914–1965) costarred in *Let's Make It Legal,* which featured starlet MM in a small role. Among Scott's other film roles are *The Southerner* (1945) and *Mildred Pierce* (1945).

***THE SCREEN GREATS: MARILYN MONROE***
Author: Tom Hutchinson
Publisher: Exeter Books
Year: 1982 (Out of print)

Yet another standard career bio on MM. However, the book does have an excellent compilation of color and black-and-white photographs to compensate for its lack of originality.

**THE SCREEN TESTS**
The following is a breakdown of the four motion picture screen tests that Marilyn Monroe is known to have made:

**Screen Test #1 (July 19, 1946), 20th Century-Fox**
The test, shot on the set of the Betty Grable movie *Mother Wore Tights* (1947), was arranged by Ben Lyon, directed by Walter Lang, and shot by Leon Shamroy. Allan Snyder did Marilyn's makeup, and Charles LeMaire selected her gown. Florence Bush reportedly did Marilyn's hair. The silent test, shot in color, called for MM to walk across the set, sit down, light a cigarette, put it out, and exit. The test resulted in Marilyn Monroe's first movie studio contract.

**Screen Test #2 (1948), Columbia**
MM reportedly tested for the Billy Dawn role in *Born Yesterday* (1950) during the term of her 1948 contract with Columbia. However, Columbia honcho Harry Cohn refused to screen the test, and Marilyn's option at the studio was dropped. The role, of course, went to Judy Holliday, who won an Oscar for her performance.

**Screen Test #3 (1950), 20th Century-Fox**
In 1950, perhaps following her success in Metro's *The Asphalt Jungle,* Fox decided to give Marilyn Monroe a second chance. In this sound test for a film called *Cold Shoulder,* MM portrayed the part of a gangster's girlfriend. The gangster was portrayed by Richard Conte. MM had lines like the following:

> (as Conte prepares to hit her) Go ahead! It won't be the first time
> I've been worked over today . . . I'm getting used to it!

The test was apparently highly successful for MM, because, on December 10, 1950, she was re-signed by 20th Century-Fox.

**Screen Test #4 (June 14, 1951), 20th Century-Fox**
Following her work in *Love Nest* (1951), MM appeared in one more sound test while at Fox. In the test, MM acted out a love scene with actor Robert Wagner, who was then just beginning his career. In all probability, the test was for *Let's Make It Legal* (1951), and was more for Wagner than for Monroe.

**SCREENWRITERS**
*See* WRITERS.

***SCUDDA HOO! SCUDDA HAY!*** ★½
1948 98 minutes Technicolor
20th Century-Fox
Directed by: F. Hugh Herbert
Produced by: Walter Morosco
Screenplay by: F. Hugh Herbert, from a novel by George Agnew Chamberlain
Photographed by: Ernest Palmer
Cast: June Haver, Lon McCallister, Walter Brennan, Ann Revere, Natalie Wood, Robert Karnes, Henry Hull, Tom Tully, Les MacGregor, Ken Christy

THE RAY VAN GOEYE COLLECTION

*Scudda Hoo! Scudda Hay!* is generally recognized as the first movie Marilyn Monroe made, although her second picture, *Dangerous Years*, was *released* first.

Despite its distinction of introducing Marilyn Monroe, *Scudda Hoo! Scudda Hay!* is a bore. The plot revolves around a farmer's son, who is obsessed with a pair of mules—or some such nonsense. And, if you're watching the film to see MM's "debut," you may as well forget it. She had one line in the film—"Hello"—which was subsequently edited out. She is not even listed in the credits for the film. As is, the twenty-one-year-old starlet can be seen in one shot, rowing on a lake. It was certainly not an auspicious start for MM, but, alas, it was a start.

Following its initial release, the inanely titled *Scudda Hoo! Scudda Hay!* was retitled *Summer Lightning* in certain markets.

**CLAIRE SEAY**

In 1951, Claire Seay was an instructor at UCLA who taught a course in "Backgrounds of Literature." One of Miss Seay's students was starlet Marilyn Monroe. Later, Miss Seay was quoted as saying about her former student: "She was so modest, so humble, so attentive, that she could have been some girl who had just come from a convent."

***THE SECRET HAPPINESS OF MARILYN MONROE***

Author: James E. Dougherty
Publisher: Playboy Press
Year: 1976 (Out of print)

Hype aside, unlike most books about Marilyn Monroe, this book actually does offer an *intimate* portrait of the girl/woman who became the biggest movie star in Hollywood.

Written by Marilyn's first husband, Jim Dougherty, *The Secret Happiness* is not so much about MM as it is about Norma Jeane Baker Dougherty—the sixteen-year-old neighbor girl whom the author courted, married, and divorced. The Norma Jeane depicted in this book is a sharp contrast to the Marilyn Monroe of later life. Here, Norma Jeane is a somewhat typical, uncomplicated Van Nuys housewife who thrives on the institution of marriage. Granted, the view presented by Dougherty tends to be a bit biased and naive. After all, if Norma Jeane really had been so happy in her domestic complacency, she never would have divorced Dougherty, and there never would have been a Marilyn Monroe.

Nonetheless, *The Secret Happiness of Marilyn Monroe* emerges as an original, provocative work—one that should prove to be worthwhile to all students of MM. In addition, Dougherty has included some very rare black-and-white photos that are presumed to be straight from the family photo album.

**"THE SECRET LOVE OF MARILYN MONROE"**

*See* "MOVIOLA: THIS YEAR'S BLONDE."

**SECRETARIES**

The following is a selective, chronological list of the secretaries that Marilyn Monroe employed during her career:

1. Peter Leonardi
2. May Reis
3. Marjorie Stengel
4. "Cherie"

**MM Trivia Quiz #41**

Marilyn Monroe portrayed a secretary in three of her movies. Name them. (Answer on page 578.)

**HARRY SEGALL**
Harry Segall (1897–1975) authored a story on which the movie *Monkey Business* (1952) was based.

**SELMA STREET SCHOOL**
Norma Jeane Baker attended the Selma Street School for a brief period, circa 1934. The Selma Street School is currently known as the Selma Avenue Elementary School (address: 6611 Selma Avenue) in Hollywood.

**MICHAEL SELSMAN**
Michael Selsman was a former colleague of Pat Newcomb at the Arthur Jacobs Public Relations agency, which represented Marilyn Monroe. According to Milo Speriglio's book, *The Marilyn Conspiracy* (Pocket Books, 1986), Selsman contends that MM had an abortion a few months prior to her death. According to Selsman, Marilyn confided to him, saying: "I just had another abortion. I don't know if it was Bobby's or Jack's."

**JACQUES SERNAS**
In the mid-1950s, Warner Brothers was busy grooming Hollywood import Jacques Sernas for movie stardom. In late 1954, Marilyn Monroe was seen with Sernas, dancing at the Crescendo Club.

***THE SEVEN YEAR ITCH* ★★★½**
1955 105 minutes De Luxe Color
20th Century-Fox
Directed by: Billy Wilder
Produced by: Billy Wilder, Charles K. Feldman
Screenplay by: Billy Wilder, George Axelrod, based on the play by George Axelrod
Photographed by: Milton Krasner
Cast: Tom Ewell, Marilyn Monroe, Evelyn Keyes, Butch Bernard, Victor Moore, Robert Strauss, Sonny Tufts

*The Seven Year Itch* was an extremely important film for Marilyn Monroe. By the time of its June 1955 release, Marilyn had not had a bona fide hit for nearly two years, since the successful opening of *How to Marry a Millionaire* in November 1953. Two years without a hit was a dangerously long period back in the 1950s. Moreover, at the time of the *Itch* release, Marilyn had been in a self-imposed exile for six months and was anything but popular in the Hollywood inner circle. She had also broken off her longtime contract with 20th Century-Fox and was facing an onslaught of legal battles. And she was threatened with the prospect of never again working in Hollywood.

But the release of *The Seven Year Itch* changed all of that. Its success was so significant that 20th Century-Fox executives were provoked to expedite and intensify their negotiations to reobtain MM—who was, once again, a hot box office commodity.

Marilyn began shooting *The Seven Year Itch* on August 10, 1954, in Hollywood. She had just completed her work on *There's No Business Like*

Bathtub scene cut from *The Seven Year Itch*, 1955

*Show Business,* and was ushered directly, without a break, into *Itch.* On November 9, 1954, MM flew to New York to shoot the exterior street scenes for the film. The infamous "Skirt Scene" was shot at 52nd Street and Lexington Avenue, in front of the Trans-Lux Theatre. It was shot after 2:00 A.M. Nevertheless, even at this late hour, a crowd of approximately four thousand New Yorkers gathered to watch MM's skirt blow up over her ears. Also present to witness the spectacle, unfortunately, was Marilyn's husband, Joe DiMaggio. It has frequently been speculated that it was this final event that precipitated the demise of the DiMaggio marriage. The day after this scene was shot, Joe DiMaggio boarded a plane and returned to California—alone. As for Marilyn, she left New York on September 15, 1954. Just over two weeks later, the famous couple officially separated. They were divorced in late October, and on Friday, November 5, MM completed her work on *The Seven Year Itch.* Secretly, she plotted to leave Hollywood, return to New York, and form her own independent production company.

Upon its completion, *The Seven Year Itch* had gone over its budget by some $150,000. Its total cost was an estimated $1,800,000, which pales considering that it initially grossed $8,000,000 (remember, this is in *1955* dollars).

The movie was a critical success as well—and deservedly so. *The Seven Year Itch* still holds up as an excellent comedy/fantasy that more than adequately displays that certain Monroe magic. Interestingly, and rewardingly, this is one of three films in which MM does *not* steal the entire picture. As her nervous, married, neighbor, Joe Normal, Tom Ewell is superb. And

Marilyn Monroe admirably pulls off the difficult trick of humanizing her molded fantasy goddess character.

Furthermore, what *The Seven Year Itch* suggests, and what *Bus Stop* (1956) later embellished, is that Marilyn Monroe could play the wanton woman/bad girl and yet come across as infinitely likable and vulnerable. To do this *believably* is a rare and much underrated talent. Marilyn Monroe accomplished it, seemingly, without even trying.

**MM Trivia Quiz #42**
What kind of plant did MM accidentally knock down onto Tom Ewell's deck in *The Seven Year Itch*? (Answer on page 578.)

**SEX**

> "She was a most responsive bride—a perfect bride in every respect—except the cooking department."
>
> Jim Dougherty on Norma Jeane's sexual responsiveness

> "Marilyn, don't try to sell this sex thing, you are sex. . . . You are the institution of sex. The only motivation you need for this part is the fact that in the movie you are as blind as a bat without glasses."
>
> Jean Negulesco, directing MM in *How to Marry a Millionaire* (1953)

> "You can't sleep your way into being a star, though. It takes much, much more. But it helps. A lot of actresses get their first chance that way."
>
> Marilyn Monroe

> "I spent a great deal of time on my knees."
>
> MM, reportedly, to Amy Greene

> "I just don't get out of sex what I hear other women do. . . . Maybe I'm . . . I'm a sexless . . . sex goddess."
>
> MM to Bob Slatzer

> "I never quite understood it—this sex symbol. I always thought symbols were those things you clash together."
>
> MM, *LIFE* magazine, 8/3/62

> "Sex is part of nature. I go along with nature."

> "I haven't taken a 'sexus'—I mean census—but sex is sex, and that's good, isn't it?"
>
> Marilyn Monroe

> "With Marilyn, you're not talking about going to bed with a woman; you're talking about going to bed with an institution. Who can handle that? And how awful to be one!"
>
> Norman Rosten on MM

> "We are all born sexual creatures, thank God, but it's a pity so many people despise and crush this natural gift."
>
> MM, *LIFE* magazine, 8/3/62

***THE SEX SYMBOL***
*The Sex Symbol* is a made-for-television movie based on the Alvah Bessie

novel *The Symbol*—both of which are thinly disguised, sensationalized, melodramatic accounts of the life and death of Marilyn Monroe.

The telepic, adapted by Alvah Bessie, was directed by David Lowell Rich and produced by Douglas S. Cramer for Columbia Pictures Television. It first aired on ABC on September 17, 1974.

There are many, many faults in this highly exploitive project. Foremost, and most obvious, however, is the absolutely preposterous casting of Connie Stevens as Marilyn Monroe. This can be equated to the absurd notion of casting Minnie Mouse as Cleopatra, Annette Funicello as Elizabeth Taylor, or Vanna White as Eleanor Roosevelt. Whoever came up with the idea should be forced to watch a nonstop marathon of old "Hawaiian Eye" episodes.

In accordance with its trashy tone and its general, all-around bad taste, *The Sex Symbol* features Shelley Winters as a Hollywood gossip columnist and Don Murray, MM's former costar, as an attractive (guess who?) U.S. senator. But, back to Connie. Perhaps it was just that every blonde movie actress in Hollywood declined the part. And that would be easy to understand. It is generally accepted in the entertainment industry that television biopics (such as those on Jayne Mansfield, Rita Hayworth, Grace Kelly, et al.) are usually bad. Well, *The Sex Symbol* does nothing to disprove that. It's about as bad as they get.

**TONY SFORZINI**

The makeup artist credited on *The Prince and the Showgirl* (1957). Nevertheless, it was Milton H. Greene who designed Marilyn's makeup for the film, and, Marilyn's favorite, Allan "Whitey" Snyder, who applied it.

**ROSE SHADE**

Rose Maria Shade cowrote *Marilyn: The Last Months* (1975), the book penned principally by Mrs. Eunice Murray—Marilyn's final housekeeper/companion.

**LEON SHAMROY**

> "When I first watched her, I thought: This girl will be another Harlow—and I still do. Her natural beauty plus her inferiority complex gave her a look of mystery."
>
> Leon Shamroy on MM's 1946 screen test, *Collier's* magazine, 9/8/51

Leon Shamroy (1901–1974) was one of the most distinguished cinematographers in the history of motion pictures. At the time of his death on July 7, 1974, Shamroy had been honored with *twenty-one* Academy Award nominations and four Oscars for *The Black Swan* (1942), *Wilson* (1944), *Leave Her to Heaven* (1946), and *Cleopatra* (1963).

In 1946, the multi-award-winning cinematographer was asked by Ben Lyon, as a favor, to shoot a screen test for an unknown starlet named Norma Jeane Dougherty. Shamroy agreed, the test was shot, and Marilyn Monroe was signed to her first studio contract. Eight years later, Shamroy worked with Marilyn again, in the splashy, Irving Berlin musical, *There's No Business Like Show Business.*

During her career, Marilyn frequently cited Leon Shamroy as one of the few men who were instrumental in her early success.

**SUE SHANNON**
Sue Shannon was Marilyn's wardrobe girl on *Monkey Business* in 1952.

**ERNEST C. SHARP**
Ernie Sharp was the manager of the Clifton Motel in Paso Robles, California, where Marilyn and Joe DiMaggio spent their wedding night on January 14, 1954.

**ARTIE SHAW**
Born Arthur Arschawsky in 1910, Artie Shaw was a famous bandleader and clarinetist who married, among others, Lana Turner and Ava Gardner.

In May 1949, while shooting what became the famous Marilyn Monroe nude calendar, photographer Tom Kelley put an Artie Shaw record on the turntable. As he explained to Marilyn's biographer, Maurice Zolotow, years later:

> "I had 'Begin the Beguine'—the Artie Shaw version—on at the time. I find it's a good number for getting a naked girl in a sexual mood. In my experience, I know of no other piece of music that can arouse sexual vibrations faster than Artie Shaw's recording of 'Begin the Beguine.' "

**SAM SHAW**
Sam Shaw, photographer and movie producer, befriended Marilyn in the mid-1950s. In 1955, Shaw was hired by 20th Century-Fox to shoot publicity stills of MM for *The Seven Year Itch.* Twenty-four years later, *The Joy of Marilyn in the Camera Eye* included those photos. Shaw's third book of MM photographs, *Marilyn: Among Friends* was published in 1987 by Bloomsbury.

In addition to his MM-related work, Shaw has produced photo essays on many film directors and movie stars. He has also served as the executive producer on the majority of films directed by his friend, John Cassavetes.

**THE SHERATON ASTOR HOTEL**
In December 1955, Marlon Brando escorted Marilyn Monroe to a champagne dinner at the Sheraton Astor Hotel on 44th Street in New York City, after the pair attended the world premiere of *The Rose Tattoo.*

**SHERMAN OAKS**
After Jim and Norma Jeane Dougherty got married in June 1942, they moved into their first jointly shared home. It was an apartment and was located on Vista del Monte Street in Sherman Oaks, California.

**THE SHERRY-NETHERLAND HOTEL**
During the 1949 *Love Happy* tour, Marilyn Monroe stayed at the Sherry-Netherland Hotel in New York City (address: 781 Fifth Avenue). Three years

later, MM returned to the Sherry-Netherland Hotel to give promotional interviews in connection with the release of *Monkey Business.*

**SHERWOOD LAKE**

In lieu of an actual honeymoon, Jim Dougherty took Norma Jeane on a fishing trip to Sherwood Lake, located in Ventura County, California. During their four years of marriage, the Doughertys occasionally revisited this lake for weekend fishing expeditions.

**MARY KARGER SHORT**

Mary Karger Short was the sister of Marilyn's early love, Fred Karger. Mary and Marilyn, who were approximately the same age, became fast and durable friends. Mary was at Marilyn's side in court when the latter obtained her October 1954 divorce from Joe DiMaggio. A month later, Mary was seen accompanying MM from Cedars of Lebanon Hospital.

And, in 1955, when she was settling down in New York City, Marilyn paid frequent visits to Mary Short's new home in New Jersey.

**FREDERICK SHROYER**

In 1965, Dr. Frederick Shroyer was the book editor of *The Los Angeles Herald Examiner.* In an article dated October 17, 1965, Shroyer attacked Arthur Miller's stage play *After the Fall*:

> Several summers ago while in New York, I saw the Arthur Miller play, *After the Fall.* That evening remains in my memory as one of the most distasteful of my life. For many hours, it seemed, those of us captive in the audience were subjected to an exhibition of whining self-justification that constituted an acutely embarrassing experience for everyone, except, one supposes, the playwright. As Miller's confessional dragged on, I asked myself what kind of man it was who could utilize the corpse of his wife as a platform for his maudlin mouthings.

**LYNN SHUBERT**

Lynn Shubert wrote the screenplay of the 1976 feature film *Goodbye Norma Jean.*

**LOUIS SHURR**

Louis Shurr was the agent who is often given credit for having arranged Marilyn's 1949 audition with producer Lester Cowan for the movie *Love Happy.*

**SIDNEY JANIS GALLERY**

In December 1967, the Sidney Janis Gallery in Manhattan (address: 110 W. 57th St.) hosted an art show in honor of Marilyn Monroe. The show, entitled "Homage to Marilyn," featured fifty works by thirty-six artists, among them William de Kooning, Rosenquist, Andy Warhol, Salvador Dali, Claes Oldenburg, John Chamberlain, George Segal, Richard Linder, and Joseph Cornell.

**LEE SIEGEL**

On April 5, 1956, while shooting *Bus Stop,* MM suffered from a virus attack that progressed into bronchitis. She was treated by Dr. Lee Siegel, who was the 20th Century-Fox doctor at that time.

**SOL C. SIEGEL**

Sol C. Siegel (1903-1982) was the 20th Century-Fox producer who made three of Marilyn Monroe's movies. They were *Monkey Business* (1952), *Gentlemen Prefer Blondes* (1953), and *There's No Business Like Show Business* (1954).

Among Siegel's other films are *Call Me Madam* (1953), *High Society* (1956), and *Les Girls* (1957).

**SIMONE SIGNORET**

> "She seemed intelligent and gracious—and resigned to playing second fiddle to this golden Hollywood star (MM) who couldn't for a minute compete with her as an actress."
>
> Dorothy Kilgallen on Simone Signoret

> "A man doesn't feel he has to confuse an affair with eternal love and make it a crisis in marriage."
>
> Simone Signoret on her husband's affair with Marilyn Monroe

> "If Marilyn is in love with my husband, it proves she has good taste."
>
> Simone Signoret, 11/60

Born Simone Kaminker on March 25, 1921, Simone Signoret was the highly acclaimed French actress who won an Academy Award for her performance in *Room at the Top* (1959). She was also the longtime wife of actor Yves Montand, whom Marilyn Monroe had an illicit affair with during the 1960 production of *Let's Make Love.*

Reportedly, prior to the shooting of *Love,* MM and SS became quite friendly, and Marilyn frequently expressed her admiration for the distinguished actress.

In 1978, Signoret's autobiography, *Nostalgia Isn't What It Used to Be* (Harper and Row, 1978), was published in America. It included Simone's recollections of her experiences with MM. Before her death on September 30, 1985, Miss Signoret also published a novel entitled *Adieu Volodia.*

**GEORGE SILK**

George Silk was a photographer whose shots of MM appeared in *LIFE* magazine in 1953.

**FRANK SINATRA**

> "I never knew what Sinatra's relationship was with her, but his invisible presence was always there, hovering over us like her guardian angel. He was very protective of her."
>
> George Masters

> "The most fascinating man I ever dated was Frank Sinatra."
>
> MM to Robert Slatzer

Not only did Marilyn Monroe date Frank Sinatra; she also, according to several sources, wanted to marry him.

The legendary entertainer/actor/producer/businessman with the baritone, bedroom voice, Francis Albert Sinatra was born in Hoboken, New Jersey, on December 12, 1915. A teenage idol in the 1940s, Sinatra pocketed an Oscar and industry respect for his "comeback" performance in the 1953 film *From Here to Eternity.* Since then, "Old Blue Eyes," as he has been affectionately tagged, has given many live concert performances, appeared on several television specials, recorded more albums, and starred in a multitude of motion pictures. Among his films are *The Man with the Golden Arm* (1956), *High Society* (1956), *Pal Joey* (1957), *The Manchurian Candidate* (1962), and *The Detective* (1968). Tough, talented, and four times married, Sinatra has remained a star of unparalleled value for over forty years.

Marilyn Monroe first met Frank Sinatra in 1954, when 20th Century-Fox had slated them to costar opposite one another in the ill-fated venture *The Girl in Pink Tights.* They began dating shortly thereafter, following MM's split from Sinatra's friend Joe DiMaggio. Reportedly, it was Sinatra's house that MM sought refuge in following her October 1954 divorce. Meanwhile, it was also at about this time that Sinatra teamed up with DiMaggio to have Marilyn followed by a private detective, presumably to "catch her in the act" with another man. However, the result turned out to be the scandalous mishap dubbed the "Wrong Door Raid," for which Sinatra was forced to testify in court in February 1957.

In the mid-1950s, during her New York period, Marilyn continued to see Sinatra on occasion. Once, while he was performing at the Copacabana Club, Marilyn showed up unexpectedly with Milton and Amy Greene in tow. MM and company had no reservations and no tickets. Worse, there were no seats available. However, when Sinatra saw Marilyn's entrance, he promptly stopped his show and told the waiter to bring a table to the foot of the stage. The waiter, of course, complied, and Sinatra proceeded to sing the entire set to Marilyn and the Greenes.

It was Marilyn's understanding, in 1958, that Frank Sinatra would be one of her costars in what would become the smash hit *Some Like It Hot.* However, Sinatra failed to show up for a meeting with the film's director, Billy Wilder, and Jack Lemmon was signed for the part. Marilyn, it would seem, was destined never to make a film with her friend Frank.

In 1960–61, following her split from Arthur Miller, MM resumed her courtship with Sinatra. In fact, upon her return to Los Angeles, Marilyn moved into Sinatra's Coldwater Canyon home for a brief period. And when she eventually settled into her Doheny Drive apartment, her neighbor was none other than Frank Sinatra. Marilyn was also an occasional visitor to the Cal-Neva Lodge, a casino and resort complex owned by Sinatra. It was during this period that Marilyn began to seriously consider marriage to Frank Sinatra.

To determine why Sinatra and Monroe never married would be pure speculation. Reportedly, she became involved with the Kennedy brothers. He, on the other hand, was romantically linked with dancer Juliet Prowse.

Nevertheless, marriage aside, the Sinatra/Monroe friendship endured until her death.

On the night that she died, as she always did, Marilyn Monroe listened to a stack of Frank Sinatra records. He was, of course, her favorite singer.

Initially, 20th Century-Fox's posthumous 1963 tribute to MM, *Marilyn,* was scheduled to be narrated by Frank Sinatra. However, and for whatever reasons, that plan failed to materialize, and Rock Hudson was called in to perform the services.

## SISTERS

### Half-Sister

Bernice Baker Miracle

### Foster Sisters

1. Beebe Goddard
2. Jody Goddard Lawrence

### Sisters-in-Law

1. Billie Dougherty Campbell
2. Frances DiMaggio
3. Mamie DiMaggio
4. Marie DiMaggio
5. Nellie DiMaggio
6. Joan Miller Copeland

## EDITH SITWELL

Born September 7, 1887, Edith Sitwell, "the first lady of English verse," was a widely admired British poetess and biographer.

While in Los Angeles, toward the end of her life, Miss Sitwell took the opportunity to meet with several prominent Hollywood figures. The most publicized of these meetings was with Marilyn Monroe. The meeting was arranged by *LIFE* magazine and took place at Miss Sitwell's Sunset Towers apartment in Hollywood. The two ladies got on extremely well and developed a friendly acquaintance. Their encounter has been vividly retold in Victoria Glendinning's biography, *Edith Sitwell, A Unicorn Among Lions.*

Miss Sitwell died of heart failure in London on December 9, 1964.

## SIXTY-FIRST STREET

Exterior location scenes for *The Seven Year Itch* were shot on East 61st Street in New York City in 1954.

## SIDNEY SKOLSKY

> "I think she's going to be one of the most popular actresses the movies have ever known."
>
> Sidney Skolsky on Marilyn Monroe, 7/16/52

Born May 2, 1905, Sidney Skolsky was a Hollywood columnist/reporter for over fifty years. He is best known for his columns in *The New York News* and the *New York Post,* the latter of which was published on a daily basis. Skolsky was also syndicated by United Features, and his column appeared in Los Angeles in the *Hollywood Citizen-News.*

Unlike his peers, Sidney Skolsky took a particular interest in the struggling unknown actors and actresses, many of whom used to frequent

Schwab's drugstore in the hope of being "discovered." Accordingly, Skolsky maintained his office on the mezzanine floor of Schwab's, where he had a view of the soda fountain patrons.

In the late 1940s, Marilyn Monroe was one of the struggling Schwab's regulars. Because he did not have a car, Skolsky was frequently driven about town by the movie star aspirants. MM was one of his chauffeurs, and Skolsky became one of Marilyn's confidants. She, of course, poured out the sob orphan story and won the columnist's early favor and support.

It was Sidney Skolsky who dubbed MM "the Girl with the Horizontal Walk." It was Skolsky who talked producer Jerry Wald into hiring MM for *Clash by Night* (1952). And it was Skolsky who kept Marilyn's name in public view. In his July 16, 1952, column, Skolsky asked Marilyn how she liked Niagara Falls, the location for (what else?) *Niagara*. Replied MM: "They just keep falling."

In 1954, Skolsky wrote and published a biography about Marilyn. It was the first of several books to be written about MM by someone who knew her. And when he wasn't writing about her, Skolsky was squiring Marilyn about town, keeping her in constant public display. Sidney Skolsky was, quite possibly, the best publicist that Marilyn Monroe ever had.

In those years of early stardom, Marilyn continued to rely on and confide in Sidney Skolsky. When paging him in a public place, Marilyn referred to herself as "Miss Caswell"—her character name from *All About Eve* (1950). When she returned from her 1954 honeymoon in the Orient with Joe DiMaggio, Marilyn reportedly confessed to Sidney Skolsky that she was secretly planning to marry Arthur Miller. And years later, Marilyn confided to Skolsky that she was having an affair with President Kennedy. As reported in Anthony Summers's *Goddess* (Macmillan, 1985), Skolsky contended:

> "I confess I still find it grim to speculate on what might have happened to me if I had tried to write about this romance in my column when it first came to my attention."

In addition to being a columnist, Sidney Skolsky was also a part-time movie producer. He produced two pictures—*The Jolson Story* (1946), which was a major, Oscar-nominated hit, and *The Eddie Cantor Story* (1953). For years, Skolsky developed *The Jean Harlow Story,* which he planned to produce as a starring vehicle for Marilyn Monroe. However, it never came to pass. According to Skolsky: "On the Sunday they found Marilyn dead, I had an appointment with her for that afternoon at four to work on *The Jean Harlow Story.*"

Sidney Skolsky never did produce *The Jean Harlow Story,* or *The Marilyn Monroe Story* for that matter. He died on May 3, 1983, the day after his seventy-eighth birthday.

**SPYROS SKOURAS**

Spyros Skouras (1893–1971) was the president of 20th Century-Fox from 1943 to 1962. He, even more than Darryl Zanuck, Chief of Production, was responsible for Marilyn Monroe's success at Fox.

Spyros Skouras first heard of Marilyn Monroe in 1948, when she was a bit player in Fox's June Haver pic *Scudda Hoo! Scudda Hay!* Skouras was approached by Marilyn's champion at that time, cinematographer Leon Shamroy, who objected to Marilyn's being edited out of the film. Skouras reportedly barked: "Zanuck knows his stars. I'm too busy to be bothered about extras!" Skouras was once again confronted with Marilyn Monroe in 1950, at the home of Joseph Schenck. But it was not until the 20th Century-Fox exhibitors' party in 1951 that Spyros Skouras took a real interest in MM. Marilyn showed up one-and-a-half hours late. But when she did arrive, she quickly became the center of attention. Spyros Skouras was reported to have asked: "Who is that girl?!" At that time, no one seemed to know. Marilyn was just another dispensable blonde studio ornament—or so they thought. When he did find out her name, Skouras is reported to have asked if MM was scheduled to appear in any upcoming Fox pictures. Said Skouras: "The exhibitors like her. If the exhibitors like her, the public likes her, no?" Skouras then took Marilyn by the arm and sat her at the head of the table by his side.

Following the exhibitors' party, word quickly spread through the studio lot that Marilyn Monroe was to be slotted into any and every Fox picture that required a sexy blonde. As a result, between 1951 and 1952, MM appeared in *seven* pictures for 20th Century-Fox alone.

**MARY SLATTERY**
*See* MARY SLATTERY MILLER.

**ROBERT SLATZER**

> "A dark horse in the MM romance derby is Bob Slatzer, former Columbus, Ohio literary critic. He's been wooing her by phone and mail, improving her mind with gifts of the world's greatest books."
>
> columnist Dorothy Kilgallen, August 1952

> "Bob and Marilyn's long relationship was an unusual one, a good one, one that I feel was good for both of them."
>
> Allan "Whitey" Snyder, *The Life and Curious Death of Marilyn Monroe* (Pinnacle, 1974)

Out of all the figures to emerge from the Marilyn Monroe story, Robert Slatzer is certainly one of the most controversial. Born in Marion, Ohio on April 4, 1927, Slatzer first met Marilyn in the summer of 1946 at 20th Century-Fox in Los Angeles. At that time, Slatzer was a struggling fan-magazine reporter, while Marilyn was a struggling model and aspiring actress, on the brink of her first movie studio contract.

> As I sat in the reception room, deeper than usual into my reading, a cute girl with brown hair sauntered in, carrying a huge portfolio. . . . Suddenly, the guard called her. It was time for her interview. She stood up, and again my eyes were riveted on her astonishing body as she took a few quick steps toward the door. Then she turned, smiling at me. "Oh, by the way, I'm Norma Jeane. Norma Jeane Mortensen."
>
> Robert Slatzer, *The Life and Curious Death of Marilyn Monroe* (Pinnacle, 1974)

According to Slatzer, he and Norma Jeane made a date for that evening, the highlight of which proved to be her nude swim in the Pacific Ocean.

The Bob Slatzer story further contends that he dated Marilyn Monroe for the next six years, during her ascent to movie stardom, and during her burgeoning romance with Joe DiMaggio. Although the alleged Slatzer/MM romance did not receive much press, it was certainly plausible. However, what *is* difficult for many of Marilyn's fans and students to accept is Slatzer's claim that he, not Joe DiMaggio, was Marilyn Monroe's second husband.

Again, according to Slatzer, the secret wedding took place on October 4, 1952, in Tijuana, Mexico. The alleged marriage ended three days later, through the coercion of Marilyn's boss at 20th Century-Fox, Darryl F. Zanuck. Said Slatzer:

> We lived together for a short time as man and wife, about three days, and then Zanuck called Marilyn into his office. He found out somehow that we were married. Marilyn was scared and asked me to go with her. He told me that he had spent thousands of dollars on her and to undo it [the marriage]. Marilyn and I went back to Mexico and found the attorney who married us and he destroyed the wedding license. Back then, you could pay the attorneys a hundred dollars or so, and they would do that.

THE ROBERT SLATZER COLLECTION

With Robert Slatzer, Mexico, 1952.

Fact or fantasy, the wedding and subsequent annullment have never been substantiated, and most observers have been divided into two camps: those who believe Bob Slatzer and those who do not.

But the Slatzer/Marilyn Monroe controversy does not end there. For the past twenty-five years, Slatzer has worked to disprove the official pronouncement that Marilyn Monroe died a "probable suicide." In fact, according to Slatzer, Marilyn was murdered. Moreover, Slatzer claims that President John F. Kennedy and his brother, Bobby (both of whom, according to Slatzer and others, Marilyn had intimate relationships with), were somehow involved in the coverup of the circumstances surrounding Marilyn's death.

In the early 1970s, when word got around that he was writing a "tell all" book about Marilyn Monroe's death, Bob Slatzer found his life in jeopardy. He received death threats, was burglarized, and was forced into hiring bodyguards. Nevertheless, Slatzer persevered, and in 1974 his *The Life and Curious Death of Marilyn Monroe* was published by Pinnacle Books. The book did much to arouse public controversy over Marilyn's death. It certainly spawned renewed interest in the Monroe case and served to reignite the Monroe legend.

As for Robert Slatzer, a self-described screenwriter/director/producer, there can be no doubt of his sincere love for Marilyn Monroe. His relationship with MM, *whatever* the extent of it, has spanned over *forty* years. He has devoted a large part of his life to Marilyn, and to the preservation of her name. In death, Marilyn Monroe has had no better friend than Robert Slatzer.

In the dedication of his book, *The Life and Curious Death of Marilyn Monroe*, Slatzer wrote:

> To Marilyn . . .
> I've told it,
> not the way they think it was,
> or the way they heard it was,
> or the way they wish it was,
> but the way it really was . . .
> the only way you'd want it told.

**SAM SLAVITT**

Sam Slavitt was Arthur Miller's attorney, who expedited the legal proceedings concerning the 1956 marriage between Miller and Marilyn Monroe.

***THE SLEEPING PRINCE***

*The Sleeping Prince* is the play by Terence Rattigan that was adapted into the 1957 MM/Olivier film vehicle *The Prince and the Showgirl.*

**MARIA SMITH**

While at the Blue Book Modeling Agency in 1945, nineteen-year-old Norma Jeane Dougherty's instructor in the basics of makeup and grooming was a woman named Maria Smith.

**EMMELINE SNIVELY**

> "She was the hardest worker I ever handled. She never missed a class. She had confidence in herself. Quit her job at the factory without anything except her confidence and my belief in her."

> "Girls ask me all the time how they can be like Marilyn Monroe, and I tell them, if they had one-tenth of the hard work and gumption that that girl had, they'd be on their way, but there will never be another like her."

> "The graduate I am most proud of is Marilyn Monroe. Not only because she is the most successful and well known of my students,

> but because she started with the least—she was cute-looking, but she knew nothing about carriage, posture, walking, sitting, or posing.
>
> "She looked a fright at first, but, my, how she worked!"
>
> "Her size twelve fitted the manufacturer's garments just fine, except in one place. They were always too tight across the front of the blouse. We advised her to give up fashion work and concentrate on photo modeling."
>
> "After Marilyn Monroe was under contract, the studio loaned her out to model in a benefit fashion show at the Ambassador. She came back to our studio, and we gave her some free advice—to brush up on her fashion modeling. I saw that fashion show, and do you know she was still a lousy fashion model?"
>
> Emmeline Snively on Marilyn Monroe

Emmeline Snively was the head of the Blue Book Modeling Agency, which signed Norma Jeane Dougherty to a contract in the summer of 1945. Miss Snively groomed Norma Jeane, enrolled her in a modeling course, and encouraged her to lighten and straighten her hair. She also advised her young student to lower her smile—a device that Marilyn Monroe later employed with quivering results.

Emmeline Snively also changed Norma Jeane's name, temporarily, to Jean Norman and obtained pictorial assignments that landed Norma Jeane on the covers of *Laff, Peek, See, U.S. Camera,* et al. Realizing—to a degree—her young protégé's potential, Emmeline Snively introduced Norma Jeane to Helen Ainsworth of the National Concert Artists Corporation, the agency that opened the doors to Norma Jeane's fledgling movie career.

In 1954, well after Marilyn Monroe had attained major stardom, Emmeline Snively visited the 20th Century-Fox set of *There's No Business Like Show Business* upon Marilyn's invitation. It is the only known instance wherein Marilyn Monroe shared her overwhelming success with her very first mentor.

**ALLAN "WHITEY" SNYDER**

Whitey Snyder was Marilyn Monroe's studio and personal makeup artist. Furthermore, over a sixteen-year period, Snyder became one of Marilyn's closest and most trusted friends. He was also one of the most dependable. Whitey Snyder was there in 1946 to do Norma Jeane's makeup for her very first motion picture screen test. He was there during the rise of her stardom and during the travails of her personal life. And he was there in 1962, at her special advance request, to do the makeup for her funeral.

Following his long working relationship with Marilyn Monroe, Whitey Snyder became the head makeup artist on many productions, including the television programs "Little House on the Prairie" and "Highway to Heaven."

**SOCIAL SECURITY NUMBER**

Marilyn Monroe's Social Security number was 563-32-0764.

**A. J. SOLDAN**

Dr. A. J. Soldan was a Lutheran pastor of the Village Church of Westwood, who conducted the services at Marilyn Monroe's 1962 funeral.

**GEORGE SOLOTAIRE**

George Solotaire, a Broadway ticket broker, was Joe DiMaggio's closest friend in New York. They were frequently seen together at Toots Shor's bar in New York City. When DiMaggio visited Marilyn Monroe during the 1953 location shooting of *River of No Return* in Canada, he was accompanied by George Solotaire. Solotaire got along quite well with MM and became a father figure, of sorts, to her.

George Solotaire was one of the select few who was invited to Marilyn Monroe's 1962 funeral.

***SOME LIKE IT HOT*** ★★★★

1959 122 minutes Black and White
United Artists
Directed by: Billy Wilder
Produced by: Billy Wilder
Screenplay by: Billy Wilder, I. A. L. Diamond, from a story by R. Thoeren and M. Logan
Photographed by: Charles Lang, Jr.
Cast: Marilyn Monroe, Tony Curtis, Jack Lemmon, Pat O'Brien, George Raft, Joe E. Brown, Billy Gray, Joan Shawlee, Nehemiah Persoff, Dave Barry, Mike Mazurki, George E. Stone

*Some Like It Hot* was Marilyn Monroe's most successful film. It was also the most popular film in America during April, May, and June of 1959. Up until that time, and eons before the era of *Ghostbusters* and Eddie Murphy, *Some Like It Hot* was the biggest comedy hit in the history of motion pictures. Moreover, it was wildly heralded by the critics as one of the best films of the year. Marilyn Monroe received uniformly excellent reviews and was awarded a Golden Globe as the best actress of the year.

Today, in reviewing the film, it seems incredible that such a warlike turmoil prevailed in this film's behind-the-scenes production. Unlike *The Misfits* in which pathos was evoked in every frame, *Some Like It Hot* appears to have been an exuberant filmmaking experience. Perhaps that is its greatest triumph—it overcame its own misery, none of which is discernible on the screen.

Marilyn Monroe was, by all accounts, impossible to work with on *Some Like It Hot*. She was late. She was absent. She didn't like the fact that it was being shot in black and white. She didn't like the fact that Frank Sinatra had been replaced by Jack Lemmon (although she did come to like Lemmon). She *didn't* like Tony Curtis. She didn't get along with Billy Wilder. She was taking drugs. She didn't like the fact that, although she was top-billed, the film's plot revolved around the antics of Lemmon and Curtis. She didn't like the casual way that her opening scene was shot. She didn't like the fact that she was

COURTESY OF THE HOTEL DEL CORONADO

On Coronado Beach with Jack Lemmon during the 1958 shooting of *Some Like it Hot*.

playing another "dumb blonde" role. But, worst of all, she couldn't remember her lines. In one scene, Marilyn was directed to rummage through a dresser drawer and search for a bottle of bourbon. While doing this, she was supposed to deliver one line: "Where's the bourbon?" After forty takes, Billy Wilder pasted the line in the dresser drawer. Another scene, in which MM was instructed to knock on a door and exclaim, "It's me, sugar," took forty-seven takes. Yet another scene took Marilyn a reported fifty-nine takes.

Naturally, the cast and crew became quite exasperated with Marilyn Monroe. The film, and the battles that resulted from it, nearly severed Marilyn's highly productive relationship with Billy Wilder. And matters became even more difficult when it was discovered, during the production, that Marilyn was pregnant. Although this news made MM very happy, it also made her already volatile condition even more sensitive.

*Some Like It Hot* began shooting at the Goldwyn Studios on August 4, 1958—four years to the day before Marilyn's death. It completed production on November 6, 1958. It went several hundred thousand dollars over budget and cost an accumulated $2,800,000. Nevertheless, it all proved to be worthwhile following the film's world premiere on March 29, 1959. Billy Wilder was later quoted as saying, "*Some Like It Hot* is the biggest hit I've ever been associated with."

The Academy of Motion Picture Arts and Sciences agreed. It honored *Hot* with five Academy Award nominations, although it won only a single Oscar, for the "Best Black and White Costume Design."

Nearly thirty years later, *Some Like It Hot* has endured as a classic American comedy. It has retained much of its original humor, invention, and creativity. As in *The Seven Year Itch* (1955), and, to a lesser extent, *Gentlemen Prefer Blondes* (1953), Marilyn Monroe does not walk away with this picture. If anyone does, it is Jack Lemmon. This is not to say that MM is not good in the movie, because she is. Reportedly, Marilyn did not like the completed *Some Like It Hot,* and it is easy to see why. Her role just isn't very big or substantial. It is surprising that a star of her magnitude was given so little to do. Still, when Marilyn *is* on the screen, it is difficult to be distracted by anything or anyone else. As Sugar Kane, the ukulele-strumming vocalist of an all-girl band, MM is funny and poignant at the same time. It's an excellent performance that suggests, sadly, potential for future greatness.

**MM Trivia Quiz #43**
Where does MM's opening scene for *Some Like It Hot* take place? (Answer on page 578.)

***SOMETHING'S GOT TO GIVE***
1962
20th Century-Fox
Directed by: George Cukor
Produced by: Henry Weinstein
Screenplay by: Nunnally Johnson and Walter Bernstein, from the 1940 film *My Favorite Wife*
Photographed by: Franz Planer, Charles Lang, Jr., William Daniels, Leo Tover
Cast: Marilyn Monroe, Dean Martin, Cyd Charisse, Wally Cox, Phil Silvers

*Something's Got to Give* would have been Marilyn Monroe's thirtieth film. The story itself was a variation of the 1940 Cary Grant/Irene Dunne comedy *My Favorite Wife,* about a shipwrecked woman, thought to be dead, who returns home after several years to discover that her husband has remarried.

The ill-fated project was besieged by setbacks from the start. The biggest mistake was that 20th Century-Fox began shooting without a final, approved script. Marilyn Monroe did not have script approval, but everyone connected with the film knew that, unless she was happy with the script, Marilyn would simply not show up on the set. To complicate matters, Marilyn had contracted a virus. And call it foreshadowing or just blatant unprofessionalism, MM showed up two hours late for a script conference with the writers and director. Once the production did start, Marilyn surprised her skeptics by showing up for the first day of shooting. However, on the second day, MM failed to appear as scheduled, which infuriated the Fox executives. Needless to mention, *Something's Got to Give* did *not* get off to an auspicious start.

As was heavily reported at the time, on June 8, 1962, Marilyn Monroe was fired from *Something's Got to Give*. Her last day of work—ever—took place on her thirty-sixth birthday, June 1, 1962. As reported by columnist Sheilah Graham, in the *Hollywood Citizen-News*:

> Marilyn Monroe will be replaced in *Something's Got to Give*. . . .
> Marilyn has been "ill" on and off ever since the picture was started five weeks ago and "the studio does not want her anymore," Henry Weinstein, who is producing the film for 20th Century-Fox, told me. "She's not ill. I have had no official notification of her illness. All I get from her is she will not be reporting. Out of 33 days of shooting Marilyn has come to the set only 12 times and will only do one page a day, which adds to a total of four days of work, only," the producer stated.
> He continued, "Every time she says she is ill and we have to close down the picture, 104 persons lose a day's pay. I'm convinced she is in willful breach of contract. She was out three weeks, returned for three days, then went to the president's birthday ball, which meant closing down again for two days. She seemed quite well last Friday when they gave her a birthday party on the set. There was a birthday cake, champagne, and caviar. She has not reported to work since. Marilyn's absence has cost the studio more than half a million dollars. We gave her everything she wanted, including Dean Martin as costar, two of her favorite cameramen, her favorite dress designer, Jean Louis, and Sidney Gilleross [sic] for her hair.
> "The fact is that the studios cannot operate with stars who do not report for work. If this sort of thing continues, there will be no movie industry at all."
> Efforts to reach Miss Monroe for comment have been unsuccessful.

After the onslaught of threatened lawsuits, 20th Century-Fox renegotiated with Marilyn Monroe and rehired her. The film was scheduled to resume production before the end of the year.

Today, in viewing the seven-and-a-half minutes of Marilyn's "usable" footage from *Something's Got to Give*, it seems a small tragedy that Marilyn never completed this film. Her presence is immediately striking and transcendent. And, despite reports to the contrary, her particular magic and beauty are evident in explosive, evocative doses.

## THE SONGS

### The Songs That MM Sang in Her Movies

***Ladies of the Chorus*** (1948)

"Anyone Can See I Love You"
"Every Baby Needs a Da-Da-Daddy"

***A Ticket to Tomahawk*** (1950)

"Oh, What a Forward Young Man You Are"

***Niagara*** (1953)

"Kiss"

***Gentlemen Prefer Blondes*** (1953)
"We're Just Two Little Girls from Little Rock"
"When Love Goes Wrong"
"Bye Bye Baby"
"Diamonds Are a Girl's Best Friend"

***River of No Return*** (1953)
"River of No Return"
"I'm Going to File My Claim"
"One Silver Dollar"
"Down in the Meadow"

***There's No Business Like Show Business*** (1954)
"After You Get What You Want You Don't Want It"
"Heat Wave"
"Lazy"
"There's No Business Like Show Business"
"A Man Chases a Girl"

***Bus Stop*** (1956)
"That Old Black Magic"

***The Prince and the Showgirl*** (1957)
"I Found a Dream"

***Some Like It Hot*** (1959)
"I'm Through with Love"
"I Wanna Be Loved by You"
"Running Wild"

***Let's Make Love*** (1960)
"Let's Make Love"
"Incurably Romantic"
"Specialization"
"My Heart Belongs to Daddy"

**The Songs That MM Sang That Were Cut from *Gentlemen Prefer Blondes***
"Four French Dances" ("Sur le Balcon," "La tentateur," "Sol taire," "Parle d'affair")
"Down Boy"
"When the Wild Wild Women Go Swimmin' Down in the Bimini Bay" *aka*
"When the Wild Wild Women Go Swimmin' Down in the Swimmin' Hole"

**The Songs That MM Sang in Public Appearances**
***At director Richard Quine's home*** (1948)
"Baby Won't You Please Come Home"

THE SABIN GRAY COLLECTION

Production number, "Four French Dances," that was cut from *Gentlemen Prefer Blondes*, 1953.

***Camp Pendleton*** (1952)

"Somebody Loves You"
"Do It Again"

***On* "The Jack Benny Show"** (1953)

"Bye Bye Baby"

***Korea*** (1954)

"Do It Again" ("Kiss Me Again")
"Diamonds Are a Girl's Best Friend"
"Somebody Love Me"
"Bye Bye Baby"

***Romanoff's Party*** (1954)

"Do It Again"

***Madison Square Garden*** (1962)

"Happy Birthday, Mr. President"
"Thanks, Mr. President" ("Thanks for the Memories")

**The Songs That MM Auditioned With For *Ladies of the Chorus*** (1948)

"Love Me or Leave Me"

**The Songs About MM**

"Marilyn" by Ervin Drake and Jimmy Shirl, performed by Ray Anthony (1952)
"Candle in the Wind" by Elton John and Bernie Taupin (1973)
"Marilyn" by Martin Mull (1974)
"Norma Jean Wants To Be a Movie Star" by J. Cunningham (1974)
"Elvis And Marilyn" by Leon Russell (1978)
"Who Killed Marilyn" by Glen Danzia (1981)

## MICKEY SONG

In 1962, twenty-two-year-old Mickey Song was the hairstylist of John and Robert Kennedy. He had gotten the prestigious presidential post via Peter Lawford, Frank Sinatra, and Eva Gabor—three satisfied, well-coiffed Song clients.

In May 1962, Song was flown from his California home to New York City to style the president's hair for his Madison Square Garden birthday appearance. According to Song:

> "When I was flown in to cut the president's hair, I learned through Bobby that Marilyn was coming, too. I asked Bobby if I could do her hair, and he said that he would find out. She *didn't* want me to do it. She wanted her own people to do it. I still wasn't sure if I was going to do her hair until the night she appeared backstage at Madison Square Garden. She came in with a jeweled scarf around her head. Her hair had been set and had clips in it, but it hadn't been combed out. She was very nervous, and I could tell she was uncomfortable with me because she didn't know me. At the time, I didn't realize how important this event was to her."

Robert Kennedy eventually convinced Marilyn Monroe to let the prodigious Mickey Song style her hair. After the job was completed, Kennedy asked Song what his impression of Marilyn Monroe was, to which Song replied: "I think she's wonderful." Bobby Kennedy reportedly retorted: "I think she was a bitch."

For his bouffant job on Marilyn Monroe, Mickey Song was paid, through the Kennedys, $50. Today, Song is a stylist at the stylish Tovar's salon in Beverly Hills. When he was asked about his experience with Marilyn Monroe, brief as it was, Song replied: "I realize now I just wanted to tell her how much I loved her. I wish I would have."

## HELENA SORELL

Helena Sorell was one of starlet Marilyn Monroe's earliest acting coaches.

## SOTHEBY PARK BERNET GALLERY

On October 21, 1973, Sotheby Park Bernet sponsored a Marilyn Monroe auction at its Los Angeles gallery (address: 7660 Beverly Boulevard). Among the items auctioned off were:

1. A letter to "Dear Norma Jeane" from "Mother"
2. A typed note to MM from producer Jerry Wald, 1952

3. A letter to "Dear Jim" [Dougherty] from Norma Jeane
4. One of Marilyn's 20th Century-Fox contracts, 1951
5. A letter to MM from the Automobile Club of Southern California, 1951
6. Several of Norma Jeane's school report cards, circa 1941–42
7. MM's MGM contract for *The Asphalt Jungle*, dated 1949
8. Several scripts, which had belonged to MM
9. A gold metallic dress, which had belonged to MM
10. Norma Jeane's junior high school diploma

MM items auctioned off at the prestigious London-based gallery (address: 3435 New Bond Street) in 1982 were:

1. A pink mesh bra, a beaded silver evening bag, a pair of long white gloves—$1,040
2. MM's *Bus Stop* costume—$836

In June 1987 Sotheby's in New York re-auctioned MM's *Bus Stop* costume for $7,975. The buyer was the Hard Rock Cafe in New York.

**JAMES SPADA**

At the age of thirteen, James Spada founded the Marilyn Monroe Memorial Fan Club. Years later, Spada coauthored the lavishly produced book, *Monroe: Her Life in Pictures* (1982). Spada is also the author of similar books on Robert Redford and Barbra Streisand.

**KATHY SPEER**

Kathy Speer cowrote the Benson segment, "Boys Night Out" that featured a Marilyn Monroe-based character. The program aired on February 4, 1983.

**MILO SPERIGLIO**

Milo Speriglio is the investigator, criminologist, and director in chief of Nick Harris Detectives, who has, for the past fifteen years, been attempting to prove to the world that Marilyn Monroe was, in fact, murdered. Speriglio's investigation has spawned two books on MM—*Marilyn Monroe: Murder Cover-Up* (1982) and *The Marilyn Conspiracy* (1986).

Initially, it was Bob Slatzer who hired Speriglio and Nick Harris Detectives (Case #72-4813) for the Marilyn Monroe case. Together, Slatzer and Speriglio have triggered and retriggered worldwide interest in the controversy surrounding the mysterious circumstances of Marilyn's death. On April 8, 1986, with the results of his lengthy investigation to support him, Milo Speriglio called a press conference and officially demanded that the Marilyn Monroe case be reopened. Thus far, Speriglio's efforts have gone unheeded.

**SAM SPIEGEL**

Sam Spiegel, born in 1901, is the noted Hollywood producer of such films as *The Stranger* (1945), *The African Queen* (1951), *On the Waterfront* (1954), *The Bridge on the River Kwai* (1957), and *Lawrence of Arabia* (1962).

In 1948, director John Huston reportedly wanted to give Marilyn Monroe a color screen test for his picture *We Were Strangers* at Columbia. However, Sam Spiegel, the film's producer, refused to test starlet MM because of the expense.

**BERNARD SPINDEL**

"The King of the Wiretappers," Bernard Spindel, was allegedly hired by Jimmy Hoffa to "bug" Marilyn Monroe's Brentwood home in 1962. Reportedly, Spindel obtained audio tapes of President Kennedy and MM in the act of "making love" and tapes that were allegedly made on the night of Marilyn's death.

In 1966, Spindel's New York home was raided by the police. In his subsequent affidavit, Spindel charged that among his missing materials were:

> ". . . tapes and evidence concerning the circumstances surrounding the causes of death of Marilyn Monroe which strongly suggest that the officially reported circumstances of her demise were erroneous."

Several years after the raid on his home, Bernard Spindel died in prison of a heart attack. He was forty-five years old. His alleged tapes have never been made public.

**JOHN SPRINGER**

In the early 1960s, John Springer was the publicist who took over Marilyn Monroe's press responsibilities so that Patricia Newcomb could devote more of her time to Marilyn.

**WILLIAM STADIEM**

William Stadiem, who was born in 1947, coauthored the book *Marilyn Monroe Confidential* (1979), which was based on the experiences of Marilyn's former New York maid and wardrobe mistress, Lena Pepitone.

***STAGE DOOR***

Reportedly, while she was a member of the Bliss-Hayden Theatre Group in Beverly Hills, movie starlet Marilyn Monroe appeared in a production of the Edna Ferber/George S. Kaufman play *Stage Door*. It ran at the Bliss-Hayden Playhouse from mid-August 1948 until September 12, 1948.

**STAMPS**

Marilyn Monroe has appeared on two postage stamps:

☆ The Republique Populaire Du Congo
☆ The Republique Du Mali

**RAYMOND G. STANBURY**

In August 1955, Raymond G. Stanbury was Marilyn's Los Angeles attorney, who settled the lawsuit filed against her by car accident victim Bart Antinora. Antinora was awarded a mere $500.

**STAND-INS**

The following is a list of actresses who are known to have served as movie stand-ins for Marilyn Monroe:

1. Irene Crosby: *Gentlemen Prefer Blondes* (1953)
2. Gloria Mosolino: *The Seven Year Itch* (1955)

3. Una Pearl: *The Prince and the Showgirl* (1957)
4. Evelyn Moriarty: *The Misfits* (1961)

**KIM STANLEY**

Kim Stanley was born Patricia Reid on February 11, 1925. After graduating from the University of Texas, Miss Stanley relocated to New York, where she became a member of the Actors Studio. Subsequently, she starred on Broadway in such productions as *Bus Stop, Picnic,* and *A Touch of the Poet.*

Reportedly, while preparing for the film version of *Bus Stop* (1956), Marilyn Monroe sat through several performances of the play to study Kim Stanley's interpretation of Cherie.

A few years later, Miss Stanley portrayed the MM-based character Rita Shawn in Columbia Pictures' *The Goddess.* The film was Kim Stanley's movie debut. She has subsequently appeared in very few films. The exceptions have been *Seance on a Wet Afternoon* (1964), *Three Sisters* (1967), *Frances* (1982), and *The Right Stuff* (1983).

Of Miss Stanley's performance in *The Goddess, The Hollywood Reporter* exclaimed:

> The time lapse of this episodic narrative is 27 years. Kim Stanley, in the leading role, is too mature to be believable in the long high school sequence and hasn't the figure to make her convincing as one of Hollywood's great glamor queens.

**BARBARA STANWYCK**

> "She was awkward. She couldn't get out of her own way. She wasn't disciplined, and she was often late, and she drove Bob Ryan, Paul Douglas and myself out of our minds . . . but she didn't do it viciously, and there was sort of a magic about her which we all recognized at once. Her phobias, or whatever they were, came later; she seemed just a carefree kid, and she owned the world."
>
> Barbara Stanwyck on early Marilyn Monroe

Tough, sultry, indomitable, Barbara Stanwyck was born Ruby Stevens on July 16, 1907. A motion picture legend, Miss Stanwyck hails from Brooklyn and began her Hollywood career in the late 1920s. She has appeared in many noteworthy films, including *Miracle Woman* (1931), *Stella Dallas* (1937), *Meet John Doe* (1941), *Double Indemnity* (1944), *The Strange Love of Martha Ivers* (1946), and *Executive Suite* (1954).

In 1952, Miss Stanwyck starred in *Clash by Night,* which featured the fast-rising star appeal of Marilyn Monroe. Five years later, Barbara Stanwyck starred in Samuel Fuller's *Forty Guns* in a role that Marilyn Monroe had reportedly wanted for herself. Some twenty-seven years later, Miss Stanwyck won an Emmy award for her performance in the television mini-series, "The Thorn Birds." She also appeared for a season (1986) on the ABC-TV soap, "The Colbys," a production that she totally outclassed.

**MAUREEN STAPLETON**

In February 1956, before members of the Actors Studio in New York, Maureen Stapleton and Marilyn Monroe performed a scene from Eugene O'Neill's

*Anna Christie.* Their presentation was an undisputed success.

Miss Stapleton, who is generally considered a fine stage actress, has appeared in such films as *A View from the Bridge* (1962), *Bye Bye Birdie* (1963), and *Reds* (for which she won a 1981 "Best Supporting Actress" Oscar).

**THE STAR OF FIRE GEM COMPANY**

In 1954, this Hollywood company, operated by Eddie LeBaron, was taken to court on charges of mail obscenity. Apparently, the Star of Fire Company had been selling, through the mail, drinking coasters that featured Marilyn Monroe's nude calendar pose.

***STARS AND STRIPES* MAGAZINE**

*Stars and Stripes,* a magazine catering to servicemen, was a chief supporter of Marilyn Monroe during her ascent to stardom in the early 1950s. In 1952, the magazine featured MM on its front page *every day* and frequently had to run "repeat" shots of MM.

**IRVING STEIN**

Irving Stein was a New York attorney involved with the formation of Marilyn Monroe Productions, circa 1954–55.

**JASON STEINBRENNER**

In August 1981, an auction dealer by the name of Charles Hamilton held an auction at the Waldorf-Astoria (MM's former residence) in New York. It was at this auction that Jason Steinbrenner shelled out $2,100 for three of MM's nude calendars, in addition to a vintage copy of *Laff* magazine that featured young Norma Jeane Dougherty.

**GLORIA STEINEM**

> "Marilyn would have been sixty this year. If the feminist movement had existed, it might have saved her life."
>
> Gloria Steinem on Marilyn Monroe, 1986

Gloria Steinem is a writer and a widely publicized leader of the feminist movement. In 1971, Ms. Steinem cofounded *Ms.* magazine. A year later, in that publication's August 1972 edition, Gloria Steinem penned an article entitled "Growing Up with Marilyn." It read, in part: "Now that women are changing their vision of themselves, they have begun to reevaluate the life of Marilyn Monroe."

In late 1986, Gloria Steinem extended that premise into a book about Marilyn Monroe. It was published by the Henry Holt & Company book publishers.

**MARJORIE STENGEL**

Marjorie Stengel replaced May Reis as Marilyn Monroe's New York secretary at the East 57th Street apartment for a brief period. Miss Stengel's name was also used on Marilyn's mailbox at her Doheny Drive apartment in Beverly Hills in 1961.

Prior to working for Marilyn Monroe, Marjorie Stengel had been employed as Montgomery Clift's secretary. She left Clift in 1960. Reportedly, he had rammed his head into her stomach.

**BERT STERN**
In the third week of June 1962, photographer Bert Stern shot what is sometimes referred to as "the last great photo session" with Marilyn Monroe. The session, which was initially shot for *Vogue* magazine, took place at the Bel Air Hotel. For his shooting with MM, Stern was equipped with his camera, a case of Dom Perignon, and a stack of Everly Brothers records—the latter, presumably, to keep her mind off of Frank Sinatra. For their first day of shooting, Marilyn was five hours late.

The session itself included a series of nudes, seminudes, and fashion shots of MM. These and other photos were published twenty years after Marilyn's death, in Bert Stern's book entitled *The Last Sitting*.

**PHIL STERN**
Phil Stern's shots of MM "sitting on a chair" at the Shrine Auditorium in 1953 still stand among the finest photos ever taken of MM. He also shot some very rare photos of a pregnant MM off the set of *Some Like it Hot* in 1958.

**CONNIE STEVENS**
In 1974, Miss Stevens *attempted* to portray Marilyn Monroe in the television biopic *The Sex Symbol*.

**SHEILA STEWART**
Reportedly, while "The Wrong Door Raid" was being perpetrated on November 5, 1954, MM was actually visiting the upstairs apartment (address: 754 Kilkea Drive, Hollywood) of her friend, Sheila Stewart. (*See* "THE WRONG DOOR RAID.")

**MARIA STINGER**
Maria Stinger was a Marilyn Monroe look-alike who served, for a period, as Miami's answer to MM. While out in public, Miss Stinger was frequently mistaken for MM. Sadly, though, she took an overdose of pills and committed suicide when she turned thirty-six years old.

**STORES**
**MM's First Department Store Charge Card:**
I. Magnin

**MM's Favorite Stores:**
1. Bloomingdale's, New York City
2. Saks Fifth Avenue, New York City
3. Saks Fifth Avenue, Beverly Hills
4. Saks Fifth Avenue, The Hamptons
5. Jax, New York City
6. Jax, Beverly Hills
7. Martha's, New York City
8. Bonwit Teller, New York City

**THE STORK CLUB**
While in New York City during the 1954 location shooting of *The Seven Year*

*Itch*, Marilyn and Joe DiMaggio dined at the famous Stork Club (address: 3 E. 53rd Street).

Today, the only existing "Stork Club" in New York City is a maternity shop, not a "hot spot."

**ROY STORK**

Roy Stork was credited with doing the makeup for two pictures in which MM appeared: *Let's Make It Legal* (1951) and *O. Henry's Full House* (1952).

**"THE STORY OF MARILYN MONROE"**

*See* "The Marilyn Monroe Story."

***THE STORY OF "THE MISFITS"***

Not actually a book about MM, *The Story of "The Misfits"* by James Goode (Bobbs-Merrill, 1963) is more of a detailed journal of the day-to-day 1960 shooting of *The Misfits*.

However, Goode's account is, ultimately, a disappointment. Totally missing from this work is the sense of doomed tragedy, the desperation that pervaded the production from start to finish. *The Misfits* was an illustrative example of just how difficult and stressful the moviemaking experience can be. It was a minor miracle, and a credit to John Huston, Arthur Miller, Marilyn Monroe, et al., that the film was ever even completed.

*The Story of "The Misfits"* as recounted by James Goode, is a superficial, presumably heavily edited look at some of the most fascinating talents of our time.

**SHIRLEY STRAHM**

Miss Strahm was Marilyn Monroe's wardrobe lady on *The Misfits* (1961).

***THE STRANGE DEATH OF MARILYN MONROE***

Author: Frank A. Capell
Publisher: Herald of Freedom
Year: 1964 (Out of print)

The Robert Slatzer book, *The Life and Curious Death of Marilyn Monroe* (Pinnacle Books), stirred public controversy in 1974 regarding the mysterious circumstances of Marilyn Monroe's death. But, *ten years before*, this magazine/pamphlet, *The Strange Death of Marilyn Monroe* by Frank A. Capell, was the first publication to confront the issue. The questions raised by Capell seem clichéd and obvious by today's standards but, back in 1964, they must have been somewhat of a revelation. The author lashes out against such individuals as Dr. Ralph Greenson, Dr. Hyman Engelberg, Patricia Newcomb, Robert Kennedy, and Lee and Paula Strasberg, and questions their possible involvement with Marilyn's demise.

It's a fascinating, though certainly slanted account and was published by *The Herald of Freedom*, an "anti-communist bi-weekly."

**ANNA STRASBERG**

In 1968, Lee Strasberg married actress Anna Mizrahi. In 1969, she gave birth to a son, Adam Lee. In 1971, she gave birth to another son, David Lee. Today, Mrs. Strasberg runs the Strasberg Institutes (though not the Actors Studio) in both New York and Los Angeles.

**JOHN STRASBERG**

John is the son of Lee and Paula Strasberg. An actor, John once appeared in a scene from *A Streetcar Named Desire* opposite Marilyn Monroe. The scene was performed in class at the Actors Studio in New York. For his eighteenth birthday, MM presented John with a black Thunderbird sports car.

**LEE STRASBERG**

> "I saw that what she looked like was not what she really was, and what was going on inside was not what was going on outside, and that always means there may be something there to work with. It was almost as if she had been waiting for a button to be pushed, and when it was pushed a door opened and you saw a treasure of gold and jewels."
>
> Lee Strasberg on MM

> "She is more nervous than any other actress I have ever known. But, nervousness, for an actress, is not a handicap. It is a sign of sensitivity."
>
> Lee Strasberg

> "All I want is to play something different—the Strasbergs say I can."
>
> Marilyn Monroe

> "If we do not see the possibilities for greatness, how can we dream of it?"
>
> Lee Strasberg

Lee Strasberg, born November 17, 1901, in Budzanow, Austria, is generally regarded as one of the most prolific acting coaches of our time.

In 1948, Lee Strasberg became the artistic director of the Actors Studio in New York. His name has been synonymous with that organization ever since. He gained worldwide recognition for his teaching of "The Method" style of acting, as well as for his impressive celebrity-studded student body.

By the spring of 1955, Marilyn Monroe had fled from Hollywood and was determined to improve her acting skills. She wanted to become a Serious Actress. Thus, it must have seemed only natural that she form an alliance with Strasberg.

Marilyn Monroe was introduced to Strasberg through the joint effort of the Actors Studio's founders, Elia Kazan and Cheryl Crawford. And she must have made a favorable impression on the formidable acting coach, because she began to take lessons from him almost immediately—not at the Actors Studio classes, like the other students, but at the eight-room Strasberg apartment on Broadway and 86th Street. For three months, Marilyn was given private instruction by Strasberg before she was deemed ready to join the regular classes at the Actors Studio.

Lee Strasberg became much more to Marilyn Monroe than a mere acting coach. He was her hero, friend, guidance counselor, savior, and, father figure. He has also been cited often, both favorably and unfavorably, as her "mentor." It was Lee Strasberg who convinced Marilyn to enter psychoanalysis. And it was Lee Strasberg who encouraged and entertained Marilyn's aspirations of acting greatness.

Strasberg was once quoted as having said that the two greatest acting talents he had ever worked with were Marlon Brando and Marilyn Monroe. There is no doubt that he was proud of MM. But perhaps even more than that, he was proud of *his* accomplishments with MM. Under Strasberg's tutelage, Marilyn Monroe had gone from *There's No Business Like Show Business* (1954) to *Bus Stop* (1956) in a period of only two years. Moreover, not only was Marilyn Monroe Lee Strasberg's most famous student; she was also, in all probability, his most malleable. MM placed her trust, friendship, career, and future in the hands of Lee Strasberg, to do with them as he wished. For him, Marilyn Monroe must have seemed the ultimate challenge.

On July 1, 1956, Strasberg "gave the bride away" at Marilyn and Arthur Miller's Jewish wedding ceremony in Katonah, New York. Six years later, on the opposite coast, he delivered the eulogy at Marilyn's funeral.

Over the next twenty years, as the Actors Studio lost some of its original prestige, Lee Strasberg the actor won acclaim for his film performances in *The Godfather Part II* (1974), *And Justice for All* (1979), and *Going in Style* (1979).

He died on February 17, 1982, leaving behind a legacy of disputed brilliance, mystery, and undeniable impact.

**PAULA STRASBERG**

> "I think we're doing Paula a disservice. For all we know, she's been holding this picture together."
>
> John Huston on Paula Strasberg and the filming of *The Misfits* (1961)

> "I feel that I have contributed to every frame of *The Misfits* and my work is on the screen."
>
> Paula Strasberg

Paula Strasberg, Lee Strasberg's wife, was the Actors Studio coach who guided Marilyn Monroe through each of her films, beginning with *Bus Stop* (1956). Mrs. Strasberg worked with Marilyn on the set, much to the aggravation of most of Marilyn's directors, and took over where Natasha Lytess, MM's previous coach, had left off.

Mrs. Strasberg, born Paula Miller in 1911, first met Marilyn Monroe in 1954, on the lot at 20th Century-Fox in Los Angeles. It was columnist Sidney Skolsky who introduced Paula to MM. The meeting proved to be a fateful one. Marilyn, who was shooting *There's No Business Like Show Business* at the time, expressed to Paula that she would one day like to study at the Actors Studio. Less than a year later, that desire was realized.

THE ALAN FRANCE COLLECTION

With Paula Strasberg on set of *Something's Got to Give*, 1962.

Paula Strasberg was not liked by most of Marilyn Monroe's moviemaking associates. Laurence Olivier, the director of *The Prince and the Showgirl* (1957), banned Paula from the set and reportedly banished her from England to New York. Others referred to Paula as "the witch in black" or "the black mushroom," because she dressed in an exclusively black wardrobe. There were also those who felt that Paula, along with her husband, had exercised undue influence over Marilyn. Others felt that the Strasbergs had been taking financial advantage of MM. For her work with Marilyn, while on a picture, Paula was paid the astronomical sum (by 1960 standards) of $3,000 a week. Moreover, following Marilyn's death, Paula filed an official request for $22,200 from the Marilyn Monroe estate.

Interestingly, Paula Strasberg was not mentioned in Marilyn Monroe's will—despite the fact that Lee Strasberg was one of Marilyn's primary beneficiaries. Also of interest is that, over the years, there has been some speculation that Marilyn had fired Paula shortly before her death. However, this report has never been substantiated. Certainly, Paula Strasberg, who died in 1966, never verified it.

**SUSAN STRASBERG**

Born in 1938, Susan Strasberg is the actress daughter of Lee and Paula Strasberg. Through her parents, Susan had the opportunity to get to know Marilyn Monroe quite well.

**THEODORE STRAUSS**

Theodore Strauss cowrote the 1966 documentary "The Legend of Marilyn Monroe." Twenty-two years later, Strauss scripted another TV documentary about MM entitled "Remembering Marilyn."

***STRAWHEAD***

*Strawhead* was a 1986 stage play about Marilyn Monroe written by—who else?—Norman Mailer. It ran for two weeks at the Actors Studio in New York. The part of MM was portrayed by Mailer's daughter, Kate Mailer. Plans to subsequently produce *Strawhead* off Broadway in April 1986 were postponed for undisclosed reasons. Of the play itself, *Vanity Fair* said: "*Strawhead* is less about Marilyn than about Mailer's quest for Marilyn."

***A STREETCAR NAMED DESIRE***

In her pursuit of acting preeminence, Marilyn Monroe portrayed Blanche DuBois in a scene from Tennessee Williams's *A Streetcar Named Desire* before members of her Actors Studio class. MM performed the difficult seduction scene in which Blanche propositions the young man from the *Evening Star* newspaper.

The demanding role of Blanche DuBois was originally portrayed by Jessica Tandy on Broadway, Vivien Leigh in the movie, and Ann-Margret in the television movie.

### *THE STRIPPER*

Marilyn Monroe was offered—and wisely rejected—the role of Lila in 20th Century-Fox's production of *The Stripper* (1963). It's easy to see why Fox suggested the film to MM. It was to be produced by Jerry Wald (his last film), the man who had hired Marilyn in 1952 for *Clash by Night.* In addition, it was based on the Broadway play *A Loss of Roses* by William Inge. Inge, of course, was the playwright of *Bus Stop,* the film version of which MM scored a major success in.

But it is even easier to see why Marilyn rejected *The Stripper.* The rather labored plot dealt with a hometown Kansas girl, raised in a foster home, who, by way of a beauty contest title, "wins" a Hollywood screen test. When the test fails, the girl is banished back to her hometown and is forced into stripping for her supper.

After MM declined *The Stripper,* which had previously been titled *A Woman In July* and *Celebration,* the role was offered to, and accepted by, Joanne Woodward. The film costarred Richard Beymer, Claire Trevor, and Carol Lynley and featured Gypsy Rose Lee. The film was directed by Franklin J. Schaffner, a television director who made his features debut with this picture. Interestingly, Miss Woodward's strip number in this film was entitled "Something's Got to Give."

### JOHN STUART

John Stuart is the creator/producer/director/writer of the Las Vegas stage show *Legends in Concert,* which features a Marilyn Monroe impersonator.

### THE STUDIO CLUB

The Studio Club in Hollywood was a residential hotel for young women from all over the country who had gone to Los Angeles with aspirations of a working career in the arts. Affiliated with the YWCA, the Studio Club was located at 1215 N. Lodi St., just a few blocks away from the Los Angeles Orphans Home Society where young Norma Jeane Baker had once lived.

In 1946, at the time of her first contract with 20th Century-Fox, Marilyn Monroe shared Room #307 at the Studio Club. She paid $12-a-week rent for her room. Later, on June 3, 1948, during her Columbia contract, Marilyn returned to the Studio Club. This time she lived by herself in Room #334. Marilyn lived there until March 13, 1949.

**Former Residents**

1. Janet Blair
2. Linda Darnell
3. Barbara Eden
4. Florence Henderson
5. Evelyn Keyes
6. Dorothy Malone
7. Marilyn Monroe
8. Kim Novak
9. Ayn Rand
10. Donna Reed
11. Gale Storm

### AL STUMP

Al Stump, a former newspaper reporter for the *Los Angeles Herald Examiner,* is another one of the individuals who has been attempting to prove, for years, that Marilyn Monroe did not commit suicide. In 1972, it was Al Stump who introduced Bob Slatzer to private investigator Milo Speriglio.

**JOHN STURGES**

Born in 1911, John Sturges was the director of such films as *Bad Day at Black Rock* (1954), *Gunfight at the OK Corral* (1957), *The Magnificent Seven* (1960), and *The Great Escape* (1963).

In 1950, Sturges directed the June Allyson/Dick Powell picture *Right Cross*, which featured starlet Marilyn Monroe in a bit part.

**JULE STYNE**

Born in London on December 31, 1905, Jule Styne is the famous stage composer of such productions as *Sugar, Funny Girl*, and *Gypsy*. Styne also cowrote some of the songs from *Gentlemen Prefer Blondes* (1953), including "Two Little Girls from Little Rock," "Bye Bye Baby," and the classic, "Diamonds Are a Girl's Best Friend." At the time of Marilyn Monroe's death, Styne had been discussing the possibility of doing a musical version of *A Tree Grows in Brooklyn* with her.

***SUGAR***

*Sugar* was an ill-fated stage musical version of the smash hit movie comedy *Some Like It Hot* (1959). Presented in 1974, *Sugar* starred Robert Morse and Larry Kent. The title role, the one that Marilyn Monroe played in the movie, was portrayed by actress Leland Palmer. The show featured music and lyrics by Jule Styne and Bob Merrill and was directed by Cyril Ritchard.

**SUICIDE**

> "Sometimes I think it would be easier to avoid old age, to die young, but then you'd never complete your life, would you? You'd never wholly know yourself."
>
> Marilyn Monroe to W. J. Weatherby, circa 1960–61

Officially, Marilyn Monroe died in 1962 from a "probable suicide." For many, this theory was easily believable because of Marilyn's history of failed suicide attempts.

- ☆ Marilyn Monroe had told writer Ben Hecht that, before her nineteenth birthday, she had attempted to commit suicide twice—once by leaving the gas on and once by swallowing sleeping pills.
- ☆ Following the 1950 death of Johnny Hyde, MM reportedly took an overdose of sleeping pills.
- ☆ Before her marriage to Joe DiMaggio, MM reportedly took an overdose of sleeping pills.
- ☆ During her marriage to Arthur Miller, Marilyn attempted suicide several times.

It had gotten to the point at which some people were *waiting* for the day when one of Marilyn's suicide attempts would succeed. Once, during the filming of *The Misfits* (1961), press agent Harry Mines received a telephone call from a New York wire service at 4:30 A.M. The caller wanted confirmation that Marilyn had committed suicide. Mines responded by saying: "Why that's impossible! She has to be on the set at 7:30 A.M.! Besides, Paula Strasberg would never stand for it!"

In the weeks following Marilyn Monroe's death, the suicide rate in Los Angeles county jumped by 40 percent. The reverberation was felt in New York as well. Wrote Gloria Steinem:

> "Within days after her body was discovered, eight young and beautiful women took their lives in individual incidents clearly patterned after Marilyn Monroe's death, some of them leaving notes to make that connection clear."

**The Suicide Investigation Team**

To investigate the cause of Marilyn Monroe's death, Theodore J. Curphey and the Los Angeles County Coroner's Office appointed a Suicide Investigation Team to conduct what was then termed a "psychiatric autopsy." The twelve-man team was headed by Dr. Robert Littman and Dr. Norman Farberow. Their "findings" were reported to the press on August 17, 1962, by Theodore J. Curphey. Said Curphey:

> "It is my conclusion that the death of Marilyn Monroe was caused by self-administered sedative drugs [and] that the mode of death is 'probable suicide.' "

## PRESIDENT SUKARNO

On May 31, 1956, Joshua Logan threw a Hollywood cocktail party for President Sukarno of Indonesia. Because Sukarno was a fan of hers, Marilyn Monroe was invited to attend the party. The two got along quite well. Said Sukarno to MM:

> "You are a very important person in Indonesia. Your pictures are the most popular of any that have ever played in my country. The entire Indonesian population is interested in my meeting you."

About a year later, when the multimarried Sukarno was in dire trouble, Marilyn Monroe wanted to offer him political refuge in her New York home. However, her husband, Arthur Miller, would not allow it, and the "rescue" never took place.

## ANTHONY SUMMERS

Anthony Summers is the writer/researcher of the superb 1985 investigative book *Goddess: The Secret Lives of Marilyn Monroe* (Macmillan Publishing Company). Mr. Summers's other books include *The File on the Tsar* and *Conspiracy.*

## SUN VALLEY, IDAHO

In 1956, the *Bus Stop* company shot some of the film's exterior scenes in Sun Valley, Idaho.

**SUTTON PLACE**

In 1955–56, Marilyn Monroe lived in an apartment at 2 Sutton Pl. in New York City. Marilyn's apartment was on the eighth floor.

**H. P. SWANTEK**

On November 21, 1954, Beverly Hills patrolman H. P. Swantek stopped Marilyn Monroe at 9200 Wilshire Boulevard for going 30 mph in a 35 mph zone. He proceeded to give her a ticket for driving without a license.

***THE SYMBOL***

*The Symbol* is a fictionalized, very thinly disguised story about Marilyn Monroe. The book was written by Alvah Bessie and was published by Random House in 1966. The heroine of this book had the following characteristics:

☆ She never knew her father.
☆ Her mother was put into a hospital.
☆ She had to be reared by an "aunt" who wasn't really an aunt.
☆ She got married at age sixteen, to a man in the Navy.
☆ She became a girlie-magazine model.
☆ She grew up to become a movie star.
☆ She married a famous football hero.
☆ She moved to New York to escape Hollywood.
☆ She then married an artist, who is forced to stand trial on communism charges.
☆ She died of a drug overdose.

*The Symbol* is obviously about Marilyn Monroe, and yet, the author and publisher had the audacity to print a disclaimer at the front of the book that read:

> Note: This story is a fiction. Neither its characters nor the situations in which they are involved are intended to represent any persons now living or dead (or both), although the milieu in which they exist has produced many like them.

In 1973, *The Symbol* was adapted into a television movie that starred Connie Stevens as the MM-based character.

# T

**NORMA TALMADGE**

In 1926, Gladys Baker Mortenson named her baby Norma Jeane after her favorite film star of the period, Norma Talmadge.

Norma Talmadge was born on May 26, 1893, in Jersey City, New Jersey. Originally one of the three Talmadge Sisters, Norma carved out a niche for herself in such silent motion pictures as *Battle Cry of Peace* (1914), *The Lady* (1925), and *Camille* (1927). Her career ended with the advent of motion picture sound.

Interestingly, Norma Talmadge was once married to producer Joseph Schenck, who later became one of starlet Marilyn Monroe's powerful benefactors. Miss Talmadge was also married to actor George Jessel. She died on December 24, 1957, in Las Vegas.

**TAR TAN**

Before she attained stardom, Marilyn Monroe appeared in a print advertisement for Tar Tan Suntan Lotion.

**DANIEL TARADASH**

Born in 1913, Daniel Taradash was the screenwriter on such productions as *Golden Boy* (1939), *From Here to Eternity* (for which he won a 1953 Oscar), *Picnic* (1956), and *The Other Side of Midnight* (1977).

In 1952, Taradash scripted *Don't Bother to Knock,* which starred rising box office commodity Marilyn Monroe.

**FRANK TASHLIN**

Frank Tashlin (1913–1972) is perhaps best known as the writer/producer/director of the two Jayne Mansfield vehicles *The Girl Can't Help It* (1956) and *Will Success Spoil Rock Hunter?* (1957).

In 1962, 20th Century-Fox initially slated Tashlin to direct the Marilyn Monroe/Dean Martin vehicle *Something's Got to Give.* However, Marilyn objected to the hiring of Tashlin, and George Cukor was given the assignment. Interestingly, thirteen years before, Tasnlin had cowritten the Marx Brothers picture *Love Happy,* which featured starlet MM in a bit part.

**BERNIE TAUPIN**

Acclaimed songwriter Bernie Taupin cowrote the 1973 song about MM "Candle in the Wind." It was recorded on the album by Elton John, *Goodbye Yellow Brick Road.*

**ELIZABETH TAYLOR**

> "I'll be happy, too, to see all those covers with *me* on them and not Liz."
>
> MM in 1962, after realizing that her nude photos would push Liz off of the worldwide magazine covers

Elizabeth Taylor was the one movie star that Marilyn Monroe felt the most competitive with. After all, not only was Elizabeth six years younger than MM; she was also far better paid. In 1962, 20th Century-Fox paid Marilyn Monroe $100,000 for *Something's Got to Give*. At the same time, the same studio shelled out $1,000,000 to Elizabeth Taylor for *Cleopatra*.

There was definitely a feud of sorts between the two most famous actresses in the world. Certainly, there was one on Marilyn's part. And by all indications, Elizabeth shared the sentiment. After Marilyn's death, Max Lerner wrote an article that claimed: "Elizabeth Taylor was a legend, but Marilyn Monroe was a myth."

THE AUTHOR'S COLLECTION

La Taylor won a 1960 Oscar for *Butterfield 8*—presumably to the irritation of MM.

Reportedly, Miss Taylor telephoned Lerner and said:

> "You have a nerve saying that Marilyn was a 'myth' and I'm just a lousy 'legend.' I'm much more beautiful than Marilyn Monroe ever was, and I'm certainly a much better actress. What the hell do I have to do to be a myth? Die young and at my own hand?"

The "rivalry" between the two ladies seemed to culminate in 1961, at the time Elizabeth Taylor was shooting *Cleopatra*. When Miss Taylor became too ill to work, causing monumental financial setbacks, Lloyds' of London, the insurance company handling the film publicly requested that Elizabeth Taylor be replaced by Marilyn Monroe. However, 20th Century-Fox and producer Walter Wanger balked. Retorted Wanger: "No Liz, no Cleo!" And rightfully so. In retrospect, the idea of Marilyn Monroe playing Cleopatra seems farfetched at the very least—regardless of how versatile an actress she had proven herself to be. Can you imagine the very idea of Elizabeth Taylor portraying Lorelei or Cherie or Sugar?

## FRANK TAYLOR

In June 1958, Arthur Miller read the first draft of his screenplay, *The Misfits,* to his friend and neighbor, Frank Taylor. At that time, Taylor was the editorial director of Dell Books. He was also Arthur Miller's former book editor. After listening to his friend's new literary work, the enthusiastically receptive Taylor suggested that John Huston be contacted to direct the project.

Such were the humble beginnings of *The Misfits* (1961), certainly one of the most artistically ambitious film productions of all time. John Huston *was* contacted and signed to direct the production. And Frank Taylor was cajoled into leaving his post at Dell Books to serve as the film's producer.

## MARK AND CURTIS TAYLOR

Mark and Curtis Taylor were the sons of Frank and Nan Taylor and were frequent visitors to the Connecticut farm owned by Arthur and Marilyn Miller.

## NAN TAYLOR

Nan Taylor was Frank Taylor's wife and a friend to both Arthur and Marilyn Miller.

## ROGER G. TAYLOR

Roger G. Taylor compiled and edited two interesting books about Marilyn Monroe—*Marilyn Monroe: In Her Own Words* (1983) and *Marilyn in Art* (1984).

## WALTER TAYLOR

In 1948, Fred Karger introduced Marilyn Monroe to Dr. Walter Taylor, an orthodontist who subsequently made a retainer to fix MM's protruding front teeth. Dr. Taylor did not charge Marilyn, and the two developed a friendly acquaintance. Reportedly, Marilyn visited the bed-ridden Taylor on the afternoon of his death.

## *THE TEAHOUSE OF THE AUGUST MOON*

One night, as a gag, during her New York period, Marilyn Monroe reportedly appeared, secretly and incognito, onstage at the Martin Beck Theatre in the Broadway production of *The Teahouse of the August Moon.* Marilyn appeared only for the performance's curtain call. She was in costume and was not recognized. At that time, her friend Eli Wallach was the star of the play.

## THE TELEPHONE

> "You know who I've always depended on? Not strangers, not friends. The telephone! That's my best friend. I seldom write letters, but I love calling friends, especially late at night, when I can't sleep."
>
> MM to W. J. Weatherby, circa 1960–61

☆ Norma Jeane's phone number at the start of her career: AR 2-2487

☆ Marilyn Monroe's phone number at the time of her death: 472-4830

☆ MM's private phone number at the time of her death: 476-1890

COURTESY OF CINEMA COLLECTORS

**MM Trivia Quiz #44**

What was the film in which MM was first heard on the telephone? (Answer on page 578.)

## TELEVISION

Marilyn Monroe started out in the movies at approximately the same time as the emergence of television. Over the years, MM has been sometimes credited with reviving, if not *saving*, the movie industry from the onslaught of television. Wrote Marjorie Rosen in her fascinating book, *Popcorn Venus* (Avon Books, 1973):

> To lure movie patrons, the industry first tried 3-D . . . [then came] Cinerama, and, in 1953, CinemaScope. But the biggest business boon was no man-made achievement. It was a natural wonder—Marilyn Monroe.

Marilyn Monroe did not particularly like television. She thought that the television screen reduced her larger-than-life image. As a result, she made very few television appearances. In fact, in 1957, one of the networks approached Marilyn's partner at the time, Milton H. Greene, with a $2,000,000 proposition for a Marilyn Monroe television series. Greene and Marilyn declined.

### MM TV Appearances

1. Royal Triton Oil Company (commercial) (1950)
2. "The Jack Benny Show" (1953)
3. "Person to Person" (1955)

### Television Series That Included a Segment About MM

1. "I Love Lucy: Ricky's Movie Offer" (1954)
2. "Eyewitness: Marilyn Monroe: Why?" (1962)
3. "The Eleventh Hour: Like a Diamond in the Sky" (1963)
4. "That's Hollywood!: Marvelous Marilyn" (1979)

5. "In Search of: The Death of Marilyn Monroe" (1980)
6. "M*A*S*H: Bombshells" (1982)
7. "Benson: Boys Night Out" (1983)
8. "Hollywood Close-Up: Marilyn, In Search of a Dream" (1983)
9. "Matt Houston: Marilyn" (1983)

**"THAT'S HOLLYWOOD!"**

On January 8, 1979, the syndicated entertainment television program "That's Hollywood!" featured a special documentary tribute to Marilyn Monroe. The segment was titled "Marvelous Marilyn." It was narrated by Tom Bosley and was written and produced by Phillip Savenick.

"Marvelous Marilyn" was essentially a compendium of Marilyn Monroe's career. Extremely well done, the segment featured film clips, newsreels, still photographs, and footage from Marilyn's last, unfinished picture, *Something's Got to Give* (1962).

**BEN THAU**

Ben Thau (1898–1983) was a powerful executive at MGM and a good friend of Johnny Hyde. After Marilyn Monroe's successful outing in Metro's *The Asphalt Jungle* (1950), Thau attempted to convince Dore Schary *not* to drop Marilyn's option. He failed. Nonetheless, he was very supportive of MM, and, in tandem with Dona Holloway and Samuel Berke, he arranged for Marilyn to attend Johnny Hyde's funeral—despite the Hyde family's objections.

**EARL THEISEN**

Starlet Marilyn Monroe posed for pinup posters that were shot by photographer Earl Theisen.

***THERE'S NO BUSINESS LIKE SHOW BUSINESS*** ★★

1954 117 minutes CinemaScope
20th Century-Fox
Directed by: Walter Lang
Produced by: Sol C. Siegel
Screenplay by: Phoebe Ephron, Henry Ephron
Photographed by: Leon Shamroy
Cast: Ethel Merman, Dan Dailey, Marilyn Monroe, Donald O'Connor, Johnny Ray, Mitzi Gaynor

*There's No Business Like Show Business* is less a movie than it is a tuneful tribute to the great composer Irving Berlin. At the time *Show Business* was shot in 1954, Marilyn Monroe was the hottest property in Hollywood. Twentieth Century-Fox exploited this, in typical fashion, by forcibly ushering MM into this all-splash, no-substance production. Marilyn has little to do in this film except scorch up the screen with a production number called "Heat Wave."

*Show Business* was the first film made while Marilyn Monroe was Mrs. Joe DiMaggio. Reportedly, Marilyn agreed to do this picture against the wishes of DiMaggio. Although she knew the script was mediocre, Marilyn finally consented because Fox had promised to give her the Broadway comedy hit *The Seven Year Itch* as her next picture. Besides, by the spring of 1954, Marilyn was going stir-crazy with the domesticity of San Francisco, and *Show Business* was her ticket back to Hollywood.

The DiMaggio-Monroe relationship began to deteriorate during the production of *Show Business*. Marilyn reportedly collapsed on the set three times. There can be little doubt that her unpleasant experience on this film and its ultimate failure contributed heavily to Marilyn's decision to flee Hollywood in pursuit of more artistically worthwhile endeavors.

**ROBERT THOEREN**

*Some Like It Hot* (1959) was based on an original story cowritten by Robert Thoeren.

**THOM McAN**

In early 1987, the Thom McAn shoe chain introduced the Marilyn Monroe line of shoes, boots, and handbags. The items were not inspired by Marilyn's movies or fashions, but were designed with a 1950s flavor.

**BOB THOMAS**

In 1951, noted Hollywood correspondent and author Bob Thomas dubbed starlet Marilyn Monroe "The Atomic Blonde." He also named her the "number one cheesecake gal of Hollywood."

In 1953, Thomas's column was used by Hollywood matriarch Joan Crawford, to publicly lambaste MM for her appearance at the *Photoplay* magazine awards. (*See* JOAN CRAWFORD.)

When interviewed thirty-four years later about the MM/Joan Crawford feud, Thomas offered the following insight:

> "Well, you have to understand that she [Crawford] was once a sex symbol and she was suddenly replaced by the new kid on the block. She spoke emotionally and very truthfully about how she felt. She had been upstaged and she was upset about it. She told Louella [Parsons] later that she thought what she told me had been off the record, but that's not true. She told me after the interview 'do be careful what you print.' And I was. I didn't print everything that she had said about Marilyn."

Of Marilyn, Thomas said:

> "She was a terrific interview. She was very bright, witty, responsive, and very easy to talk to. She was an interviewer's dream!"

As of 1987, Mr. Thomas was based in Encino, California, and was still the Hollywood correspondent for the Associated Press.

**FLORENCE THOMAS**

Marilyn Monroe's former housekeeper.

**J. LEE THOMPSON**

At the time of Marilyn Monroe's death, director J. Lee Thompson had been negotiating with her to do a picture called *What a Way to Go*. Thompson had already signed Gene Kelly for the male lead, and he had an appointment with Marilyn on August 7, 1962, to finalize her deal. Obviously, the deal never materialized, and Thompson eventually made the picture with Shirley MacLaine.

J. Lee Thompson was born in England in 1914 and is best known for his Charles Bronson movies, as well as for his other action-adventure pictures. Among his credits are *The Guns of Navarone* (1961), *The Greek Tycoon* (1978), and *Ten to Midnight* (1983).

**DAME SYBIL THORNDIKE**

> "I thought, surely she won't come over, she's so small scale, but when I saw her on the screen, my goodness—how it came over!"
>
> Dame Sybil Thorndike on MM

When nearly everyone on the set of *The Prince and the Showgirl* (1957) was infuriated by Marilyn Monroe's lack of professionalism, it was actress Dame Sybil Thorndike who rushed to MM's defense. Said Dame Sybil to the all-English cast: "We need her desperately. She's the only one of us who really knows how to act in front of a camera."

Mostly known as a distinguished actress on the British stage, Dame Sybil Thorndike (1882-1976) has appeared in such films as *Nicholas Nickleby* (1947) and *Alive and Kicking* (1958).

***A TICKET TO TOMAHAWK*** ★

1950 90 minutes Technicolor
20th Century-Fox
Directed by: Richard Sale
Produced by: Robert Bassler
Screenplay by: Mary Loos, Richard Sale
Photographed by: Harry Jackson
Cast: Dan Dailey, Anne Baxter, Rory Calhoun, Walter Brennan, Will Wright, Connie Gilchrist, Arthur Hunnicutt, Otis Howlin, Chief Yowlachie

Stupid, mildly entertaining stagecoach western with bland performances, Technicolor scenery, and vintage Marilyn Monroe in a bit as the pretty blonde chorus girl in the yellow dress.

*A Ticket to Tomahawk* took MM back to the Fox lot, after she had been discarded by the studio just a short time before. Marilyn began shooting *Ticket* on August 15, 1949, almost immediately after the *Love Happy* tour had disbanded. The film was released in May 1950 and did little to further Marilyn's career.

**TOM TIERNEY**

In 1979, businessman Tom Tierney marketed the Marilyn Monroe Paper Doll. The set came complete with thirty-one costumes from twenty-four of Marilyn's movies.

### CHARLENE TILTON

Five-foot-tall Charlene Tilton, formerly Lucy Ewing on the "Dallas" television show, portrayed Marilyn Monroe at a Hollywood fund-raiser in October 1980. Tilton even wore *the* same dress that Marilyn made famous twenty years before in *Some Like It Hot.*

### THE TIME-LIFE BUILDING

Marilyn Monroe assisted in "breaking the ground" for the Time-Life Building (address 1271 Avenue of the Americas), near Rockefeller Center in New York City, on July 2, 1957. Marilyn was two hours late for the festivities—but everyone, including Laurence Rockefeller, waited for her.

### *TIME* MAGAZINE

> Her acting talents, if any, finish a needless second to her moist come-on look, half-closed eyes, and moist half-open mouth.
>
> *Time* magazine on MM's acting aspirations

> The urge to go nude was her most public whim. "I dreamed I was standing up in church without any clothes on," she recalled, "and all the people there were lying at my feet." Years later, she posed nude for Christendom's most famous calendar, and from that moment on, she was the only blonde in the world.
>
> *Time* magazine on MM

*Time* has published the following articles on MM:

☆ 8/11/52: "Something for the Boys"
☆ 2/23/53: "Go Easy"
☆ 11/30/53: "Portrait"
☆ 1/25/54: "Storybook Romance"
☆ 2/15/54: "Walker"
☆ 10/18/54: "Out at Home"
☆ 1/24/55: "Dostoyevsky Blues"
☆ 1/16/56: "Winner"
☆ 1/30/56: "Who Would Resist?"
☆ 2/20/56: "Co-Stars"
☆ 5/14/56: "To Aristophanes and Back"*
☆ 7/9/56: "People"
☆ 7/30/56: "Conquest"
☆ 4/29/57: "Executive Sweet"
☆ 8/8/60: "Marilyn and the Mustangs"
☆ 11/21/60: "Popsie and Poopsie"
☆ 2/17/61: "Marilyn's New Role"
☆ 8/17/62: "Thrilled with Guilt"
☆ 5/31/63: "Marilyn, My Marilyn"
☆ 12/15/67: "People"
☆ 8/7/72: "Still Magic"
☆ 7/16/73: "Two Myths Converge: NM Discovers MM"*

☆ 5/7/78: "Marilyn Without Makeup" (excerpted from *Nostalgia Isn't What It Used to Be*, by Simone Signoret)
☆ 1/24/83: "The Manufacture of Marilyn"

---

**Time* covers that MM appeared on.

**TINKER BELL**
It's a little-known fact that Marilyn Monroe was actually the inspiration for the final model of Walt Disney's most famous fairy, Peter Pan's companion character, Tinker Bell. Marilyn was honored by the animated homage and refused to be paid for her likeness.

**TOBEY BEACH**
Tobey Beach is twenty-three miles east of New York City and is located in the town of Oyster Bay, on the North Shore of Long Island.

In 1949, photographer Andre de Dienes shot his pink-and-white-swimsuit, beachside photos of Marilyn Monroe. At that time, MM was in New York to promote the Marx Brothers picture *Love Happy*.

**MIKE TODD**
Showman/producer Mike Todd was born Avrom Goldenborgen in 1907. He gained fame and fortune for his productions of Broadway spectaculars, as well as for the much heralded film *Around the World in 80 Days* (1956). In February 1957, Todd married actress Elizabeth Taylor. The following year, on March 22, 1958, he was tragically killed when his personal airplane exploded in mid-flight.

In 1955, Marilyn Monroe rode atop a pink elephant at Madison Square Garden to benefit Mike Todd's Arthritis and Rheumatism Foundation.

**TOKYO**
*See* JAPAN.

**RAY TOLMAN**
In 1962, Marilyn Monroe employed carpenter Ray Tolman to construct the cabinets in the kitchen of her new Brentwood home. Tolman also built MM a breakfast table and a set of black walnut benches.

***TOMMY***
Ken Russell's 1975 film adaptation of the Who's rock opera includes a sequence that graphically illustrates the pop-saint status that Marilyn Monroe has attained since her death in 1962. In the scene, Ann-Margret takes her mute son, Tommy, to a chapel to be cured by goddess apostle MM, "the plastic miracle healer," while Eric Clapton sings the song "Eyesight to the Blind."

**TOOTS SHOR'S**
Once referred to as "a gymnasium with room service," Toots Shor's was a

New York City bar/restaurant that typically catered to "men's men"—sports figures, newspaper writers, and assorted other characters from the theatre, public relations, and advertising worlds.

In the early 1950s, Toots Shor's (address: 51st Street between 5th and 6th Avenues, before it moved up a block to 52nd Street) was Joe DiMaggio's favorite hangout. He was frequently seen there with his cronies, George Solotaire, Lefty O'Doul, and, of course, Toots Shor himself. During the course of their relationship, Marilyn Monroe frequently accompanied DiMaggio on his visits to Toots Shor's. In fact, it was here that DiMaggio threw a surprise birthday party for his ex-wife on June 1, 1955, following the screening of *The Seven Year Itch*. However, the attempt at reconciliation failed, the couple ended up in a fight, and DiMaggio was left alone at the bar stool.

Toots Shor, the bar's owner, was a celebrated character in his own right, a hard drinker who died in 1976. Today, his establishment is still in existence and has been relocated to 233 West 33rd Street in New York City. Not surprisingly, Joe DiMaggio is no longer a "regular" at Toots Shor's.

**MEL TORME**

Melvin Howard Torme was born on September 13, 1925. A prominent musician and jazz vocalist, Torme has appeared in such motion pictures as *Higher and Higher* (1943), *Good News* (1947), and *The Patsy* (1964).

In the mid-1950s, there was some speculation that Torme was having an affair with none other than Marilyn Monroe.

**LEO TOVER**

Leo Tover (1902–1964) was the cinematographer of such films as *The Snake Pit* (1948), *The Heiress* (1949), and *Journey to the Center of the Earth* (1959).

In 1952, Tover shot *We're Not Married*, which featured Marilyn Monroe in a supporting role. Ten years later, Tover was one of the four cinematographers who worked on the uncompleted *Something's Got to Give*.

**TOYS**

According to Agnes Flanagan, as told to writer Anthony Summers, on the day of August 4, 1962, Marilyn Monroe received, via messenger, a mysterious package at her Brentwood home. The package contained a stuffed toy tiger that, according to Miss Flanagan, left MM in an inexplicable state of depression. It is not known whom the package was from.

**THE TRANS-LUX THEATRE**

Marilyn Monroe shot her famous "skirt scene" from *The Seven Year Itch* outside of the Trans-Lux Theatre, which, in 1954, was located near 52nd Street and Lexington Avenue in New York City. Today, the Trans-Lux Theatre is situated at 1221 Avenue of the Americas.

**WILLIAM TRAVILLA**

Catalina Island-born William Travilla is one of the best and most respected

COURTESY OF TRAVILLA

Wardrobe illustration, *There's No Business Like Show Business*, 1954.

COURTESY OF TRAVILLA

Wardrobe illustration, *Gentlemen Prefer Blondes*, 1953.

COURTESY OF TRAVILLA

With Travilla at Tiffany's, Los Angeles, circa 1953.

costume designers of film and television. He was also the man who costumed Marilyn Monroe in most of her movie hits, including *Don't Bother to Knock* (1952), *Monkey Business* (1952), *Gentlemen Prefer Blondes* (1953), *How to Marry a Millionaire* (1953), *River of No Return* (1954), *There's No Business Like Show Business* (1954), *The Seven Year Itch* (1955), and *Bus Stop* (1956).

When questioned recently about the nature of his relationship with MM, Travilla admitted that he had dated Marilyn, despite the fact that he had been married at the time. "She would make any guy feel like a king. She only looked at you. She would never look around at anyone else," he recalled. Naturally, this put some pressure on his marriage. According to Travilla, Marilyn would telephone him at 3:00 A.M. and plead: "Please come over, I need you." Understandably, Travilla's wife was more than slightly jealous; but, just as understandably, Travilla went to Marilyn, anyway. On dressing his famous subject, Travilla admitted that MM *was* displeased with one of his creations. "It was a beige wool jersey dress [for *Monkey Business,* 1952] with a pleated full circle skirt, and she hated it!"

Travilla, who was one of MM's personal fashion designers, once named her "the easiest person I ever worked with." Among the other famous ladies he has designed for over the years are Ann Sheridan, who established him at Warner Brothers in 1948; Joanne Woodward in *The Stripper* (1963); Faye Dunaway in *Evita Peron* (1982); Jaclyn Smith as Jacqueline Kennedy Onassis; and Ann-Margret in *A Streetcar Named Desire.* He won an Oscar for his work in *The Adventures of Don Juan* (1949) and Emmys for *Moviola* (1980) and *Evita Peron.* Currently, Travilla designs the costumes for both "Dallas" and "Knots Landing."

The last time William Travilla saw Marilyn Monroe was in 1962, just a week before her death. Said Travilla:

> I was having dinner with a friend at a restaurant and I saw a woman across the room. She was very thin, and had no makeup on. My friend commented that the woman looked like Marilyn Monroe, and I said, "She wishes! It would take a lot of makeup [to make her look like MM]! Then I heard her laugh. I went over to say 'hi,' and she looked at me with no recognition at all. She was with Peter Lawford, his wife, and someone else, a woman. Then all of a sudden, she said 'Billy!' I left the table very hurt and upset. I was going to write her a nasty letter, but she was dead a few days later. I'm so glad I didn't write that letter.

### *A TREE GROWS IN BROOKLYN*

On August 9, 1962, Marilyn Monroe had an appointment with Jule Styne in New York to discuss the possibility of appearing in a film musical version of *A Tree Grows in Brooklyn.*

Directed by Elia Kazan in 1945, *A Tree Grows in Brooklyn* was a successful motion picture starring Peggy Ann Garner, James Dunn, Dorothy McGuire, and Joan Blondell. It was based on the novel by Betty Smith. In

1974, 20th Century-Fox finally remade *Tree,* though not in musical form, but as a television movie. It starred Cliff Robertson and Diane Baker.

**DIANA TRILLING**

Noted writer Diana Trilling was born on July 21, 1905, in New York City. In *McCall's* magazine, July 1982, Ms. Trilling penned an article about MM entitled "Marilyn Monroe: The Meaning of Her Life and Death." Of Marilyn, Trilling wrote:

> This was one of the most painful feelings that I and many other women had at her death—that we would have been glad to help her. But we weren't there, she didn't know about us. She couldn't look to us for help.

**LAMAR TROTTI**

Lamar Trotti (1900–1952) was the writer/producer of such films as *The Ox-Bow Incident* (1942), *Wilson* (1943), and *With a Song in My Heart* (1952).

Trotti also wrote and produced *As Young as You Feel,* the 1951 Fox comedy that featured Marilyn Monroe in a supporting role, and he adapted the O. Henry stories for the 1952 picture *O. Henry's Full House,* in which MM appeared. Trotti was also given a story credit for the Irving Berlin tribute *There's No Business Like Show Business* (1954), in which Marilyn costarred.

**"THE TRUTH ABOUT ME"**

"The Truth About Me" was a series of articles, authored by Marilyn herself, "as told to" Hollywood writer Liza Wilson. The articles commenced their run in the November 16, 1952, edition of *American Weekly* magazine. In defense of herself, MM wrote:

> I think that in view of some of the surprising—even vicious—untruths that have been printed about me since I became a movie star, it is high time that I come out and tell the truth.

Ultimately, and unfortunately, though, "The Truth About Me" failed to deliver its promise. Instead of providing "truth," the series succumbed to sugar-coated studio bio material that covered the gamut from poor little orphan girl to fast-rising new movie star.

***TURN ON THE HEAT***

*Turn on the Heat* was a 1967 stage play about Marilyn Monroe that was produced at the Hole in the Wall Theatre in Perth, Australia. The play dealt exclusively with the last hours of Marilyn's life. It was written by Gerry Glaskin, and featured actress Judy West as MM.

### *TV GUIDE*

Marilyn Monroe appeared on the cover of *TV Guide* only once. It was the January 23–29, 1953, issue.

Reprinted with permission from *TV Guide®* Magazine. Copyright © 1953 by Triangle Publications, Inc., Radnor, PA.

THE ALAN FRANCE COLLECTION

### 20th CENTURY-FOX

In 1935, Joseph Schenck and Darryl Zanuck spearheaded the formation of 20th Century-Fox (address: 10201 W. Pico Boulevard), which, over fifty years later, has remained one of the major production forces in Hollywood.

In 1942, Schenck and Zanuck were joined by Spyros Skouras, who, for the next twenty years, served as the company's president. Over the years, Fox has been responsible for such stars as Shirley Temple, Alice Faye, Tyrone Power, Will Rogers, Betty Grable, and, of course, Marilyn Monroe. Fox has also produced such classic films as *The Grapes of Wrath* (1940), *How Green Was My Valley* (1941), *Gentleman's Agreement* (1947), and *All About Eve* (1950).

> "Most of what I did while I was at Fox that first time was pose for stills. Publicity made up a story about how I was a babysitter who'd been babysitting for the casting director. . . . You'd think they would have had me at least [be] a daddy-sitter."
>
> MM to Pete Martin,
> *Will Acting Spoil Marilyn Monroe* (Doubleday, 1956)

Based on a color, silent screen test, as well as the recommendation of the studio's head of talent, Ben Lyon, 20th Century-Fox signed Marilyn Monroe to a standard player contract on August 24, 1946. Six months later, the studio renewed Marilyn's option for another six-month term. At that time, it was thought by Fox that MM had the possibility of becoming the studio's third-string blonde, following Betty Grable and June Haver. During this period, Marilyn was cast in two Fox pictures: *Scudda Hoo! Scudda Hay!* (1948) and

*Dangerous Years* (1947). However, after Marilyn failed to make much of an impact in either of these films, her option was dropped on August 25, 1947.

Within the next three years, as a free agent, Marilyn Monroe returned to 20th Century-Fox for three more pictures, two of which were strictly incidental: *A Ticket to Tomahawk* (1950) and *The Fireball* (1950). However, the other picture, the "important" one, landed Marilyn her second contract with Fox. The film was *All About Eve* (1950). Reportedly, when Zanuck saw Marilyn's rushes from that film, he promptly re-signed her to the studio for another six-month term. The contract, negotiated by Marilyn's agent/manager/lover, Johnny Hyde, was implemented on December 10, 1950.

> Amid a slowly gathering hush, she stood there, a blond apparition in a strapless black cocktail gown, a little breathless as if she were Cinderella, just stepped from a pumpkin coach.
>
> *Collier's* magazine on MM's appearance at the Fox exhibitors' party, 1951

THE SYLVIA BARNHART COLLECTION

Publicity still, circa 1947.

In 1951, at an exhibitors' party held at the Cafe de Paris, aka the Fox commissary, Marilyn Monroe cemented the stability of her moviemaking future. In attendance that evening were such studio luminaries as Susan Hayward, Jeanne Crain, June Haver, Anne Baxter, Gregory Peck, and Tyrone Power. However, Marilyn, who arrived at the function one-and-a-half hours later, was easily the evening's center of attention. And not only did she snatch the fickle spotlight from the veteran actors and the marquee "names"—she also landed the prime dinner spot at the number-one table, seated on the right-hand side of Fox president Spyros Skouras.

Following the exhibitors' party, Marilyn Monroe's short-term contract was extended to a seven-year term. Not only did this contract, which commenced on May 11, 1951, give Marilyn financial security; it also made her, for better or worse, the "property" of 20th Century-Fox. As a result, Fox began to hype its new acquisition as the "Cinderella of Hollywood." She was given the full-scale star buildup, which consisted of publicity, photographs, posters, personal appearances, and seven pictures in a one-year period!

The hype worked. Moreover, Marilyn Monroe had an indescribable, luminous on-screen presence that quickly found favor with the moviegoing public. Twentieth Century-Fox kept a weekly tab in its mailroom of which studio stars were receiving the most mail. Even before her breakthrough picture, *Niagara* (1953), Marilyn Monroe was the most popular star on the Fox lot.

And then she became the most popular movie star in the world. In 1953, the overwhelming back-to-back wallop of *Niagara, Gentlemen Prefer Blondes,* and *How to Marry a Millionaire* sent Marilyn Monroe's star and 20th Century-Fox's profits ascending through the proverbial roof and into some stellar, previously uncharted galaxy of riches.

Accordingly, one would have thought that 20th Century-Fox would have gone out of its way to accommodate its newest and biggest financial commodity. Instead, Fox executives continued to treat Marilyn Monroe as if she were just another busty, blonde, two-bit bit player. After all, as they may or may not have reasoned, MM was, by means of that 1951 contract, *bound* to them for at least another five years! Thus, Marilyn continued to be paid the minuscule salary that had been negotiated for her when she was still a starlet. Moreover, she was forced to appear in any production of Fox's choosing, including such mediocre pictures as *River of No Return* (1954), which is generally regarded as Marilyn's worst post-stardom film.

Thus, it was inevitable that Marilyn Monroe would rebel against the not-so-friendly forces at Fox. On December 15, 1953, just a month after the highly successful release of *How to Marry a Millionaire,* Marilyn refused to show up for work on a picture named *The Girl in Pink Tights.* As a result, MM was suspended, for the first time, by her studio bosses. However, within a few months, Marilyn and Fox made amends—temporarily—and MM agreed to appear in the Irving Berlin musical tribute, *There's No Business Like Show Business.* However, by the end of 1954, there was more dissension between the studio and the star. This time, Marilyn refused to appear in *How to Be Very, Very Popular.* Moreover, not only did MM leave Fox; she also fled Hollywood. By the beginning of 1955, Marilyn Monroe had moved to New York, disavowed her contract with Fox, and formed her own production company.

Following MM's defection and her declaration of independence, an irate 20th Century-Fox issued the following statement to the press:

> No one can handle her. No one can give her advice. She has always decided everything for herself. We're getting 200 letters a day demanding we get rid of her, but we have $2,000,000 tied up in this picture [*The Seven Year Itch*], and we're trying to protect that."
>
> *The Los Angeles Mirror,* 1/17/55

> Since she has been at 20th Century-Fox, Miss Monroe was given every consideration, surrounded by the finest creative talent

Publicity still, 1954. COURTESY OF CINEMA COLLECTORS

available, cast only in multimillion-dollar productions and given a careful and worldwide publicity campaign. . . . [Fox] has a firm contract for her exclusive services until August 8, 1958 . . . the studio will use every legal means to see that she lives up to every provision of it.

*Los Angeles Herald-Examiner*, 1/55

And an "unnamed" 20th Century-Fox stockholder told syndicated columnist Hedda Hopper:

"It's disgusting. She's had four or five years' training—enough to produce ten competent actresses—and she still can't act!"

For the next six months, the two opposing sides battled it out, in the negotiations and in the press. However, after the extremely successful opening of *The Seven Year Itch* in June 1955, 20th Century-Fox accelerated its effort to re-sign Marilyn Monroe to a mutually acceptable agreement. On September 6, 1955, the industry trade paper *Variety* reported that Fox had succumbed to Marilyn's contractual demands that she be given story approval and director approval. However, it was not until December 31, 1955, that MM actually signed her fourth and final Fox contract.

The contract awarded MM privileges that were considered revolutionary and unprecedented at that time. It called for Marilyn to make four nonexclusive pictures for Fox in a period of seven years. For her services, Marilyn was to be paid no less than $100,000 per film. Moreover, she was granted the right to make one independent film and six television appearances a year. Also, as a fringe benefit, while working on a Fox film she was to be given the services of a personal maid and an additional $500 a week for incidental expenses. But, most importantly, the new contract stipulated that any picture Marilyn appeared in had to be considered (by MM's criteria) a "Class A" production. On top of that, Marilyn was given the then rarely given rights of director and cinematographer approval.

In February 1956, the "new" Marilyn Monroe returned to 20th Century-Fox with a significant victory to her credit. Marilyn's first film, under her new Fox agreement, was the prestigious William Inge play *Bus Stop*. The film offered MM her most substantial role to date and was produced by Buddy Adler, who had recently replaced Darryl F. Zanuck as the head of production at Fox.

Over the next six years, Marilyn Monroe and the 20th Century-Fox executives got along quite amicably. However, by 1962, MM had made only two out of the four required pictures that she contractually owed to 20th Century-Fox. And she had only a year left on the term of that contract. Thus, to fulfill her obligation, MM agreed to star in the Fox comedy *Something's Got to Give*. But, as time would tell, there was nothing at all funny about the making of that picture.

By 1962, 20th Century-Fox was in deep financial distress. Due to the looming tragedy and gargantuan cost of *Cleopatra*, the executives at Fox were in a perpetual state of panic. To compensate for its losses, the studio was forced to sell much of its original "back lot" real estate to a developer named the Alcoa Company. (Today, the old Fox lot has been transformed into the massive, upscale complex of offices, shops, restaurants, and theatres known as Century City.) Furthermore, Buddy Adler had been replaced as the head of production by Robert Goldstein, who had, in turn, been replaced by former advertising man Peter Levathes. Such were the unstable conditions at 20th Century-Fox when Marilyn Monroe returned there in April 1962 to shoot *Something's Got to Give*.

To compound matters, Marilyn was sick with a virus. As a result, out of the thirty-three days of shooting, Marilyn appeared on the set a total of twelve days. A few years earlier, the studio might have tolerated MM's absenteeism, but by 1962 the front office at 20th Century-Fox was exasperated, frustrated, and sick of unhealthy movie actresses (Elizabeth Taylor's illness on *Cleopatra* had escalated that film's already enormous budget). Thus, desperately fighting to retain some semblance of control over his organization, Peter Levathes did what no man before him had done—he fired Marilyn Monroe. Furthermore, he also threatened to slap a $500,000 breach-of-contract lawsuit on her.

Reportedly, Fox president Spyros Skouras later overrode Levathes's decision to fire MM and shelve *Something's Got to Give*. Thus, on June 28, and again on July 12, 1962, MM met 20th Century-Fox officials to discuss negotiations to restart production of the film. Reportedly, all parties eventually resolved their differences, and *Something's Got to Give* was slated to commence shooting by the end of 1962.

But that was not to be the case. Nineteen sixty-two proved to be a pivotal year for 20th Century-Fox. By the end of the year, Fox lost the services of its president of twenty years, Spyros Skouras, who had resigned. Skouras was replaced by none other than Darryl Zanuck. In addition, Fox lost and regained and lost one of the biggest stars in its history, Marilyn Monroe.

The lot at 20th Century-Fox was hometown to Marilyn. Fox had first hired her when she was twenty, nurtured her to stardom, and fired her when she was thirty-six. It was also Fox that had been saved from financial depression when MM registered, resoundingly, at the box office in the 1950s. It is particularly sad and disappointing, then, that today the 20th Century-Fox lot has no reminders of or tributes to its former golden girl, Marilyn Monroe. There is no physical evidence that she was once the reigning queen of this fairytale domain. There is not a statue constructed in her memory. There is not a street named in her honor. There is not even a hamburger named after her at the studio commissary.

**THE 20TH CENTURY LIMITED**

In 1949, on the *Love Happy* tour, MM traveled aboard the 20th Century Limited locomotive, en route from Chicago to New York City.

**"20/20"**

> When the decision came down, Barbara Walters, Geraldo Rivera and Hugh Downs stood together on the set of ABC's "20/20." Linking arms to symbolize their unanimity, the trio of TV news personalities vowed to protest the network's last-minute decision to kill an investigative segment of the mysterious circumstances surrounding the 1962 death of Marilyn Monroe, complete with interviews about the movie queen's alleged affairs with both John and Bobby Kennedy.
>
> *People* magazine, 10/21/85

> "[The segment] was more carefully documented than anything any network did during Watergate."
>
> Hugh Downs, *The New York Times*

Over twenty years after her death, Marilyn Monroe is still creating scandals. This particular controversy arose in October 1985, when, at the last minute,

ABC news chief Roone Arledge questionably killed a "20/20" segment about Marilyn's involvement with John and Robert Kennedy.

Initially, the segment was twenty-six minutes in length and was scheduled to air on September 26, 1985. However, by the rescheduled October 3, 1985, air date, the segment had been chopped, at Arledge's request, to thirteen minutes. Then, at the last minute, just before it was scheduled to air, Arledge decided to pull the segment altogether.

A controversy erupted. As it turned out, the top brass at ABC News had more than its share of Kennedy family affiliations. Roone Arledge was a longtime, close personal friend of Ethel Kennedy; ABC vice-president David Burke had been a former top aide to Ted Kennedy; and Arledge's assistant, Jeff Ruhe, was married to Courtney Kennedy—Bobby and Ethel Kennedy's daughter.

The segment, which took over three months and $150,000 to produce, was to have been reported by Sylvia Chase. It was produced by Stanhope Gould and Ene Riisna. As a result of the "20/20" Marilyn Monroe controversy, Geraldo Rivera lost his job at ABC, and Miss Chase resigned from her post shortly thereafter.

The segment has never been aired.

**MM Trivia Quiz #45**

"20/20" abruptly replaced its MM segment with a segment about what? (Answer on page 578.)

## PAUL ULLMER

Photographer Lawrence Schiller took his 1962 nude shots of Marilyn Monroe to Paul Ullmer at the Life Laboratory on Wilshire Boulevard in Los Angeles to be processed.

## UNDERWEAR

> "All those lines and ridges in undergarments, girdles and brassieres are unnatural, and they distort a girl, so I never wear them."
>
> MM to Earl Wilson, in his syndicated column, 8/27/52

> "Somebody, somewhere, had told her that if she always wore a bra her boobs wouldn't sag and she insisted on it. She slept with a bra on. She told me she'd finish making love with someone and then, zoom, on with the bra."
>
> Amy Greene to Anthony Summers, *Goddess* (1985)

> "When she was dressed she wore no bra or panties. If she had to wear a brassiere, it was always a skimpy affair with two strings and a sheer half-cup called a no-no bra. But usually she wore none. She didn't have a huge bust. She looked good with no bra; not vulgar or trashy but different."
>
> George Masters on MM

THE AUTHOR'S COLLECTION

Uncharacteristically demure, MM donned *two* pairs of underpants for the 1954 shooting of *The Seven Year Itch*.

"I never wear girdles, and bras as rarely as possible. I feel encumbered by them. Anyway, I dress for men, not for other women, and men like to *see* a woman when they look at one. Not a boy. When I wear a girdle, it flattens me out. Can you give me one good reason why I should flatten myself out?"

MM to columnist Mike Connolly,
*The Hollywood Reporter*, 1952

Reporter: Do you wear underwear?
MM: Men seldom jump hurdles
for girls who wear girdles.

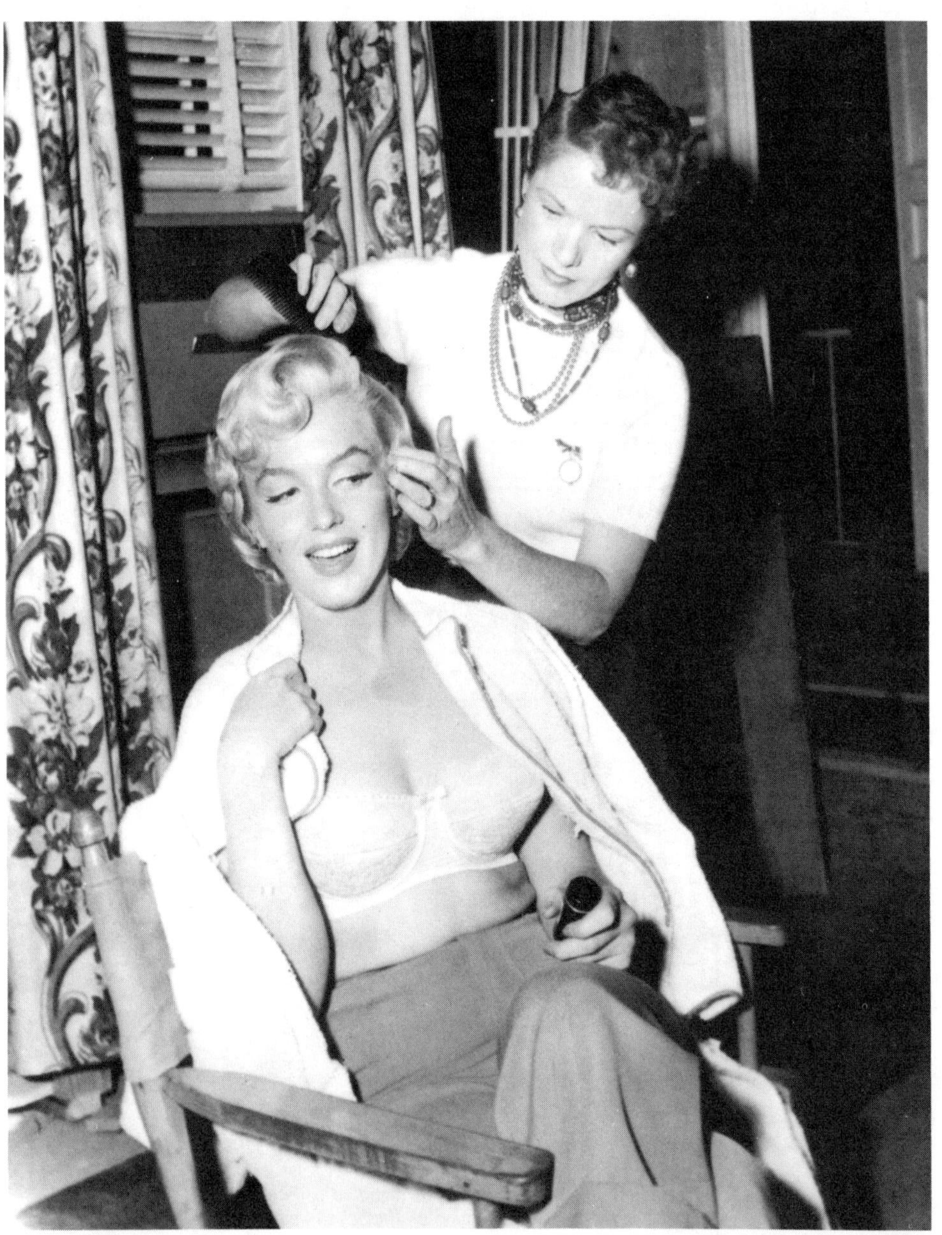

THE RAY VAN GOEYE COLLECTION

Marilyn Monroe did *not* like underwear. As a result, she rarely wore any. She particularly despised underpants. In her later years, Marilyn sometimes wore bras that were specially designed to prevent sagging. However, most of the time she avoided the constriction of underwear entirely.

**MM Trivia Quiz #46**
In *The Seven Year Itch*, where did MM store her underwear? (Answer on page 578.)

**UNEMPLOYMENT**
In August 1947, after her option was dropped by 20th Century-Fox, Marilyn Monroe filed for, and got, unemployment compensation from the state of California.

**UNITED ARTISTS**
The United Artists Corporation was founded in 1919 by Mary Pickford, Douglas Fairbanks, Charlie Chaplin, and D. W. Griffith. In 1959, UA (address: 1918 S. Vermont, Hollywood) released Marilyn Monroe's most successful picture, *Some Like It Hot.* UA also financed and distributed Marilyn's last completed film, *The Misfits* (1961).

THE ALAN FRANCE COLLECTION

**THE UNITED STATES ARMY**

In 1952, the U.S. Army drew embarrassing attention to itself by banning a photograph of Marilyn Monroe in which she was posed with a WAC, a WAVE, a WAF, and a lady Marine. The army felt that the dress MM was wearing in the photo exposed a bit too much cleavage and that the photo might give parents an incorrect conception of what life was like in the service.

However, much to the chagrin of the U.S. Army officials, the banning of the MM photograph created a stir, and subsequently the photo was published in nearly every newspaper in the country. As for Marilyn, she explained herself with the following statement to the national press:

> "That dress I wore was designed for eye-level—*not* for photographers who stand on a balcony and shoot downward. I'm embarrassed and hurt."

**THE UNITED STATES POST OFFICE**

In September 1954, the U.S. Post Office banned the Fire Gem Company from selling, via the mail, drinking coasters that featured Marilyn Monroe's nude calendar photo. The post office charged that the coasters were "obscene, lewd, lascivious, and indecent." However, when the case went to court, federal judge William M. Byrne ruled that the coasters were not obscene, and he restored the mailing privileges to the Fire Gem Company.

**UNIVERSITY HIGH SCHOOL**

In 1942, shortly before her marriage to Jim Dougherty, Norma Jeane Baker attended University High School in West Los Angeles for a brief period. Today, the school is called University Senior High (address: 11800 Texas Ave.).

**UNIVERSITY OF CALIFORNIA AT LOS ANGELES**

In February 1951, starlet Marilyn Monroe enrolled in the adult extension program at the University of California at Los Angeles (address: 405 Hilgard Ave., in Westwood). While at UCLA, Marilyn took an art appreciation course and a "Background in Literature" course.

**THE U.S. NAVY *NAUTILUS***

The U.S. Navy *Nautilus* was the world's first-known atomic submarine. In April 1956, the *Nautilus* generated some additional publicity when its crew members hung a pin-up poster of Marilyn Monroe inside the ship for morale.

**"USO WHEREVER THEY GO!"**

Marilyn Monroe narrated the film footage of her 1954 USO Tour of Korea for the television special "USO Wherever They Go!" that aired on NBC-TV's "Dupont Show of the Week" on October 8, 1961.

**THE U.S.S. *BENHAM***

Toward the end of 1951, as a publicity gimmick, Marilyn Monroe represented the *Los Angeles Daily News* as a hostess and entertainer aboard the U.S.S. *Benham* destroyer.

**JOHN VACHON**

John Vachon was a photographer who was present at the 1953 location shooting of *River of No Return* in Banff, Canada. During that period, Vachon shot two great photographs of Marilyn Monroe. One of them featured MM alone, wearing a very tight sweater. The second one was of MM and Joe DiMaggio sitting together on a window sill. In the photograph, Marilyn is leaning toward DiMaggio with her forehead touching his.

**MAMIE VAN DOREN**

In the 1950s, Mamie Van Doren was a blonde bombshell of the strictly B-picture variety. Born Joan Lucille Olander in Rowena, South Dakota, in 1933, Mamie started out as a secretary before she became a model and an actress. Among her films were *The Second Greatest Sex* (1955), *High School Confidential* (1960), and *The Navy Versus the Night Monsters* (1966).

For a period, Mamie Van Doren was Universal Studio's "answer" to Marilyn Monroe. As it turned out, Mamie was not much of an answer. However, over the years, she has garnered somewhat of a cult following. Today, she is still alive, still attractive, and, for the past several years, she has been threatening to make a comeback.

**MM Trivia Quiz #47**

Which one of Mamie Van Doren's husbands wrote a song in tribute to MM? (Answer on page 578.)

**RAY VAN GOEYE**

Ray Van Goeye saw his first Marilyn Monroe movie, *How to Marry a Millionaire,* at a Kalamazoo, Michigan, picture palace in 1954. For the past thirty-three years, Ray has translated his admiration for Monroe into an impressive tribute, a collection which presently includes over a thousand still photographs, a multitude of MM magazine covers and lobby cards, and extensive video and literary libraries. Employed as a shipping clerk, Ray is also a member of the Marilyn Remembered Fan Club in Los Angeles.

**VAN NUYS, CALIFORNIA**

Shortly after she was released from the orphanage in 1937, Norma Jeane Baker went to live with her "Aunt" Ana Lower at Aunt Ana's house on Odessa Avenue in Van Nuys, California. For the next eight years of her life, Norma Jeane lived in Van Nuys, at various residences, on and off.

**VAN NUYS HIGH SCHOOL**

Norma Jeane Baker entered Van Nuys High School in September 1941. She left there in February 1942, when she transferred to University High School in West Los Angeles.

Today, Van Nuys Senior High School is located at 6535 Cedros Avenue in Van Nuys, California.

**FRANKIE VAUGHAN**

Born Frank Abelsohn in 1928, singer Frankie Vaughan costarred in the 1960 comedy *Let's Make Love,* which featured Marilyn Monroe and Yves Montand in the starring roles.

Among Vaughan's other film appearances were *These Dangerous Years* (1957) and *It's All Over Town* (1964).

***VENUS AT LARGE***

On April 12, 1962, while Marilyn Monroe was still alive, a play named *Venus at Large* opened at the Morosco Theatre on Broadway. The attempted comedy was written by Henry Denker and was directed by Rod Amateau. The cast included David Wayne, Sally Gracie, Leon Janney, and Joyce Jameson. Miss Jameson portrayed the MM-based character Olive Ogilvie. Said *The New York World-Telegram and Sun*:

> She [Jameson] is built like Marilyn Monroe, talks like her and, in this role, enrolls at the Actors Studio to become a real dramatic actress and not just a movie star. The plot also has her fall in love with a tall, lean, Arthur Miller type writer.

The play itself was generally panned by the New York critics.

**GWEN VERDON**

Born Gwyneth Evelyn in 1925, Gwen Verdon is the famous Broadway actress/dancer who was once married to film and stage director Bob Fosse. Among Miss Verdon's films are *Meet Me After the Show* (1951), *The I Don't Care Girl* (1953), and *Damn Yankees* (1958).

In 1953, Miss Verdon served as the assistant choreographer on *Gentlemen Prefer Blondes,* which starred Marilyn Monroe and Jane Russell.

**VICENTE PHARMACY**

The Vicente Pharmacy (address: 12025 San Vicente Boulevard) in Brentwood, California, is where Marilyn Monroe filled most of her prescriptions in 1962. It was at the Vicente Pharmacy that Marilyn obtained the lethal dose of drugs that allegedly killed her. On August 3, 1962, MM had two prescriptions filled at the Vicente Pharmacy—they were numbered #20857 and #20858 and were for Phenergan and Nembutal, respectively.

**VIDEOS**

In the 1980s, Marilyn Monroe invaded the home video market. Not only are many of her film titles available to rent and buy; there are also the movies made *about* her and the compilation tapes that include her. The following is the Marilyn Monroe videography:

**MM Movies Available on Home Video:**
*All About Eve* (Magnetic Video)
*The Asphalt Jungle* (MGM/UA)
*Bus Stop* (FOX)
*Clash by Night* (Command Performance VCI)
*Gentlemen Prefer Blondes* (FOX)
*How to Marry a Millionaire* (FOX)
*Let's Make Love* (CBS/Fox)
*Love Happy* (Republic)
*The Misfits* (CBS/FOX)
*Monkey Business* (CBS/FOX)
*Niagara* (CBS/FOX)
*The Prince and the Showgirl* (Warner Brothers)
*River of No Return* (CBS/FOX)
*The Seven Year Itch* (FOX)
*Some Like It Hot* (CBS/FOX)
*There's No Business Like Show Business* (FOX)

**Documentaries and Movies About MM Available on Home Video:**
*The Goddess* (RCA/Columbia)
*Goodbye Norma Jean* (Thorn EMI/HBO)
*Marilyn Monroe* (Karl Video)
*Marilyn, Say Goodbye to the President* (Key Video)

**Home Videos That Include MM**
*45/85 America & The World: Volume II 1953–1960* (Vestron Video)
*Hollywood Home Movies* (MalJack Production, Inc.)
a.k.a. *Ken Murray Shooting Stars* (Cinemagreats)
*Hollywood Out-Takes and Rare Footage* (RCA/Columbia)
*Hollywood Without Make-Up* (Hollywood Home Theatre*)
*The Love Goddesses* (Embassy)

---

*Inactive

## THE VILLA CAPRI RESTAURANT

Marilyn Monroe and Joe DiMaggio sometimes dined at the Villa Capri restaurant in Hollywood. A modest Italian restaurant, run by the D'Amore family, the Villa Capri was also the favorite eatery of James Dean, who reportedly ate there the night before his death. And, on November 13, 1954, MM and Joe were seen at the Villa Capri with Joe's brother Dominic. This led some reporters to speculate that the DiMaggios, who had been divorced less than a month before, were going to attempt a reconciliation.

The Villa Capri closed down in 1982. Today, KFAC Radio station (address: 6735 Yucca Street) is located where the Villa Capri once entertained some of Hollywood's finest.

## THE VILLA NOVA RESTAURANT

The Villa Nova Restaurant was a popular Italian restaurant located on the Sunset Strip (address: 9015 Sunset Boulevard) in Hollywood. It was at the

Villa Nova, in March 1952, that David March arranged the first date between Marilyn Monroe and Joe DiMaggio. The date was set for 6:30 P.M. on a Saturday night. Marilyn, who was shooting *Monkey Business* at the time, did not arrive until 8:30 P.M.. During the evening, very little was said between MM and Joe, although Joe was instantly struck by Marilyn, and she, in turn, was pleasantly surprised by DiMaggio's reserved demeanor. The dinner ended at approximately 10:00 P.M.

The Villa Nova Restaurant was sold in 1972, and today it is known as the Rainbow Bar and Grill.

**DOUG VILLIERS**

Doug Villiers was the owner of the Antiquarius Antique Market in Beverly Hills, who offered a $150,000 reward for Marilyn Monroe's long-lost diary, which allegedly contained references to her affairs with both John and Robert Kennedy. Reportedly, Villiers wanted the diary for his Antique Market, not for his personal collection. However, much to his disappointment, the missing diary has never been retrieved.

**VINE STREET SCHOOL**

Norma Jeane Baker attended elementary school at the Vine Street School in Hollywood September 1932–June 1934 and September 1935–June 1937. During the latter period, Norma Jeane was a resident at the nearby Los Angeles Orphan's Home Society.

Today, the Vine Street School is still in existence and is known as the Vine Street Elementary School (address: 955 N. Vine St.) in Hollywood.

**MICHAEL VINER**

Michael Viner was a former aide to Robert Kennedy. In March 1976, Viner claimed that he had once, through his relationship with Kennedy, had access to Marilyn Monroe's infamous, long-lost diary. According to Viner, the diary contained evidence of Marilyn's relationships with both John and Robert Kennedy.

**VIOLATIONS OF THE CHILD MARILYN MONROE**

Author: Her Psychiatrist Friend
Publisher: Bridgehead Books
Year: 1962 (Out of print)

Penned by "Her Psychiatrist Friend," this book is *not* about Marilyn Monroe, or about Marilyn's relationship with one of her psychiatrists (which *would* have been interesting). Instead, it is about an intimate relationship Marilyn allegedly shared with a mysterious, unnamed doctor whom she met at a Hollywood party. The text includes recollections of MM telling "her psychiatrist friend" labored stories of how she had been abused by boys and men since she was a child.

Published the year of Marilyn's death, *Violations of the Child Marilyn Monroe* is slight on facts and insight, and totally devoid of taste.

**VIRGINIA CITY, NEVADA**

In 1960, during a break from shooting, members of *The Misfits* company used to spend some of their free time in Virginia City, Nevada, a ghost town outside of Reno.

**VISTA DEL MONTE STREET**

After their marriage on June 19, 1942, Jim and Norma Jeane Dougherty moved into a brand-new, one-room studio apartment at 4524 Vista del Monte Street in the San Fernando Valley. The newlywed Doughertys lived at the Vista del Monte apartment for a few months before they moved into more spacious quarters.

***VOGUE* MAGAZINE**

> She has given a warm delight to millions of people, made them smile affectionately, laugh uproariously, love her to the point of caring deeply—often aggressively—about her personal happiness. That she withstood the incredible, unknowable pressures of her public legend as long as she did is evidence of the stamina of the human spirit."
>
> *Vogue* magazine, in its 9/1/62 tribute to Marilyn Monroe

*Vogue* has published the following articles on MM:

☆ 7/56: "Portrait"
☆ 9/1/62: "Marilyn Monroe"
☆ 9/73: "Norman Mailer's Marilyn Monroe"
☆ 8/82: "Natalie Wood, Marilyn Monroe . . . & the Hollywood Risk"
☆ 9/82: "The Last Sitting" (Excerpts from the book, *The Last Sitting* by Bert Stern)

**THE VOLTAIRE APARTMENTS**

In late 1954, following her divorce from Joe DiMaggio, Marilyn Monroe was secretly planning to "quit" 20th Century-Fox, flee Hollywood, and move to New York. Upon advice from her attorneys, MM went into hiding until she was ready to make the big move. Los Angeles-area newpapers queried, "Where Is Marilyn?" As it turned out, MM was living at the Voltaire Apartments with her friend, Mrs. Anne Karger. Interestingly, at that time, the Voltaire was owned by none other than Spyros Skouras, the president of 20th Century-Fox.

Today, the Voltaire is known as the Granville and is located at 1424 N. Crescent Heights Boulevard in West Hollywood.

### *A WAC IN HIS LIFE*

*A Wac in His Life* was the original title of *Love Nest* (1951), which starred William Lundigan, June Haver, and Marilyn Monroe.

### LUTEVA RISHEL WADSWORTH

Luteva Rishel Wadsworth was Norma Jeane Baker's kindergarten teacher at the Ballona Elementary and Kindergarten School in Hawthorne, California, from September 14, 1931, until June 17, 1932.

### EDWARD WAGENKNECHT

Born in Chicago in 1900, Edward Wagenknecht is a distinguished author who has published over forty biographical and critical books. Among his works are *Mark Twain, The Man and His Work* (1935), *The Seven Worlds of Theodore Roosevelt* (1958), *The Personality of Shakespeare* (1972), and *Fifty Great American Silent Films* (1980).

In 1969, Wagenknecht edited and wrote the excellent compilation study, *Marilyn Monroe: A Composite View* (Chilton Books).

### ROBERT WAGNER

On June 14, 1951, Marilyn Monroe costarred opposite Robert Wagner in his screen test for 20th Century-Fox. The pair also appeared together in the film *Let's Make It Legal* (1951). Since his screen test, Wagner has appeared in such films as *With A Song in My Heart* (1952), *Titanic* (1953), and *The Longest Day* (1962). However, he has garnered most of his popularity from his successful television ventures, "It Takes a Thief" (1965–1969) and "Hart to Hart" (1979–1984).

### JERRY WALD

> "Her sexuality, well, it's something she has corked up in a bottle. She opens the bottle and uses some when she needs it for a scene and then she puts the cork back in the bottle and puts the bottle away until she needs it again."
>
> Jerry Wald on Marilyn Monroe, *Marilyn Monroe* by Maurice Zolotow (Harcourt Brace, 1960)

> "It doesn't make any difference where a kid like Marilyn comes from. The shortest distance to stardom is from the screen to the seats in the first row of a movie theatre. She's traveled it—and her background doesn't make any difference. She has inner illumination, temper but not temperament, everything it takes, including a native talent, to be big box office."
>
> Jerry Wald on Marilyn Monroe, in Hedda Hopper's syndicated column, 5/4/52

"She is the greatest farceuse in the business, a female Chaplin. In the right kind of picture she is superb and the public will go to see her. It is only when she plays a serious role that she has trouble. The audience doesn't believe her."

Jerry Wald on Marilyn Monroe, *Show Business Illustrated,* 1962

Born Jerome Irving Wald in New York City, Jerry Wald (1911-1962) was the Hollywood producer of such films as *Mildred Pierce* (1945), *Johnny Belinda* (1948), *Peyton Place* (1957), and *Sons and Lovers* (1960).

In 1952, it was Jerry Wald who hired starlet Marilyn Monroe for his picture *Clash by Night.* It was an important picture for MM—one that elevated her to costarring status and placed her in such heavyweight company as Barbara Stanwyck, Paul Douglas, and Robert Ryan.

Eight years later, Jerry Wald also produced MM in *Let's Make Love* (1960). Unlike *Clash,* it was not a particularly successful picture for either Wald or Monroe.

**MARVIN WALD**

Marvin Wald scripted the half-hour, 1963 television special "The Marilyn Monroe Story," which was narrated by Mike Wallace. The documentary special is currently available on home video under the title "Marilyn Monroe."

**FRED WALDEMAR**

In 1950, Fred Waldemar was Johnny Hyde's chauffeur. Hyde, of course, was Marilyn Monroe's agent/manager/lover at that time.

**WALDORF-ASTORIA TOWERS**

In April 1955, Marilyn Monroe subleased a three-room apartment at the exclusive Waldorf-Astoria Towers (address: 301 Park Avenue) in New York City. The apartment cost Milton H. Greene and Marilyn Monroe Productions $1,000 a week in rent.

**THE WALK**

"The way she giggled, the way she stood in the corner flirting with the camera, and especially the way she walked, for with every step her derriere seemed to wink at the onlooker. It is incredible that 20th Century-Fox had had her under contract for many years and had never thought of photographing her from behind."

Photographer Philippe Halsman, *The Celluloid Sacrifice* by Alexander Walker (Hawthorn Books, 1966)

"She walks as if the whole earth were a tightrope on which she has to balance."

Gavin Lambert, *Marilyn Monroe: A Composite View* by Edward Wagenknecht (Chilton Books, 1969)

"She can squeeze more meaning out of a few steps than most actresses can get out of six pages of dialogue."

Director Harmon Jones, *Marilyn Monroe* by Maurice Zolotow (Harcourt Brace, 1960)

COURTESY OF CINEMA COLLECTORS

"I've never deliberately done anything about the way I walk. People say I walk all wiggly and wobbly, but I don't know what they mean. I just walk. I've never wiggled deliberately in my life, but all my life I've had trouble with people who say I do."

Marilyn Monroe, *Marilyn Monroe: Her Own Story* by George Carpozi, Jr. (Belmont Books, 1961)

"I use walking just to get me around."

Marilyn Monroe, *LIFE* magazine, 4/7/52

It has frequently been commented upon that it was Marilyn Monroe's 116-foot walk in *Niagara* (1953), one of the longest walks in cinema history, that cemented her path to stardom. Marilyn actually introduced "the walk" in the 1950 Marx Brothers picture *Love Happy*. But it was after *Niagara* that everyone was aware of the exaggerated MM wiggle. Author Pete Martin and columnist Sidney Skolsky dubbed MM "the girl with the horizontal walk," and Emmeline Snively, Norma Jeane's modeling instructor was quoted as saying about early MM:

"The first thing we tried to do was change that horrible walk. That wiggle wasn't good for fashion models but it was Marilyn and we couldn't change it. I'm glad now, of course."

*The Los Angeles Mirror*, 1/21/54

**ALEXANDER WALKER**

Alexander Walker is the author of, among other things, *The Celluloid Sacrifice*, published by Hawthorn Books in 1966. The book contains an excellent, well-written chapter entitled "Body & Soul," which compares Marilyn Monroe to Jean Harlow.

**MIKE WALLACE**

In 1963, Mike Wallace narrated a half-hour documentary television special entitled "The Marilyn Monroe Story." The special has since been adapted to the home video market and is available under the title "Marilyn Monroe."

Mike Wallace, born on May 9, 1918, has gained fame and recognition as a television news correspondent for CBS-TV, particularly for his work on the hit magazine-format show, "60 Minutes."

**ELI WALLACH**

Actor Eli Wallach, born December 7, 1915, in Brooklyn, was one of Marilyn Monroe's closest friends from the Actors Studio. Also a friend of Arthur Miller, Wallach was cast in the "dream" production of *The Misfits* (1961). However, during the turbulent production of that picture, the friendship between MM and Wallach reportedly deteriorated.

Eli Wallach, married to actress Anne Jackson, has been, over the years, one of the strongest proponents of the Actors Studio's "Method" style of acting. Among his films are *Baby Doll* (1956), *The Magnificent Seven* (1960), *How the West Was Won* (1962), and *The Tiger Makes Out* (1967).

**SEYMOUR WALLY**

Seymour Wally is a photographer who shot a series of photos of Marilyn Monroe with her dog Hugo, circa 1956.

**CHRIS WALSH**

Chris Walsh was the company doctor on the production of *The Misfits* (1961).

**WARNER BROTHERS**

Founded in 1923 by the four Warner Brothers, this studio entered into a distribution deal with Marilyn Monroe Productions in 1956 to release the film *The Prince and the Showgirl* (1957). Fifteen years later, Warner Brothers purchased all rights to the film from the Marilyn Monroe estate and from Laurence Olivier Productions. For the film, the MM estate was paid the paltry sum of $96,049.27.

**JACK WARNER**

Born Leonard Warner in Ontario, Canada, Jack L. Warner (1892–1978) was the longtime ruler of Warner Brothers and the man who pioneered the invention of talking pictures with *The Jazz Singer* in 1927.

On March 1, 1956, Jack Warner held a press conference with Marilyn Monroe to announce the distribution deal between Warner Brothers and Marilyn Monroe Productions for the film *The Prince and the Showgirl* (1957).

**HAZEL WASHINGTON**

Hazel Washington was Marilyn Monroe's personal studio maid.

**WASHINGTON ELEMENTARY SCHOOL**

In 1931, Norma Jeane Baker began attending this elementary school (address: 4339 W. 129th Street, Hawthorne, California). However, back then, the school was named the Ballona Elementary and Kindergarten School.

**THE WATERGATE THEATRE CLUB**

On September 9, 1956, while in England, Marilyn Monroe became one of the founding members of the Watergate Theatre Club. The organization was formed to squeeze banned plays past Britain's theatrical censor. Marilyn's admission fee into the club was 70¢. The first play presented by the organization was Arthur Miller's *A View from the Bridge*.

**WAX**

Marilyn Monroe has been immortalized in wax at two of the most famous wax museums in existence:

- ☆ The Hollywood Wax Museum (address: 6767 Hollywood Boulevard): MM in "the skirt scene" from *The Seven Year Itch* (1955)
- ☆ Madame Tussaud's Waxworks (address: Baker Street Station, London): MM as Elsie Marina in *The Prince and the Showgirl*

**DAVID WAYNE**

Born Wayne McKeekan in 1914, David Wayne appeared in four films with Marilyn Monroe—more than any other actor. The films were *As Young as You Feel* (1951), *We're Not Married* (1952), *O. Henry's Full House* (1952), and *How to Marry a Millionaire* (1953).

Among Wayne's other films are *Adam's Rib* (1949), *With A Song in My Heart* (1952), and *The Three Faces of Eve* (1957).

**W. J. WEATHERBY**

W. J. Weatherby was a noted journalist who covered the 1960 shooting of *The Misfits* for the prestigious *Manchester Guardian.* Following the shooting of that film Weatherby met with Marilyn Monroe several times at a New York bar on Eighth Avenue. He subsequently recorded their sessions in a book entitled *Conversations with Marilyn,* which was published by Mason/Charter in 1976.

**LOIS WEBER**

In 1955–56, Lois Weber was Marilyn Monroe's publicist, from the Arthur Jacobs Agency in New York. Miss Weber worked for MM before and after *Bus Stop* (1956) and during the stressful period of Marilyn's wedding to Arthur Miller.

**WEDDINGS**

**James Dougherty**

Date: June 19, 1942
Location: The Chester Howell residence (432 Bentley Avenue, Los Angeles)

Twenty-five guests attended the wedding of Jim Dougherty and Norma Jeane Baker. Present were Albert Wayne and Ida Bolender, Norma Jeane's former foster parents. Norma Jeane's maid of honor was one of her girlfriends from University High School; Jim's best man was his brother, Marion Dougherty. The bride was given away by Norma Jeane's "Aunt" Ana Lower. The service was performed by Reverend Benjamin Lingenfelder of the Christian Science Church. Neither Gladys Baker, Norma Jeane's mother, nor Grace Goddard, Norma Jeane's guardian, was able to attend. Norma Jeane was dressed in a white embroidered gown, sewn by Ana Lower. Jim Dougherty wore a rented white tuxedo. The wedding took place at 8:30 P.M.

**Robert Slatzer**

Date: October 4, 1952
Location: Tijuana, Mexico

The details about Marilyn Monroe's alleged marriage to Robert Slatzer are sketchy, at best. According to Slatzer, the only witness present was his friend, "Kid" Chissell. Also according to Slatzer, the service was performed by an unnamed Tijuana lawyer and cost $5.

**Joe DiMaggio**
Date: January 14, 1954
Location: San Francisco City Hall

About a dozen of Joe DiMaggio's friends witnessed his long-delayed marriage to Marilyn Monroe. The event took place in the chambers of Judge Charles S. Peery, who performed the services. Present were best man Reno Barsocchini and his wife; Lefty and Jean O'Doul; and Joe's brother, Tom DiMaggio, and his wife. Also present were over a hundred photographers and reporters. MM wore a chocolate-brown suit with a high ermine collar and a corsage of three white orchids. DiMaggio wore a dark blue suit with the same polka-dotted tie that he wore the night he met MM. The wedding took place at 1:48 P.M.

**Arthur Miller #1**
Date: June 29, 1956
Location: White Plains, New York

Judge Seymour Robinowitz performed the civil wedding ceremony between Arthur Miller and Marilyn Monroe at the White Plains Court House in Westchester County. Present were Arthur's cousin, Morton Miller, and his wife, Florence; Milton H. Greene; Lee and Paula Strasberg; and John Moore. MM wore a casual sweater and skirt combination. The ceremony took place at 7:21 P.M.

**Arthur Miller #2**
Date: July 1, 1956
Location: The Kay Brown residence (Katonah, New York)

The official, double-ring Jewish wedding ceremony between Arthur Miller and Marilyn Monroe was conducted by Rabbi Robert Goldberg. All of MM's New York friends were in attendance. Conspicuously absent were all of Marilyn's Hollywood friends and the intrusion of photographers and reporters. Lee Strasberg gave the bride away. The matrons of honor were Hedda Rosten, Amy Greene, and Judy Kantor. Marilyn wore a beige wedding dress and a matching veil. Reportedly, MM had dyed the veil in brewed coffee in order for it to match her gown.

**MM Trivia Quiz #48**
In what film was MM a matron of honor? (Answer on page 578.)

## WEIGHT
Marilyn usually weighed between 115 and 120 pounds. However, particularly during her marriage to Arthur Miller, MM had a tendency to put on weight. In the last months of her life, though, following her divorce from Miller, Marilyn lost a good deal of weight. At the time of her death, she weighed 117 pounds.

## WEIGHTLIFTING
Marilyn Monroe was way ahead of her time when it came to female

bodybuilding. As early as 1943, Norma Jeane Dougherty was being trained to lift weights. And, as a Hollywood starlet in 1951, Marilyn Monroe had a regular exercise routine that consisted of forty minutes of calisthenics and a workout with two five-pound dumbbells.

**SIDNEY S. WEINBERG**

Dr. Sidney S. Weinberg is a forensic pathologist who, regarding Marilyn Monroe's alleged suicidal overdose of drugs, stated:

> "There is no way Marilyn Monroe could have orally taken the drugs she allegedly took, without some of them being present in her system. And they were not present, according to the toxicologist's report."

Dr. Weinberg's statement cast even further doubt as to the credibility of the official coroner's report about the death of Marilyn Monroe.

**HENRY WEINSTEIN**

Henry Weinstein, the producer of *Something's Got to Give* (1962), initiated steps to fire Marilyn Monroe after she jaunted off to New York to sing "Happy Birthday" to John F. Kennedy. After Marilyn was fired, Weinstein released the following statement to the press:

> [Marilyn Monroe] completely flouted professional discipline and is responsible for putting 104 crew members out of work. It seems she's taking the bread right out of the mouths of men who are depending on this picture to support their families.
>
> *The Hollywood Citizen-News*; 6/1962

***WE'RE NOT MARRIED* ★★**

85 minutes Black and White
20th Century-Fox
Directed by: Edmund Goulding
Produced by: Nunnally Johnson
Screenplay: Nunnally Johnson, from a story by Gina Kaus and Jay Dratler
Photographed by: Leo Tover
Cast: Ginger Rogers, Fred Allen, Victor Moore, Marilyn Monroe, David Wayne, Eve Arden, Paul Douglas, Eddie Bracken, Mitzi Gaynor, Louis Calhern, Zsa Zsa Gabor, James Gleason, Paul Stewart, Jane Darwell

Mildly amusing compendium about five couples who find out, surprisingly, that they were never legally married. It's a fun premise that is stretched and overworked into a frequently dull feature that is heavy on the marquee bait and, unfortunately, light on creativity.

Marilyn Monroe portrayed, rather attractively, Annabel Norris, a beauty queen contestant in both the Mrs. Mississippi and Miss Mississippi beauty pageants. Said *Variety* about MM's performance:

> The Monroe-Wayne sequence is pretty lightweight, but shows off the Monroe form to full advantage in a bathing suit, offering certain exploitation for film.

*We're Not Married* was released in June 1952, a few months after MM's nude calendar story was reported and half a year before MM attained major stardom.

## WESTERN LITHOGRAPH COMPANY

The Western Lithograph Company (address: 600 E. Second Street) in Los Angeles was one of the original buyers of one of the MM nude calendar shots. Western Lithograph paid photographer Tom Kelley a mere $200 for the shot. And, although the photo was not *the* famous one, it earned a fortune, nonetheless.

THE T. R. FOGLI COLLECTION

## WESTMORES OF HOLLYWOOD

In 1953, MM appeared in ads for Tru-Glo makeup and lipstick made by the Westmores of Hollywood.

## WESTON, CONNECTICUT

In early 1955, Marilyn Monroe lived with Milton and Amy Greene at their barnlike home on Fanton Hill Road outside of Weston, Connecticut.

**EDWARD WESTON**

Edward Weston reportedly spent ten years collecting some of the finest photographs ever taken of Marilyn Monroe. In 1982, to commemorate the twentieth anniversary of MM's death, Weston took his MM collection on a nationwide tour.

**WESTSIDE HOSPITAL**

On August 17, 1960, Marilyn Monroe suffered from a physical and emotional breakdown on the set of *The Misfits,* was flown from Reno to Los Angeles, and was admitted into the Westside Hospital. MM recuperated at Westside for a week before she flew back to Reno to rejoin the production of *The Misfits.*

**WESTWOOD MEMORIAL CEMETERY**

Marilyn Monroe is buried at Westwood Memorial Cemetery, aka Westwood Memorial Park (address: 1218 Glendon Avenue, Westwood, CA). Also buried at Westwood Memorial is actress Natalie Wood. Visiting hours are 9:00 A.M. to 5:00 P.M.

**WESTWOOD VILLAGE MORTUARY CHAPEL**

On August 8, 1962, funeral services for Marilyn Monroe were held at the Westwood Village Mortuary Chapel (address: 1218 Glendon Ave., Westwood, CA). At that time, the Westwood chapel was brand-new. Marilyn Monroe's service was only the second one to be conducted there.

***WHAT A WAY TO GO***

*What A Way to Go* was a film comedy that Marilyn Monroe planned to make following the completion of *Something's Got to Give* (1962). Following MM's death, it was eventually filmed by Fox in 1964 with Shirley MacLaine, Bob Cummings, Dick Van Dyke, Robert Mitchum, Gene Kelly, and Paul Newman. J. Lee Thompson directed.

**"WHERE WERE YOU IN 1962?"**

On February 6, 1982, ABC-TV aired "Where Were You in 1962?" a special documentary that included, among many other things, a segment on Marilyn Monroe's death and funeral. The program was hosted by Larry Carroll.

**JON WHITCOMB**

Jon Whitcomb penned "Marilyn Monroe: The Sex Symbol vs. the Good Wife," an article that was published in *Cosmopolitan* magazine in December 1960.

**LESTER WHITE**

Lester White was the cinematographer of *The Fireball,* a 1950 film for 20th Century-Fox that featured, in a bit role, starlet Marilyn Monroe.

***THE WHITE WHORE AND THE BIT PLAYER***

*The White Whore and the Bit Player* was Tom Eyen's off-off-Broadway play, freely inspired by the life and death of Marilyn Monroe. It was first staged in

1964 and has been revived many times since. However, it received its most complete presentation when it opened at the St. Clement's Theatre in New York on February 5, 1973.

The plot, set in a madhouse, featured the split personality of a Hollywood star (guess who?). One side of the star's personality was "the white whore"—the star as she was seen by others. The other side was "the bit player"—a nun and the way the star saw herself.

*The White Whore and the Bit Player* was written by Tom Eyen, directed by Manuel Martin, and featured female impersonator Candy Darling as the whore. Upon opening, the play received a generally lukewarm response.

**JAMES WHITELEY**

James Whiteley was the producer of the 1974 British stage play about MM entitled *Legend.*

**GLADYS WHITTEN**

*See* GLADYS RASMUSSEN.

***WHO KILLED MARILYN?***

Author: Tony Sciacca aka Anthony Scaduto
Publisher: Manor Books/Woodhill
Year: 1976
$1.75 paperback, 224 pages (ISBN 0-532-17124-1)

Ultimately, this book does *not* answer the question so provocatively asked in its title. Instead it states, adamantly, that Marilyn Monroe did *not* kill herself. It also provides a roster of names that might or might not include Marilyn's killer, among them, John and Robert Kennedy, Jimmy Hoffa, Fidel Castro, Frank Sinatra, and Sam Giancana. Scaduto depicts Marilyn Monroe as a cunning, ambitious woman who was killed after she attempted to force Robert Kennedy into marriage.

*Who Killed Marilyn?* is certainly not without interest. However, its subject matter is outdated and overexploited.

***WHO KILLED MARILYN MONROE?***

Author: Charles Hamblett
Publisher: Leslie Frewin Publishers, Ltd.
Year: 1966 (Out of print)

Over the years, and, despite its misleading title, *Who Killed Marilyn Monroe?* by Charles Hamblett has been incorrectly referred to as a book about MM. In truth, however, it is a book about *many* film stars, with a single chapter ("Whispers of Heavenly Death") about Monroe. Furthermore, it's not a very good chapter at that. More interesting is Hamblett's material on Elizabeth Taylor, Jayne Mansfield, Sophia Loren, Kim Novak, Gregory Peck, Ginger Rogers, Humphrey Bogart, et al.

**RICHARD WIDMARK**

Richard Widmark was born on December 26, 1914, in Sunrise, Minnesota. He has appeared in many motion pictures, including *Kiss of Death* (1947), *Judgment at Nuremberg* (1961), *The Bedford Incident* (1965), and *Madigan* (1968), the last of which was spun off into a television series.

In 1952, Widmark costarred opposite Marilyn Monroe in *Don't Bother to Knock*. Years later, in 1986, Widmark narrated the cable television documentary "Marilyn Monroe: Beyond the Legend."

**DAN WILCOX**

Dan Wilcox coscripted the 1982 "M*A*S*H" segment, "Bombshells," that featured a story line involving Marilyn Monroe.

**HARRY J. WILD**

Harry J. Wild was the cinematographer of *Gentlemen Prefer Blondes* (1953).

**BILLY WILDER**

Billy Wilder was, with the possible exception of John Huston, the best director Marilyn Monroe ever worked with. Certainly he was the best director of comedy, which was what MM was most adept at. In addition to being a great director/producer/writer, Wilder is also one of the most outstanding wits ever to come out of Hollywood. Of MM, his star of *The Seven Year Itch* (1955) and *Some Like It Hot* (1959), Billy Wilder has said:

> The question is whether Marilyn is a person at all, or one of the greatest DuPont products ever invented. She has breasts like granite and a brain like swiss cheese, full of holes. The charm of her is her two left feet.
>
> *LIFE* magazine, 8/7/64

> I can tell you my mouth is watering to have her in another picture. The idea that she may be slipping is like saying marble is out of fashion when 100 sculptors are just waiting to get their chisels in a choice piece.
>
> *Show Business Illustrated,* 1962

> There has never been a woman with such voltage on the screen, with the exception of Garbo.
>
> *Norma Jean: The Life of Marilyn Monroe* by Fred Lawrence Guiles (McGraw-Hill 1969)

> I'm the only director who ever made two films with Monroe. I think the Screen Directors Guild owes me a purple heart.
>
> *Billy Wilder in Hollywood* by Maurice Zolotow (Putnam, 1977)

> God gave her everything. The first day a photographer took a picture of her she was a genius.
>
> *Marilyn Monroe* by Maurice Zolotow (Harcourt Brace, 1960)

> The greatest thing about Monroe is not her chest. It is her ear. She is a master of delivery. She can read comedy better than anyone else in the world.
>
> *Show Business Illustrated,* 1962

COURTESY OF CINEMA COLLECTORS

With Billy Wilder and Sidney Skolsky on set of *The Seven Year Itch*, 1954.

They're trying to elevate Marilyn to a level where she can't exist. She will lose her audience. She is a calendar girl with warmth, charm, great charm, and she's compared to Duse! Marilyn's whole success is she can't act. She's going through a bad evolution. If she takes it serious, it is the end of Monroe.

*The Fox Girls* by James Robert Parish (Arlington House, 1971)

If she sets out to be artistic and dedicated, and she carries it so far that she's willing to wear sloppy-Joe sweaters and go without makeup and let her hair hang straight as a string, this is not what has made her great to date. I don't say that it's beyond her realm of possiblility that she can establish herself as a straight dramatic actress—but it will be another career for her, a starting over.

*Will Acting Spoil Marilyn Monroe?* by Pete Martin (Doubleday, 1956)

She has become a better actress, even a deeper actress, since Strasberg. But I still believe she was developing herself naturally and would have become greater as she matured, even without him. I still say she was encouraged in bad habits.

*Marilyn Monroe* by Maurice Zolotow (Harcourt Brace, 1960)

Every movie star has a certain voltage. It is as if one were to hold up a light meter to the screen and certain stars will register more than others. Well, Marilyn has the highest voltage. You can't watch any other performer when she's playing a scene with somebody else.

*Marilyn Monroe* by Maurice Zolotow (Harcourt Brace, 1960)

It used to be you'd call her at 9:00 A.M. and she'd show at noon. Now, you call in May and she shows up in October.

*Marilyn in Art* by Roger Taylor (Salem House, 1984)

I have discussed this project with my doctor and my psychiatrist, and they tell me I'm too old and too rich to go through this again.

Wilder to Joe Hyams on whether he'd make a third film with MM

I knew it wasn't going to be a simple third act for her. I just couldn't visualize Monroe in a rocking chair or in the motion picture relief home, or married to somebody who was a pilot for United Airlines.

*Marilyn in Art* by Roger Taylor (Salem House, 1984)

Hollywood didn't kill Marilyn Monroe. It's the Marilyn Monroes that are killing Hollywood. Marilyn was mean. The meanest woman I have ever met around this town. I have never met anybody as mean as Marilyn Monroe, nor as utterly fabulous on the screen. And that includes Garbo.

*The Show Business Nobody Knows* by Earl Wilson (Bantam, 1971)

I miss her. It was like going to the dentist, making a picture with her. It was hell at the time, but after it was over, it was wonderful."

*The Show Business Nobody Knows* by Earl Wilson (Bantam, 1971)

Maybe she was tough to work with. Maybe she wasn't even an actress. But it was worth a week's torment to get those three luminous minutes on the screen.

*The Los Angeles Herald Examiner*, 8/8/62

> Never a week passes when I don't wish she was still around.
>
> *Marilyn in Art* by Robert Taylor (Salem House, 1984)

As is apparent from these and other quotes, Billy Wilder had ambivalent feelings about Marilyn Monroe. Following the labored shooting of *Some Like It Hot* in 1958, Wilder and MM were barely speaking. In fact, at the "wrap party" hosted by Wilder at his apartment on November 6, 1958, not only was Marilyn Monroe not present, she was not invited. By the end of the *Hot* shooting, Wilder was under such enormous stress that he contracted painful muscle spasms in his back and, reportedly, had to sleep in a chair. Shortly after the completion of the film, Wilder told a reporter that he could now "look at my wife again without wanting to hit her because she was a woman." When word of Wilder's verbal assault on Marilyn went public, Arthur Miller responded, via telegram, by saying that MM was "the salt of the earth." Wilder in turn responded, via telegram, by saying, "The salt of the earth told an assistant director to go fuck himself." However, it was Wilder who ended the telegram wars by sending Arthur Miller one last cable that read:

> Dear Arthur
> In order to hasten the burial of the hatchet I hereby acknowledge
> that good wife Marilyn is a unique personality and I am the beast
> of Belsen but in the immortal words of Joe E. Brown nobody is
> perfect unquote
> Sincerely Billy Wilder

Shortly thereafter, Billy Wilder and Marilyn Monroe reportedly kissed and made up at a party celebrating the successful release of Wilder's *The Apartment* in 1960. At that time, and until her death, Marilyn Monroe and Billy Wilder considered making another film together. One of the possible projects was *Irma La Douce,* which Wilder ended up shooting in 1963 with Shirley MacLaine.

Billy Wilder is one of the most prolific directors in cinema history. Born Samuel Wilder on June 22, 1906, in Vienna, Wilder has masterminded such films as *Double Indemnity* (1944), *The Lost Weekend* (for which he won 1945 Oscars for direction and screenplay), *Sunset Boulevard* (for which he won a 1950 Oscar for screenplay), *Stalag 17* (1953), *Sabrina* (1954), *The Seven Year Itch* (1955), *Witness for the Prosecution* (1958), *Some Like It Hot* (1959), *The Apartment* (for which he won 1960 Oscars for best film, direction, and screenplay), *One Two Three* (1961), and *The Private Life of Sherlock Holmes* (1970).

**MM Trivia Quiz #49**
What film did Billy Wilder pay tribute to MM with? (Answer on page 578.)

**W. R. WILKERSON**
See *The Hollywood Reporter.*

**THE WILL: THE LAST WILL AND TESTAMENT**
Marilyn Monroe's last will and testament was filed in New York's Surrogate

Court on August 17, 1962. However, in late October of that year, a controversy arose over the legality of the will. On October 25, 1962, *The Los Angeles Times* reported that Marilyn's will, which was then estimated at disposing of an estate worth $1 million, was being contested by Inez Melson, MM's former business manager. Miss Melson felt that the will was made under the undue influence of either Lee Strasberg or Dr. Marianne Kris. Miss Melson was represented in her claim by attorney Allen Stein. However, on October 30, 1962, surrogate Judge S. Samuel DiFalco ruled against Inez Melson and admitted the will into probate. Nevertheless, due to further controversy and a reported lack of funds, the first payment made to a beneficiary wasn't made until December 1971.

**The Beneficiaries**

1. Bernice Miracle: $10,000
2. Norman and Hedda Rosten: $5,000 (for the education of their daughter, Patricia)
3. Xenia Chekhov: $2,500 a year
4. Gladys Baker: $5,000 a year (from a $100,000 trust fund)
5. May Reis: $10,000 plus 25% of the balance (not to exceed $40,000)
6. Dr. Marianne Kris: 25% of the balance (to be donated to the psychiatric institution of her choice)
7. Lee Strasberg: 50% of the balance (in addition to all of Marilyn's personal effects and clothing)

*Note:* According to Robert Slatzer, Marilyn Monroe had an appointment with her attorney, Mickey Rudin, on August 6, 1962, to change her will. According to Slatzer, Marilyn wanted to include Joe DiMaggio, Joan Greenson, and Slatzer.

### *WILL ACTING SPOIL MARILYN MONROE?*

Author: Pete Martin
Publisher: Doubleday
Year: 1956 (Out of print)

In 1955, Marilyn Monroe was at a crossroads in her career. Determined to become a Serious Actress, Marilyn had traded in Hollywood for New York. She severed her ties with 20th Century-Fox, employed the coaching services of Lee Strasberg, learned "The Method" style of acting, and courted the friendship of the New York intellectual community. Pete Martin's book *Will Acting Spoil Marilyn Monroe?* captures this period of MM's life.

Although it is low on facts, this partially fictionalized work was based on an interview session with Marilyn herself and is therefore not without interest. The book also includes some rare black-and-white photographs that are worth a look—particularly the photos of the Martin/Monroe interview.

### *WILL SUCCESS SPOIL ROCK HUNTER?*

On October 13, 1955, George Axelrod's stage comedy *Will Success Spoil Rock Hunter* opened at the Belasco Theatre on Broadway. Axelrod's previous stage hit, *The Seven Year Itch* had recently been released as a smash film vehicle for Marilyn Monroe. Thus, it was only appropriate that Axelrod pay tribute to

MM with his follow-up play. The production featured, among other things, the enormous assets of Jayne Mansfield as the kewpie doll MM-based character, Rita Marlowe. The rest of the cast included Orson Bean, Walter Matthau, and Tina Louise (who would later impersonate MM for her role as Ginger in television's "Gilligan's Island"). The play was produced by Jule Styne, and opened to less than enthusiastic critical response.

In 1957, a movie based on the play was made, featuring a repeat performance by Jayne Mansfield as the Marilyn Monroe-based character Rita Marlowe. The film was produced by 20th Century-Fox, directed by Frank Tashlin, and costarred Tony Randall, Betsy Drake, Joan Blondell, and Mickey Hargitay.

The familiar plot featured a famous blonde movie star/sex goddess who flees Hollywood in favor of New York. Upon arrival in New York City, she meets an intellectual-type advertising man named Rock Hunter.

*Will Success Spoil Rock Hunter* was a modest film success, particularly for Jayne Mansfield, whose talents were bountifully displayed throughout.

### *WILL YOU LOVE ME IN DECEMBER?*

*Will You Love Me in December?* was the original title of *As Young as You Feel* (1951), which featured Monty Woolley, Jean Peters, Thelma Ritter, Albert Dekker, Constance Bennett, and, in a brief role, Marilyn Monroe.

### THE WILLIAM MORRIS AGENCY

For years, the William Morris Agency has been the most powerful talent agency in Hollywood. Through the influence of Johnny Hyde, an executive at William Morris, Marilyn Monroe was signed to the agency circa 1949-1950. However, after Hyde's death in December 1950, MM became increasingly dissatisfied with the agency.

By the middle of 1953, Marilyn Monroe was, perhaps, the biggest star on the 20th Century-Fox lot. And yet, according to the contract she signed in 1951, she was making only $1,500 a week and would not be receiving another increase for at least five years! Thus, MM took her case to her agents at the William Morris Agency and asked that they renegotiate her contract with 20th Century-Fox. When they were unable or unwilling to do this, MM left the agency and transferred to the Famous Artists Agency.

In 1950, the William Morris Agency was located at 202 North Canon Drive in Beverly Hills. In 1954, the agency relocated to its present site, 151 El Camino Drive in Beverly Hills.

### FLORENCE WILLIAMS

Florence Williams was the managing director of the Studio Club in Hollywood in the late 1940s, when Marilyn Monroe was a resident.

### GAYLORD ELMO WILLIAMS

Gaylord Elmo Williams coproduced the unsuccessful stage musical *Marilyn!*, which opened at the Adelphi Theatre in London on March 17, 1983.

**TENNESSEE WILLIAMS**

Next to Arthur Miller, of course, Tennessee Williams was Marilyn Monroe's favorite playwright. In fact, while in class at the Actors Studio, Marilyn once had the opportunity to portray Blanche DuBois from Williams's *A Streetcar Named Desire*. Marilyn was actually introduced to Williams by Miller. Reportedly, Tennessee used to tease MM by belittling Arthur.

Born Thomas Lanier Williams on March 26, 1911, Tennessee Williams is generally regarded as the finest American playwright of our time. His stage works included: *The Glass Menagerie* (1945), *A Streetcar Named Desire* (1947), *The Rose Tattoo* (1950), *Cat on a Hot Tin Roof* (1955), *Suddenly Last Summer* (1958), and *Sweet Bird of Youth* (1959). Williams died on February 15, 1983.

**LASZLO WILLINGER**

Laszlo Willinger was a noted photographer who, in 1946, shot a calendar photo of MM wearing a gold bathing suit. Willinger used early MM for other modeling jobs as well.

**WILSHIRE BOULEVARD, LOS ANGELES**

For approximately the first twelve days of her life, Norma Jeane Mortenson lived with her mother, Gladys Baker at 5454 Wilshire Boulevard, in Los Angeles, California. Following her short residence there, baby Norma Jeane was sent to live with a foster family, Ida and Wayne Bolender, in Hawthorne, California.

**EARL WILSON**

Syndicated columnist and author Earl Wilson was born on May 3, 1907, in Rockford, Ohio. Among Wilson's entertaining books are *Earl Wilson's New York* (1964), *The Show Business Nobody Knows* (1971), *Show Business Laid Bare* (1974), and *Sinatra* (1976).

Earl Wilson first met Marilyn Monroe in July 1949, when she was in New York to promote the Marx Brothers picture *Love Happy*. The subsequent interview took place at the Sherry-Netherland Hotel on July 24, 1949. At that time, Wilson dubbed MM the "Mmmmmmm Girl." Wilson's column read:

> Over the years Hollywood has given us its "It Girl," its "Oomph Girl," its "Sweater Girl," and even "The Body." Now we get the "Mmmmmmm" Girl." Miss Monroe still wasn't sure what an "Mmmmmmm Girl" has to do when I talked to her. "But, I'm sure none of the girls ever got hurt by being called such names," she said. Miss Monroe is probably right. They don't get hurt, but they get mighty tired, even sick, of the tags. Miss Monroe, who is practically an unknown; is a twenty-one-year-old blonde from Van Nuys, California. She has a nice flat waist that rises to an (MMMMM!) 36½ bra line. She also has long pretty legs. "But, why do they call you the 'Mmmmmmm Girl?'" I asked her. "Well," she said, "it seems it started in Detroit where they were having a sneak preview of my picture." "But, why?" [Wilson asked.] "Well," she said, doubtless remembering it just as the press agent told her to, "it seems some people couldn't whistle so they went 'Mmmmmmm.' " "Why couldn't they whistle?" I asked, "Well," she said, "some people just can't whistle." "Maybe they couldn't whistle because

> they had their mouths full of popcorn," I suggested. Personally, we think the whole thing was dreamed up by the publicist—but, the fact remains that these appellations have helped to make a few girls pretty famous.

Over the years, Earl Wilson and Marilyn Monroe developed a friendly and durable acquaintance. Wilson frequently peppered his columns with items about MM. Once, in September 1955, when MM was dating Arthur Miller, Wilson asked her if she had any current love interests. Marilyn, who was trying to keep her affair with Miller secret, replied: "No serious interests, but I'm always interested." A few years later, on September 12, 1960, Earl Wilson was the first columnist to break the news about Marilyn's impending divorce from Arthur Miller.

As a token of their friendship, Marilyn Monroe once presented Earl Wilson with an autographed copy of her nude calendar. The inscription read: "I hope you like my hairdo."

Earl Wilson died of Parkinson's disease on January 17, 1987 in New York City.

**JACQUES WILSON**
Jacques Wilson was responsible for the book and lyrics of the poorly received 1983 British stage play, *Marilyn*, which was presented at the Adelphi Theatre in London.

**LIZA WILSON**
Liza Wilson was a Hollywood writer who collaborated with Marilyn Monroe on a series of autobiographical articles entitled "The Truth About Me." The articles appeared in the *American Weekly* magazine, beginning on November 16, 1952.

**WALTER WINCHELL**
Television commentator and syndicated newspaper columnist Walter Winchell (1897–1972) was present in September 1954 when Marilyn Monroe shot the infamous "skirt scene" from *The Seven Year Itch* on a New York City street. Winchell, who was accompanied by his friend, Joe DiMaggio, witnessed the highly exploitive scene, which reportedly put DiMaggio in a rage.

***WINGED VICTORY***
For her July 1946 screen test, Norma Jeane Dougherty/Marilyn Monroe was going to read from the script *Winged Victory. Winged Victory* had been a 1944 20th Century-Fox film that starred Lon McCallister and Jeanne Crain. Previously, actress Judy Holliday had successfully used the *Winged Victory* script to audition. However, and for whatever reason, Ben Lyon, the head of talent at Fox, decided to test MM without sound, thus, the *Winged Victory* script was never read by MM.

**GARY WINOGRAND**
Gary Winogrand was a photographer who shot a series of photographs of Marilyn Monroe for the December 1954 edition of *Pageant* magazine.

**ARCHER WINSTEN**

In the 1950s, Archer Winsten was an influential critic for *The New York Post.* He was also an early and staunch supporter of Marilyn Monroe.

***WINTER KILLS***

This 1974 novel by Richard Condon attracted considerable interest for fictionalizing the assassination of John F. Kennedy. Published by Dial Press, the complex plot included a character rather obviously based on Marilyn Monroe. Five years later, the novel was the basis of a movie written and directed by William Richert. *Winter Kills* (1979) was a mediocre, mangled mess of a film. The confused plot, which was freely "inspired" by the assassination of John F. Kennedy, featured Jeff Bridges as the slain President's younger brother, who is determined to confront his brother's assassin. The film also included, in a small part, actress Belinda Bauer as "Yvette Malone," a fading MM-based movie star who was sexually linked with the Bridges character.

**SUZETTE WINTER**

Suzette Winter coproduced the 1986 cable television documentary "Marilyn Monroe: Beyond the Legend."

**SHELLEY WINTERS**

Born Shirley Schrift on August 18, 1922, in St. Louis, Missouri, actress Shelley Winters met starlet Marilyn Monroe in the late 1940s. According to Miss Winters, the two became friends, and in 1951 they shared a $227-a-month apartment on Holloway Drive in Hollywood.

Over the years, Miss Winters has appeared in an abundance of films that have ranged in quality from superior (*A Place in the Sun,* 1951) to slop

COURTESY OF CINEMA COLLECTORS

Shelley Winters and MM once compared lists of men they wished to sleep with.

(*Bloody Mama*, 1970). Her other films include *Red River* (1948), *A Double Life* (1948), *The Big Knife* (1955), *The Diary of Anne Frank* (for which she won a 1959 supporting actress Oscar), *A Patch of Blue* (for which she won a 1965 supporting actress Oscar), *What's the Matter with Helen?* (1970), *Who Slew Auntie Roo?* (1971), and *The Poseidon Adventure* (1972).

Miss Winters is also known for her marriages and divorces to and from actors Vittorio Gassman and Anthony Franciosa, as well as for her telling autobiography, *Shelley: Also Known as Shirley* (Ballantine, 1980).

**CAROL WIOR**
Carol Wior was the fashion designer who developed the Marilyn Monroe clothing line for the Bloomingdale's chain of stores in 1983.

**"THE WISDOM OF EVE"**
Writer Mary Orr originated the story "The Wisdom of Eve," on which the original screenplay of *All About Eve* (1950) was based.

**JOE WOHLANDER**
In 1959, Joe Wohlander was an executive with the Arthur Jacobs Agency, a New York-based public relations firm that represented Marilyn Monroe. Reportedly, Marilyn once gave Wohlander an interview in the nude.

**RAPHAEL WOLFF**
Raphael Wolff is the photographer who is responsible, to some degree, for Marilyn Monroe's being the most famous *blonde* in the history of motion pictures. It seems that it was Wolff who hired model Norma Jeane Dougherty for a series of Lustre-Creme Shampoo ads, circa 1946. However, Wolff's stipulation at that time was that Norma Jeane bleach her brownish-colored hair to a "blonde/blonde." Norma Jeane reluctantly relented and was paid $10 an hour for a six-hour shoot.

**SONIA WOLFSON**
In the early 1950s, Sonia Wolfson was a publicist at 20th Century-Fox—one whose interest was courted by ambitious Fox starlet Marilyn Monroe. In March 1952, Miss Wolfson was present in the room when Marilyn made her semihistoric nude calendar confession to reporter Aline Mosby.

**DAVID L. WOLPER**
Born on January 11, 1928, in New York City, former documentarist David L. Wolper has, in the past ten years, gained a reputation as being "the showman of the spectacular." In 1977, Wolper produced the landmark television miniseries *Roots*. In 1984, he was the principal architect of the lavishly extravagant opening and closing ceremonies of the Los Angeles Summer Olympics. And, not to be overshadowed by his previous work, in 1986 he masterminded his Technicolor opus, the Statue of Liberty unveiling and celebration.

However, back in 1966, David L. Wolper was just another television and documentary producer. One of his projects at that time was "The Legend of

Marilyn Monroe," a one-hour documentary about MM that had been completed in August 1964, but was not aired until November 1966. Fourteen years later, David Wolper produced another television special about Marilyn Monroe. This one was the 1980 telepic *Moviola: This Year's Blonde,* which featured Constance Forslund as Marilyn Monroe.

**"WOLVES I HAVE KNOWN"**

In 1952, rising star Marilyn Monroe wrote a series of three articles, "as told to" columnist Florabel Muir. The articles were published in the *Los Angeles Mirror* beginning on September 22, 1952. Wrote Marilyn:

> First I want to say that this would be a very uninteresting world if there weren't any wolves, but a girl has to learn how to handle them or she'll run into a bushel of trouble. There are many types of wolves. Some are sinister, others are just good-time Charlies trying to get something for nothing, and others make a game of it. This last type is the most interesting.
>
> I didn't have much trouble brushing them off. I found out in those days if I looked sort of stupid and pretended I didn't know what they were talking about, they soon gave up in disgust.
>
> Whether a girl survives among a pack of wolves depends entirely on her. If she is trying to get something for nothing she often winds up giving more than she bargained for. If she plays the game straight she can usually avert unpleasant situations, and she gains the respect of even the wolves.

**NATALIE WOOD**

Born Natasha Gurdin on July 20, 1938, Natalie Wood was the former child actress who, in the 1950s and 1960s became a major movie star.

When she was ten years old, Natalie costarred in 20th Century-Fox's *Scudda Hoo! Scudda Hay!* (1948), which is generally recognized as Marilyn Monroe's film debut. Among Miss Wood's other films: *Miracle on 34th Street* (1947), *Rebel Without a Cause* (1955), *Marjorie Morningstar* (1958), *Splendor in the Grass* (1961), *West Side Story* (1961), *Gypsy* (1962), *Love with the Proper Stranger* (1964), and *Bob and Carol and Ted and Alice* (1969).

On November 19, 1981, Natalie Wood drowned in an accident off Catalina Island. Today, she is buried at Westwood Memorial Cemetery, not far from the vault that contains Marilyn Monroe's body.

**BILLY WOODFIELD**

In 1962, photographer Billy Woodfield shot Marilyn Monroe's nude swimming sequence on the set of *Something's Got to Give.* Woodfield and his partner, photographer Lawrence Schiller, subsequently sold the exclusive and lucrative MM nudes to a multitude of magazines from around the world.

**JOANNE WOODWARD**

> "Marilyn is quite a product of our generation and it would be an honor for any girl to be able to emulate her."
>
> Joanne Woodward, *The Los Angeles Herald-Examiner,* 6/24/62

After Marilyn Monroe rejected *The Stripper* (1963), the role was accepted by actress Joanne Woodward.

Joanne Gignilliat Woodward was born on February 27, 1930, in Thomasville, Georgia. Over the years, she has appeared in many films and has given a variety of excellent performances—both in motion pictures and in television. However, she seems eternally confined to being best known as the wife of Paul Newman. Among her films are *The Three Faces of Eve* (for which she won a 1957 Oscar), *Rachel, Rachel* (1968), *The Effect of Gamma Rays on Man-in-the-Moon Marigolds* (1972), and *Summer Wishes Winter Dreams* (1973). Miss Woodward's television movies include *Sybil* (1977), *The Shadow Box* (1981), and *Do You Remember Love?* (1985).

**MONTY WOOLLEY**

Edgar Montillion Woolley, aka Monty Woolley (1888–1963) was the popular comedy actor who appeared in such films as *The Man Who Came to Dinner* (1941), *Holy Matrimony* (1943), and *Night and Day* (1946). In 1951, Woolley starred in *As Young as You Feel,* which featured starlet Marilyn Monroe in a small part.

**P. L. WORKMAN**

At Christmas 1962, a large white floral wreath, set upon an easel, was delivered to Marilyn Monroe's crypt site at Westwood Memorial Cemetery. The wreath was sent by Marine Sergeant P. L. Workman. The attached card read:

> My memories of 1953 will always remain, as the heavens gain another angel.

**THE WORLD DOLL COMPANY**

In 1982, the World Doll Company, a Brooklyn-based firm, began to manufacture Marilyn Monroe dolls. The vinyl MM dolls were marketed for $80; the porcelain dolls sold for $400. The original model for the dolls was sculpted out of clay by artist Joyce Christopher.

**"THE WORLD OF MARILYN MONROE"**

"The World of Marilyn Monroe" was the original title of the 1963 20th Century-Fox tribute to MM, "Marilyn," which was narrated by Rock Hudson.

**MICHAEL WOULFE**

Michael Woulfe was credited with designing the costumes for *Clash by Night* (1952) which costarred Marilyn Monroe.

**FRANK LLOYD WRIGHT**

In 1957, Marilyn Monroe made an appointment with architect Frank Lloyd Wright at his residence in the Plaza Hotel in New York. Marilyn, it seems, wanted Wright to design and build a house in Roxbury, Connecticut, for her and Arthur Miller. However, the plans never materialized, and Mr. Wright died on April 9, 1959.

**LLOYD WRIGHT**

Lloyd Wright was Marilyn Monroe's attorney at the time of her 1954 marriage to Joe DiMaggio. At that time, Wright lent his mountain retreat to the famous newlyweds for their honeymoon getaway.

**WRITERS**

**The Writers Who Wrote Non-Fiction Books About MM**

| *AUTHOR* | *BOOK* | *YEAR* |
|---|---|---|
| Janice Anderson | *Marilyn Monroe* | 1983 |
| Eve Arnold | *Marilyn Monroe: An Appreciation* | 1987 |
| Frank A. Capell* | *The Strange Death of Marilyn Monroe* | 1964 |
| George Carpozi, Jr. | *Marilyn Monroe: Her Own Story* | 1961 |
| David Conover | *Finding Marilyn: A Romance* | 1981 |
| Michael Conway | *The Films of Marilyn Monroe* | 1964 |
| Lawrence Crown | *Marilyn: At Twentieth Century Fox* | 1987 |
| Andre de Dienes | *Marilyn Mon Amour* | 1986 |
| James E. Dougherty | *The Secret Happiness of Marilyn Monroe* | 1976 |
| Joe Franklin | *The Marilyn Monroe Story* | 1953 |
| Fred Lawrence Guiles | *Norma Jean: The Life of Marilyn Monroe*<br>*Legend: The Life and Death of Marilyn Monroe* | 1969<br>1984 |
| Charles Hamblett** | *Who Killed Marilyn Monroe?* | 1966 |
| Her Psychiatrist Friend | *Violations of the Child Marilyn Monroe* | 1962 |
| Neal Hitchens | *The Unabridged Marilyn: Her Life from A–Z* | 1987 |
| Edwin P. Hoyt | *Marilyn: The Tragic Venus* | 1965 |
| James A. Hudson | *The Mysterious Death of Marilyn Monroe* | 1968 |
| Tom Hutchinson | *The Screen Greats: Marilyn Monroe* | 1982 |
| Roger Kahn | *Joe & Marilyn: A Memory of Love* | 1986 |
| John Kobal | *Marilyn Monroe: A Life on Film* | 1974 |
| Hans Jorgen Lembourn | *Diary of a Lover of Marilyn Monroe* | 1979 |
| Guus Luijters | *Marilyn Monroe: A Never Ending Dream* | 1987 |
| Norman Mailer | *Marilyn*<br>*Of Women and Their Elegance* | 1973<br>1980 |
| Pete Martin | *Will Acting Spoil Marilyn Monroe?* | 1956 |
| Joan Mellen | *Marilyn Monroe* | 1973 |
| Marilyn Monroe | *My Story* | 1974 |
| Robin Moore | *Marilyn & Joe DiMaggio* | 1977 |
| Eunice Murray | *Marilyn: The Last Months* | 1975 |
| Joel Oppenheimer | *Marilyn Lives!* | 1981 |
| Laurie Palmer | *The Marilyn Monroe Story* | 1953 |
| Bob Patrick* | *Marilyn: Screen Greats Vol II* | 1980 |

| | | |
|---|---|---|
| Lena Pepitone | *Marilyn Monroe Confidential* | 1979 |
| Mark Ricci | *The Films of Marilyn Monroe* | 1964 |
| Randall Riese | *The Unabridged Marilyn: Her Life From A–Z* | 1987 |
| Carl E. Rollyson, Jr. | *Marilyn Monroe: A Life of the Actress* | 1986 |
| Norman Rosten | *Marilyn: An Untold Story* | 1973 |
| | *Marilyn: Among Friends* | 1987 |
| Gene Schoor | *Marilyn & Joe DiMaggio* | 1977 |
| Tony Sciacca (aka Anthony Scaduto) | *Who Killed Marilyn?* | 1976 |
| Sam Shaw | *Marilyn Monroe as the Girl: The Making of "The Seven Year Itch"* | 1955 |
| | *The Joy of Marilyn in the Camera Eye* | 1979 |
| | *Marilyn: Among Friends* | 1987 |
| Sidney Skolsky* | *Marilyn* | 1954 |
| Robert Slatzer | *The Life and Curious Death of Marilyn Monroe* | 1974 |
| Milburn Smith* | *Marilyn: Barven Screen Greats No. 4* | 1971 |
| James Spada | *Monroe: Her Life in Pictures* | 1982 |
| Milo Speriglio | *Marilyn Monroe: Murder Cover-Up* | 1982 |
| | *The Marilyn Conspiracy* | 1986 |
| William Stadiem | *Marilyn Monroe Confidential* | 1979 |
| Gloria Steinem | *Marilyn* | 1986 |
| Bert Stern | *The Last Sitting* | 1982 |
| Anthony Summers | *Goddess: The Secret Lives of Marilyn Monroe* | 1985 |
| Roger Taylor | *Marilyn Monroe: In Her Own Words* | 1983 |
| | *Marilyn in Art* | 1984 |
| Edward Wagenknecht | *Marilyn Monroe: A Composite View* | 1969 |
| W. J. Weatherby | *Conversations with Marilyn* | 1976 |
| George Zeno | *Monroe: Her Life in Pictures* | 1982 |
| Maurice Zolotow | *Marilyn Monroe* | 1960 |

---

*These writers are responsible for cover-to-cover magazines about Marilyn Monroe. Their names are included here because, over the years, they have been incorrectly credited with having written books about MM.

**Over the years, *Who Killed Marilyn Monroe?* by Charles Hamblett has been referred to as a book about Marilyn Monroe. In actuality however, and, despite its title, only one chapter of this book is devoted to MM. It is being included here for clarification.

### The Writers Who Wrote Movies That MM Appeared In

| *SCREENWRITER* | *MOVIE* | *YEAR* |
|---|---|---|
| George Axelrod | *The Seven Year Itch* | 1955 |
| | *Bus Stop* | 1956 |
| Arnold Belgard | *Dangerous Years* | 1947 |
| Mac Benoff | *Love Happy* | 1950 |
| Walter Bernstein | *Something's Got to Give* | 1962 |

| | | |
|---|---|---|
| Charles Brackett | *Niagara* | 1953 |
| Richard Breen | *Niagara* | 1953 |
| Joseph Carol | *Ladies of the Chorus* | 1948 |
| I. A. L. Diamond | *Love Nest* | 1951 |
| | *Let's Make It Legal* | 1951 |
| | *Monkey Business* | 1952 |
| | *Some Like It Hot* | 1959 |
| Henry Ephron | *There's No Business Like Show Business* | 1954 |
| Phoebe Ephron | *There's No Business Like Show Business* | 1954 |
| Frank Fenton | *River of No Return* | 1954 |
| Tay Garnett | *The Fireball* | 1950 |
| Alfred Hayes | *Clash by Night* | 1952 |
| Ben Hecht | *Monkey Business* | 1952 |
| F. Hugh Herbert | *Scudda Hoo! Scudda Hay!* | 1948 |
| | *Let's Make It Legal* | 1951 |
| John Huston | *The Asphalt Jungle* | 1950 |
| Nunnally Johnson | *We're Not Married* | 1952 |
| | *How to Marry a Millionaire* | 1953 |
| | *Something's Got to Give* | 1962 |
| Norman Krasna | *Let's Make Love* | 1960 |
| Charles Lederer | *Monkey Business* | 1952 |
| | *Gentlemen Prefer Blondes* | 1953 |
| Mary Loos | *A Ticket to Tomahawk* | 1950 |
| Ben Maddow | *The Asphalt Jungle* | 1950 |
| Joseph Mankiewicz | *All About Eve* | 1950 |
| Horace McCoy | *The Fireball* | 1950 |
| Arthur Miller | *The Misfits* | 1961 |
| Arthur Pierson | *Hometown Story* | 1951 |
| Terence Rattigan | *The Prince and the Showgirl* | 1957 |
| Walter Reisch | *Niagara* | 1953 |
| Richard Sale | *A Ticket to Tomahawk* | 1950 |
| Harry Sauber | *Ladies of the Chorus* | 1948 |
| Charles Schnee | *Right Cross* | 1950 |
| Daniel Taradash | *Don't Bother to Knock* | 1952 |
| Frank Tashlin | *Love Happy* | 1950 |
| Lamar Trotti | *As Young as You Feel* | 1951 |
| | *O. Henry's Full House* | 1952 |
| Billy Wilder | *The Seven Year Itch* | 1955 |
| | *Some Like It Hot* | 1959 |

### The Writers Who Wrote Plays About MM (or Plays That Featured a Major MM-Based Character)

| *PLAYWRIGHT* | *PLAY* | *YEAR* |
|---|---|---|
| George Axelrod | *Will Success Spoil Rock Hunter?* | 1955 |
| David Butler | *Legend* | 1974 |
| Henry Denker | *Venus at Large* | 1962 |
| Tom Eyen | *The White Whore and the Bit Player* | 1973 |
| Gerry Glaskin | *Turn on the Heat* | 1967 |
| John Guare | *Cop Out* | 1969 |
| Anthony Ingrasia | *Fame* | 1974 |
| Terry Johnson | *Insignificance* | 1982 |
| Cliff Jones | *Hey, Marilyn* | 1979 |
| Garson Kanin | *Come on Strong* | 1962 |
| Norman Mailer | *Strawhead* | 1986 |
| Patricia Michaels | *Marilyn: An American Fable* | 1983 |
| Arthur Miller | *After the Fall* | 1964 |
| Roger Newman | *Public Property* | 1979 |
| | *The Hardest Part of It* | 1978 |
| Robert Patrick | *Kennedy's Children* | 1975 |
| Jacques Wilson | *Marilyn!* | 1983 |

### The Writers Who Wrote Movies About MM (or Movies That Featured a Major MM-Based Character)

| *SCREENWRITER* | *MOVIE* | *YEAR* |
|---|---|---|
| Larry Buchanan | *Goodbye, Norma Jean* | 1976 |
| Paddy Chayefsky | *The Goddess* | 1958 |
| Terry Johnson | *Insignificance* | 1985 |
| Harold Medford | *Marilyn* | 1963 |
| Arthur Miller | *The Misfits* | 1961 |
| Lynn Shubert | *Goodbye, Norma Jean* | 1976 |
| Frank Tashlin | *Will Success Spoil Rock Hunter?* | 1957 |
| Vernon Zimmerman | *Fade to Black* | 1980 |

### The Writers Who Wrote TV Movies About MM (or TV Movies That Featured a Major MM-Based Character)

| *TELEWRITER* | *TV MOVIE* | *YEAR* |
|---|---|---|
| Alvah Bessie | *The Sex Symbol* | 1974 |
| Gene Feldman | *Marilyn Monroe: Beyond the Legend* | 1986 |
| James Lee | *Moviola: This Year's Blonde* | 1980 |
| Arthur Miller | *After the Fall* | 1974 |

| | | |
|---|---|---|
| Christopher Olgiati | *The Last Days of Marilyn Monroe* | 1985 |
| Terry Sanders | *The Legend of Marilyn Monroe* | 1966 |
| Lionel E. Siegel | *Hoover vs. The Kennedys* | 1987 |
| Theodore Strauss | *The Legend of Marilyn Monroe*<br>*Remembering Marilyn* | 1966<br>1988 |
| Marvin Wald | *The Marilyn Monroe Story* | 1963 |
| Suzette Winter | *Marilyn Monroe: Beyond the Legend* | 1986 |
| Dalene Young | *Marilyn: The Untold Story* | 1980 |

## The Writers Who Wrote Books, Plays, or Other Source Material That Became a Movie That MM Appeared In

| *WRITER* | *MOVIE* | *YEAR* |
|---|---|---|
| Zoe Akins | *How to Marry a Millionaire* | 1953 |
| Katherine Albert | *How to Marry a Millionaire* | 1953 |
| Charlotte Armstrong | *Don't Bother to Knock* | 1952 |
| George Axelrod | *The Seven Year Itch* | 1955 |
| Mortimer Braus | *Let's Make It Legal* | 1951 |
| W. R. Burnett | *The Asphalt Jungle* | 1950 |
| George Agnew Chamberlain | *Scudda Hoo! Scudda Hay!* | 1948 |
| Paddy Chayefsky | *As Young as You Feel* | 1951 |
| Scott Corbett | *Love Nest* | 1951 |
| Jay Dratler | *We're Not Married* | 1952 |
| Dale Eunson | *How to Marry a Millionaire* | 1953 |
| Joseph Fields | *Gentlemen Prefer Blondes* | 1953 |
| William Inge | *Bus Stop* | 1956 |
| Gina Kaus | *We're Not Married* | 1952 |
| Louis Lantz | *River of No Return* | 1954 |
| Doris Lilly | *How to Marry a Millionaire* | 1953 |
| M. Logan | *Some Like It Hot* | 1959 |
| Anita Loos | *Gentlemen Prefer Blondes* | 1953 |
| Harpo Marx | *Love Happy* | 1950 |
| Clifford Odets | *Clash by Night* | 1952 |
| Mary Orr | *All About Eve* | 1950 |
| William Porter | *O. Henry's Full House* | 1952 |
| Terence Rattigan | *The Prince and the Showgirl* | 1957 |
| Harry Sauber | *Ladies of the Chorus* | 1948 |
| Harry Segall | *Monkey Business* | 1952 |
| Robert Thoeren | *Some Like It Hot* | 1959 |
| Lamar Trotti | *There's No Business Like Show Business* | 1954 |

**MM Trivia Quiz #50**
In what film did MM have an affair with a writer? (Answer on page 578.)

**THE "WRONG DOOR RAID"**
The infamous "Wrong Door Raid" scandal involving Marilyn Monroe, Joe DiMaggio, Frank Sinatra, et al., took place on November 5, 1954, at 8112 Waring Avenue in Hollywood. On that day, Marilyn was reportedly visiting her friend, Sheila Stewart, who lived at one of the apartments in the Waring building complex.

During that period, and for his own personal reasons, Joe DiMaggio was having his ex-wife MM followed by a private detective, Barney Ruditsky. Well, on this particular day in November, Joe DiMaggio got word that Marilyn was inside one of the Waring Avenue apartments. With Frank Sinatra at his side, DiMaggio arrived at the site, where he was met by Ruditsky and another private detective, Phil Irwin.

Once the stage was set, however, everything misfired for DiMaggio and his company of would-be investigators. Instead of catching Marilyn "in the act" (if that was indeed the intention) or some other such feat, the detectives broke into the wrong apartment, much to the horror of that apartment's tenant, Florence Kotz.

In May 1957, Florence Kotz Ross (she had gotten married) filed suit against DiMaggio, Sinatra, et al., to the tune of $200,000. However, she eventually settled out of court for the sum of $7,500.

**SOL WURTZEL**
Sol Wurtzel was the producer of *Dangerous Years* (1947), which featured starlet Marilyn Monroe in a small part, as a waitress named Eve.

**JANE WYMAN**
Jane Wyman was *not* one of Marilyn Monroe's best friends. It was Miss Wyman who married the man that Marilyn considered to be the first love of her life: Fred Karger. Not only that: Jane Wyman married him *twice!* Marilyn once sought revenge against her rival by planting a life-size cutout of herself, from *The Seven Year Itch* (1955), on the front lawn of Miss Wyman's home in the Holmby Hills area of Los Angeles. Presumably, Marilyn reveled in flaunting her youth and beauty in the older woman's face. The prank didn't get her Karger back, but it must have provided her with a good laugh and a sense of temporary fulfillment.

Born Sarah Jane Faulks in 1914, Jane Wyman actually started her film career as a blonde ingenue before she went on to serious, more respectable roles. Her films include *The Lost Weekend* (1945), *Johnny Belinda* (for which she won a 1948 Oscar), *Magnificent Obsession* (1954), and *Pollyanna* (1960). She later gained additional success as Angela Channing in the prime-time television soap "Falcon Crest." Miss Wyman also has the distinction of being the former wife (1940–1948) of President Ronald Reagan. Her marriages to Fred Karger lasted from November 1, 1952, to December 7, 1954; and from March 11, 1961, to March 9, 1965.

# Y

### *YANK* MAGAZINE

Norma Jeane Dougherty's first magazine feature as a model was shot by Army photographer David Conover and appeared in *Yank* magazine in the mid-1940s.

### "THE YANKEE CLIPPER"

"The Yankee Clipper" was one of baseball great Joe DiMaggio's professional nicknames. It was also the name of the DiMaggio cabin cruiser, which Joe and Marilyn would sometimes take refuge aboard.

### *YOU WERE MEANT FOR ME*

Reportedly, contract player Marilyn Monroe was an extra in this 1948 20th Century-Fox musical production. It was produced by Fred Kohlmar, directed by Lloyd Bacon, and starred Jeanne Crain, Dan Dailey, and Oscar Levant.

### DALENE YOUNG

Dalene Young scripted the teleplay of the 1980 ABC biography *Marilyn: The Untold Story* which starred Catherine Hicks as MM. The TV biopic was based on Norman Mailer's book *Marilyn* (Grosset & Dunlap, 1973).

### MAX YOUNGSTEIN

Born in 1913, Max Youngstein was an executive at United Artists who was shown an early cut of *The Misfits* (1961), a movie that United Artists had financed. Reportedly, upon seeing the film, Youngstein was quite disappointed by the results. So much so, in fact, that the film's director, John Huston, opted to shoot some additional scenes for the film. However, this decision was subsequently vetoed by the film's star, Clark Gable, who had script approval. Thus, no additional scenes were shot.

# Z

**TOMMY ZAHN**

Former "Muscle Beach" lifeguard, Tommy Zahn, was a contract player at 20th Century-Fox in 1946—at the same time MM was under contract to that studio. Reportedly, the pair became lovers for a short period.

**LENORE ZANN**

Lenore Zann was the actress who portrayed Marilyn Monroe in the stage play *Hey, Marilyn* at the Citadel Theatre in Edmonton, Alberta, Canada, circa 1979-1980.

Of her performance, *Variety* said:

> Lenore Zann is outstanding as Marilyn. Although this is her first role, she has authority and presence, despite the limitations of her material.

**DARRYL F. ZANUCK**

> "One day, a great friend of mine, Joseph M. Schenck, brought over to my home in Palm Springs this very beautiful girl who was also on the plump side. I didn't jump up and say, 'Oh, this is a great star,' or anything like that. Later on, Joe said, 'If you can work her in some role or something, some, you know, supporting role, do so.' I did, but I didn't think that I had found any gold mine. John Huston gave her a hell of a good role in *The Asphalt Jungle* (1950). Jesus, she was good in it. I thought, it must have been the magic of Huston, because I didn't think she had all that in her. But then I put her in *All About Eve* (1950), and she was an overnight sensation."
>
> Darryl F. Zanuck, *LOOK* magazine, 11/3/70

Darryl Francis Zanuck first signed Marilyn Monroe to a 20th Century-Fox studio contract on August 26, 1946. Thus commenced what would eventually evolve into a love-hate relationship between the studio executive and the star.

In 1950, Zanuck produced the superb Joseph Mankiewicz picture *All About Eve*. The film featured, amid a stellar company, starlet Marilyn Monroe. Sufficiently impressed, Zanuck signed MM to another six-month contract. Then, in May 1951, due to the "suggestion" of Fox president Spyros Skouras, Zanuck signed Marilyn to a seven-year contract and proceeded to groom her for stardom.

Nevertheless, Marilyn Monroe was convinced, throughout the duration of her career, that Zanuck did not like her. She did not give Zanuck the credit for making her a star. Instead, she credited the public. Said MM:

> "Mr. Zanuck had never seen me as an actress with star quality. He thought I was some kind of freak. Studio bosses are jealous of their

power. They are like political bosses. They want to pick out their own candidates for public office. They don't want the public rising up and dumping a girl they consider 'unphotogenic' in their laps."

*Marilyn Monroe*, by Maurice Zolotow (Harcourt Brace, 1960)

Still, in 1951, Darryl Zanuck issued a statement to the press that read: "Miss Monroe is the most exciting new personality in Hollywood in a long time."

Zanuck saw Monroe as a personality, *not* as a talent. He cast her, repeatedly, in vacuous roles that demanded minimum acting skills and maximum cleavage. When Zanuck first saw the rushes from *Gentlemen Prefer Blondes* (1953), he refused to believe that MM had done her own singing in the film. To prove her vocal point, Marilyn sang privately for her boss. And, perhaps for the first time, Darryl Zanuck became convinced that he had a major star on his hands.

But stardom did not bring Zanuck and Monroe closer. If anything, it achieved the opposite effect. After the stunning consecutive successes of *Niagara, Gentlemen Prefer Blondes,* and *How to Marry a Millionaire,* all in 1953, Marilyn Monroe began to demand, only naturally, to be treated like a star. However, Zanuck refused to renegotiate her contract and continued to treat her in a manner far short of reverence. He also cast her in two mediocre productions that were far short of her new status: *River of No Return* (1954) and *There's No Business Like Show Business* (1954). As a result, Marilyn rebelled. Toward the end of 1954, she went into hiding. Zanuck responded with a manipulative ploy—a press statement that read:

There has been so much talk about Marilyn Monroe that there is now a danger that women moviegoers will say, "So, she makes men excited—enough of her." In the future she will make only two films a year and there will not be so many photographs of her sent around.

*The Los Angeles Mirror*, 11/25/54

In actuality, though, Zanuck was attempting to humble his insubordinate star by minimalizing her appeal and by threatening to limit the quantity of MM publicity and product.

However, Zanuck's ploy did not work. In a heated legal battle, Marilyn Monroe severed her ties with 20th Century-Fox—until she was given the contract provisions and respect that she demanded. It is interesting to note that Marilyn returned, triumphantly, to Fox in February 1956. A month later, Zanuck resigned from his post and was replaced by Buddy Adler.

Darryl F. Zanuck did not return to 20th Century-Fox until 1962—which, of course is the year that MM was fired from Fox. Zanuck replaced Spyros Skouras as the company's president. At the time of Marilyn Monroe's death, Darryl Zanuck was in Paris. He released the following statement to the worldwide press:

I disagreed and fought with her on many occasions, but in spite of the fact that I have not seen her for six years, we were always

> personal friends. Like everyone who knew Marilyn Monroe or worked with her, I am shocked. Marilyn was a star in every sense of the word. I do not claim to have discovered Marilyn Monroe. Nobody discovered her. She discovered herself. I was merely an instrument that provided her with the vehicles in which she was able to reach the theatregoing public of the world.

Born in 1902, Darryl Zanuck cofounded 20th Century-Fox Productions in 1933 and merged the company to form 20th Century-Fox in 1935. He was affiliated with Fox, on and off, until his death in 1979.

**GEORGE ZENO**

> His father was a Betty Grable fan. So it was only natural that George Zeno would fall for the next generation's blond bombshell, Marilyn Monroe.
>
> *LIFE* magazine, 10/81

George Zeno has been a Marilyn Monroe fan and collector for over thirty years. Four of those years were spent as the vice president of the Marilyn Monroe Memorial Fan Club. In 1981, *LIFE* magazine featured Zeno in its tribute to "Marilyn Mania." And the following year Zeno coauthored the book *Monroe: Her Life in Pictures,* which was published by Doubleday.

**GUS ZERNIAL**

Gus Zernial was a baseball player for the Chicago White Sox. In 1951, Zernial posed for a publicity photo with starlet Marilyn Monroe at a Pasadena, California, ballpark. It was this photo that piqued the interest of baseball legend Joe DiMaggio. He reportedly asked, "Who's the blonde?"

**MAURICE ZOLOTOW**

Biographer Maurice Zolotow first met Marilyn Monroe at a 1953 dinner honoring Walter Winchell. He had his first in-depth interview with her in July 1955, at her apartment in the Waldorf-Astoria Towers in New York City. In all, Zolotow had three sittings with MM in July 1955. The results were published in a series of articles for *American Weekly* magazine, beginning in its September 25, 1955, edition. The material also served as the impetus for Zolotow's impressive, definitive biography, *Marilyn Monroe* (Harcourt Brace, 1960). Seventeen years later, Zolotow penned "Joe and Marilyn: The Ultimate LA Love Story," an article for the February 1979 issue of *Los Angeles Magazine.*

Maurice Zolotow was born on November 23, 1913, in New York City. His subsequent writing career has produced such works as *Never Whistle in a Dressing Room* (1944), *The Great Balsamo* (1946), *No People Like Show People* (1951), *Stagestruck: The Romance of Alfred Lunt and Lynn Fontanne* (1965), *Shooting Star: A Biography of John Wayne* (1974), and *Billy Wilder in Hollywood* (1977).

# BIBLIOGRAPHY

## ON MARILYN MONROE


1. Anderson, Janice. *Marilyn Monroe.* (The Hamlyn Publishing Group Ltd., 1983)
2. Capell, Frank A. *The Strange Death of Marilyn Monroe.* (Herald of Freedom, 1964)
3. Carpozi, George, Jr. *Marilyn Monroe: Her Own Story.* (Belmont Books, 1961)
4. Conover, David. *Finding Marilyn: A Romance.* (Grosset & Dunlap, 1981)
5. Conway, Michael, and Mark Ricci. *The Films of Marilyn Monroe.* (Citadel Press, 1964)
6. de Dienes, Andre. *Marilyn Mon Amour.* (Sidgwick and Jackson, 1986)
7. Dougherty, James E. *The Secret Happiness of Marilyn Monroe.* (Playboy Press, 1976)
8. Franklin, Joe, and Laurie Palmer. *The Marilyn Monroe Story.* (Rudolph Field, 1953)
9. Guiles, Fred Lawrence. *Norma Jean: The Life of Marilyn Monroe.* (McGraw-Hill, 1969)
10. Guiles, Fred Lawrence. *Legend: The Life and Death of Marilyn Monroe.* (Stein and Day, 1984)
11. Hamblett, Charles. *Who Killed Marilyn Monroe?* (Leslie Frewin Publishers, Ltd., 1966)
12. Her Psychiatrist Friend. *Violations of the Child Marilyn Monroe.* (Bridgehead Books, 1962)
13. Hoyt, Edwin P. *Marilyn: The Tragic Venus.* (Chilton Books, 1965)
14. Hudson, James A. *The Mysterious Death of Marilyn Monroe.* (Volitant Books, 1968)
15. Hutchinson, Tom. *The Screen Greats: Marilyn Monroe.* (Exeter Books, 1982)
16. Kahn, Roger. *Joe and Marilyn: A Memory of Love.* (William Morrow and Company, Inc., 1986)
17. Kobal, John, with an introduction by David Robinson. *Marilyn Monroe: A Life on Film.* (Exeter Books, 1974)
18. Lembourn, Hans Jorgen. *Diary of a Lover of Marilyn Monroe.* (Arbor House, 1979)
19. Mailer, Norman. *Marilyn.* (Grosset & Dunlap, 1973)
20. Mailer, Norman. *Of Women and Their Elegance.* (Simon and Schuster, 1980)
21. Martin, Pete. *Will Acting Spoil Marilyn Monroe?* (Doubleday, 1956)
22. Mellen, Joan. *Marilyn Monroe.* (Pyramid Publications, 1973)
23. Monroe, Marilyn. *My Story.* (Stein and Day, 1974)
24. Moore, Robin, and Gene Schoor. *Marilyn & Joe DiMaggio.* (Manor Books, 1977)
25. Murray, Eunice, with Rose Shade. *Marilyn: The Last Months.* (Pyramid Books, 1975)
26. Oppenheimer, Joel. *Marilyn Lives!* (Delilah Books, 1981)
27. Patrick, Bob, ed. *Marilyn: Screen Greats Vol. II.* (Starlog, 1980)
28. Pepitone, Lena, and William Stadiem. *Marilyn Monroe Confidential.* (Simon and Schuster, 1979)
29. Rollyson, Carl E., Jr. *Marilyn Monroe: A Life of the Actress.* (UMI Research Press, 1986)
30. Rosten, Norman. *Marilyn: An Untold Story.* (Signet/New American Library, 1973)
31. Sciacca, Tony, aka Anthony Scaduto. *Who Killed Marilyn Monroe?* (Woodhill Books, 1976)
32. Shaw, Sam. *The Joy of Marilyn in the Camera Eye.* (Exeter Books, 1979)
33. Shaw, Sam, with a foreword by George Axelrod. *Marilyn Monroe as the Girl: The Candid Picture-Story of the Making of* The Seven Year Itch. (Ballantine Books, 1955)
34. Skolsky, Sidney. *Marilyn.* (Dell Publishing Company, 1954)
35. Slatzer, Robert. *The Life and Curious Death of Marilyn Monroe.* (Pinnacle Books, 1974)
36. Smith, Milburn, ed. *Marilyn, Barven Screen Greats No. 4.* (Barven Publications, 1971)
37. Spada, James, with George Zeno. *Monroe: Her Life in Pictures.* (Doubleday, 1982)
38. Speriglio, Milo A. *Marilyn Monroe: Murder Cover-up.* (Seville Publishers, 1982)

39. Speriglio, Milo A. *The Marilyn Conspiracy*. (Pocket Books, 1986)
40. Steinem, Gloria. *Marilyn*. (Henry Holt and Company, 1986)
41. Stern, Bert, with Annie Gottlieb. *The Last Sitting*. (William Morrow and Company, Inc., 1982)
42. Summers, Anthony. *Goddess: The Secret Lives of Marilyn Monroe*. (Macmillan, 1985)
43. Summers, Anthony. *Goddess: The Secret Lives of Marilyn Monroe*. (A chapter has been added to the original text.) (New American Library, 1986)
44. Taylor, Roger. *Marilyn in Art*. (Salem House, 1984)
45. Taylor, Roger. *Marilyn Monroe: In Her Own Words*. (Delilah/Putnam, 1983)
46. Wagenknecht, Edward, ed. *Marilyn Monroe: A Composite View*. (Chilton Books, 1969)
47. Weatherby, W. J. *Conversations with Marilyn*. (Mason/Charter Books, 1976)
48. Zolotow, Maurice. *Marilyn Monroe*. (Harcourt Brace, 1960)


## GENERAL


1. Adams, Cindy. *Lee Strasberg: The Imperfect Genius of the Actors Studio*. (Doubleday, 1980)
2. Bacall, Lauren. *By Myself*. (Knopf, 1979)
3. Bacon, James. *Hollywood Is a Four Letter Town*. (Avon, 1976)
4. Baker, Carroll. *Baby Doll: An Autobiography*. (Arbor House, 1983)
5. Berle, Milton. *Milton Berle: An Autobiography*. (Delacorte, 1974)
6. Blackwell, Earl. *Celebrity Register*. (Simon and Schuster, 1973)
7. Blackwell, Earl. *Celebrity Register*. (Times Publishing Group, 1986)
8. Bosworth, Patricia. *Montgomery Clift*. (Harcourt Brace, 1978)
9. Bronaugh, Robert Brett. *The Celebrity Birthday Book*. (Jonathan David Publishers, Inc., 1981)
10. Bronner, Edwin J. *The Encyclopedia of the American Theatre 1900–1975*. (A. S. Barnes and Company, Inc., 1980)
11. Brown, Les. *Encyclopedia of Television*. (New York Times Book Company, 1977)
12. Brown, Peter Harry. *Kim Novak: Reluctant Goddess*. (St. Martin's Press, 1986)
13. Capote, Truman. *Music for Chameleons*. (Random House, 1980)
14. Collier, Peter, and David Horowitz. *The Kennedys*. (Summit, 1984)
15. Curti, Carlo. *Skouras: King of Fox Studios*. (Holloway House, 1967)
16. Dalton, David. *James Dean: American Icon*. (St. Martin's Press, 1984)
17. Dick, Bernard F. *Billy Wilder*. (Twayne Publishers, 1980)
18. Edwards, Anne. *Judy Garland: A Biography*. (Simon and Schuster, 1975)
19. Edwards, Anne. *Vivien Leigh*. (Simon and Schuster, 1977)
20. Fein, Irving A. *Jack Benny: An Intimate Biography*. (G. P. Putnam's Sons, 1976)
21. Godfrey, Lionel. *Paul Newman Superstar: A Critical Biography*. (St. Martin's Press, 1978)
22. Goode, James. *The Story of* The Misfits. (Bobbs-Merrill, 1963)
23. Graham, Sheilah. *Hollywood Revisited*. (St. Martin's Press, 1985)
24. Greif, Martin. *The Gay Book of Days*. (Lyle Stuart, Inc., 1982)
25. Griffith, Richard, and Arthur Mayer. *The Movies*. (Simon and Schuster, 1957)
26. Guild, Leo. *Zanuck: Hollywood's Last Tycoon*. (Holloway House, 1970)
27. Halliwell, Leslie. *Film Guide*. (Granada, 1979)
28. Halliwell, Leslie. *Halliwell's Film Goers Companion*. (Charles Scribner's Sons, 1984 and 1985)
29. Harris, Warren. *The Other Marilyn*. (Arbor House, 1985)
30. Heilman, Joan. *Kenneth's Complete Book on Hair*. (Doubleday, 1972)
31. Herndon, Venable. *James Dean: A Short Life*. (Doubleday, 1974)
32. Hirschhorn, Clive. *Gene Kelly: A Biography*. (Henry Regnery, 1970)
33. Huston, John. *John Huston: An Open Book*. (Knopf, 1980)

34. Josefsberg, Milt. *The Jack Benny Show.* (Arlington House, 1977)
35. Kael, Pauline. *Reeling.* (Warner Books, 1976)
36. Kelley, Kitty. *Elizabeth Taylor: The Last Star.* (Simon and Schuster, 1981)
37. Leigh, Janet. *There Really Was a Hollywood.* (Doubleday, 1984)
38. Linet, Beverly. *Susan Hayward: Portrait of a Survivor.* (Atheneum, 1980)
39. Lloyd, Ann, Graham Fuller, and Arnold Desser, eds. *The Illustrated Who's Who of the Cinema.* (Macmillan, 1983)
40. Mann, May. *Jayne Mansfield: A Biography.* (Drake Publishers, 1973)
41. Martin, Ralph G. *A Hero of Our Times: An Intimate Story of the Kennedy Years.* (Macmillan, 1983)
42. Marx, Kenneth S. *Star Stats.* (Price/Stern/Sloan, 1979)
43. Masters, George, and Norma Lee Brown. *The Masters Way to Beauty.* (E. P. Dutton, 1977)
44. McBride, Joseph, ed. *Howard Hawks.* (Prentice-Hall, 1972)
45. McIntosh, William Currie, and William Weaver. *The Private Cary Grant.* (Sidgwick and Jackson, 1983)
46. Miller, Arthur. *After the Fall.* (Viking, 1964)
47. Morella, Joe, and Edward Z. Epstein. *Brando: The Unauthorized Biography.* (Crown Publishers, 1973)
48. Mosley, Leonard. *Zanuck: The Rise and Fall of Hollywood's Last Tycoon.* (Little Brown and Company, 1984)
49. Olivier, Laurence. *Laurence Olivier: Confessions of an Actor.* (Simon and Schuster, 1982)
50. Parish, James Robert. *The Fox Girls.* (Arlington, 1971)
51. Pitts, Michael R., and Louis H. Harrison. *Hollywood on Record: The Film Stars Discography.* (Scarecrow Press, 1978)
52. Roberts, Glenys. *Bardot.* (St. Martin's Press, 1984)
53. Robertson, Patrick. *Movie Facts and Feats.* (Sterling Publishing, 1980)
54. Robyns, Gwen. *Princess Grace.* (W. H. Allen, 1982)
55. Romero, Gerry. *Sinatra's Women.* (Manor Books, 1976)
56. Rosen, Marjorie. *Popcorn Venus.* (Avon Books, 1973)
57. Russell, Jane. *Jane Russell: My Paths and My Detours.* (Franklin Watts, 1985)
58. Russo, Vito. *The Celluloid Closet.* (Harper and Row, 1981)
59. Saxton, Martha. *Jayne Mansfield and the American Fifties.* (Houghton Mifflin, 1975)
60. Sheppard, Dick. *Elizabeth: The Life and Career of Elizabeth Taylor.* (Doubleday, 1974)
61. Shipman, David. *The Great Movie Stars: The International Years.* (Hill and Wang, 1980)
62. Signoret, Simone. *Nostalgia Isn't What It Used to Be.* (Harper and Row, 1978)
63. Skinner, John Walter. *Who's Who on the Screen.* (Madeleine Productions, 1983)
64. Skolsky, Sidney. *Don't Get Me Wrong, I Love Hollywood.* (G. P. Putnam's Sons, 1975)
65. Smith, Ella. *Starring Miss Barbara Stanwyck.* (Crown Publishers, 1974)
66. Steinberg, Cobbett. *Film Facts.* (Facts on Film, Inc., 1980)
67. Thomas, Bob. *King Cohn: The Life and Times of Harry Cohn.* (Putnam, 1967)
68. Truitt, Evelyn Mack. *Who Was Who on the Screen.* (R. R. Bowker Company, 1984)
69. V. ed. *Who's Who of American Women.* (Marquis, 1958)
70. V. ed. *Who's Who 1984.* (Marquis, 1984)
71. V. ed. *Who's Who 1985.* (Marquis, 1985)
72. Walker, Alexander. *The Celluloid Sacrifice.* (Hawthorn Books, 1966)
73. Wallace, Irving. *The Intimate Sex Lives of Famous People.* (Dell, 1982)
74. Warren, Doug. *Betty Grable.* (St. Martin's Press, 1981)
75. Wilson, Earl. *The Show Business Nobody Knows.* (Cowles Book Company, 1971)
76. Winters, Shelley. *Shelley: Aka Shirley.* (Ballantine, 1980)
77. Zolotow, Maurice. *Billy Wilder in Hollywood.* (G. P. Putnam's Sons, 1977)

## MAGAZINES


1. *American Classic Screen*. "How a Cinema Legend Was Born," by James Haspiel, 11–12/77.
2. *American Weekly*. "The Truth About Me," by Liza Wilson, 11/16/52, 11/23/52; "The Mystery of Marilyn Monroe," by Maurice Zolotow, 9/25/55.
3. *California*. "The Case of the Purloined Diary," by Steve Oney, 10/82; "The Day Marilyn Monroe Needed 47 Takes To Remember To Say, 'Where's the Bourbon?'," by I. A. L. Diamond, 12/85.
4. *Cavalier*. "Carl Sandburg Talks About Marilyn Monroe," by Julian Scheer, 1/63.
5. *Collier's*. "Hollywood's 1951 Model Blonde," by Robert Cahn, 9/8/51; "Marilyn Monroe Hits a New High," by Robert Cahn, 7/9/54.
6. *Connoisseur*. "Isozaki," by Phil Patton, 11/86.
7. *Cosmopolitan*. "Marilyn Monroe: The Sex Symbol vs. the Good Wife," by Jon Whitcomb, 12/60.
8. *Esquire*. "Making *The Misfits* or Waiting for Monroe or Notes from Olympus," by Alice T. McIntyre, 3/61; "Marilyn Monroe's Last Picture Show," by Walter Bernstein, 7/73; "The Redecade," by Tom Shales, 3/86; "What Ever Happened to Geraldo Rivera? Who?" by Geraldo Rivera, 4/86.
9. *Film Comment*. "Baby Go Boom," by David Stenn and David Thomson, 9–10/82.
10. *Films in Review*. "Her Tragedy Was Allowing Herself To Be Misled Intellectually," by Robert C. Roman, 10/62; The Letters Section, 11/62; "The Harlow/Monroe Connection," by Jim Haspiel, 3/79; "The Marilyn Monroe Dress," by Jim Haspiel, 6–7/80.
11. *Focus*. "Marilyn Monroe: She Breathes Sex Appeal," 12/51.
12. *Good Housekeeping*. "Remembrance of Marilyn," by Flora Rheta Schreiber, 1/63; "The Hidden Years of Marilyn Monroe," by Cindy Adams, 1/80.
13. *Hollywood Studio*. "Marilyn Monroe's Twin," by Jim Haspiel, 2/80; "The Decline and Fall of the Blonde Sex Symbol," by Patrick Agan, 5/80; "If Marilyn Were Still Alive," by Lee Graham, 12/81; "Jim Haspiel Uncovers Marilyn Monroe's Stage Career," by Jim Haspiel, 9/84.
14. *House and Garden*. "Marilyn Monroe Meets Frank Lloyd Wright," by Bruce Brooks Pfeiffe, 12/85.
15. *Hustler*. "Marilyn Monroe Was Murdered: An Eyewitness Account," by James E. Hall, 5/86.
16. *Interview*. "Sidney Guilaroff's Hollywood Hair," by Beauregard Houston-Montgomery, 9/85; "Travilla," by Beauregard Houston-Montgomery, 7/86.
17. *LIFE*. "Eight Girls Try Out Mixed Emotions," 10/10/49; The Letters Section, 10/31/49; "Hollywood Topic A-Plus," 4/7/52; "They Fired Marilyn: Her Dip Lives On," 6/22/62; "Marilyn Monroe Lets Down Her Hair About Being Famous," by Richard Meryman, 8/3/62; "Last Long Talk with a Lonely Girl," by Richard Meryman, 8/17/62; "What Really Killed Marilyn," by C. B. Luce, 8/7/64; "Behind the Myth the Face of Norma Jean," by Richard Meryman, 11/4/66; "Ann-Margret, Suddenly Blooming," by P. F. Kluge, 8/6/71; "Mania for Marilyn," by Jim Watters, 10/81.
18. *Los Angeles*. "The Strange Case of Marilyn Monroe Versus the Government," by C. Robert Jennings, 8/66.
19. *LOOK*. "Zanuck: Last of the Red Hot Star Makers," by Henry Ehrlich, 11/3/70.
20. *McCall's*. "Marilyn Monroe: The Meaning of Her Life and Death," by Diana Trilling, 7/82.
21. *Modern Screen*. "The True Life Story of Marilyn Monroe," by Elyda Nelson, 12/52.
22. *MS*. "Growing up with Marilyn," by Gloria Steinem, 8/72.
23. *The Nation*. "Marilyn Monroe: 1926–1962," by Lincoln Kirstein, 8/25/62.
24. *Newsweek*. "A Constellation Is Born," 10/31/60; "Newsmakers," by Susan Cheever Cowley, 6/6/67; "The Star Crossed Kennedys," by Jennet Conant with Tenley-Ann Jackson, 11/14/85.

25. *People*. "MM's First Husband Waxes Nostalgic," 5/31/76; "He Makes Sure DiMaggio's Roses Are There," by D. Wallace, 8/9/82; "Marilyn Monroe-Mania Hits the Stores and a New Generation Discovers Wearing Marilyn's Dress Is a Breeze," 2/21/83; "The Time Marilyn Monroe Hid Out at Our House," by Olie and Joe Raul, 8/8/83; "The Monroe Report," by William Plummer, 11/21/85.
26. *Photoplay*. "Marilyn Monroe Was My Wife," by Jim Dougherty, 3/53; "Marilyn to Wed Again?" by Bob Dean, 5/61; ". . . So That the Memory of Marilyn Will Linger On," by Adele Whiteley Fletcher, 9/65.
27. *Picture Week*. "Marilyn Monroe's Tragic Final Hours," 10/14/85.
28. *Playboy*. "The Celebrity Sex Register," by Shirley Seay, 6/82; "Marilyn Monroe Remembered," 1/64; "Marilyn," by Hugh Hefner, 1/87.
29. *Popular Photography*. "Marilyn Monroe: The Image and Her Photographers," by Ralph Hattersley, 1/66.
30. *Quick*. "The New Jean Harlow," 11/19/51.
31. *Redbook*. "So Far To Go Alone," by Jim Henaghan, 6/52; The Letters Section, 7/52; "Marilyn Monroe's Marriage," by Robert J. Levin, 2/58; "Marilyn Monroe: A Good Long Look at Myself," by Alan Levy, 8/62.
32. *Rolling Stone*. "Say Goodbye to Camelot: Marilyn Monroe and the Kennedys," by C. D. B. Bryan, 12/5/85.
33. *The Saturday Evening Post*. "The New Marilyn Monroe," by Pete Martin, 5/5/56, 5/12/56, 5/19/56.
34. *Show*. "A Memory of Marilyn," by Joshua Logan, 9/72.
35. *Show Business Illustrated*. "Marilyn Monroe: Star at Turning Point," by Joe Hyams, 2/62.
36. *Time*. "The Walker," 2/15/54; "Marilyn Monroe: To Aristophanes and Back," 5/14/56; "Popsie and Poopsie," 11/21/60; The People Section, 12/15/67; "Madonna on Madonna," 5/27/85.
37. *Vanity Fair*. "The First Sitting," by James Atlas, 2/86.
38. *Vogue*. "Marilyn Monroe," by The Editors, 9/1/62.
39. *Woman's Day*. "Beauty Isn't Everything—It's the Only Thing!" by George Masters, 5/3/77.

## NEWSPAPERS

Much of the research for *The Unabridged Marilyn* was accomplished by reading and studying back issues of many daily newspapers. In some cases, nearly *forty years* of material was examined; thus the individual titles of the articles would be far too numerous to index here. However, the publications that were used are listed below by city.

### Chicago

*Chicago Sun-Times*
*Chicago Sunday Tribune Magazine*
*Chicago Tribune*

### Los Angeles

Beverly Hills Citizen
Hollywood Citizen News
Hollywood Reporter
Los Angeles Citizen News
Los Angeles Daily News
Los Angeles Examiner

Los Angeles Herald Examiner
Los Angeles Herald Express
Los Angeles Mirror
Los Angeles Times
Variety

**New York**
New York Daily News
New York Daily Mirror
New York Herald Tribune
New York Post
The New York Times
New York World Telegram & Sun

# TRIVIA QUIZ ANSWERS

1. b) The Betty Grable Story
2. *How to Marry a Millionaire*
3. Cuba
4. *Don't Bother to Knock*
5. *Clash by Night*
6. None
7. *Ladies of the Chorus*
8. *We're Not Married*
9. *Right Cross*
10. *Legend*
11. *The Misfits*
12. *How to Marry a Millionaire*
13. *Ladies of the Chorus*, Rand Brooks
14. "Thank you ever so"
15. *Some Like It Hot*
16. *River of No Return*
17. Little Rock, Arkansas
18. *Don't Bother to Knock*
19. "Men aren't attentive to girls who wear glasses"
20. *Gentlemen Prefer Blondes*
21. Rhinestones
22. The Blue Dragon Cafe
23. Camp Pendleton, The Marine Corp Air Station in El Toro
24. Diamonds
25. Elizabeth Taylor, by nearly five years
26. *Niagara*
27. *Ladies of the Chorus*
28. *We're Not Married*, *Gentlemen Prefer Blondes*, *How to Marry a Millionaire*
29. Rand Brooks
30. Miss Mississippi
31. *The Seven Year Itch*, "Chopsticks"
32. Boy George
33. The Rainbow Cabins
34. Carroll Baker, *Baby Doll*; Ingrid Bergman, *Anastasia*; Katharine Hepburn, *The Rainmaker*; Nancy Kelly, *The Bad Seed*; Deborah Kerr, *The King and I*
35. Philippe Halsman
36. *Aged in Wood*
37. *Niagara*

38. La Scala
39. Terry Moore
40. Miss Caswell
41. *Hometown Story, As Young as You Feel, Monkey Business*
42. Tomato plant
43. A train station
44. *The Asphalt Jungle*
45. Drug-sniffing dogs
46. The freezer
47. Ray Anthony
48. *How to Marry a Millionaire*
49. *Kiss Me Stupid*
50. *All About Eve*

THE ALAN FRANCE COLLECTION

**THF LAST WORDS**

Question: What were Marilyn Monroe's last words on a movie screen?
Answer: "How do you find your way back in the dark?"

—*The Misfits,* 1961